Marketing Channels

SEVENTH EDITION

MARKETING CHANNELS

Anne T. Coughlan

Associate Professor of Marketing
Northwestern University

Erin Anderson

John H. Loudon Chaired Professor of
International Management
INSEAD

Louis W. Stern

John D. Gray Distinguished Professor Emeritus of Marketing
Northwestern University

Adel I. El-Ansary

Donna L. Harper Professor of Marketing
Coggin College of Business
University of North Florida

PEARSON
Prentice
Hall

Upper Saddle River, NJ 07458

Library of Congress Cataloging-in-Publication Data

Marketing channels / Anne T. Coughlan . . . [et al.].—7th ed.
    p. cm.
  Includes bibliographical references and index.
  ISBN 0-13-191346-8 (casebound : alk. paper)
  1. Marketing channels. I. Coughlan, Anne T.
  HF5415.129.M365 2006
  658.8'7—dc22

                                                    2005030008

VP/Editorial Director: Jeff Shelstad
Acquisitions Editor: Katie Stevens
Project Manager: Melissa Pellerano
Editorial Assistant: Christine Ietto
Marketing Manager: Ashaki Charles
Marketing Assistant: Joanna Sabella
Associate Director: Judy Leale
Managing Editor: Renata Butera
Production Editor: Suzanne Grappi
Permissions Coordinator: Charles Morris
Manufacturing Buyer: Michelle Klein
Production Manager, Manufacturing: Arnold Vila
Cover Design Manager: Jayne Conte
Composition: Laserwords
Full-Service Project Management: BookMasters, Inc.

Typeface: 10/12 New Baskerville

Credits and acknowledgments borrowed from other sources and reproduced, with permission, in this textbook appear on appropriate page within text.

Pearson Education LTD.   Pearson Education Australia PTY, Limited
Pearson Education Singapore, Pte. Ltd   Pearson Education North Asia Ltd
Pearson Education, Canada, Ltd   Pearson Educación de Mexico, S.A. de C.V.
Pearson Education–Japan   Pearson Education Malaysia, Pte. Ltd

ISBN 0-13-191346-8

Brief Contents

Contents

This book is meant for an international audience of practicing managers and managers under formation. It is written in the English of international business. Our subject is marketing channels, the companies that come together to bring products and services from their point of origin to their point of consumption. Marketing channels, the company's routes to market, are the downstream part of a value chain. It is through marketing channels that the originator of goods or services gains access to a market. Channels of distribution are a critical element of business strategy.

This book relies on examples taken from all over the world. The ideas it presents apply to any channel for any product or service in any market. The generality of the book is shown in its many examples, which cover a wealth of different products and services sold to businesses and consumers, selected from the worldwide business press, research, and consulting. Some examples are:

> Books, music, Taiwanese tea, pharmaceuticals, computers, online bill payment, reverse logistics, furniture, pet food, luxury products, grocery stores, Kmart, African breweries, sunglasses, toys, plumbing supplies, athletic shoes, construction equipment, express shipping services, soft drinks, meat packing, hardware stores and cooperatives, McDonald's and Truffaut Garden Centers as franchise businesses, and apparel.

The variety of the list reinforces the generality of the principles. As is appropriate for an international readership, we present each example as though the reader is unfamiliar with the product/market in question. We cover the highlights needed to frame the problem, then cover the channel issues in the examples. Detailed examples are broken out in sidebars to improve the readability of the main text.

Each chapter is designed to stand on its own. The chapters may be read in any order, and any chapter may be omitted. Each chapter is of a length that can be assigned for a single class or read in one sitting with a single issue in mind. The chapters are designed modularly. Essential definitions are repeated where necessary, so that the reader is free to choose one chapter and defer or omit another. The reader is referred to other chapters where appropriate to explore further any topic raised in the chapter at hand. In this way, the reader can select how deeply to delve into all the sections of the book that most closely fit the problem under consideration.

The content of each chapter comes from the best of current research and practice. We cover a vast and varied literature, bringing in findings, practice, and viewpoints from multiple disciplines (marketing, strategy, economics, sociology, law, political science) and from the best practices of channel managers worldwide. In presenting these works, we set aside the technical aspects of the research. Instead, we focus on framing the problem and its solution in the language of business. We introduce technical vocabulary where it is appropriate for the manager. We do not go into detail on the theory, data, and methods that underlie the content of this book. Instead, we liberally note the relevant references and tie them to the content, so that the interested reader may delve further into specific points.

The text is organized into four parts. Part I, Introduction, introduces the basic ideas and concepts underlying channel analysis. It explains why specialized institutions and agencies have emerged to assist in the task of making goods and services available for industrial, institutional, and household consumption. Among the more critical concepts introduced in Chapter 1 are the notions of service outputs and marketing flows on which we rely heavily throughout the remainder of the book. Chapter 1 also provides a coherent framework for building, maintaining, and analyzing channel structure and function. It includes demand-side analysis, supply-side analysis of both channel flows and channel structures, the analysis of gaps on the demand and supply sides, and responses by channel managers concerning the creation or modification of channel structures to meet target segments' needs. It also emphasizes the importance of ongoing management and coordination of the channel through the use of channel power sources and the recognition and management of channel conflict. This framework unifies the discussion throughout the rest of the book and forms the basis for the book's approach to channel design and management.

Part II, Channel Design: Demand, Supply, and Channel Efficiency, develops the framework for channel creation or modification. Chapter 2 focuses on the demand side by discussing how to appropriately segment a market for the purposes of channel design, using the core concept of service output demands. Chapter 3 turns to the supply side of the channel, introducing the concept of channel flows to describe the work done by channel members. This chapter emphasizes the importance of distributing flow responsibilities to channel members who can perform them most efficiently. Not only is the allocation of flows important, however; so are the issues of channel structure and intensity of distribution, the topics of Chapter 4, which discusses the types of firms that can and should be included in the channel, how broadly distributed the channel's products should be, and who specifically should be a member of the channel. Chapter 5 brings together the demand and supply sides through a discussion of gap analysis, where gaps can exist on the demand side, the supply side, or both. Sources of gaps, types of gaps, and methods of closing channel gaps are all discussed. The next part of the book covers how to create such a midrange solution.

Part III, Channel Implementation, is about how to get all the members of a channel to work in concert with each other. Concerted or coordinated action does not happen naturally in a marketing channel. This section covers how to overcome this problem, crafting channels that function smoothly in pursuit of common goals. Power is the subject of Chapter 6, which covers how to obtain the potential for influence—and how to use it. Of course, channels are full of conflict, the subject of Chapter 7. Here, the emphasis is on how to diagnose the true sources of conflict and how to direct conflict to use it as a constructive force for change. Power, conflict, and intensity of distribution all turn on how to influence channel members. The ultimate form of influence is to forge a strategic alliance in a channel, the subject of Chapter 8. Chapter 9 discusses a key issue in channel structure: whether or not to vertically integrate the channel. This chapter covers the make-or-buy issue in channels, as well as the decision concerning whether to adopt an intermediate solution. These are options that blend the features of make and of buy. Because efforts to coordinate often run afoul of the law, the legal environment (Chapter 10) closes Part III on channel coordination and implementation.

Part IV, Channel Institutions, describes and evaluates the institutional forms that predominate at each level of a marketing channel. The retailing level has a great variety of forms. The major issues and challenges confronting them are discussed in Chapter 11. This chapter discusses all types of retailing, including physical stores, online stores, and direct selling. Further up in the value-added chain is the wholesaling sector, the subject of Chapter 12. Chapter 13 deals with the fascinating, complex, inherently contradictory channel institution of franchising, discussing how, when, and why franchising works. Finally, Chapter 14 discusses supply chain management, an important bridging topic between marketing and operations; managing upward in the supply chain is viewed as part of a continuum along with managing downstream through the marketing channel.

The seventh edition differs slightly from the sixth edition in its organization of material but not in its philosophical underpinning. The framework for analysis is presented first, followed by institutionally oriented chapters, as in the sixth edition. The framework continues to be developed over several chapters, each of which can be the focus of a single course session. We continue and expand the international focus of the book from the sixth edition, reflecting the importance of channel management issues throughout the world, including in emerging economies. In this edition, we include e-commerce examples throughout the book, rather than discussing them in a separate chapter.

Support materials for this textbook are available to adopting instructors at our instructor's resource center (IRC) online. Please visit www.prenhall.com/coughlan for more information.

ACKNOWLEDGMENTS

The structure and content of this book have been deeply influenced by many people. Each author appreciates the contributions of a distinct (but sometimes overlapping) set of people, whereas a fourth set of individuals has influenced us all.

Anne Coughlan thanks Charles B. Jameson for his unflagging support and patience. C. J. and Catherine Anne frequently commented on ideas about channels brought up at the dinner table, and their budding insights into marketing problems refined the thinking for this book. This work is also dedicated to the memory of Catherine M. Coughlan and John M. Coughlan, who have been an inspiration to excellence. Finally, her colleagues and students in the marketing community deserve recognition for their many insights that have shaped her thinking over the years.

Erin Anderson expresses her appreciation to Alberto Sa Vinhas, Rupinder Jindal, Vincent Onyemah, and Frédéric Dalsace. Their penetrating insights and many ideas have been invaluable. Peter Kimurwa, Deanna White, and Neeraj Mehrotra provided valuable research assistance. Sandra Kanel and Françoise Brachain were invaluable in editing and production.

Louis Stern is indebted to his wife, Rhona, whose encouragement, humor, support, and affection have been sources of inspiration to him. He is also indebted to all of his colleagues at Northwestern who have, over the years, supplied such enormous intellectual leadership to the marketing field. He is especially grateful for the opportunity he has been given to work with so many outstanding doctoral students, both at Northwestern and at Ohio State, where he previously taught.

Adel El-Ansary would like to acknowledge the encouragement and support of a number of marketing scholars. Many thanks to all, particularly those who have been personally supportive and encouraging over the years. A special debt is owed to Louis W. Stern, William R. Davidson, and the late Bert C. McCammon, Jr.

The inputs of many colleagues, both in academia and business, have improved the book. We thank in particular Adam Fein, Enver Yücesan, Bob Trinkle, Rajesh Iyer, Howard Hoffman, Joyce A. Young, John Fraedrich, and Nita L. Paden. We especially thank the many MBA students who offered comments and encouragement during the process of writing the book.

We are also especially indebted to the large number of authors whose work we cite throughout the text. Without their efforts, we could not have written this book.

Anne T. Coughlan
Evanston, Illinois

Erin Anderson
Fontainebleau, France

Louis W. Stern
Evanston, Illinois

Adel I. El-Ansary
Jacksonville, Florida

Marketing Channels

Structure and Functions

Learning objectives

After reading this chapter, you will know:

- What a marketing channel is
- Why manufacturers choose to use intermediaries between themselves and end-users
- What marketing flows define the work of the channel
- Who the members of marketing channels are and the flows in which they can specialize
- The elements of a framework for marketing channel design and implementation

Marketing channels are the routes to market used to sell every product and service that consumers and business buyers purchase everywhere in the world. Why should you be excited about learning what marketing channels are, how they are designed and how they work, and how to manage them? There are several reasons:

> First, the channel is a *gatekeeper* between the manufacturer and the end-user. This means that failing to understand and proactively manage the actions of one's channel partners can lessen the effective reach and attractiveness of the manufacturer's products or services. For example, the biggest driver of a movie's success is the number of movie-theater screens on which the movie is shown upon its release. It is therefore in the interests of a movie producer to understand how theaters decide to screen movies, for how long, and on how many screens.

> In addition, the channel is an *important asset* in the company's overall marketing and positioning strategy, often serving as the main differentiator of the company's market offering from those of its competitors. Basic marketing courses teach that differentiation is fundamental in building and maintaining a competitive advantage. But differentiation of what? Often, the emphasis is on *product* or *feature* differentiation, which leads manufacturers to focus on research, development, and innovation as keys to success. But what if the firm is selling a commodity or mature product line (indeed, the very products that were the innovative technology leaders of the past)? Is there a successful sales path for such products, or must the marketer abandon them in favor of perpetual searches for new products? We would argue that the product is just one part of the total purchase bundle for the end-user and that the

services rendered by channel members are not only also part of the total bundle but are often the deciding factor in what to buy. This means that effective differentiation need not be defined only through product features but can also occur through innovative channel offerings.

➤ Third, the *channel experience* strongly affects the end-user's overall perception of a brand's image and, hence, end-user satisfaction. For example, in the auto market, research has shown that consumers who take better care of their autos actually perceive the cars' quality to be higher and that purchasers of higher quality cars tend to have them serviced more at the dealership. These findings imply that the dealer's postsale service inputs are crucial to the long-term quality image of the auto (and, hence, its resale price, as well as future consumer quality perceptions of the auto brand).[1]

➤ Amazingly, *awareness* of the channel as a key strategic marketing asset is low in many firms and industries. The distribution process is seen (erroneously) as simply a necessary and costly evil that gets the company's products to the hands of eager end-users. In this sort of competitive environment, the manufacturer that sees the value of positioning through effective channel design and of investing in cost efficiencies in that design beats its rivals handily.[2]

➤ Finally, even when aware of the value of careful channel design and management, companies often *find it hard* to create and maintain a well-working channel design. It is, therefore, useful to develop a framework for thinking about the problem that will help companies at every level of the channel operate more profitably and do a better job of meeting end-users' demands and preferences.

In short, a strong channel system is a competitive asset that is not easily replicated by other firms and is, therefore, a strong source of sustainable competitive advantage. Further, building or modifying the channel system involves costly and hard-to-reverse investments. This means that making the effort to do it right the first time has great value and, conversely, making a mistake may put the company at a long-term disadvantage.

This book explains how to build, modify, and maintain efficient and effective channel structures in both consumer goods markets and business-to-business markets for products and services within one country and across national borders. Our first chapter defines the concept of a marketing channel and then discusses the purpose of using marketing channels to reach the marketplace, the functions and activities that occur in marketing channels, membership in marketing channels, and how a framework for analysis can improve the channel decisions made by an executive acting as a channel manager or designer.

WHAT IS A MARKETING CHANNEL?

The rich array of institutional possibilities in marketing channels is impossible to convey briefly, but consider the examples in Sidebar 1.1 illustrating how commonly bought products are distributed. These examples, among many others, suggest our basic definition of a marketing channel:

A marketing channel is a set of interdependent organizations involved in the process of making a product or service available for use or consumption.

Our definition of a marketing channel bears some explication. It first points out that a marketing channel is a *set of interdependent organizations*. That is, a marketing

Sidebar 1.1

Channel options for three product types

- *Apparel:* Department stores were once the primary retail outlets through which branded clothing was sold in the United States. They offered a wide variety and deep assortment of men's, women's, and children's clothing and accessories, attractively displayed, with full service from in-store employees, who would help a shopper find what he or she needed, complete the sale, and if necessary arrange for gift wrapping, home delivery, or other services. Clothing designers and manufacturers relied heavily on the department stores as their major high-quality channel partners, supporting a brand image that manufacturers sought to convey to consumers. Today, such department stores still exist, but they have lost significant market share to other retail competitors, and their service levels are widely believed to have diminished over time. One department store competitor is the focused specialty store, which itself may operate multiple different store formats to appeal to different clienteles (e.g., The Gap targets teenagers to young adults, but Gap Kids offers a full array of casual children's clothing for boys and girls; Ann Taylor operates Ann Taylor stores targeting the "successful, relatively affluent career woman" and also Ann Taylor Loft targeting "value conscious women with a more relaxed lifestyle both at work and at home"[3]). Department stores also face competition from full-price retail outlets run by the same manufacturers whose clothing those department stores distribute, such as Tommy Hilfiger (which operates 7 of its own full-service retail stores in the United States, 15 in Canada, and 13 in Europe, in addition to a network of independently franchised Tommy Hilfiger stores[4]) or Polo Ralph Lauren (which operates 40 of its own stores in the United States and 121 outside the United States[5]).

  These manufacturers often also operate their own outlet stores (Tommy Hilfiger has 122 U.S. outlet stores[6]; Ralph Lauren has 130 U.S. outlet stores[7]; and Jones New York, owned by Jones Apparel Group, has 127 North American outlet stores[8]). Indeed, outlet stores housed in outlet malls are not just a U.S. phenomenon but have spread to Europe, Japan, and the Middle East due to high demand from value-conscious (but less service-sensitive) consumers around the world.[9] Finally, discount and mass merchandisers like Kohl's and Wal-Mart in the United States are gaining in retail apparel sales against department stores; one study reports that discounters accounted for $70.2 billion of an estimated $182 billion U.S. retail apparel market, or 38.6 percent, in 2003.[10] Meanwhile, shopping malls, long the home of department stores, are suffering: they accounted for only 19 percent of U.S. retail sales in 2003, down from 38 percent in 1995. Although department store companies are responding by opening off-mall outlets to appeal to time-starved shoppers, those that remain at traditional malls are suffering.[11]

- *Books:* The standard marketing channels for books have always included authors, publishers, book wholesalers, and finally bricks-and-mortar bookstores selling to end-users. In today's marketplace, however, standard retailers like Barnes & Noble and Borders find it necessary to sell online as well. Barnes & Noble's online bookstore, www.barnesandnoble.com, opened in 1997 and was taken public as a separate business in 1999. Meanwhile, Borders' online offering, www.borders.com, has been handled since August 2001 through an e-commerce alliance with Amazon.com, under which Amazon.com provides technology services, site

  (continued)

Sidebar 1.1 (cont.)

Channel options for three product types

content, product selection, and customer service, with Borders receiving a percentage of sales in return.[12] Since November 2002, the service has also offered in-store pickup for online orders if the consumer wishes. These active competitive moves are being pursued despite the persistent lack of profitability of online bookselling.[13] Barnes & Noble's 2003 Annual Report adds: "Barnes & Noble.com also validates our belief that all twenty-first century retailers, especially booksellers, should have a viable multi-channel service for customers. . . . We are convinced that Barnes & Noble.com adds value to our brand."[14] These developments threaten some standard book wholesalers but create new opportunities for shipping and logistics companies that can handle many small shipments, such as UPS and FedEx.

- *Pharmaceutical products:* Prescription drugs reach the end-user in several different ways. The pharmaceutical manufacturer typically uses an employee sales force (but may also use contract salespeople who are not employees) to make sales calls on physicians, hospitals, distributors, and insurance companies. Most health insurance companies in the United States have *formularies*, lists of approved drugs

that may be prescribed for particular conditions, and sales effort is used to convince the insurance companies to put new drugs on their lists (or to keep existing ones on them). The prescription drugs themselves may pass through the hands of independent distributors on their way to a retail, hospital, or online pharmacy. Even the physician plays a role by actually prescribing the pharmaceutical that the patient finally uses. In cases where the patient's health care coverage includes prescription drug coverage, payment may flow not from the patient directly to the pharmacy but from the insurance company to the pharmacy. To further complicate this complex channel structure, many U.S. patients have been buying their prescription drugs from non-U.S. outlets because the pharmaceutical companies typically maintain premium prices in the U.S. market. This raises profitability issues for the pharmaceutical companies, which have heretofore sought to recover the very high costs of drug research and development through premium pricing in U.S. pharmaceutical channels, counterbalanced by lower pricing in other national markets whose nationalized health services impose strict price controls on pharmaceuticals.[15]

channel is not just one firm doing its best in the market—whether that firm is a manufacturer, wholesaler, or retailer. Rather, many entities typically are involved in the business of channel marketing. Each channel member depends on the others to do their jobs.

What are the channel members' jobs? Our definition makes clear that running a marketing channel is a *process*. It is not an event. Distribution frequently takes time to accomplish, and even when a sale is finally made, the relationship with the end-user usually is not over (think about a hospital purchasing a piece of medical equipment and its demands for postsale service to see that this is true).

Finally, what is the purpose of this process? Our definition claims that it is *making a product or service available for use or consumption*. That is, the purpose of channel marketing is to satisfy the end-users in the market, be they consumers or final business buyers. Their goal is the use or consumption of the product or service being sold. A manufacturer who sells through distributors to retailers who in turn serve final consumers may be tempted to think that it has generated sales and developed happy customers when its sales force successfully places product in the distributors' warehouses. Our definition argues otherwise. It is of critical importance that all channel members focus their attention on the end-user.

The marketing channel is often viewed as a key strategic asset of a manufacturer. Gateway, a personal computer maker in the United States, announced the acquisition of eMachines in late January 2004, with retail channel access a major factor in the acquisition (it completed the acquisition in March 2004). Prior to the acquisition, Gateway reached consumers directly through online sales and phone sales and through its own network of retail stores. Gateway retail stores provided very high service levels to consumers who wanted help choosing the right set of components for a computer system. Gateway introduced an extended line of consumer electronics products including plasma televisions, digital cameras, DVD player/recorders, MP3 players, and home theater systems in late 2003 to bolster sagging sales in its retail stores, but the move did not improve the company's profitability. Meanwhile, eMachines sold only through third-party retailers and had strong relationships with retailers like Best Buy, Circuit City, Costco, and Wal-Mart, as well as a 20 percent market share in computer sales in Europe and Japan (markets that Gateway had previously abandoned in a cost-cutting effort). Further, eMachines had slashed the costs of running its business, while Gateway's expenses were high. Thus, the acquisition combined Gateway's expanded consumer electronics line with eMachines' broad distribution access and low-cost management style. In early April 2004, just after the acquisition, Gateway announced the closing of the remainder of its retail store network, seeking to focus on third-party sales of its Gateway and eMachines product lines. Channel conflict had been a threat (what retailer would want to sell Gateway products or, perhaps, even eMachines products, when it was competing with Gateway at retail?), but the closing of the retail network eliminated this problem as well as Gateway's relatively high retailing cost structure. As a result, the company's losses narrowed in the first quarter of 2004. Gateway branded products are now sold online directly by the company and through Costco, while eMachines branded products are sold through such major retailers as Circuit City, Best Buy, and Wal-Mart in the United States, as well as overseas. The crucial role of improved channel access (combined with the need to minimize costs due to operating an expensive owned retail network) in motivating this acquisition shows that marketing channel decisions are strategically important in the overall presence and success a company enjoys in the marketplace.[16]

WHY DO MARKETING CHANNELS EXIST AND CHANGE?

The preceding examples all include intermediaries who play some role in distributing products or services, and some are examples of markets whose marketing channel activities or structures have changed over time. This raises the fundamental questions of why marketing channels exist and why they change. Why, for example, do not all manufacturers sell all products and services that they make directly to all end-users? Further, once in place, why should a marketing channel ever change or new marketing channels ever emerge?

We focus on two forces for channel development and change, demand-side and supply-side factors. Although it did not use the demand-side and supply-side terminology, Wroe Alderson's early work in this area has significantly influenced thinking on this topic, and the discussion here builds on Alderson's original framework.[17]

Demand-Side Factors

Facilitation of Search

Marketing channels containing intermediaries arise partly because they facilitate *searching*. The process of searching is characterized by uncertainty on the part of both end-users and sellers. End-users are uncertain where to find the products or services they want, while sellers are uncertain how to reach target end-users. If intermediaries did not exist, sellers without a known brand name could not generate many sales. End-users would not know whether to believe the manufacturers' claims about the nature and quality of their products. Conversely, manufacturers would not be certain that their promotional efforts were reaching the right kind of end-user.

Instead, intermediaries themselves facilitate search on both ends of the channel. For example, Cobweb Designs is a top-quality needlework design firm headquartered in Scotland. It is the sole licensee for designing needlework kits relating to the royal family, the National Trust for Scotland, the architect Charles Rennie Mackintosh, and the great socialist writer and designer William Morris. Although Cobweb's needlework kits are available at all of the National Trust for Scotland's retail outlets, as well as on the company's Web site (www.cobweb-needlework.com), its proprietor, Sally Scott Aiton, recognizes the potential untapped market for her kits outside the United Kingdom. The challenge, of course, is how to reach the large but dispersed market of potential buyers in markets like the United States. Scott Aiton therefore purposefully seeks retail placement in gift shops at major art museums and botanic gardens throughout Europe and the United States. Gaining shelf space in the gift shop of a museum like the Smithsonian Institution in Washington, D.C., or the Art Institute of Chicago would greatly enhance the company's sales reach because American consumers who do not frequently travel to the United Kingdom could still find its designs (indeed, they might become aware of the company's designs for the first time). These retailers' images facilitate the search process on the demand side: Consumers seeking museum-reproduction needlework kits know they can find them at museum shops.

Similarly, from Cobweb's point of view, museum shops have images that are consistent with the high quality of Cobweb Designs' kits and, hence, attract visitors who are likely to be in the potential target market for Cobweb's products. This virtually guarantees access to a broad base of potential viable buyers. Again, search is facilitated, this time from the manufacturing end of the channel. In short, the retailer (here, the museum shop) becomes the matchmaker that brings together buyer and seller.

Adjustment of Assortment Discrepancy

Independent intermediaries in a marketing channel perform the function of *sorting goods*. This is valuable because of the natural discrepancy between the assortment of goods and services made by a given manufacturer and the assortment demanded by the end-user. This discrepancy results because manufacturers typically produce a large quantity of a limited variety of goods, whereas consumers usually demand only a limited quantity of a wide variety of goods.

The sorting function performed by intermediaries includes the following activities:

1. *Sorting.* This involves breaking down a heterogeneous supply into separate stocks that are relatively homogeneous (e.g., a citrus packing house sorts oranges by size and grade.)
2. *Accumulation.* The intermediary brings together similar stocks from a number of sources into a larger homogeneous supply. (Wholesalers accumulate varied goods for retailers, and retailers accumulate goods for their consumers.)
3. *Allocation.* This refers to breaking down a homogeneous supply into smaller and smaller lots. (Allocating at the wholesale level is referred to as *breaking bulk.*) For example, goods received in carloads are sold in case lots. A buyer of case lots in turn sells individual units.
4. *Assorting.* This is the building up of an assortment of products for resale in association with each other. (Wholesalers build assortments of goods for retailers, and retailers build assortments for their consumers.)

In short, intermediaries help end-users consume a combination of product and channel services that are attractive to them. Intermediaries can thus be viewed as *creating utility* for the end-user. In particular, by having a product in their assortments in a certain place and at a certain time, intermediaries can create *possession*, *place*, and *time* utilities that are all valuable to the target end-user.

Supply-Side Factors

Routinization of Transactions

Each purchase transaction involves ordering of, valuation of, and payment for goods and services. The buyer and seller must agree on the amount, mode, and timing of payment. These costs of distribution can be minimized if the transactions are made routine; otherwise, every transaction is subject to bargaining, with an accompanying loss of efficiency.

Moreover, routinization leads to standardization of goods and services whose performance characteristics can be compared and assessed easily. It encourages production of items that are more highly valued. In short, routinization leads to efficiencies in the execution of channel activities. For example, *continuous replenishment programs (CRP)* are an important element of efficient channel inventory management. First created by Duane Weeks, a product manager at Procter & Gamble, in 1980 to automatically ship Pampers diapers to the warehouses of Schnuck's, a St. Louis grocer, without requiring Schnuck's managers to place orders, the system was brought to Wal-Mart in 1988 by Ralph Drayer (then P&G's vice president of customer services) and has spread since then. Under CRP, manufacturing and retailing partners share inventory and stocking information to ensure that the right array of retail products is stocked on the retail shelf and is neither understocked nor overstocked. Shipments typically increase in frequency but decrease in size. This leads to lower inventories in the system and higher turnaround, both sources of increased channel profitability. A routinized and mature relationship between channel partners is a necessity to make CRP succeed; Ralph Drayer says, "First, you have to have a trusting business relationship with your counterpart before you'll get very far in collaboration and, specifically, in establishing jointly managed processes. . . . Trust means you have a working relationship with your trading partner, where you have confidence that they will use information that is given to them and not share it with competitors."[18]

Reduction in Number of Contacts

Without channel intermediaries, every producer would have to interact with every potential buyer in order to create all possible market exchanges. As the importance of exchange increases in a society, so does the difficulty of maintaining all of these interactions. As an elementary example, a small village of only ten specialized households would require 45 transactions to carry out decentralized exchanges (i.e., exchanges at each production point: 10 times 9, divided by 2). Intermediaries reduce the complexity of this exchange system and thus facilitate transactions. With a central market consisting of one intermediary, only twenty transactions would be required to carry out centralized exchange in our village example (10 plus 10).

Implicit in the preceding example is the notion that a decentralized system of exchange is less efficient than a centralized network using intermediaries. The same rationale can be applied to direct selling from manufacturers to retailers, relative to selling through wholesalers. Consider Figure 1.1. For example, given four manufacturers and 10 retailers who buy goods from each manufacturer, the number of contact lines is 40. If the manufacturers sold to these retailers through one wholesaler, the number of necessary contacts would be reduced to 14.

The number of necessary contacts increases dramatically as more wholesalers are added, however. For example, if the four manufacturers in our example used two wholesalers instead of one, the number of contacts would rise from 14 to 28, and if the manufacturers used four wholesalers, the number of contacts would be 56. Thus, employing more and more intermediaries diminishes returns simply from the point of view of number and cost of contacts in the market.

Note that in this example we assume the cost and effectiveness of any contact—manufacturer to wholesaler, wholesaler to retailer, or manufacturer to retailer—is the same as any other contact. This is clearly not true in the real world, where selling through one type of intermediary can incur very different costs from those of selling through another. Further, not all intermediaries are equally skilled at selling or motivated to sell a particular manufacturer's product, and this certainly affects the choice of which and how many intermediaries to use. The example also assumes that each retailer contacts each of the wholesalers used by the manufacturers. If a retailer prefers some wholesalers over others, restricting the number of wholesalers used can prevent the manufacturer from reaching the market served by that retailer, suggesting the value of using multiple wholesalers.

Nevertheless, judiciously used intermediaries do, indeed, reduce the number of contacts necessary to cover a market, and this principle guides many manufacturers seeking to enter new markets without engaging in high-cost direct distribution with an employee sales force. The whole trend toward rationalizing supply chains by reducing the number of suppliers is also consistent with the concept of reducing the number of contacts in the distribution channel. It is interesting in this context, then, to ponder how manufacturers can efficiently sell their wares directly online because Internet selling implies *disintermediation* (i.e., the shedding of intermediaries rather than their use). Indeed, companies like Levi Strauss, the jeans maker, once sold direct online but discontinued doing so and now steer online shoppers to third-party retailers such as Target and Wal-Mart both for efficiency reasons and to reduce channel conflict (by not competing with their retailer partners for end-user sales). The benefits of interacting directly with one's end-users that direct selling brings (information on consumer

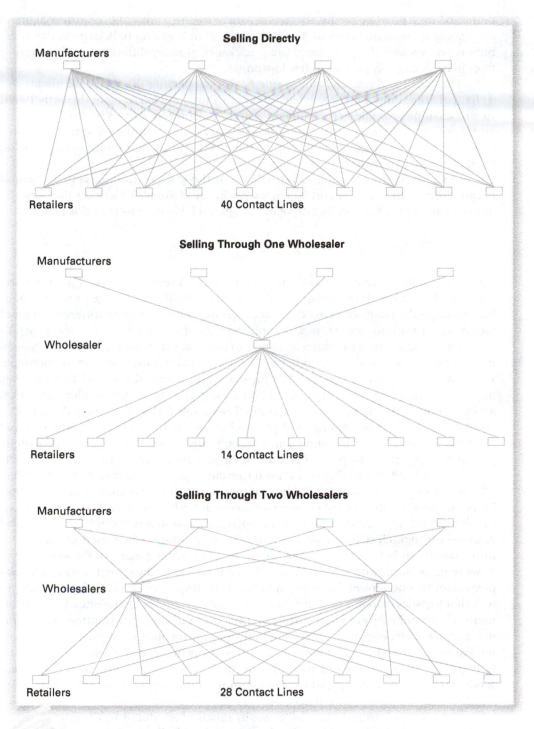

Figure 1.1 Contact costs to reach the market with and without intermediaries

demands and sources of dissatisfaction, for example) must be counterbalanced against the incremental costs of doing so (the cost of breaking bulk early in the distribution process and shipping many small packages to many different locations rather than making large shipments to few locations).

These demand-side and supply-side factors supporting the use of middlemen in a channel are exemplified in Sidebar 1.2 on the Taiwanese tea trade in the early 1900s. In this example, middlemen facilitated search, performed various sorting functions, and significantly reduced the number of necessary contacts in the channel. Their success even prevented a government-supported direct-sale auction house from surviving as an alternative route to market.

In summary, intermediaries participate in the work of the marketing channel because they both *add value* and *help reduce cost* in the channel. This raises the question of what types of work are in fact done in the channel. We turn next to this issue.

WHAT IS THE WORK OF THE MARKETING CHANNEL?

The work of the channel includes the performance of several *marketing flows*. We use the term *flows* rather than *functions* or *activities* to emphasize that these processes often flow through the channel, being done at different points in time by different channel members. In institutional settings, one often hears of the need to carry inventory, to generate demand through selling activities, to physically distribute product, to engage in after-sale service, and to extend credit to other channel members or to end-users. We formalize this list in Figure 1.2, showing eight universal channel flows as they might work in a hypothetical channel containing producers, wholesalers, retailers, and consumers. As the figure shows, some flows move forward through the channel (physical possession, ownership, and promotion), while others move up the channel from the end-user (ordering and payment). Still other flows can move in either direction or are engaged in by pairs of channel members (negotiation, financing, risking).

We have left out of Figure 1.2 an important flow that permeates all the value-added activities of the channel: the flow of *information*. Information can and does flow between every possible pair of channel members in both routine and specialized ways. Retailers share information with their manufacturing suppliers about sales trends and patterns through electronic data interchange relationships; when used properly, this information can help better manage the costs of performing many of the eight classic flows (e.g., by improving sales forecasts, the channel can reduce total costs of physical possession through lower inventory holdings). So important is the information content that logistics managers call this flow the ability to "transform inventory into information." Manufacturers share product and salesmanship information with their distributors, independent sales representatives, and retailers to improve these intermediaries' performance of the promotion flow. Consumers give preference information (when asked!) to the channel, improving the channel's ability to supply valued services. Clearly, producing and managing information well is at the core of developing distribution channel excellence.

Although we discuss channel flows in much more detail in Chapter 3, a few remarks are in order here. First, the flows presented in Figure 1.2 may be managed in different ways for different parts of a company's business. Spare-parts distribution very commonly is handled by a third-party distributor who is not involved in

Sidebar 1.2

Tea selling in Taiwan:
The key roles of tea middlemen

The Taiwanese tea industry started when tea trees were imported from China and planted in the Taiwanese hills in the mid-1800s. By the late 1920s, there were about 20,000 tea farmers in Taiwan, who sold their product (so-called *crude tea*) to one of about 280 tea middlemen, who in turn sold the tea to the 60 tea refineries located in Ta-tao-cheng on the oceanfront, ready for commercial sale and exportation. The tea middlemen journeyed into the hills of Taiwan to search for and buy tea and then bring it down to the dock areas to sell to refineries.

Tea middlemen had a bad reputation among both farmers and refineries. They were accused of exploiting the market by buying low and selling high; critics suggested that a simple direct trading system could instead be instituted to bypass the tea middlemen completely. Accordingly, the governor general of Taiwan set up a tea auction house in 1923 in Ta-tao-cheng. Farmers could ship their tea directly to the auction house, where a first-price sealed-bid auction would determine the selling price for their products to refineries. The auction house's operating costs were covered by farmers' membership fees, trading charges, and subsidies by the governor general, so that the remaining tea middlemen had to compete with the auction house. Despite this, the middlemen survived, and eventually the auction house was closed. How could this happen if, indeed, the middlemen were just exploiters of the buy-sell situation?

The answer lies in the key roles played by the Taiwanese tea middlemen. First, the middlemen *facilitated search* in the marketplace. A middleman would visit many farms, finding tea to sell—thus searching upstream for product supply. Then, the middleman would take his samples of tea to a series of refineries and ask for purchase orders. Visiting multiple refineries was necessary because the same variety and quality of tea could fetch very different prices from different refineries depending on the use to which they would put the tea. In addition, the middlemen had to repeat the search process every season because any given refinery's offer changed from season to season. The middlemen thus found both buyers for the farmers' harvest and tea supplies for the refineries.

Second, tea middlemen performed various *sorting* functions. Crude tea was a highly heterogeneous product because even the same species of tea tree was cultivated on many different farms with resulting quality variations. Further, 25 different species of tea trees grew in the Taiwanese hills. The appraisal process both at the middleman and refinery levels, therefore, required considerable skill. Refineries hired specialists to appraise the tea brought to them by middlemen. Middlemen aided in this process by *accumulating* the tea harvests of multiple farmers into homogeneous lots for sale to the refineries.

Third, tea middlemen served to *minimize the number of contacts* in the channel system. With 20,000 tea farmers and 60 refineries, up to 1,200,000 contacts would have to be made for each farmer to market his product to get the best refiner price (even if each farmer cultivated only one variety of tea tree). Instead, each farmer tended to sell to just one middleman, making for about 20,000 contacts at the farmer-to-middleman level of the channel. Thus if an average middleman collected n varieties of tea, letting each of the 280 middlemen negotiate on average middleman collected n varieties of tea, letting each of the 280 middlemen negotiate on behalf of the farmers with the 60 refineries would result in [$60 \times 280 \times n$] negotiations

(continued)

Sidebar 1.2 (cont.)

Tea selling in Taiwan: The key roles of tea middlemen

between middlemen and refineries. Then the total number of negotiations throughout the channel in the presence of intermediaries was [20,000 + 16,800 × n]. This would exceed 1,200,000 negotiations only if the number of tea varieties exceeded 70 (shown by equating [20,000 + 16,800 × n] to 1,200,000 and solving for n). However, Taiwan had only 25 tea varieties at this time, so intermediaries reduced the number of contacts from over 1 million to about 440,000.

These value-added activities were ignored in the attacks on the tea middlemen as exploiters. The resulting failure of the government-sanctioned and government-subsidized auction house suggests that, far from merely exploiting the market, tea middlemen were efficiency-enhancing market-makers. Clearly, in this situation, the intermediation of the channel through the use of tea middlemen both added value and reduced costs.[19]

the distribution of original products. For example, three manufacturers—Ingersoll-Rand International Bobcat, Clark Material Handling, and the Spicer Division of Dana Corporation—use a German third-party logistics (3PL) firm, Feige, to handle all non-U.S. distribution of spare parts. Feige simplifies the otherwise difficult job of managing spare-parts inventories to be shipped quickly to several countries using

Figure 1.2   Marketing flows in channels

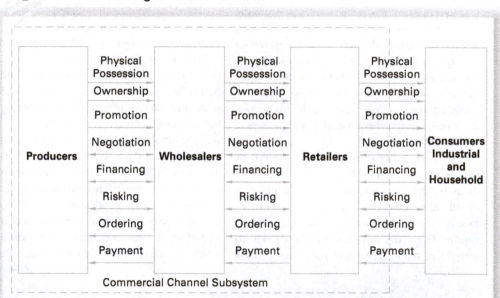

different languages. Feige not only receives, stores, and ships spare parts but also provides debt and credit accounting services and cash management for its manufacturer clients. Dealers in turn can order from Feige online and track their orders after first checking to verify that the desired parts are in stock. Feige's information technology systems produce a 95 percent in-stock result for its dealer customers. Given customers' demands for quick delivery of spare parts, using a separate intermediary to handle them efficiently is a superior strategy both from a cost-control perspective and a demand-satisfaction perspective.[20] In situations like this, the channel manager may well want to represent these two physical possession activities (original equipment versus spare parts) separately because they represent important but different flows in moving products to the market.

In addition, not every channel member need participate in every flow. Indeed, specialization in the performance of channel flows is the hallmark of an efficiently operating channel. Figure 1.2 depicts a channel where, for example, physical possession of product moves from the manufacturer to wholesalers to retailers and finally to end-users. An alternate channel might involve not stocking wholesalers but manufacturers' representatives, who generally do not participate in the physical possession or ownership flows. In short, they do not handle physical product. In such a case, the physical possession flow might be performed by the manufacturer and retailer but not by other intermediaries on its way to the end-user. In general, flows should be shared only among those channel members who can add value or reduce cost by bearing them. However, specialization increases interdependencies in channels, and thus requires close cooperation and coordination in channel operations.

It is also important to note that the performance of certain flows is correlated with that of other flows. For instance, any time inventories are held and owned by one member of the channel system, a financing operation also is underway. Thus, when a wholesaler or retailer takes title and assumes physical possession of a portion of a manufacturer's output, the intermediary is financing the manufacturer. This is consistent with the fact that the largest component of carrying cost is the cost of capital tied up when inventories are held dormant (i.e., not moving toward final sale). (Other carrying costs are obsolescence, depreciation, pilferage, breakage, storage, insurance, and taxes.) If that intermediary did not have to tie up its funds in inventory holding costs, it would instead be able to invest in other profitable opportunities. Capital costs are thus the opportunity costs of holding inventory.

The foregoing discussion suggests that given a set of flows to be undertaken in a channel, a manufacturer must either assume responsibility for all channel flows itself or shift some or all of them to the various intermediaries populating its channel. This implies an important truth about channel design and management: one can eliminate or substitute *members* in the channel, but the *flows* performed by these members cannot be eliminated. When channel members are eliminated from the channel, their flows are shifted either forward or backward in the channel and, therefore, are assumed by other channel members. The obvious reason to eliminate a channel member from a channel is that the flows performed by that channel member can be handled as effectively and at least as cheaply by other channel members. Thus, the channel manager should not expect cost savings from eliminating a channel member merely because that member's profit margin will revert to the rest of the channel but, rather, because the flows performed by that channel member will be managed more efficiently in another channel design.

WHO BELONGS TO A MARKETING CHANNEL?

The key members of a marketing channel are *manufacturers, intermediaries* (wholesale, retail, and specialized), and *end-users* (who can be business customers or consumers). The presence or absence of particular types of channel members is dictated by their ability to perform the necessary channel flows to add value to end-users. Often there is one channel member that can be considered the "channel captain." The channel captain is an organization that takes the keenest interest in the workings of the channel for this product or service and that acts as a prime mover in establishing and maintaining channel links. The channel captain is often the manufacturer of the product or service, particularly in the case of branded products. However, this is not universally true, as the following examples show.

Manufacturers

By *manufacturer* we mean the producer or originator of the product or service being sold. Frequently a distinction is drawn between branded and private-label manufacturing:

> ➤ Some manufacturers brand their products and thus are known by name to end-users even if they use intermediaries to reach those end-users. Examples include Coca-Cola, Budweiser beer (Anheuser-Busch), Mercedes-Benz, or Sony.

> ➤ Other manufacturers make products but do not invest in a branded name for them. Instead, they produce *private label* products, and the downstream buyer (either a "manufacturer" or a retailer) puts its own brand name on the products. For example, Multibar Foods, Inc., focuses on making private-label products for the neutraceuticals marketplace (health, diet, and snack bars), and its brand clients include Dr. Atkins' Nutritionals and the Quaker Oats Co. Multibar prides itself on research and development expenditures that make it valuable to the brand companies that hire it to make their products.[21] Even branded-goods manufacturers sometimes choose to allocate part of their production capacity to the production of private-label goods; in some markets, such as the United Kingdom, where private label accounts for half the goods sold in most leading supermarkets, private label is a strong option for some manufacturers.[22]

In today's retail marketplace, the ownership of the brand can belong to the manufacturer (e.g., Mercedes-Benz) or to the retailer (e.g., Arizona clothing at J. C. Penney). Indeed, the retailer may even *be* the brand (e.g., The Gap).

A manufacturer can be the originator of a service as well as the manufacturer of a product; for example, tax preparation services like H&R Block (a franchiser) or insurance companies like State Farm or Allstate. No physical product is sold to the end-user. The manufacturer in these cases creates a family of services to sell (tax preparation services and financial management services in the case of H&R Block, and life, health, disability, medical, and other insurance products in the case of the insurance companies), which is its "manufacturing" function. Its marketing channel functions typically focus on promotional and risking activities: H&R Block promotes its services in the United States, Canada, Australia, and the United Kingdom on behalf of itself and its franchisees and guarantees to find the maximum tax refund allowed by law or the client's tax return is free. In the case of an insurance company, again because physical product handling is not a major issue, some of the key channel flows are promotion (on behalf of its independent agents in the marketplace) and risking (due to the specific nature of the product, risk management is at the heart of the insurance business). The absence of a physical product to move through the channel thus does not mean that a services company has no channel design or management issues!

These examples also suggest that the manufacturer need not be the channel captain. For manufacturer branded and produced goods like Mercedes-Benz automobiles, the manufacturer is the channel captain; its ability and desire to proactively manage channel efforts for its products is intimately tied to its investment in brand equity for those products. But a private-label apparel or neutraceuticals manufacturer like those already described does not own the brand name in the end-user's eyes; another channel member (in these cases, the retailer) does.

The manufacturer's ability to manage a production operation does not always extend to a superior ability to manage other channel flows. An apparel manufacturer certainly need not be a retailing or logistics expert; Ingersoll-Rand International Bobcat is clearly less competent at managing spare-parts distribution outside the United States than is Feige, its channel partner. This reinforces the notion that intermediaries add value to the channel through their superior performance of certain channel flows and that manufacturers voluntarily seek out such intermediaries to increase their reach in the end-user market.

All of the physical product manufacturers are involved in physical possession and ownership flows until the product leaves their manufacturing sites and travels to the next channel member's site. Manufacturers also engage in negotiation with the buyers of their products to set terms of sale and merchandising of the product. The manufacturer of a branded good also participates significantly in the promotion flow for its product.

Intermediaries

The term *intermediary* refers to any channel member other than the manufacturer or the end-user (individual consumer or business buyer). We differentiate among three types of intermediaries: wholesale, retail, and specialized.

Wholesale intermediaries include merchant wholesalers or distributors, manufacturers' representatives, agents, and brokers. A wholesaler sells to other channel intermediaries, such as retailers, or to business end-users but not to individual consumer end-users. Merchant wholesalers take both title to and physical possession of inventory, store inventory (frequently of many manufacturers), promote the products in their line, and arrange for financing, ordering, and payment with their customers. They make their profit by buying at a wholesale price and selling at a marked-up price to their downstream customers, pocketing the difference between the two prices (of course, net of any distribution costs they bear). Manufacturers' representatives, agents, and brokers typically do not take title to or physical possession of the goods they sell. The major flows in which they take part are promotion and negotiation in that they work on selling the products of the manufacturers they represent and negotiating terms of trade. Some of these intermediaries (such as trading companies or import-export agents) specialize in international selling, whether or not they take on title and physical possession flows. Chapters 12 and 14 focus in depth on these intermediaries' roles in logistics and wholesaling activities.

Retail intermediaries assume many forms today, including department stores, mass merchandisers, hypermarkets, specialty stores, category killers, convenience stores, franchises, buying clubs, warehouse clubs, catalogers, and online retailers. Unlike purely wholesale intermediaries, they sell directly to individual consumer end-users. Although their role historically has focused on amassing an assortment of goods that is appealing to their consumer end-users, the role of today's retailers often goes much farther. As discussed above, they may contract for private label goods, effectively vertically integrating upstream in the supply chain. They may sell to buyers other than consumer end-users: Some "retailers," such as Office Depot, have very significant sales to businesses (in the case of Office Depot, about one-third of its sales are to businesses, not consumer end-users), although their storefronts nominally identify them as retailers. Office Depot's Business Services Group has more than 60 local sales offices in the United States, 22 domestic delivery centers, 13 regional call centers, more than 1,200 trucks, 1,500 drivers, and 1,400 account managers, and it sells to businesses through contracts, direct mail, and the Internet. The company offers these business-to-business sales services in the United Kingdom, the Netherlands, Japan, France, Ireland, Germany, Italy, and Belgium as well.[23] Chapter 11 discusses retailing in depth, and Chapter 13 discusses franchising.

Specialized intermediaries are brought into a channel to perform a specific flow and typically are not heavily involved in the core business represented by the product sold. These intermediaries include insurance companies, finance companies, credit card companies (all involved in the financing flow), advertising agencies (participating in the promotion flow), logistics and shipping firms (participating in the physical possession flow), information technology firms (who may participate in ordering or payment flows), and marketing research firms (generating marketing intelligence that can be useful for the performance of any of the flows).

End-Users

Finally, end-users (either business customers or individual consumers) are themselves channel members. We classify consumers as marketing channel members because they can and frequently do perform channel flows, just as other channel members do. Consumers who shop at a hypermarket like Costco, Sam's Club, or Carrefour and stock up on paper towels are performing physical possession, ownership, and financing flows because they are buying a much larger volume of product than they will use in the near future. They pay for the paper towels before they use them, thus injecting cash into the channel and performing a financing flow. They store the paper towels in their house, lessening the need for warehouse space at the retailer and thus taking on part of the physical possession flow. They bear all the costs of ownership as well, including pilferage, spoilage, and so forth. Naturally, consumers expect a price cut when they shop at such a store to compensate for the channel flow costs they bear when buying through this channel relative to buying a single package of paper towels at the local grocer.

Channel Formats as Combinations of Channel Members

The various channel participants can combine in many ways to create effective marketing channels. The range and number of channel members are affected by the nature of demand by end-users, and the captaincy of the channel can vary from situation to situation. Appendix 1A summarizes different possibilities for channel formats that are manufacturer-based, retailer-based, service-provider-based, and others.

A FRAMEWORK FOR CHANNEL ANALYSIS

Now that we have established what a marketing channel is, how it can be organized and why it includes intermediaries, and who can be its members, we need to ask how we can use this knowledge to do a better job of designing and managing marketing channels. Channel managers need a comprehensive framework for analysis to guide them through both the initial design of the channel and its ongoing management over time. Without such a framework, they may ignore important elements of the design or management processes, resulting in inappropriately constructed or managed channels. The concept of interdependence is critical in this regard. Because of the extreme interdependence of all channel members and the value of specialization in channels, attention must be paid to all the design and management elements to ensure a well-working marketing channel. For instance, even the best-designed channel is completely unproductive if the retailer neglects to stock product on the retail shelf. Consumers will not buy what they cannot see in the store!

The marketing channel challenge involves two major processes: (1) designing the right channel, and (2) implementing that design. The *design* process involves segmenting the market, choosing which segment(s) to target, and producing channel service outputs for the target end-users in the most efficient way possible. The efficiency imperative implies a need to understand what the work of the channel is, in order to choose the kinds of intermediaries to include in the channel, their specific identities, and their number and to allocate the work of the channel optimally among them. In short, the design process implies the need to match the demand and supply sides of the channel to meet target end-users' demands at the minimum possible cost. Because a preexisting channel may already be in place, the design process also allows for an examination of the gaps that may exist in current channel operations and suggestions for their control or elimination. The *implementation* process requires an understanding of each channel member's sources of power and dependence, an understanding of the potential for channel conflict, and a resulting plan for creating an environment where the optimal channel design can be effectively executed on an ongoing basis. This outcome is called channel coordination.

Figure 1.3 depicts the channel design and implementation framework. The framework is useful both for creating a new channel in a previously untapped market and for critically analyzing and refining a preexisting channel. The rest of this book is organized around that framework.

Channel Design: Segmentation

One of the fundamental principles of marketing is the *segmentation* of the market. Segmentation means the splitting of a market into groups of end-users who are (a) maximally similar within each group, and (b) maximally different between groups. But maximally similar or maximally different based on what criterion? For the channel manager, segments are best defined *on the basis of demands for the outputs of the marketing channel*. A marketing channel is more than just a conduit for product; it is also a means of adding value to the product marketed through it. In this sense, the marketing channel can be viewed as another production line engaged in producing not the actual product that is sold but the ancillary services that define *how* the product is sold. These value-added services created by channel members and consumed by

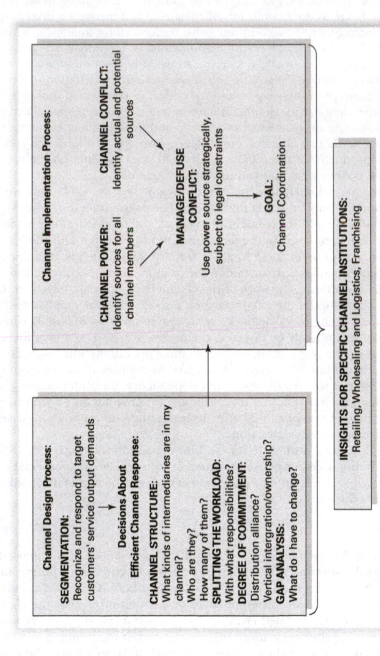

Channel Design Process:

SEGMENTATION:
Recognize and respond to target customers' service output demands

↓

Decisions About Efficient Channel Response:

CHANNEL STRUCTURE:
What kinds of intermediaries are in my channel?
Who are they?
How many of them?
SPLITTING THE WORKLOAD:
With what responsibilities?
DEGREE OF COMMITMENT:
Distribution alliance?
Vertical intergration/ownership?
GAP ANALYSIS:
What do I have to change?

Channel Implementation Process:

CHANNEL CONFLICT:
Identify actual and potential sources

CHANNEL POWER:
Identify sources for all channel members

↘ ↙

MANAGE/DEFUSE CONFLICT:
Use power source strategically, subject to legal constraints

↓

GOAL:
Channel Coordination

INSIGHTS FOR SPECIFIC CHANNEL INSTITUTIONS:
Retailing, Wholesaling and Logistics, Franchising

Figure I.3 Framework for channel design and implementation

end-users along with the product purchased are called service outputs.[24] Service outputs include (but may not be limited to) *bulk-breaking, spatial convenience, waiting and delivery time, assortment and variety, customer service,* and *product/market/usage information provision.*

End-users (be they final consumers or business buyers) have varying demands for these service outputs. Consider, for example, two different buyers of books: consumers browsing for some entertaining best-sellers to take on an upcoming vacation and students buying textbooks for college. Table 1.1 outlines the differences in service output demands between the two segments of buyers. The vacationers highly value a broad assortment of books from which to choose, in-store amenities like a coffee bar, and salesperson advice. But they do not care as intensely about bulk-breaking (because they intend to buy several books), can easily shop among bookstores, and have some time before vacation begins and thus are willing to wait to get some good books. The student textbook buyers have almost the opposite demands for service outputs of the retail book channel: They want just one textbook per class, cannot travel far to get it, and need it virtually immediately. On the other hand, the students do not value the ability to browse (because the professor has dictated the book to be bought) and, therefore, do not need information about what book to buy; nor do they need customer service or in-store amenities while shopping.

Clearly, a different marketing channel meets the needs of these two segments of shoppers. The vacationers will be well satisfied shopping at a large, well-stocked bookstore somewhere in town, such as a Border's or a Barnes & Noble bookstore. The students will favor the university bookstore close to campus that caters to student book needs. Interestingly, a subsegment of college students with less intense demands for quick delivery (perhaps because they plan ahead or know their reading lists in advance) increasingly chooses to buy textbooks from online booksellers. These booksellers deliver to the student's home or college residence (thus providing an extremely high level of spatial convenience), can do so in less than a week (thus providing a moderate, if not high, level of quick delivery), and can deliver the exact number and titles of books the student needs (thus satisfying demands for bulk-breaking and assortment and variety). They may not excel in customer service or information provision, but because the college student does not intensely demand these services, their absence is not missed. Note that the vacationer, who highly values in-store customer service and information provision, might not find the online bookstore as satisfying as a bricks-and-mortar shop (although amazon.com seeks to counteract the information provision problem by providing inside looks at many of its books online, so that the buyer can resolve uncertainty about the book's contents before purchasing it).

This example shows how different segments of end-users can demand the same type of product with widely varying sets of service outputs, resulting in very different product-plus-service-output bundles. An analysis of service output demands by segment is thus an important input into a manufacturer's marketing plan and can help increase the reach and marketability of a good product to multiple market segments.

Consumer analysis for marketing channel design is the topic of Chapter 2.

Channel Design: Channel Structure Decisions

Knowing the intensity of demands for service outputs by different segments in the market, the channel analyst can identify the most efficient and effective channel structure to satisfy these demands. A different channel may (indeed, probably will) be

Table 1.1 Service output demand differences

An example of segmentation in the book-buying market

	Browser Buying Best-Sellers to Take on Vacation		Student Buying Textbooks for Fall Semester at College	
	Descriptor	Service Output Demand Level	Descriptor	Service Output Demand Level
Bulk-breaking	"I'm looking for some 'good read' paperbacks to enjoy."	Medium	"I only need one copy of my marketing textbook!"	High
Spatial convenience	"I have lots of errands to run before leaving town, so I'll be going past several bookstores."	Medium	"I don't have a car, so I can't travel far to buy."	High
Waiting and delivery time	"I'm not worried about getting the books now.... I can even pick up a few when I'm out of town if need be."	Low	"I just got to campus, but classes are starting tomorrow and I'll need my books by then."	High
Assortment and variety	"I want the best choice available, so that I can pick what looks good!"	High	"I'm just buying what's on my course reading list."	Low
Customer service	"I like to stop for a coffee when book browsing."	High	"I can find books myself, and don't need any special help."	Low
Information provision	"I value the opinions of a well-read bookstore employee; I can't always tell a good book from a bad one before I buy."	High	"My professors have already decided what I'll read this semester."	Low

required by each segment's set of service output demands, and this channel's design involves three main elements. First, the channel designer must decide who are to be the members of the channel. For example, will an ethnic food manufacturer sell its grocery products through small independent retailers with in-city locations or through large chain stores that operate discount warehouse stores? Or will it use an outlet such as EthnicGrocer.com, an online seller of ethnic foods and products from various countries that operates no retail stores at all? Moving up the channel from the retail level, the channel designer must decide whether to use independent distributors, independent sales representative companies (called reps or rep firms), independent trucking companies, financing companies, export management companies, and any of a whole host of other possible independent distribution channel members that could be incorporated into the channel design.

A second element of channel design is deciding the exact identity of the channel partner to use at each channel level. For example, if it is advisable to sell a line of fine watches through retail stores, should the manufacturer choose more upscale outlets, such as Tiffany's, or family-owned local jewelers? The choice can have implications both for the efficiency with which the channel is run and the image connoted by distributing through a particular kind of retailer. In a different context, if a company seeks distribution for its products in a foreign market, the key decision may be which distributor is appointed to carry the product line into the overseas market. The right distributor may have much better relationships with local channel partners in the target market and can significantly affect the success of the foreign market entry.

Third, the channel manager must decide how many of each type of channel member to include in the channel. This is the channel intensity decision. In particular, should the channel for a consumer good include many retail outlets (intensive distribution), just a few (selective distribution), or only one (exclusive distribution) in a given market area? The answer to this question depends both on efficiency and on implementation factors. More intensive distribution may make the product more easily available to all target end-users but may create conflict among the retailers competing to sell it.

The questions of what kinds of intermediaries to use, their exact identities, and the intensity of distribution in the channel are dealt with in Chapter 4.

Channel Design: Splitting the Workload

The optimal channel is determined by the channel flows that must be performed to satisfy the specific target segment's service output demands. Channel flows include all the activities of the channel that add value to the end-user. In enumerating channel flows, we go beyond the concept of the mere handling of the product to include issues of promotion, negotiation, financing, ordering, payment, and the like (see Figure 1.2). For instance, our college student looking for textbooks (see Table 1.1) has a high demand for spatial convenience and a minimal tolerance for out-of-stock product. This means that the physical-possession channel flow (the physical holding of inventory, in particular at the college retail bookstore) takes on great importance for such end-users. Each product or service selling situation can have its own unique set of service output demands for each segment, implying that the differential importance of different sets of channel flows depends on the segment.

The type, identity, and intensity of channel members should be decided keeping in mind the goal of minimizing channel flow costs. That is, each channel member is assigned a set of channel flows, and ideally the allocation of activities results in the reliable performance of all channel flows at minimum total cost. This is a nontrivial task, particularly because it involves comparing activities across different member companies in the channel. Intuitively, an activity-based costing (or ABC) analysis is useful to establish the best allocation of channel flows.[25]

The issue of how to distribute the channel's workload, building on a discussion of channel flows, is the topic of Chapter 3.

Channel Design: Degree of Commitment

Even after the identities of channel members and their roles and responsibilities are defined in a channel structure, a question remains concerning channel structure: How deeply committed to this channel of distribution should the channel members be? At one end of the spectrum, channel members can engage in distribution-related transactions without any commitment at all to each other. Such relationships are inherently transactional rather than being built on a strong underlying commitment between parties. There is no guarantee that a company's supplier (or buyer) in a transactional channel will continue to do business with that company in the future, and it is similarly easy for the company in question to find a different source of supply or downstream market for its goods or services.

An intermediate step that involves more commitment between channel members is the creation of a distribution alliance. In such a situation, the channel members involved typically have an enduring set of connections that can span multiple functions throughout the companies. As a result, a well-working alliance is characterized by partners that act according to a single, overarching interest rather than merely following their own individualized goals. Such committed partners may make seemingly irrational short-term sacrifices that in fact improve the long-term viability and success of the distribution alliance.

At the other end of the commitment spectrum is the choice to vertically integrate, or own, strategic distribution functions, resources, and entities. Vertical integration is essentially the "make" choice in the "make versus buy" decision that is frequently discussed in business strategy circles. Manufacturers may decide to vertically integrate forward into wholesaling and/or retailing when other options do not exist (e.g., the best local distributor is in an exclusive marketing relationship with one's competitor); when the manufacturer can perform the wholesaling and/or retailing functions as efficiently as an independent channel partner could; or when the independent channel partner is not sufficiently committed to the channel relationship to guarantee adequate performance of its designated channel flows and functions. Important to the channel structure concept is the insight that a channel manager can choose to vertically integrate *some*, but not *all*, channel functions and flows into its organization. Vertical integration is, therefore, a matter of degree in channel structure.

Distribution alliances are discussed in more depth in Chapter 8, and vertical integration of channel functions or of the entire channel is the topic of Chapter 9.

Channel Design: Gap Analysis

At this stage of the analysis, the channel manager is equipped to decide what segments to target. This also means that the channel manager is now equipped to decide what segments *not* to target! Knowing what segments to ignore in one's channel design and management efforts is very important because it keeps the channel focused on the key segments from which it plans to reap profitable sales.

Why not target *all* the segments identified in the segmentation analysis? The answer requires the channel manager to consider the channel's internal and external environments. Internally, *managerial bounds* may constrain the channel manager from implementing the optimal channel (e.g., top management of a manufacturing firm may be unwilling to allocate funds to build a series of regional warehouses that would be necessary to provide spatial convenience in a particular market situation). Externally, both *environmental bounds* and *competitive benchmarks* may suggest some segments as higher priority than others. For example, legal practices can constrain channel design and, hence, targeting decisions. To protect small shopkeepers whose sales would be threatened by larger retailers, many countries restrict the opening of large mass-merchandise stores in urban areas.[26] Such legal restrictions can lead to a channel design that does not appropriately meet the target segment's service output demands and may cause a channel manager to avoid targeting that segment entirely.

Knowing the optimal channel to reach each targeted segment and the bounds that might prevent implementing that optimal channel design, the channel manager is free to establish the best possible channel design if no channel for this segment currently exists. If a channel already exists in the market, however, the channel manager should now perform a *gap analysis*. The differences between the optimal and actual channels constitute gaps in the channel design. Gaps can exist on the demand side or the supply side.

On the demand side, gaps mean that at least one of the service output demands is not being appropriately met by the channel. The service output in question may be either undersupplied or oversupplied. The problem is obvious in the case of undersupply: members of the target segment are likely to be dissatisfied because they want more service than they are getting. The problem is more subtle in the case of oversupply. Here, target end-users are getting all the service they desire—and then some. The problem is that service is costly to supply, and therefore, supplying too much of it leads to higher prices than the target end-users are likely to be willing to pay. Clearly, more than one service output may be a problem, in which case several gaps may need attention.

On the supply side, gaps mean that at least one flow in the channel of distribution is carried out at too high a cost. This not only lowers channel profit margins but can result in higher prices than the target market is willing to pay, leading to reduced sales and market share. Supply-side gaps can result from a lack of up-to-date expertise in channel flow management or simply from waste in the channel. The challenge in closing a supply-side gap is to reduce cost without dangerously reducing the service outputs being supplied to target end-users.

When gaps are identified on the demand or supply sides, several strategies are available for closing the gaps. Once a channel is in place, however, closing these gaps may be very difficult and costly. This suggests the strategic importance of initial channel design. If the channel is initially designed in a haphazard manner, channel members may have to live with a suboptimal channel later on, even after recognizing channel gaps and making their best efforts to close them.

We discuss the gap analysis and mechanisms for closing gaps in more depth in Chapter 5.

Channel Implementation: Identifying Power Sources

Assuming that a good channel design is in place in the market, the channel manager's job is still not done. The channel members now must *implement* the optimal channel design and, indeed, must continue to implement an optimal design through time. The value of doing so might seem self-evident, but remember that a channel is made up of multiple entities (companies, agents, individuals) who are interdependent but who may or may not all have the same incentives to implement the optimal channel design.

Incompatible incentives among channel members would not be a problem if the members were not dependent upon each other. But by the very nature of the distribution channel structure and design, specific channel members are likely to *specialize* in particular activities and flows in the channel. If all channel members do not perform appropriately, the entire channel effort suffers. For example, even if everything else is in place, a poorly performing transportation system that results in late deliveries (or no deliveries) of product to retail stores prevents the channel from succeeding in selling the product. The same type of statement could be made about the performance of any channel member managing any of the flows in the channel. Thus, it is apparent that inducing *all* of the channel members to implement the channel design appropriately is critical.

How, then, can a channel captain implement the optimal channel design in the face of interdependence among channel partners, not all of whom have the incentive to cooperate in the performance of their designated channel flows? The answer lies in the possession and use of *channel power*. A channel member's power "is its ability to control the decision variables in the marketing strategy of another member in a given channel at a different level of distribution."[27] These sources of channel power can, of course, be used to further one channel member's individual ends. If channel power is used instead to influence channel members to do their jobs as the optimal channel design specifies, the result will be a channel that more accurately delivers demanded service outputs at a lower cost.

Chapter 6 develops the concept of power in depth.

Channel Implementation: Identifying Channel Conflicts

Channel conflict is generated when one channel member's actions prevent the channel from achieving its goals. Channel conflict is both common and dangerous to the success of distribution efforts. Given the interdependence of all channel members, any one member's actions influence the overall success of the channel effort and thus can harm total channel performance.[28]

Channel conflict can stem from differences between channel members' goals and objectives (*goal conflict*), from disagreements over the domain of action and responsibility in the channel (*domain conflict*), and from differences in perceptions of the marketplace (*perceptual conflict*). These conflicts directly cause a channel member to fail to perform the flow tasks that the optimal channel design specifies for them and, thus, inhibit total channel performance. The management problem is twofold. First, the channel manager must be able to *identify* the sources of channel conflict and, in particular, to differentiate between poor channel design (which can, of course, also inhibit channel performance) and poor performance due to channel conflict. Second, the channel manager must decide what (if any) action to take to manage and reduce those channel conflicts.

In general, channel conflicts are reduced by applying one or more sources of channel power. For example, a manufacturer may identify a conflict in its independent-distributor channel; the distributorship is exerting too little sales effort on behalf of the manufacturer's product line and, therefore, sales of the product are suffering. Analysis might reveal that the effort level is low because the distributorship makes more profit selling a competitor's product than selling this manufacturer's product. Thus, there is a *goal* conflict. The manufacturer's goal is the maximization of profit over its own product line, but the distributorship's goal is the maximization of profit over *all* of the products that it sells—only some of which come from this particular manufacturer. To resolve the goal conflict, the manufacturer might use some of its power to reward the distributor by increasing the distributor's discount, thus increasing the distributor's profit margin on the manufacturer's product line. Or the manufacturer may invest in developing brand equity and thus pull the product through the channel. In that case, its brand power will induce the distributor to sell the product more aggressively because the sales potential for the product has risen. In both cases, some sort of leverage or power on the part of the manufacturer is necessary to change the distributor's behavior and thus reduce the channel conflict.

Channel conflict is discussed in detail in Chapter 7.

Channel Implementation: The Goal of Channel Coordination

After following the framework for channel design and implementation in Figure 1.3, the channel will have been designed with target end-user segments' service output demands in mind, and channel power will be applied appropriately to ensure the smooth implementation of the optimal channel design. When the disparate members of the channel are brought together to advance the goals of the channel rather than their own independent (and likely conflicting) goals, the channel is said to be *coordinated*. This term is used to denote both the coordination of interests and actions among the channel members who produce the outputs of the marketing channel and the coordination of performance of channel flows with the production of the service outputs demanded by target end-users. This is the end goal of the entire channel management process. As conditions change in the marketplace, the channel's design and implementation may need to respond; thus, channel coordination is not a one-time achievement but an ongoing process of analysis and response to the market, the competition, and the abilities of the members of the channel.

Channel Design and Implementation: Insights for Specific Channel Institutions

Our framework for channel design and implementation unites the activities and efficiencies of multiple companies and entities in a holistic approach to satisfying end-users' demands for the services of the channel along with the products they buy. It is also instructive to consider individual channel members and their institutions because they play important roles in their own right in the economy as well as in the channels in which they take part. Retailing is the connecting point between the channel and the end-user, and the multiplicity of retailing modes in today's world market is testimony to the many different segments of end-users seeking different concatenations of service outputs. Wholesaling is distribution's "back room," moving and holding product both efficiently (i.e., to minimize cost) and effectively (i.e., to create spatial convenience and

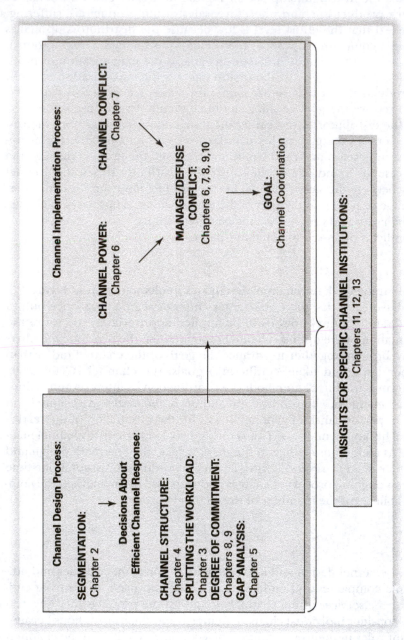

Channel Design Process:

SEGMENTATION:
Chapter 2

Decisions About
Efficient Channel Response:

CHANNEL STRUCTURE:
Chapter 4
SPLITTING THE WORKLOAD:
Chapter 3
DEGREE OF COMMITMENT:
Chapters 8, 9
GAP ANALYSIS:
Chapter 5

Channel Implementation Process:

CHANNEL POWER:
Chapter 6

CHANNEL CONFLICT:
Chapter 7

**MANAGE/DEFUSE
CONFLICT:**
Chapters 6, 7, 8, 9, 10

GOAL:
Channel Coordination

INSIGHTS FOR SPECIFIC CHANNEL INSTITUTIONS:
Chapters 11, 12, 13

Figure I.4 Organization of the text

quick delivery for target end-user segments). Logistics firms are specialists that coordinate the activities of the marketing channel (and frequently participate in some key activities themselves, as FedEx does in package shipping). Supply chain issues involve looking *upstream* toward vendors, not just downstream toward end-users, in an effort to improve service and efficiency throughout the entire chain from raw material to end-user product consumption. Finally, franchising is an important worldwide method of selling that allows small businesspeople to operate retail product and service outlets with the benefits of a large-scale parent company's (the franchiser's) knowledge, strategy, and tactical guidance.

We discuss these channel institutions in Chapters 11, 12, 13, and 14.

ORGANIZATION OF THE TEXT

The organization of the text is summarized in Figure 1.4, which restates Figure 1.3 with annotations for chapters dealing with each element of channel management. Chapters 2 through 5 lay out the basic framework for the channel design process; Chapters 6 and 7 discuss channel power and conflict. Chapters 8 and 9 focus on channel structures that represent different levels of commitment—alliances and vertical integration—and show how they imply varying channel structures as well as varying tools for managing and defusing channel conflict. Chapter 10 focuses on legal factors that influence implementation of channel designs. Finally, Chapters 11 through 13 apply the channel analytic framework to an understanding of important institutions in marketing channels, including retailing, wholesaling and logistics, and franchising.

Throughout we provide tools for analysis of the channel to guide the student or channel manager in the channel management process. After studying the book, the reader will have a firm grasp both of the necessary elements of channel analysis and management and of the specific institutions that comprise marketing channels in today's worldwide marketplace.

SUMMARY

In this introductory chapter, we define the concept of a marketing channel and explain why channels exist. The chapter explains how channels work and what functions and activities are performed inside a channel. The manufacturer and intermediaries between it and the end-user share the work of the channel, sometimes specializing in the performance of certain channel flows to which they are uniquely suited. The chapter uses these building-block concepts to develop an analytic framework for channel design, modification, and implementation that we follow throughout this book.

The framework, summarized in Figure 1.3, encompasses all of the elements necessary for effective channel management: an analysis of demand factors in the marketplace and their importance for distribution channel design; the responsive design process that characterizes the optimal distribution channel to reach target segments of end-users; the recognition that preexisting channels may exhibit gaps on either the demand side or the supply side that may be closed, subject to bounds on channel activities; and the issues surrounding effective implementation of the optimal channel design.

The discussion in this chapter suggests that all of these analytic elements are important in generating a well-designed and well-working marketing channel. None of the elements can be safely ignored. Ignoring the segmented nature of demands for service outputs leaves the channel manager with no guidelines for optimal channel design. Ignoring the costs of channel flows leads to channels that operate at too high a cost. Failing to close demand-side or supply-side gaps leaves the channel open to competitive challenges. And failing to recognize the threats of channel conflict or the leverage that channel power confers on the channel manager can leave a well-designed channel open to poor performance in the marketplace because of improper implementation of the design. In contrast, being aware of these elements can give the channel manager a checklist to evaluate points of challenge or weakness in the channel system and, thus, a guide for strategies to improve performance and avoid failure. In short, although good channel performance is not the only necessary condition for a successful marketing strategy, poor channel performance guarantees less than optimal strategic outcomes for the product and its manufacturer.

Take-Aways

- A marketing channel is a set of interdependent organizations involved in the process of making a product or service available for use or consumption.
- Both demand-side and supply-side factors affect the development of channels and provide reasons to change channels through time.
  - Demand-side factors include:
    - Facilitation of search
    - Adjustment of assortment discrepancy
  - Supply-side factors include:
    - Routinization of transactions
    - Reduction in number of contacts
- Marketing flows are the elements of work that are done by members of the marketing channel. Eight universal channel flows are:
  - Physical possession
  - Ownership
  - Promotion
  - Negotiation
  - Financing
  - Risking
  - Ordering
  - Payment
  - Information, not listed as one of the eight universal flows, nevertheless permeates the entire channel's efficiency and affects the ways in which the eight flows are performed and by whom.
- A channel member can be eliminated from a channel, but the flows performed by that member typically cannot be eliminated; thus, before eliminating a

channel member, the channel manager should consider the cost of replacing the performance of that member's channel flows.

- The key members of marketing channels are manufacturers, intermediaries (wholesale, retail, and specialized), and end-users (whether business customers or consumers).
- A framework for analysis of (a) channel design and (b) channel implementation is crucial to help the channel manager create effective (i.e., demand-satisfying) and efficient (i.e., cost-effective) routes to market, whose members continue to be willing to perform the channel flows designed for them to perform through time. Figures 1.3 and 1.4 provide the framework around which the rest of the book's analysis is centered.
- The goal of the channel manager is to achieve *channel coordination*, a state where channel members act to further the goals of the channel, rather than their own independent goals.

DISCUSSION QUESTIONS

1. The marketing channel for Mary Kay Cosmetics is called a direct selling channel. The company uses a sales force of over 1,000,000 Independent Beauty Consultants around the world. These consultants are not employees of Mary Kay Corporation; they buy cosmetics from the company at a wholesale price and sell to end-users at a retail price. They maintain personal relationships with their end-user consumers and deliver product to them after it is ordered; it is a high-service purchasing relationship from the consumer's point of view. Consultants thus act as both distributors and retailers.
   a. To what extent does an Independent Beauty Consultant participate in the eight universal marketing flows?
   b. How might these flows be shifted, either among the members now in the channel or to different agencies or institutions not presently included? What do you think would be the implications of such shifts? (Think about how cosmetics are sold through department stores or through drugstore chains, for example.)
   c. Within each of these distribution systems, specify the consumer's role from a flow-absorption perspective. Contrast this with the consumer's role when buying cosmetics from a department store or a drugstore chain.
2. Should advertising agencies and financial institutions be considered channel members? Why? Why not? Is it more useful from a managerial perspective to think of consumers as members of the channel or as end-users consuming the services of the channel?
3. According to Alderson, "the number of intervening marketing agencies tends to go up as distance increases." Distance, in his conception, is measured in terms of "the time and cost involved in communication and transportation." What factors, then, would tend to increase (or decrease) distance? What is the impact of the Web and marketing in cyberspace on "distance" as discussed by Alderson?
4. Why is it that "small, medium, and large" is not as strong a segmentation scheme for service outputs as it might be for product attributes? Use a business-to-business product or market in your answer; for example, steel, semiconductors, fax machines sold to sheet metal fabricators, computer companies, or insurance agents.

5. Explain how the shopping characteristics for the following consumer and industrial goods affect the channels for them:

CONSUMER GOODS	INDUSTRIAL GOODS
Bread	Computer printer ink cartridges
Breakfast cereal	Uranium (for nuclear power plants)
Women's hats	Cement
Refrigerators	Data-processing equipment

6. Describe how the necessary channel flow performance differs when selling and servicing an ultrasound machine (a piece of medical equipment) when targeting two different segments of buyers: (a) a hospital emergency room and (b) an academic medical researcher on a tight government-funded budget using the machine for laboratory research.

7. Should a channel manager always seek to target the maximum possible number of segments to sell to? Why or why not?

8. The service on high-end automobiles is of very good quality: timely and done by polite and competent professionals at service facilities that give the auto owner access to many amenities (free refreshments, free loaner cars, etc.). In what sense can there be a demand-side gap in this service channel?

9. Explain how not keeping up with advances in distribution channel technology (e.g., information technology advances, warehouse management techniques, database management tools, etc.) can cause an otherwise well-working channel to develop a supply-side gap.

10. Why is it important to understand channel power sources and channel conflict sources? Why can we not simply design a zero-based channel and be done with the channel analysis process?

ENDNOTES

1. Conlon, Edward, Sarv Devaraj, and Khalil F. Matta (2001), "The Relationship Between Initial Quality Perceptions and Maintenance Behavior: The Case of the Automotive Industry," *Management Science* 47, no. 9 (September), pp. 1191–1202.

2. See Wise, Richard and Peter Baumgartner (1999), "Go Downstream: The New Profit Imperative in Manufacturing," *Harvard Business Review*, September–October, pp. 133–141, for a comprehensive discussion of this.

3. investor.anntaylor.com/letter.cfm (accessed August 2005) is a company profile on the Ann Taylor Web site's "Investor Relations" page, profiling the Ann Taylor and Ann Taylor Loft store concepts and consumer targets.

4. See www.tommy.com (accessed August 2005).

5. See stores.polo.com/locator/featured.asp (accessed August 2005).

6. See www.tommy.com (accessed August 2005).

7. See stores.polo.com/locator/outlet.asp (accessed August 2005).

8. Jones Apparel Group 2003 Annual Report, available at www.jny.com (accessed August 2005).

9. Coughlan, Anne T. and David A. Soberman (2004), "A Survey of Outlet Mall Retailing, Past, Present, and Future," working paper, Northwestern University, April; *Focus Japan* (1999), "New Retail Centers Boom Despite Slump" 26, no. 6 (July–August), pp. 3–5; Thomson, Simon (2002), "Outlet Malls on the Horizon: A View from the Middle East," *Real Estate Issues* 27, no. 3–4 (Fall), pp. 102–106.

10. Troy, Mike (2003), "Study: Top 10 Own 70% of Apparel Biz," *DSN Retailing Today* 42, no. 20 (October 27), pp. 6, 66. See also "Looking at 2004: Mass Takes More Share," *DSN Retailing Today* 42, no. 22 (November 24, 2003), p. 16.

11. McKinley, Ed (2004), "Study: Off-Mall Sales Increasing at Expense of Malls," *Stores* 86, no. 1 (January), p. 141; Stringer, Kortney (2004), "Abandoning the Mall: To Attract Busy Customers, Department-Store Chains Open Stand-Alone Outposts," *Wall Street Journal*, March 24, p. B1.

12. "Amazon.com Extends E-Commerce Agreement with Borders Group," Borders Group, Inc., press release, November 13, 2003, available at phx.corporate-ir.net/phoenix.zhtml?c=65380&p=irol-news (accessed August 2005).

13. www.bn.com (accessed August 2005).

14. 2003 Barnes & Noble Annual Report, p. 3.

15. See, for example, Lueck, Sarah (2002), "Senators Push Drug-Reimportation Bill," *Wall Street Journal*, June 3, p. A4; "The Drugs Industry: Where the Money Is," *The Economist* 367, no. 8321 (April 26, 2003), pp. 53–54; "Canadian Pharmacies Turning to Europe," *Chicago Tribune*, April 14, 2004, Section 3, p. 3; and Sherman, Mark (2004), "Governor Objects to FDA's 'Hardball' on Canada Drugs," *Chicago Tribune*, April 15.

16. For some business press articles covering the Gateway-eMachines acquisition, see: PR Newswire (2004), "Gateway to Acquire eMachines," January 30; Chuang, Tamara (2004), "EMachines Joins Rival Gateway in Deal Valued at $266 Million," *Knight Ridder Tribune Business News*, January 31, p. 1; McWilliams, Gary (2004), "Gateway Buys eMachines to Boost Its Own Electronics Sales," *Wall Street Journal*, February 2, p. B1; Olenick, Doug (2004), "Gateway Alters CE, Retail Plans With eMachines," *TWICE* 19, no. 4 (February 9), p. 1; Heller, Laura (2004), "Gateway Points and Clicks with eMachines," *DSN Retailing Today* 43, no. 4 (February 23), p. 3; Olenick, Doug (2004), "Gateway Closes eMachines Merger," *TWICE* 19, no. 7 (March 22), p. 48; "Gateway Will Close Remaining Retail Stores," *Wall Street Journal*, April 2, 2004, p. 1; Flynn, Laurie J. (2004), "Gateway to Lay Off 2,500 with Closing of 188 Retail Stores," *New York Times*, April 2, Business, p. 6; "Gateway Inc.: About 40% of Jobs Will Be Cut; First-Quarter Loss Narrowed," *Wall Street Journal*, April 30, 2004, p. B6; and "Best Buy to Sell Limited Quantity of Gateway Products," *New York Times*, June 12, 2004, p. 2.

17. Alderson, Wroe (1954), "Factors Governing the Development of Marketing Channels," in Richard M. Clewett (ed.), *Marketing Channels in Manufactured Products* (Homewood, IL: Richard D. Irwin), pp. 5–22.

18. See, for example, Gordon, Todd (1995), "Streamline Inventory Management Via Continuous Replenishment Program," Information Access Company (a Thomson Corporation Company), *Automatic I.D. News*, April, p. 62; Zwiebach, Elliott (1995), "Reconstruction: Firms in Grocery Industry Streamline Operations for More Efficient Business," Information Access Company (a Thomson Corporation Company), *Supermarket News*, May 8, p. 32; Purpura, Linda (1997), "Vendor-Run Inventory: Are Its Benefits Exaggerated?" Information Access Company (a Thomson Corporation Company), *Supermarket News*, January 27, p. 59; Raghunathan, Srinivasan and Arthur B. Yeh (2001), "Beyond EDI: Impact of Continuous Replenishment Program (CRP) Between a Manufacturer and Its Retailers," *Information Systems Research* 12, no. 4 (December), pp. 406–419; Koch, Christopher (2002), "It All Began with Drayer," *CIO* 15, no. 20 (August 1), p. 1; and Mishra, Birendra K. and Srinivasan Raghunathan (2004), "Retailer- vs. Vendor-Managed Inventory and Brand Competition," *Management Science* 50, no. 4 (April), pp. 445–457.

19. See Koo, Hui-Wen and Pei-yu Lo (2004), "Sorting: The Function of Tea Middlemen in Taiwan during the Japanese Colonial Era," *Journal of Institutional and Theoretical Economics* 160, no. 4 (December), pp. 607–626, for more details on this example.

20. See "Outsourcing: A Global Success Story," *Logistics Management* 42, no. 2 (February 2003), pp. 60–63.

21. Fuhrman, Elizabeth (2003), "Multibar Multi-Tasking," *Candy Industry* 168, no. 6 (June), pp. 28–32.

22. Ritson, Mark (2003), "Wise Marketers Know When to Throw in the Towel on Own-Label," *Marketing*, April 17, p. 18. Ritson refers to Heinz as "working with, rather than against, the own-brand threat."

23. See www.officedepot.com (accessed August 2005) and the company's 2003 annual report, which reports that 46 percent of Office Depot's sales are from North American retail, 32 percent are from the Business Services Group, and 22 percent are from international (combining retail and business sales outside the United States).

24. Louis P. Bucklin defines service outputs in *A Theory of Distribution Channel Structure* (Berkeley, CA: IBER Special Publications, 1966) and *Competition and Evolution in the Distributive Trades* (Englewood Cliffs, NJ: Prentice Hall, 1972), pp. 18–31. See also Etgar, Michael (1974), "An Empirical Analysis of the Motivations for the Development of Centrally Coordinated Vertical Marketing Systems: The Case of the Property and Casualty Insurance Industry," unpublished doctoral dissertation, the University of California at Berkeley, pp. 95–97.

25. For information on activity-based costing, see, for example, Balachandran, Bala (1994), "Strategic Activity Based Accounting," *Business Week Executive Briefing Service*,; Yates, Ronald E. (1993) "New ABCs for Pinpoint Accounting," *Chicago Tribune*, January 24, p. 1; Cooper, Robin and Robert S. Kaplan (1991), "Profit Priorities from Activity-Based Costing," *Harvard Business Review* 69, no. 3 (May–June), pp. 130–135; and Rotch, William (1990), "Activity-Based Costing in Service Industries," *Journal of Cost Management*, (Summer), pp. 4–14.

26. The Large Scale Retail Store Law in Japan requires retailers wanting to open a store larger than 5,000 square meters to follow a complicated bureaucratic process that tends to prevent large stores from opening in town commercial centers. Other legal constraints exist in some European markets, where "green belts" are sometimes created around cities and inside of which large retailers may not open stores. For a viewpoint on the perceived threat imposed by outlet mall developers in Europe, see Beck, Ernest (1997), "Europeans Fear a Mauling by Outlet Malls," *Wall Street Journal Europe*, September 16, p. 4.

27. El-Ansary, Adel I. and Louis W. Stern (1972), "Power Measurement in the Distribution Channel," *Journal of Marketing Research* 9 (February), p. 47. Other related definitions and implications of channel power are discussed in depth in Chapter 8.

28. See Stern, Louis W. and J. L. Heskett (1969), "Conflict Management in Interorganization Relations: A Conceptual Framework," in Louis W. Stern (ed.), *Distribution Channels: Behavioral Dimensions* (Boston, MA: Houghton Mifflin Co.), pp. 288–305; Rosenberg, Larry J. and Louis W. Stern (1971), "Conflict Measurement in the Distribution Channel," *Journal of Marketing Research* 8, no. 4 (November), pp. 437–442; Etgar, Michael (1979), "Sources and Types of Intrachannel Conflict," *Journal of Retailing* 55, no. 1 (Spring), pp. 61–78; Cadotte, Ernest R. and Louis W. Stern (1979), "A Process Model of Dyadic Interorganizational Relations in Marketing Channels," in Jagdish N. Sheth (ed.), *Research in Marketing*, vol. 2 (Greenwich, CT: JAI Press); and Reve, Torger and Louis W. Stern (1979), "Interorganizational Relations in Marketing Channels," *Academy of Management Review* 4, no. 3 (July), pp. 405–416.

Alternate Channel Formats

DEFINITIONS AND EXAMPLES

Alternate channel formats may be based in any of the three sections of the traditional distribution pipeline—manufacturer, distributor, or customer—but they may also have other bases. The following material summarizes in detail a variety of channel formats and the characteristics on which they rely for strategic advantage, and it gives examples of specific companies or types of companies or product categories using that channel format. By comparing each of your markets to this information, you can identify opportunities and vulnerabilities.

Manufacturer-Based Channel Formats

1. **Manufacturer Direct.** Product shipped and serviced from manufacturer's warehouse. Sold by company sales force or agents. Many manufacturer-direct companies also sell through wholesaler-distributors.

   Example: Wide variety of products for customers with few service needs and large orders

2. **Manufacturer-Owned Full Service Wholesaler-Distributor.** An acquired wholesale distribution company serving the parent's and other manufacturers' markets. Typically, these diverse product lines in an industry support synergies between a company's manufacturing and distribution operations. Due to customer demand, some companies also distribute other manufacturer's products.

   Examples: Revlon, Levi Strauss, Kraft Foodservice, GESCO, clothing and apparel products

3. **Company Store/Manufacturer Outlets.** Retail product outlets in high-density markets; often used to liquidate seconds and excess inventory. They often sell branded consumer products.

   Examples: Athletic footwear, bakery goods

4. **License.** Contracting distribution and marketing functions through licensing agreements, usually granting exclusivity for some period of time. Often used for products in the development stage of the life cycle.

   Examples: Mattel, Walt Disney, importers

5. **Consignment/Locker Stock.** Manufacturing ships product to point of consumption, but title does not pass until consumed. Risk of obsolescence and ownership is with manufacturer until used. Concerned with high-priced/high-margin items and emergency items.

   Examples: Diamonds, fragrances, tool cribs, and machine repair parts

6. **Broker.** Specialized sales force contracted by manufacturer; the sales force carries other comparable product lines and focuses on a narrow customer segment; product is shipped through another format such as the preceding. Typically used by small manufacturers attempting broad coverage.

   Examples: Frozen foods, paper goods, lumber, newer product lines

Retailer-Based Channel Formats

1. **Franchise.** Product and merchandising concept is packaged and formatted. Territory rights are sold to franchisees. Various distribution and other services are provided by contract to franchisees for a fee.

   Examples: Blockbuster Video, McDonald's

2. **Dealer Direct.** Franchised retailers carry a limited number of product lines supplied by a limited number of vendors. Often big-ticket items needing high after-sales service support.

    Examples: Heavy equipment dealers, auto dealers

3. **Buying Club.** Buying services requiring membership. Good opportunity for vendors to penetrate certain niche markets or experiment with product variations. They also often provide buyers with a variety of consumer services. Today they are largely consumer-oriented.

    Examples: Compact disc/tape clubs, book clubs

4. **Warehouse Clubs/Wholesale Clubs.** Appeal is to price-conscious shopper. Size is 60,000 square feet or more. Product selection is limited, and products are usually sold in bulk sizes in a no-frills environment.

    Examples: Pace, Sam's Club, Price Club, Costco

5. **Mail Order/Catalog.** Nonstore selling through use of literature sent to potential customers. Usually has a central distribution center for receiving and shipping direct to the customer.

    Examples: Lands' End, Spiegel, Fingerhut

6. **Food Retailers.** Will buy canned and boxed goods in truckloads to take advantage of pricing and manufacturing rebates. Distribution centers act as consolidators to reduce the number of trucks received at the store. Pricing is not required because manufacturer bar codes are used. Typically includes full line of groceries, health and beauty aids, and general merchandise items. Some food retailers have expanded into additional areas, such as prescription and over-the-counter drugs, delicatessens, bakeries, etc.

    Examples: Publix, Safeway

7. **Department Stores.** These stores offer a wide variety of merchandise with a moderate depth of selection. The typical product mix includes both soft goods (such as clothing, food, linens) and hard goods (such as appliances, hardware, sporting equipment). Distribution centers act as consolidators of both soft goods and hard goods. Quick response for apparel goods demands direct link with manufacturer. Having stores on a national basis motivates retailers to handle their own distribution.

    Examples: J. C. Penney, Mervyn's, R. H. Macy & Co., Dayton Hudson Corp., Federated Stores

8. **Mass Merchandisers.** Similar to department stores, except product selection is broader and prices are usually lower.

    Examples: Wal-Mart, Kmart, Target

9. **Specialty Stores.** Offer merchandise in one line (e.g., women's apparel, electronics) with great depth of selection at prices comparable to those of department stores. Due to the seasonal nature of fashion goods, partnership with the manufacturer is essential. Manufacturer will ship in predetermined store assortment and usually will price the goods. Retailer in some cases has joint ownership with the manufacturer.

    Examples: The Limited, The Gap, Kinney Shoes, Musicland, Zales

10. **Specialty Discounters/Category Killers.** Offer merchandise in one line (e.g., sporting goods, office supplies, children's merchandise) with great depth of selection at discounted prices. Stores usually range in size from 50,000 to 75,000 square feet. Buys direct in truckloads. Manufacturer will ship direct to the store. Most products do not need to be priced. National chains have created their own distribution centers to act as consolidators.

    Examples: Toys "R" Us, Office Max, Drug Emporium, F&M Distributors

11. **Convenience Store.** A small, higher-margin grocery store that offers a limited selection of staple groceries, nonfoods, and other convenience items; for example, ready-to-heat and ready-to-eat foods. The traditional format includes those stores that started out as strictly convenience stores, but they may also sell gasoline.

    Examples: 7-Eleven, White Hen Pantry

12. **Hypermarket.** A very large food and general merchandise store with at least 100,000 square feet of space. Although these stores

typically devote as much as 75 percent of the selling area to general merchandise, the food-to-general merchandise sales ratio typically is 60/40.

Examples: Auchan, Carrefour, Super Kmart Centers, Hypermarket USA

Service Provider-Based Channel Formats

1. **Contract Warehousing.** Public warehousing services provided for a fee, typically with guaranteed service levels.

   Examples: Caterpillar Logistics Services, Dry Storage

2. **Subprocessor.** Outsourcing of assembly or subprocessing. Usually performed with labor-intensive process or high fixed-asset investment when small orders are needed for customer. These channel players are also beginning to take on a traditional wholesale distribution role in some cases.

   Examples: Steel processing; kitting of parts in electronics industry

3. **Cross Docking.** Trucking companies service high-volume inventory needs by warehousing and back hauling product on a routine basis for customer's narrower inventory needs. Driver picks up inventory and delivers to customer.

   Examples: Industrial repair parts and tools, various supply industries

4. **Integration of Truck and Rail (Intermodal).** Joint ventures between trucking and rail companies to ship large orders door-to-door from supplier to customer with one waybill.

   Examples: Becomes very economical for large orders, or from manufacturer to customer for a manufacturer with a broad product line.

5. **Roller Freight.** Full truckload is sent from manufacturer to high-density customer markets via a transportation company. Product is sold en route, and drivers are directed to customer delivery by satellite communication.

   Examples: Lumber products, large moderately priced items, with commodity-like characteristics that require routine orders.

6. **Stack Trains and Road Railers.** Techniques to speed movement and eliminate handling for product to be shipped by multiple formats. For example, importer loads containers directed to specific customers on a truck body in Hong Kong, ships direct, and unloads onto railcars. This can eliminate 2 to 3 days' transit time. Large customer orders using multiple transportation techniques.

   Examples: Importers

7. **Scheduled Trains.** High-speed trains leave daily at prescribed times from high-density areas to high-density destinations. Manufacturer "buys a ticket" and hooks up his railcar, and product is picked up at the other end by the customer.

   Examples: High-density recurring orders to large customers with limited after-sales service needs

8. **Outsourcing.** Service providers sign a contract to provide total management of a company's activities in an area in which the provider has particular expertise (computer operations, janitorial services, print shop, cafeteria, repair parts, tool crib). The outsourcer then takes over the channel product flow for products associated with outsourced activity (janitorial supplies). Outsourcing has spread to virtually every area of the business (repair part stockroom, legal, and accounting department) and may not use merchant wholesaler-distributors. Wide variety of applications and growing.

   Examples: ServiceMaster, ARA, R. R. Donnelly

9. **Direct Mailer.** Direct mail advertising companies expanding services in conjunction with market research database services in order to direct market narrower line products. Product logistics and support are either performed by manufacturer or outsourced to a third party.

   Examples: Big ticket consumer products, high-margin, low-service-requirement industrial and commercial equipment

10. **Bartering.** Service provider, usually an advertising or media company, signs a barter arrangement with a manufacturer to

exchange product for media advertising time or space for product. Bartered product is then rebartered or redistributed through other channels.

Examples: Consumer and commercial products that have been discontinued or for which demand has slowed considerably

11. **Value-Added Resellers (VARs).** Designers, engineers, or consultants for a variety of service industries that joint venture or have arrangements with manufacturers of products that are used in their designs. The VARs often get a commission or discount to service the product later and often carry inventory of high-turn items.

Examples: Computer software companies that market hardware for turnkey products; security system designers that form joint ventures with electronics manufacturers to sell turnkey products

12. **Influencers/Specifiers.** Similar to a VAR, but these firms generally design highly complex, large projects (commercial buildings), do not take title to product, and have a group of suppliers whose products can be specified into the design. Selling effort is focused on both the ultimate customer and the specifier. Distribution of product is handled through other channel formats.

Examples: Architects, designers, consultants

13. **Financial Service Providers.** These formats have historically been initiated by joint venture with financial service companies to finance margin purchases for customers or dealers (such as floor planning). They have been expanded to allow manufacturers to initiate distribution in new markets and assess these markets (with the help of the financial provider). High-capital, highly controlled distribution channel for one or two suppliers.

Examples: Branded chemicals, construction equipment

Other Channel Formats

Door-to-Door Formats. To some extent these are variations on the channel formats previously listed. These formats have existed in the United States since pioneer days in situations in which a product has a high personal sales cost and high margins and is sold in relatively small orders (encyclopedias, vacuum cleaners, and so forth). A wide range of variations (e.g., the home-party format) attempt to get many small buyers in one location to minimize the sales cost and provide a unique shopping experience. Variations of the format have also spread to the industrial and commercial markets to capitalize on similar market needs (e.g., Snap-On Tools uses a variation of the home-party system by driving the product and salesmen to the mechanic's garage and selling to the mechanics on their lunch hour). Each format is different and needs to be analyzed to understand its unique characteristics. A brief summary of the more identifiable formats follows.

1. **Individual On-Site.** Very effective for generating new business for high-margin product requiring a high level of interaction with customers.

Examples: Fuller Brush, Electrolux, bottled water, newspapers

2. **Route.** Used for servicing routine repetitious purchases that do not need to be resold on each call. Sometimes price is negotiated once and only changed on an exception basis. This concept was historically more prevalent in consumer lines (e.g., milk deliveries) but has recently spread to a variety of commercial and industrial segments.

Examples: Office deliveries of copier paper and toner

3. **Home Party.** Similar to individual on-site sales, this format takes the product to a group of individuals, as outlined in the introduction.

Examples: Tupperware, Snap-On Tools

4. **Multi-Level Marketing.** Salesperson not only sells product but recruits other salespeople who become a leveraged sales force that gives the original salesperson a commission on sales. Channel can be used for

"high-sizzle," high-margin, fast-growth opportunities in branded differentiated products.

Examples: Amway, Shaklee, NuSkin, plumbing products, cosmetics, other general merchandise

5. **Service Merchandising/Rack Jobbing.** Similar to a route but expanded to provide a variety of services with the product. Originally, the rack jobber sold small consumer items to grocery stores, merchandised the product, and owned the inventory, merely paying the retailer a commission for the space. This concept is expanding to the commercial, industrial, and home market in a variety of niches: maintaining a stockroom of office supplies, maintaining repair parts stock, servicing replenishable items in the home such as chemicals, purified water, salt, and so on.

Examples: Specialty items and gadgets or novelties, paperback books, magazines

Buyer-Initiated Formats. These are formats that have been built on the concept of all buyers joining together to buy in large quantities at better prices. This concept has expanded to give these buyers other securities and leverage that they might not be able to obtain on their own (e.g., private labeling and advertising design). As with the door-to-door concepts, variations of this concept are proliferating to meet individual buyers' needs.

1. **Co-Op.** Companies, usually in the same industry, create an organization in which each member becomes a shareholder. The organization uses the combined strength of the shareholders to get economies of scale in any number of areas of its business, such as purchasing, advertising, or private label manufacturing. This format is generally designed to allow small companies to compete more effectively with large companies. Although wholesaler-distributors can form or join co-ops, in their use as an alternate channel format co-ops may be direct buyers from nonwholesalers-distributors.

Example: Topco

2. **Dealer-Owned Co-Op.** Similar to the co-op format except the co-op may perform many of the functions rather than contracting them with third-party suppliers (e.g., it may own warehouses). Shareholders/members are generally charged a fee for usage, and all profits in the co-op at year-end are refundable to the shareholders on some prorated basis. In many instances, this format has elements of a franchise.

Example: Distribution America

3. **Buying Group.** Similar to the co-op except the relationship is usually much less structured. Companies can be members of several buying groups. The loose affiliation format usually does not continually commit the members to performance. This format is being used throughout the economy and has taken on a host of roles. A group can buy through the wholesale distribution channel or direct from manufacturers. Often, wholesaler-distributors are members of buying groups for low-volume items.

Examples: AMC, May Merchandising

Point-of-Consumption Merchandising Formats. This concept has grown from the practice of strategically placing vending machines where the demand is predictable and often discretionary and the cost of selling through a full-time salesperson would be too high. This format has spread into commercial, industrial, and home markets for products and services never before imagined. The increased use of technology and telecommunications has opened this channel to even more products and services.

1. **Vending/Kiosks.** Kiosks historically have been very small retail locations that carry a very narrow product line. Through interactive video, online ordering technology, and artificial intelligence, this format has been significantly enhanced and can operate unattended. It is also being used for point-of-use dispensing of maintenance supplies and tools. Purchases are recorded in a log

by the computer to control inventory shrinkage and balance inventory levels.

Examples: Film processing, candy, tobacco, compact discs, tapes

2. **Pay-Per-Serving Point of Dispensing.** Product is prepared or dispensed by vending machine at the time of purchase. Vending machines for soup and coffee, soft drinks, and candy or food are usual uses of this format, but it is expanding to include such foods as pizza and pasta.

Examples: Beverages, food

3. **Computer Access Information.** Many of the computer access information formats have not necessarily altered the product flow (products are not available online), but they have significantly altered the service and information flow by uncoupling them from the product. This allows the product to pass through less expensive channels.

Examples: Online information services, cable movies, newswire services, shopping services for groceries

Third-Party Influencer Formats. These formats are designed around the concept that an organization that has a relationship with a large number of people or companies can provide a channel format to these entities for products and services not traditionally associated with the organization (e.g., a school selling candy to the community by using the school children as a sales force). Here again, the concept has broadened across both the commercial and industrial sectors and deepened in terms of the products and services offered.

1. **Charity.** This format typically involves sales of goods and services in which the sponsoring charitable organization receives a commission on the sale. All types of products can be included and can be shipped direct or outsourced. Sales force may be unpaid volunteers.

Examples: Market Day, World's Finest Chocolate

2. **Company-Sponsored Program.** Employers contract with companies for products and services for their employees or segments of employees on an as-needed basis. The provider has access to the employee base.

Examples: Health care and drug services, car maintenance

3. **Premium and Gift Market.** Companies buy products customized with company logos or names for sale or distribution

Examples: Pens, plaques, awards, T-shirts, novelties

4. **Product Promotion Mailing with Normal Correspondence.** Promotion of products is done by mailing to customers with letters and perhaps phone call follow-up. Typically involves promotional inserts with credit card and other billings. Logistics and order fulfillment activities may be handled by others.

Examples: American Express, VISA, MasterCard

5. **Customer List Cross-Selling.** An unusual format in that the customer list is sold by one company to another. In effect, the marketing function is circumvented. Started in the customer industry but is migrating to the commercial and industrial segments.

Examples: Catalog companies, credit card companies

Catalog and Technology-Aided Formats. The time-honored catalog marketing channel dates from use by department stores to extend their merchandising ability to the predominantly rural U.S. population of the late 1800s. Catalog use has expanded dramatically to follow the buying habits of consumers and institutions. Although it continues to be a growing threat to the traditional merchant wholesaler-distributor through mail order and linkage to technology, it should be pointed out that catalogs are also a sales tool used by some wholesaler-distributors. Some of the adaptations below illustrate the need to evaluate this format very carefully in all sectors of the market.

1. **Specialty Catalogs.** Uses catalogs to promote a narrow range of special products or services. Mailings are made to potential and

repeat customers. Orders come in by mail or phone.

Examples: Eddie Bauer, Bass Pro Shops, Williams Sonoma

2. **Business-to-Business Catalogs.** Similar to specialty catalogs except that the product and customer focus is on business.

Examples: Moore Business Forms, Global, CompuAdd, Damart

3. **Television Home Shopping and Satellite Networks.** Heavily dependent on technology, these offer shopping in the comfort of your own home. Also has business application. Orders are placed by phone.

Example: Home Shopping Network

4. **Interactive Merchandising.** Could embody many of the attributes of television home shopping and satellite networks except that this format allows extensive interactive in-store capabilities as well as online ordering. It may offer inventory checking or physical modeling capabilities and unusually extensive communication linkages.

Examples: Florsheim, kitchen planning computers in do-it-yourself home centers

5. **Third-Party Catalog Services.** Catalog selling format in which one or more suppliers provide a combined catalog for a group of customers frequenting a certain place.

Examples: Airline in-flight magazines and catalogs, in-room hotel publications

6. **Trade Shows.** A format used in some segments for direct sales order activities. Suppliers sell from booths at major trade shows or conventions. Also used for retail applications.

Examples: Boats, cars, hardware/software applications

7. **Database Marketing.** Databases of customer buying habits and demographics are analyzed to enable the company to target customers for future mailing. Also used for retail applications.

Examples: Large grocery/consumer products companies, telephone companies

Segmentation for Marketing Channel Design

Service Outputs

Learning objectives

After reading this chapter, you will:

■ Understand the central role played by end-users and their demands in the design of marketing channels

■ Know what service outputs are and how to identify and analyze them

■ Be able to divide a market into channel segments for the purposes of designing or modifying a marketing channel

■ Be able to evaluate when and whether to try to meet all expressed service output demands in the short run in a particular market

■ Understand the relationship between service output demands and solutions to overall channel design problems

Marketing channel system design and management, like the management of any other marketing activity, requires starting with an analysis of the end-user. This is true even for a channel member that does not sell directly to an end-user. For example, a manufacturer selling through a distributor to business-to-business end-users may book a sale when the distributor buys inventory, but it is the end-user who holds the ultimate power of the purse, and therefore, the manufacturer's demand from the distributor is only a derived demand from ultimate end-users. Only after first understanding the nature of end-users' demands can the channel manager design a well-working channel that meets or exceeds those demands. The most useful demand-side insights for marketing channel design are not about *what* end-users want to consume but about *how* end-users want to buy and use the products or services being purchased. We will thus take as given a product's viability for the market and concern ourselves with the understanding of *how* to sell it rather than what to sell.

This chapter focuses on the demand side of the marketing channel design problem, first by describing end-user behavior. In *all* markets, end-users will have differential preferences and demands for *service outputs* that reduce their search, waiting time, storage, and other costs. Grouping end-users in the market by demands for service outputs (as opposed to preferences for physical product attributes, for example) helps us define potential target market segments for which to design specific marketing channel solutions. We then ask under what marketplace conditions it is most important to meet all service output demands and how to link this demand-side analysis with the supply-side decisions required when designing a channel. Appendix 2A presents the service output demands template, a tool for analyzing segmented demands for service outputs.

END-USER CHANNEL PREFERENCES

End-users (both business-to-business buyers and individual consumers) purchase products and services of every sort. Yet it seems that more than just the product itself is important to the buyer. This chapter's sidebars on corporate personal computer (PC) purchases (Sidebar 2.1) and online bill payment (Sidebar 2.2) illustrate this idea. In these examples, a particular product or service can be bought in multiple ways. It is not the product that changes but the method of buying and selling the product and the associated services that accompany the product. For the small- to medium-sized corporate buyer in the corporate personal computer purchases example, one essential difference between buying PCs directly from the manufacturer versus buying them through a corporate supplier like CDW lies in CDW's varying kinds of customer service tailored specifically to this segment of buyer; this and other service outputs offered through the CDW channel create a product-plus-service output bundle that the targeted customer highly values.

The online bill payment example suggests that introducing a new technology requires an understanding of consumers' service output demands and how the current technology is (or is not) meeting them. The surprise in the online bill payment story is that consumers in fact do *not* prefer an apparently dominant new technology; the financial services industry did not initially understand that what seems dominant from a *supply* perspective may not be best from a *demand* perspective, and therefore, if the new technology is to be adopted in the market, better serving the service needs of the end-user is crucial.

These examples suggest the need to identify *how* the end-user wants to buy as well as *what* the end-user wants to buy. Further, they suggest that different end-users have different demands and that understanding and responding to those demands can create new business opportunities for manufacturers (and failing to understand them can short-circuit these same new business opportunities). We turn next to a discussion of the *how* of distributing products by defining the concept of *service outputs in the channel.*

Sidebar 2.1

CDW and PC purchases by small/medium business buyers[1]

Personal computers are by now virtually a commodity *product*. The technology is well enough established that buyers know they can purchase a computer with a given combination of characteristics (amount of memory, weight, speed, monitor quality, etc.) from a number of manufacturers. In a market like this, two questions immediately emerge: First, how can any manufacturer differentiate itself from the competitive crowd so that it can gain disproportionate market share and/or margins higher than purely competitive ones; and second, what role could an intermediary possibly play when the product purchase appears to be a straight commodity one? CDW (which was formerly known by the expanded name Computer Discount Warehouse) has risen to the challenge, creating an enduring role as a valued intermediary to some specific market segments in the PC marketplace, particularly small and medium business buyers, government, and education. In the process, it has also attracted the attention and business of major computer makers.

CDW recognizes that the small/medium business buyer is not purchasing just a PC (or a set of PCs) but rather the products *with ancillary valued services accompanying them*. The CEO observed in 2003 that "We're kind of the chief technical officer for many smaller firms" (Schmeltzer 2003). What does this mean in terms of demand for and supply of service outputs along with the product purchased?

- CDW is the key provider of *advice and expertise* to the buyer, about everything from the appropriate configuration of products to buy to the setting up of a local area network for the buyer. CDW is also available after the purchase if any customer service problems arise.

- CDW prides itself on its *speed of delivery* of orders; 99 percent of orders are shipped the day they are received. The company can do this because of an investment in a 400,000-square-foot warehouse, which permits it to hold significant speculative inventory and avoid stockouts.

- CDW offers different *customer service* options: a customer can buy online without a great deal of sales help, but CDW also assigns a salesperson to every account—even small online purchase accounts. This gives the CDW small/medium business buyer access to a person to talk to if any questions or problems arise and increases the buyer's flexibility of choice in how to shop. The salesperson has no incentive to be overly aggressive, however, because a sale results in the same commission whether the customer orders online or through the salesperson. CDW salespersons go through four months of training before being allowed to serve customers, so their level of expertise and professionalism is high enough to serve the customer well.

- CDW offers its customers broad *assortment and variety*. A small/medium business buyer can, of course, buy directly from a manufacturer, such as Dell, Gateway, or Hewlett-Packard. But in so doing, the buyer is restricting itself to one manufacturer's product line. Buying through CDW gives the buyer access to many different brands, which can be useful when assembling components in the optimal computer system. CDW enhances the effective assortment available by also reconfiguring products to the specific demands of the business buyer before shipping them.

How does CDW compare to the competition? After all, offering great levels of service outputs is good to do, but the question is always how well a channel performs against other

Sidebar 2.1 (cont.)

CDW and PC purchases by small/medium
business buyers

routes to market through which a customer can buy. In 2004, CDW faced a strong challenge from Dell Computer, which offered 0 percent financing for the first time, along with free shipping and rebate programs. Dell also cut the prices of printers in half in a direct challenge to Hewlett-Packard, CDW's biggest supplier. In short, the competitive challenge was based mainly on price elements. Any individual buyer must then ask how much CDW's extra service outputs are worth to the company. For the buyer that values quick delivery, assortment, and CDW's targeted customer service, the apparent price premium is well worth the money because it saves the buyer the cost of acquiring those services in another way (or the cost of not getting the desired level of service at all). Given that the market for small/medium business buyers, government, and educational buyers was about $125 billion in the United States in 2004 and CDW's sales in 2003 were just $4.7 billion, considerable room for growth remains for more than one competitor.

It is also important to consider the value that CDW brings to a manufacturer in its ability to produce and deliver valued service outputs

to targeted customer segments. Evidence of CDW's performance is Gateway's decision in May 2003 to sign a reseller agreement with CDW, allowing CDW to sell Gateway computer equipment. This agreement was noteworthy because of Gateway's prior strategy of selling direct (either online or through its then-existing network of wholly-owned retail outlets). CDW brought value to Gateway through its reach to small- and medium-sized business owners and its strong reputation for service (the agreement stipulated that CDW would perform post-sale service on the Gateway machines it sold). Gateway management recognized that CDW now served as the computer purchasing arm for some of Gateway's desired customers, saying, "There are customers who like to buy from CDW. There is a suite of value-added service that CDW provides that gives customers a choice."

In sum, CDW's strategy of (a) focusing on a particular subset of all computer buyers and (b) providing valued service outputs to them, as well as quality product, not only has helped them cement relationships with these buyers but also has made them a preferred intermediary channel partner to key manufacturers.

SERVICE OUTPUTS

A framework for codifying and generalizing how the end-user wants to buy a particular product was proposed by Bucklin as a basis for determining channel structure.[2] We use his original theory here as a foundation to our approach for segmenting the market for marketing channel design purposes.

Bucklin argues that channel systems exist and remain viable through time by performing duties that reduce end-users' search, waiting time, storage, and other costs. These benefits are called the service outputs of the channel. Other things being equal (in particular, price and physical product attributes), end-users will prefer to deal with a marketing channel that provides a higher level of service outputs. Bucklin specifies four generic service outputs: (1) bulk-breaking, (2) spatial convenience, (3) waiting or delivery time, and (4) product variety. We add two other service outputs to this list: (5) customer service and (6) information provision. While this list is generic and can

Sidebar 2.2

Online bill payment[3]

Paying bills is an activity shared by billions of people around the world. Most view it as a tedious rather than an enjoyable task. In the United States, consumers have historically received paper bills through the mail and paid them with hand-written checks sent back through the mail. So, when electronic bill payment was made broadly available to consumers in about 2001, the financial services industry widely anticipated that e-bill payments would quickly replace paper bill payments. Ancillary business declines were predicted for the U.S. Post Office's first-class mail and for businesses that print paper checks, among others. Yet consumers were very slow to adopt e-bill payment (see Table 2.1), surprising the pundits who predicted its quick adoption. Why was this? The answer lies in a host of reasons that we will explore in this chapter as well as in Chapter 3 on channel flows and Chapter 5 on gap analysis. Here, we will focus on the *consumer demand* issues that contributed to the slow penetration of electronic bill payment in the United States.

First, consider what electronic bill payment is, particularly in comparison to paper bill payment processes. A consumer could (and can today) choose from two main ways in which to pay a bill electronically: directly at the biller's Web site, or through a third-party bill paying intermediary, such as the consumer's bank or an independent firm such as Quicken. Whether paying a bill by paper, directly at the biller's Web site, or via a third party, four common steps are involved in bill payment:

1. A *set-up process* to make it possible to pay bills in this way.
2. Bill presentment to the consumer. *Presentment* is the term used in the banking/ billing industry to mean that the consumer can actually see the full bill with information on all charges.

3. *Bill review and payment authorization* by the consumer. Here, the consumer (presumably!) checks the bill's contents for accuracy before payment and then arranges for payment to actually occur.
4. *Confirmation of payment* to the consumer, either by the biller or by the third-party payment intermediary.

Table 2.2 details the specific elements of each of these four steps for the three payment alternatives. It also summarizes the *costs* of using each of the payment alternatives. Note that some of the costs are not direct monetary costs but also include the cost of learning to pay in each particular way, as well as any probabilistic costs related to the risk of nonpayment (despite the consumer's completion of the payment process).

While Table 2.2 describes how each payment process works, it does not provide insight into what consumers *demand* from a payment process in the way of service outputs. Only through comparing what is *supplied* (as detailed in Table 2.2) and what is *demanded* can we start to identify the demand-side reasons for lack of quick adoption of electronic bill payment.

When paying bills, the typical consumer demands an easy-to-use process, reliability, speed (both in carrying out the payment steps and in the time until actual recording of the bill as paid), and responsive customer service in the event of failure of the payment submission process. *Ease of use* implies that the consumer has ready access to all the information needed to accomplish bill payment and, thus, further implies a high demand for the information service output if the bill paying technology is new (which has been the case for electronic bill payment). It also implies that most or all bills can be paid in one way or at one site—in effect, offering a broad assortment and variety

Sidebar 2.2 (cont.)

Online bill payment

Table 2.1   Estimated number of U.S. consumers using online bill payment, various years

Year	# U.S. Consumers Paying at Least One Bill Online (Millions, Est.)	% of U.S. Population (Est.)
1998	3.4	1.3%
1999–2000	—	—
2001	20.4	7.3%
2002	25.5	9.1%
2003	35	12.5%
2004	65	23%

Notes:

1998: in 1998, just 2% of U.S. households used online bill payment, according to Tower Group (Bielski 2003). From U.S. Census data, in 1998 there were 100 million households in the United States, with an average of 1.7 adults per household; thus, 2 million households or 3.4 million adults were using online bill payment in 1998.

2001: A Forrester Research report said that nearly 17 million U.S. households would pay bills online in 2002, up 41 percent from 2001 numbers (Higgins 2002). Thus, in 2001, 12 million U.S. households paid bills online. From U.S. Census data, there were 108 million households in the United States, with an average of 2.58 adults per household; thus, 20.4 million adults were using online bill payment in 2001.

2002: The same Forrester Research report said that nearly 17 million U.S. households would pay bills online in 2002 (Higgins 2002), while a Tower Group report said that 13.7% of U.S. households did pay bills online in 2002 (Bielski 2003). The table, therefore, reports the numbers from Bielski. There were 109 million households in the United States in 2002; thus, 15 million households paid bills online. Further, there were an average of 2.58 adults per household in the United States in 2002 (from U.S. Census data), yielding the estimate of 25.5 million adult online bill payers in 2002.

2003 and 2004: A Gartner study cited 65 million U.S. consumers paying at least some bills online, and reported that was almost twice as many as in 2003 (Park, Elgin et al. 2004). We therefore estimate that 35 million U.S. consumers paid bills online in 2003.

Sources: Higgins, Michelle (2002), "Honest, the Check Is in the E-Mail: To Lock in Customers, Banks Step Up Push to Get You to Pay Bills Online; "Making It Automatic," *Wall Street Journal*, September 4, p. D1; Bielski, Lauren (2003), "Hard to Get the Online Habit," *ABA Banking Journal* 95, no. 2 (February), 79–86; Park, Andrew, Ben Elgin, and Timothy J. Mullaney (2004), "Checks Check Out: with Online Bill Payment and Processing, Use of Paper Checks Is Headed for a Steep Decline," *Business Week* 10, p. 83.; U.S. Census data.

(continued)

Sidebar 2.2 (cont.)

Online bill payment

Table 2.2 Online bill payment: The consumer experience

Option	Paper Bill Payment	Direct Biller Online Pay	Third-Party Online Bill Payer (e.g., Bank, Quicken)
Set-up Process	None	Consumer logs on to biller's Web site; enters information about account, name, bank account from which payment will be made, etc.; picks a password *specific to this Web site* to gain access in future. Activation usually occurs within 24 hours.	Consumer logs on to third-party Web site; enters information about *each account individually*; picks a password *specific to this site but common across all bills paid at this site* to gain access in future.
Bill Presentment to Consumer	Consumer receives bill through U.S. mail in envelope containing summary of bill charges and due date, payment stub, and payment envelope.	Either through U.S. mail (see paper bill) or electronic bill presentment through e-mail alert; both note payment due date.	Arrival of electronic bill noted through e-mail alert; third party may or may not offer actual bill presentment.
Consumer Bill Review and Payment Authorization	Consumer reconciles bill with paper receipts; fills out payment stub; writes paper check; inserts check and stub in envelope; puts U.S. first-class stamp on envelope; mails payment.	Consumer reconciles bill with receipts; visits biller Web site's payment page; enters amount and date of payment; Web site indicates how fast payment will be made.	Consumer visits third party's Web site to view bill (if no presentment by third party) and reconcile; enters amount and date of payment (may need up to 5 days to clear payment).

Option	Paper Bill Payment	Direct Biller Online Pay	Third-Party Online Bill Payer (e.g., Bank, Quicken)
Confirmation of Payment to Consumer	Only when next bill is received does consumer learn if previous payment was received in time (unless consumer telephones biller).	Typically, e-mail confirmation of payment receipt the day payment is recorded.	Typically, e-mail confirmation that payment was made.
Cost to Consumer	Cost of first-class stamp; no cost to learn system; cost of time to process bill and write check; cost of paper check; risk-adjusted cost of late payment (perceived very low); no monthly fee for payment processing.	No stamp; initial learning time for *each biller's system*; cost of time to check bill's accuracy; no check writing or cost; risk-adjusted cost of late payment (perceived low); no monthly fee for payment processing.	No stamp; initial learning time once for *whole system*; cost of time to check bill's accuracy; no check writing or cost; risk-adjusted cost of late payments (moderate: up to 5 days to clear payment); may be a monthly fee (e.g., Quicken: $9.95/month for up to 20 bills, plus $2.49 per 5 bills thereafter; many banks now do not charge for service); may be low cost to integrate with home financial records (e.g., Quicken financial software program).

(continued)

Sidebar 2.2 (cont.)

Online bill payment

of bills that can be paid. *Reliability* is important because a bill-paying process that fails (even sporadically) results in high late fees for the consumer. This service element is most closely related to the quick delivery service output (because poor performance here implies that payment is in fact late). *Speed* (also a measure of quick delivery) has two relevant service output dimensions in the case of bill payment: first, the consumer's ability to get his/her part of the bill payment process done quickly, and second, the speed with which the rest of the channel consummates the payment of the bill after the consumer directs that it should be done. Finally, *responsive customer service* is the consumer's assurance that if a bill or payment is mislaid somewhere in the process, the biller will resolve any complaints expeditiously and fairly. While different consumers could clearly place different levels of importance on these service outputs, just as clearly they are all more important than bulk breaking or spatial convenience for bill payers.

Given these typical consumer demands, how does paper bill payment compare to e-bill payment?

- *Ease of use:* Paper bill payment was clearly better than electronic payment methods for at least the first two to three years that e-bill payment was offered. This was not only because e-bill payment systems were in their infancy, so that the technologies were not always transparently easy to learn, but also simply because there was *no* need to incrementally learn when paying a bill via paper—it was the status quo. Further, at many bank sites, a consumer could *pay* bills but could not *see* them, so while payment was electronic and seamless, presentment was not.

- *Reliability:* The evidence was a bit more mixed but still favored paper bill payment

for most Americans in the early 2000s. The U.S. Postal Service has an extremely high reliability record for delivery of first-class mail, so few consumers would expect the mail to be a poor delivery system for a paper check. Meanwhile, many consumers still did not fully trust the reliability of an electronic payment system, where there might be no tangible evidence that payment had been made.

- *Speed:* This was expected to be a big reason for adoption of e-bill payment; it was expected that consumers would resent the time needed to handwrite a check, prepare an envelope, and put it in the mail, when the same payment ostensibly could be made with a few mouse clicks on the computer. However, consumers did not find paper payment times onerous, nor did they find electronic bill payments saved much time (particularly when, as novices, consumers were not as adept at the process as experts would be).

- *Responsive customer service:* Consumers who were not comfortable with e-bill payment technology worried that their lack of knowledge would result in inadvertent mispayments or nonpayments, which would be viewed as their fault rather than as a customer-service opportunity. Cases where e-bill payments were inappropriately made—for whatever reason—were viewed as poor customer service encounters, compared to the status quo paper-based payment systems, making them unpopular with consumers.

Even these reasons might not have prevented quick adoption of e-bill paying if the *consumer cost* of paying electronically were much lower than that of paying with paper. Here too, however, many consumers preferred paper bill paying. The main observable cost of paying a paper bill is the cost of a first-class

Sidebar 2.2 (cont.)

Online bill payment

stamp, which e-bill pay avoids. But the more significant costs of paying bills electronically are the initial learning costs and the risk-adjusted cost of a possible mispayment or nonpayment of a bill—both of which were considerably higher for e-bill payment systems than for paper bill payment. To add insult to injury, most banks and third-party bill consolidation and payment services charged consumers for using their e-bill payment systems! The full cost of using these systems, new and untried as they were, was simply too great, particularly given the lack of compelling service output superiority. This sort of demand-based analysis illustrates how a seemingly great new technology can fail in the market, not because it does not work or is not cost effective (neither of which is true in this case), but because the demand-side

case is simply not compelling enough for consumers to abandon their tried-and-true status quo method of getting the job done.

Conversely, the provider who helps the consumer conquer these hurdles can gain tremendous consumer loyalty. One Bank of America consumer who finally decided to adopt electronic bill payment through her bank had trouble adding the names of her billers to her software at home. Upon calling the bank, she was amazed that the branch manager made a house call, spent 45 minutes at her computer, and fixed the problem so that she could get started with e-bill pay. Her response: "I will never leave my bank"—is evidence of the very great weight such novice consumers place on the service output of customer service.[4]

be customized to any particular application, these six service outputs cover the major categories of end-users' demands for different channel systems.

Bulk-breaking refers to the end-users' ability to buy their desired (possibly small) number of units of a product or service even though they may be originally produced in large, batch-production lot sizes. When the marketing channel system allows end-users to buy in small lot sizes, purchases can more easily move directly into consumption, reducing the need for the end-user to carry unnecessary inventory. However, if end-users must purchase in larger lot sizes (i.e., benefit from less bulk-breaking), some disparity between purchasing and consumption patterns will emerge, burdening end-users with product handling and storage costs. Consequently, the more bulk-breaking the channel does, the smaller the lot size end-users can buy and the higher the channel's service output level to them. This, in turn, can lead to a higher price for the end-user to cover the costs of providing small lot sizes.

The common practice of charging a lower per-unit price for larger package sizes in frequently purchased consumer packaged goods at grocery stores is an example of this pricing phenomenon. Consider how a family buys laundry detergent when at home versus when renting a house on vacation. At home, the family is likely to buy the large, economy size of detergent, perhaps at a supermarket or even at a hypermarket, because it can be easily stored in the laundry room at home and there is no question that, eventually, the family will use up that large bottle of detergent. Naturally, the large bottle is comparatively inexpensive per fluid ounce. But on vacation for a week at a rental cottage, the family prefers a small bottle of detergent—even if it is much more expensive per fluid ounce—because they do not want to end the week with a large amount left over (which they will probably have to leave at the cottage). Most vacationers are not at all surprised, or even reluctant, to pay a considerably higher price per ounce for the convenience of buying and using a smaller bottle of detergent, and indeed, unit prices for such products very commonly are much higher in resort towns' supermarkets than in supermarkets or hypermarkets serving permanent residents.

Spatial convenience provided by market decentralization of wholesale and/or retail outlets increases consumers' satisfaction by reducing transportation requirements and search costs. Community shopping centers and neighborhood supermarkets, convenience stores, vending machines, and gas stations are but a few examples of channel forms designed to satisfy consumers' demand for spatial convenience. Business buyers value spatial convenience too: The business PC buyers value the fact that CDW delivers PCs directly to their place of business and comes to pick up computers that need service.

Waiting time is the time period that the end-user must wait between ordering and receiving goods or postsale service. The longer the waiting time, the more inconvenient it is for the end-user, who is required to plan or predict consumption far in advance. Usually, the longer that end-users are willing to wait, the more compensation (i.e., the lower the prices) they receive. Conversely, quick delivery is associated with a higher price paid. This trade-off is evident in CDW's positioning to the small and medium business buyer: In response to queries about the threat of lower-priced computers from Dell Computer, the CEO of CDW said, "We are seldom below Dell's price, but we get it to you faster"—shipping in 1 day versus in 10–12 days from Dell.[5]

The intensity of demand for quick delivery may also vary between the purchase of original equipment (where it may be lower) versus the purchase of postsale service (where it is frequently very high). Consider, for example, a hospital purchasing an ultrasound machine. The purchase of the original machine is easily planned for, and therefore, the hospital is unlikely to be willing to pay a high price premium for quick delivery of the machine itself. However, if the ultrasound machine breaks down, the demand for quick repair service may be very intense, and the hospital may, therefore, be willing to pay a high price for a service contract that promises speedy service. In such cases, the sophisticated channel manager prices the sale of product versus postsale service very differently to reflect the different concatenation and intensity of demands for service outputs.

An example that offers combined insights into demands for bulk-breaking, spatial convenience, and delivery time is the beer market in Mexico. Here, understanding market demands requires an understanding of the market's and consumers' environmental characteristics and constraints. A market with limited infrastructural development, for instance, usually will be characterized by consumers with high demands for service outputs like spatial convenience (because the consumers cannot travel very easily to remote retail locations), minimal waiting time for goods, and extensive bulk-breaking (because consumers will not have sufficiently high disposable income to keep backup stocks of goods at their homes in case of retail stock-outs). In the Mexican market, major beer manufacturers sell through grocery stores, liquor stores, and hypermarkets, as well as through restaurants. However, they also sell beer through very small local distributors—apartment residents who buy a small keg of beer and resell it by the bottle to neighborhood buyers who cannot afford a six-pack of beer. These buyers provide their own bottles (frequently washed, used beer bottles) that the distributor fills. The manufacturer values this channel because the other standard retail channels do not meet the intense service output demands of this lower-end consumer.

Fourth, the wider the *breadth of variety* or the greater the *depth of product assortment* available to the end-user, the higher the output of the marketing channel system and the higher the overall distribution costs, because offering greater assortment and variety typically means carrying more inventory. *Variety* describes generically different classes of goods making up the product offering, that is, the *breadth* of product lines. The term *assortment*, on the other hand, refers to the *depth* of product brands or models offered within each generic product category. Discount department stores like Kohl's or Wal-Mart have limited assortments of fast-moving, low-priced items across a wide variety of household goods, ready-to-wear, cosmetics, sporting goods, electric appliances, auto accessories, and the like. In contrast, a specialty store dealing primarily in home audiovisual electronic goods, such as Tweeter, would have a very large and complete line of radios, tape recorders, and high-fidelity equipment, offering the deepest assortment of models, styles, sizes, prices, and so on.

Not only is the extent of the product array important, however; *what* assortment of goods is offered to the target consumer is also important. J. C. Penney, the American midscale department store retailer, has been seeking to change its image from "your grandmother's store"—and a downscale one at that—to a trendy fashion boutique. It signed an exclusive distribution agreement in 2003 with Michele Bohbot, the designer of the Bisou Bisou clothing line previously sold only in boutiques and upscale department stores. Penney has also hired David Hacker, a trend expert who looks for emerging fashion trends to attract the desired target, the so-called Holy Grail of retail: 25- to 35-year-old women, who account for $15 billion in annual clothing revenue. This is a much younger, fashion-forward shopper than Penney's traditional buyer, who is a 46-year-old woman. Indeed, a Bisou Bisou fashion show in a Bronx, New York, J. C. Penney store attracted almost 100 young women. One of them, laden with J. C. Penney shopping bags, said, "I guess I'm going to have to start coming to J. C. Penney now. Wow!"[6]

The right assortment and quick delivery is the winning service output combination for another retailer, Hot Topic. This chain of 450 stores across the United States targets teen girls; its 41-year-old CEO, Elizabeth McLaughlin, goes to rock concerts to see popular new trends that can be turned into new merchandise for the store. Hot Topic can roll out a new line of product (like t-shirts with a popular band's logo) in just eight weeks, very speedy in comparison to competitor Gap, Inc., which can take up to nine months to bring new product to its store shelves. This speed is critical when the right assortment is fueled by fads, which flame and fade very quickly. Hot Topic's responsiveness to the market helped it grow revenue 37 percent annually and to grow profit 35 percent annually for the years 2001 through 2003.[7]

Fifth, *customer service* refers to all aspects of easing the shopping and purchase process for end-users as they interact with commercial suppliers (for business-to-business [B2B] purchases) or retailers (for business to consumer [B2C] purchases). The discussion of CDW in Sidebar 2.1 outlines several different types of customer service valued by the small/medium business buyer, encapsulated in the statement, "We're the chief technical officer for many smaller firms." The online banking example in Sidebar 2.2 also shows that excellent customer service can sway the consumer to adopt what might otherwise be perceived as a risky new method of paying bills and can even result in broader consumer loyalty.

Excellent customer service can translate directly into greater sales and profit. One U.S. industry that has been plagued by poor customer service is cable- and other pay-TV services. In a 2003 American Customer Satisfaction Index (ACSI) survey, three cable-TV operators were noted for earning some of the lowest customer satisfaction scores for any company or industry in the entire survey. Customer service in this industry typically is outsourced to third-party providers (another channel partner) that offer low pay and poor training to their employees. But one provider, DirecTV, ranks at the top of its industry in customer satisfaction and as a result enjoys a high average monthly revenue from its customers, as well as a very low churn rate (the rate of turnover of end-users buying its service)—even though it uses the same outsourced customer service companies as some of its competitors. How does it accomplish this? It stations an employee at each of its outsourced call centers, thus providing more control; it pays the call centers more for customer service, which translates into better service provided; it provides better information to the customer service reps, due to an overhauled information system; and it gives the customer service reps various non-monetary forms of compensation, such as free satellite TV. DirecTV views these channel expenses as money well spent: It estimates that every one-tenth of a percentage point of market share represents 120,000 customers per year, and its churn rate had dropped from 1.7 percent in 2000 to 1.5 percent in 2003, below the industry average of 2.5 percent. The company estimates this saves it up to $120 million annually in customer acquisition costs.[8]

The type of customer service offered must be sensitive to the targeted end-user. Cabela's, a small chain of stores catering to the outdoorsman, succeeds by knowing the key fact about its target market: These are men who hate to shop. To appeal to them, Cabela's makes their stores a showcase of nature scenes and waterfalls populated by stuffed and mounted animals. It staffs its departments liberally with well-trained salespersons who have to pass tests showing their knowledge of its products. It offers outdoor kennels (for dogs) and corrals (for horses) to cater to customers who visit in the middle of a hunting trip (perfect, given the store's rural locations). Cabela's augments this targeted customer service with a carefully thought-out assortment of products: Its depth of assortment in most categories is six to ten times as great as competitors' like Wal-Mart, and it stocks high-end product, not just low-priced, low-quality goods. Further, it stocks products appealing to other members of the family, providing an assortment that draws women and children as well as men. Cabela's understands that rural shoppers want more than Wal-Mart can provide and that they care about service, fashion, and ambiance, not just price; as a result, they routinely draw shoppers willing to travel hours to reach the store (showing their willingness to trade spatial convenience for superior customer service and assortment).[9]

Finally, *information provision* refers to education of end-users about product attributes or usage capabilities, or prepurchase and postpurchase services. In both of our sidebars, the provision of information is a crucial service output to the consumer. The business PC buyer values presale information about what products to buy, in what combinations, with what peripheral computer devices attached, and with what service packages, as well as postsale information if and when components or systems fail. In the online bill payment situation, consumers may not even perceive information provision as a *demand*, but it is certainly a necessary service output to provide in order to explain to consumers the greater value they can enjoy from online bill payment. This example suggests that when innovating new channel technologies or processes end-users may simply be unaware of the benefits of adoption, and it is then up to the channel members to offer the relevant information to sway those end-users.

Some manufacturers and retailers now classify information provision at retail as solutions retailing and view it as crucial in generating new sales as well as upgrade sales from end-users. Home Depot offers do-it-yourself classes in all sorts of home improvement areas, and now computer and software companies like Hewlett-Packard and Microsoft have followed suit, setting up "experience centers" in retail stores to increase sales of complicated products whose benefits consumers may simply not yet understand, such as Media Center PCs, digital cameras that print on computers, personal digital assistants, and the like. For example, one collaboration between Microsoft and Hewlett-Packard offers through various retailers a series of educational programs designed to increase sales of H-P Media Center PCs. One section of the display, called Create, shows consumers how to use a Media Center PC as a digital-photography center with Microsoft software. Other associated displays show the consumer how to use the PC for home office applications, as part of a home-office network, and as a music center. Miniclasses are run by a third-party firm that staffs the retail store booths. Hewlett-Packard finds that purchase intent increases by as much as 15 percent among consumers who see these product demonstrations and believes the programs also strengthen the products' brand image and brand equity. Information dissemination of this type is a costly proposition; interestingly, Microsoft and Hewlett-Packard bear the costs of these retail efforts, not the retailers themselves.[10] However, they view these efforts as both crucial in the short run and redundant in the long run because the relevant information eventually diffuses into the broader consumer population.[11]

In general, the greater the level of service outputs demanded by meaningful segments of end-users, the more likely it is that intermediaries will be included in the channel structure. For example, if targeted end-users wish to purchase in small lot sizes, there are likely to be numerous intermediaries performing bulk-breaking operations between mass producers and the final users. If waiting time is to be reduced, then decentralization of outlets must follow, and therefore, more intermediaries will be included in the channel structure. Intermediaries that are closer to the end-user are also attractive additions to a manufacturer's channel structure by virtue of their precise targeting of specific desired end-user segments, as in the case of Gateway using CDW as a route to the small/medium business marketplace. Chapter 4 focuses in depth on the reasons for various channel structures.

Service outputs are produced through the costly activities of channel members (i.e., the *marketing flows* performed by them, discussed in depth in Chapter 3). For example, CDW's low waiting time for its business customers (whether or not they buy online) can be offered only with the help of the significant inventory holdings at their 400,000-square-foot distribution center. Thus, CDW engages in costly physical possession of inventory in order to produce the service output of low waiting time. As service outputs increase, therefore, costs undoubtedly will increase, and these higher costs will tend to be reflected in higher prices to end-users.

End-users sometimes have a choice between a low-service-output, low-price channel on the one hand and a channel offering high-service-output, high-price channel on the other. For example, a particular pair of running shoes is priced at $108.75 at a bricks-and-mortar New Balance running store in Chicago, but the same pair of shoes costs only $80.90 at zappos.com, an online shoe store. How can the pricier New Balance retail store survive against such price competition? The answer, of course, is that the New Balance store offers more than a specific pair of running shoes at a high price. It also offers custom fitting; the ability to see, touch, and try on the shoes before buying them; advice and in-store service from running pros; and easy returns. By contrast, zappos.com offers spatial convenience (how much more convenient can shopping be than from home!) but fails to offer the service outputs that the New Balance store does. Because zappos.com does not bear the high costs of running a chain of bricks-and-mortar stores, it can afford to offer the shoe at a lower retail price. A certain type of runner—the dedicated, reasonably serious one—values the in-store service offerings highly enough to return to the higher-priced, higher-service outlet again and again. Coexisting with them in the market, of course, are runners who are more price-sensitive and place lower value on the personalized service and touch-and-feel benefits of in-store purchasing; this segment of buyers finds the zappos.com offering (product plus service output bundle, for a given price) superior.

The more service-sensitive buyer may, of course, be able to "free ride" on the high-service retailer by consuming presale service such as seeing and touching the product before purchase and then buying the product itself at a lower-priced outlet such as an online store. This is common end-user behavior when consumption of valued service outputs is *alienable* from the purchase of the product itself, as in the prepurchase collection of product information. Free-riding becomes difficult or impossible when consumption of key service outputs is inextricably tied to, or *inalienable* from, the purchase of the product—as is true for postsale installation, consulting, or maintenance services. In the case of running shoes, many of the valued service outputs are alienable from the shoe purchase itself (e.g., prepurchase fitting advice, the ability to try on shoes before buying, and presales advice from professional runners in the store), but others are not (e.g., easy returns and postsale interaction with the professional running community). The continued survival of high-service running-shoe stores suggests the existence of a segment of buyers whose valuation for the *inalienable* service outputs is great enough to keep them buying at the high-service retailer.

Note that *price* has not been listed as a service output. This is because price is what is paid to *consume* the bundle of product plus service outputs; price is not a service that is itself consumed. That said, end-users routinely make trade-offs among service outputs, product attributes, and price and weigh which product/service bundle (at a specific price) provides the greatest overall utility or satisfaction. Because of this trade-off, marketing researchers often do investigate the relative importance of price along with service outputs and physical product attributes in statistical investigations like conjoint analysis. This is consistent with our conceptual view of price as something different from a service output—just as a physical product attribute is not a service output yet still affects an end-user's overall utility.

The six service outputs discussed here are wide-ranging, but may not be exhaustive in all situations. Therefore, one should not be inflexible in defining service outputs because different product and geographic markets may naturally demand different service outputs.[12]

A multiplicity of different channels can survive in a single market because of the variations in service output demands by different groups of end-users. Further, because an ideal channel often does not exist for a given end-user segment, the end-user typically must trade off service output bundles when deciding from which channel to buy or mix and match by patronizing multiple types of outlets and channels. One Manhattan journalist illustrated this principle by experimenting with shopping for the same dinner party ingredients from two very different grocery retailers: the hypermarket Costco, and the specialty grocer Stew Leonard's, both located outside Manhattan proper. Her experience showed that, while one could buy the relevant bundle of *products* at either of these places as well as at the usual inside-Manhattan grocery outlets, the service outputs accompanying each varied widely. Shopping inside Manhattan offered the greatest spatial convenience and also a broad variety of choices but suffered from a lack of some customer service amenities like convenient parking; it was also the most expensive option. Costco was much less expensive but did not offer bulk-breaking, spatial convenience (being outside Manhattan), broad assortment, or intensive customer service. Stew Leonard's offered customer service via an intensely interesting shopping experience described as a "theme park for shoppers" more than as a plain grocery store. Its other draws were fresh products and an element of assortment and variety, but like Costco, it was spatially inconvenient to the Manhattan shopper. The journalist's conclusion: Costco excels for buying staples; Stew Leonard's for seeking a shopping experience; but neither totally replaces the standard Manhattan grocery store.[13]

SEGMENTING THE MARKET BY SERVICE OUTPUT DEMANDS

Service outputs clearly differentiate the offerings of different marketing channels, and the success and persistence of multiple marketing channels at any one time suggests that different groups of end-users value service outputs differently. Thus, to effectively apply the concept of service outputs to channel design, we must consider the issue of channel segmentation according to service output demands. This means segmenting the market into groups of end-users who differ not in the product(s) they want to buy but also in *how* they want to buy them.

At the very high end of service valuation in any market is a (usually small) segment of buyers who are both very service-sensitive and very price-*in*sensitive and who can, therefore, be profitably served through a specialized channel. One such product category is men's clothing. Albert Karoll, a custom tailor in the Chicago area, sells fine custom men's clothing by visiting his customers rather than making them visit him as most fine clothiers normally would do. Karoll takes fabric, buttons, and all the makings of the clothes to customers, helps them choose the clothing they want, fits them, and then has the clothing made before returning to the client to deliver the finished goods for any final alterations. His target buyer segment clearly has a very high demand for *spatial convenience*, as stated by one of his loyal suburban customers: "For me to travel downtown is very hard to do. I'd much rather have him come here. It saves me time and money, and I get the same quality that I'd get going downtown to his store." The target customer also values custom clothing made to order—the ultimate in assortment and variety. Karoll also provides quick service and delivery, both pre- and postsale; he once even flew from Chicago to Birmingham, Alabama, to alter some clothing sent to a client there, just two days after the client received the clothes and found they needed alterations. Ultimately, Karoll's target customer is a man whose most scarce asset is *time*, and from this flow the customer's extremely high demands for service outputs and his correspondingly low price sensitivity. Note that Karoll does not seek to serve every man who would like to buy a suit; instead, he has carefully crafted a business centered around the provision of service rather than just the sale of a high-end piece of business clothing, and he knows both who *is* in his target segment and who is *not*. In this sense, the targeting decision when applied to channel design can be seen as a choice of whom *not* to pursue just as much as of whom *to* pursue.[14]

From a marketing research perspective, it is essential to generate a comprehensive understanding of all the relevant service outputs demanded by different end-users. This is accomplished by conducting qualitative focus groups and/or one-on-one exploratory interviews to generate an unbiased list of all the service outputs that apply to the particular product and market in question.[15] This research results in a full set of service outputs that might be demanded by some or all groups of end-users in the market.

Once the list of possible service outputs is identified, the market can be segmented in two different ways. It can be divided into a priori segments (such as those often used in product or advertising decisions) and then analyzed in order to see whether those segments share common purchasing preferences. Alternatively, research can be designed and conducted from the start to define channel segments that best describe end-users' service output demands and purchasing patterns. It is much better to follow this latter path because end-users' preferred shopping and buying habits rarely correlate highly with their preferences for product features, their media habits, their lifestyles, or other common segmentation schemes that management and advertising agencies usually employ. In general, the channel segmentation process should be carefully designed to produce groups of buyers who (a) are maximally similar *within* a group, (b) are maximally different *between* groups, and (c) differ on dimensions that *matter* for building a distribution system. For example, IBM France serves thousands of end-users through their reseller network. They seek to segment their end-users by the ways in which those end-users want to purchase computer hardware and software (i.e., their service output demands), but these dimensions are not easily observable. Instead, IBM France uses flags, or indicators of service output preference, which are rough descriptions of the buyers (e.g., florist, doctor, travel agent) that correspond to data found in publicly available business directories. The result is an end-user segmentation of 46 segments in 10 market divisions in the French market. IBM France uses this segmentation to customize promotional campaigns that help its reseller partners find customers; it finds that many small prospects are responsive to web promotions, for instance, and this increases the effectiveness of the promotional effort.[16]

Traditional marketing research techniques like conjoint analysis, hybrid modeling, or constant-sum scales are useful in quantitative calibration of the importance of various service outputs to different channel segments. It is not enough to ask respondents their preference for various service outputs. Given free choice, most individuals are likely always to prefer more of *all* the service outputs. To obtain information that ultimately will be useful in designing marketing channels to meet the key needs of target segments, it is essential to understand how end-users are likely to actually behave in the marketplace. Researchers can do this by making respondents trade off one attribute of the channel for another (e.g., locational convenience versus low price versus extensive product variety versus expert sales assistance). Research tools like those mentioned here can be carefully used to create the necessary trade-off data.[17]

Table 2.3 shows how this type of channel analysis using constant-sum scales can help to identify relevant segments of the business marketplace for a new high-technology product. The service outputs (references and credentials, financial stability and longevity, product demonstrations and trials, etc.), along with price sensitivity, are listed down the left hand side of the table. The columns represent the segments (lowest total cost, responsive support, full-service, and references and credentials) that emerge from a cluster analysis. The names assigned to the segments were derived from the strength of the preferences for specific service outputs. For example, the lowest total cost segment assigned 32 out of 100 points to the service output of lowest price but only 8 points to that of responsive problem solving after sale, while the responsive support segment allocated 29 points to responsive problem solving after sale, but only 8 points to lowest price. Finally, the percentage of respondents in each segment is given at the bottom of each column, indicating that the majority of respondents (and thus of the population of customers at large, assuming the sample is representative) are in the full-service segment. This study allows a trade-off between price and service outputs in recognition of the fact that a segment's demands for service outputs really reflect its willingness to pay for them—hence the pricing connection.

Some interesting insights can be generated from Table 2.3. First, marketing channels serving any of the specific segments will be required to deliver more of some service outputs than others. This means that any one channel solution likely will not be able to satisfy the needs of all segments. For example, lowest price is highly valued only in one segment (the lowest total cost segment, representing only 16% of respondents), suggesting that the majority of the market is not driven primarily by price considerations. This information is invaluable in designing channel solutions that respond to the service output needs of customers, even if doing so implies higher prices than a no-frills solution. Further, all segments value installation and training support at least moderately highly; therefore, this support capability must be designed into every channel solution. Similar insights can be gathered by inspecting the rows of Table 2.3 to discern contrasts among segments on other specific service output demands.

These insights were then used to propose channel structure solutions to fit each segment's particular needs (for more discussion of the channel structure decision, see Chapter 4). The proposed channel structure is pictured in Figure 2.1. The full service segment (largest at 61% of respondents in Table 2.3) is best served through two possible channels, one including value-added resellers (VARs) and one including dealers as intermediaries. These intermediaries are capable of providing the specific and high levels of service outputs demanded by the full service segment. At the other end of the spectrum, the lowest total cost segment can be served suitably through a third-party supply channel that outsources most functions. This low-cost, low-service output channel provides precisely the combination these customers desire. The responsive support segment and the references/credentials segment can be served through similar channels, but the latter segment's desire for validation of the seller makes the additional use of associations, events, and awareness efforts a valuable addition to the channel offering.

The constant-sum scale approach is typically the most useful in determining which service outputs are relatively most important in driving the ultimate behavior of each unique segment. It forces the respondents to trade off one service output for another because only 100 points are available to allocate among the service outputs.

Table 2.3   Business-to-business channel segments for a new high-technology product

Possible Service Output Priorities	Lowest Total Cost/ Presales Info Segment	Responsive Support/ Postsales Segment	Full-Service Relationship Segment	References and Credentials Segment
References and Credentials	5	4	6	25
Financial Stability and Longevity	4	4	5	16
Product Demonstrations and Trials	11	10	8	20
Proactive Advice and Consulting	10	9	8	10
Responsive Assistance During Decision Process	14	9	10	6
One-Stop Solution	4	1	18	3
Lowest Price	32	8	8	6
Installation and Training Support	10	15	12	10
Responsive Problem Solving After Sale	8	29	10	3
Ongoing Relationship with a Supplier	1	11	15	1
Total	100	100	100	100
% Respondents	16%	13%	61%	10%

Respondents allocated 100 points among the following supplier-provided service outputs according to their importance to their company:

■ = Greatest Discriminating Attributes   ■ = Additional Important Attributes

Source: Reprinted with permission of Rick Wilson, Chicago Strategy Associates, © 2000.

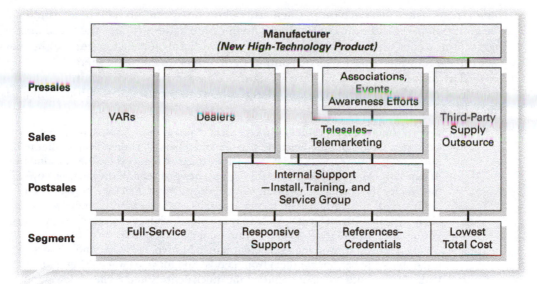

Figure 2.1   Ideal channel system for business-to-business segments buying a new high-technology product

Source: Reprinted with permission of Rick Wilson, Chicago Strategy Associates, © 2000.

However, this analysis alone does not tell the full story of the differences between segments of end-users. Also important is the determination of how highly the various segments of end-users value *overall* the service outputs. For example, in Table 2.3, it might be true that the full-service relationship segment values all service outputs more highly than does the lowest total cost segment. Put another way, an end-user in the lowest total cost segment is willing to pay less for a given level of support/maintenance/reliability than is a relationship segment end-user, and this can be true for all service outputs. A constant-sum scale analysis could even produce equal weights for service outputs between two segments, suggesting that the two segments are really just one segment, when, in fact, end-users in the two segments differ in their *overall* valuation of the channel's service outputs. In short, both *relative* weights and *absolute valuation* matter in segmenting a market for marketing-channel design.

While gauging how much end-users are willing to pay for each desired service output is a difficult part of the research process, it is nevertheless important. This knowledge helps in the evaluation of alternative channel approaches to meeting service output demands as the overall system is designed.

MEETING SERVICE OUTPUT DEMANDS

One of the basic precepts in marketing is that the seller should seek to identify and then meet the needs of its end-users in the marketplace. In the marketing channel strategy context, this means creating and running a marketing channel system that produces the service outputs demanded by targeted end-user segments. However, being responsive to service output demands when designing marketing channels can be very expensive and time-consuming. The question arises whether there are market conditions under which a channel manager can profitably serve a segment in the market *without* fully meeting the service output demands characterizing them.

The answer has multiple parts by nature. The key factors determining whether and how quickly to respond to knowledge about unmet service output demands include:

> **Cost:** Sometimes it is prohibitively expensive (from a supply perspective) to meet expressed service output demands. Channel members must then decide whether or not to provide the service, and if so, whether to cover that cost for the consumer or to explicitly charge the consumer for high service provided. If the channel covers the cost for the consumer, its profit per sale drops, but if it charges consumers for the high cost of providing high service levels, its customer base and sales volume are likely to drop. Channel members have to decide which is the lesser of the two evils. For instance, consider a loyal Lands' End catalog/online shopper who is an American currently working as an expatriate in Mexico. He likes Lands' End's tailored shirts. He has bought them from Lands' End for years when living in the United States, and has always enjoyed the quick delivery and relatively low shipping charges Lands' End offers in the United States. But he discovers that having the same shipment of shirts shipped to him in Mexico will cost much more than it used to, as Table 2.4 shows.[18] Note that the fastest shipping option to a Mexican address, UPS, takes 1 to 2 weeks, so delivery to a Mexican address in 3 to 5 days is not offered at *any* shipping charge; it is just not feasible, given Lands' End's shipping arrangements outside the United States. Further, even giving up on quick delivery still means paying a premium for shipping. Lands' End is likely to lose some of its sales to such loyal customers as a result—but it is still probably the right decision, given the very high cost of serving them.

> **Competitive:** The question here is whether existing competitors can beat this channel's current service output provision levels. It may be that *no* competitor currently in the market exceeds this channel's service output levels, and therefore, the added cost of improving service would not lead to any change in market share from current market sales for the channel in question (although it could lead to an increase in total market sales by attracting new buyers who were not willing to buy at the previously lower overall service levels). The online bill payment example in Sidebar 2.2 provides a graphic comparison of competitive service output offerings and shows that online bill payment offered little competitive threat to standard paper-based

Table 2.4   Shipping charges for $150 purchase of shirts from Lands' End

Buyer's Location	Shipping Method	Shipping Charge	Time to Delivery
United States	Standard UPS	$11.95	3 to 5 business days
Mexico	Surface Mail	$20.00	8 to 12 weeks
Mexico	Priority Air	$30.00	2 to 4 weeks
Mexico	UPS	$50.00	1 to 2 weeks

Source: www.landsend.com (accessed August 2005).

bill payment in terms of service outputs delivered for the fees charged. The poorer service level and higher cost of online bill payment were contributing factors in its slow adoption in the United States.

➤ **Ease of entry:** Competition comes not just from firms currently in operation but also from *potential* competitors, or entrants to the industry. A channel that fails to meet end-user segments' demands for service outputs may find itself surprised by the incursion of new competition with better technologies for meeting those demands. If entry is somehow blockaded, the existing competitors can continue in their current channel strategies. But if entry is easy, providing parity service to the market may not be sufficient. This is precisely the challenge facing distributors of music CDs in today's market, where entrants offering online downloads of music provide not only quicker delivery and more spatial convenience (downloads *now*, done *at home*), but also offer precisely the assortment the consumer wants (it is possible to download just the song or songs the consumer wants without having to buy an entire album). As a result, retail sales of recorded music dropped from $13 billion in 1999 (when Napster was launched) to approximately $10.6 billion in 2003; the Wherehouse retail chain and Tower Records both filed for bankruptcy in the interim, while Musicland Group, the second-largest retailer, closed more than 20 percent of their stores.[19]

➤ **Other elements of excellence in the marketing offering:** The marketing channel is one part of the overall marketing mix. A truly superior product or a tremendously low price can lead end-users to buy through a channel that does not quite meet their service output demands. For example, even very time-constrained, wealthy consumers may spend large amounts of time searching for just the right addition to their home décor. Such end-users find it necessary to do so because of the lack of a good alternative means of buying the specific products they want (i.e., a deficiency of *assortment*). However, the existence of an unmet service output demand means that there is a potential threat to the channel that offers some, but not all, elements of a marketing mix tailored to the target end-user's demands.

The key insight here is that none of these arguments alone is sufficient to guarantee protected markets and sales if the channel fails to offer the level of service outputs demanded by target end-users. Where there is a market opportunity, the chances are that rivals (either those currently competing against this channel or potential entrants) will sooner or later figure out how to exploit that opportunity. Thus, in the short run it certainly is possible to maintain a strong market share, and even loyal end-users, with a less than stellar service output demand provision. But over the longer run, the chances of success with this course of action diminish because of the overwhelming incentive to compete for these end-users' sales.

THE ROLE OF SERVICE OUTPUT DEMAND ANALYSIS IN MARKETING CHANNEL DESIGN

After segmenting the market and identifying each channel segment's distinct service output demands, the channel manager can integrate these insights into the overall marketing channel design and management plan. In particular, this information should be used to *assess segment attractiveness, target a subset of the segments identified,* and *customize the marketing channel system solution used to sell to each targeted segment.*

Targeting a channel segment means focusing on that segment, with the goal of achieving significant sales and profits from selling to it—just as Albert Karoll, the custom men's suit seller described previously, has done. He recognizes that his target end-users "are business executives, men who are short on time, who work their brains out."[20] Note that this description *excludes* most buyers of business suits and, further, that Karoll's segmentation definition hinges not on product purchased but on the services that accompany it. Therefore, Karoll's high-service (and high-price) offering will *not* meet the demands of most suit buyers—but it is ideal for Karoll's identified target buyers.

More generally, if the channel segmentation exercise has been properly done, targeting multiple channel segments for channel system design purposes will imply a need to build different marketing channels for each targeted segment. Because this can be costly and hard-to-manage, channel managers are likely to target the most attractive subset of all the identified segments. This implies a corollary to the targeting concept: *targeting means choosing which segments* not *to target.* This can be a difficult challenge for a channel management team because all segments offer the potential for revenue dollars (although not always for profits). Segmented-service-output-demand information, however, will help the channel manager decide which segments offer the greatest relative growth and profit opportunities for targeting. Even though other segments also may have some potential, only the best should be chosen for targeting. *Best*, of course, has different meanings for different companies and should include the size and sales potential of the targeted segment, the cost to serve it, and the intensity of competition for its business, among other factors.

The information on the targeted segments is then used either to design new marketing channels to meet its needs or to modify existing marketing channels to better respond to its demands for service outputs. Service output demand analysis can identify a new market opportunity that leads to the development of entirely new ways to sell to a particular segment. One example of this idea is fandango.com, a business formed by seven of the ten largest movie exhibitors in the United States to sell movie tickets through a different channel: online (or by phone).[21] Instead of going to a movie theater the evening one wants to see a particular movie, standing in line, and often finding out that the showing of that movie is sold out, the buyer can go online at fandango.com and purchase in advance a ticket for a particular showing of a particular movie at a particular movie theater for a small fee per ticket. Tickets can be printed at home or picked up at the theater at convenient kiosks, saving time and lessening uncertainty for the consumer. This new channel for purchasing theater tickets provides the consumer a lower waiting/delivery time (because there is no wait at the theater), higher spatial convenience (because buyers can search for and buy theater tickets online), and a very broad assortment and variety (because fandango.com sells tickets to nearly 70% of all theaters in the United States that are enabled for remote ticketing). Clearly, fandango.com is not for every moviegoer, at least in part because of the extra charge per ticket it imposes for the extra service provided. But fandango.com can both allow theaters to take market share in the target segment of time-constrained moviegoers from non-fandango-capable theaters and also expand the total market for in-theater movie watching because of the greater convenience it offers.

Similarly, consider an advertisement for bn.com, the online arm of the Barnes & Noble bookstores and, thus, its second major route to market. Table 2.5 lists the

Table 2.5   Copy from an advertisement for BN.com

Advertising Copy	Service Output Offered
"Really free shipping": Offers free shipping if two or more items are purchased. "We make it easy and simple."	Customer service.
"Fast & easy returns": End-user can return unwanted books to a bricks-and-mortar Barnes & Noble bookstore. "Just try and return something to a store that isn't there."	Quick delivery (for returns), spatial convenience; note implicit comparison with Amazon.com, the pure-play online bookseller.
"Books not bait": Promises no additional sales pitches to buy nonbook products.	Assortment/variety: Just books (targeting the book lover). Again, note implicit comparison with Amazon.com.
"Same day delivery in Manhattan": Delivery by 7:00 p.m. on any item(s) ordered by 11:00 a.m. that day. "No other online bookseller offers that."	Quick delivery: The offer is possible because of Barnes & Noble's warehouses in New Jersey, near Manhattan. Note direct comparison with other online booksellers (notably, amazon.com).
"The gift card that gives more": Can be used either online or in the bricks-and-mortar bookstores nationwide.	Spatial convenience, assortment/variety: When buying a gift for a friend, this provides virtually limitless assortment and does so anywhere the recipient lives in the United States.
"bn.com—1,000,000 titles; amazon.com—375,000 titles"	Assortment/variety: Direct comparison with amazon.com, offering a broader assortment of titles to the consumer.

Source: Advertisement for BN.com in *Wall Street Journal*, November 20, 2002, p. A11.

promises made in the advertisement and maps those promises to the effective service outputs offered. Note that the advertisement does not trumpet specific *books* (i.e., not the *products* to be bought) but the *way in which they are to be bought* as the offering for sale. Further, it contrasts the offer of this combination of service outputs with those from competitors (primarily amazon.com) to convince the buyer that bn.com is the place to buy books online. Finally, note that the advertisement clearly targets the segment of end-users who specifically love books in great variety and does so in a way that clearly differentiates it from the competition.

Ideally, the service output demand analysis performed by the channel manager should be used for both positioning (channel design) and targeting purposes. Indeed, pursuing a targeting and channel design policy without this information is risky because one cannot be sure of having executed properly without knowing what the marketplace wants in its marketing channel. Given the expense of setting up or modifying a marketing channel, it is prudent to perform the demand-side analysis before proceeding to the supply-side decisions that are also critical to a successful channel policy. Done correctly, an analysis of target segments' service output demands can be the foundation of higher profits that come from high-margin sales to intensely loyal end-users.

With this understanding of the demand side of the marketing channel design problem, we can turn to the supply side in Chapter 3 to see how a marketing channel operates to produce service outputs through the concerted efforts of all its members.

Take-Aways

- An end-user's decision about where to purchase a product (or service) depends not just on *what* the end-user is buying but also on *how* the end-user wants to buy it.
- The elements of *how* the product or service is bought are called *service outputs*: Service outputs are the productive outputs of the marketing channel, over which end-users have demand and preference.
- A general list of service outputs, customizable to particular marketplace contexts, is:
  - Bulk-breaking
  - Spatial convenience
  - Waiting time (or quick delivery)
  - Variety and assortment
  - Customer service
  - Information provision
- To make their final purchase decision, end-users make trade-offs among different combinations of (a) product attributes, (b) price, and (c) service outputs offered by different sellers.
- Segmenting the market by service output demands is a useful tool for channel design because the resulting groups of end-users are similar (within each group) in terms of the channel that best serves their needs.
- Cost, competitive, ease of entry, and compensatory service output provision factors can mitigate the need to excel in providing service outputs to the target market.
- The ultimate purpose of service output demand analysis is to assess segment attractiveness, target a subset of the segments identified, and customize the marketing channel system solution used to sell to each targeted segment.

DISCUSSION QUESTIONS

1. For each of the three scenarios below, categorize the demand for bulk-breaking, spatial convenience, waiting/delivery time, and assortment/variety as high, medium, or low. In each case, explain your answers.
   a. A woman in an emerging-market country of Southeast Asia wishes to buy some cosmetics for herself. She has never done so before and is not entirely sure of the occasions on which she will wear the cosmetics. She does not live near a big city. She is too poor to own a car but has a bit of extra money for a small luxury.

b. A manufacturer uses a particular industrial chemical in one of its large-scale production processes and needs to buy more of this chemical. The rest of the raw materials for its plant operations are delivered in a just-in-time fashion.

c. Before you visit certain parts of the world, you are required to get a yellow fever vaccine. Many travelers let this slip until the last minute, forgetting that it is advisable (or avoiding an unpleasant shot as long as possible). But they definitely realize they need the shot, and they do not want to have to cancel their trip at the last minute because they did not get it. They often find themselves making a long trip to a regional medical center because they did not plan ahead.

2. For the three scenarios in Question 1, describe a marketing channel that would meet the target end-user's demands for service outputs.

3. Describe three different buying situations with which you are familiar and the SODs of the buyers in each one. Do you think the SODs being supplied are close to those being demanded? Why or why not?

4. Give an example of a service output demand that goes beyond the standard ones of bulk-breaking, spatial convenience, waiting/delivery time, assortment/variety, customer service, and information provision.

5. Give an example of market segmentation that is appropriate for the purposes of product design but inappropriate for the purposes of marketing channel design. Conversely, give an example where the product-design segmentation is also useful for marketing channel design purposes. Explain your answers.

ENDNOTES

1. Information for this sidebar is drawn from: Campbell, Scott (2003), "CDW-G Calls on VARs," *Computer Reseller News*, November 17, p. 162; Campbell, Scott (2004), "CDW Snags Companywide Cisco Premier Status: Relationship Advances Reseller's Bid to Build Services Business," *Computer Reseller News*, April 12, p. 12; Gallagher, Kathleen (2002), "CDW Computer Remains Afloat Despite Market's Choppy Waters," *Milwaukee Journal Sentinel*, September 29, Business Section, p. 4D; Jones, Sandra (2004), "Challenges Ahead for CDW; Dell Deals Make Inroads in Already Difficult Market," *Crain's Chicago Business*, June 28, p. 4; Kaiser, Rob (2000), "Vernon Hills, Ill., Computer Products Reseller Has an Approach to Win Business," *Chicago Tribune Online Edition*, August 16; McCafferty, Dennis (2002), "Growing Like Gangbusters: Sales at Chicago-Area CDW-Government Shot Up 63 Percent from 2000 to 2001," *VAR Business* online, July 8; Moltzen, Edward (2003), "Looking for SMB Traction, Gateway Inks Reseller Pact with CDW," *Computer Reseller News*, May 26, p. 55; O'Heir, Jeff (2003), "CDW Teams with Small VARs to Access Government Biz," *Computer Reseller News*, August 25, p. 6; O'Heir, Jeff (2003), "Time to Move On," *Computer Reseller News*, October 20, p. 98; Schmeltzer, John (2003), "CDW Pulls Out the Stops to Reach Small Business," *Chicago Tribune Online Edition*, September 8; and Zarley, Craig and Jeff O'Heir (2003), "Seeking Solutions: CDW, Gateway and Dell Come Calling on Solution Providers for Services Expertise," *Computer Reseller News*, September 1, p. 16.

2. Bucklin, Louis P. (1966), *A Theory of Distribution Channel Structure* (Berkeley, CA: IBER Special Publications); Bucklin, Louis P. (1972), *Competition and Evolution in the Distributive Trades* (Englewood Cliffs, NJ: Prentice Hall); and Bucklin, Louis P. (1978), *Productivity in Marketing* (Chicago: American Marketing Association), pp. 90–94.

3. More information about the growth and nature of online bill payment systems is available from the following sources: *Information Week* (2001), "Online Invoicing Ready For Business-To-Business Users,"

Information Week, November 12, p. 80; Ip, Greg and Jacob M. Schlesinger (2001), "Questions of Security: Even Temporary Disruption in Delivery of Mail Could Be Another Economic Blow," *Wall Street Journal*, October 23, p. A10; Rosen, Cheryl (2001), "Seamless B-to-B Online Payment Systems Readied," *Information Week* September 10, p. 54; Adler, Jane (2002), "Suddenly, Security," *Credit Card Management* 14, no. 11 (January), pp. 30–35; Bruno, Mark (2002), "Charge Customers to Pay Bills On-Line? Forget It," *USBanker* 112, no. 7 (July), pp. 19–20; Higgins, Michelle (2002), "The Dark Side of Online Billing: Missed Payments, Glitches Drive Many Back to Checks," *Wall Street Journal*, October 17, p. D1; Higgins, Michelle (2002), "Honest, the Check Is in the E-Mail: To Lock in Customers, Banks Step Up Push to Get You to Pay Bills Online; Making It Automatic," *Wall Street Journal*, September 4, p. D1; Hoffman, Karen Epper (2002), "Electronic Bill Payment Comes of Age," *Community Banker* 11, no. 7 (July), pp. 16–21; Rombel, Adam (2002), "Electronic Billing Catches On," *Global Finance* 16, no. 3 (March), pp. 49–50; Rombel, Adam (2002), "Businesses Tell Their Suppliers: Present Your Invoices Online," *Global Finance* 16, no. 8, July/August, pp. 22–24; Varon, Elana (2002), "To Bill or Not to Bill (Online): Digital Invoicing Is the Next Big Step in E-Business Transactions," *CIO* 16, no. 3 (November 1), p. 1; Webster, John (2002), "Moving Beyond Just Paying the Bills," *Computerworld* 36, no. 42 (October 14), p. 40; *ABA Bank Marketing* (2003), "Consumers Pay More Bills Online, But the Check Habit Persists," *ABA Bank Marketing* 35, no. 3 (April), p. 8; Bernstel, Janet B. (2003), "Bill Pay: Where's the Payoff?" *ABA Bank Marketing* 35, no. 6 (July/August), pp. 12–17; Bielski, Lauren (2003), "Hard to Get the Online Habit," *ABA Banking Journal* 95, no. 2 (February), pp. 79–86; Brooks, Rick and Charles Forelle (2003), "Despite Online-Banking Boom, Branches Remain King," *Wall Street Journal*, October 29, p. B1; Forrester Research (2003), "Few U.S. Consumers Pay Bills at Bank Sites," *Forrester First Look: Research Highlights*, September 18; Gonsalves, Antone (2003), "E-Bill Paying a Hit with Consumers," *Insurance and Technology* 28, no. 5 (May), p. 43; Gutner, Toddi (2003), "Online Bill Payment," *Business Week*, October 20, p. 162; Higgins, Michelle (2003), "How to Break Up with Your Bank: Direct Deposit, Online Billing Make Switching an Ordeal; Some Ways to Make It Easier," *Wall Street Journal*, August 14, p. D1; Martin, Steven (2003), "Who Needs Cash?" *Information Week*, December 22–29, p. 20; Nelson, Kristi (2003), "E-Payment Competition Heats Up," *Bank Systems & Technology* 40, no. 7 (July), p. 35; Scheier, Robert L. (2003), "The Price of E-Payment," *Computerworld* 37, no. 21 (May 26), pp. 25–26; Dean, Teresa J. (2004), "Getting Customers to Try: Online Bill Payment," *Community Banker*, Annual Buyers Guide pp. 22–24; Lankford, Kimberly (2004), "Why It's Time to Pay Bills Online," *Kiplinger's Personal Finance*, April, pp. 84–87; Ng, David (2004), "On-Line Bill Payment: Cost-Benefit Ratio Still Not Clear Among Respondents," *Bank Technology News* 17, no. 6 (June 1), p. 20; Park, Andrew, Ben Elgin, and Timothy J. Mullaney (2004), "Checks Check Out: With Online Bill Payment and Processing, Use of Paper Checks Is Headed for a Steep Decline," *Business Week*, May 10, p. 83; Ramsaran, Cynthia (2004), "AOL Introduces Free Online Bill Payment Service," *Bank Systems & Technology* 41, no. 6 (June), p. 56.

4. Lankford, Kimberly (2004), "Why It's Time to Pay Bills Online," *Kiplinger's Personal Finance*, April, pp. 84–87.

5. Jones, Sandra (2004), "Challenges Ahead for CDW: Dell Deals Make Inroads in Already Difficult Market," *Crain's Chicago Business*, June 28, p. 4.

6. Daniels, Cora (2003), "J. C. Penney Dresses Up," *Fortune*, June 9, pp. 127–130.

7. Weintraub, Arlene (2003), "Hotter than a Pair of Vinyl Jeans," *Business Week*, June 9, pp. 84–86.

8. Parks, Bob (2003), "Where the Customer Service Rep Is King," *Business 2.0* 4 (June), pp. 70–72.

9. Helliker, Kevin(2002), "Retailer Scores by Luring Men Who Hate to Shop," *Wall Street Journal Online,* December 17, online.wsj.com/article/ 0,,SB1040076142891025818,00.html (accessed August 2005).

10. This example raises a twofold issue: first, identifying which service outputs to provide (here, information provision) and, second, which channel member(s) should provide them. In this case, it is worth it to the suppliers (Hewlett-Packard and Microsoft) to bear the cost of information provision because the retailer is not willing to do so despite the apparent value. The retailer's unwillingness stems from its ability to sell many other products without bearing high information provision costs, among other things. Issues regarding which channel member should bear which channel flow costs are dealt with in depth in Chapter 9 on vertical integration.

11. Saranow, Jennifer (2004), "Show, Don't Tell," *Wall Street Journal Online,* March 22, online.wsj.com/article/ 0,,SB107956027620658292,00.html (accessed August 2005).

12. Rangan, V. Kasturi, Melvyn A. J. Menezes, and E. P. Maier (1992), "Channel Selection for New Industrial Products: A Framework, Method, and Application," *Journal of Marketing* 56, no. 3 (July), pp. 72–73, define five service outputs in their study of industrial goods. These are product information, product customization, product quality assurance, after-sales service, and logistics. Some of these are simply specific examples of the generic service outputs defined by Bucklin (e.g., logistics refers to the spatial convenience and waiting/ delivery time outputs). Their work does

highlight the value of being aware of the specific application, however.

13. Hesser, Amanda (2002), "The Truth About My Dinner Party," *New York Times Online,* October 9, query.nytimes.com/gst/ abstract.html?res=F10913FD3A5F0C7A8CD DA90994DA404182 (accessed August 2005).

14. Stanek, Steve (2003), "Custom Tailor Finds House Calls Often Worth the Trip," *Chicago Tribune Online Edition,* July 13, Transportation section, page 1, ISSN: 10856706, available from pqasb.pqarchiver.com/chicagotribune(ac cessed August 2005).

15. Such data sometimes already exist. For example, in the computer industry, data on service outputs valued by end-users are collected by firms like IntelliQuest, Incorporated, and International Data Group.

16. Brouillet, Sylvie (1998), "IBM Segmente, Détecte, Chasse Sa Clientèle," *Action Commerciale,* no. 43, p. 178.

17. See Green, Paul E. (1984), "Hybrid Models for Conjoint Analysis: An Expository Review," *Journal of Marketing Research,* 21, no. 2 (May), pp. 155–169. See also Churchill, Gilbert A. Jr. (1987), *Marketing Research,* 4th ed. (Chicago: The Dryden Press), pp. 364–376.

18. www.landsend.com (accessed August 2005).

19. Keegan, Paul (2004), "Is the Music Store Over?" *Business 2.0 Online,* March 2004, www.business2.com/b2/web/articles/ 0,17863,591734,00.html (accessed August 2005).

20. Stanek, Steve (2003), "Custom Tailor Finds House Calls Often Worth the Trip," *Chicago Tribune Online Edition,* July 13, Transportation section, page 1, ISSN: 10856706, available from pqasb.pqarchiver.com/chicagotribune (accessed August 2005).

21. See www.fandango.com (accessed August 2005) for more details.

The Service Output
Demands Template

TOOLS FOR ANALYSIS

Table 2.5 shows a completed service-output-demands analysis in the market for telecommunications equipment and services. This analysis rests on the collection of sophisticated marketing research data. The marketing channel manager is in general well advised to do marketing research to determine what end-users really want in the way of service outputs because the cost of guessing wrong is very high in the channels context.

In this appendix, we discuss what to do in filling out the service output demands (SOD) template in Table 2A.1 (an empty and generic version of that in Table 2.5). We will not assume here that the channel manager has detailed, quantitative marketing research data but will try instead to give an intuitive idea of how to perform such an analysis and what to do with the information thus codified. The service output demands template is designed to help the reader (a) segment the market, (b) in ways that matter for distribution channel design, and (c) to report on the segments' different demands for service outputs.

The first task is to identify the segments in the market being served. Standard segmentation measures may or may not be appropriate in the channel management context. The key criterion in assessing whether segmentation has been done properly is whether the resulting groups of buyers require different sets of service outputs. For example, we could identify two segments for buyers of laptop computers: men and women. This might be a valid segmentation criterion for some purposes

(e.g., choosing advertising media through which to send promotional messages), but it is unlikely to be useful in a channel design and management context because there is no discernible difference in the service outputs demanded by men and women. A better segmentation might be, for example, (a) business buyers, (b) home buyers, and (c) student buyers.

The next step is to fill in information about the service output demands of each of the identified segments on the SOD template. While more information is always better, in the absence of detailed marketing research data it can be useful to simply identify demands as being low, medium, or high. It is then often useful to note how the service output demands are expressed. Here are a few prototypical examples:

- A business buying laptop computers wants to buy more units than does a home or a student buyer. Since breaking bulk (i.e., providing a smaller lot size) requires an effort, we would say that the business segment has a low demand for the bulk-breaking service output, while the home buyer and the student have a high demand for the bulk-breaking service output (because they typically want to buy only one computer at a time).

- Spatial convenience may be important to all three segments but for different reasons. Here, it may be important to note that the sale of a laptop computer is not over when the unit is initially purchased; postsale service is a critical factor that affects initial purchase decisions and, of course, also affects subsequent satisfaction of the end-user. With that in mind, one might argue

Table 2A.1 The service output demands (SOD) template

Segment Name/Descriptor	Bulk Breaking	Spatial Convenience	Delivery/ Waiting Time	Assortment/ Variety	Customer Service	Information Provision
			Service Output Demand:			
1.						
2.						
3.						
4.						
5.						

Instructions: If quantitative marketing-research data are available to enter numerical ratings in each cell, this should be done. If not, an intuitive ranking can be imposed by noting for each segment whether demand for the given service output is high, medium, or low.

that the home and student buyers have a relatively low demand for spatial convenience at the point of initial purchase but might have a high demand for spatial convenience when it comes to getting a faulty unit fixed or getting technical service. Conversely, the business buyer may have a high demand for spatial convenience at the initial point of purchase (may, for example, require a salesperson to visit the company rather than having a company representative go to a retail store), but a large enough company may even have in-house computer repair and consulting facilities and, hence, might have a low demand for spatial convenience for postsale service.

- The demand for delivery/waiting time is said to be high when the end-user is unwilling to wait to get the product or service. Impulse purchases are a classic product category for which almost all segments of end-users have a high demand for the delivery/waiting time service output. What can we say in the case of our laptop computers? Again, we can differentiate between the delivery/waiting time demands at initial purchase and those at the postsale service step. At initial purchase, the home buyer probably has a low demand for delivery/waiting time because when the machine arrives probably is not crucial. A student may have a very high demand for quick delivery, however, particularly if the unit is purchased to match the beginning of the school year. A business buyer may have a very high demand for this service output as well if the lack of the laptops means lower sales force productivity, for example.

    At the postsale service stage, home buyers may also have a low demand for the delivery/waiting time service output because they may be willing to put up with a delay in getting technical service or repairs—their use of the computer may not be a life-or-death matter. Students, however, have a very high demand for the delivery/waiting time service output on the postsale service side because their cost of downtime is very high (cannot get homework done without the unit). Interestingly,

business buyers may have a low demand for this service output for two reasons: (a) they may have internal service facilities and, hence, may not depend on the manufacturer's technical service or repair facilities; and (b) they may have excess units in inventory that can be swapped for a faulty unit until it is fixed.

- Assortment/variety demands refer to the segments' preference for a deep assortment in a given category and for a wide variety of product category choices. In our laptop example, we can rephrase this statement to ask, how intense are our segments' demands for assortment of computer brands, and how intense are their demands for a variety of computers, peripherals, software, and so forth? Business buyers probably have a very precise demand for brand of computer because they typically want conformity across the units in use in the company. Hence we would say they have a low demand for assortment. Note, however, that aggregated across the entire population of business buyers, our laptop marketer may observe considerable diversity in brand preference. Thus, we sometimes see a different variety demand when we look at the market from a micro perspective (customer-specific level) versus from a macro perspective (market-wide level). Business buyers may have a moderate to high demand for variety (e.g., software to do word-processing, spreadsheets, and database management; printer ports, PC cards, etc., on the demanded list of peripherals), depending on the variety of tasks they want the laptop to perform. Among home computer buyers the demand for variety is probably the lowest because they may be the least sophisticated laptop users and may, therefore, demand only the most basic word-processing and game software. However, their demands for assortment (brand choice) may be high because unsophisticated consumers typically want to see a selection of models and brands before making a purchase decision. Student buyers probably fall between the other two segments in their demand for assortment/variety: This segment may have more applications or uses for the laptop, necessitating more peripherals and software programs, but may or may not need to see a wide assortment of brands before making the purchase (indeed, the relevant brand set may be quite small if the school has dictated which brands are preferred).

- Customer service demands will differ widely among the business, home, and student buyers. Even the *types* of customer service demanded could differ across the segments. For instance, a student buyer probably values home delivery very highly, as few students have cars to carry large items back from the store where they are purchased. A home buyer may not care about home delivery but may value in-home installation services to network multiple computers. A business buyer might not care about either of these benefits but might highly value trade-in options on older machines.

- Information provision demands in the laptop purchase example can be separated into presale and postsale information elements. Before purchase, a buyer may need information not only about differences in physical product attributes but about how components fit together in a system and how to use the new state-of-the-art features a new computer provides. After purchase, the buyer may have questions about what add-on peripheral devices can be used with the computer and how to use them or about what version of certain software programs to buy to use with the machine. Home buyers are likely to place the highest value on both presale and postsale information provision from channel members because they are the least likely to have a support group in place to provide key information about what, how, and where to buy. A student buyer is likely to have informational needs postpurchase more than prepurchase, particularly if the student's school recommends a certain subset of laptops. An individual business buyer is likely

to have relatively lower informational demands than the other two groups, both pre- and postpurchase, particularly if the company is large enough to (a) prespecify approved laptop models and (b) support them after purchase. However, the procurement specialist at the company is likely to have significant presale informational needs at the time decisions are being made about which laptop models to support.

Once the SOD template is filled out, the information it codifies has several strategic uses:

1. It may help reveal why sales tend to cluster in one segment to the exclusion of others. If postsale service is poor, for example, it may be difficult to sell to home and student buyers.

2. It may suggest a new channel opportunity to build sales to an underserved segment. Perhaps a channel structure can be designed that is ideally suited to the needs of student buyers. Doing so would lock out the competition that otherwise would fight on the basis of price alone for these sales.

3. It may identify commonalities among segments previously thought to be totally distinct. Home and student buyers may share enough similarities that both can be served with only minor variations on a single channel theme.

4. This template can suggest which channel form would best suited to serve each segment. Thus, it provides inputs to match segments to channels.

It is important to remember that this list of service output demands may not completely characterize demands in a specific market. The customer service demand, for example, is sometimes broken out into presale and postsale service elements, as is the information provision service output demand.

Supply-Side Channel Analysis

Channel Flows and Efficiency Analysis

Learning objectives

After reading this chapter, you will:

- Be able to define the eight generic channel flows that characterize costly and value-added channel activities

- Understand how the efficiency template helps codify channel flow performance by channel and by channel participant

- Understand the role of channel flow allocation in designing a zero-based channel

- Understand how channel flow performance leads to appropriate allocation of channel profits among channel members using the Equity Principle

- Be able to place the channel flow analysis in the overall channel audit process

- Know how to use the efficiency template with little available information

The channel management schematic in Figure 1.3 of Chapter 1 specifies that efficient channel response to the recognition of end-users' service output requires several tasks, including deciding on a channel structure, splitting the workload of the channel among the available channel members, creating and fostering the desired degree of commitment in the channel system, and updating channel design to minimize gaps in channel performance. A basic understanding of how the work of a marketing channel gets done is fundamental to answering all of these questions, and that is the focus of this chapter. Manufacturers, wholesalers, and retailers participate in marketing channels to create the service outputs (bulk-breaking, quick delivery, spatial convenience, and assortment and variety) demanded by their target end-users. Just as a production plant produces physical products, the members of a marketing channel are also engaged in productive activity. This is so even if what they produce is intangible. The productivity derives from the value end-users place on the service outputs resulting from channel efforts. The activities or functions that produce the service outputs demanded by end-users are our specific topic here. We call these activities *channel flows*.

Identifying *what channel flows* are performed in the marketing channel, *by whom*, and *at what levels* is helpful in several aspects of channel management. First, detailed knowledge of the flow performance in the channel helps the channel manager diagnose and remedy shortcomings in the provision of service outputs. Second, the concept of channel flows can be used to design a new channel or revise an existing channel to minimize the cost of providing desired service outputs. Third, knowing which channel members have incurred the cost of performing what flows helps in allocating the profits of the channel equitably. This may help channel members preserve a sense of fairness and cooperation and thus avert channel conflicts (the topic of Chapter 7).

We carry over in this chapter our discussion of CDW and online bill payment, first discussed from a service output perspective in Chapter 2 (Sidebars 3.1 and 3.2). We add to this a discussion of reverse logistics, the process by which returned merchandise is handled by the channel (Sidebar 3.3). This chapter's discussion focuses on channel flow identification and performance in these channels as well as how channel specialists, who focus on particular channel flow activities, can reduce total channel costs.

CHANNEL FLOWS DEFINED

Eight Generic Channel Flows

Section 1.3 in Chapter 1 introduces the concept of channel flows (see particularly Figure 3.1, which reproduces Figure 1.2). As that discussion points out, specific channel members may specialize in performing one or more flows and may not participate at all in the performance of other flows. Further, it may be tempting to remove a particular channel member from the channel (i.e., to change the channel *structure*), but the flows performed by that channel member cannot be eliminated. When a channel member is removed from the channel, its functions need to be shifted to some other channel member to preserve service output provision in the channel. The only exception to this rule would occur if the eliminated channel member were performing flows that were already being performed elsewhere in the channel, so that its contributions to service output provision were redundant and hence unnecessary. For example, an employee salesperson and an independent distributor sales representative might call on the same customer, resulting in wasted effort and cost. The channel is better off using one or the other, but not both, salespeople in this case.

Every flow not only contributes to the production of valued service outputs but also carries an associated cost. Figure 3.1 gives examples of the channel cost-generating activities associated with each flow. For instance, physical possession refers to all channel activities concerned with the storage of goods, including their transportation between two channel members. The costs of running warehouses and of transporting product from one location to another are thus physical possession

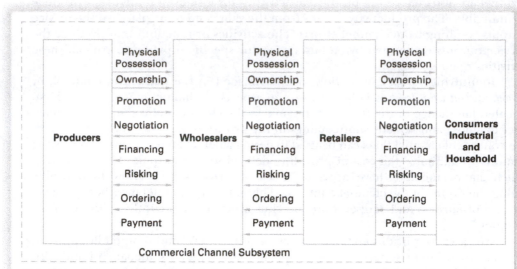

The arrows above show flows of activity in the channel (e.g., physical possession flows from producers to wholesalers to retailers to consumers). Each flow carries a cost. Some examples of cost of various flows are given below:

Market Flow	Cost Represented
Physical possession	Storage and delivery costs
Ownership	Inventory carrying costs
Promotion	Personal selling, advertising, sales promotion, publicity, public relations costs
Negotiation	Time and legal costs
Financing	Credit terms, terms and conditions of sale
Risking	Price guarantees, warranties, insurance, repair, and after-sales service costs
Ordering	Order-processing costs
Payment	Collections, bad debt costs

Figure 3.1   Marketing flows in channels

costs. In the case of commercial PC purchases, Sidebar 3.1 on CDW shows that CDW's intermediary role involves significant physical possession investments, including running a 400,000-square-foot warehouse and buying product from manufacturers in large volumes.

In the case of a *service* like online bill payment, physical possession costs are incurred by channel members who host the data (i.e., those who own, operate, and maintain the computer hardware and software systems necessary to provide ready access to the financial data in the system). While this might seem a trivial channel flow, given that this is a services market, it is in fact both costly and crucial to the channel's success.

When we consider the example of product returns (whether in the consumer-good or industrial-good context), physical possession and how it is managed is the driving channel flow in shaping how the reverse channel is run, who its members might be, and where the ultimate destination for the product will be. Figure 3.2 in Sidebar 3.3 shows some probable pathways for the physical movement of product.

Sidebar 3.1

CDW and PC purchases by small/medium
business buyers
Channel flow and equity principle insights[1]

Sidebar 2.1 profiles computer systems reseller CDW and its success in serving small and medium business buyers through its superior provision of service outputs. Clearly, its ability to do this rests on its performance of key channel flows in a more efficient (lower-cost) and effective (better at producing service outputs) manner than other channel partners could do. The channel flows in which CDW plays a key role include physical possession, promotion, negotiation, financing, and risking. CDW also offers flexibility to its buyers, so that not all buyers have to pay for and consume all of the flows CDW can offer. Through this mechanism, CDW effectively offers differentiated packages of flow performance to the market through basically one umbrella channel structure. Also noteworthy is that in all of its operations CDW makes significant investments in information— not considered a channel flow per se but a facilitator of efficient performance of many other functions in the channel, as we will see here.

CDW'S ROLE IN BEARING CHANNEL FLOW COSTS

Table 3.1 summarizes CDW's participation in key marketing channel flows. Each of these has specific implications for channel efficiency (cost management) and/or channel effectiveness (minimizing total channel-wide costs subject to maintenance of desired service output levels).

As a channel intermediary, one of the key flows that CDW performs is physical possession. The entries in Table 3.1 for this flow indicate that CDW takes on a significant portion of the costly burden of holding inventory (through its 400,000-square-foot warehouse and its large volume purchases). The entries also suggest,

however, that CDW's participation in the physical possession flow lowers the total channel cost of inventory holding. In particular, the fact that CDW ships 99 percent of orders the day they are received suggests that CDW is expert at interpreting demand forecasts for minimal inventory holding costs. CDW's investment in asset tagging for its government buyers also constitutes a costly channel flow investment that is designed to reduce later physical possession costs through its ability to provide quick information to both CDW and its buyers about the location of inventory (for example, to schedule routine service and maintenance calls and to reduce product theft or loss). CDW's large-volume purchases also reduce system-wide inventory holding costs. Interestingly, they are accompanied by reduced wholesale prices from suppliers, a fact about which smaller wholesale buyers (so-called solution providers) have complained. In response to these complaints, one journalist commented: "Can anyone say that price [paid by CDW] is not deserved? The company receives about eight trailers full of products from each of those distributors every day. They are bulk loads, stripped of the value-added services the distributors usually tack on to the smaller sales of their general solution provider customers."[2] The implication, of course, is that taking large volumes of product at once actually lowers the supplier's cost of selling into the market, improving channel efficiency.

CDW's *promotional* investments in the channel are also extensive, as Table 3.1 demonstrates. CDW trains its salespeople for several months when they start on the job, thus providing its channel partners with experienced promotional agents to sell their products. CDW

(continued)

Sidebar 3.1 (cont.)

CDW and PC purchases by small/medium business buyers

Table 3.1   CDW's participation in various channel flows

Channel Flow	CDW's Investment in Flow
Physical possession	(a) CDW has a 400,000-square-foot warehouse.
	(b) CDW ships 99 percent of orders the day they are received.
	(c) CDW has instituted an asset tagging system that lets government buyers track what product is going where; product is scanned into both buyer and CDW databases for later ease in tracking products (e.g., for service calls).
	(d) CDW buys product in *large volumes* from manufacturers, taking in approximately eight trailer-loads of product from various suppliers every day. Loads are received in bulk, with few added services.
Promotion	(a) CDW devotes a salesperson to every account (even small, new ones!), so that an end-user can talk to a real person about technology needs, system configurations, postsale service, etc.
	(b) Salespeople go through 6 1/2 weeks of basic training, then 6 months of on-the-job coaching, then a year of monthly training sessions.
	(c) New hires are assigned to small-business accounts to get more opportunities to close sales.
	(d) Salespeople contact clients not through in-person sales calls (too expensive) but through phone/e-mail.
	(e) CDW has longer-tenured salespeople than its competitors.
Negotiation	(a) CDW-G started a small-business consortium in 2003 to help small firms compete more effectively for federal IT contracts.
	(b) What CDW-G gives the small business partner: lower prices on computers than they could otherwise get; business leads; and access to CDW's help desk and product tools.
	(c) CDW also handles shipping and billing, reducing the small business partner's channel flow burden.
	(d) What the small business partner provides: access to contracts CDW otherwise could not get.
Financing	(a) CDW collects receivables in just 32 days.
	(b) CDW turns its inventories two times per month.
	(c) CDW has no debt.
Risking	(a) "We're a kind of chief technical officer for many smaller firms."
	(b) In April 2004, CDW was authorized as a Cisco Systems Premier (CSP) partner in serving the commercial customer market.

Sidebar 3.1 (cont.)

CDW and PC purchases by small/medium business buyers

also devotes a salesperson to every account—even small, new accounts that initially generate low revenues. The company recognizes it cannot afford to have salespeople call on such accounts in person, so it serves them through phone or e-mail contacts (thus controlling promotional channel flow costs). But the salesperson is available for any question the customer might have and is the (well-trained) conduit to expanding sales from each of these accounts. A customer that has a relationship in place with a CDW salesperson is likely to buy more from CDW because of the relatively high-touch relationship it enjoys given the initially small purchase levels. Because of these investments, CDW reaps reduced promotional costs through its long-tenured sales force: The company finds that a salesperson with three or more years of tenure on the job generates approximately $30,000 in sales per day on average, twice as much as someone with two years of experience and ten times as much as a salesperson with less than six months of experience!

An interesting example of clever management of negotiation flow costs in Table 3.1 comes from CDW's government arm (called CDW-G), which established a small-business consortium in 2003 to help small computer services firms compete for U.S. government information-technology contracts. These small firms benefit from a government directive to seek to award 23 percent of its procurement contracts to small businesses (this means that the small firms already have a *negotiation* advantage with the government); however, the small firms still must offer competitive price bids, which is difficult to do when buying small quantities of product to put into their systems solutions. CDW's contribution to this process was to provide both expertise and more competitive

wholesale prices for computer equipment to the small firms, enabling them to compete in price as well as in category of provider. In this sense, CDW offers superior negotiating capability to its small-firm partners so that they, in turn, can generate greater sales. CDW of course benefits from this, because CDW itself would not qualify for the small-business preference in government contracting. This arrangement is thus a fine example of complementary inputs that jointly generate superior negotiating power for the channel partners.

CDW also performs financing flows efficiently, as Table 3.1 demonstrates. It does so through its creditable inventory turn rate of twice per month (inventory turn rate measures how frequently a bit of shelf space, here in the CDW warehouse, empties and is replenished with inventory). CDW is also efficient at collecting payment, with just a 32-day average receivable figure (which in turn helps it minimize the total financing cost borne in the channel), and the company has no debt (reducing the financing cost of capital).

Finally, CDW's extensive investments in expertise and information serve not only to reduce other channel flow costs, but also to reduce risk for its buyers. One manager quoted in Table 3.1 says, "We're a kind of chief technical officer for many smaller firms"; in short, the small buyer relies on the expertise and knowledge offered by CDW to guarantee that the right systems solutions are chosen. Similarly, in serving commercial customers in general, CDW's authorization as a Cisco Systems Premier (CSP) partner signals its expertise in providing full solutions for its commercial customers, not just computer components. A CDW executive explains that this authorization lets CDW act as a "trusted adviser" for the customer so that

(continued)

Sidebar 3.1 (cont.)

CDW and PC purchases by small/medium business buyers

CDW can "really talk technical about what a customer is trying to accomplish and really add value to the sale, as opposed to just sending out a box."[3] The channel-wide efficiency in managing the cost of risk comes because CDW can learn relevant information and then apply it for many customers, rather than each customer's having to invest in the knowledge individually; in short, customers can benefit from the economies of scale generated by CDW in information gathering.

CDW also offers its customers a choice of how intensively they wish to transfer channel flow costs onto CDW's shoulders. The discussion here suggests that CDW routinely performs significant channel flows, but when serving an end-user with a technical service capability of its own and/or a direct relationship with the computer manufacturer, CDW is willing to lessen its participation in channel flows. One example of this is CDW's role in serving the Kellogg School of Management at Northwestern University. The Kellogg School uses CDW as its provider of laptop and desktop computers for students, faculty, and staff. Kellogg specifies IBM as its laptop computer provider in order to limit the number of stock-keeping units (SKUs) it has to support. Once machines are purchased from CDW (i.e., once CDW passes physical possession over to the Kellogg buyer), the product warranty is with IBM directly, not with CDW, and repairs are also done by IBM. Kellogg Information Systems (KIS) has the technical capability to handle some repairs in-house and offers loaner machines to faculty and staff when it must ship their computers back to IBM for servicing. Further, CDW is not responsible for the post-sale services that Kellogg students and faculty enjoy when they buy the Kellogg-sanctioned laptop. Instead, it is KIS that installs the Kellogg-customized software images on the machines and tests them before handing them over to the ultimate buyer. In this example, then, we see a buyer that can itself perform certain important channel flows, and CDW responds flexibly by offering tiered service levels to let the end-user spin off to them only those channel flows that the end-user cannot or does not want to perform.

CDW'S USE OF THE EQUITY PRINCIPLE IN FLOW MANAGEMENT AND INCENTIVE CREATION

There are two notable ways in which CDW acts in accordance with the Equity Principle in its channel flow participation and in the rewards it offers to its channel partners. The first is its decision to compensate its employee salespeople through commissions that are the same, whether the customer's sale is generated person-to-person through the salesperson or via online ordering (both of which CDW offers). Recall from the preceding discussion of the promotion flow that every customer is assigned a CDW salesperson, in the hope that more promotional (sales force) contact will generate a higher lifetime value of these customers. But suppose that a customer interacts with the CDW salesperson periodically for major purchases but buys replacement components (e.g., printer cartridges) and smaller routine purchases online. Is it fair to award sales commissions to the salesperson for these online purchases? CDW believes it is indeed fair, because these online purchases resulted at least in part from the initial sales efforts of the salesperson in building the customer relationship. Further, CDW recognizes that it is not only how costly the inputs were that matters; it is also

---

Sidebar 3.1 (cont.)

CDW and PC purchases by small/medium
business buyers

how the customer wants to buy that matters. If the customer prefers to make certain purchases online, for instance because that method is easier than contacting a salesperson, then CDW wants to create an internal incentive system that supports the customer's freedom of choice among purchasing channels. Through its equal-commission policy, CDW avoids creating a pernicious incentive in the salesperson to force the customer to buy in person rather than online.

Another way in which CDW obeys the Equity Principle is by offering a separate fee to smaller solution providers with which it partners to serve some ultimate end-users. In these situations, CDW relies on the solution provider to do on-site work for the end-user, such as installation, software or hardware customization, provision of postsale customer service, and the like. The Equity Principle suggests that these solution provider partners would be unwilling to undertake these costly activities unless they knew they would be compensated for doing them, and the fee structure offered by CDW gives them adequate reward for doing so. This is a straightforward example of "paying them what they're worth," the heart of the Equity Principle.

The sidebar also emphasizes that controlling physical possession costs—through such means as holding inventory in the channel for a shorter time—is a powerful tool for improving overall channel profitability because of the enormous costs of handling product returns.

Note that the costs of physical possession are distinct from the costs of ownership, the second flow. When a channel member takes title to goods, it bears the cost of carrying the inventory; capital is tied up in product (the opportunity cost of which is the next highest-valued use of the money). In many distribution systems, such as commercial personal computer sales, physical possession and ownership commonly move together through the channel, but this need not be so. In consignment selling, for example, product is physically held by a retailer (e.g., an art gallery owner) but is owned by the manufacturer (e.g., the painter or sculptor). The manufacturer gives up ownership of the product only when it is sold to the final buyer. Separation of ownership from physical possession occurs when a manufacturer contracts with a third-party reverse logistics specialist such as Channel Velocity (www.channelvelocity.com); the specialist handles the reverse flow of the product, but ownership rests with the manufacturer, distributor, or retailer that hires the specialist. The specialist in cases like this receives payment through a fee for service or a percentage split of the ultimate resale revenue for the returned merchandise. Similarly, the data hosting company in the online bill payment situation does not actually own the data that it holds.

Despite the fact that physical possession and ownership by definition are separate channel flows, they travel together in many channel systems. A common term to designate the combined costs is *inventory holding costs*. Inventories in this sense are

Sidebar 3.2

Online bill payment
Channel flows and channel performance insights

We have already introduced the concept of electronic bill presentment and payment (EBPP) in the consumer context in Chapter 2 (see Sidebar 2.2).[4] Here, we build on that discussion by focusing on the supply side of the process: how channel members produce online bill payment for their customers and how bill payers, as well as billers themselves, act as channel members bearing (and seeking to manage) the costs of invoicing and paying. Because electronic bill payment is a technology for managing the payment flow in business-to-business (B2B) and business-to-consumer (B2C) contexts, the discussion here will refer to both.

Introducing EBPP technologies into a channel system changes the way several channel flows are performed, sometimes in unexpected ways. Consider the following:

- *Physical possession:* Online bill payment and invoicing involves using state-of-the-art technology including specialized computers and software. Who in the channel is (or should be) responsible for holding that equipment, and just as importantly, the data housed on those computers and accessed by that specialized software? As a concrete example, consider a biller (say, a credit card company) that uses a bank's services to issue electronic bills (invoices) to consumers, which consumers then pay electronically. The bank itself usually chooses to retain a specialized intermediary (called an applications service provider, or ASP) that runs the relevant software and warehouses the data to accomplish electronic bill payment. These ASPs then can be said to bear significant physical possession costs in the channel. They have sufficient scale of operations across all their banking clients to be able to offer these services even to small community banks—something these smaller

banks could not efficiently offer themselves. Alternatively, a company could choose to develop its own technology and infrastructure to offer these services, in which case it would be responsible itself for holding and managing all invoicing and payment data.

- *Promotion:* It is less expensive to engage in promotion to consumers who use electronic payment services. AT&T Wireless Services, Inc., has found that customers who use e-billing and other online services stay longer with the company than those who do not. Similarly, bank customers who pay their bills online through the bank are more than two times as likely to stay with the bank. Further, they are more profitable customers, retain higher bank balances, and are in the highest household income brackets. These *loyalty* benefits directly imply a less intense need to extend promotional efforts to these customers than to those who do not use e-bill payment services.

- *Negotiation:* Especially in the contexts of B2B invoicing and payment, one of the demonstrated benefits of electronic payment systems is the lower cost of processing and resolving billing disputes. One study[5] claims that up to 85 percent of the benefits of electronic invoice presentment and payment result from the elimination of manual resolution of billing disputes. Similarly, a study by Gartner Research in 2002 estimated that 15 percent of invoices issued by large businesses result in a dispute, each of which costs between $20 and $40 to resolve by nonelectronic means. Considerable savings are possible with electronic technologies.

- *Risking:* Several elements of risk and its management bear mention in the context of electronic invoicing and payment.

Sidebar 3.2 (cont.)

Online bill payment

We have already mentioned one key obstacle to the adoption of e-bill payment by consumers: a concern about the integrity of the payment process relative to that of paper bill payment. In the channel flows context, we can translate this into the insight that (a) the consumer is, in fact, a channel member, and (b) the consumer perceives that adopting e-bill payment carries with it an increased risk that the bill will be paid incorrectly or not paid at all. In effect, perceptually, a channel flow cost (that of risk) is thrust upon the consumer, with an insufficient level of compensating benefit. There are other elements of risk, as well. In the B2B context, adopting EBPP requires authentication software that guarantees that trading partners are who they say they are (i.e., protects against a computer hacker breaking into the invoicing and payments system), as well as guaranteeing their creditworthiness. Incorporation of these software elements into EBPP systems has been a key risk-management tool that enhances the attractiveness of the systems both for the biller and the payer. Finally, executed properly, EBPP (whether offered to business or consumer end-users) can reduce the risk of billing errors in the system. Clearly, the total (true plus perceived) cost of the risking flow in an e-payments system balances negative and positive effects; over time, the perceptual increase in risk that consumers have expressed is likely to fall significantly, producing a net reduction in total risking costs in the e-payment channel system.

- *Ordering:* From the bill payer's perspective in a B2B system, electronic invoicing and bill payment can greatly reduce ordering costs—if the EBPP system is integrated with other systems inside the payer's organization, such as purchasing, accounts payable, and order management. Investment in such integration systems has lagged behind the investment in systems to issue bills electronically; in the B2B arena, creating cost reductions for *both* seller and buyer is key to generating wide adoption of EBPP.

- *Payment:* Clearly, this is the key channel flow activity affected by electronic invoice presentment and payment. From the biller's perspective, EBPP can generate faster payments as well as reducing the administrative and postage costs of issuing bills. From the payer's perspective, it is true that e-payment may reduce the float in bill payment—that is, the ability to delay payment while bills are being processed. But this is counterbalanced by the lower costs of issuing payment when it can be done electronically. On net, payment costs tend to fall throughout the channel system under e-invoicing and payment.

These are the major effects of introducing electronic bill payment technologies on channel flow performance. The net effect clearly is to reduce ongoing channel flow costs through EBPP's salutary effects on several channel flows. But how much does it cost to establish an electronic payment system, and when does a firm reach the breakeven point on investments made in instituting EBPP in its channel system? There is general agreement that processing paper bills is much more expensive than processing electronic ones; the U.S. Treasury estimated in 2001 that the cost of consummating a paper-based payment is 22.5 times as high as that of the corresponding electronic payment. Further, paper-based payments can involve literally dozens of intermediaries.

There are several different estimates of the fixed cost to establish an e-billing and payments system with its associated time to break even on that investment. The initial set-up costs can range from a few hundred thousand dollars to

(continued)

Sidebar 3.2 (cont.)

Online bill payment

over one million dollars; one study of 100 major online billing companies reported an average of $1.1 million spent on their e-billing systems, but because the marginal cost of processing these bills is so much lower, the system can break even in a reasonable amount of time. On a per-bill basis, the estimates are that e-bill payment saves between $5.00 and $8.00 per invoice; one study by Gartner consultants estimates that a business that sends out 66,000 invoices per month can save $7.25 per bill sent and paid online. To take a specific example, if the system costs $600,000 to set up but saves $6.00 per electronically processed invoice, the break-even point occurs when 100,000 bills are paid online. Clearly, the very smallest firms would not find this financially attractive, but the benefits are significant for medium to large-scale enterprises.

Specialized intermediaries have sprung up to manage electronic bill presentment and payment so that the very channel structure has changed with the advent of the new technology. For example, Xign (founded in 2000; www.xign.com) markets electronic order delivery, invoicing, and payment services to companies engaging in B2B sales. Over 12,000 suppliers (i.e., billers) participate in its network, offering one-stop payment systems to payers such as Payless ShoeSource, Bristol-Myers Squibb, and Sprint. Xign's systems integrate with the payer's internal systems to save costs to the payer and are also linked with financial services firms to provide seamless money transfer services between payer and biller. Such intermediaries help make the market by bringing together all the functions necessary to generate cost savings throughout the channel; without them, it is unlikely that the potential benefits of electronic invoicing and payment could be achieved.

stocks of goods or the components used to make final goods. Inventories exist for several reasons:[6]

> ➤ Demand surges outstrip production capacity. To smooth production, factories produce to meet the anticipated surge. Inventory results. The demand surge may be natural (e.g., ice cream demand rises in summer), or it may be due to marketers' actions, such as short-term promotions. The discipline of supply-chain management developed in the grocery industry mainly because retailers stockpile goods to take advantage of manufacturer promotions. The result is high inventory carrying costs, including the cost of obsolescence.

> ➤ Economies of scale exist in production or in transportation. Inventory then results from batch-processing orders to make a long production run or from stockpiling goods to fill containers, trucks, ships, and planes.

> ➤ Transportation takes time because of the distances between points of production and points of consumption. Downstream channel members keep inventories (pipeline stock) to hold them over until a shipment arrives and can be unpacked and put out to use.

> ➤ Supply and demand are uncertain. Buyers are uncertain how long it will take to be resupplied (lead time)—if they can get the stock at all. Thus, they acquire safety stock (the excess of inventory over the best estimate of what is needed during an order cycle) as a hedge against uncertainty. That uncertainty is often in the form of ignorance about what will sell (demand uncertainty).

Sidebar 3.3

Reverse logistics
Channel flows for returned merchandise[7]

Product returns generate a whole host of costs that are often ill-understood (or completely ignored) by the manufacturers, distributors, or retailers accepting the returned goods. Among the costs are freight (not just for the outgoing initial sale but for the incoming return), handling, disposal or refurbishment, inventory holding costs, and the opportunity cost (or foregone value) of lost sales. The scope of the problem is very large, as Table 3.2 shows.

Furthermore, returns are very significant in many industries. In a survey of over 300 reverse logistics managers in 1998, researchers found the ranges for return percentages shown in Table 3.3. While the percentage returns vary widely by industry, returns clearly are a significant headache in many industries.

Given the high cost of handling returns, some retailers have put tighter controls on consumers seeking to return merchandise. For example, Target, Best Buy, and CompUSA charge restocking fees of 10 percent to 15 percent on returned electronics products. This means that a consumer who purchases a $500.00 camera and then returns it will get back only $425.00 to $450.00. Similarly, Baby Mine Store, Inc., a baby apparel and accessories store, charges a 10% restocking fee for returned product. These policies are designed to curtail consumer returns and thereby help control the overall cost of returns through the channel. But they also reduce the quality of the experience the consumer enjoys and can lead to a poorer brand reputation and lower sales. Given this potential for negative demand-side effects, managing returns well becomes even more imperative for firms at all levels of the channel.

WHAT HAPPENS TO A RETURNED PRODUCT?

When an end-user returns a product, that unit can end up in one of many places (see Figure 3.2). One survey found that retailers and

Table 3.2   **Product returns**

A large-scale problem

Costs and Scope of Product Returns

- The value of returned goods is close to $60–100 billion annually in the United States.
- Web returns alone had value between $1.8 and $2.5 billion in 2002.
- Estimates are that the cost of processing those Web returns is twice as high as the merchandise value itself!
- U.S. companies are estimated to spend from $35 billion to more than $40 billion per year on reverse logistics.
- The average company takes 30–70 days to move a returned product back into the market.
- The estimated number of packages returned in 2004 is 500 million.

(continued)

Sidebar 3.3 (cont.)

Reverse logistics

Table 3.3   Product returns
Percentage ranges

Industry	Return % Ranges
Magazine publishing	50%
Catalog retailers	18–35%
Book publishers	20–30%
Greeting cards	20–30%
CD-ROMs	18–25%
Computer manufacturers	10–20%
Book distributors	10–20%
Mass merchandisers	4–15%
Electronic distributors	10–12%
Printers	4–8%
Auto industry (parts)	4–6%
Consumer electronics	4–5%
Mail order computer manufacturers	2–5%
Household chemicals	2–3%

manufacturers variously disposed of products by sending them to a central processing facility, reselling them as is, repackaging them and selling them as new products, remanufacturing or refurbishing them before selling, selling to a broker, selling at an outlet store, recycling them, dumping them in landfills, or donating them to charity. In general, retailers appear to have invested more heavily in reverse logistics management technologies than have manufacturers using automated handling equipment (31 percent versus 16 percent), bar codes (63 percent versus 49 percent), computerized returns tracking (60 percent versus 40 percent) and entry (32 percent versus 19 percent), EDI (31 percent versus 29 percent), and RFID (radio frequency identification) (37 percent versus 25 percent).

One perhaps surprising example of refurbishment is in the greeting-card industry. U.S. greeting-card companies instruct their retailers to box up their unsold cards (for example, the day after Valentine's Day or Mother's Day) and send them to a return center in Mexico, where they are checked for resellability, refurbished if possible (with smoothed envelopes and card edges), and readied for the next year's holiday. Such a process may work well in industries where inventory holding costs are low (storing a card for a year takes up almost no space), but may be too costly otherwise.

A newer channel for reselling returned products is eBay, the online auction house. Some manufacturers resell their returned product directly on eBay: Dell can recover up to 40 percent of a returned computer's value when it resells it on eBay, but only 20 percent of the value when it resells it through other channels. Other firms use dedicated third-party reverse logistics firms, such

Sidebar 3.3 (cont.)

Reverse logistics

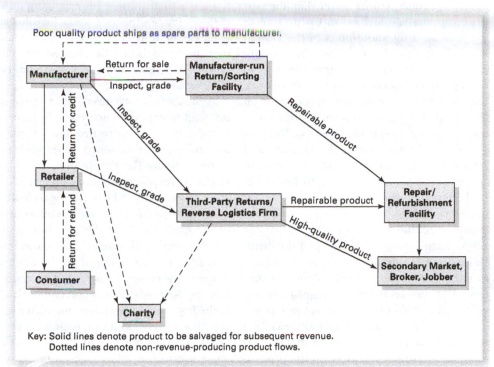

Figure 3.2   **Possible pathways for returned product**

as Channel Velocity (www.channelvelocity.com). Channel Velocity provides complete returns and reverse logistics services, including receiving returned product directly at its dedicated Atlanta warehouse, checking and refurbishing returned product, repackaging product, and running the eBay auction for the product, all for a percentage fee. Other companies offer software-only solutions to manufacturers, but these often require significant customization and investment by the manufacturer—cost that the manufacturer may be reluctant to incur.

More generally, a third-party independent specialist in reverse logistics can engage in a 360-degree management process combining state-of-the-art flow management both for outbound initial shipments and subsequent returns. This includes investments in efficient shipping (both ways), expertise for assessing which returned products are salvageable and which should be disposed of, repairs/refurbishment, repackaging, and returning inventory for resale.

In the case of the pharmaceutical drug industry, a third-party outsourcer often can

(continued)

Sidebar 3.3 (cont.)

Reverse logistics

manage product returns better than the best drug wholesalers. McKesson Corp., one of the leading drug wholesalers in the United States, with annual sales of over $57 billion, chose to outsource the returns function to third-party logistics company USF Processors, Inc. McKesson encourages its downstream channel partners (such as retail pharmacies or hospital pharmacies) to use USF as well. One of USF's valued capabilities is the evaluation of returned product for appropriate allocation of credits to the pharmacies that returned them. Each returned item must be checked by lot number and expiration date to verify whether or not a refund is due and to provide for appropriate disposal or recycling of the items. USF maintains a database of drugs categorized as hazardous or nonhazardous for this purpose. USF also keeps track of regulations specific to individual states to ensure appropriate treatment of pharmacies in each region of the country. Even though product returns in pharmaceuticals are low compared to the percentages noted previously—only 1 to 3 percent of units are returned—the benefits of using a dedicated and efficient third-party outsourcing company can be substantial.

MANAGEMENT OF THE PROCESS IS CURRENTLY VERY POOR IN MANY COMPANIES, LEADING TO HIGH CHANNEL FLOW COSTS

Many manufacturers process returns on paper (manually) rather than through any sort of computerized system, incurring very high costs of managing them.

In many cases, reverse logistics costs are not reported in any unified way, so it is difficult for the manufacturer to see how high the costs actually are. Further, company managers may

not put a high priority on managing returns through state-of-the-art reverse logistics practices. Common reasons given for not making these investments include a low priority placed on reverse logistics and a lack of systems capability for handling them.

Although manufacturers and retailers may not want to expend much effort in managing returns, in some industries and/or markets they are (or are threatened to be) likely to be forced to do so. The European Union imposes very strict recycling programs on manufacturers of all kinds of products, from glass bottles to computer equipment, and forces adherence to them. While the United States has not uniformly backed such "green" (i.e., environmentally friendly) proposals, there is interest in doing so for computer parts and components in states like Massachusetts and California. One of the key issues in implementing such a policy is paying for it; various proposals include a fee assessed from the buyer at the point of purchase to cover recycling costs or the development of a national financing system jointly funded by manufacturers, retailers, consumers, and government.

The many differences in the way reverse logistics occur versus forward logistics (i.e., the initial shipment of new product forward through the channel) help explain why channel members are not completely adept at managing returns. As outlined in Table 3.4, this suggests that many channel flow costs for handling returns are high and also require special decisions on the part of the manufacturer.

- *Physical possession:* The manufacturer has several decisions to make concerning the physical flow of returned product. It must decide where to permit the returned goods to go, whether from end-user

Sidebar 3.3 (cont.)

Reverse logistics

directly back to the manufacturer or from end-user back to the retailer or reseller from which they were bought, and then back to the manufacturer or whether they will flow back to a third-party reverse logistics specialist. Failing to make this decision may result in returned product simply sitting in a retailer's back room or, worse, being put back on a sales shelf without proper evaluation. Any decision to have returned product shipped back to the manufacturer or a third party incurs reverse freight charges that the manufacturer likely will bear. Some manufacturers believe that they can use their outbound distribution center to handle inbound returns as well, but this typically does not work well because forward logistics is usually large-scale in nature and generates economies of scale, while returns come back on mixed pallets with few or no economies of scale. Warehouse personnel in a combined forward and reverse logistics

warehouse are likely to prioritize outbound shipments first, leaving returns as an afterthought, but a dedicated returns warehouse will handle returns more quickly (and efficiently, if the scale is great enough).

- *Ownership:* When product is returned to a retail store, the consumers no longer own it—they get a refund. The manufacturer must set a policy regarding the retailer's right to return the merchandise for a refund. This policy varies widely across firms and industries. In bookselling, for example, retailers are allowed to return product freely (this is viewed as a means to get retailers to carry sufficient inventory to meet possibly high demand). If product ownership flows back to the manufacturer, however, the manufacturer must plan for this cost. If return rates are high, this can wreak havoc with planning.

- *Promotion:* Often, the manufacturer or a third-party returns specialist refurbishes

Table 3.4   Differences between forward and reverse logistics

Factor	Difference Between Forward and Reverse Logistics
Volume forecasting	More difficult for returns than for original sales of new product.
Transportation	Forward: ship in bulk (many of one SKU), with economies of scale. Reverse: ship many disparate SKUs in one pallet, no economies of scale.
Product quality	Forward: uniform product quality. Reverse: variable product quality, requiring costly evaluation of every returned unit.
Product packaging	Forward: uniform packaging. Reverse: packaging varies with some like-new, some damaged—no economies of scale in handling.
Ultimate destination	Forward: clear destination—to retailer or industrial distributor. Reverse: many options for ultimate disposition of product, necessitating separate decisions.
Accounting cost transparency	Forward: high. Reverse: low, because activities are not consistently tracked on a unified basis.

(continued)

Sidebar 3.3 (cont.)

Reverse logistics

the returned product and may also repackage it to look different from the new product. For example, reverse logistics specialist Channel Velocity refurbished one company's returned electric dog fences. To differentiate the returned product from new product in upscale pet stores, Channel Velocity rekits the products, putting the components together in slightly different combinations than are available in the new-product market, repackages the refurbished products in slightly different boxes, and sells them through a different channel, the eBay auction. These promotional efforts, of course, cost money but are viewed as important investments to (a) make the returned product sellable again, and (b) differentiate it sufficiently from the new product to minimize cannibalization.

- *Negotiation:* The manufacturer may need to negotiate with its retailer or distributor over the amount to refund on returned merchandise (i.e., net of any restocking fees) and even the maximum number of units the retailer is permitted to return.

- *Financing:* Financing costs rise with product returns because a given unit of inventory has to be financed twice rather than being shipped out when new, sold, and kept by the end-user. One study reports that it takes the average company between 30 and 70 days to get a returned product back into the market—days during which the manufacturer must finance this temporarily unsellable inventory.

- *Risking:* Increased channel risk is the heart of the problem with reverse logistics and product returns. Manufacturers and retailers do not know with certainty the demand they will face, and poor demand forecasting leads to much greater uncertainty about the expected volume of returns. This

means that poor demand forecasting, which leads to returns, is a risking cost.

- *Payment:* Decisions must be made about what restocking fee to charge the retailer or consumer who returns a product (e.g., cameras often bear a 15 percent restocking fee, and wallpaper companies often assess 30 percent to 40 percent restocking fees); once decided upon, these restocking fees must be managed and processed.

TOOLS FOR MANAGING/LOWERING THE COST OF REVERSE LOGISTICS

There are multiple tools for managing reverse logistics costs, above and beyond contracting with a third-party reverse logistic specialist firm. One is investments in customer service to pre-screen customer orders to lower subsequent return rates. For example:

- Lands' End's online store offers Web tools to help consumers determine which size is right for them before purchasing; this minimizes the ordering of multiple units of one item, in adjacent sizes, which results in high returns per unit sale.

- W. W. Grainger, the huge industrial products distributor, hires customer service personnel to help buyers choose the right products. In some cases, the cost of handling returns is so high that Grainger simply tells the buyer to keep or dispose of the unwanted product and sends the right product to the customer. In light of this possibility, bearing the cost of extra employees to avoid returns becomes financially very sensible.

Another possibility is for the manufacturer to invest in better demand forecasting and improve customer service. After all, one sure way to get rid of the channel costs of product returns

Sidebar 3.3 (cont.)

Reverse logistics

is to undertake other channel investments that reduce the incidence of those returns!

BENEFITS OF A WELL-MANAGED PROCESS: BOTH LOWER COST AND, POSSIBLY, HIGHER CONSUMER SATISFACTION

A well-managed returns and reverse logistics channel can generate multiple benefits for the firm, including recovering significant lost sales, improving the quality of all sales, and controlling customer relationships. Consider the manufacturer that refuses to accept returns (leaving unsold product with the retailer or downstream distributor) or accepts them and immediately sells them to a broker. In both cases, the manufacturer may believe it has cleverly minimized returns costs. In fact, it may have succeeded instead in creating a "gray market" for these products because the retailers or the brokers will themselves try to sell those units in another market as quickly as possible. The firm that instead takes a proactive stance in managing returns, whether by itself or with the partnership of an expert third-party reverse logistics provider, reduces both the cost of returns and the possibility of inadvertently creating a cannibalizing competitor.

How much inventory a channel member should hold is thus a very difficult question. Many models in the operations research field have been developed to solve this problem. They vary in the assumptions they make to render the inventory problem mathematically tractable. The EOQ (economic order quantity) model is the oldest and best known.[8]

Promotion flows in marketing channels can take many forms, including personal selling by an employee or outside sales force (such as the brokers and registered investment advisors in the mutual fund channel), media advertising, sales promotions (either to the trade or at retail), publicity, and other public relations activities. Promotional activities are designed to increase awareness of the product being sold, to educate potential buyers about the products' features and benefits, and to persuade potential buyers to actually purchase. A third-party reverse logistics specialist helps manufacturers achieve this promotional goal when it refurbishes returned products and sells them through new channels like eBay so as to target new buyer segments and differentiate the refurbished units from new products sold through standard channels. Promotional efforts may also have the goal of increasing the overall brand equity of the product, which could increase sales in the future. The positive effect of online bill payment on sales of other banking services described in Sidebar 3.2 is such an example. Clearly, any channel member can be involved in promotion, not just the retailer or the manufacturer. For example, CDW is a distributor, but its sales force investments and its resulting sales force longevity help it reduce the total costs of promotion for its computer equipment manufacturers.

The negotiation flow occurs whenever terms of sale or of the maintenance of the ongoing relationships with the market are discussed and decided. The costs of negotiation are measured mainly in the cost of personnel time spent in negotiating and (in the case of legal contractual arrangements) the cost of legal counsel. CDW's consortium with small businesses to serve the government market discussed in Sidebar 3.1 is an example of using both channel members' capabilities to jointly enhance the negotiation power of the channel with the buyer: CDW's negotiation abilities allow it to get product at low prices, while small businesses have a negotiation edge in landing government contracts. Sidebar 3.2 on online bill payment illustrates how the use of a new technology can reduce negotiation costs via a reduced need for high-cost dispute resolution.

Financing costs are inherent in the terms of sale from one level of the channel to another or from the channel to the end-user. Typical financing terms on a business-to-business purchase require payment within 30 days. Sometimes a discount is offered for early payment. If, for example, a 2 percent discount is offered for payment within 10 days, the terms of sale are said to be 2-10 net 30, meaning a 2 percent discount for payment in 10 days, but the net (full) payment amount is due in 30 days. Regardless of the specific payment terms, the key issue is that the seller essentially agrees to finance the buyer's purchase for a period of time (here, 30 days) after the product actually is delivered to the buyer, and thus the seller bears a financial cost—the cost of the foregone income achievable by putting that money to use in an alternative investment activity. Financing flow costs may be borne by the manufacturer or an intermediary or even by an outside channel member that specializes in these activities, such as a bank or credit card company. CDW, as a distributor, buys product from computer products manufacturers and, therefore, finances that inventory until receiving payment from its customers; Sidebar 3.1 notes its efficiency at performing this flow, exemplified by its good inventory turn rate and low number of days of receivables. On the other end of the financing efficiency spectrum would be a manufacturer with high product return rates that it does not manage well; Sidebar 3.3 notes that the average company finances returned product for 30–70 days before moving it back into the market.

Many sources of risking exist in the marketing channel. Long-term contracts between a distributor and a business end-user may specify price guarantees that lock in the distributor to a certain price, for instance. Should the market price for that product rise during the course of the contracting period, the distributor will lose revenue because it still will be forced to sell at the previously agreed-upon lower price. Price guarantees are sometimes offered to intermediaries who hold inventory in case the product's market price falls before the inventory is sold. Such a practice moves risk from the intermediary's shoulders to those of the manufacturer. Warranties, insurance, and after-sales service activities also represent costs due to risky, unforeseeable future events (such as parts failures or accidents). In general, either a manufacturer or a reseller may bear the cost of these activities. Sometimes one of a channel intermediary's key functions is as a risk manager, as in Sidebar 3.1 on CDW. When a CDW manager says, "We're kind of chief technical officer for many smaller firms," he is referring to the company's expertise in computer products and systems. The small business customer faces a much lower risk of buying an inappropriate or poorly working system if it buys from CDW rather than relying on its own limited knowledge. Interestingly, an increase in consumers' perceived risk (compared to the status quo) is one reason for slow diffusion of electronic bill payment, as Sidebar 3.2 notes, suggesting the value of identifying and seeking to control risking costs throughout a channel.

Ordering and payment flow costs are the total costs incurred in the actual purchase of and payment for the product. Many innovations are occurring today in the performance of these flows, unglamorous though they may seem, as Sidebar 3.2 demonstrates. Automatic replenishment, for instance, is an automated reordering system used by many retailers in which a computer system tracks levels of inventory in the retailer's system and automatically sends a replenishment order to the manufacturer when stock reaches a previously agreed-upon low level. This process reduces ordering costs as well as improving in-stock percentages.

Because of the cost associated with performing channel flows, it is important not to perform unnecessarily high levels of any of the flows. Thus, knowing which service outputs are demanded by target end-users and at what intensity helps the channel manager control the total cost of running the channel through the performance of only those flow levels that create valued service outputs.

Customizing the List of Flows for a Particular Channel

Just as we pointed out in our discussion of service outputs in Chapter 2, it is important to customize the list of flows to the particular channel being analyzed. This can mean, for example, combining two of the eight generic flows. In some channels, for instance, it can make sense to consider the costs of physical possession and of ownership jointly if they are always incurred by the same channel members at the same time.

Conversely, it can make sense either to add to the list of eight flows or to expand one of the flows into more than one element. For example, the promotion flow could be considered to be several different flows, each with its own cost: The cost of running an employee sales force to engage in personal selling, the cost of creating and running advertisements with an outside advertising agency, and the cost of running a public relations program all could be considered distinct flow processes worthy of separate categorization. Or the channel manager might categorize physical possession into two flows, one for the storage and delivery costs to sell an original product and one for the storage and delivery of spare parts. Sidebar 3.3 on reverse logistics suggests that most manufacturers treat outgoing new goods very differently from incoming returned product.

Finally, the channel manager conceivably could wish to minimize the effort to understand and measure the costs of certain flows that are not very important in the channel. For example, negotiation activities may be negligible in channels of long-standing relationships with long-term contracts and, hence, not as worthy of close scrutiny as are other activities and flows.

Why should the channel manager expend so much effort to categorize channel activities into specific flows? The key to this process is to generate a list that:

- Has names that channel members can recognize and use
- Matches the ways in which channel costs are incurred and measured by channel members
- Accounts for all the relevant costly flow activities of the channel

Characterizing channel flows in terms of names that are recognizable to channel members is important because it helps the channel manager communicate information about the workings of the distribution operation. If channel members are not comfortable with terms like *physical possession* but easily recognize the terms *storage* or *warehousing*, obviously the names in the list of flows should change to represent that familiarity.

Channel flow descriptions also need to match the ways in which channel costs are incurred. If, for example, parts inventorying for postsale service is carried out in a different profit center of a distributor's company than is presale product inventorying, then representing these as two separate flows will best help track the costs of running the channel. These data become useful later on if the channel manager is considering reallocating flows within the channel to minimize channel costs.

Who Does Which Channel Flows?

The previous two sections discuss what channel flows are and how to create a list of channel flows that fits the particular channel's nature and functions. It is crucially important that the description of channel flows measure *all* the costs incurred in running the channel. In the near term, the channel manager needs an accurate accounting of the channel's activities in order to evaluate the efficiency and effectiveness of flow performance. In the longer term, failure to recognize costly but valuable channel flow performance by any channel member can lead to inappropriate rewarding of channel flow performance and eventually to serious channel conflicts.

Further, *which channel member(s) is/are involved in the performance of what channel flow(s)* is not always obvious. We can characterize this situation by imagining a news headline reading Channel Member Performs Surprising Flow! (an extremely compelling headline to anyone involved in channel management!). Sidebar 3.4 tells a story of online furniture buying that could have just such a headline.

Yet another problem arises when the channel captain fails to recognize channel flow performance either by a channel intermediary or, in fact, by end-users. This possibility could be captured in a news headline reading, End-Users Are Channel Members Too! The electronic bill payment example of Sidebar 3.2 illustrates this headline in terms of consumers' risk-bearing activities if they adopt online bill payment.

DESCRIBING THE CURRENT CHANNEL WITH THE EFFICIENCY TEMPLATE

The first use to which we will put the concepts of channel flows is to describe the productive activities of a currently operating channel. To do this, we introduce here the efficiency template, a tool to measure the costs borne and the value added by each channel member in its performance of channel flows. A detailed description of the application of the efficiency template to a real-world channel appears in Appendix 3A. Here, we discuss the elements of the efficiency template and its uses.

The efficiency template is used to describe (a) the types and amounts of work done by each channel member in the performance of the marketing flows, (b) the importance of each channel flow to the provision of demanded consumer service outputs, and (c) the resulting share of total channel profits that each channel member

Sidebar 3.4

"Channel member performs surprising flow!"

An online furniture seller planned its business without thinking very hard about the problem (and cost) of returned merchandise (see Sidebar 3.3 for details on this problem). This sidebar tells a true story of how an unlikely channel member performed a surprising (and highly valued) channel flow and what channel managers can learn from it.

Buying a piece of furniture online takes considerable time. Take the example of a woman who buys a kitchen table for her home. She first visits the online furniture company's Web site (its so-called electronic storefront) and finds a table she thinks will be appropriate. She uses her credit card to pay for and order the table online; thus far, using the Web site has been her only interaction with the furniture company.

Time passes. . . . In fact, eight to twelve weeks pass, because furniture delivery is a long process due to the commonality of batch production processes whereby many pieces of one type of furniture are made at a time before the production equipment is retooled to make another type of furniture. At last, the long-awaited day comes when the woman's kitchen table is delivered to her home. Who delivers the furniture? A truck driver employed by a third-party trucking and delivery company hired by the online furniture retailer. The truck driver is, indeed, the only human being the woman has met thus far who represents the seller of the kitchen table!

The truck driver/delivery man brings the box containing the table parts into the woman's kitchen, and he assembles the table for her on site (something he has been trained to do and for which he is paid by the trucking company, which in turn is paid by the online furniture company). Once he has assembled the table in the consumer's kitchen, she looks at the table, ponders it, and pronounces: "You know, I don't think this is the table I ordered!"

The next likely event in this scenario is, of course, the return of the kitchen table. But amazingly, the woman ends up keeping the kitchen table—willingly! What happens to change her mind? The truck driver talks to the woman about the table and after perhaps fifteen or twenty minutes convinces her that the table looks fine in her kitchen and that whether or not it is the actual table she ordered, it is the right table for the kitchen.

Let's consider what happened in this situation, what types of channel costs were borne by whom, and what potential channel costs were averted. Clearly, the channel member responsible for averting the return of the kitchen table is none other than . . . the truck driver! A less likely channel member to perform this flow would be difficult to imagine. Yet the truck driver is the only actual person with whom the woman interacts; if not him, then who could possibly do it?

What flow does the truck driver perform in convincing the woman to keep the table? It is the promotion flow. In effect, the truck driver closes the sale in much the same way that an automobile salesperson gets a customer to buy a car. Again, it is highly unlikely that any online company records in its business plan that truck driver/delivery personnel will serve sales force roles and be important in closing the sale; yet in this example, this is precisely what has happened. Hence, our headline for this story: Channel Member Performs Surprising Flow!

How much does it cost the truck driver to perform this promotional flow? At one level, the answer is the value of fifteen to twenty minutes of his time—the amount of time he talks to the woman before she decides to keep the table. But this calculation measures only the gross cost borne by the truck driver, not the net

(continued)

Sidebar 3.4 (cont.)

"Channel member performs surprising flow!"

cost. The net cost is the cost left over after accounting for any costs the truck driver himself avoids by inducing the woman to keep the table. Consider what the truck driver would have to do if she were to return the table: he would have to disassemble the table, reinsert all the parts into their shipping box (almost impossible, particularly without losing parts), and then truck the reboxed table back to the warehouse where he picked it up. All of this likely takes at least 15 to 20 minutes—suggesting that, in net, the truck driver bears little or no incremental cost due to the time he spends averting the return.

Given this logic, how much would the Equity Principle dictate the truck driver should be paid for averting the return? At one level, the answer is nothing! After all, the truck driver in essence bears no incremental cost himself for taking the time and effort to talk to the woman, so why should he be paid any sort of reward for averting returns? But this logic misses another important point: not only the costs the truck driver avoids are relevant but also the channel costs the online furniture retailer avoids in deciding whether an incremental reward or bonus is due to the truck driver. Any such costs avoided by the online furniture retailer can be seen equivalently as incremental value created in the channel, holding other costs constant. And as Sidebar 3.3 makes abundantly clear, the costs of taking

back returns are very large. Because it is the truck driver's efforts that create this extra channel value (by avoiding large channel costs), the Equity Principle implies that some payment or reward is due him—not because he must be reimbursed for any extra net cost borne, but in order to create a positive incentive for him to (constructively) avert returns in the future.

This raises the crucial question of how to create an appropriate reward system. A naïve furniture company might simply announce a bonus plan, offering an incremental payment to any truck driver/delivery person who averts a return. Imagine the response: savvy truck drivers would suddenly be announcing many averted product returns because they would see an opportunity to get a bonus without the furniture company's being able to discern who is telling the truth and who is not. Thus, to create an appropriate incentive system to reward the performance of desired channel flows, the furniture company must have a monitoring system in place to measure when the incremental beneficial activity is being performed. Here, the furniture company probably should measure baseline levels of returns, by truck driver route, to create a database of reasonable returns rates by region. Then the company is in a position to reward returns rates that are lower than the baseline levels with some expectation that this both rewards the desired behavior and avoids rewarding any other behaviors.

should reap. Figure 3.3 shows a blank efficiency template. The rows list the channel flows. The efficiency template has two sets of columns: one set for determining the importance weights for the flows and another set for listing the proportional performance of each flow by each channel member.

Consider first the three columns in Figure 3.3 determining the importance weights to be associated with each channel flow. The idea here is to account for both the cost of performance of that flow and the value added through the performance of that flow. The entries in the cost column should be percentages adding up to 100 percent across all the

	Weights for Flows:			Proportional Flow Performance of Channel Member:				
	Costs*	Benefit Potential (High, Medium, or Low)	Final Weight*	1	2	3	4 (End-User)	Total
Physical Possession**								100
Ownership								100
Promotion								100
Negotiation								100
Financing								100
Risking								100
Ordering								100
Payment								100
Total	100	N/A	100	N/A	N/A	N/A	N/A	N/A
Normative Profit Share***	N/A	N/A	N/A					100

Figure 3.3   The efficiency template

Entries in column must add up to 100 points.

** *Entries across row (sum of proportional flow performance of channel members 1 through 4) for each channel member must add up to 100 points.*

*** *Normative profit share of channel member i is calculated as: (final weight, physical possession)*(channel member i's proportional flow performance of physical possession) + ... + (final weight, payment)*(channel member i's proportional flow performance of payment). Entries across row (sum of normative profit shares for channel members 1 through 4) must add up to 100 points.*

flows. For example, if the costs of promotion accounted for 23 percent of all channel flow costs, the analyst would enter the number *23* in the cost cell for the promotion flow. One technique for generating quantitative cost weights is an activity-based cost (ABC) analysis of the channel. Activity-based costing is an accounting tool to measure the cost of performing activities within one organization.[9] Here, the task is more comprehensive: To get good quantitative measures of costs, the cost of all the activities of all the channel members must be measured. Of these total costs, the question is then (for example), what proportion of all channel costs is accounted for by promotional activities?

If strict quantitative measures of cost are not available, the analyst can still use more qualitative techniques to get an estimate of the cost weights to use. A Delphi-type research technique can be applied, for example, with several of the best-informed managers in the channel developing a best estimate of the cost weights to use.[10] Again, the output of such an exercise is a set of weights adding up to 100 that measure the proportion or percentage of total channel *costs* accounted for by each flow.

Beyond measuring the cost of performing flows, it is also useful to consider the value created by the performance of each flow. This is a more intuitive process, as it links the performance of flows to the generation of demanded service outputs. The extra value created (i.e., channel cost avoided) by the truck driver/delivery man in Sidebar 3.4 who averts the return of a kitchen table is not captured by measuring his cost of averting the return (which is itself very small). In a case like this, the channel analyst would want to rate the promotion flow as having a high value (as well as record-ing the [small] promotional cost borne by the delivery man).

The cost weight can then be adjusted to achieve a final set of importance weights for each flow in the channel. The adjustment process is judgmental but generally involves increasing the weight on flows rated as generating high value added in the channel and demoting the value placed on flows with a low value added. Remember that the final weights themselves must add up to 100, so if some flow weights are increased, others *must* decrease. Again, a Delphi analysis can help channel members arrive at a final set of weights that accurately represent both the cost borne and the value created through the performance of a given channel flow.

The other columns in the efficiency template in Figure 3.3 require the channel ana-lyst to allocate the total cost of each flow across all the channel members. Again, the ana-lyst enters figures adding up to 100 to represent the proportion of the total cost of a given flow borne by a particular channel member. That is, if a channel consists of a manufac-turer, a distributor, a retailer, and an end-user, the costs of physical possession must be spread across these channel members, and so the cost proportions must add up to 100.

Not all channel members must bear all costs. For example, a manufacturer may use independent sales representatives to aid in selling its product. These sales reps do not inventory any product, nor do they take title to product; they specialize in promo-tional and sometimes order-taking activities. Hence, the sales rep's cost proportion entry in the physical possession row would be zero because it does not do physical pos-session of inventory at all.

The end-user is also a member of the channel for the purposes of channel flow performance. Any time end-users buy a larger lot size than they really need in the short term (i.e., forego bulk-breaking, for example, by stocking up on paper goods at a hypermarket), they are performing part of the physical possession flow, as they will have to inventory the as yet unused product themselves. Similarly, such a consumer bears inventory carrying costs and, hence, shares in the costs of ownership in the channel. If the end-user pays for the whole lot at the time of purchase, financing is also being borne, since payment is being made early. Thus, there are many ways in which end-users can participate in the channel flows, and as with any other channel member, these costs borne can and should be measured. This is particularly useful when contrasting one segment of end-users versus another because it helps shed light on such issues as why it costs more to serve some end-users than others (they perform fewer costly chan-nel flows themselves, thrusting this cost back onto other channel members).

With weights assigned to each flow and cost proportions allocated for the per-formance of each flow across all the channel members, the channel analyst can then calculate a weighted average for each channel member measuring that member's con-tribution to the cost borne and value created in the channel. This weighted average is calculated (weight times cost proportion) for each flow, summed across all the flows. In our example of the building materials company profiled in Appendix 3A, the manufacturer's weighted average is 28 percent (equal to $[(.35 \times .30) + (.15 \times .30) + (.08 \times .20) + (.04 \times .20) + (.29 \times .30) + (.02 \times .30) + (.03 \times .20) + (.04 \times .20)]$). Similarly, a retailer in the channel contributes 39 percent of the cost/value in the channel, and a customer contributes 33 percent.

These final percentages have a special meaning. Consider the total profit avail-able to the whole channel (i.e., channel contribution), when selling product at full-service list prices. This is equal to the total revenue (were all units sold at list prices), minus all costs of running the channel. Then the data on the building materials company in Appendix 3A say that the manufacturer's channel flow performance is responsible for generating 28 percent of the channel contribution from selling through the retail channel; the retailer's efforts are responsible for generating 39 percent; and the customer's shouldering of channel flow costs is worth 33 percent. That is, these percentages measure the proportionate value creation of each channel member. We call these percentages the normative profit shares of each channel member. Note that being responsible for a large proportion of a low-value flow does not create as much overall value as does performing most of a highly valued flow. Thus, a channel member's being busy should not always signal high value creation for the channel. We will return to this meaning in our discussion of the Equity Principle later in this chapter.

What does it mean for an end-user (in this example, a buyer of cement at retail) to generate channel profits in our example in Appendix 3A? These end-users buy reasonably large quantities and store them for use after the time of purchase. They thus pay in advance for product that they will use only later, and they also are willing to store it on their own property rather than forcing the retailer or manufacturer to warehouse it. Thus, the end-user is, in fact, performing valued channel flows that are costly to it, just as they would be costly to any other channel member. The performance of these flows merits some reward. In general, the reward given to a segment of end-users who perform valued channel flows is a reduction in price from full-service list price levels. Thus, the end-user should be counted as a channel member for the purpose of measuring performance of channel flows because different segments of end-users perform different quantities and sorts of channel flow activities and, thus, lift the cost of performing those flows off the shoulders of other channel members.

It is important to note that a separate efficiency template should be created for each channel used to distribute the product. (One really should create a separate efficiency template also for each market segment that buys through each channel because multiple segments may patronize one channel but buy in different ways.) Thus, in the building materials company's case, there could be a separate efficiency template for the retailer channel than the one created for a direct channel serving building contractors. This is necessary because a channel member involved in selling to retail customers (e.g., the retailer) does not contribute to the bearing of channel flow costs when selling to building contractors who buy direct.

Finally, suppose that full financial data on the costs borne by each channel member are lacking. Thus, precise ratings cannot be entered in the efficiency template because it is not known precisely how much of a given flow's cost is borne by each particular channel member. Must we discard the efficiency template in this situation? No, as long as some ranking data are available to calibrate relative intensity of performance of each flow. Appendix 3A details how the channel analyst can use even rough ranking data to get a reasonably good approximation of the relative value created by each channel member. As with any approximation system, the more rough the approximations, the more rough the estimates of value created, but as the example in Appendix 3A shows, the approximations are often much better than no consideration at all of the relative value added by each channel member.

In sum, the efficiency template is a very useful tool for codifying the bearing of cost and adding of value to the channel of each channel member. The efficiency template should be channel-specific; that is, a separate efficiency template must be created for each channel used to sell the product. The efficiency template accounts for channel flow costs borne by end-users as well as other channel members. Its uses are many. It reveals how the costs of particular flows are shared among channel members. It shows how much each channel member contributes to the overall value creation in the channel. It reveals how important each of the flows is to total channel performance. It can be a powerful tool in explaining current channel performance and justifying changes that channel managers wish to make to currently operating channels. In cases where the product is sold through multiple channels, the efficiency templates can be compared to see differences in costs of running the different channels. This may lead to insights about how to decrease costs without compromising the provision of desired service output levels in the target market.

There are, of course, many situations where a marketing channel does not already exist for a product. Any time a manufacturer seeks to sell its product in a new market or country, it needs to create a new marketing channel through which to sell the product. The next section describes how to use flow concepts and the efficiency template to design a new marketing channel.

USING CHANNEL FLOW CONCEPTS TO DESIGN A ZERO-BASED CHANNEL

What would a channel manager do if given the luxury of being able to design an optimal channel from scratch, without a preexisting channel structure to hamper the design? We call such a channel the zero-based channel, and define it as follows:

> A zero-based channel design is one that (a) meets the target market segment's demands for service outputs, (b) at minimum cost of performing the necessary channel flows that produce those service outputs.

Notice that there is an unavoidable tension in this concept. On the one hand, the channel manager of course wants to minimize the cost of running the marketing channel in order to preserve profit margins. On the other hand, enough must be spent on performing channel flows to guarantee the generation of the desired service outputs. Spending too little (or making poor decisions about how to spend money in running the channel) will result in insufficiently low provision of service outputs. Competitors may take advantage of the hole in service output provision by offering a superior combination of product plus service outputs. This can lead to loss of market share and profitability. However, spending too much will produce a higher level of service outputs than the target market values and will unnecessarily increase the cost basis of the channel, again reducing profitability. Achieving the right balance is a continuously demanding task, given the changes occurring in the marketplace.

Consider the task of managing inventory holding costs. A key question in cost control in channels is how inventory can be reduced. Some obvious methods are to avoid items that turn slowly, to lengthen the life of goods (e.g., add preservatives to foods), to find a vendor who resupplies faster, or to locate a cheaper warehouse. Some less obvious methods are to develop better ways to forecast demand or to alter factory processes to attain scale economies at lower levels of production. Advances in manufacturing practice have done a great deal to achieve this latter goal.

A powerful way to cut inventory is to simplify, that is, to cut variety. Of course, this can be a powerful way to cut sales as well! The key is to find those offerings no one will really miss—in other words, to rationalize the product line in a way that preserves the service output level of assortment and variety for the target consumer. Another way is to design products to be modular and then design manufacturing processes to fit the principle of postponing as late as possible the point of differentiating a product for a customer or customer base. For example, Hewlett-Packard redesigned a line of laser printers so as to make a standard subassembly. This subassembly (only) is shipped to a distribution center. The center procures and then adds in those elements needed to tailor the printer to its destination market: power supplies, packaging, and manuals, all of which are tailored to the language and infrastructure of each national market. This involves assembly and light manufacturing, thereby expanding the role of the marketing channel. As a result, manufacturing costs are slightly higher, in part because this sort of redesign often necessitates upgrades in the materials used. But total costs (manufacturing, shipping, and inventory) are 25 percent lower.[11]

One of the major reasons inventory accumulates is demand uncertainty, and one of the major causes of demand uncertainty is poor communication between members of marketing channels. Even a simple product, such as beer, can serve as a good example of the so-called bullwhip effect.[12] Imagine a supply chain ending with a beer drinker and going back through the retailer who sells the beer, the wholesaler who supplies the retailer, and the brewer who makes the beer. Each party must forecast end-user demand and then take production, shipping, and stocking delays into account to plan how much to order to meet its own level of demand (the retailer, hence the wholesaler) or how much to brew and, therefore, what ingredients to order (the brewer). Because each player sees only its link in the supply chain, demand uncertainty obliges all of them to guess. The result is that inventories of beer and ingredients oscillate, going up and down in dramatic surges, then plunges. The graph of inventories resembles the path a bullwhip cuts through the air (see Figure 3.4). In particular, small changes in end-user demand magnify into ever larger changes upstream. This is costly in terms of both stockouts (unfilled orders or back orders) and excessive inventory holding costs. Aiming for a zero-based channel in the presence of these uncertainties is a major theme of supply chain management.

Even with a preexisting channel, the channel manager should be asking whether the current channel design is zero-based or not. Chapter 5, dealing with gap analysis, tackles this question. The growth of reverse logistics as a separate channel discipline in Sidebar 3.3 and the emergence of electronic channels for bill payment in Sidebar 3.2 are pertinent here: both emerge in response to the recognition that legacy systems were and are inefficient.

Figure 3.4   **The bullwhip effect**

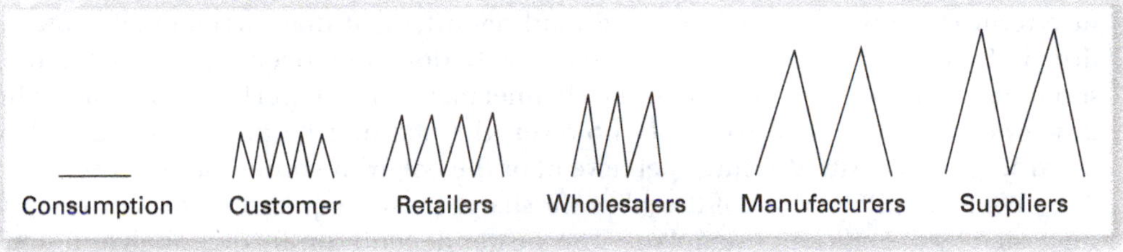

Consumption   Customer   Retailers   Wholesalers   Manufacturers   Suppliers

Source: Based on the lecture notes of Enver Yücesan at INSEAD.

In short, the establishment of a zero-based channel involves a recognition of what level of channel flows must be performed to generate the service outputs demanded (demands that are frequently unmet) in the market.

MATCHING NORMATIVE AND ACTUAL PROFIT SHARES: THE EQUITY PRINCIPLE

The normative profit shares calculated from the efficiency template for a currently operating channel give a measure of the share of total channel profits each channel member's efforts are responsible for generating. This share and the actual share of total channel profits garnered by each channel member should be related, as the following rendering of the Equity Principle indicates:

> Compensation in the channel system should be given on the basis of the degree of participation in the marketing flows and the value created by this participation. That is, compensation should mirror the normative profit shares for each channel member.

The Equity Principle states that it is appropriate to reward each channel member in accordance with the value that the member creates in the channel. Doing so creates the right incentives among channel members to continue to generate that value in the future, just as CDW's equal commission rates for either online purchases or salesperson-handled purchases safeguards the salesperson's incentive to maintain and try to build the client account no matter how the client wants to buy. Conversely, trying to deprive a channel member of its rewards for effort expended and value created can result later in underperformance of necessary channel flows. This creates serious channel conflicts and sometimes even the dissolution of the channel. U.S. consumers' reluctance to adopt electronic bill payment, as described in Sidebar 2.2 and Sidebar 3.2, given the adequacy of the legacy (paper) bill channel and the increased risk they perceived from electronic bill payment technology, reflects their belief that the rewards of electronic bill payment simply were not worth the effective cost of the incremental flows being thrust upon them.

To live by the Equity Principle, channel members must know what costs they have actually incurred and have an agreed-upon estimate of the value created in the channel. Otherwise, channel members are open to disagreements about the value each one actually adds to channel performance. Worse, these disagreements are likely to be shaped more by each channel member's perception of its own contribution than by the facts of the case. It takes effort to amass the information necessary to complete the efficiency analysis, but the payoffs are worth the effort. Measuring the incremental value added and cost avoided by the truck driver of Sidebar 3.4, who averts the furniture return, can only be accomplished (and rewarded!) if that incremental contribution is first recognized, something that likely does not occur in many channel situations. This does not mean that the channel member who performs the high-value flow does not recognize its value; however, the channel member who should be rewarding this activity also must perceive it, or the behavior cannot be reinforced.

What should be done if actual profit shares do not equal the normative shares suggested by the efficiency template? The answer depends on further analysis not just of the channel situation but also of the external competitive environment. There can be competitive situations where, despite a channel member's contributions to channel performance, that member makes less profit than the efficiency template would suggest. This is because the availability of competitors who could easily take this channel member's place limits the profits that the channel member can command.

As an example, think of a supplier of commodity cookware to Wal-Mart. Wal-Mart's announcement in 2005 that its suppliers would have to adopt RFID (radio frequency identification) technology to improve stock management forces a significant cost of adopting the new technology onto the cookware supplier's shoulders. The supplier not only has to buy appropriate equipment to make the tags but also must buy the tags themselves (a consumable) on an ongoing basis and train employees to handle the tags, affix them to product, and program the their contents. Significant cost savings are expected ultimately from the adoption of RFID technology in retailing, and importantly, these savings cannot be achieved without the cooperation of suppliers as well as Wal-Mart. It might seem that the supplier has to bear more than its fair share of the technology's cost. Although this is a violation of the Equity Principle, the supplier has little recourse. If it refused to pay the cost of maintaining the RFID system inside its firm, Wal-Mart would simply drop it as a supplier because in the competitive marketplace Wal-Mart would be able to replace this supplier. Thus, competitive pressures can cause deviations from the Equity Principle that do not necessarily imply the need to change channel reward systems.

However, in the long run it behooves channel members to adhere to the Equity Principle. Channel partners who do not receive rewards commensurate with their perceived contributions to the channel will not remain highly motivated for long. Should competitive conditions change in the future, they are likely to leave the relationship or, at the very least, bargain hard for a more favorable change in terms. In addition, a firm that treats its channel partners poorly develops a bad reputation that hurts its ability to manage other channel relationships in the future. These problems are a major cause of channel conflict (discussed in more depth in Chapter 7). The astute channel manager carefully balances the risk of such events against the immediate gain to be had by garnering a greater share of channel profits today. If competitive conditions do not give one channel member profit leverage over another, rewards should at least roughly mirror the level of flow performance in the channel.

SUMMARY: CHANNEL FLOW ANALYSIS AS PART OF THE OVERALL CHANNEL AUDIT PROCESS

Understanding the concept of channel flows is critical to the channel manager's ability to design and maintain a well-working channel. Channel flows are the activities and processes in which marketing channel members engage that both are costly and at the same time add value to the channel. The performance of channel flows results in the generation of service outputs for end-users in the marketplace. With an understanding of the segment(s) of the market that the channel will target, the channel manager can use an analysis of channel flows to evaluate the cost-effectiveness of channel activities.

We introduced the concept of the efficiency template to aid in this analysis. The efficiency template codifies information about the importance of each channel flow in both cost and value terms, as well as about the proportion of each flow performed by each channel member. An efficiency template analysis can be done for a preexisting channel or can be the basis for the development of a new channel. In either case, the efficiency template produces a metric called the normative profit share for each channel member, a measure of the proportionate value added to the total channel's performance by each channel member.

If there are no intervening adverse competitive conditions, the normative profit shares should mirror at least approximately the actual shares of total channel profits enjoyed by each channel member. This is the Equity Principle. In the short run, it is possible to diverge from the Equity Principle, particularly when one channel member is in a very competitive industry. Even though that channel member generates considerable value through its performance of necessary channel flows, it may not be able to reap a proportionate share of channel profits because other possible channel members stand ready to take its place if it demands too high a proportion of total channel profits. In the long run, however, reasonable adherence to the Equity Principle helps ensure the continued good efforts of all channel members.

This chapter has focused on the actual channel flows. We turn in the next chapter to a discussion of the overall channel structure—the identity and numbers of various channel members—through which the channel flows are allocated.

Take-Aways

- Just as a production plant produces physical products, the members of a marketing channel also are engaged in productive activity. We call the channel's activities channel flows.

- Detailed knowledge of the flow performance in the channel improves service output provision, helps in channel design or redesign, helps in deciding rewards to channel members, and can help manage channel conflicts.

- Every channel flow not only contributes to the production of valued service outputs but is also associated with a cost.

- The generic list of channel flows includes physical possession, ownership, promotion, negotiation, financing, risking, ordering, and payment.

- The drive to minimize the cost of channel management implies that it is important not to perform unnecessarily high levels of any of the flows; knowing what service outputs are demanded by target end-users is the key to knowing what flow levels will create the right level (not too low or too high) of service outputs valued by target end-users.

- The channel manager should customize the generic list of channel flows to generate a list that (a) has names that channel members can recognize and use, (b) matches the ways in which channel costs are incurred and measured by channel members, and (c) accounts for all the relevant costly flow activities of the channel.

- Recognizing explicitly which channel member(s) perform which channel flow(s) is difficult but necessary if the channel manager wants to adequately reward channel flow cost-bearing and performance.

- The efficiency template is used to describe (a) the types and amounts of work done by each channel member in the performance of the marketing flows,

(b) the importance of each channel flow to the provision of demanded consumer service outputs, and (c) the resulting share of total channel profits that each channel member should reap. This involves an activity-based cost (ABC) analysis of the channel, with the goal of measuring as accurately as possible the cost of all the activities of all the channel members.

- End-users are also channel members in the sense that they (like any other channel member) may bear the cost of various channel flows. When they do, they typically expect to be compensated for doing so via lower prices than they would pay for full-service purchasing.
- A separate efficiency template should be created for each channel used to distribute the product and, ideally, for each market segment that buys through each channel.
- A zero-based channel design is one that (a) meets the target market segment's demands for service outputs (b) at a minimum cost of performing the necessary channel flows that produce those service outputs.
- Comparing a zero-based efficiency analysis with the current channel's efficiency analysis informs the channel analyst of situations where a channel member may be busy (bearing high channel flow costs) but not adding commensurate value to the channel's overall operation.
- The Equity Principle states that compensation in the channel system should be given on the basis of the degree of participation in the marketing flows and the value created by this participation. That is, compensation should mirror the normative profit shares for each channel member.

DISCUSSION QUESTIONS

1. Give an example where a channel member performs only one flow for the channel yet is an important member in making the channel work well. Give another example of a channel member who participates in all eight channel flows and describe how the channel member does so.
2. Many consumer-goods and industrial-goods companies both sell original product and provide service after the sale. Relative to a system where only product is sold (but no service is necessary), how would you suggest describing the list of channel flows performed by various members of the channel?
3. If a consumer buys an item through a catalog over the phone with a credit card, is the credit card company a channel member? If the product is delivered by FedEx, is FedEx a channel member? If yes, what flows do they perform?
4. Explain how the shopping characteristics for the following consumer and industrial goods affect the channels for them:

CONSUMER GOODS	INDUSTRIAL GOODS
Bread	Laser printer toner cartridges
Breakfast cereal	Uranium for nuclear power plants
Women's hosiery	Cement
Refrigerators	Medical machinery (e.g., ultrasound machines)

5. A channel can be zero-based when targeted at one segment and not zero-based when targeted at another segment. True or false? Explain your answer.

6. Suppose that a set of channel participants decides to spare no expense in meeting all the service output demands of their target market. Assuming they indeed do meet those expressed demands, under what conditions might their channel still not be zero-based?

7. In the Wal-Mart example in Section 3.4, the argument is that in the short run, deviations from the Equity Principle can occur due to competitive reasons. What might make this statement untrue in the long run?

ENDNOTES

1. Information for this sidebar is drawn from: Campbell, Scott (2003), "CDW-G Calls on VARs," *Computer Reseller News*, November 17, p. 162; Campbell, Scott (2004), "CDW Snags Companywide Cisco Premier Status: Relationship Advances Reseller's Bid to Build Services Business," *Computer Reseller News*, April 12; Gallagher, Kathleen (2002), "CDW Computer Remains Afloat Despite Market's Choppy Waters," *Milwaukee Journal Sentinel*, September 29, Business Section, p. 4D; Jones, Sandra (2004), "Challenges Ahead for CDW; Dell Deals Make Inroads in Already Difficult Market," *Crain's Chicago Business*, June 28, p. 4; Kaiser, Rob (2000), "Vernon Hills, Ill., Computer Products Reseller Has an Approach to Win Business," *Chicago Tribune*, August 16, online; McCafferty, Dennis (2002), "Growing Like Gangbusters: Sales at Chicago-Area CDW-Government Shot up 63 Percent from 2000 to 2001," *VAR Business*, July 8, online; Moltzen, Edward (2003), "Looking for SMB Traction, Gateway Inks Reseller Pact with CDW," *Computer Reseller News*, May 26, p. 55; O'Heir, Jeff (2003), "CDW Teams with Small VARs to Access GovernmentBiz," *Computer Reseller News*, August 25, p. 6; O'Heir, Jeff (2003), "Time to Move On," *Computer Reseller News*, October 20, p. 98; Rose, Barbara and Mike Highlett (2005), "Balancing Success with High Stress," *Chicago Tribune*, June 5, online; Schmeltzer, John (2003), "CDW Pulls Out the Stops to Reach Small Business," *Chicago Tribune*, September 8, online; and Zarley, Craig and Jeff O'Heir (2003), "Seeking Solutions: CDW, Gateway and Dell Come Calling on Solution Providers for Services Expertise," *Computer Reseller News*, September 1, p. 16.

2. O'Heir, Jeff (2003), "Time to Move On," *Computer Reseller News*, October 20, p. 98.

3. Campbell, Scott (2004), "CDW Snags Companywide Cisco Premier Status: Relationship Advances Reseller's Bid to Build Services Business," *Computer Reseller News*, April 12.

4. See the references for Channel Sketch 2.2 for more detail on online invoicing and payment systems, and particularly *Information Week* (2001), "Online Invoicing Ready For Business-to-Business Users," *InformationWeek*, November 12, p. 80; Rosen, Cheryl (2001), "Seamless B-to-B Online Payment Systems Readied," *InformationWeek*, September 10, p. 54; Hoffman, Karen Epper (2002), "Electronic Bill Payment Comes of Age," *Community Banker* 11, no. 7 (July), pp. 16–21; Rombel, Adam (2002), "Electronic Billing Catches On," *Global Finance* 16, no. 3 (March), pp. 49–50; Rombel, Adam (2002), "Businesses Tell Their Suppliers: Present Your Invoices Online," *Global Finance* 6, no. 8 (July/August), pp. 22–24; Varon, Elana (2002), "To Bill or Not to Bill (Online): Digital Invoicing Is the Next Big Step in E-Business Transactions," *CIO* 16, no. 3 (November 1), p. 1; Webster, John (2002), "Moving Beyond Just Paying the Bills," *Computerworld* 36, no. 42 (October 14), p. 40; Bernstel, Janet B. (2003), "Bill Pay: Where's the Payoff?" *ABA Bank Marketing* 35 no. 6 (July/August), pp. 12–17; Gonsalves, Antone (2003), "E-Bill Paying a Hit With Consumers," *Insurance and Technology* 28, no. 5 (May), p. 43; Scheier, Robert L. (2003), "The Price of E-Payment," *Computerworld* 37,

no. 21 (May 26), pp. 25–26; Park, Andrew, Ben Elgin, and Timothy J. Mullaney (2004), "Checks Check Out: With Online Bill Payment and Processing, Use of Paper Checks Is Headed for a Steep Decline," *Business Week*, May 10, p. 88.

5. Scheier, Robert L. (2003), "The Price of E-Payment," *Computerworld* 37, no. 21 (May 26), pp. 25–26.

6. van Ryzin, Garrett (1997), "Analyzing Inventory Cost and Service in Supply Chains," *Technical Note*, Columbia Business School, New York.

7. Background references for this sidebar include: Andel, Tom (2004), "How to Advance in the Reverse Channel," *Material Handling Management* 59, no. 2 (February), pp. 24–30; Coia, Anthony (2003), "Channeling E-Tail Resources," *Apparel Magazine* 44, no. 12 (August), pp. 18–20; Cottrill, Ken (2003), "Dumping Debate," *TrafficWORLD*, March 17, p. 1; Cottrill, Ken (2003), "Remedying Returns," *Commonwealth Business Media Joint Logistics Special Report 2003*, p. L-19; Enright, Tony (2003), "Post-Holiday Logistics," *TrafficWORLD*, January 6, p. 20; Gooley, Toby B. (2003), "The Who, What, and Where of Reverse Logistics," *Logistics Management* 42, no. 2 (February), pp. 38–44; Hughes, David (2003), "Reverse Thinking in the Supply Chain," *Focus*, September, pp. 30–36; Rogers, Dale S. and Ronald S. Tibben-Lembke (1998), *Going Backwards: Reverse Logistics Trends and Practices*, Reverse Logistics Executive Council, University of Nevada, Reno: Center for Logistics Management; Spencer, Jane (2002), "The Point of No Return: Stores from Gap to Target Tighten Refund Rules; a 15% 'Restocking Fee,'" *Wall Street Journal*, May 14, p. D1; Tibben-Lembke, Ronald S. and Dale S. Rogers (2002), "Differences Between Forward and Reverse Logistics in a Retail Environment," *Supply Chain Management* 7, no. 5, pp. 271–282; and Zieger, Anne (2003), "Reverse Logistics: The New Priority?" *Frontline Solutions* 4, no. 11 (November), pp. 20–24.

8. See Chopra, Sunil and Peter Meindl (2003), *Supply Chain Management*, 2nd ed. (Upper Saddle River, NJ: Prentice Hall); and Stock, James R. and Douglas M. Lambert (2001), *Strategic Logistics Management*, 4th ed. (Homewood, IL: McGraw-Hill), for a discussion of EOQ models.

9. We will not discuss in depth activity-based costing in this text. However, the interested reader is referred to the following sources for further information: Cooper, Robin and Robert S. Kaplan (1991), "Profit Priorities from Activity-Based Accounting," *Harvard Business Review* 69, no. 3 (May–June), pp. 130–135; Balachandran, Bala (1994), "Strategic Activity Based Accounting," *Business Week Executive Briefing Service* 5, pp. 1 ff.; O'Guin, Michael (1990), "Focus the Factory with Activity-Based Costing," *Management Accounting* 68, pp. 36–41; Rotch, William (1990), "Activity-Based Costing in Service Industries," *Journal of Cost Management* 4, no. 4 (Summer), pp. 4–14; and Yates, Ronald E. (1993), "New ABCs for Pinpoint Accounting," *Chicago Tribune*, January 24, pp. 1–2.

10. See, for example, Forsyth, Donelson R. (1983), "An Introduction to Group Dynamics," (Monterey, CA: Brooks/Cole). The Rand Corporation is credited with developing the Delphi technique in the 1950s to forecast where the Soviet Union would attack the United States if they were to launch an offensive. Rand originally assembled generals and other Kremlinologists in a room to discuss the issue and made very little progress. As a result, they developed the Delphi technique to arrive at an orderly consensus.

11. Feitzinger, Edward and Hau L. Lee (1997), "Mass Customization at Hewlett-Packard: The Power of Postponement," *Harvard Business Review* 75, no. 1 (January–February), pp. 116–121.

12. Lee, Hau L., V. Padmanabhan, and Seungjin Whang (1997), "The Bullwhip Effect in Supply Chains," *Sloan Management Review* 38, no. 3 (Spring), pp. 93–102.

The Efficiency Template

This appendix will focus on how to complete the efficiency template for the current channel structure. Completing the efficiency template for the zero-based channel follows an analogous process. Contrasts between the two templates will be pointed out. Please refer to Figure 3.3, which shows a blank efficiency template.

This template is designed to help you understand (a) who is doing what functions and flows in the channel, (b) how much of the combined cost and value each channel member is responsible for, and (c) whether each channel member is being fairly compensated for the performance of these flows. The outputs of understanding these issues are: (a) a strengthened ability to defend the allocation of total channel profits among channel members (based on an in-depth analysis rather than on ad hoc rationales or inertia), (b) a set of recommendations regarding alteration of the split of channel profits, (c) a set of recommendations regarding future emphasis to be placed on the performance of particular flows in the channel.

The template should be filled out separately for each channel used in the market. For example, IBM uses a direct sales force as well as VARs (value added resellers) to sell its personal computers. These are two distinct channels and require two distinct efficiency templates.

The first step in filling out the efficiency template is deciding what weights each of the channel flows should have. Your final assessment of weights should take into account (a) the cost of performing this channel flow in

the entire channel as a proportion of total channel operation costs and (b) the value generated by performing this channel flow. If possible, the costs column of the efficiency template should reflect financially sound data collected through a process like activity-based costing to assess the proportion of total channel costs allocated to each flow. The benefit potential column should reflect the judgmental inputs of managers who are knowledgeable about the channel concerning the potential for good performance of the channel's flow to create highly valued service outputs. Because these inputs are judgmental, a qualitative input, such as a low/medium/high ranking, should be used. These rankings should then be used to adjust the purely cost-based weights in the costs column to arrive at final weights for each flow. Particularly when a flow's benefit potential gets a high rating, it should receive more weight than its pure cost-based weight would suggest because it is important not just on the cost side but also on the service output generation side. The sum of the importance weights is 100. Thus, if you wished, for example, to increase the weight of the promotion flow, you would have to take some points away from some other flow, presumably one (or more than one) that received a low benefit potential ranking.

Once you have decided on weights, you will need to fill in the share of cost of each flow borne by each channel member. Consider the example of promotion on laptop computers in a retail channel. The relevant channel members may include (a) the manufacturer, (b) the retailer, and (c) the consumer. The consumer probably does not do any of the promotional flow (unless word-of-mouth plays a big role in this market); this implies that the consumer should get a zero in the promotions row. Both the manufacturer and the retailer perform promotional flows: the manufacturer does national advertising of the laptops, primarily in print media, while the retailer uses floor salespeople to promote the product to consumers who walk in the door. Parceling out the costs, suppose that we discover that the manufacturer bears 65 percent of total promotional costs in the channel and the retailer bears 35 percent. Thus, the sum of the three numbers (promotional costs borne by the manufacturer, retailer, and consumer) is 100 percent. You will need to replicate this exercise for each of the channel flows in the template.

Can consumers perform channel flows and, hence, get any entries other than zero in this template? Yes. Consider consumers shopping for groceries at a hypermarket in France. These consumers buy in large bulk—for example, they buy six weeks' worth of paper goods in one visit to the hypermarket. In so doing, they bear physical possession flows (storing inventory in their home instead of going to the store every time they need more paper goods), ownership flows (purchasing the paper goods and, hence, owning them sooner than they need to), financing flows (paying for the goods when they take ownership, thus improving upstream channel members' cash flow positions), and so on. Contrast this with shoppers who buy only what they need on a daily or biweekly basis. These consumers will typically buy in smaller lot sizes, will not store inventory in the home, and therefore, will not perform the previously mentioned flows. The consumer who shops at the hypermarket typically gets a lower price than the one who shops daily at a regular grocery store. Why? Precisely because the hypermarket shopper is bearing the cost of several channel flows. Thus, we can see a direct relationship between the bearing of

channel flows and the garnering of channel profits (in the consumer's case, getting a lower price).

This brings us to the "bottom line" of this template. Once you have filled in both the weights and the proportionate shares of flow performance on the template, you can calculate a weighted average for each channel member as described at the bottom of Figure 3.3. You can write the results in the bottom row of the efficiency template, and they should sum to 100 percent horizontally across the row.

What do these numbers mean? They tell you what proportion of total channel profits each channel member should get, given the current channel structure. We call this the normative profit share of channel member i in the current channel. It is very important to note that the normative profit share may or may not equal the actual profit share. When these two numbers are not equal, you need to ask why. Some reasons for a divergence between normative and actual profit shares include:

1. Profits are misallocated in the channel, and should be reallocated.
2. Competitive conditions force a particular channel member to take a lower profit share than its normative flow performance would indicate; its "economic rents" were essentially competed away in the market.
3. External constraints such as government regulation confer economic rents on a channel member beyond their performance of channel flows. This can be a particularly thorny issue in international channel management.

Finally, it is relevant to ask what these profit shares actually are. Consider total retail sales of your product: that would be the retail price times the total units sold. Now, subtract from this total revenue the total costs of running the channel and the cost of goods sold (to net out the part of costs accrued in the manufacturing process). What remains is total channel profits. So, to get a really good handle on the allocation of profits among channel members, you need to do your best to do something like an activity-based costing analysis of the channel.

Now consider some of the contrasts between a template describing the current channel and one describing a zero-based channel:

1. The weights do not necessarily have to be the same in the two templates. You may decide that the current channel underemphasizes the importance of promotion, and you may, therefore, decide to increase the proportion of total channel costs spent on promotion in the zero-based channel, for instance. That will change the weights allocated to the other flows accordingly.

2. The ratings in the template can be different. You may decide that in the zero-based channel, it makes more sense to have your distributor take care of all inventory-handling functions, and thus, physical possession flow costs will be borne much more heavily by the distributor in the zero-based channel than in the current channel. If this is the case, the physical possession row will show different percentages in the zero-based template than in the current template.

3. The column headings themselves may be different in the two templates. You may decide that the zero-based channel is a vertically-integrated channel, so the zero-based template may lack a column heading for the distributor that you now use.

Finally, remember that managers in particular firms may think about this list of flows differently than we have enumerated them here. For example, managers may clump physical possession and ownership together into an inventorying function. This is fine if physical possession and ownership always go hand in hand. But if they do not (for example, if some sales are consignment sales), then the flows need to be separated out.

As an example, consider an efficiency analysis done on a European building materials company. Data were collected from top managers of the company, who were expert in the workings of their channels. Table 3A.1 shows the efficiency template for this company's channel for serving small- and medium-sized end-users (specifically, contractors) who buy through retailers. Because the building materials are bulky and expensive to transport, physical possession costs are the largest part of the total channel costs and, hence, account for 30 percent of channel costs in total. Financing is also a significant channel cost, accounting for 25 percent of the total. Other flows have smaller associated costs . In the benefit potential column, physical possession is again listed as the main benefit-conferring channel flow. This is because end-users of these building materials require product to be provided in a spatially convenient way (to minimize their own transportation costs) and with minimal time delays. Thus, the final weight allocated to the physical possession flow for this company in this channel was 35 percent, with ownership and financing also increased in importance somewhat. The other flows' final weights are reduced somewhat from their pure cost-based levels.

The channel consists of the manufacturer, who sells direct to retailers, who in turn sell directly to end-users. Small contractors, who are a major portion of this segment, buy product in advance and hold small inventories themselves; they thus participate in 40 percent of the physical possession flow, with the manufacturer and retailer each taking 30 percent. The retailers are very active channel members, particularly in their performance of the promotional, negotiation, ordering, and payment flows, because they buffer the manufacturer by dealing with all the many small customer orders that come in. End-users do none of the promotional flow but participate in a small way in other flows. For their efforts,

Table 3A.1   Building materials company efficiency template for channel serving end-users through retailers

Undisguised data

	Weights for Flows:			Proportional Flow Performance of Channel Member:			
	Costs	Benefit Potential (High, Medium, or Low)	Final Weight	Mfgr.	Retailer	End-User	Total
Physical Possession	30	High	35	30	30	40	100
Ownership	12	Medium	15	30	40	30	100
Promotion	10	Low	8	20	80	0	100
Negotiation	5	Low/Medium	4	20	60	20	100
Financing	25	Medium	29	30	30	40	100
Risking	5	Low	2	30	50	20	100
Ordering	6	Low	3	20	60	20	100
Payment	7	Low	4	20	60	20	100
Total	100	N/A	100	N/A	N/A	N/A	N/A
Normative Profit Share	N/A	N/A	N/A	28%	39%	33%	100

these end-users deserve one-third of the channel profits, which translates into a price lower than the list price that would be charged to an individual buyer (e.g., a do-it-yourself homeowner). The retailer earns a normative channel profit share of 39 percent, while the manufacturer earns a normative channel profit share of 28 percent. Specifically, one calculates the manufacturer's normative channel profit share as:

$$(.35)*(.3) + (.15)*(.3) + (.08)*(.2) + (.04)*(.2) + (.29)*(.3) + (.02)*(.3) + (.03)*(.2) + (.04)*(.2).$$

This analysis was done after careful estimation of the total costs of performing all flows in this particular channel. But suppose that the company had not determined exact percentage shares for all the flows done by all channel members. Instead, suppose the data were very rough, with only

ratings of zero, low, medium, and high. Further, suppose that if the true rating were zero, a zero would be reported; if the true rating were between 1 and 29 percent, a low would reported; if the true rating were between 30 and 69 percent, a medium would be reported; and if the true rating were between 70 and 100 percent, a high would be reported. Let us code a zero as a 0, a low as a 1, a medium as a 2, and a high as a 3. (The coding scheme is linear; if there is a strong reason to believe that a nonlinear scheme would be better, it is possible, of course, to use that as well.) We would then get an efficiency template that looks like Table 3A.2.

To translate this into percentages, we look at these rank-order data for a given flow and ask, "What proportion of the costs of performing this flow is borne by the manufacturer? By the retailer? By the final end-user?" For the case of physical possession,

Table 3A.2   Building materials company efficiency template for channel serving end-users through retailers
Rank-order data

	Weights for Flows:			Proportional Flow Performance of Channel Member:			
	Costs	Benefit Potential (High, Medium, or Low)	Final Weight	Mfgr.	Retailer	End-User	Total
Physical Possession	30	High	35	2	2	2	100
Ownership	12	Medium	15	2	2	2	100
Promotion	10	Low	8	1	3	0	100
Negotiation	5	Low/Medium	4	1	2	1	100
Financing	25	Medium	29	2	2	2	100
Risking	5	Low	2	2	2	1	100
Ordering	6	Low	3	1	2	1	100
Payment	7	Low	4	1	2	1	100
Total	100	N/A	100	N/A	N/A	N/A	N/A
Normative Profit Share	N/A	N/A	N/A	?	?	?	100

each entry is a 2 (medium). Thus, the point total is 6, of which each channel member has one-third of the points. We, therefore, can allocate 33 percent of the channel flow costs of physical possession to each channel member. In another example, consider the rank-order data for the promotion flow. Here, the manufacturer gets a ranking of 1 (low), the retailer gets a 3 (high), and the end-user gets a 0. Thus, of the 4 total points in the promotion flow, 25 percent (and hence an estimated 25 percent of the channel flow costs of promotion) are borne by the manufacturer, and 75 percent are borne by the retailer, with 0 percent borne by the end-user.

These transformed data produce percentages similar to those in the original efficiency template, but they are based on rougher data inputs (a four-point scale rather than a 100-point scale). The transformed efficiency template appears as Table 3A.3. From this analysis, the manufacturer gets a normative channel profit share of 32 percent; the retailer gets 38 percent; and end-users get 29 percent. These correspond well with the 28 percent, 39 percent, and 33 percent from the true data in Table3A.1. Since it is not always easy to do a full activity-based costing analysis of channel flow performance, the rank-order data inputs suggested here may provide reasonable estimates.

Table 3A.3   Building materials company efficiency template for channel serving end-users through retailers
Transformed rank-order data

	Weights For Flows:			Proportional Flow Performance of Channel Member:			
	Costs	Benefit Potential (High, Medium, or Low)	Final Weight	Mfgr.	Retailer	End-User	Total
Physical Possession	30	High	35	33	33	33	100
Ownership	12	Medium	15	33	33	33	100
Promotion	10	Low	8	25	75	0	100
Negotiation	5	Low/Medium	4	25	50	25	100
Financing	25	Medium	29	33	33	33	100
Risking	5	Low	2	40	40	20	100
Ordering	6	Low	3	25	50	25	100
Payment	7	Low	4	25	50	25	100
Total	100	N/A	100	N/A	N/A	N/A	N/A
Normative Profit Share	N/A	N/A	N/A	32%	38%	29%	100

Supply-Side Channel Analysis

Channel Structure and Intensity

Learning objectives

After reading this chapter, you will be able to do the following:

- Describe the idea of selectivity as the negotiated and often reciprocal limitation of the number of trading partners in a market area

- Explain why manufacturers prefer more coverage, especially in fast moving consumer goods, while preferring the downstream channel member to limit its assortment in their product category

- Explain why downstream channel members prefer less coverage, while preferring more assortment in the manufacturer's product category

- Explain why limited distribution is preferable for brands with a high-end positioning or a narrow target market

- Explain the mechanism by which limiting the number of trading partners raises motivation and increases power

- Describe selectivity as a way to reassure trading partners against the threat of opportunism

- Forecast when either side (upstream or downstream) will concede to a limitation of the number of their trading partners

- Describe means of maintaining intensive coverage while containing its destructive effects on the channel

- Describe the special challenges of multiple formats and of dual distribution (parallel usage of third-party and company-owned channels)

The legal implications of these topics are covered in depth in Chapter 10.

INTRODUCTION

Chapters 2 and 3 cover the first steps of channel design: understanding the end-user's service output demands and what channels flows must be undertaken to meet them. The next step in channel design is deciding on the channel structure.

> A description of the channel structure summarizes the types of members that are in the channel, the intensity or number of members of each type that coexist in the market, and the number of distinct channels that coexist in the market.

Channel design presents three challenges. The first is to determine the level of intensity needed: How much coverage should the producer have, in any form? Put differently, how easy should it be for a prospect to find the brand and buy it? Most of this chapter focuses on this pivotal issue. The second challenge comes from combining different channel types by going to market in multiple ways, mixing different formats (such as stores, kiosks, and the Web). The third design challenge is to decide whether the manufacturer should simultaneously go to market via its own channels and via third parties (called dual distribution or concurrent distribution). Although this may seem like a manufacturer-centered way to consider channel structure, it is not because the key issues turn on the downstream channel member's concerns and strategies. We consider the downstream channel member's interests in composing its portfolio of suppliers. We discuss when the downstream channel member should demand that suppliers limit their degree and variety of market coverage and when the downstream member should be willing to limit its own brand assortment.

Intensive distribution means that a brand can be purchased through many of the possible outlets in a trading area (at saturation, every possible outlet). The opposite is exclusive distribution, whereby a brand can be purchased only through one vendor in a trading area, so that the vendor has a local monopoly on the brand. Both saturation and exclusivity are out of the ordinary. Typically, a brand is distributed with some degree of intensity, achieving partial coverage of available outlets in a market area. Degree of channel intensity (alternatively, degree of selectivity) is a major factor driving the manufacturer's ability to implement its channel programs.[1]

The more intensively a manufacturer distributes its brand in a market, the less the manufacturer can influence how channel members perform marketing channel flows. To control the performance of flows, a manufacturer must refrain from blanketing or saturating a trading area's distribution outlets. Yet by limiting coverage, the manufacturer may be giving up sales and profits to its competitors. Naturally, manufacturers prefer to maximize coverage and actively resist the idea of deliberately restricting the availability of their brands. When and why should a manufacturer limit coverage?

The upstream member (manufacturer) considers how many outlets to pursue (degree of selectivity). The downstream member (e.g., the reseller) considers the mirror-image question: how many competing brands to carry in a product category (category selectivity). Both sides consider limiting their number of channel partners.

This complex decision is frequently seen as a strong player imposing unwanted restrictions on a weak one. This is a limited and often misleading viewpoint. A more useful way to frame the decision is as the outcome of a negotiation that reflects patterns of trade-offs and reciprocity. This chapter presents selectivity as a negotiated settlement and covers how selectivity influences a channel member's ability to implement its channel strategy.

COVERAGE VERSUS ASSORTMENT: FRAMING THE DECISIONS OF UPSTREAM AND DOWNSTREAM CHANNEL MEMBERS

Why More Coverage Is Better for Manufacturers of Convenience Goods

When it comes to availability of a brand in a trading area, more is always better—or so it would seem. It is almost a truism to say that the more outlets carry a brand, the more it will sell. Not only does coverage make it easier for prospects to find brands, but in addition, if prospective purchasers encounter a vigorous sales effort for the brand in every outlet they visit, and if many outlets carry the brand, the prospect must surely surrender to the combined persuasion of all these outlets. How could it *not* be true that more coverage is better?

The answer hinges first on the nature of the product category. Many categories of product or service are routine, low-involvement purchases that the buyer considers minor and low risk (so that making a significant error is unlikely). Fast moving consumer goods (FMCG), such as juice or facial tissues, fall into this category, as do many products, such as office supplies, purchased by businesses. These convenience goods[2] are the stuff of everyday life. Given an acceptable brand choice, buyers will tend to take what is offered, rather than search for their favorite brand.

One indication of this phenomenon is that FMCG brand market share is disproportionately related to distribution coverage (see Figure 4.1 for examples of such relationships).

After a certain threshold of coverage has been reached, securing a few more points of distribution coverage is frequently associated with a sharp upturn in market share. One reason this occurs is that for many mundane products most consumers will not leave one store to visit another if they cannot find their preferred brands. They tend to buy from the set of brands they find if at least some brands are acceptable to them. Small retailers, constrained by space, stock only the top one or two brands, knowing that will suffice for most of their customers on most of the purchase occasions the small outlet serves. Collectively, small retailers move large amounts of merchandise, and in these stores, consumers have very little brand choice. Hence, coverage over a threshold level boosts coverage in small outlets, which rapidly boosts a brand's market share disproportionately. This creates a spiral: The higher the brand's market share, the greater the likelihood that other small stores will adopt that brand, which increases share, and so on (the rich get richer).[3]

Thus, for convenience goods, all else being constant, higher degrees of distribution intensity will always boost sales. For anything other than convenience goods, this statement does not hold.

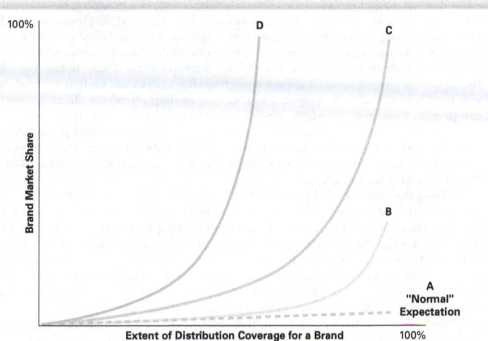

Function A is an example of the type of relationship that would ordinarily be expected between distribution coverage and market share.

Functions B, C, and D are convex and are examples of approximate relationships often found in FMCG markets.

A brand can achieve 100% market share at less than 100% coverage because not every possible outlet will carry the product category. For example, convenience stores sell food but not every category of food.

Figure 4.1   Sample representations of the coverage/market share relationship for fast moving consumer goods.

Source: Based on Reibstein, David J. and Paul W. Farris (1995), "Market Share and Distribution: A Generalization, A Speculation, and Some Implications," *Marketing Science*, 14, no. 3; pp. G190–G202.

Why Downstream Channel Members Dislike Intensive Distribution

From the downstream channel member's perspective, more coverage for a given brand is a negative, not a positive. Among other factors, channel members differentiate themselves by offering unique assortments. Intensive distribution means that a channel member's competitors have the same brand, thereby eroding the outlet's uniqueness. Each downstream channel member would prefer exclusivity. This clash of interests between manufacturers and downstream players builds a permanent source of conflict into the channel.

When a market is saturated (all possible outlets carry a brand), a channel member cannot present the brand as a reason why a buyer should visit that outlet rather than a competing outlet. Once the buyer does appear, the outlet must give the buyer a reason to purchase on the spot. Inertia may be one such reason: A prospect will buy to avoid the nuisance of shopping elsewhere, particularly for a minor purchase like toothpaste or tomato sauce. But for a more important purchase, such as a digital camera, the buyer will delay a decision and continue to shop unless the channel member can present some reason—usually a price cut—to buy now. This sets up channel members directly against each other, thereby driving ferocious intrabrand price competition (i.e., price competition between sellers of the same brand, as contrasted with interbrand competition, which is the more standard competition between different brands in a product category).

From the manufacturer's perspective, intrabrand price competition at the retail level (but not, of course, at the wholesale level!) is desirable—in the short term. Channel members will move more product by charging lower prices and are likely to fund it by slashing their own margins. The manufacturer realizes higher volume at the same wholesale price. For example, many retailers offer Coca-Cola soft drinks as promotions. The larger super- and hypermarkets often carry a large product variety (size, multipaks, flavors), which can take up a large amount of shelf space. To induce shoppers to buy the products, the stores offer low promotional prices.

But this situation cannot go on indefinitely. Channel members, realizing the brand is unprofitable for them, will press for relief in the form of lower wholesale prices. If wholesale prices are not cut, the problem of low margins persists; however, even if wholesale prices are cut, the problem may still persist. Resellers will be obliged to compete away the higher margin at resale, thereby failing to resolve their profitability problem.[4] In the example of Coca-Cola products, the stores may not incur accounting losses on the drinks, but they may incur significant opportunity costs that come with end-of-aisle displays and advertising to accompany the promotions. This will make channel members reconsider their brand support.

Except for the most powerful brands, the likely outcome is that some channel members will drop the brand. If enough of them do so, the brand declines to a lower degree of distribution intensity, and the problem of intrabrand competition is resolved. Of course, it is the channel members, not the manufacturer, who decide the marketing channel structure. The manufacturer likely will lose many of its preferred outlets and keep many inferior outlets. This is because the best outlets have the most alternatives.

Channel members drop a brand in three ways. First, they may do so overtly by discontinuing the saturated brand and substituting another that is less intensively distributed in their trading areas. For very strong brands, the clientele will not accept the substitution, but for more typical brands, this strategy is likely to succeed. Second, channel members may discontinue the entire product category if they cannot find a satisfactory substitute brand and the category is not essential. Third, a channel member may appear to carry a brand by offering nominal stock and display but attempt to convert prospective customers to a different brand once they are on site. Thus, a brand actually can have poor coverage even though it appears to have high coverage because that coverage is merely nominal.

The most flagrant form of this behavior is to advertise one brand to bring customers to the site (bait), and then persuade them to buy another brand (switch). Bait-and-switch tactics are most common for brands with high buyer recognition because such brands are attractive bait. For example, an electronics store may run advertisements promoting a Sony television, but at the store the sales assistant may guide the buyer to a different, perhaps lesser-known brand on which the store earns higher margins.

All too often, manufacturers fail to ask themselves whether it is in the channel member's interest to do more for their brands. Frequently, it is not. Sidebar 4.1 explains how Royal Canin makes itself appealing to retailers by limiting availability (and also by focused targeting of the desirable segment buyer: one who is loyal and has low price sensitivity). This example is striking because it is about what many buyers consider a convenience good—dog and cat food.

Another factor is also at work, the problem of free riding. Imagine you are a retailer selling consumer entertainment durables and pursuing a high-quality strategy. To implement this strategy, you invest heavily. Your store is well located and appealing. In the speaker category, you stock the full product line of a hypothetical speaker brand called Johanson. To support this brand, you carry substantial inventory (even of slow moving items), devote showroom space, advertise on behalf of Johanson, maintain a well-stocked repair facility, and offer extended warranties. You retain a large and well trained sales staff to explain each category of product (speakers, home cinema systems, etc.), to point out the myriad features of each brand and model, to explain how features translate into benefits, to help prospects discover what trade-offs they prefer, and to help prospects match their preferences to their options.

Your strategy is to attract an appreciative clientele who will compensate you for your high costs by paying higher prices and becoming loyal clients. This strategy has worked well for you. Your store has a reputation, which it lends to every brand it carries.[5] Your clientele views you as their purchasing agent and trusts you to screen products for them.

Recently, Johanson hired a new distribution manager who has aggressively pursued competing outlets of various types and has gained a considerable increase in coverage. Now your salespeople are complaining that they are spending their time on browsers, who end lengthy interactions about Johanson speakers with "I'm going to think about it." They leave the store with an informed decision about what they want. Then they visit other stores or Web sites and bargain for a better price on the precise model they have selected—as a function of your assistance to them. Other sellers can offer a better price because they do not offer your level of support. Nor do they need to, thanks to your assistance to their customers. These stores are free riding on you. You bear the costs. They gain the benefits.

As the store manager, your inclination is to discontinue the Johanson brand. This may, however, be costly. Your parts and merchandise inventory may not be returnable for full credit. The knowledge your personnel have gained about Johanson will be rendered worthless. Your advertising on behalf of Johanson not only will be wasted but will raise embarrassing questions about why you no longer carry the brand. Your Johanson-specific investments are not readily redeployable to another brand.

Hence, you may continue to sell Johanson, but an acrimonious relationship with the manufacturer is now a certainty. Hence, even though you are an ethical retailer,

Sidebar 4.1

Royal Canin

Royal Canin is an independent company that holds the leading position in Europe for dog and cat food with an 18 percent market share. This leads the brands of the multinationals, such as Nestle (Friskies, Fido), Mars (Pal, Whiskas), and Colgate (Hills). Royal Canin began in 1966 when a French veterinarian, Henri Lagarde, noticed that many of his canine patients had dull fur and eczema. The cause was poor nutrition. Lagarde began making dog food in a biscuit form, cooking the biscuits in an oven in his garage. When his patients recovered their glossy coats and healthy skin, Lagarde decided to close his practice and go into the pet food business.

Lagarde's first customers were dog breeders and other veterinarians. His first salespeople were the owners whose dogs he had cured. Lagarde built a strong business by cultivating breeders. From breeder endorsements, Lagarde built a strong business (people who buy puppies from a breeder do not dare to change the recommended brand). Over the years, Royal Canin invested heavily in research and development and built a very sophisticated and complete product line. The product range is enormous, offering food for every type and age of dog or cat and every level of activity. A color coding system and a strict store planogram (outlining how the shelf should be filled) helps the owner find the right product quickly. A key to the brand's success is loyalty: Owners begin with puppy or kitten food, then follow the Royal Canin color-coded line through all the stages of their pet's life.

A key to the brand's excellent results (13% margins and a very successful entry into the stock market) is distribution. Initially, the brand sold only to breeders. Then Lagarde switched to hypermarkets, but the brand was displayed in the midst of inexpensive competitors, and the line was not properly presented.

Early in the 1990s, Royal Canin switched to selling through specialty outlets: garden stores with pet departments, as well as pet stores. These outlets account for the bulk of the brand's sales today. These specialists, as opposed to (people) food stores, are more welcoming to salespeople. They will take time to talk with Royal Canin "counselors," generally student veterinarians, who explain the line and offer advice about animal health. These stores send their floor salespeople to Royal Canin seminars, and they stock the full line, displayed as suggested by the supplier. They reach a buyer who is willing to pay a substantial premium over the ordinary pet food available in food stores. Why? Lagarde explains it thus: "People feel guilty if they don't give the best to their animals."

The result for Royal Canin is high market share, high margins, fast growth, and a high valuation on the Paris stock exchange. These results are due to astute marketing of a superior product. Limiting distribution has proven to be a key element. That pet owners are willing to go to pet and garden stores to buy Royal Canin rather than buying another brand where they buy their own food is an indication that even for a convenience good the right presentation and sales assistance make a difference.[6]

you will not consider it dishonorable to engage in a certain degree of bait-and-switch as long as you can switch to a brand you feel comfortable endorsing. This will not pose an obstacle because there are multiple excellent brands of audio speakers. One day, you will become irritated enough to contact the sales representatives of some of Johanson's competitors. As a retailer, you will not tolerate free riding indefinitely.

Can the Manufacturer Sustain Intensive Distribution?

Intensive distribution often creates lackluster sales support, defection of downstream channel members, and even bait-and-switch tactics. How can the manufacturer remedy this situation?

One solution is contractual: The manufacturer can attempt to impose on the channel member a contract demanding certain standards of conduct (for example, barring bait-and-switch) and then bring legal action against offenders. This is an expensive route: It requires documentation (e.g., of recurring bait-and-switch tactics) as well as legal resources. This muscular method of implementation is likely to alienate other channel members and to generate unfavorable publicity for the brand.

Another solution is to invest in a pull strategy to build brand equity. Customer preference may then oblige the channel member to carry the brand, pay a high wholesale price, charge a low retail price, and make up the low gross margin elsewhere. This strategy frequently is used to great effect in fast moving consumer goods.[7] The consumer demand for either Coca-Cola or Pepsi forces most channel members to carry one if not both of these brands. Similarly, in consumer entertainment durables, Sony's brand equity enables the supplier to offer its goods in many types of channels and forces almost all members of any type of channel to carry them because consumers would question whether an electronics outlet that does not carry Sony is a legitimate seller. In general, channel members surrender and carry those intensively distributed brands that have high brand equity. However, this strategy is extremely costly, requiring the manufacturer to make continuing, massive investments in advertising and promotion.

Even this strategy has its limits. It is tempting for a manufacturer with a sought-after brand to overproduce and then load up channel members with more product than they can sell (channel stuffing). Inevitably, the brand ends up in too many places and too many different types of places. The brand's positioning becomes unclear. Downstream channel members slash prices to move stock. Ultimately, the brand dilutes its equity, which can topple the heads of companies. For example:

> ➤ The Barbie doll's phenomenal brand equity prompted its maker to expand its 90 Barbie models to 450 in fifteen years and to increase production capacity. This avalanche of product caused market saturation in both the number and the variety of outlets. Overloaded retailers, seeing that Barbie was available even in supermarkets and on cable television, dumped their stocks, cutting prices by as much as 75 percent. As the brand's price tumbled, so did Mattel's stock price, and the company's president, the architect of the policy, was forced to resign.[8]

> ➤ Similarly, the CEO of Warnaco was fired after the apparel company produced so much product that it became available almost anywhere at distress prices. Warnaco made clothing under license from brand owners, such as Calvin Klein and Ralph Lauren. Seeking to maximize coverage, Warnaco sold not only through many retailers, but through many types of retailers. Department stores were alienated by sales in discount generalist stores, such as Wal-Mart, and the licensors were angered by what they saw as the cheapening of their brand images.[9]

In some countries, a third solution is possible: resale price maintenance (RPM). This means the manufacturer can legally set a price floor below which channel members cannot charge their own customers. RPM permits the manufacturer to limit the normal pricing behavior of its resellers.[10] The legality of RPM varies widely in world markets: It has been illegal in the United States but is now governed under a rule of reason (see Chapter 10 for more details).[11] Where RPM is allowed, manufacturers can use it to set minimum resale prices high enough so that all channel members have an acceptable margin, even at high levels of distribution intensity. Thus, RPM enables artificially high levels of coverage. For the purchaser, the good news is that the brand is easy to find and resellers will compete on a nonprice basis (selling services, amenities, and so forth). The bad news is that it is difficult to get a discount: Resellers are obliged to disguise discounts and are subject to legal action for so doing, even if they do not have a formal contract with the manufacturer.

The fourth and generally most applicable solution for the manufacturer with low sales support is to bow to the inevitable and limit its market coverage; that is, to elect some degree of selectivity in its distribution. One advantage of this approach is that the manufacturer has the opportunity to target desired channel members rather than merely settling for those who do not eliminate themselves when intrabrand competition becomes too intense for channel members to realize adequate profits on a particular brand. Another advantage is better working relationships. See Sidebar 4.2 for an example. We develop these arguments later in this chapter.

The critical question is how much coverage should a manufacturer aim to achieve? Curiously, the answer hinges on a seemingly unrelated question: In a given product category, how many brands should a downstream channel member carry? We will turn to this issue and then return to the manufacturer's coverage problem.

Degree of Category Exclusivity: The Downstream Channel Member's Decision

Let us consider a distributor and take the example of an industrial supply house. The supply house sells consumables (and some durables) to manufacturing plants of all kinds and to some offices in a trading area. Due to the generality of the demand, the distributor must carry thousands of stock-keeping units in hundreds of product categories. For any given product category, say, metalworking fluids, the industrial supply house must decide how many brands to carry.

For simplicity, the distributor might prefer to carry one brand. However, it is likely to carry many more, partly to benefit from competition, even limited competition,[12] but largely to meet the assortment demands of its customer base.[13] Part of the appeal of an industrial supply house is that whatever the buyer might want is there, in stock. Keeping a broad assortment satisfies customers (although it drives up inventory-related costs).

For each product category, the distributor must decide how large its brand assortment will be: very broad (all brands) or narrower, even a single brand (i.e., giving a brand category exclusivity, otherwise known as exclusive dealing).[14] A priori, the importance of assortment leads the distributor (more generally, a downstream channel member) to resist giving a manufacturer category exclusivity. Of course, manufacturers generally prefer not to be presented alongside their competitors, creating another built-in source of permanent channel conflict.

Thus, we have two conflicts. First, manufacturers want to blanket a trading area with outlets, but the outlets prefer the reverse. Second, downstream channel members prefer to have multiple brands to offer in a category, but manufacturers prefer the reverse. Here are the makings of a negotiated settlement. We have yet a third conflict: Manufacturers want downstream channel members to support their brands vigorously

Sidebar 4.2

Appliances makers shun hypermarkets

It is widely believed in France that retail coverage must include hypermarkets. Giant stores that sell groceries, other FMCG, and specialty items (including durables), hypermarkets are a fixture on the French retail scene. Suppliers dread dealing with the handful of chains that dominate, all of which are known for tough negotiating tactics, yet they feel obliged to sell to hypermarkets because these are "destination stores" or "habitual stores." Customers go to them regularly (e.g., for groceries), then browse and purchase unrelated items. One category in which hypermarkets have become very strong is small electrical appliances, which they dominate in terms of category volume and category profit.

Nonetheless, specialist retailers have been gaining ground at the hypermarkets' expense. They have countered the hypers' influence through a number of steps, such as improved merchandising and better supply-chain management. This has allowed specialists to capitalize on supplier discontent with hypermarkets, which have redeployed their shelf space to other product categories.

Market research done by suppliers shows that one quarter of prospects who plan to purchase a small appliance walk out empty handed either because they cannot find the product they came in to buy (a stockout, which is a failure of supply-chain management) or they cannot find an appealing product at all (a failure of assortment or merchandising). Importantly, this rate of lost sales for hypermarkets is double what it is for specialists. One reason for this is that hypermarkets not only have chronic stockouts but have few sales staff to steer consumers

to something else and persuade them to buy the substitute.

Another reason for the gain in specialist share is that manufacturers are increasingly choosing to work with specialists rather than hypermarkets. There is considerable market potential in newer, high-end models, for which the prospects want advice and selection. Further, although small appliances are usually considered specialty products for which customers will search, research shows that 10 percent of all purchases are impulse. These, in turn, are heavily influenced by merchandising and sales support. Specialist stores offer better-trained salespeople and more of them, plus better merchandising.

To take advantage of these conditions, suppliers are increasingly choosing to award some models exclusively to specialists. Indeed, some suppliers sell everything they make exclusively through specialists. For example, Nespresso, maker of a proprietary home system for making café-quality cups of coffee, refuses to sell through any hypermarket, in part to avoid becoming dependent on hypermarkets. Nespresso's machines use a proprietary system of coffee capsules, over which Nespresso itself is the monopoly supplier. The capsules are a lucrative business. Nespresso anticipates that hypermarkets would demand the right to distribute the capsules once they were to build a large business in the coffee machines. Thus, Nespresso avoids the problem by not starting down the path to depending on hypermarkets. In return for protection from hypermarkets, specialist chains give the machines favored treatment—thereby growing the capsule market.[15]

and take low margins, but channel members prefer lower costs and higher margins. Here again is an opportunity to trade one's way to a mutually satisfactory arrangement.

The rest of this chapter concerns how, when, and why a trade-off among competing interests comes about.[16]

STRIKING A DEAL: HOW MUCH SELECTIVITY TO TRADE AWAY

The Threat of Complacency

To this point, we have focused on one reason to cover a market intensively, which is to make it easy for a prospect to find the brand. Another reason to seek higher degrees of distribution coverage is driven not by customer behavior but by channel-member behavior. Whenever coverage of a brand is highly selective, the manufacturer faces a difficult circumstance. When a small set of channel members carries the brand, intrabrand competition is low. This is a dangerous situation. When competition is insufficient, even channel members with the very best intentions will be inclined not to give their most vigorous efforts to the brand. Quasi monopoly in distribution (as in any other activity) encourages complacency and, hence, inadequate performance.

A certain degree of intrabrand competition in a market area is beneficial to the manufacturer. It brings forth each channel member's best efforts without going so far as to put the channel member in a losing situation. Best Buy, a giant electronics retailer, acquired Future Shop, a competitor in Canada. Rather than shutting down Future Shop stores or converting them to the Best Buy name, the parent company actually left both names and both stores in place—even when they had stores literally across the street from each other. The two chains serve to block a third entrant—and to stimulate each chain to perform better.[17] Companies often use the strategy of competing head-to-head with themselves at the brand/product level on the theory that it is better to be cannibalized by another division than to be bankrupted by another company. Best Buy elevates this logic to the channel level.

One of the greatest drawbacks of selective distribution is the danger that selectivity fosters lackluster representation. Attaining enough coverage to create the optimal degree of intrabrand competition, however, can clash with other objectives. The rest of this chapter will cover how to balance the risk of complacency that inevitably accompanies selective distribution by creating other methods of motivating channel members to give their best efforts when coverage has been limited. Sidebar 4.3 details how a boat builder, Bénéteau, skillfully avoided this risk after acquiring a rival, Jeanneau.

The Nature of the Product Category

In deciding how much selectivity to grant to channel members in a market area, the manufacturer should begin with service output demands that are likely to be common to the product class. As noted earlier, buyers will not expend much effort to purchase convenience goods such as milk or copier/printer paper. They will demand high spatial convenience and quick delivery (therefore, they will not tolerate stockouts). To fit buyer behavior, convenience goods should be distributed as intensively as possible. For shopping goods such as a small appliance, buyers will do some comparison of brands and prices across outlets, suggesting an intermediate degree of selectivity is desirable. For specialty goods such as a home cinema system or production machinery, buyers will expend considerable effort to make the "right choice." For this, they will make an effort to find outlets they can trust, suggesting that highly selective, even exclusive distribution is acceptable, indeed desirable, to the buyer. This generalization applies to both industrial and consumer products and services.[18]

Sidebar 4.3

Bénéteau acquires Jeanneau

A fierce rivalry existed for decades between two French builders of pleasure boats, Bénéteau and Jeanneau, the "enemy brothers of the coast." In 1995, Jeanneau was in serious financial trouble. Management reluctantly accepted an offer of acquisition by rival Bénéteau. Observers criticized the move, arguing that Jeanneau's situation was desperate and that Bénéteau, which had its own problems, was not strong enough to salvage its acquisition. Today, the critics have retracted their judgments. Bénéteau-Jeanneau is prosperous, growing, and making an impression with its new products at boat shows.

Shortly after the acquisition, such an outcome seemed unlikely. The rivalry was so strong that the head of Bénéteau, Annette Roux, hesitated to visit Jeanneau. Roux is the granddaughter of Bénéteau's founder and was concerned that her presence would only inflame the old feud. How did the fusion succeed?

The key was achieving economies of scale while preserving the identities of the two brands. Bénéteau's image is one of risk, innovation, sportiness, and stylishness. The brand is avant garde, and its customers are elitist, even for the boating industry. Jeanneau, in contrast, is conservative, comfortable, classic, and reassuring. This said, there is some overlap in the companies' clientele, leading the two to compete fiercely. Boat owners used this rivalry and the fact that towns that had a Jeanneau dealer also had a Bénéteau dealer to play the two brands against each other and drive down prices.

Annette Roux astutely found selected economies of scale in production, personnel management, financing, accounting, and purchasing. Yet, she ensured that the two brands did not become similar in any way the customer could detect. A small point is typical and telling: teak, a traditional wood for boats, is reserved exclusively for Jeanneau, while mahogany, a more daring and unusual wood for boats, is reserved exclusively for Bénéteau. In her drive for economies of scale in sharing operations, however, Roux surprised and angered many observers by refusing to alter either brand's channels.

Why this contradiction? Why preserve two channels generally competing in exactly the same markets? Observers, managers, and dealers all expected Bénéteau dealers to acquire the Jeanneau line. Roux rejected this idea, arguing that each brand needed to pursue its own strategy and that fusing the dealerships would lessen interbrand competition too much. The managing director of Bénéteau puts it like this:

> First, I'm convinced that people defend their own flag better than an ensemble imposed by headquarters. Second, if the dealers for Bénéteau and Jeanneau had merged, we would have left an empty site in every port—for the competition!

Time has proved the wisdom of keeping two distribution channels and letting them compete with each other. Each brand is prosperous. Customers are unable to use one dealer to drive down the prices of the other because the brands are well differentiated (much better than they were as independent companies). Headquarters steers the marketing of each brand in different directions to lessen cannibalization, and each dealer network then drives each brand hard, aiming at potentially the same customer without making any effort to steer the customer to one brand or the other.[19]

While a useful starting point, these ideas are somewhat difficult to operationalize because it is not always evident when buyers are willing to search and to what degree. One indication of a search good is that a category is new; for both industrial and consumer products, new categories often require considerable channel member support to induce prospects to become customers.[20] New-to-the-world categories do not even start out as search goods because no one is searching for them yet.

To distribute specialty goods and, to a lesser degree, shopping goods, to have many outlets is less important than to have the right outlets. Manufacturers should carefully select, cultivate, and support the correct outlets in a trading area. This is a policy of selective distribution.

It is important to separate selective distribution from poor coverage. A brand has poor coverage when few outlets will take it or when the right outlets will not carry it. Merely examining the percentage of outlets carrying the brand in a trading area does not indicate whether a manufacturer's coverage is selective or whether it is mediocre.

Brand Strategy: Quality Positioning and Premium Pricing

Thus far, we have covered product class factors in determining what degree of selectivity a manufacturer should grant in a market area, as well as cost factors that apply to distributing any good or service. We now turn to a class of factors that apply to a given brand and its marketing strategy.

The first consideration is the brand's positioning on the quality dimension. In any product category, the strategy of a given brand may be to attempt to position as high quality. Mercedes-Benz automobiles and Cabasse audio speakers are examples of brands positioned as high quality. Operationally, this means conveying an image that the brand has superior ability to perform its functions, or more simply, that it is so superior as to be excellent. This position, typically accompanied by a premium price, is difficult to achieve. To do so, the manufacturer must pay particular attention to the image or reputation of the channel member representing the brand because this image will be imparted to everything the channel member sells. Therefore, the manufacturer should prefer channel members that themselves excel in handling high-end brands.

By definition, excellence is scarce. Manufacturers will be obliged to focus on the subset of channel members that matches the brand's intended image. Selective distribution is called for to support the high-quality positioning. This is particularly the case when premium pricing is part of the positioning: higher-priced products are usually limited in their distribution availability.[21] Broadening coverage to other outlets will dilute the brand's positioning of superior quality. Sidebar 4.4 describes the experience of luxury goods maker Louis Vuitton Moet Hennessy (LVMH) with a prestigious brand of clothing, Donna Karan, that violated this rule.

Of course, these high-end-image channel members will be in great demand and have their choice of brands to represent. Inducing them to carry any given brand, even one positioned as premium, can be difficult. Even though the manufacturer will not seek intensive coverage, it will need a capable sales force to convince the target channel members to carry and support the brand. Of course, there must be a segment of buyers interested in high quality, convinced the brand is high quality, and willing to exert effort to make a high-quality purchase. Put differently, the high-quality brand's marketing strategy must be correct if the channel is to succeed in implementing it.

Sidebar 4.4

LVMH acquires Donna Karan

Louis Vuitton Moet Hennessy (LVMH) is a French luxury goods maker with brand names in many product categories. Desirous of entering the luxury clothing business, the firm moved swiftly when it learned that Donna Karan (maker of DKNY and other prestigious labels) was available for sale. LVMH paid what is now viewed as a considerable price for its acquisition, only to learn that the brand was feeling the effects of overly intensive distribution. Management had boosted production to the point that it was obliged to liquidate merchandise at very high discounts and to take on channels that did not fit its upscale image. Consequently, the flagship DKNY brand suffered. For example, prestigious department store Neiman Marcus refused to take on DKNY because it was also available, piled high on tables under fluorescent lights, at discount chain TJ Maxx. For the same reason, Bloomingdale's, another prestigious department store, cut the line back from 16 stores to one, and revised the terms of trade to sell only on consignment (leaving Donna Karan with the cost of unsold merchandise).

LVMH apparently learned how serious the situation was only after the acquisition, even though customers surely knew how widely the brand was available. And Donna Karan's management had been planning to accelerate the volume push for the coming year. Said one executive after seeing the audited books,

> Unless you are inside a company, you don't know how much inventory they bought for the next season. The strategy was to push

the sales figures, to push the sales, no matter what. Any company is at risk when it orders two times more than was sold.

Giuseppe Brusone, the newly installed head of Donna Karan, vowed, "We have to suffer in the beginning" to rectify the situation. LVMH decided to close company-owned stores, cut back production, restructure the business, and dramatically reduce coverage. This, in turn, required weaning management off the strategies it used to stuff the channels, such as markdown money to share with channels the costs of unsold goods, special discounts, and consignments. Managers were told to encourage department stores (the targeted channel) only to buy merchandise they could sell at full price. As a visible gesture, Donna Karan gave up $18 million in annual profits by reducing its business with TJ Maxx. Brusone described the new outlook to his subordinates like this:

> Don't worry about the volume. I prefer they sell less with a good healthy margin. They can make more money without any agreement on special discounts, consignments, and things like that.

Going forward, a major challenge is to rebuild the confidence of department stores to the point that they rearrange their floors and their purchasing routines to welcome the line again. LVMH reports the reorganization is producing improved results, but now Donna Karan must displace the competitors that stepped in while the firm moved volume to discounters.[22]

Of course, brands not positioned as high quality are not presented as low quality. They are instead positioned as adequate (but not superior) in quality. Often the brand will be featured on other attributes, frequently convenience or low price. Either of these is consistent with a more intensive distribution policy.

A variation on the theme of high quality is the theme of scarcity. Some manufacturers deliberately create product shortages. The idea is that scarcity can be appealing (if not everyone can get the product, it may be psychologically more desirable). Artificial scarcity is a marketing strategy that is coupled with selective distribution in order to increase the illusiveness, hence the allure, of the product. Harley-Davidson pursues this strategy, underproducing its motorcycles and limiting distribution to a few outlets (many of them company owned). This creates long waiting lists and holds up a Harley's mystique (and resale value).

The producer of a brand positioned as high quality faces a difficult circumstance. Coverage has been restricted. Now that only a restricted set of channel members carries the brand, intrabrand competition is low, and the threat of channel complacency is high. Yet, attaining enough coverage to motivate channel members can put the brand into outlets that clash with its intended high-quality positioning. How can the manufacturer balance selectivity in distribution with the need for channel members to exert extra effort to support the brand?

One method is to ask channel members to sign unusually demanding contracts in order to represent the brand and in return to grant them protection from their competitors. This is common practice in the selling of stereo speakers, for example. These restrictive contracts curtail the channel member's freedom of choice in managing the brand. For example, they may contain clauses detailing channel member obligations with respect to displays, promotions, and sales goals, or they may specify conditions under which the manufacturer may terminate the arrangement without further obligation. (In contrast, it is common for contracts to reflect only a broad and general understanding—if, indeed, there is a contract at all.) For example, French speaker maker Cabasse, known for ultrahigh performance in sound reproduction, holds resellers to a certification program, obliges store personnel to take product training, obliges stores to maintain a customized auditorium, and insists that sellers pass on consumer opinion to Cabasse management. In return for these concessions, Cabasse covers the large French market with only 750 points of sale.[23]

Another form of restrictive contract is an agreement to meet demanding goals. For example, J. E. Ekornes is a Norwegian manufacturer of home furniture. Ekornes saturated the French market with 450 furniture dealers, making it difficult for any of them to make money on the brand. Ekornes completely redesigned its channel, pulling back to 150 dealers and asking them to help redraw territories so as to guarantee exclusive distribution to each one. In return for this concession, Ekornes's surviving dealers signed contracts committing them to ambitious sales goals. Indeed, the 150 dealers committed to figures that significantly improved on the actual results achieved by the original 450 dealers. They more than met these goals. In three years, Ekornes's sales tripled.[24]

Why are restrictive contracts effective? Manufacturers can use restrictive contracts as a way of screening out resellers who are reluctant to support the brand. This is because channel members who are inclined to dishonor promises of brand support will be reluctant to sign a restrictive contract. Knowing this, some managers of high-end brands couple a policy of selective distribution with a policy of insisting on restrictive contracts for all downstream channel members. These manufacturers broaden their distribution coverage somewhat beyond the level they would choose if they employed lenient contracts or no contracts. They do so because they can be confident that the additional resellers will uphold the brand's image.

Without contracts, Ekornes, for example, might have reduced intensity to 120 dealers that it was sure were willing to uphold the image of its Stressless brand. Ekornes would have relied on its own judgment in culling from 450 to 120. But the

150 dealers willing to commit in a legal document to very ambitious goals were a self-selected group. Each of these dealers sent Ekornes a credible signal that they were the right dealers in which to invest. The contract provided dealers a way to signal Ekornes and provided Ekornes an effective way to screen them.

Brand Strategy: Target Market

Some brands target a niche market, that is, a narrow and specialized band of buyers. One might expect that manufacturers would seek broad coverage in this case to maximize the probability of finding these customers. In practice, the reverse occurs. Producers of brands targeting a narrow spectrum of the market will target a narrow spectrum of outlets. The more restricted the target market, the more selective the distribution.

To some extent, this policy is not a matter of choice: channel members are less interested in niche brands than in brands with broader appeal. In addition, niche markets are not necessarily difficult to access. Often, the target buyers are a homogeneous group with common shopping patterns. Only a select band of resellers is necessary (or perhaps even appropriate) to reach them.

A good example of a specialty group is pregnant women who are searching for maternity clothing. Often they are interested in making minimal investments in a wardrobe that they will wear for only a limited time. They may be very price sensitive and sacrifice the better quality fabrics and styles and designer labels that they typically would choose for clothing purchases. This is why producers of most maternity clothes accept limited coverage. They offer women a selection of basic quality maternity clothes at reasonable, even low, prices, and are satisfied with small floor space and being available in relatively few clothing stores.

Of course, one can pursue a niche strategy, providing a superior quality brand to a specialty group. A Pea in the Pod (www.peainthepod.com) is an example, also in maternity clothing. Through its boutiques in the United States, the company sells premium-priced maternity clothes that cater to professional women desiring business attire, as well as fashion-conscious women who want maternity clothes that follow the current trend. The generalization that a restricted target segment implies selective distribution applies to any narrowly focused brand, regardless of its quality positioning.

Many manufacturers seek more influence over channel members, regardless of their brand strategy. We now turn to another motivation, apart from strategy, for selectivity. This motive is simply to gain influence downstream.

BARGAINING FOR INFLUENCE OVER CHANNEL MEMBERS

Many manufacturers desire to have inordinate influence over their downstream channel members. Rather than accepting the premise that market outcomes are efficient and channel members know best, these manufacturers have strong views about how channel members should handle their brands. They do not believe that market incentives will lead the channel member to perform channel flows appropriately for their brands. These interventionist manufacturers would like to manage their channels as they manage their subsidiaries.

A manufacturer wishing to direct a channel member can "purchase" a certain amount of cooperation (really, acquiescence) by the skillful use of selective distribution. The reason is that selective distribution allows a downstream channel member to achieve higher margins *and* higher volume on a given brand. Further, selectivity allows a channel member, such as a reseller, to differentiate its assortment, creating strategic advantage. Hence, a higher degree of selectivity is an extremely powerful incentive. Manufacturers can use selective distribution to buy considerable influence over a downstream channel member. Indeed, manufacturers that grant exclusivity do make more efforts (of any kind) to influence their channel members' behavior.[25] They do not give up coverage only to sit back and let market forces operate freely. Their influence is an expensive purchase because low coverage carries a considerable opportunity cost. Which manufacturers find the purchase worthwhile? When is influence over a channel member's behavior worth the opportunity cost of limited market coverage?

One answer that has already been suggested is that the investment is worthwhile when the brand has a premium quality position. To maintain the premium, manufacturers must be sure the brand is presented and supported appropriately, which limits the set of resellers. The next section goes into other producer rationales for effectively trying to direct channel member behavior. The principle is that the more direction the manufacturer needs to exert, the more it must restrict its distribution in order to gain the channel member's acquiescence.

Desired Coordination

Some producers wish to influence reseller decisions and activities in great detail. Inevitably, this drive to control the downstream channel member will lead the manufacturer into conflict because it will pressure the channel member to do something that it would not have done otherwise. For example, the producer may wish to dictate prices, promotional activities, displays, how the brand is presented by salespeople, and stocking levels, or it may wish to limit the channel member's ability to resell to a customer of its own choosing. This is outright interference in the management of the reseller's business. The reseller will resist, and the manufacturer will need power to overcome that resistance. By offering protection from intrabrand competition, the manufacturer exerts reward power. In general, all else being constant, the more the manufacturer wishes to coordinate activities with the channel member (that is, to direct the channel member's activities to align them with the manufacturer's preferences), the more selectively the manufacturer should distribute.

This is effective not only because it increases the manufacturer's reward power over a given player. It also reduces the number and variety of players. With a large and heterogeneous group of players, it is difficult for the producer to exert influence over them all primarily because managers have limited resources. The manufacturer's ability to give the proper time, attention, and support is strained when there are many channel members. One person can only handle so much, and hiring more people creates coordination problems internally. A smaller channel is a simpler channel to manage. Simplicity enhances control.

Nonetheless, many arguments for selectivity are elaborations of the fundamental idea that selectivity creates reward power, which in turn creates influence. Such arguments for the manufacturer's side might include:

> ➤ Because exclusive or limited market coverage means higher average reseller margins, the manufacturer should be able to attract better resellers.

> ➤ Paradoxically, the manufacturer may attract more resellers under a selective regime. This is because under an intensive regime, each reseller may estimate that margins will be too low to be worthwhile; hence, no reseller bids for the business.

➤ With a small but dedicated group of resellers, the manufacturer may enjoy more vigorous overall market efforts, albeit from a smaller group of channel partners.

➤ If each reseller competes vigorously, the manufacturer may actually reach a greater range of customers and reach them more effectively.

➤ This is particularly important when the manufacturer needs a more motivated selling effort, for example, for a new market or when selling a new product.[26] Motivated resellers may be willing to take a greater risk on behalf of the manufacturer, for example, by carrying more stock, or investing in building a new brand name.

➤ This in turn encourages market entry (entrants trade some degree of exclusivity for strong representation).

➤ Finally, this raises the overall level of competition across brands at the product category level.

Sidebar 4.5 shows how Linn Products applied this reasoning to boost sales *and* margins.

The reasoning here may seem perverse, as it reduces to the dubious argument that local monopolies are desirable. Clearly, an opportunity cost must offset all this purported benefit. A local monopoly can be desirable only under limited circumstances.

Fundamentally, the argument can be made that intensive distribution creates a large but ineffective army (i.e., a huge number of indifferent channel members), each of which represents the brand but only in a desultory fashion. By limiting coverage, the manufacturer creates a small strike force composed of elite soldiers. When is a large army preferable to an elite strike force? The coordination rationale is, at root, a family of arguments for an elite strike force; that is, limiting the number of trading partners in order to gain more influence over each one.

These arguments may be employed in reverse for the downstream channel member. If the organization represents only a handful of suppliers, it can offer greater rewards to each supplier, thereby gaining influence over each. This influence can be used to induce the manufacturer to do a better job of supporting the downstream channel member, for example, by offering lower prices, promotional materials, or better credit terms. The downstream channel member weighs the advantages of an army of potentially indifferent suppliers versus an elite strike force of more motivated suppliers.

Manufacturer-Specific Investments by Downstream Channel Members

Earlier, we introduced a hypothetical retailer of Johanson stereo speakers and described the retailer's Johanson-specific investments. These are assets that are not readily redeployable to the service of another brand. They become sunk costs if the relationship ends. Most of the investments a downstream channel member would make in a manufacturer are not specialized: they can be reused (transferred to another brand), but some brands demand that a reseller or agent acquire capabilities and commit resources that have no alternative use. This is particularly the case for industrial goods and services. The major categories of these specific investments are:

➤ *Idiosyncratic knowledge:* To the extent that a brand's applications and features are unique, the sales staff must learn about them to sell effectively.

➤ *Unusual handling or storage:* A brand may require this, for example, if it is shipped on nonstandard pallets that require custom shelving and possibly even specialty forklifts.

Sidebar 4.5

Reducing coverage to increase sales and margins

Linn Products, Ltd., based in Waterfoot, Scotland, produces top-quality (and expensive) high-fidelity equipment. Linn's products command 10 to 20 times the prices of the comparable cheapest stereo components on the market.

At one time, Linn had high coverage given the niche appeal of its brand. Then Linn's management introduced a new selling and service strategy that placed heavy demands on its resellers. Under the new plan, Linn required each reseller to demonstrate products before each sale and to stock a minimum level of inventory. Linn's dealers were outraged. As a result, 82 retailers in the United Kingdom alone refused to continue selling the brand, leaving the company with only 55 U.K. resellers. At the time of the change in policy, Linn's annual sales dropped from £11 million to £9 million. However, management remained confident that establishing a selective distribution network eventually would increase sales through greater market share and through propagation by loyal customers, either from upgrades or referrals of new customers. Linn also wanted to expand into different geographic markets and believed its selectivity strategy would position the company to do so.

Five to six years after the shift in its distribution policy, Linn's sales were approaching £20 million. Indeed, with the product demonstrations and personalized service, an average sale to a single customer increased, and previous customers were coming back to upgrade a single component at a time. Clearly Linn will remain a niche player in the stereo market, but by adopting a selective distribution strategy, the company boosted its sales and gained control over the presentation of its products to the marketplace.[27]

➤ *Brand-specific parts and know-how:* These may be needed for servicing the brand postsale.
➤ *Customer training:* Brand-specific instructions may be required.
➤ *Mingling the identity of buyer and seller:* Joint promotions can make it difficult to disentangle the downstream channel member and the brand.

In consumer goods channels, these kinds of investments are particularly heavy when the end-user buys from a contractor-dealer. These are dealers who assemble and install technical products or those requiring substantial customization. The dealer incorporates the supplier's product into systems to meet each buyer's needs. These dealers specify, assemble, and install to a degree that makes them look (to the consumer) more like a manufacturer than a reseller. Contractor-dealers handle such products as swimming pools, climate control (heating and cooling), fireplaces, metal buildings, greenhouses, security systems, garage doors, solar energy, and custom doors and windows.[28]

In short, for some brands or product categories, manufacturer-specific assets are necessary to distribute the brand effectively. Naturally, however, downstream channel members prefer not to commit these assets. The investments are expensive in themselves. More importantly, they raise the reseller's dependence on the manufacturer.[29] Hence, they make the reseller vulnerable to manufacturer opportunism (deceptive seeking of one's self-interest). A rational reseller would hesitate to make these investments and incur the subsequent dependence on the producer. Therefore, the producer must induce the reseller to make these investments. Offering a degree of selectivity is an effective means of doing this because it increases the rewards the reseller can gain from the brand. However, what is to prevent the manufacturer from reneging on its agreements (i.e., dropping the resellers) once the reseller has made brand-specific investments? The manufacturer must give assurance that it will not exploit the reseller's vulnerability once the investments are in place.

An effective way to reassure the reseller who contemplates making brand-specific investments is to limit distribution. This is because the fewer channel partners the manufacturer has in a market area, the more difficult it is to shift resources away from a given reseller. At the limit, an exclusive agent, distributor, or retailer is extremely difficult to replace. Manufacturers that limit distribution thereby increase their own dependence on their downstream channel members. They have counterbalanced the dependence resellers incur by making manufacturer-specific investments.

In short, a policy of selective distribution in a market area can be understood as a means of balancing dependence in a distribution channel. By limiting its coverage, the manufacturer accepts being dependent on the downstream channel. Because this is not to be done lightly, the manufacturer will do it in exchange for the reseller's acquisition of brand-specific assets. The manufacturer negotiates, exchanging limited distribution coverage for the reseller's acquisition of brand-specific assets. One vulnerability is offset by another. Selective distribution is currency that the manufacturer can use to induce the reseller to make brand-specific investments.

Dependence Balancing: Trading Territory Exclusivity for Category Exclusivity

The idea of balancing dependence is instrumental to understanding how channel members, upstream and downstream, use selectivity as a strategic tool to enhance their business interests.[30] The principle is that no one wishes to be dependent on another channel member because this gives the other party power and, therefore, creates vulnerability (covered in detail in Chapter 6). However, to distribute effectively often requires one side (for illustration, the reseller) to accept some degree of dependence on the other side (the manufacturer). This dependence is unlikely to be incurred: The reseller will resist. One way to overcome reseller resistance is for the manufacturer to create an offsetting dependence of its own upon the reseller. This calculated mutual dependence, or mutual vulnerability (which has been likened to a sort of balance of terror in international politics), is designed to bring stability to a relationship by making it unprofitable for either side to exploit the other. This reasoning is explored in more depth in Chapter 8.

Selective distribution has been presented as a currency with which the manufacturer purchases reseller investments in brand-specific assets. This section presents an even more direct exchange of currency. It is the exchange of some degree of territory exclusivity for some degree of category exclusivity. In general, the more the manufacturer limits its coverage of a market area, the more a reseller limits its coverage of the associated product category.

At the extreme, each side trades exclusivity for exclusivity. Resellers offer the manufacturer exclusivity in its product category. In return, manufacturers offer the reseller exclusivity in its market area. This is a swap of category exclusivity for territory exclusivity. Of course, this is the extreme case. It is more common to exchange some degree of selectivity without going so far as to eliminate other brands (for the reseller) or other resellers (for the manufacturer). Returning to the case of the industrial supply house, management might agree to reduce its line to four instead of six of the ten brands offered by metalworking fluids manufacturers. In exchange, the manufacturer who requested this reduction authorizes ten instead of twenty distributors in the supply house's territory. Exchanging (market) selectivity for (category) selectivity is frequent, particularly in business-to-business marketing. Each side voluntarily limits the number of its trading partners.

For the manufacturer, trading selectivity for selectivity is a means to influence how the downstream channel member composes and displays its brand portfolio. This is important for manufacturers that wish to influence the competitive set in which their brands are presented.[31] This idea—influence downstream assortment and display—is one of the most important upstream reasons to be selective. The manufacturer cares about the channel's assortment because the end user's perception of its offering is highly dependent on the context in which the end user encounters it. This is a function of other brands and how they are displayed. For example, if a retailer carries medium-quality merchandise (assortment) and shows it next to high-quality merchandise (display), the buyer will assimilate the two quality grades, thereby upgrading the medium grade—and, similarly, will downgrade the medium grade if it is embedded in a display of low quality.[32] Assortment and display are so important that they even influence not only perceived quality but even what the buyer thinks the product is.[33] For example, a granola bar appears to be a breakfast food, a snack food, or an exercise food, depending on which aisle of a supermarket (breakfast cereals, packaged snacks, or sports food and drink) it occupies.

The need to be embedded in the right assortment displayed in a particular way leads LVMH to a policy of selling only through a combination of company-owned stores (in which the assortment is rigidly controlled and exclusively LVMH) and highly selective distribution. LVMH wants to ensure its products are displayed with what it considers to be complements (e.g., purses with shoes) in a manner that puts the products to best advantage. For example, LVMH has been able to do well in France with two-story stores connected only by a staircase. It has done so by insisting that the ground floor be a shoe store with purses demoted to the top of the stairs. The reason: Browsers will enter the store for shoes and then climb the stairs to continue shopping for purses—but not vice versa.[34] The idea that the assortment should be dominated by shoes is not one that an independent retailer might naturally adopt. The reward of selective distribution elicits cooperation on this critical assortment decision (as well as the decision of where to place the merchandise).

For suppliers, the assortment and selectivity decisions are intricately linked. If the assortment is small, it needs to be embedded in a larger context. See Sidebar 4.6 for how Mercedes-Benz addressed this problem for its new Smart division.

On the other hand, if the assortment is too big, a brand cannot differentiate itself. For example, up until 1993 Volkswagen obliged its Audi and Volkswagen divisions to sell in Europe through the same dealers in order to draw customers with a sufficiently large assortment. Audis were built on the same platforms as VWs and looked somewhat similar. Displayed side by side, the lower-priced VW cannibalized Audi, in part because dealers created a self-fulfilling prophecy that an Audi prospect would

Sidebar 4.6

The Smart: A tiny car makes a miniature assortment

Mercedes-Benz launched its tiny city car, the Smart, via an independent division and as a stand-alone product.[35] Its independent dealers, who committed to selling only Smart, needed to be sure they would get all the Smart business in a territory to justify their investments. However, because the product line was quite narrow, Smart not only had to give its dealers exclusivity but had to make the territories very large. They turned out to be too large: Buyers were unwilling to travel up to 150 kilometers to buy a car, let alone to get it serviced. In desperation, management switched strategy: Instead of differentiating the Smart from Mercedes, it tried to add the Smart to the lines of existing Mercedes dealers.

In France, some 50 Mercedes dealers added "Smart corners," only to discover that a Mercedes buyer was not interested in the tiny car, while a Smart prospect would not walk into a Mercedes dealership. Once again, the assortment was wrong: this time, it was too big. Most Mercedes dealers have discontinued the Smart.

This undercoverage is one reason why Smart has never been successful. Management is preparing to repeat the same error (giving dealers selling only Smart exclusive territories and then making the territories so big that dealerships are too far from prospects, in order to compensate the dealers for the small assortment) when it enters the U.S. market.[36]

ultimately prefer a VW. Starting in 1993, Audi was allowed to create its own separate dealerships. Audi awarded its dealerships territory exclusivity in return for close cooperation with management. It turned out the Audi assortment was, indeed, big enough by itself to attract a clientele. Audi dealers with nothing else to sell discovered how to develop an Audi clientele distinct from Volkswagen. They also gave Audi management valuable feedback that helped the division refine its marketing strategy. For example, through dealer feedback, management developed a successful ad campaign that drew in women drivers interested in practical yet sporty vehicles. The result is that Audi today is highly successful and is increasingly differentiated from VW even though the brands continue to share some platforms.[37]

For the downstream channel member, bargaining selectivity for selectivity is a means of influencing the set of carriers in its market area; hence, the set with which it can be compared readily. For example, two venerable Parisian department stores, Galeries Lafayette and Printemps, are located in the same neighborhood and compete vigorously with each other. The competition is fierce, in part because each store closely watches and then imitates the other. Printemps gains a unique advantage by cultivating selected clothes designers. Its strategy is to give these designers extraordinary consideration in how their goods are presented in the massive store. In return, Printemps negotiates exclusivity and boasts that of its 47 brands, three quarters are exclusives (meaning no other Parisian *department store* has them, although some other formats in Paris do carry the same brands).[38] This is a good example of how exclusivity is negotiable based on both sides' differing perceptions. These brands are willing to concede exclusivity as long as Printemps is willing to perceive that department stores are its major competition.

How will the relentless increase in sales via the Web influence the selectivity calculation? Some evidence indicates that as the Internet penetrates product categories, it becomes more important than ever for resellers to gain exclusives on differentiated goods. An experiment in selling wine is revealing here.[39] Wine is not only highly differentiated but highly confusing. Wine stores guide buyers by providing information and composing meaningful, appealing assortments. What happens when wine stores go online, offering their advice and exposing their complete assortment to site visitors? Much depends on the store's ability to get exclusives. For wines that are widely distributed, wine stores that counsel consumers find that their customers will use the information to become more price sensitive and shop (if necessary, elsewhere) for bargains. These sellers find that when they offer the same merchandise as is available elsewhere, providing counsel pays for them only if they are the cheapest seller. However, for sellers with a differentiated assortment (two thirds exclusives and one third available elsewhere), browsers actually become less price sensitive and more attentive to the differences among wines. Further, they report having more fun wine shopping—and purchase more wine.

The lesson is that, for differentiated categories, only low-cost, low-price sellers can do well with intensively distributed brands. Other sellers will lose the competition by providing information support on such brands to prospects. Hence, a supplier that wants a retailer to provide information support will need to reciprocate by limiting coverage. By helping the seller differentiate its offering, the supplier helps the seller get a return on its investment in customer information support. While this has always been the case, the Internet accelerates the phenomenon.

Reassurance: Using Selectivity to Stabilize Fragile Relationships

In the negotiations between upstream and downstream channel members, both sides are preoccupied with concerns about what will happen once an agreement has been struck. The more vulnerable party fears that the other side will misuse its power.[40] These fears destabilize the relationship, thereby reducing channel effectiveness. Therefore, the stronger party may need to reassure the vulnerable party of its good faith. In general, a stronger party that offers selectivity to a weaker party is balancing the other side's dependence.

A frequent example in B2B markets occurs when a brand has a favorable position, or pull, with the customer base. Naturally, a distributor may be concerned that the manufacturer will use its brand name pull first to create distributor dependence and then to supplant or exploit the distributor. To reassure the distributor, strong brands frequently limit their coverage, thereby increasing their downstream dependence (dependence balancing). On the face of it, this behavior is puzzling. The stronger the brand, the easier it is to increase coverage. Yet, many manufacturers voluntarily refrain from maximizing coverage.

In the same vein, many manufacturers sell some fraction of their products direct (i.e., bypass their channels for selected orders, selling directly to the channel's customer base). Sometimes direct selling is explicitly negotiated with downstream channel members (in which case, it is not opportunism because there is no deception or bad faith). More often, the practice is simply carried out, frequently with attempts to disguise it (which *is* opportunism).

To restore confidence, industrial suppliers tend to offset direct selling by offering selectivity. In a given trading area, the more direct selling they do, the more they are likely to limit the number of channel members in the area. This can be interpreted as if it were a tacit understanding: "I reserve the right to go to your customers, but in return I will not sell through as many of your competitors as I would otherwise." This encourages channel members to set aside their concerns and represent the brand vigorously in spite of the supplier's direct selling.

The logic of offsetting sources of relationship instability also applies to the downstream channel member. Some distributors, for example, have a loyal customer base so staunch that the distributor heavily influences brand choice.[41] Here, the distributor is powerful, and the manufacturer may reasonably fear the distributor's opportunism. To allay this concern, distributors with loyal customers often limit brand assortment in a product category. Although these distributors can represent anyone, they limit their number of trading partners, which serves to balance the manufacturer's dependence on them.

The Price of the Concession: Factoring in Opportunity Cost

In bargaining away the right to have an unlimited number of trading partners, the manufacturer is making a concession to the downstream channel member. Two circumstances are crucial to assess the price of the concession: the importance of the market area and the competitive intensity of the product category.

For markets that are major to the manufacturer, the opportunity cost of lower coverage is substantial. Hence, the manufacturer will bargain harder, perhaps even refusing to limit coverage. For a minor market area, the manufacturer will concede selectivity more readily. This negligible concession often leads to a source of conflict that grows over time. Eventually, the manufacturer may reassess and conclude the market is actually a major one—especially if the downstream channel member appears to be doing very well with its products. Hence, the manufacturer may try to renege on its implicit or explicit agreement to practice selectivity.[42]

For product categories that are intensely competitive, manufacturers are more reluctant to limit the number of their downstream trading partners. Here again, the reason is the opportunity cost of this concession to downstream channel members. Manufacturers fear that prospective buyers will not be motivated to make the effort to seek out a limited set of points of purchase when the competition at the category level is fierce. Hence, lower coverage appears to be a very risky proposition.

A source of conflict arises in these circumstances due to differing perceptions. It is easy for the manufacturer in an intensely competitive product category to be doing poorly because of the competition but to misattribute its disappointing performance to insufficient coverage. This sometimes leads to a spiral of marketing-channel mediocrity. Rather than addressing the reasons for competitive disadvantage in the first place, a manufacturer may instead seek a quick remedy: higher sales via more coverage. To get the coverage, it may lower its standards, distributing through inferior downstream channel members. This in turn may provoke the original channel members to withdraw support for the brand, leaving the manufacturer even worse off in spite of being available through more outlets. The idea that some degree of selectivity is a bargaining chip for the manufacturer is summarized in Figure 4.2.

FOR THE MANUFACTURER

Limited coverage is currency
More selectivity = more money
Exclusive distribution =

Manufacturers use the money to "pay" the Channel Members for:

- limiting its own coverage of brand in product category
  (gaining exclusive dealing is *very* expensive)

- supporting premium positioning of the brand

- finding a narrow target market

- coordinating more closely with the manufacturer

- making supplier-specific investments
  ○ new products
  ○ new markets
  ○ differentiated marketing strategy requiring downstream implementation

- accepting limited direct selling by manufacturer

- accepting the risk or becoming dependent on a strong brand

Manufacturers need to "pay more" when:

- the product category is important to the Channel Member

- the product category is intensely competitive

Figure 4.2   Selective coverage: The manufacturer's considerations

Turning to the other side of the relationship, a downstream channel member will hesitate to limit its number of brands in a product category when the category is a major one in the channel member's assortment. Thus, an industrial supply house that does little business in metalworking fluids will agree more readily to limit its brand selection than will a competitor to whom metalworking fluids are an important category. To that latter business, the opportunity cost of limiting assortment is too great.

Downstream channel members also hesitate to grant selectivity in categories that are intensely competitive. This is an expensive concession: Prospective buyers may lose interest when they realize that many brands are missing from the assortment. Competitive intensity makes it more likely that buyers will be aware of alternative brands, will have strong preferences, and will insist on presentation of a more complete assortment. The idea that some limitation of brand assortment is a bargaining chip for the downstream channel member is summarized in Figure 4.3.

In short, for either side, selectivity is an expensive concession when the object of negotiation is important (for the manufacturer, a market area, and for the reseller, the product category). Selectivity is also expensive when the object of negotiation (market

FOR THE DOWNSTREAM CHANNEL MEMBER

Limited brand assortment is currency
Fewer brands = more money
Exclusive dealing =

Downstream Channel Members use the money to "pay" the supplier for:

• limiting the number of competitors who can carry the brand in the
  Channel Member's trading area

• providing desired brands that fit the Channel Member's strategy

• working closely to help the Channel Member achieve competitive advantage

• making Channel-Member-specific investments
  ○ new products
  ○ new markets
  ○ differentiated Channel Member strategy requiring supplier cooperation

• accepting the risk of becoming dependent on a strong Channel Member

Downstream Channel Members need to "pay more" when:

• the trading area is important to the supplier

• the trading area is intensely competitive

Figure 4.3   Category selectivity: The downstream channel member's considerations

area or product category) is intensely competitive. These concessions are expensive because the opportunity cost of limiting the number of trading partners is great.

BACK TO THE BASICS: CUTTING COSTS AND RAISING SALES

To this point, we have focused on strategic reasons why channel members (upstream and downstream) might limit the number of trading partners. We close our treatment of this issue by addressing two basic questions: All else being constant, does selectivity in representation cut costs in any significant way, and does intensity of representation really increase sales? We have saved these issues for last in order to disentangle them from more strategic reasons for selectivity, whose cost and revenue implications are indirect and difficult for an accountant to estimate.

Saving Money By Limiting the Number of Trading Partners

Earlier, we noted that many manufacturers think more coverage is always better because it creates higher sales. Of course, there are associated costs. For a manufacturer, each outlet is an account, and each account requires sales attention and support. Fulfilling each account's orders entails costs of ordering, shipping, financing, and so forth. Many manufacturers carry accounts whose orders do not justify even the accounting costs of serving them, let alone the opportunity costs of serving them. (Some estimates are that manufacturers, once they put sophisticated activity-based costing systems into place, discover that up to one quarter or one third of their accounts are unprofitable.[43]) At some point, many accounts cost more to serve than the coverage-based benefits they offer.

One way around this obstacle to achieving greater distribution intensity is to serve outlets via master distributors,[44] which achieve economies of scope and scale in serving their clientele. Of course, the manufacturer loses control and information in going this route, but the additional coverage is often worthwhile.

What is at issue here is a simple and fundamental reason for some degree of selectivity, which is that it costs money to secure representation per se. Note that the rationale here is not to gain more influence by increasing one's reward power. It is simply to cut costs by dealing with fewer entities. As discussed in Chapter 1, one of the reasons to use intermediaries is to reduce the cost of contacts. For example, Michelin used master distributors in Italy simply because there are so many small tire dealers there, for several reasons:

> Manufacturers limit the number of trading partners to keep their selling expenses down. By not serving marginal resellers, they reduce the number of salespeople and/or the expenses (travel, entertainment, samples, and so forth) associated with a large account base.

> Manufacturers that offer high levels of support to each channel member as a matter of policy tend to distribute more selectively in order to limit the total costs of channel support.

> To the extent that fewer resellers means lower turnover, there is less opening, training, and servicing of new resellers.

> Fewer channel partners often means fewer but larger transactions on a regular basis, reducing inventory holding costs and other processing costs.

> Fewer but larger orders imply more accurate forecasting of demand, which in turn enables better production planning and lower inventories.

From the reseller's standpoint, dealing with a smaller number of brands can also offer important economies. Consolidating demand into a smaller number of brands may facilitate forecasting and improve inventory practices. Dealing with a smaller number of suppliers may economize on the expenses of running the reseller's purchasing function.

Do More Trading Partners Really Mean More Revenue?

Many managers think it goes without saying that brands will sell more when they are carried by more downstream channel members. What evidence exists concerning the coverage-sales relationship fits prevailing beliefs. While the evidence is not conclusive, it does appear that, in general, brands that are more widely available do, indeed, have higher sales, hence higher market share.

But why is this so? It is tempting to conclude that more outlets cause more sales. If so, seeking wider coverage would appear to be always a desirable policy. Yet, why we see more sales accompanying more intensive distribution is not at all clear. The relationship may be spurious (i.e., caused by a third factor driving both sales and coverage).[45] For example, a brand backed by excellent marketing will sell more due to the marketing plan. Well-marketed brands also appeal to the trade. Hence, good marketing will create both higher sales and greater coverage. Rather than more coverage raising revenue, more coverage and more revenue may both be results of superior marketing.

Perhaps more importantly, most of the rationales for limiting coverage have to do with increasing profit. Increasing revenue may not increase total profit.

This said, it would be simplistic to argue that limited coverage always raises a brand's image and, therefore, always increases unit margins. Limited coverage may not increase per-unit margins. A good counterexample is "twin" automobiles. Car twins are essentially identical physically (often made in the same factory) but are marketed under different brand names. Rational, well-informed consumers should refuse to pay more for one brand than another, and yet, frequently they do pay the higher price.[46] In particular, consumers pay more for one brand of a pair of twins when that brand has greater coverage (more dealers). It is not clear why this is so. Consumers may infer that a brand with more dealers is more reputable, or they may pay a premium to be closer to a service facility, or they may reason that a somewhat more widely distributed brand will be easier to resell. Whatever the reasons, coverage actually increases margins for car twins. (Note that most car twins do not appear in the luxury segment, where it is essential to limit the number of dealerships in order to cultivate an upscale image.)

In short, it does appear that more coverage tends to accompany more sales. However, this does not mean a manufacturer should always seek the broadest coverage. More coverage may not be the actual cause of more sales. Further, there is a limit to how much coverage a market will support, and this limit depends on the nature of the product category and of the brand.

What of the reseller's side of the issue? Do more brands mean more sales? Here, evidence is sparse. And again, the causality of any relationship can be questioned. If a dealer carrying more brands has higher revenue, is it because the dealer carries more brands or because a superior dealer (who would sell more under any circumstances) can attract more brands?

A Caution on the Issue of Limiting the Number of Trading Partners

We caution the reader not to simplify the issue to cutting costs and raising revenues. Fewer trading partners do mean lower accounting costs per partner, on the whole, but the opportunity cost of fewer partners often dwarfs their accounting costs. Although more trading partners are often associated with greater sales, it is not clear whether this is a cause-and-effect relationship or other factors are at work. Fundamentally, the choice of how many trading partners turns not just on accounting costs and benefits but also on strategic costs and benefits. These are usually more important, although more difficult to estimate.

SIMULATING THE BENEFITS OF SELECTIVITY WHILE MAINTAINING INTENSIVE COVERAGE

Selective distribution has the benefit of increasing the manufacturer's ability to motivate and to control downstream channel members at the cost of reducing healthy intrabrand competition and making it more difficult for the prospective purchaser to find the brand. Covering a market intensively makes the opposite trade-off. Some manufacturers experiment in search of ways to gain most of the benefits of selective distribution while retaining intrabrand competition and making it easy for the prospect to become a buyer. There is little systematic evidence about how successful these experiments are. What evidence exists is anecdotal and is probably skewed to the positive side because manufacturers do not publicize their failures. Here we present some methods that may (or may not) be effective (or efficient) means of gaining the best of both worlds (intensive *and* limited coverage).

One method, noted earlier, is to invest in brand building, so as to generate so much brand equity that downstream channel members will tolerate high intrabrand competition and not destroy the brand by such tactics as bait-and-switch. This method is highly expensive. It appears particularly effective for fast moving consumer goods (think of Coca-Cola, for example), because the channel member's ability to change a strong brand preference is already limited by the low-involvement nature of the product category.

Another method is to couple information sharing with frequent introduction of new products that have a low failure rate. Perhaps the best-known exemplar of this approach is 3M, famous for its competence in new-product development.[47] Channel members are willing to maintain ties with 3M that are unusually close, considering how intensively the company distributes. The steady stream of well-marketed new products, coupled with information, is a welcome and rather scarce combination that appears to overcome channel members' reluctance to coordinate activities with 3M.

An intriguing and lesser-known approach is to offer branded variants. These are variations of models of a branded product.[48] The key feature is that some of the variations (that is, combinations of levels of attributes) are made available only to certain resellers, not to the entire channel. For example, watches carrying the Seiko brand vary in terms of the color of the watchband, whether the watch is digital or analogue, and the type of the watch's hands (size and luminosity). The key to the branded variant strategy is that certain combinations are made available only to selected channel members, thereby giving them a sort of exclusivity.

This strategy is effective for strong brand names of shopping goods, for which the consumer feels some involvement in the product category. Durables and semi-durables fit this description well if they are not yet commodities. The customer feels a certain level of risk due to the importance of the category and the sense that products are not interchangeable. The purchase of a mattress and box springs fits this situation. In these categories, strong brand names can attract a retailer, and differentiating by creating a variant builds some level of retailer commitment to the brand. Sealy manufactures mattresses that are sold in bedding, furniture, and department stores throughout the United States. For its various resellers Sealy takes a particular product having the same characteristics (durability, firmness, padding, and number of springs) and makes variants differing by color, covering style, and the made-for label for each set of resellers.

Evidence to date, although not definitive, suggests that manufacturers that pursue a branded variants strategy induce more stores to carry the brand and induce the stores holding the variant to put more service (such as stocking and displaying many models of the brand and offering sales assistance) behind the brand. Why does the strategy work? It may be because busy consumers invest time to develop a preference within the store's considerable selection of the brand name's models. The power of the brand name assures them that it is worthwhile to examine alternatives within the brand's line. Warned by salespeople that other stores do not have an identical selection (a credible statement, given the store's large offering in the brand), many consumers are unwilling to take the time to visit another store and to take the risk that the variant they favor is not there. Hence, they conclude their purchase without shopping further.

A different approach is to focus on mitigating the buyers' costs of selective distribution. For example, many durable goods require manufacturer-specific service. Traditionally, this is offered at the point of sale. To induce resellers to invest in service facilities, manufacturers are obliged to be more selective in coverage, which in turn inconveniences the customer. One solution is to decouple sales and service. This can be done by establishing separate service-only facilities. Relieved of the service burden, more stores will be qualified to offer sales.

When General Electric decided to adopt more intensive distribution for its small electrical ("traffic") appliances, it found that it could not obtain adequate service from its expanded retail network. The company had to institute a nationwide, company-owned chain of service centers to solve this significant marketing problem. Eventually, it sold off its entire traffic appliance business to Black & Decker. To some extent, the widespread availability of consumer electronics in superstores and discounters, such as Circuit City, Best Buy, and Wal-Mart, is a major reason why these retailers offer virtually limitless return policies to customers. Rather than investing in repair facilities, they merely ship the returned merchandise (defective or not) back to the manufacturer for credit against future purchases.[49]

In short, there are ways to distribute more intensively while retaining at least some of the benefits of distributing selectively. These methods are expensive and are not easy to duplicate, which may explain why they are not commonly practiced. Whether and when the costs outweigh the benefits is an open question.

GOING TO MARKET VIA MULTIPLE TYPES OF CHANNELS

Thus far, we have focused on the consequences of high coverage, no matter how it is achieved. A department store wants to make sure other department stores do not have the same merchandise. Problems can be acute when two very different types of channels have the same merchandise, such as a prestigious department store and a discount seller or mass merchandiser. The reason is that these types of channels offer prospects different service outputs and perform different flows. These are distinct processes of selecting, purchasing, ordering, and receiving product.[50] These processes can differ based on ownership (company owned or independent), which we cover in the next section, or they can be based on different location (e.g., in-store versus at-home), different technology (e.g., catalog versus Web), or different type of intermediary (e.g., mass merchandisers versus drug stores, grocery stores, or club stores). In general, different formats appeal to specific clienteles and are strongly associated in buyers' minds with certain product categories.[51]

The tendency in developed economies is for manufacturers to add multiple types of channels in the hope of connecting with ever-more-finely segmented customers. In so doing, manufacturers raise the variety of their coverage, though not necessarily its overall level. When manufacturers do this, however, suppliers frequently assume (or perhaps simply hope) that these channels will not collide. Their assumption is that customers will not cross-shop the channels. For B2B products, this assumption is somewhat tenuous because purchasing agents make their living by finding ways to extract value from sellers. Even for B2C products, consumers may refuse to stay in their expected channels. The result is often cannibalization. Sidebar 4.7 considers the example of Tupperware.

Unlike the Tupperware example, adding a new format can have unexpected positive side effects, especially for consumers. For example, U.S. car buyers have become accustomed to using the Web to replace dealer salespeople as a source of information about cars. The result has been salutary for consumers. They spend less time (on average, 15 hours total rather than 18 in the pre-Internet era) to gather the necessary information to decide. They enter the dealership well informed, hence negotiate better.[52] Here, the online automobile channel serves as an "infomediary" that provides information that the consumer then takes to the dealership and uses to bargain—to the detriment of the dealer's margins.

Buyers (both individuals and businesses) often confound the producer's intentions in setting up multiple channels. Buyers use the supposed multiple routes to market together to consummate the sale, cherry-picking certain service outputs from one channel and other service outputs from another. This takes us back to the concepts of service outputs (Chapter 2) and the costly flows necessary to meet service output demands (Chapter 3). When different channels are set up to specialize in the performance of particular flows, these flows produce service outputs that are valued by prospective buyers. Those prospective buyers may seek to consume those service outputs from the high-support channel. But they may consummate the actual purchase in another channel. In effect, prospects are free riding (taking benefits from one channel member without paying for them, just as Johanson's prospects wanted to do when shopping for speakers in our earlier example in this chapter). Downstream channel members must be compensated for the flows they perform and will not tolerate free riding indefinitely. If producers want their prospects to continue to be able to meet their service output demands in one place but reward another place with their patronage, then producers must find a way to compensate these service providers (for example, by fees or by overrides on business booked with another channel).

Some customers use the Web not only to gather information but actually to negotiate their purchase (in the United States, the law provides that a dealer must be involved in the actual sale, so even if the consumer uses a Web agent to negotiate, they literally must buy from a dealer). Consumers' groups have long suspected that in the United States some demographic groups pay more when they shop for a car in person, regardless of their socioeconomic status or preparedness (previsit information search). But customers who engage a Web agent (such as Autobytel.com) to shop and purchase for them enjoy anonymity. Autobytel negotiates directly with the dealers without revealing the demographics of the customer on whose behalf they

Sidebar 4.7

Tupperware's retail channels cannibalize the party channel

Tupperware is a maker of plastic storage goods of premium quality and price, available in a huge assortment of models. For decades, Tupperware has been famous in North America for its party channel. Independent dealers (Tupperware Ladies) organized social events in private homes, where they presented and sold the full line. This system worked extremely well, partly because the sellers were doing business within their social network and partly because they ably presented the line, persuading buyers that many sizes and types were useful and worth their price.

Over time, sales fell as women entered the labor force and fewer women had the time, energy, or interest to host or attend Tupperware parties. In response, Tupperware added booths in malls and moved to the Internet. Rather than cannibalizing the agents, these new formats revived interest in the party format. Encouraged by its revival, Tupperware extended coverage to over 1,000 retail discount stores in the Target chain. Dealers were invited to demonstrate product in the Target aisles in the belief that new parties would result from these encounters.

This move was disastrous. Tupperware dealers in the Target aisles found that few customers were willing to stop and talk. And because Tupperware was easy to find, interest in Tupperware parties plummeted. Further, Target sales did not replace the lost party sales.

Displayed next to relatively narrow assortments of inexpensive plastics made by competitors, Tupperware's many finely distinguished items appeared overpriced and superfluous. With no one to explain why this impression was wrong, the goods stayed on the shelves. Although Target proclaimed it was satisfied with the partnership, Tupperware lost customers and dealers and ended its Target coverage. But the damage had been done, particularly to the dealer network.

What this fiasco showed management was that its dealers played a massive role in creating sales but needed the party setting and atmosphere to be effective. Parties are typically given in private houses, where the seller can manage the ambiance with music, wine, cooking demonstrations, and the like. The events become social to the point that dealers report having to send buyers home at midnight. Typically, they write a substantial amount of business before so doing. The Target format destroyed the ambiance and attracted a clientele that was not in the right mood. Further, a Tupperware dealer is willing to give parties until midnight because "when I leave the party, I feel great." When dealers left Target at closing time (usually late at night), they simply felt tired.

Ironically, the party format that Tupperware considered inadequate is being copied by makers of other products with great success.[53]

are negotiating. The result is that, on average, women, Hispanics, and African Americans pay substantially less than they would if they made the purchase in person at the dealer.[54]

The Internet is often viewed as an inherently cannibalistic channel. But this need not be the case. Adding Web distribution can create new business without taking business from existing channels. For example, newspapers sell in multiple types of outlets.[55] When they add Web distribution, it can work well, raising long-term growth rates in revenue from circulation or advertising—except when the content is identical or very close (operationally, 78% overlap vs. 45% overlap). Given nonoverlapping content, Web distribution brings in an audience that does not read the paper or advertise in it. (For newspapers, adding new content is not difficult, because syndicates—essentially distributors of information goods, such as TV shows, films, news stories, comic strips, or software—make it easy to gather, pay for, and publish diverse content from multiple sources.[56]) Adding the Internet even raises the firm's stock price—unless the firm already has many different types of channels, which makes it difficult even for a newspaper to put enough different content into its Web version

DUAL DISTRIBUTION: GOING TO MARKET VIA INDEPENDENT CHANNELS AND SELF-OWNED CHANNELS

On the face of it, dual distribution (going to market via third parties and via one's own distribution divisions) appears to be just a variation on the theme of multiple formats. But there is a special issue here. When third parties compete, the manufacturer can claim to be neutral, letting the market decide who will win. But when the manufacturer competes against its own customers by running employee-staffed channel operations in parallel, the claim of neutrality is not credible. Independent channels are quick to suspect the manufacturer is favoring its own people.

Inherent Rivalry

For example, when AT&T was at the peak of its market position in the 1990s, the capital equipment manufacturer (which no longer operates under this name) distributed telecommunications hardware and software via third party distributors (VARs, or value added resellers) and its own employees.[57] VARs regularly complained that AT&T discretely favored its division with better terms of trade, product availability, and service. Although AT&T claimed to be evenhanded, large B2B customers went to the board of directors and obliged the manufacturer to better serve its resellers. Why? Customers had strong relationships with VARs, who understood their businesses, and wanted to funnel their purchases through these resellers.

Managing dual systems is challenging and fraught with the risk of dysfunctional conflict.[58] B2B customers are quick to play in-house and outside channels against each other, and the two channels tend to view each other with some suspicion and treat each other as rivals. This is why CyberGuard, a maker of IT products, adopted a draconian policy: Any of its salespeople who book business themselves that should go to a reseller will not receive a commission on that business.[59]

Nonetheless, dual channels (make and buy) can offer customers valued variety and can allow the manufacturer readily to match costs and benefits to each segment.[60] Further, dual channels offer the manufacturer information (one channel can be used to benchmark the other) and flexibility (business can be shifted from one channel to the other if need be).[61]

The Demonstration Argument

The demonstration value in having some company outlets is often cited as a reason for dual distribution. The rationale here is that company outlets can show independents the potential in a brand and suggest better ways to sell it. For example, Swatch operates flagship stores in expensive locations that carry exclusively Swatch watches in an unusual depth of assortment. The reasoning is that independents would hesitate to mount such an operation but are impressed by the profitability of these stores and, thus, more inclined to stock Swatch and to carry more models.[62]

Guy Degrenne and Baccarat are French makers of premium products. Degrenne makes a full line of tableware, while Baccarat is a venerable maker of crystal.[63] Both have seen demand decline as consumers adopt a more casual lifestyle and forego formal dinnerware and dining room décor. As retailers shrank their displays and demoted the merchandise to distant corners of their stores, both firms countered by opening their own stores. The idea is to show retailers that, stocked and displayed as recommended by the manufacturer, these products have far greater sales potential than is currently believed. This strategy has worked well.

In a similar example, Sony's market research convinced the company that electronics retailers do a poor job of selling to women in the United States.[64] To demonstrate its ideas, Sony has opened small Sony stores in upscale malls near other stores that attract females. Sony "boutiques" follow a merchandising plan thought to appeal to women. For example, models are arranged to look like a living room rather than being aligned in a row. Aisles are wide to accommodate strollers. Shoppers are greeted at a "concierge desk" and directed to salespeople. Television sets are never tuned to sports events. Whether in spite of or because of these policies, Sony reports its stores are doing much better business with females (and with upscale customers) than do typical "big-box" electronic retailers located in outdoor strip malls. Sony hopes this demonstration will encourage its channels to reconsider their approach.

CARRIER-RIDER RELATIONSHIPS

One last channel structure deserves mention: carrier-rider relationships. Sometimes the most appropriate channel member to carry one's products to market is another manufacturer's owned sales force and distribution abilities, a relationship called piggybacking. In a piggybacking channel, the rider is the firm in need of distribution for its product; the carrier is the other manufacturer who has excess capacity in its distribution system to accommodate the rider's product. The benefit to the rider is the avoidance of the cost of hiring a large employee sales force or finding an independent channel member. The benefit to the carrier is the fee earned by carrying the rider's product, along with any synergies that result from adding a complementary product to its line.[65] This arrangement is found among pharmaceutical companies, consumer packaged goods companies, and financial services companies.

The issue of coordination is just as important as that of efficiency, however. Consider a specific piggybacking example. Dove International, a maker of super-premium ice cream products in the United States, is a part of the M&M/Mars company, which also makes a wide variety of candy products. The M&M/Mars distribution channel did not specialize in freezer trucks for transporting ice cream, so Dove signed on an ice cream company, Edy's (also a superpremium ice cream maker), to physically distribute Dove products to grocery stores.[66] The match was clearly a good one from the perspective of availability of the right distribution channel resources. Because the arrangement appeared to be working so well, Dove signed a permanent contract with Edy's for distribution of its products. At that point, effort by Edy's began to erode, and without reliable physical distribution, Dove's sales and profits dropped. The moral of the story is that it is difficult to expect a piggybacking partner to maintain effort when the extra product carried is a direct competitor to the carrier's own line, particularly without retaining any leverage through the contracting process.

If the possibility for an unfavorable outcome is so great, who would be a good piggybacking partner? One way to pick a partner who is likely to exert good-faith efforts on behalf of the rider is to find a firm that makes complementary, rather than directly competitive, products. Such a partner is more likely to want to do a good job representing the rider's product because sales of its own products may actually increase as a result. However, there is a latent danger: The carrier could decide the rider's product is such a good complement that it brings out its own version and displaces the rider's brand. Carrier-rider relationships are thus inherently fragile.

A common technique to strengthen them is to engage in reciprocal piggybacking, where each firm sells both its own products and those of the partner, so that the rider in one relationship is the carrier in the other. Mattel, an American toy manufacturer, and Bandai, a Japanese toy maker, signed a reciprocal piggybacking agreement in which Bandai pledged to sell Mattel toys in Japan (where Mattel previously had trouble selling on its own), while Mattel pledged to sell Bandai toys in Latin America (where Bandai has no presence). As part of the agreement, Mattel agreed to buy 5 percent of Bandai's stock. This is part of a potentially much more extensive relationship between the two companies.[67] The deal is Mattel's third try at setting up a distribution system in Japan, after a partnership with a British marketing firm failed, as did an attempt to set up its own employee sales network. In a reciprocal arrangement like Mattel-Bandai's, neither partner would want to exert weak selling effort for fear that its own product would suffer the same fate at the hands of the other. Each relationship serves as a hostage to protect the other (see Chapter 8: for more on using mutual hostages to strengthen channel alliances).

SUMMARY

The decision of how thoroughly to cover a market area is, for the manufacturer, a critical policy choice, for it has a substantial influence on how well the manufacturer can implement its channel plans. This is because the intensity of coverage drives how much reward power the manufacturer has over downstream channel members and how much it depends on its downstream counterparts.

At first glance, the issue is deceptively simple from the manufacturer's viewpoint. The manufacturer's sales force would like the freedom to open as many accounts (sign up as many channel members) as possible. The customer would like to find an outlet nearby, especially for convenience goods. Channel members will be pressured by market forces to sell more (for example, by cutting prices) if at least some of their competitors carry the brand. All these factors suggest that more coverage is better. The corporate lawyer, concerned about incurring allegations of restricting competition, is likely to approve. On the manufacturer's side, only the corporate accountant, adding up the costs of servicing many outlets placing small orders, is likely to object.

But the issue is far more complex. Channel members will object vigorously. Unable to differentiate themselves and to maintain margins in the face of withering intrabrand competition, channel entities will ask the manufacturer for relief. If their competition is not reduced, they will withdraw their efforts, perhaps even use the brand to bring in traffic—to be diverted to another brand. Other entities will refuse to join the manufacturer's channel. And they will refuse to undertake actions to support the brand unless those efforts can be readily redeployed to another brand. In general, the manufacturer will experience a lack of cooperation. Implementation problems rise exponentially when coverage is too high for downstream channel members to earn a reasonable return on the brand.

There exists a multitude of ways to cope with the implementation problems created by intensive distribution. All are expensive, and some are difficult to implement. These include creating so much brand equity as to exercise pull over the channel's customers (effectively obliging the channel to carry the brand), imposing and enforcing a restrictive contract, practicing resale price maintenance (where legal), offering branded variants, decoupling sales and service, and frequently introducing new products that have low failure rates.

A more direct and often cheaper and more effective way to influence the channel is to limit one's coverage. This move raises the manufacturer's dependence upon its resellers, as each becomes more important and would require more effort to replace. In return, the manufacturer can reassure channel members that it will not be opportunistic. For example, the manufacturer can allay fears that it will exploit resellers making brand-specific investments once those investments are in place. The manufacturer can allay fears that it will abuse a strong brand position or that it will undercut channel members by unreasonable levels of direct selling.

Apart from allaying fears of opportunism, the manufacturer can use limited distribution to induce the channel member to make concessions of its own. Prime among these is limiting brand assortment (offering some degree of category selectivity, even going so far as offering category exclusivity or exclusive dealing). More generally, by limiting coverage the manufacturer is able to offer greater rewards to each channel member. Manufacturers can use this influence to attract only the best resellers (important for a high-quality positioning) and to attract only resellers matching a particular customer profile (important when the target segment is very focused). Manufacturers may also use reward power to exercise greater influence over how channel members market their brands (important for manufacturers that, for whatever reason, are reluctant to let market forces dictate outcomes).

In short, the manufacturer can increase its influence over channel members and its ability to motivate them by limiting coverage. In the process, the corporate accountant can be appeased by the cost savings due to serving a smaller but more active account base. The same argument applies in reverse to a downstream channel member: Representing fewer brands can increase leverage over a manufacturer while reducing costs.

Will the customer be better off? Yes, if the manufacturer's choice of channel members and ideas of how to control them lead to outcomes that meet the customer's needs (e.g., needs for product safety, repair services, sales efforts, etc.). The customer may not necessarily pay a higher price: To the extent that limited intrabrand competition fosters vigorous interbrand competition, the customer may actually pay a lower price. The customer will be inconvenienced by lesser availability (which will be a minor factor for specialty goods in any case).

A trend in both B2B and B2C markets is to create multiple routes to market by mixing different formats (combinations of flows and service outputs). Achieving greater coverage by adding more different types of channel members can be highly effective—if customer segments gravitate to different formats. If they do not, cannibalization and conflict are highly likely. Free riding is a major issue and must be addressed because downstream channel members will not tolerate being victimized indefinitely.

Another trend is toward dual distribution using wholly owned and independent channels to serve prospective customers. Dual distribution can be highly effective if, indeed, the company's channels and independent channels meet different service output demands. The danger is that firms will be seen as biased toward their own channels. Further, both the employee and the third-party channels may view each other as rivals and compete more vigorously with each other than with other brands. Firms need to take steps to ensure that each format perceives it is being treated fairly. When designed and managed well, dual distribution can provide valuable information (benchmarking) and can give the manufacturer leverage over both channels. Demonstration sites also serve these purposes and signal independent channel members that underserved demand may exist.

Carrier-rider relationships are inherently unstable, even if the products involved are complements rather than substitutes. The dangers are that the carrier may frustrate the rider by failing to represent the product well—or may find the product desirable enough to copy it. One way to motivate the carrier to make best efforts with the rider's products is reciprocal piggybacking.

Fundamentally, this chapter is about limiting intrabrand competition for the purpose of increasing interbrand competition. This can be achieved by attracting the right channel partners, motivating them highly, and gaining their cooperation with the manufacturer's initiatives. If these initiatives are well considered (or if the manufacturer skillfully uses channel feedback to improve its ideas), the result will be a well-executed marketing plan that facilitates the manufacturer's competitive efforts vis-à-vis other brands.

Take-Aways

- Selective distribution is a strategic choice not to be confused with the inability to attract channel members to carry the brand.
- Manufacturers tend to think that more coverage is always better. Conflict is, therefore, inherent because channel members prefer the manufacturer to offer less coverage.
  - In general, the manufacturer will experience a lack of cooperation when coverage is too high for downstream channel members to earn a reasonable return on the brand. The manufacturer will have poor coverage in spite of having high coverage.

- There exists a multitude of ways to cope with the implementation problems created by intensive distribution. All of them are expensive and some of them are difficult to implement.

- A more direct and often cheaper and more effective way to influence the channel is to limit one's coverage. This raises the manufacturer's dependence upon its resellers because each becomes more important (and would require more effort to replace). But in return, the manufacturer can reassure channel members that it will not be opportunistic.

- For convenience goods, more coverage is usually better because buyers purchase impulsively or refuse to exert effort to find the brand. For shopping goods or experience goods, selective distribution is feasible and may even be desirable.

- The decision to be selective should reflect the marketing strategy of the brand, given the nature of the product category. Selectivity makes sense

  - To support a premium positioning

  - To pursue a narrow target market

  - To pursue a niche strategy (premium positioning in a narrow target market)

- The manufacturer can use limited distribution to induce the channel member to make concessions of its own, such as limiting brand assortment.

- Manufacturers can use the reward power of selective distribution to attract only the best resellers or only resellers matching a particular customer profile. Manufacturers may also use reward power to exercise greater influence over how channel members market their brands and save costs by serving a smaller but more active account base.

- The same arguments apply in reverse to a downstream channel member: Representing fewer brands can increase leverage over a manufacturer while reducing costs.

- The customer will be better off if the choice of channel members and ideas of how to control them lead to desirable outcomes (for example, needs for product safety). To the extent that limited intrabrand competition fosters vigorous interbrand competition, the customer may actually pay a lower price. The customer will be inconvenienced by reduced availability.

- Achieving greater coverage by adding more different types of channel members can be highly effective—if customer segments gravitate to different formats. If they do not, cannibalization and conflict are highly likely.

- Dual distribution can also be highly effective, but the danger is that firms will be seen as biased toward their own channels.

- Carrier-rider relationships are inherently unstable, which may be remedied by reciprocal piggybacking.

DISCUSSION QUESTIONS

1. Which is preferable, intrabrand or interbrand competition? Can there be one without the other? Where do you stand on the issue of intrabrand competition: Is it necessary in order for there to be viable general competition from a macro perspective? Discuss these questions in the context of resale restrictions and the granting of exclusive territories.

2. An industrial supply house carries only a single brand of a grease-cutting compound used to clean the concrete floors of factories. That brand is prominent and is well

viewed by the clientele. What are all the possible reasons why the distributor would carry only one brand? Is this normal behavior? What do you expect the distributor's relationship with the manufacturer of this brand to be like? What would you expect is this manufacturer's degree of intensity of coverage in this distributor's market area?

3. Apple, as a computer company, has struggled over the years with the assortment problem. Company-owned Apple stores offered only Apple computers. Although management liked having control of the assortment, customers wanted side-by-side comparisons with other brands, eventually driving Apple to close many of its own stores. Apple also has had difficulty influencing how independent computer outlets stock and display its products. Apple is now using the success of its music download-ing systems (iPod and variations) to compose larger assortments—and is reopening company-owned stores.[68] Is this a good idea? What, if anything, would you recom-mend to Apple as an alternative strategy to improve its products' coverage and sales?

4. Why do greater sales and greater coverage go together? Should manufacturers always seek greater coverage? Conversely, should resellers always seek to carry more brands in their assortment for a given product category? Why or why not?

5. "A brand can never be available in too many places." Debate this statement.

6. "A distributor should stock as many brands as possible for each product category demanded by its clients." Debate this statement.

7. If you were a new brand entering the market for a consumer durable, how much cov-erage would you seek? What arguments would you give to channel entities as to why they should carry your brand? What questions and objections are they likely to have? To convince them to stock your product, would you pursue a branded variants strategy?

ENDNOTES

1. Frazier, Gary L., Kirti Sawhney, and Tasadduq Shervani (1990), "Intensity, Functions, and Integration in Channels of Distribution," in *Review of Marketing, 1990*, V. A. Zeithaml, ed., (Chicago: American Marketing Association), pp. 263–300.

2. The terminology of convenience, shop-ping, and specialty goods refers to con-sumer markets and was developed in Copeland, Mervin (1923), "Relation of Consumers' Buying Habits to Marketing Methods," *Harvard Business Review* 1, no. 2 (March–April), pp. 282–289.

3. Reibstein, David J. and Paul W. Farris (1995), "Market Share and Distribution: A Generalization, a Speculation, and Some Implications," *Marketing Science* 14, no. 3 (Summer), pp. G190–G202.

4. Narus, James A. and James C. Anderson (1996), "Rethinking Distribution," *Harvard Business Review* 96, no. 4 (July–August), pp. 112–120.

5. Chu, Wujin and Woosik Chu. (1994), "Signaling Quality By Selling Through a Reputable Retailer: An Example of Renting the Reputation of Another Agent," *Marketing Science* 13, no. 2 (Spring), pp. 177–189.

6. Bialobos, Chantal (1999), "Le Sacre de Royal Canin," *Capital* 10, no. 12 (December), pp. 50–51. Quotation from p. 51.

7. Steiner, Robert L. (1993), "The Inverse Association Between the Margins of Manufacturers and Retailers," in *Review of Industrial Organization* 8, no. 6 (December), pp. 717–740.

8. Chapdelaine, Sophie (2000), "Les malheurs de la Famille Barbie," *Capital* 11 (March), pp. 38–40.

9. *The Economist* (2001), "The Wrong Trousers," *The Economist*, June 16, p. 74.

10. Breit, William (1991), "Resale Price Maintenance: What Do Economists Know and When Did They Know It?" *Journal of Institutional and Theoretical Economics* 147, no. 1 (March), pp. 72–90. Fabricant, Ross A. (1990), "Special Retail Services and Resale Price Maintenance: The California Wine Industry," *Journal of Retailing* 66, no. 1 (Spring), pp. 101–118.

11. Sheffet, Mary Jane and Debra L. Scammon. (1985), "Resale Price Maintenance: Is It Safe to Suggest Retail Prices?" *Journal of Marketing* 49, no. 4 (Fall), pp. 82–91.

12. Chatterjee, Sharmila C., Saara Hyvönen, and Erin Anderson (1995), "Concentrated vs. Balanced Sourcing: An Examination of Retailer Sourcing Decisions in Closed Markets," *Journal of Retailing* 71, no. 1 (Spring), pp. 23–46.

13. Corey, E. Raymond, Frank V. Cespedes, and V. Kasturi Rangan (1989), *Going to Market: Distribution Systems for Industrial Products* (Boston, MA: Harvard Business School Press).

14. Marvel, Howard P. (1982), "Exclusive Dealing," *Journal of Law and Economics* 25, no. 1 (April), pp. 1–25. Exclusive dealing is also sometimes referred to as exclusive purchasing.

15. Thouanel-Lorant, Patricia and Francis Lecompte (2002), "Petit Electromenager: Les Hypers en Perte de Vitesse," *LSA* 34, no. 9 (September), pp. 52–60.

16. Comprehensive references for this material are: Fein, Adam J. and Erin Anderson (1997), "Patterns of Credible Commitments: Territory and Category Selectivity in Industrial Distribution Channels," *Journal of Marketing* 61, no. 2 (April), pp. 19–34; and Frazier, Gary L. and Walfried M. Lassar. (1996), "Determinants of Distribution Intensity," *Journal of Marketing* 60, no. 4 (October), pp. 39–51.

17. Cora Daniels (2003), "Canadian Double," *Fortune*, March 17, p. 42.

18. Miracle, Gordon E. (1965), "Product Characteristics and Marketing Strategy," *Journal of Marketing* 29, no. 1 (January), pp. 18–24; and Murphy, Patrick E. and Ben M. Enis (1986), "Classifying Products Strategically," *Journal of Marketing* 50, no. 3 (July), pp. 24–42.

19. Cantin, Anne (1999), "Bénéteau-Jeanneau, Fusion Modele," *Management* 10, no. 11 (November), pp. 32–34. Quotation from p. 33.

20. Rangan, V. Kasturi, Melvyn A. J. Menezes, and E. P. Maier (1992), "Channel Selection for New Industrial Products: A Framework, Method, and Application," *Journal of Marketing* 56, no. 3 (July), pp. 69–82.

21. Tellis, Gerard J. (1988), "The Price Elasticity of Selective Demand: A Meta-Analysis of Econometric Models of Sales," *Journal of Marketing Research* 25, no. 4 (November), pp. 331–341.

22. All information in this sidebar comes from Agins, Teri and Deborah Ball (2002), "Fashion Faux Pax: Donna Karan Deal May Not Fit LVMH," in *Wall Street Journal Europe*, March 25, pp., B1, B8.

23. Scherrer, Matthieu (2003), "Cabasse Reprend du Volume," *Management* 15, no. 11 (November), pp. 39–40.

24. Kumar, Nirmalya (1996), "The Power of Trust in Manufacturer-Retailer Relationships," *Harvard Business Review* 60, no. 6 (November–December), pp. 92–106.

25. Celly, Kirti Sawhney and Gary L. Frazier (1996), "Outcome-Based and Behavior-Based Coordination Efforts in Channel Relationships," *Journal of Marketing Research* 33, no. 2 (May), pp. 200–210.

26. Rangan, V. Kasturi, Melvyn A. J. Menezes and E. P. Maier. (1992), "Channel Selection for New Industrial Products: A Framework, Method, and Application," *Journal of Marketing* 56, no. 3 (July), pp. 69–82.

27. Southam, Hazel (1993), "Turning the Tables at Linn," *Marketing*, May 20, pp. 20–21; Murdoch, Adrian (1997), "Music Man," *Chief Executive* 17, no. 130 (December), p. 24; Linn Products, Ltd., at www.linn.co.uk (accessed August 2005).

28. Magrath, Allan J. and Kenneth G. Hardy (1988), "Working with a Unique Distribution Channel: Contractor-Dealers," *Industrial Marketing Management* 17, no. 4 (November), pp. 325–328.

29. Buchanan, Lauranne (1992), "Vertical Trade Relationships: The Role of Dependence and Symmetry in Attaining Organizational Goals," *Journal of Marketing Research* 29, no. 1 (February), pp. 65–75.

30. Heide, Jan B. and George John (1988), "The Role of Dependence Balancing in Safeguarding Transaction-Specific Assets in Conventional Channels," *Journal of Marketing* 52, no. 1 (January), pp. 20–35.

31. Heide, Jan B., Shantanu Dutta, and Mark Bergen (1998), "Exclusive Dealing and Business Efficiency: Evidence from Industry Practice," *Journal of Law and Economics* 41, no. 2 (October), pp. 387–407.

32. Buchanan, Lauranne, Carolyn J. Simmons, and Barbara A. Bickart (1999), "Brand Equity Dilution: Retailer Display and Context Brand Effects," *Journal of Marketing Research* 36, no. 3 (August), pp. 345–355.

33. Shocker, Allan D., Barry L. Bayus, and Namwoon Kim (2004), "Product Complements and Substitutes in the Real World: The Relevance of 'Other Products,'" *Journal of Marketing* 68, no. 1 (January), pp. 28–40.

34. Grundahl, Marie-Pierre (2000), "Vuitton: Les Secrets d'une Cash Machine," *Management* 11, no. 9 (September), pp. 22–26.

35. Chabert, Patrick (2005), "Smart, La Mauvaise Etoile de Mercedes," *Capital* 15, no. 3 (March), pp. 42–44.

36. Taylor, Alex (2003), "Mercedes Hits a Pothole," *Fortune*, October 27, pp. 44–49.

37. Chabert, Patrick (2004), "Audi, le Seigneur des Anneaux," *Capital* 12, no. 11 (November), pp. 38–42.

38. Bialobos, Chantal (2004), "Le Match Galeries Lafayette-Printemps," *Capital* 12, no. 12 (December), pp. 62–64.

39. Lynch, John G. and Dan Ariely (2000), "Wine Online: Search Costs Affect Competition on Price, Quality, and Distribution," *Marketing Science* 19, no. 1 (Winter), p. 83.

40. This section is based on Fein and Anderson (1997) and Frazier and Lassar (1996), both already cited.

41. Butaney, Gul and Lawrence H. Wortzel (1988), "Distributor Power Versus Manufacturer Power: The Customer Role," *Journal of Marketing* 52, no. 1 (January), pp. 52–63.

42. McAfee, R. Preston and Marius Schwartz (1994), "Opportunism in Multilateral Vertical Contracting: Nondiscrimination, Exclusivity, and Uniformity," *American Economic Review* 84, no. 1 (March), pp. 210–230.

43. Bowman, Douglas and Das Narayandas (2004), "Linking Customer Management Effort to Customer Profitability in Business Markets," *Journal of Marketing Research* 16, no. 4 (November), pp. 433–447.

44. Narayandas, Das and V. Kasturi Rangan (2004), "Building and Sustaining Buyer-Seller Relationships in Mature Industrial Markets," *Journal of Marketing* 68, no. 3 (July), pp. 63–77.

45. Farley, John U. and Harold J. Leavitt (1968), "A Model of the Distribution of Branded Personal Products in Jamaica," *Journal of Marketing Research* 5, no. 4 (November), pp. 362–368.

46. Sullivan, Mary W. (1998), "How Brand Names Affect the Demand for Twin Automobiles," *Journal of Marketing Research* 35, no. 2 (May), pp. 154–165.

47. Frazier and Lassar, already cited.

48. Bergen, Mark, Shantanu Dutta, and Steven M. Shugan (1996), "Branded Variants: A Retail Perspective," *Journal of Marketing Research* 33, no. 1 (February), pp. 9–19.

49. Timothy L. O'Brien (1994), "Unjustified Returns Plague Electronics Makers," *Wall Street Journal*, September 26, p. B1.

50. Frazier, Gary L. and Tasadduq A. Shervani (1992), "Multiple Channels of Distribution and Their Impact on Retailing," in *The Future of U.S. Retailing: An Agenda for the 21st Century*, Robert A. Peterson, ed. (Westport, CT: Quorum Books), pp. 217–238.

51. Inman, J. Jeffrey, Venkatesh Shankar, and Rosellina Ferraro (2004), "The Roles of Channel-Category Associations and Geodemographics in Channel Patronage,"

Journal of Marketing 68, no. 2 (April), pp. 51–71.

52. Ratchford, Brian T., Myung-Soo Lee, and Debabrata Talukdar (2003), "The Impact of the Internet on Information Search for Automobiles," *Journal of Marketing Research* 40, no. 2 (May), pp. 193–209.

53. Brooks, Rick (2004), "Sealing Their Fate: A Deal with Target Put Lid on Revival at Tupperware," in *Wall Street Journal*, February 18, 1–2.

54. Morton, Fiona Scott, Florian Zettelmeyer, and Jorge Silva-Risso (2003), "Consumer Information and Discrimination: Does the Internet Affect the Pricing of New Cars to Women and Minorities?" *Quantitative Marketing and Economics* 1, no. 1, pp. 65–92.

55. Deleersnyder, Barbara, Inge Geyskens, Katrijn Gielens, and Marnik G. Dekimpe (2002), "How Cannibalistic Is the Internet Channel? A Study of the Newspaper Industry in the United Kingdom and the Netherlands," *International Journal of Research in Marketing* 19, no. 4 (December), pp. 337–348 and Geyskens, Inge, Katrijn Gielens, and Marnik G. Dekimpe (2002), "The Market Value of Internet Channel Additions," *Journal of Marketing* 66, no. 2 (April), pp. 102–119.

56. Werbach, Kevin (2000), " Syndication: The Emerging Model for Business in the Internet Era," *Harvard Business Review* 78, no, 3 (May–June), pp. 54–62.

57. Torode, Christina (2003), "Partners: AT&T Lives by Channel Playbook," *CRN News*, September 2, pp. 6–7.

58. Vinhas, Alberto Sa (2003), "Dual Distribution Channels in Business-to-Business Marketing: A Transaction Interdependencies View," Ph.D. dissertation, INSEAD, Fontainebleau, France.

59. Neel, Dan (2004), "CyberGuard to Direct-Sales Force: No Commission If You Sell Direct," *CRN News* July 7, p. 15.

60. Moriarty, Rowland T. and Ursula Moran (1990), "Managing Hybrid Marketing Systems," *Harvard Business Review* 68, no. 6 (November–December), pp. 146–150.

61. Dutta, Shantanu, Mark Bergen, Jan B. Heide, and George John (1995), "Understanding Dual Distribution: The Case of Reps and House Accounts," *Journal of Law, Economics, and Organization* 11, no. 1 (April), pp. 189–204.

62. Aoulou, Yves (2005), "L'héritier Inattendu de Monsieur Swatch," *Management* 13 (March 6), 18–22.

63. Gava, Marie-Jose (1999), "Guy Degrenne N'est Pas le Cancre de la Distribution," *Management* 5, no. 4 (April), p. 16; and Bouyssou, Julien (2004), "Le Deuxième Souffle de Baccarat," *Management* 5, no. 2 (February), pp. 28–30.

64. Spagat, Elliot (2004), "Sony Makes Big Changes with Small Stores," *Marketing News*, November 15, p. 12.

65. Terpstra, Vern and Bernard L. Simonin (1993), "Strategic Alliances in the Triad: An Exploratory Study," *Journal of International Marketing* 1, no. 1, pp. 4–26.

66. Edy's ice cream is marketed by Dreyer's (www.dreyers.com, accessed August 2005). The same ice cream is sold as Dreyer's west of the Rocky Mountains in the United States and as Edy's east of the Rocky Mountains.

67. "Mattel Forms Toy Alliance with Bandai of Japan," *Wall Street Journal*, July 22, 1999, p. A20; "Execution of a Letter of Intent Regarding an Alliance Between Bandai Co., Ltd. and Mattel, Inc.," Bandai Web site at www.bandai.co.jp (accessed August 2005); "Mattel, Inc. and Bandai Co., Ltd. Establish Global Marketing Alliance," Mattel Web site at www.mattel.com (accessed August 2005).

68. Krauss, Michael (2003), "Apple Takes Branding Cue from Bob Dylan," *Marketing News*, September 15, pp. 11, 14; *Economist* (2005), "Crunch Time for Apple," January 7, pp. 53–54.

Gap Analysis

After reading this chapter, you will:

- Be able to define a channel gap as either a shortfall or an oversupply of service outputs demanded (a demand-side channel gap) or as an overly high total cost of running the channel (a supply-side channel gap)

- Understand that the sources of channel gaps are channel bounds, which can be either environmental or managerial in nature

- Be familiar with the different types of channel gaps both on the demand side and the supply side

- Be able to identify strategies for closing the various types of channel gaps

- Be able to use the gap analysis templates to summarize the knowledge about channel gaps in a given channel situation and suggest means of closing the gaps

Using the analysis of service output demands, marketing channel flows, and channel structure described in Chapters 2, 3, and 4, the channel planner has a good idea of the ideal channel structure to meet target segments' needs. The obvious next step is to build the channel that both meets service output demands and does so at a minimum cost of performing the necessary channel flows. We call such a channel the zero-based channel.

The zero-based channel may not exist or may seem difficult to build. Consider the following questions that should be answered when structuring the ideal channel system:

➤ What nonvalued functions (e.g., excessive sales calls) can be eliminated without damaging customer or channel satisfaction?

➤ Are there likely to be any redundant activities? Which of them could be eliminated to result in the lowest cost for the entire system?

➤ Is there a way to eliminate, redefine, or combine certain tasks in order to minimize the steps in a sale or reduce its cycle time?

➤ Is it possible to automate certain activities in a way that reduces the unit cost of getting products to market even though it will lead to increased fixed costs?

➤ Are there opportunities to modify information systems to reduce the costs of prospecting, order entry, or quote generation activities?[1]

In cases of new channel design, where no previous channel is present in the market, the planner may face managerial or environmental bounds that seem to prevent the establishment of the zero-based channel. In cases where a channel already exists in the marketplace, it may not be zero-based. In either situation, we say that one or more

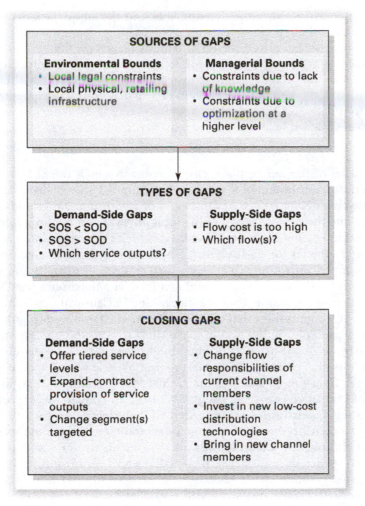

Figure 5.1   The gap analysis framework

channel gaps exist.[2] This chapter's purpose is to discuss the sources of channel gaps and the types of channel gaps that exist, along with techniques for closing channel gaps. We use the framework in Figure 5.1 to organize our discussion of channel gaps, covering sources of gaps, types of gaps, and techniques for closing gaps.

SOURCES AND TYPES OF CHANNEL GAPS

Sources of Gaps

Gaps in channel design can come about simply because management has not thought carefully about target end-users' demands for service outputs or about managing the cost of running their channel. The advice in this situation is simple: Channel managers must pay attention to both the demand side and the supply side in designing their channel to avoid these gaps.

But gaps also can arise because of bounds placed on the best-intentioned channel manager. That is, managers seeking to design a zero-based channel for the company's product may face certain constraints on their actions that prevent the establishment of the best channel design. Before diagnosing the types of gaps, then, it is useful to discuss the bounds that create these gaps. We concentrate on two such sources: *environmental bounds* and *managerial bounds.*

Environmental Bounds

Characteristics of the marketplace environment in which the channel operates can constrain the establishment of a zero-based channel.[3] These environmental bounds in turn create channel gaps. Two key instances of environmental bounds are local legal constraints and the sophistication of the local physical and retailing infrastructure.

For example, manufacturers of electric vehicles are constrained as to where they can sell their vehicles for on-street use. These vehicles are like electric golf carts but can be equipped with doors, seat belts, turn signals, headlights and taillights, and other systems for the driver's safety and comfort. The maximum legal speed of these vehicles is 35 miles per hour. They are widely used in California, Arizona, and Georgia, particularly in communities that border golf courses; families own golf carts not only to use on the golf course but also to make short trips to the grocery store, school, or other nearby destinations. This product might seem like a great solution to today's problems of traffic, pollution, and parking. But electric vehicles are not legal for on-street use in 10 of the 50 states of the United States, meaning that they can only be used off of regular streets (e.g., on golf courses, on college or corporate campuses, etc.). This legal constraint has prevented Global Electric Motorcars (GEM), a subsidiary of DaimlerChrysler, from getting distribution for its vehicles through auto dealerships in Illinois, for example, and of course, no dealer wants to invest in the capability to service these vehicles. While GEM seeks permission for its vehicles to be driven on streets whose speed limit is less than 35 miles per hour, the current legal environment effectively bars entry for this product.[4]

Legal conditions in the marketplace affect which channel partners a company chooses, even if they do not totally prevent the company's access to the market. Recall our example of CDW, the computer reseller (first introduced in Sidebar 3.1; gap analysis insights are the focus of Sidebar 5.1 in this chapter). CDW's penetration of the government market is limited by the government's stated goal of 23 percent of vendors being small- or medium-sized businesses. Its small-business and minority-business partners program matches it with these independent companies, whose size fits the governmental bound perfectly; this program thus creates a channel structure for CDW that is mainly the result of the imposition of the legal bound.

Beyond environmental bounds due to governmental dictates, the physical and infrastructural environment may prevent the establishment of certain types of distribution channel structures.[5] The challenges of rolling out online bill payment systems, profiled in Sidebar 5.2 (and examined from demand and supply sides in Sidebars 2.2 and 3.2), are largely in the development of systems that can communicate between different levels of the channel and can manage information consistently through time. Not only must a bill be payable by the payer electronically, but it must also be electronically presentable in a common-database system. For many bill payers (business

Sidebar 5.1

CDW and PC purchases by small/medium business buyers: Gap analysis insights[6]

Sidebars 2.1 and 3.1 profile computer systems reseller CDW from both demand (service output) and supply (channel flow) perspectives. These discussions implicitly suggest that CDW itself faces certain limitations (i.e., bounds) to its ability to operate in the marketplace; that it identifies gaps faced by potential suppliers; and that it helps other companies close their gaps through its particular positioning and capabilities. These are all gap analysis insights, as the discussion here makes clear.

Channel bounds are evident in CDW's minority-partner initiative aimed at building government business. CDW itself faces an environmental bound in targeting government contracts because it is not categorized as a small business and, hence, cannot take advantage of the government's goal of awarding 23 percent of its procurement contracts to small businesses. If CDW had not taken any action, this bound would essentially prevent it from targeting this part of the government market. Meanwhile, small-business vendors may not face that environmental bound, but they face managerial bounds due to their small size: their costs of negotiation are higher than those facing larger firms. In addition, small businesses face a promotional managerial bound because their small size prevents them from being well known to potential buyers. One vendor remarked, "There are a million other IT shops out there, but when I say I'm a CDW-G partner, they immediately know who I am."

In the face of these (different) bounds facing each partner, the CDW-G initiative to partner with small business explicitly takes account of the bounds to craft a set of alliances that minimize their effects on either side. CDW gains access to sales and business it otherwise would not be able to get, and the small business partners gain access to both competitive component prices and borrowed brand equity that help close their gaps. Note that the solution involves giving up some control on both sides; CDW-G and the small business partner must trust each other because they do not have an equity relationship that helps one of them control the other's actions. This cost (the loss of control) must in general be balanced against the gain from closing channel gaps. Evidently, CDW-G views the trade-off as an excellent bargain; it expanded the Small Business Consortium program in Fall 2003 to add more reseller solutions providers who can extend CDW-G's reach beyond federal government business into state, local, and educational accounts. Its goal is to partner with woman-, minority-, or veteran-owned VARs (value-added resellers) in several states that provide special business access to these vendors. As in the earlier program aimed solely at federal contracts, the new consortium members receive sales leads from CDW-G and have access to CDW-G's software design tools and help desk. In return, CDW-G gains access to sales it could not otherwise hope to bid for.

CDW's success lies partly in its ability as a channel intermediary to close the gaps that would plague its current channel partners were they not to use CDW as a channel partner. One example of how CDW helps the channel close demand-side gaps comes from Sidebar 2.1: Gateway's decision to sell its computers through CDW at a time it had concentrated mainly on direct selling through owned channels. Gateway management's recognition of the demand-side gap facing it is epitomized by the statement, "There are customers who like to buy from CDW. There is a suite of value-added service that CDW provides that gives customers a choice." If Gateway did not partner with CDW, it recognizes that it would forego access to a desired target

(continued)

segment, one that demands service outputs of choice and service that Gateway by selling direct cannot provide. This suggests more generally that successful intermediaries survive through their continued ability to narrow the gaps that their channel captains would face otherwise.

Similarly, CDW closes supply-side gaps for its buyers, as Sidebar 3.1 illustrates in the statement that CDW is recognized as the "chief technical officer for many smaller firms." If these small business buyers bought direct from a suite of computer-products suppliers rather than using CDW, their managers realize the risk of a poor choice would significantly increase. Thus, CDW closes a supply-side risking gap for small- and medium-sized business buyers. Its ability to close gaps like this is the cornerstone of its profitability; buyers that gain efficiencies from using a competent intermediary must be, and are, willing to share in the gains from trade.

In a different realm, CDW itself faces a supply-side challenge to the efficiency with which it performs the promotion flow. Sidebar 3.1 notes the extensive sales force training program CDW provides for each salesperson it hires. The obvious benefit to rigorous training like this is that CDW's salespeople are among the most knowledgeable about computer lines in the industry. This is a terrific selling advantage when serving business customers. However, CDW also faces a 25 percent turnover rate in its sales force, meaning that each year, about one fourth of the sales force leaves the company. This means that one-fourth of training expenses are unproductive—a very high cost to bear. The CEO counts this as both a business challenge and a human resources challenge for the company. In terms of channel gap analysis, this situation illustrates that even for companies whose channel efforts are managed very well overall, there always remain some gaps to work on; it is virtually impossible to create and maintain a true zero-based channel system.

and consumer), the real value of electronic bill payment involves the ability to integrate the payment with the payer's own database of information (back-office activities for business payers and home budgeting information for consumers). Limitations on the integration of all these electronic data sources limits the possible spread of electronic payments throughout the market.

Similarly, even companies that want to manage returned product more efficiently may not be able to develop the capacity to do so themselves or to find an intermediary that can handle the company's specific problems. Sidebar 5.3 expands on our channel-flows-based discussion of reverse logistics in Chapter 3 (see Sidebar 3.3) with a focus on the retail book industry. One industry executive claims, "The most expensive thing we do in our warehouse is process returns."[7] The legacy in the industry of allowing free returns from retail to the publishers appears to be a hard habit to break, creating an effective environmental bound even for those who want to change the system.

In sum, environmental bounds occur outside the boundary of the companies directly involved in the channel and constrain channel members from establishing a zero-based channel either because of an inability to offer an appropriate level of service outputs or because the constraints impose unduly high costs on channel

Sidebar 5.2

Online bill payment: Channel bounds, resulting demand-side and supply-side gaps, and efforts to close them

Sidebars 2.2 and 3.2 outline the basics of electronic bill presentment and payment (EBPP) from a demand-side and a supply-side perspective, respectively.[8] The conundrum has been that, despite the evident channel-wide cost savings of paying bills electronically, EBPP has been slow to penetrate the financial landscape in the United States. Resolving this conundrum requires an understanding of the bounds facing EBPP implementation, the resulting demand-side and supply-side gaps, and investments being made to close the gaps that are finally resulting in higher adoption rates for electronic bill payment.

Figure 5.2 depicts these three elements of the gap analysis.

The main channel bounds that have slowed the adoption of e-bill payment are environmental: specifically, a lack of the necessary technological infrastructure. As with any new family of technologies, it is extremely difficult to make every component work seamlessly from the beginning. In the case of EBPP technologies, it was necessary first to build software applications that provided for electronic bill payment (even if the bill was presented on paper to the payer). Once these were in place, however, the full infrastructure was still not in place, either for business-to-business (B2B) or business-to-consumer (B2C) bill presentment and payment. Thus, the initial buzz about online bill payment oversold the promise of the technology as it currently stood; it initially only replaced paper check writing with electronic funds transfers. Nevertheless, this was the necessary first step to creating a full-fledged EBPP system.

The second step was to expand the technological infrastructure by developing electronic presentment of bills; this meant that not only could a payer electronically pay a bill that was received through another medium but could electronically receive and see the bill, too. In the best systems, this combination occurs all on one site—either the biller's site or a third party's site (such as that of a bank offering online bill payment). As pointed out in Sidebar 2.2, the benefit of presentment along with payment on a third party's site is the ability to see and pay for multiple bills in one place—in effect, an assortment and variety service output benefit. But as of the mid-2000s, this combination of presentment and payment capabilities, along with broad assortment of bills that could be paid on one site, was not universally available for consumer bill payment, again limiting the attractiveness of the technology.

A third step is necessary to maximize the benefits of EBPP in the B2B context: the ability of the payer to integrate the electronic information contained in the system with its own back-office activities, specifically accounts payable, ordering, and other bookkeeping tasks. Without this end-to-end capability, the biller would still find an EBPP system attractive, but the payer would find it considerably less so. Thus, until the advent of connected software technologies to link all levels of the channel in the billing and payment management process, the infrastructure simply prevented the adoption of an ostensibly superior way of dealing with the bill payment flow in B2B channels.

This lack of immediate availability of all the necessary technologies is not at all unusual. The complexity of the software systems makes it impossible to seamlessly and quickly bring all of them to market. This is why we categorize these limitations as environmental bounds: They have characterized the environment in

(*continued*)

Sidebar 5.2 (cont.)

Online bill payment: Channel bounds, resulting demand-side and supply-side gaps, and efforts to close them

BOUNDS	GAPS	CLOSING THE GAPS
Environmental Technology infrastructure: • takes time to fully develop • initially endowed benefits more on _billers_ than on _payers_ • is not universally available • is characterized by high fixed set-up costs, but low marginal implementation costs and thus is not attractive unless significant scale is achieved	**_Demand-side_** • Assortment/variety (one-stop bill payment site not available) • Waiting time too long (some e-bills took 5 days to pay) • Information provision poor (thus e-bill payment viewed as risky) **_Supply-side_** • Clear lowering of many channel flow costs • But consumer (as a channel member) bears more _perceived_ risk, with no compensating price cut • Cost cuts initially much more available to _biller_ than to _payer_ (asymmetric cost efficiencies that hamper adoption)	**_Relax environmental bounds_** • Build software applications to generate back-office benefits for B2B players • Presentment technology eventually developed to improve assortment/variety for consumer payers _Increase promotional efforts → generate information for consumers_ _Add new specialist channel members_ _New specialists develop new technology to provide integrated benefits to consumers and B2B payers_

Figure 5.2   Online billing and payment: Gap analysis

Sidebar 5.2 (cont.)

Online bill payment: Channel bounds, resulting demand-side and supply-side gaps, and efforts to close them

which billers and payers operate, at least for the short to medium term, in a way that cannot be simply overturned.

This set of environmental bounds directly created both demand-side gaps and supply-side gaps that hampered the adoption of electronic bill payment. As outlined in Sidebar 2.2, the level of service output provision in electronic bill payment systems of the early 2000s (in assortment and variety of bills that could be paid at one site, in quick delivery of the payment once the payer completed it, and in information provision to resolve uncertainties about the process), combined with their high cost and high perceived risk, made them a poor alternative to the very robust status quo of paper-based bill payment. These demand-side insights illustrate how the market will not embrace a new offering through a new channel merely because it is new, even if it offers parity product quality on average. It must actually beat the competition to earn marketplace acceptance, and in this case the competition was simply the tried-and-true paper bill payment methods.

Further, as Sidebar 3.2 showed, good EBPP implementation generates cost reductions in several key channel flows. Promotion, negotiation, risking, ordering, and payment costs all can be significantly reduced. Adoption of electronic billing and payment is, therefore, not hampered by supply-side gaps nearly as much as by demand-side gaps driven by the environmental bounds of a slow infrastructure build-up.

Are these bounds being relaxed and the resulting gaps being closed? Absolutely. There is little doubt that the world economy is moving toward paperless invoicing and bill payment. Indeed, in many countries it is already the norm (due to a variety of factors, including faster

implementation of financial system innovation and a less-attractive paper-based alternative). The extremely high reliability of the U.S. Postal Service, combined with relatively low costs of first-class mail, makes paper-based bill payment an easy and transparent method for U.S. consumers to use and, thus, creates a high hurdle for new technologies to jump. But jump the hurdle they will, as is already evident in many markets. In the United States, the increasing adoption of e-bill payment is facilitated by the growth and success of specialized intermediaries that build and maintain the hardware and software systems behind EBPP. Thus, the solution involves both the insertion of new intermediaries into the channel and the development and refinement of new technologies to make payments faster, easier, and less risky. As these advances occur, the perceived consumer cost of adopting e-bill payment is also falling, so that a "virtuous cycle" of adoption is occurring, as Figure 5.3 illustrates. As more consumers and businesses pay bills online, the economies of scale available to the channel players (EBPP technology intermediaries, banks, and billers themselves) producing the services expand, making the cost savings from implementing it even greater. These cost savings in turn prompt providers like banks to lower or eliminate the charges for using them to their consumers, which increases their adoption even further. In short, removing the bounds to electronic invoicing and bill payment naturally leads to a system where most bills will be offered and paid electronically because the entire system is more efficient under this technology. The current lack of complete acceptance of electronic bill payment is more an indication of the continued existence of the bounds on the system than of the inferiority of the idea.

(continued)

Sidebar 5.2 (cont.)

Online bill payment: Channel bounds, resulting demand-side and supply-side gaps, and efforts to close them

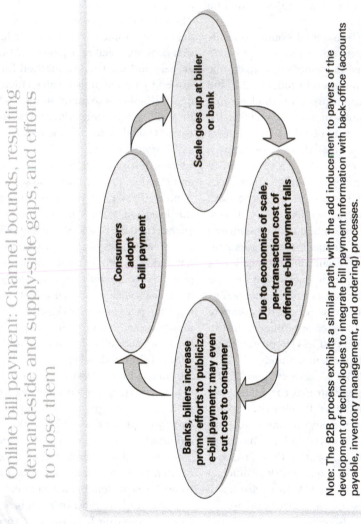

Scale goes up at biller or bank

Due to economies of scale, per-transaction cost of offering e-bill payment falls

Banks, billers increase promo efforts to publicize e-bill payment; may even cut cost to consumer

Consumers adopt e-bill payment

Note: The B2B process exhibits a similar path, with the add inducement to payers of the development of technologies to integrate bill payment information with back-office (accounts payable, inventory management, and ordering) processes.

Figure 5.3   Online billing and payment: A virtuous cycle

Sidebar 5.3

Reverse logistics: Gap analysis insights[9]

Sidebar 3.3 highlights the reverse logistics problem in channel management from a channel flows perspective. That discussion leads naturally to a realization that significant supply-side gaps exist in the management (or nonmanagement) of product returns, sometimes themselves leading to demand-side gaps. Figure 5.4 summarizes the gap analysis insights from this example. The retail book market provides a specific product example of the general issues.

The fact that a supply-side gap exists is clear from Table 3.2: Managing product returns in the United States alone costs an estimated $35 to $40 billion annually (above and beyond the returned-goods value of $60 to $100 billion annually!), and returned product sits in retail back rooms and manufacturer warehouses for 30 to 70 days. In the book market in particular, 34 percent of adult hardcover books were returned from retailers to publishers in 2003, with a wholesale value of $743 million. The problem has been accelerating: The wholesale value of returns was just over $200 million in 1990. Clearly, the management of that cost and the minimization of time spent in the reverse channel are challenges that many companies have not yet fully met.

Where does the gap come from—that is, what bounds on channel management create these inefficiencies? There are both managerial and environmental bounds at play here. Managerially, one can argue for bounds due both to a lack of knowledge and to (an attempt to) optimize at a higher level. The lack of knowledge problem exists because many manufacturers are not aware of the scope of the problem or the true accounting costs of reverse logistics in their channels. Survey evidence shows that reverse logistics is still considered a low priority in many companies. But some companies would argue that allowing for a

certain percentage of returned products is good business because it means that there is enough product in the channel for end-users to find (i.e., there are no stockouts and hence the quick delivery service output is provided) and because a generous returns policy provides good customer service, another service output that may be highly valued. If the revenue productivity of high service output levels on these dimensions more than covers the cost of the resulting returns, then the policy may be optimal at a higher level—that is, a level that accounts for prevention of service output deficiencies as well as for cost control in returns. If this is the case, then the main issue is maximizing the efficiency with which returns are handled rather than trying to stop or lower the frequency of returns. That said, there is not much evidence that manufacturers either appreciate this trade-off or are able to measure its effects financially.

Environmentally, bounds exist in the lack of widespread sophisticated systems for handling returns. While some reverse logistics specialists are springing up, the infrastructure for handling returns is still in development, preventing easy access to state-of-the-art techniques for managing returned product. The CEO of Holtzbrinck Publishers, owners of publishing imprints like Farrar, Straus and Giroux and St. Martin's Press, says "The most expensive thing we do in our warehouse is process returns." One executive at Time Warner Book Group refers to the "happy" warehouse (the one that ships out 60 million new books for the first time to bookstores) and the "sad" warehouse (the one that receives, holds, and processes 20 million returned books per year). The description of the voyage traveled by a copy of "The Perricone Promise," a best-seller by Nicholas

(*continued*)

Sidebar 5.3 (cont.)

Reverse logistics: Gap analysis insights

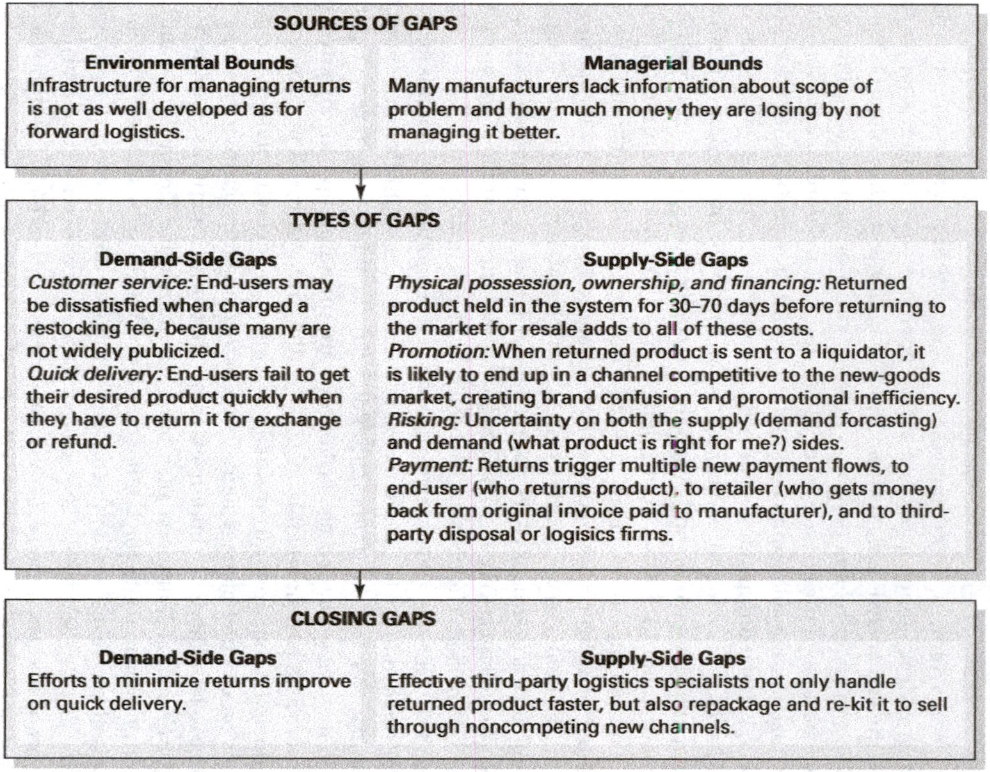

SOURCES OF GAPS

Environmental Bounds
Infrastructure for managing returns is not as well developed as for forward logistics.

Managerial Bounds
Many manufacturers lack information about scope of problem and how much money they are losing by not managing it better.

TYPES OF GAPS

Demand-Side Gaps
Customer service: End-users may be dissatisfied when charged a restocking fee, because many are not widely publicized.
Quick delivery: End-users fail to get their desired product quickly when they have to return it for exchange or refund.

Supply-Side Gaps
Physical possession, ownership, and financing: Returned product held in the system for 30–70 days before returning to the market for resale adds to all of these costs.
Promotion: When returned product is sent to a liquidator, it is likely to end up in a channel competitive to the new-goods market, creating brand confusion and promotional inefficiency.
Risking: Uncertainty on both the supply (demand forcasting) and demand (what product is right for me?) sides.
Payment: Returns trigger multiple new payment flows, to end-user (who returns product), to retailer (who gets money back from original invoice paid to manufacturer), and to third-party disposal or logisics firms.

CLOSING GAPS

Demand-Side Gaps
Efforts to minimize returns improve on quick delivery.

Supply-Side Gaps
Effective third-party logistics specialists not only handle returned product faster, but also repackage and re-kit it to sell through noncompeting new channels.

Figure 5.4   Applying the gap analysis framework to reverse logistics

Sidebar 5.3 (cont.)

Reverse logistics: Gap analysis insights

Perricone in 2004, is representative of the problem:

- 525,000 copies were shipped to retail booksellers
- The book hit the United States' major best-seller lists and was considered a "hot book" of 2004
- Retailers sold about 70 percent of the book's publication run—meaning that about 225,000 copies were unsold

Each of the 225,000 unsold copies, of course, travels its own route, but the specific geographic path one of those copies travels is as follows (see Figure 5.5 for a geographic depiction of the "voyage" of this book):

- The book ships out of Time Warner's (happy) warehouse in Lebanon, Indiana, to a Barnes & Noble bookstore in Marina del Rey, California, 2,100 miles away.
- The book is unpacked and displayed in the bookstore.
- Unsold, the book is repacked into a box several weeks later, picked up by a trucking company, and shipped 2,800 miles to Barnes & Noble's national distribution center in Jamesburg, New Jersey.
- Barnes & Noble processes the book, and sends it back 700 miles to Time Warner's (sad) warehouse in Lebanon, Indiana.
- The book sits for as long as 12 to 18 months before being sold to bargain

Figure 5.5   Path followed by a Copy of *The Perricone Promise*

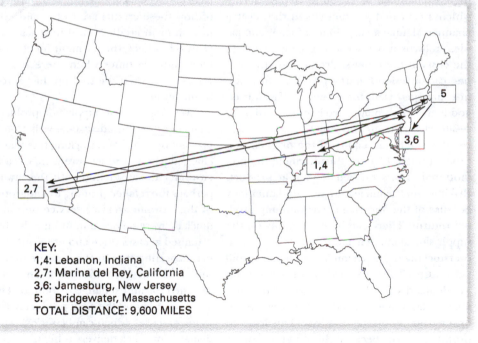

KEY:
1,4: Lebanon, Indiana
2,7: Marina del Rey, California
3,6: Jamesburg, New Jersey
5:   Bridgewater, Massachusetts
TOTAL DISTANCE: 9,600 MILES

(continued)

Sidebar 5.3 (cont.)

Reverse logistics: Gap analysis insights

book wholesale buyer Strictly-By-The-Book, Inc., and received into its warehouse in Bridgewater, Massachusetts, 1,000 miles away.

- Then, the book is sold *back* to Barnes & Noble as a bargain book to be priced at $7.98 (instead of the cover price of $27.95), with a 3,000-mile trip through Barnes & Noble's Jamesburg distribution center back to the Marina del Rey bookstore. The book's total voyage has been 9,600 miles!

The resulting gaps are primarily supply-side in nature: that is, because returns are so pervasive and so ill-managed, the cost of performing many channel flows is much higher than it needs to be. Sidebar 3.3 suggests that almost all channel flows are implicated. Physical possession, ownership, and financing costs are too high, exemplified by the 30 to 70 days during which a returned product sits in the reverse channel. Manual management of many companies' returns processes also greatly increases the costs of these flows. Promotion effectiveness can be seriously hurt if product returns are not managed well; for example, if returned goods are simply plowed back into a third-party resale channel, such as eBay or some other retailer, the brand equity of the original new product might be hurt, thus harming the promotional efforts on behalf of that product. Risking inefficiencies arise fundamentally because of the uncertainty surrounding product returns. There can be uncertainty on the supply side about demand forecasts, leading to overstocking in the channel and, hence, product returns. There can also be uncertainty on the demand side when end-users are not sure about what to buy (e.g., what size of sweater to order from an online retailer). This leads to product returns because the end-user either

unintentionally buys the wrong item and must return it or the end-user intentionally buys multiple sizes of the same product to ensure getting one that fits—leading again to product returns (of all the sizes that did not fit!). This uncertainty thus leads to risk-minimizing behavior by end-users that increases channel flow costs. In the book industry, uncertainty about demand for a given title leads to overproduction and overstocking in bookstores, just to avoid the possibility of stocking out of a blockbuster. Further, payment is much more costly to manage when there are returns. End-users have to be issued credits for the products they return; there are costs of monitoring restocking fees to ensure that end-users get back only the proportion of the original purchase price to which they are entitled. When retailers return product to manufacturers, manufacturers must issue credits back to the retailers, raising issues of how these credits are to be paid, whether in cash or in credit toward next season's purchases. In effect, the payment function is handled multiple times when there is a return, versus once when the sold product is retained by the buyer.

Even worse, these supply-side problems can engender demand-side gaps as well. Consumers may not be aware of restocking fees that will be charged when product is returned, leading to customer dissatisfaction with the brand and perhaps the retailer (leading to underprovision of the customer-service service output). The quick delivery service output may also be compromised in cases when end-users order a product, expecting it to arrive (and be useful) but find it is not what they want and must be returned for an exchange or refund. This creates a delay before the right product is available to the end-user, which can be serious when the demand for quick delivery is high.

Sidebar 5.3 (cont.)

Reverse logistics: Gap analysis insights

Notice that closing these gaps through seeking to minimize the frequency of returns themselves is itself costly. Indeed, the general truth is that no gap can be closed at zero cost. As described in Sidebar 3.3, Lands' End's online sizing service is costly, as is the personnel cost incurred by W. W. Grainger to talk to buyers before they take delivery of ordered product in order to minimize returns. When W. W. Grainger instructs a buyer to discard unwanted merchandise instead of returning it, it is seeking the "best of a bad lot" of solutions. On the one hand, telling an end-user to destroy unwanted product is a loss to the channel system, as this product can never again generate revenue. On the other hand, taking back the unwanted product itself triggers costs that W. W. Grainger has already decided are too high. It recognizes that the best (not optimal, but best) solution involves bearing some cost but trying to minimize that cost. In the case of the book industry, Steve Riggio, CEO of Barnes & Noble, suggests that retailers should stop returning books to publishers and simply mark them down at retail and sell them off. But others argue that this strategy would decrease retailers' incentives to take on new or untried authors' works, reducing variety in the industry; or that consumers would simply learn to wait for the marked-down price on the books rather than paying full price.

Closing the gaps in reverse logistics involves using several of the tools mentioned in Figure 5.1. The use of third-party reverse logistics specialists, such as Channel Velocity, is an example of closing supply-side channel gaps through the insertion of a new channel member into a previously existing channel system. The new channel partner is a specialist that will ideally bear many flow costs, not just the physical movement and disposal of returned product; thus, insertion of this new channel member into the channel system also implies a shifting of channel flow responsibilities for the other legacy channel members (e.g., returned product may no longer be held at retailer warehouses for a period of time and then shipped back to manufacturer warehouses; instead, returned product may be immediately shipped to the warehouse of the third-party logistics specialist). The best outcomes arise from a reverse logistics specialist that is able to screen returned product to find units that can be rekitted and resold and is able to create appropriate packaging and new forward routes to market for the refurbished product. Channel Velocity's operations epitomize this set of valued channel activities. The result to the manufacturer that uses a third party of this type is (a) avoided cost of holding on to unwanted returned merchandise, thus freeing warehouse space for more productive uses, and (b) newly found sources of incremental profit.

members. In contrast, managerial bounds may also constrain channel design but emanate from within the channel structure itself or from the orientation or culture of specific channel members. We turn to this issue next.

Managerial Bounds

Managerial bounds refer to constraints on distribution structure arising from rules within a company. The most typical managerial bounds exist inside the company manufacturing the product to be sold through a channel. Sometimes a desire to control the customer or simply a lack of trust among channel members prevents management from implementing a less bounded channel design.

The bound imposed by management may be due to a lack of knowledge of appropriate levels of investment or activity in channel flow performance. One computer company whose primary route to market was online sales found its returns rates were very high. In a (misguided) effort to minimize returns, it promulgated a policy that refunds would be offered on returned product only if the product was broken (the logic being that if the consumer received the product in good condition, it should be kept, but that, of course, a product that arrived at the buyer's doorstep broken should be taken back for a full refund or exchange). Despite the company's best intentions, returns percentages did not fall at all. Now, however, all of the returned product was . . . *broken*, of course! The company had unwittingly created a managerial bound by instituting a policy that was even worse than the original problem. Fortunately, management realized the problem within a short time and reversed the policy. This example suggests that some managerial bounds are obvious enough, and easily enough reversed, not to cause persistent malfunctioning of the channel.

Similarly, the lack of focus in many companies on managing the costs of returned product detailed in Sidebar 5.3 on reverse logistics is often driven not by a perverse desire to incur high costs but simply from ignorance of what those costs are and what resources might be available to try to control them. Here, however, we see a confluence of the managerial bound (we do not see the value of focusing on reverse logistics) with a back-up environmental bound (once we realize it is worth focusing on, the solution is not easily contrived). It is still good to recognize all of the self-imposed managerial bounds and to attack them wherever possible; as we will see later in this chapter, attacking bounds has to start with the realization that they exist.

CDW's small-business partners profiled in Sidebar 5.1 face a somewhat different managerial bound: that of size. Their small size constrains their abilities to negotiate as aggressively as their larger competitors for favorable supply prices for product or to promote their products' quality and availability in the market. In other markets of this type, companies often seek mergers or strategic alliances to increase their bargaining strength; the company that does not choose this route faces the limitations of small size.[10]

The computer company example is one of miscalculation on the part of management. But this is not always the reason for a managerial bound. In many cases, a conscious choice not to optimize the distribution activities at one level of the organization is made in favor of a greater common good. Sidebar 5.3 on reverse logistics highlights that even with optimal control of shipments to minimize returns, some level of flexibility in the retail system is still desired because of the need to satisfy target end-users' demands for quick delivery and assortment and variety. Allowing book retailers to freely return books to the publisher is one means to preserve that flexibility in the face of persistent and high uncertainty about the future demand for a new book.

Whether channel gaps arise because of managerial bounds, environmental bounds, or a lack of attention to the well-being of the channel, they can profoundly affect either side of a zero-based channel: the demand or the supply side. We turn to a taxonomy of channel gaps from a demand- and supply-side perspective next.

Types of Gaps: Demand-Side Gaps

If gaps exist on the demand side, they create what we call a service-value gap. These gaps can arise in two ways. Let us think about a single service output. A demand side gap can exist either when the amount of a service output supplied is less than the amount demanded (for shorthand we can say SOS < SOD) or when the amount supplied is greater than the amount demanded (SOS > SOD).

In the first case, too low a level of the service output is produced for the target market (SOS < SOD). Sidebars 2.2 and 5.2 on online bill payment highlight the limited assortment of bills that could be paid through one online bill payment site, the surprisingly slow payment speed (i.e., the lack of quick delivery), and the poor level of information provision as key factors in the slow diffusion of this channel-efficiency-increasing set of technologies. Similarly, Sidebar 5.4 on recorded music retailing shows how too low a level of bulk-breaking and assortment/variety have limited the success of standard music retailers, particularly given the rise of online alternatives.

Note that, in contrast to the online bill payment and music store examples, a demand-side gap may exhibit a low-service-output offering accompanied by a low price (e.g., Dollar Stores are discount stores where everything is priced at one dollar; they offer low prices but also relatively poor assortment and service). In such a case, even though the price may be low, some segments of end-users may not perceive sufficient value (i.e., utility for the price paid). As a result, the bundle consisting of the product plus its service outputs will likely not be purchased. In short, the service-value gap can arise on the demand side because the level of service is too low, even controlling for a possibly lower price, to generate a reasonable amount of value for the end-user.

In the second case, too high a level of the service output is produced for the target market (SOS > SOD). Sidebar 5.4 on retail music sales shows that in one target segment (younger popular music buyers who are well-versed in using the Internet), the standard music retail outlet's provision of customer service is simply too high; they would prefer a do-it-yourself downloading channel to the attention of possibly poorly informed in-store personnel (especially as the relevant information on what popular music is "hot" is available most quickly on the Internet itself, not in stores). More generally, many people are familiar with the retail shopping experience of the overly helpful store clerk; at first the attention may be welcome, but eventually, it becomes irritating and distracting. These are examples of overinvestment in service outputs that decrease, rather than increase, the end-user's satisfaction, even while they also cost money to provide—a double penalty!

The key insight here is, of course, that erring on either side is a mistake for the channel manager. Providing too high a level of a service output is just as bad as providing too low a level. On the one hand, channel costs (and hence prices) rise too high for the value created, while on the other hand, the channel skimps on providing service outputs for which the target market would be willing to pay a premium. Profit opportunities are lost on both sides.

A demand-side gap can exist in more than one service output. Indeed, it is possible for the level of one service output to be too low while the level of another is too high, as our sidebar on music retailing makes clear (SOS < SOD for bulk-breaking and assortment/variety, but SOS > SOD for customer service). The channel manager might actually believe that such combinations balance out, that in some sense the extra amount of one service output can compensate for a shortfall of another. But service outputs may not be good substitutes for each other, and when they are not, no excess of one service output compensates for too little of another. For example, a small neighborhood variety store offers extremely high spatial convenience but may not offer as much assortment and variety as a hypermarket and may charge higher prices.

Sidebar 5.4

Music retailing: Are music stores a dying breed?[11]

The channel system for music sales has gone through an enormous transition in the last several years. Once a standard system involving manufacturers (the record/CD production houses) selling albums (today, CDs) to retailers at wholesale prices and retailers marking up those albums to suggested list prices, today it presents consumers with a myriad of routes to market. In addition to music stores, consumers can now get CD albums from electronics stores like Best Buy or from online stores like Amazon.com or cdnow.com. But the consumer can now also download individual songs from Napster or Apple's iTunes services for about 99 cents per song—and there is still significant downloading or song sharing among consumers without payment for songs as well. The growth of these alternative channels for music prompts one magazine to ask, "Is the Music Store Over?" To answer the question requires an investigation of consumers' demands for service outputs in music markets and a recognition of how standard music stores fare versus the newer routes to market in meeting these service output demands; in short, an analysis of the gaps in the standard music channel.

There is cause for concern. Consider that retail sales of recorded music fell from $14.6 billion in the United States in 1999 (the year that Napster launched its free downloading service) to $11.8 billion in 2003 (see Table 5.1). Meanwhile, many retail music store chains' businesses fell on hard times. Wherehouse, a 405-store chain in 2002, filed for bankruptcy in 2003; it was purchased by Trans World Entertainment in late 2003 and shrank to just 113 stores by late 2004. Musicland Group, owner of Sam Goody, Media Play, and Suncoast Stores, was purchased by Best Buy in 2001, closed over 250 stores in 2003, and was again sold to Sun Capital Partners in 2003. It decreased its number of stores from 1,331 in 2001 to 914 in 2004. Tower Records had 215 stores in the United States and overseas in 2002 but was forced to sell all of its non-U.S. stores and to downsize inside the United States when it filed for bankruptcy in 2003; it has since emerged from bankruptcy and closed over half of its stores.

Industry participants at both the retail and CD production levels attributed the huge decline in retail sales to illegal piracy of music through free download services like Napster. But this alone does not explain the current plight of the music retailer because downloaded music continues to be very attractive even though

Table 5.1   U.S. retail music sales, 1999–2003

Year	Sales in $ Billion
1999	$14.6
2000	$14.3
2001	$13.7
2002	$12.8
2003	$11.8

Sidebar 5.4 (cont.)

Music retailing: Are music stores a dying breed?

Napster has "gone legal," offering a for-fee download service instead of its initial free downloads. Apple also launched the iTunes fee-based music download service in 2003 to complement sales of its fabulously successful iPod MP3 players. Even at about one dollar per song, the fee-based download business is booming; one report predicts that online music downloads can increase to one third of music sales by 2009.

If piracy can explain some, but not all, of the decline in the fortunes of music retailers, what other reasons can be found? Consider consumers' demands for service outputs. Three key service outputs were provided at the wrong levels: bulk-breaking, assortment/variety, and customer service:

- Before the advent of downloadable music, consumers' only real music purchase choice was buying a full album of music; interest in singles was low. But once single-song downloads became available, consumers were able to get just the song(s) they wanted without having to buy a whole album's worth of songs. With CDs priced at $15.00 to $20.00 apiece, the alternative of paying about a dollar for the one song the consumer wanted seemed a much better deal. In short, bulk-breaking became a key service output demand, and retailers selling album-sized CDs were providing more songs per purchase than consumers wanted to buy (thus, the demand for bulk-breaking exceeded the supply, which we can denote by SOD > SOS).

- No bricks-and-mortar store can match online music sellers for assortment and variety, making standard music stores relatively less and less attractive as consumers became increasingly comfortable with "virtual"

music purchasing—either of CDs from Amazon.com or of downloadable music from Napster (thus, again SOD > SOS).

- One of the ways a bricks-and-mortar store can beat online purchase outlets is in personalized customer service. The end-user can talk to a real person at a store, get advice, and also touch and feel the product before buying it. While these are valued service outputs in some markets, they became increasingly less valuable as consumers' ability to shop at online sellers increased; online, they could listen to sample tracks of music and visit chat rooms to get the latest information on popular music to download. Here, unlike in the other two service outputs, the problem is oversupply of customer service (so that SOS > SOD in this instance).

Against this backdrop of mismatched service output provision and the increasing use of electronic channels for music by consumers, one music manufacturer, Vivendi Universal, decided to take action. In September 2003, Universal cut the suggested retail price of almost all of its CDs to $12.98 from the prior level of $16.98 to $18.98. Universal also cut its top wholesale price to retailers to $9.09 from $12.02 (with the exception of a handful of top music artists' work, which would carry a wholesale price of $10.10). Universal made this decision after considerable market research indicating that the $12.98 price would generate maximum sales lift. Management also indicated that the price cuts were driven by widespread piracy of music among online downloaders and further pointed out that recent significant price cuts on movie DVDs made CD prices look too expensive by comparison.

(continued)

Sidebar 5.4 (cont.)

Music retailing: Are music stores a dying breed?

Consider the implications of this move inside the bricks-and-mortar music channel. Wholesale prices were cut by about 24 percent. Wholesale margins dropped considerably as well. Meanwhile, Universal's decreased suggested retail price implied a drop in retail prices of almost 32 percent, with a higher implied percentage drop in retail margins. Universal further dropped all cooperative advertising payments to retailers and required that they allocate 25 percent of their bin space and 33 percent of prime retail space (kiosks and displays), to Universal products in order to get the lower wholesale price. These percentages were approximately equal to Universal's market share at the time—about 30 percent. For this strategy to break even financially, Universal estimated it would need an increase in unit sales of about 21 percent.

The move failed miserably. Some retailers—particularly mass merchandisers like Wal-Mart and Best Buy—welcomed the lower wholesale prices, as they had for some time been discount-pricing CDs to build store traffic. But in these stores, total volume did not respond as much as was needed for breakeven because of the already-low prices prevailing before the change (see Tables 5.2 and 5.3 for average pricing and market share information in the industry). Meanwhile, small- and medium-sized retailers were outraged at the extreme cuts in their margins, and many of them failed to pass along the wholesale price cuts to consumers in lower retail prices. Even though Universal put stickers on their CDs advertising the lower retail prices, these retailers simply covered them with larger stickers with higher prices on them. Retail prices on average fell by only 5 percent in the year after the price cuts, instead of the 30 percent planned by Universal. Unit sales volume increased not 21 percent, but only 8 to 13 percent on average. Further, competitors did not lower their prices in response to Universal's move, making it difficult to maintain the lower pricing strategy. As a result, Universal

Table 5.2   Average retail CD prices in the United States

Time Period	Average Price
2002 (Q1)	$13.90
2002 (Q2)	$13.90
2002 (Q3)	$13.60
2002 (Q4)	$13.90
2003 (Q1)	$13.80
2003 (Q2)	$13.70
2003 (Q3)	$13.50
2003 (Q4)	$13.55
2004 (Q1)	$13.25

Sidebar 5.4 (cont.)

Music retailing: Are music stores a dying breed?

Table 5.3   **Share of albums sold by channel, 2002**

Channel	Share of Albums Sold
Music chain stores	51.0%
Mass merchants	33.8%
Independents	11.9%
Other	3.3%

Notes: 680.9 million albums were sold in total in 2002. Mass merchant channel includes Best Buy, Kmart, Wal-Mart, Costco, and Target.

scaled back the price-cutting initiative in June 2004.

Looking at this chain of events from a channel management perspective suggests that the price-cutting strategy was simply the wrong one to follow because it did not attack the core demand-side gaps plaguing the bricks-and-mortar music channel. Cutting price is always attractive to consumers, but competing against a price of "free" is usually not profitable for a manufacturer. The real issue is that consumers did not want to pay even $12.98 for an entire album of songs when the one song they wanted was available for download for 99 cents (or free, if they were willing to violate copyright). Bulk-breaking was not offered at an improved level. The price cuts also did not improve the variety and assortment offered by bricks-and-mortar retailers. Even worse, the high-cost small- and medium-sized retailers found their margins cut by Universal; even though the service produced with those costly inputs might not have been highly valued by consumers, retailers could not instantaneously respond by lowering their costs. Instead, they simply shifted their efforts and assets to other music companies' offerings that offered higher margins. Thus, the price cut neither increased underproduced service outputs nor controlled the cost of overproduced ones; it only generated increased conflict from the retailers. This is an example of how *fixing the wrong gap problem can make channel matters worse, not better.*

Indeed, today some of the surviving retailers are joining the bandwagon of online music downloading rather than trying to fight it. A consortium of major music retailers launched its own downloading service called Echo in late 2004; some retailers also offer Internet-connected kiosks or portable Wi-Fi devices so that consumers can sample music as they tour the store. It remains to be seen whether initiatives like these will be enough to keep the standard music store profitable and thriving as electronic music acquisition continues to grow.

The decline of these small variety stores in many urban and suburban areas in the United States suggests that consumers are not willing to trade a poor assortment and variety offering for extreme spatial convenience. It is important to get the combination of service outputs just right.

It is also important to note that, ideally, one should check for demand gaps both service output by service output and segment by segment. Our retail music store sidebar shows a shortfall in provision of some service outputs (bulk-breaking, assortment and variety), along with a surfeit of another (customer service). But service output elements that result in a demand-side service gap for one target segment may be exactly right for another target segment. The retail music store may not ultimately die; it may instead serve a smaller set of target end-users well and continue to focus on them.

Segmentation helps identify those clusters of potential buyers for which demand-side gaps exist, rather than suggesting a need for global changes in channel strategy. We will see later that knowing the segment for which one's service output offering is correct can be useful when deciding how to close demand-side gaps.

Types of Gaps: Supply-Side Gaps

A supply-side gap exists when the total cost of performing all channel flows jointly is too high. This can occur only when one or more channel flows are performed at too high a cost—that is, holding the level of service outputs constant when there is a lower-cost way of performing the channel flow in question. Note that it is meaningless to say that flows are performed at too low a cost, as long as demanded service outputs are being produced. A supply-side gap can result from high-cost performance of any of the relevant channel flows, from physical possession to payment.

Sidebar 5.1 on CDW illustrates supply-side gaps in the performance of the promotional flow (specifically, in the cost of training salespeople and managing sales force turnover). CDW puts its newly hired salespeople through a rigorous training program so that they can provide excellent customer education and service, which are service outputs that are highly valued by small- and medium-sized business customers. However, the question is how costly it is to generate this superior level of service outputs, and CDW's sales force turnover rate of 25 percent per year means that one fourth of the newly hired (and expensively trained) salespeople leave the company. Those salespeople's training costs are wasted investments and, even worse, may give one of CDW's competitors a well-trained salesperson if the turnover leads to employment with that competitor. If before embarking on costly training CDW could determine which types of salespeople are most likely to leave the company early, it could lessen promotional (sales training) costs while not compromising the delivery of valued service outputs.

Sidebars 3.2 and 5.2 on electronic bill presentment and payment (EBPP) illustrate the supply-side gaps before the onset of the new technology as well as after. Before EBPP technologies spread through the United States, the costs of several key channel flows, including promotion, negotiation, risking, ordering, and payment were all higher than necessary to effectively pay bills. There is no doubt that when adopted throughout the system, from presentment to final bill payment and reconciliation, channel costs are significantly reduced. However, one interesting facet of this situation is that the very introduction of the improvements itself led to other supply-side gaps. In particular, bill payers themselves—who, as Chapter 3 makes clear, are channel members too—perceived the risk of electronic bill payment to be much higher than that of paper bill payment. Thus, a reduction in some channel flow costs for other channel members was replaced by higher channel flow costs for a crucial channel member—the end user—without whose cooperation the new technologies could not successfully spread. Further, bill paying end-users typically were not compensated for the time, effort, and risk associated with adopting the new technology, so this supply-side flow shift was not offset with a shift in payments in the channel. This vignette illustrates that shifting channel flows (even perceptually) will create a gap unless the channel member to whom the flows are shifted actually agrees to perform them; if that channel member is not compensated for doing so, the chances of compliance and successful implementation are slim.

In our discussion of reverse logistics in Sidebar 5.3, all channel flow costs are raised when returned product is not handled efficiently. Physical possession, ownership, and financing costs are too high, exemplified by the 30 to 70 days during which a returned product sits in the reverse channel; promotional effectiveness is hurt when returned merchandise turns up in uncontrolled third-party channels at distressed prices; risking is endemic in the system, arising from uncertainties in both demand for original new goods and in the percentage of those new-good sales that are returned; and payment involves repetitive costs due to the multiple times the product is handled and paid for. In this situation, then, a single apparent problem in the channel gives rise to many sources of higher cost.

The criterion defining a supply-side gap expressly states that the total cost of performing all flows jointly is higher than need be. This means that a supply-side gap may not exist, even if one flow is performed at an unusually high cost, as long as this minimizes the total cost of performing all flows jointly.[12] For example, one electrical wire and cable distributor expanded across the United States and internationally, acquiring many other independent distributors and eventually building an international network of warehouses. Some of the products it stocked and sold were specialty items, rarely demanded but important to include in a full-line inventory (i.e., end-users demanded a broad assortment and variety). To stock these specialty items in every warehouse around the world was very costly. Thus, the distributor chose to stock such items in just one or two warehouses. This minimized the cost of physical possession of inventory (in the warehousing sense). However, sometimes an end-user located far from the warehouse but valuing quick delivery very highly demanded the specialty product. To meet that service output demand, the distributor chose to air-freight the required product to the end-user, incurring what seems like an inefficiently high transportation cost to ship the product. However, the key here is that the high transportation cost is still lower than the cost of stocking the specialty product in all possible warehouses while awaiting the rare order for that product. Such a situation does not present a true supply-side gap because the total cost of performing channel flows is minimized.

For the electrical wire and cable distributor, it makes abundant economic sense to incur high shipping costs because much lower inventory-holding costs result. Further, both of those costs are borne by the same channel member: the distributor itself. The optimal allocation of channel flow activities and costs is not so easy when different channel members perform the two flows. Imagine that our wire and cable distributor were to bear the inventory-holding cost, but another intermediary (say, a broker) were to bear the shipping costs to the end-user. In this case, without close coordination and cooperation between the channel members, the distributor likely would benefit from lower warehousing costs at the expense of the broker, who would have to bear higher shipping costs. Even though the entire channel system might benefit from this method of inventory holding and shipping, the optimal solution (involving high shipping costs but low inventory-holding costs) is unlikely to occur unless the distributor and broker make an explicit arrangement to share the total costs and benefits fairly.

In sum, a supply-side gap occurs whenever channel flows are performed in a jointly inefficient (high-cost) way. Sometimes, one or more flows may appear to be performed inefficiently, but channel members purposefully trade off inefficiency in one flow for superefficiency in another flow, resulting in overall lower costs. Inefficiently high costs of performing flows are usually a strong signal of supply-side gaps. Further, a supply-side gap can occur even when there is no evidence from the demand side of any problem in channel performance. End-users may be delighted with the level of service they get along with the products they buy. The price for the (product-plus-service-outputs) bundle may even be perceived as reasonable. However, if a supply-side gap is accompanied by a price that is reasonable in the end-user's eyes, it is a good bet that at least some channel members are not receiving the level of profit that adequately compensates them for the flows they are performing. This is because a supply-side gap inflicts costs on channel members that are higher than they have to be. Either end-users pay for that increased cost through higher prices, or channel members pay for it through decreased profit margins. A true zero-based channel both offers the right level of service outputs and does so at minimum total cost to run the channel.[13]

Combined Channel Gaps

Our taxonomy of demand-side and supply-side gaps produces six possible situations, depicted in Figure 5.6, only one of which is a no-gap condition. The figure illustrates several points. First, it is important to identify the source of the gap. If the gap arises from the cost side but the right amount of service outputs are being produced, for example, then it is important not to reduce or increase service output provision while reducing cost. Alternatively, if a demand-side gap with too high a level of a particular service output produced and a supply-side gap (flows are performed inefficiently) are both present, then reducing the level of service outputs offered without also increasing efficiency will not fully close the gap. Even worse, if a demand-side gap with too low a level of service outputs provided is present with a high-cost supply-side gap, the temptation may be to cut service provision in an attempt to reduce channel costs. The result would be doubly disastrous: not only would service levels suffer even more, but efficiency on a flow-by-flow basis would not improve. Thus, if the source of the gap is not properly identified, the solution may be worse than the original problem.

To use Figure 5.6 completely in a typology of channel gaps, the channel manager must specify whether demand gaps exist (and of which type) for each particular service output valued in the marketplace. This enables the manager to identify both over-availability and underavailability of each service output in a single framework. Further, Figure 5.6 is target segment-specific. That is, the figure should be analyzed separately for each segment targeted in the market because a demand gap with one segment may not be a gap at all in another segment (or the gap may go in the opposite direction).

Cost Performance Level	Demand-Side Gap (SOD > SOS)	No Demand-Side Gap (SOD = SOS)	Demand-Side Gap (SOS > SOD)
No Supply-Side Gap (Efficient Flow Cost)	Price/value proposition = right for a less demanding segment!	*No Gaps*	Price/value proposition = right for a more demanding segment!
Supply-Side Gap (Inefficiently High Flow Cost)	Insufficient SO provision, at high costs: Price and/or cost too high, value too low.	High cost, but SOs are right: Value is good, but price and/or cost is high.	High cost *and* SOs = too high: No extra value created, but price and/or cost is high.

Figure 5.6   **Types of gaps**

Combinations of supply-side and demand-side gaps are also possible because of the interlinking between supply-side (allocation of channel flows) decisions and the provision of service outputs on the demand side. The principle of postponement and speculation, developed by Louis P. Bucklin, is a good example of this phenomenon.[14] Postponement refers to the desire of both firms and end-users to put off incurring costs as long as possible. For a manufacturing firm, postponement often means delaying production until orders are received, thereby avoiding differentiation of inputs like raw materials into finished goods (e.g., iron ore into carbon steel). Postponement minimizes the manufacturer's risk of selling what is produced and eliminates the cost associated with holding relatively expensive inventory, thus helping to control total channel costs. But suppose that end-users have a high demand for quick delivery; in other words, they too want to postpone (that is, they want to buy at the last minute). In this situation, manufacturers engaging in postponement cannot meet the service output demands of the target end-users, and while they may not face a supply-side gap, they most certainly will face a demand-side gap.

End-users with high demands for quick delivery thus make the successful channel lessen its reliance on postponement in favor of an increased level of speculation. Under speculation, goods would be produced in anticipation of orders rather than in response to them. Frequently, the lowest-total-cost channel that employs speculation uses a channel intermediary. Intermediaries specialize in holding finished inventories for the manufacturer (such as a retailer holding finished goods for consumers) in anticipation of sales to end-users. Although speculation is risky and creates costs associated with holding finished goods inventory, it also permits economies of scale in production because it allows the manufacturer to make product in large batch lot sizes. This is something that postponement does not do. Nevertheless, as demand for quick delivery increases, eventually total channel costs rise. This generally results in a higher total price paid for a product supplied speculatively.

The retail music business faces exactly this trade-off in the apparent progression from speculative sales of CDs (which involves guessing in advance which CDs will sell well, and how well, in order to stock the right number of units in stores) to postponement sales through instant online downloads of just the music tracks an individual listener wants to hear. The tension between postponement and speculation is also evident in Sidebar 5.3 on reverse logistics and the book industry: Book publishers still favor speculation (i.e., the supply of many copies of potential bestsellers to retail bookstores), over postponement, which would mean waiting to get an order before shipping a book to a customer. In the book business, the most apt example of postponement selling today is electronic book downloading, where a consumer with the right hardware and software can download books from the Internet on demand to read electronically. Book publishers rely on speculation because of their beliefs that consumers still prefer paper books to electronic ones and that they are not willing to wait to get the book they want if it is not immediately available in a bookstore, leading to lost sales opportunities. That is, publishers believe that even though postponement might save on channel costs (notably physical possession, ownership, and financing costs), it compromises the delivery of too many service outputs on the demand side to be profitable on a net basis.

Under some conditions, of course, end-users are willing to speculate, such as when offered a particularly good price, or "deal," on a product (e.g., stocking up on grocery items when a promotion is offered at the supermarket). When end-users speculate, however, they also tie up their capital in household inventory and run the risk of obsolescence, pilferage, or breakage (e.g., the teenagers in the house may use up all the toilet paper decorating the tree branches of friends' houses as a prank, or extra meat or fruits may spoil before they are used).

Clearly, the optimum amount of speculation in inventory holding in the channel depends jointly on the costs of speculation and the intensity of demand for quick delivery by end-users (measured by their willingness to pay a price premium for ever quicker delivery). One solution that Bucklin suggests is to minimize the total cost of offering a particular delivery time to the end-user. This total cost includes the most efficient level of channel costs and the cost to the end-user of waiting that long for the inventory. Figure 5.7 depicts this solution. The curve ABC depicts the lowest possible cost of delivering product to end-users as a function of the required delivery time. The longer the delivery time allowed, the lower cost the methods the manufacturer can use. In particular, postponement, possible only with long delivery times, is a lower-cost method of delivering product than is speculation. The curve ABC might encompass not just the move along the speculation-postponement continuum but also the switch to different technologies and channel structures that provide the particular delivery time in the lowest cost way.

Meanwhile, curve DE in Figure 5.7 depicts the end-user's cost of holding goods as a function of the delivery time offered. Very short delivery times (i.e., very quick delivery) incur no cost of inventory-holding. As delivery times increase, however, the end-user must speculate and buy safety stocks of product in advance of their usage, and hence, the end-user's inventory holding costs increase. Finally, curve AFG is the sum of the channel's and the end-user's cost of acquiring product offered with a particular delivery time. On the premise that the end-user must pay for all channel costs (plus some profit margin for the channel members) in the end, it is desirable to seek

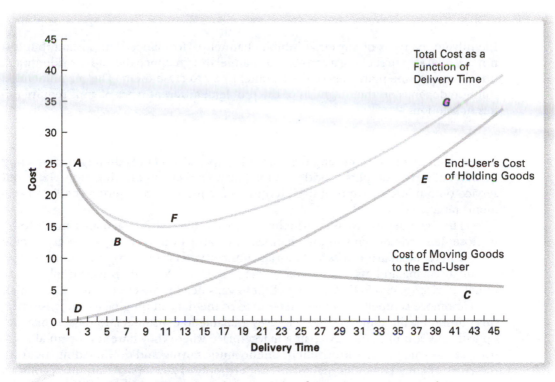

Figure 5.7   Channel costs and the principle of postponement-speculation

Source: Adapted from Louis P. Bucklin, *A Theory of Distribution Channel Structure* (Berkeley, CA: IBER Publications, University of California, 1966), pp. 22–25.

the lowest-total-cost method of inventory-holding. Thus, a cost-minimization orientation would direct the channel to seek the combination of postponement and speculation that corresponds with point F in Figure 5.7 because this minimizes total channel costs of providing a particular delivery time.

The same type of analysis could be applied to the marketing flow costs associated with providing other service outputs, for example, availability, bulk-breaking, product variety, and information provision. A more complete set of criteria would include not just total cost minimization but would also appropriately factor in the utility or benefit accrued by the end-user in receiving these service outputs. Clearly, focusing on efficiency—that is, cost minimization—inside the channel itself will not provide a channel solution that minimizes gaps for the channel, and attention to the relative value placed on postponement and speculation by both channel members and end-users helps highlight the sources of some channel gaps.

Given the multidimensional nature of our gap analysis, it is no wonder that there are persistent gaps in channel design in many selling situations. Careful identification of the type of gap present and which segment is affected prevents mistakes in gap resolution. The next section discusses more precisely the tools available to the channel manager to close the gaps that have been identified in the channel design.

CLOSING CHANNEL GAPS

Identifying the types of gaps that inhibit channel performance is important, but it is not the final step in seeking a zero-based channel design. Once the gaps are identified, it is then up to the managers of the channel to try to close them. The recommended solution depends on the diagnosis of the problem; different types of gaps require different solutions.

Closing Demand-Side Gaps

Three main methods of closing demand-side gaps exist: (1) expanding or retracting the level of service outputs provided to the target market; (2) offering multiple, tiered service output levels to appeal to different segments; and (3) altering the list of segments targeted.

The first question to ask is whether and when the channel manager needs to try to close demand-side gaps in the channel. Sidebar 5.4 on music retailing gives some insight here. Standard bricks-and-mortar music retailers suffer from an undersupply of bulk-breaking and assortment and variety (SOD > SOS) but an oversupply of customer service (SOS > SOD). Do any of these gaps need to be closed, and if so, which ones are more compelling than others? One of the determining factors in answering this question is the number of alternatives available to consumers. End-users may put up with this sort of poor service in a marketplace where they have few or no alternatives, as was true before the advent of online music buying and downloading, but with the entry of competing channel forms, undersupply of key service outputs becomes a serious threat, leading to loss of sales and market share. This highlights the fact that channel managers do not need to worry about demand-side channel gaps if they meet those service output demands as well as competition. But when the competition can provide higher levels of the desired service output, the threat is great.

Certainly, this insight is relevant when the demand-side gap is such that SOD > SOS. On the other hand, it is more difficult to see how oversupplying customer service could be a big problem. After all, is more service not always better? How could this lead to sales declines? The answer lies in the fact that providing these high levels of service is costly. Indeed, the standard wholesale and retail prices for a CD were about $12 and $19, respectively, for a CD that might have 12 or so songs on it. This pricing was driven partly by historical norms; once a particular level of margins is established in the industry, it is hard to challenge them to achieve lower retail prices for consumers. But it is also necessary to charge a retail price high enough to generate retail profits that cover the costs of running bricks-and-mortar stores. If customers do not highly value the in-store services created through bearing these costs and have an alternative channel through which they can buy more cheaply (but still get adequate levels of their key service outputs), then oversupplying customer service becomes a serious drawback.

Given that the channel manager, indeed, decides to close demand-side channel gaps, one strategy would to be increase (or decrease) service output provision, depending on whether the gap arises from a lack or an excess of service output provision. Because service outputs are produced directly through the performance of channel flows, either the intensity of flow performance will change (without changing the identity of channel members performing the flows), or there will be some change in the responsibility for flow performance. This change in responsibility can be accomplished by shifting flow responsibility within the current set of channel members or by actually changing the structure of the channel itself. This situation often occurs when a company introduces a new, complex product to the market. The natural channel choice for the new product is to sell it through a preexisting channel; but that channel may not be ideal for the new, unfamiliar product. Sidebar 5.5 describes this type of problem through the example of the Microsoft Media Center PC. While the new product is a personal computer, it also is much more than that; the challenge for Microsoft (the designer of the operating system software) and its hardware partners is to use existing retail channels for computers to sell the new concept. Existing computer retailers are good "box-movers," but are not inherently designed for a high-touch consumer contact; indeed, one high-touch retailer, Gateway, closed all of its retail stores in April 2004 because it could not be profitable with a high-service model. Microsoft and Hewlett-Packard's response to the situation was not to discard the existing channel but to take over the educational promotion flow in the retail stores through their design of "experience centers."

Second, offering a menu of service output levels from which the end-user can choose can help close demand gaps when the product is targeted at multiple segments with differing service output demands. Sidebar 5.1 on CDW documents the company's positioning as the "chief technical officer for many smaller firms," suggesting a very high level of customer service provision. But CDW also offers lower service levels to more sophisticated corporate customers that may have their own in-house systems integration experts because it recognizes that not every end-user has the same service output demands and not every end-user has the same high willingness to pay for customer service. Sometimes channel conflict (see Chapter 7) arises from customers who persist in wanting high service levels but at a lower price than paid by a customer consuming less service. Ideally, these separate channels would be completely self-contained to eliminate overlap in customer sets, but in the real world, some mixing of segments and channels is likely.

Third, channel managers may simply decide that rather than trying to change the level of service output provision, modifying or fine-tuning the actual segment targeted would be easier and more profitable. The responses of small specialty food retailers in the Chicago market to the entry and success of Trader Joe's (a primarily private-label specialty food retailer that buys in bulk and operates larger stores than the stand-alone specialty retailers against which it competes) are representative of this strategy. Trader Joe's private-labels many of the same products that are sold under the manufacturer's label at other, smaller specialty grocers in Chicago. Some of these smaller retailers welcome Trader Joe's because they believe it raises the market awareness of specialty and gourmet foods and all specialty retailers benefit thereby. Others, however, notice that their volumes have dropped since the entry of Trader Joe's into their neighborhoods, and some say that they educate consumers only to see them go to Trader Joe's for the lower prices. A spokesman from the National Association for the Specialty Foods Trade advises that when Trader Joe's comes to a specialty grocer's neighborhood, the response should be to "stress what you do well already. . . . Just keep plugging away at what they do best." Stand-alone specialty grocers respond by continuing to differentiate elements of customer service to retain their loyal customers, such as hosting gallery shows and late-night food tastings or simply emphasizing personalized service.[15]

Sidebar 5.5

Microsoft Windows Media Center PC: Supply-side gaps in new product launches

New product launches—even when rolled out through preexisting channels—pose special challenges to channel managers because channels that may produce minimal channel gaps for existing products can nevertheless be problematic for the new product. The Microsoft Windows Media Center PC is such a new product, and its launch strategy is an example of how specific, foresighted channel efforts are necessary to try to minimize these gaps.[16]

What is the Media Center PC? The fact that this is a sensible question at the time this book is being written highlights exactly the problem: End-users do not know what the new product really is, and more importantly, do not know how using it can be a great experience. Clearly, from the product name, we know it is a personal computer, and most of us are quite familiar with PCs by now. Does this therefore mean that Microsoft and its PC hardware partners like Hewlett-Packard can simply produce these machines and induce retailers like Best Buy and CompUSA to stock them (as they do the other PCs already in the market) and expect them to sell?

Far from it. The Media Center PC is a personal computer that operates on a variant of the Microsoft Windows operating platform called (naturally enough) Microsoft Windows Media Center Operating System. A Media Center PC looks like, and can act like, a high-powered regular Windows operating-system PC. But it has much more capability than that. It also has a television tuner so that it can play cable TV as well as operate as a PC. Users can watch as well as record TV programming, watch DVDs, listen to music, organize their digital music file collection, and view photos and video clips. The PC operates with a keyboard and mouse, *or* with a remote control like those

for TVs. A special device called a Media Extender can be used along with the Media Center PC to turn a single computer into a networked system of Media Center PCs throughout the house, with access by all the "spoke" computers to the "hub" Media Center PC and its audio and video file capabilities. Microsoft Xbox, the company's video game console, can be connected to a Media Center network as well. In short, the Media Center PC is a multimedia home entertainment hub and spoke system as well as a fully functional personal computer. In some ways, it is a computer. But to call it merely a computer is to miss the broad suite of benefits it can provide to the end-user, whether that end-user is a person operating a home office, a family that combines computing and entertainment in its household, or a college student in a dorm room.

The Media Center PC is thus significantly differentiated from standard PCs. It is also more expensive than a PC with similar personal-computing features. Consequently, it would not sell well through standard, big-box computer retailers. End-users would simply not understand why this machine that looks just like all the other computers is actually worth many hundreds of dollars more. In short, from a channels perspective, there is a supply-side gap in the promotional flow if this new product is sold through standard channels with a standard split of channel activities among the current channel members. Poor execution of the promotional flow leads to uninformed end-users, who get insufficient customer service (a demand-side gap), and are therefore not motivated to buy the product.

When Microsoft and its hardware partners wanted to take the Media Center PC to market, they realized that more was needed than the

Sidebar 5.5 (cont.)

Microsoft Windows Media Center PC: Supply-side gaps in new product launches

standard channel efforts. Microsoft partnered with Hewlett-Packard (HP) to design and set up 15-by-15 foot "experience centers" inside retailers like Circuit City, CompUSA, and selected specialty computer and home video stores. The experience centers are paid for by Microsoft and HP, not by the retailers. They are staffed with instructors from a third-party firm that trains them to demonstrate the benefits of the products and run lessons at half-hour intervals. The centers focus on four "experiences": Create (a photo exhibit), Perform (the home-office scenario), Connect (on setting up a home wireless network), and Play (focusing on digital music enjoyment). By focusing on how the product will be used rather than on its technical features, Microsoft and HP hope to offer a higher-quality promotional experience that excites the consumer and raises sales.

Indeed, the approach does seem to work: HP reports an increase of up to 15 percentage points in intent to purchase at retailers with the experience centers, suggesting that the correlating demand-side gap is closing. The companies view the centers as overall brand-building exercises as well. They do not have to rely on the retailer's sales force, which is often made up of short-term, high-turnover, poorly-trained employees. Given the core need to improve upon the baseline promotional flow, the experience center (run by HP and Microsoft, not by the retailers) represents the reallocation of channel flows among channel members. This is particularly important as computer retail outlets become more and more commoditized. As higher-service retailers find it harder and harder to survive in the computer market (creating environmental bounds for manufacturers of innovative software/hardware combinations), gaps like the promotional one highlighted here become more and more common, and closing them necessitates creative solutions like the experience center.

Closing Supply-Side Gaps

Channel gaps arising from high-cost channel flow performance on the supply side can also be managed through multiple means: (1) changing the roles of current channel members, (2) investing in new distribution technologies to reduce cost, or (3) bringing in new distribution function specialists to improve the functioning of the channel.

The channel manager may not find it necessary to take extremely drastic action and may, therefore, follow the first route, which involves keeping the current roster of channel members but changing their roles and channel flow responsibilities to improve cost efficiency. Simply shuffling flow responsibilities among the current channel members may not be sufficient to achieve flow cost efficiencies, however. The second avenue for action provides for the channel members to invest in new technologies that reduce the cost of flow performance. Our sidebar on Media Center PCs exhibits this solution strategy. Microsoft and Hewlett-Packard have kept the same channel members but have shifted flow responsibilities so that they bear the promotional/educational costs of the "experience centers" in major retailers like Circuit City and CompUSA in a bid to maximize the effectiveness of the promotional effort.

A third option to reduce supply-side gaps is to alter the channel structure to bring in members who specialize in state-of-the-art performance of one or more flows. This solution is the cornerstone of our sidebars about online bill payment and reverse logistics. Improving the efficiency of online bill payment inherently involves introducing new channel members who specialize in various aspects of database management, Web site design, and software integration to make the system work from bill presentment to payment and reconciliation. Similarly, in the case of managing returned merchandise, specialists like Channel Velocity make it possible for manufacturers to recover profit from seemingly worthless returns that add channel cost through their weeks spent in inventory. Even though these newly introduced channel specialists take a portion of channel profits, they increase the size of the channel profit pie sufficiently to more than pay their way.

As a final caution, it is extremely important not to fix the wrong gaps. Sidebar 5.4 on music retailing highlights the possible problems. Thinking that the reason for dropping retail sales of music was primarily high price, Vivendi Universal tried to force price cuts at both the wholesale and retail levels of the standard bricks-and-mortar channel. From a cost-focused perspective, this might have seemed sensible because the wholesale margins on CD manufacturing are very high, due to the low marginal cost of producing a CD. However, focusing on a cost-driven pricing strategy ignored the fact that the real gaps were on the demand side. Cutting price would not close gaps in bulk-breaking and assortment and variety for target music buyers. Even worse, closing a nonexistent gap did not just have a neutral effect on channel effectiveness but had a distinctly negative one because retailers rebelled against the forced retail gross margin cuts. The resulting channel conflict and ultimate need to withdraw the policy were worse than if Universal had never taken action. Channel managers can avoid these difficulties by carefully diagnosing the actual gaps (demand- versus supply-side, for which channels, and affecting which target segments) in their channels and taking actions to close only the identified gaps.

Challenging Gaps Produced by Environmental or Managerial Bounds

The preceding discussion of closing demand-side and supply-side gaps implicitly assumes that it is not only in the channel manager's power to identify these gaps but it is also in the manager's power to take the necessary actions to close the gaps. This is certainly true when the source of the gaps is managerial oversight, errors in judgment, or there is willingness to change in the face of a changing marketplace. But what if the source of gaps is a set of environmental or managerial bounds that remain after other channel improvements have been made?

Some bounds simply cannot be relaxed completely, making it impossible to achieve a true first-best channel design outcome. Our sidebar on Microsoft's Media Center PC exemplifies this situation: At least in the short to medium run, it is impossible to transform a mass merchandiser in the computer retail arena (like CompUSA or Circuit City) into a high-service, high-touch retailer. Indeed, this would be contradictory to these retailers' core positioning in the market. Nor is it immediately possible to distribute Media Center PCs through high-end computer retailers, particularly in a market where such retailers are going out of business (viz., Gateway closing its retail stores in April 2004). While it might have been optimal to entrust all retail-level educational promotion channel flows to the retailer, in this case that was not possible. The next best response for Microsoft and Hewlett-Packard is to step in and perform those flows themselves.

However, many bounds can be and routinely are challenged. CDW's consortium programs with small business partners and minority business partners effectively challenges the government's bound on purchasing from large vendors by altering channel structure to create a solution that satisfies the bounds. Our reverse logistics sidebar provides a more aggressive form of challenging of bounds: Surmounting managerial indifference to the costs of returned merchandise means breaking down this managerial bound completely. The next step after managerial recognition of the importance of the problem is to adapt the channel's mechanisms for handling returned product, but this redesign of the system (i.e., the closing of supply-side channel gaps) would not be possible without first challenging the managerial bound of ignorance.

Other suggestions for challenging bounds, particularly managerial bounds, include the following:

- ➤ "Buy-in" should be achieved across the organization. Participation and voice in the channel design process must be given to all relevant functions and levels.
- ➤ An energetic champion should be found to manage the change process. The champion must have power, credibility, political skills, and most important, tenacity.
- ➤ Who or which group in the organization is responsible for channels should be made clear as soon as possible in the process. Task forces comprised of key individuals from various interest groups help buy-in if they are involved with the process from the outset.
- ➤ The approach must be truly customer-driven because then the results are very difficult to dispute. Opposing the suggested design identifies the critic as being opposed to delivering customer satisfaction. Nevertheless, patience and persistence are required because movement toward the optimal system will not be immediate, given the tradition-bound ideas that generally surround channel decisions.
- ➤ The design must include a mechanism that permits the organization to stay in touch with the end-users of its products or services.[17]

Two major points are worth mentioning here. The first is that where you invest your marketing dollars matters. You can invest them in changing the ground rules of engagement in the market in such a way that enables you to assemble a channel structure that is closer to the zero-based model. The second is that challenging channel bounds and closing associated channel gaps costs money. Channel managers should not expect to transform the rules of engagement or the existing channel design without exerting costly effort. The ultimate gains can be well worth the initial investment, however; conversely, failing to attack channel bounds or close channel gaps can mean significant forgone revenue and market share.

PULLING IT TOGETHER: THE GAP ANALYSIS TEMPLATE

We have described what channel gaps are, where they come from, and what types of gaps exist on both the demand and supply sides. We have also suggested means of closing these gaps in various situations. Figure 5.8, the demand-side gap analysis template, is a means of explicitly identifying demand-side gaps by targeted end-user segment. Figure 5.9, the supply-side gap analysis template, builds on the information from

	SERVICE OUTPUT LEVEL DEMANDED (SOD) VERSUS SERVICE OUTPUT LEVEL SUPPLIED (SOS)					
Segment Name/ Descriptor	Bulk Breaking	Spatial Convenience	Delivery/ Waiting Time	Assortment/ Variety	Customer Service	Information Provision	Major Channel for This Segment
1.						
2.						
3.						
4.						
5.						

Notes and directions for using this template:
• Enter names and/or descriptions for each segment.
• Enter whether SOS > SOD, SOS < SOD, or SOS = SOD for each service output and each segment. Add footnotes to explain entries if necessary. If known and relevant, footnotes can record any supply-side gaps that lead to each demand-side gap.
• Record major channel used by each segment (i.e., how does this segment of buyers choose to buy?).

Figure 5.8   Demand-side gap analysis template

Channel (Targeting Which Segment[s]?)	Channel Members and Flows They Perform	Environmental/ Managerial Bounds	Supply-Side Gaps (Affecting Which Flow[s]?)	Planned Techniques for Closing Gaps	Do/Did Actions Create Other Gaps?
1.					
2.					
3.					
4.					
5.					

Notes:
- Record routes to market in the channel system. List should include all channels recorded in Figure 5-4 above. Note the segment or segments targeted through each channel.
- Summarize channel members and key flows they perform (ideally, link this to the efficiency template analysis in Chapter 3).
- Note any environmental or managerial bounds facing this channel.
- Note all supply-side gaps in this channel, by flow or flows affected.
- If known, record techniques currently in use or planned for use to close gaps (or note that no action is planned, and why).
- Analyze whether proposed/actual actions have created or will create other gaps.

Figure 5.9 Supply-side gap analysis template

To be used in conjunction with Demand-side Gap Analysis Template, Figure 5-8.

Figure 5.8 to identify supply-side gaps, the bounds that give rise to them, and proposed (or ongoing) actions to close gaps. Importantly, Figure 5.9 also allows for entries denoting whether the planned or ongoing actions also create other, unintended gaps (think about our sidebar on music retailing; there, a misguided effort to close demand-side gaps by reducing CD prices merely created other gaps on the supply side rather than solving the problem). Ideally, after a suitable period of time, the analysis should be revisited to see whether the predicted results have, in fact, been achieved—that is, the analyst should be held accountable for the suggested changes in the channel.

Figures 5.10 and 5.11 show an analysis of the CDW situation (using information from Sidebars 2.1, 3.1, and 5.1) using the gap analysis template. The information suggests that service output demands differ significantly across three key segments: small business, large business, and government buyers. Further, spatial convenience and waiting/delivery time demands need to be broken out by those for original equipment versus those for postsale service; small business buyers need high levels of these outputs for postsale service but less for original equipment purchases (because they have no in-house servicing capabilities), while the opposite relative relationship holds for large business buyers (because they do have in-house servicing personnel). Figure 5.10 also points out that all three segments buy from CDW, and thus, CDW is part of the route to market for multiple segments of buyers. However, the government buyer is constrained to use multiple channels, given the government's goal of using small business vendors for 23 percent of purchases. Finally, Figure 5.10 points out key service outputs where CDW's offerings are either too little (SOS < SOD) or too much (SOS > SOD) for the target segment. In general, demand-side gaps are due to overprovision rather than underprovision of service; this is a common phenomenon in channel systems where the channel targets multiple segments of buyers and tries to at least satisfy every segment. Because segments do differ in their demands for various service outputs, overprovision to some segments is inevitable in this situation.

Given the demand-side information in Figure 5.10, Figure 5.11 identifies environmental and managerial bounds facing CDW. These have to do with CDW's own acknowledged difficulty in prescreening sales-force recruits for longevity and with external governmental dictates about approved vendor sizes. Ensuing supply-side gaps plague CDW's promotion and negotiation flows in particular. The channel analyst is encouraged to note any direct linkages from bounds to demand-side gaps as well. Finally, in CDW's case, actions taken to close gaps do not obviously create new ones, but it is important to consider in each case whether they do or not.

When all is said and done, the final channel structure may be close to the zero-based design but not actually zero-based. That is, some environmental or managerial bounds may not have been lessened, and this constrains the final channel solution. The end product is the best that the channel manager can produce but still deviates from the first-best or zero-based channel. We can thus call it a second-best channel design, with the understanding that the first-best design is not always attainable.

Finally, we should point out that the process of gap analysis is never done. Not only do environmental bounds change over time, but end-users' demands for service outputs, as well as the available distribution technology, also change over time. This propensity for change creates a never-ending opportunity for channel design innovation to pursue the moving target of the zero-based channel for each targeted segment in the market.[18]

Segment Name/ Descriptor	Bulk Breaking	Spatial Convenience	Delivery/ Waiting Time	Assortment/ Variety	Customer Service	Information Provision	Major Channel for This Segment
SERVICE OUTPUT LEVEL DEMANDED (SOD: L/M/H) VERSUS							
SERVICE OUTPUT LEVEL SUPPLIED BY CDW (SOS)							
1. Small business buyer	H (SOS = SOD)	Original equiptment: M (SOS = SOD) Postsale service: H (SOS = SOD)	Original equiptment: M (SOS > SOD) Postsale service: H (SOS = SOD)	M (SOS > SOD)	H (SOS = SOD)	H (both presale and postsale) (SOS = SOD)	Value-added reseller like CDW, or retailer
2. Large business buyer	L (SOS > SOD)	Original equiptment: H (SOS = SOD) Postsale service: L (SOS > SOD)	Original equiptment: M (SOS > SOD) Postsale service: L (SOS > SOD)	M/H (SOS = SOD)	M (SOS > SOD)	L (SOS > SOD)	Manufacturer direct, or large reseller like CDW
3. Government/ education	L (SOS > SOD)	Original equiptment: H (SOS = SOD) Postsale service: H (SOS = SOD)	Original equiptment: M (SOS > SOD) Postsale service: M (SOS > SOD)	M/H (SOS = SOD)	H (SOS = SOD)	H (both presale and postsale) (SOS = SOD)	Manufacturer direct, or reseller; 23% from small business (VARs)

Figure 5.10   Demand-side gap analysis template: CDW example

Channel (Targeting Which Segment[s]?)	Channel Members and Flows They Perform*	Environmental/ (E) / Managerial (M) Bounds	Supply-Side Gaps (Affecting Which Flow[s]?)	Planned Techniques for Closing Gaps	Do/Did Actions Create Other Gaps?
1. CDW direct to buyer (→ small business buyer)	Manufacturer; CDW; Small Business Buyer	(M): No screening of recruits for expected longevity with firm	Promotion (sales force training/ turnover)	Better screening of new recruits	No Buying from CDW *closes* gap for customer in *Risking*
2. CDW direct to buyer (→ large business buyer, government)	Manufacturer; CDW, CDW-G; Large Business Buyer or Government Buyer	(E): Government requires 23% of purchases from small vendors (M): No screening of recruits for expected longevity with firm	*Promotion* (sales force training/ turnover) *Negotiation* (cannot close 23% of deals with government]	Better screening of new recruits; Rely on consortium channel structure (below)	No
3. CDW + small buiness VAR consortium member (→ government)	Manufacturer; CDW-G; small VAR; Consortium Partner Government Buyer	(E): Government requires 23% of purchases from small vendors; (M): VAR's small business size (M): No screening of recruits for expected longevity with firm	*Promotion* (sales force training/ turnover) *Negotiation* (only a gap for a small VAR not in the CDW alliance)	Better screening of new recruits; *Negotiation* gap above is closed through consortium with small VARs	No

*Notes: All channel members perform all flows to some extent. Key channel flows of interest are *promotion, negotiation,* and *risking.*

Figure 5.11 Supply-side gap analysis template: CDW example

To be used in conjunction with Demand-Side Gap Analysis Template, Figure 5-10.

Take-Aways

- The channel that both meets service output demands and does so at minimum cost of performing the necessary channel flows is called the zero-based channel.
- A channel system that is not zero-based has either demand-side gaps, supply-side gaps, or both.
- Channel gaps arise as a result of bounds that prevent the channel captain from optimizing the channel structure.
  - Environmental channel bounds are constraints imposed from outside the channel itself, for example, due to legal restrictions or due to a lack of adequate infrastructural capabilities in the market to support the optimal channel structure.
  - Managerial channel bounds are constraints imposed from inside the channel itself, due to a lack of knowledge on the part of channel managers about the full implications of channel actions or due to optimization at a higher level than the channel itself.
  - The channel structure can be optimized subject to these constraints, but this second-best solution will not be quite as efficient or will not satisfy target end-users' service output demands quite as well as would the unconstrained channel.
- Demand-side channel gaps can arise either because a particular service output is provided to a particular target segment of end-users at too low a level (so that service outputs demanded exceed service outputs supplied, or in shorthand, SOD > SOS) or because a particular service output is provided to a particular target segment of end-users at too high a level (so that service outputs supplied exceed service outputs demanded, or in shorthand, SOD > SOS).
  - When SOD < SOS, it is a sign that the channel is operating inefficiently because consumers are not willing to pay for the high level of service offered to them due to their low valuation of that service.
  - In general, demand-side channel gaps may not need to be closed when the competition is no better at providing the service outputs in question. However, persistent demand-side gaps provide an ideal opportunity for a channel to build overall market demand, as well as to steal market share, by investing in improved service output levels.
- Supply-side channel gaps arise when one or more channel flows are performed at too high a cost. This implies that a superior technology exists to decrease the cost of performing that flow without compromising service output provision.
  - Supply-side gaps can exist in one or more channel flows simultaneously.
  - Supply-side gaps may exist in one of a company's channels without existing in all of them.
- Supply-side channel gaps can (but do not always) give rise to demand-side channel gaps. When this happens, closing the supply-side gaps can both decrease the cost of running the channel and improve service output provision to target end-users.
- Demand-side channel gaps can be closed by:
  - Expanding or retracting the level of service outputs provided to the target market
  - Offering multiple, tiered service output levels to appeal to different segments
  - Altering the list of segments targeted

- Supply-side channel gaps can be closed by:
  - Changing the roles of current channel members
  - Investing in new distribution technologies to reduce cost
  - Bringing in new distribution function specialists to improve the functioning of the channel
- The gap analysis templates provide a tool with which to codify your knowledge of both the demand-side and the supply-side gaps facing you in your channel management tasks.

DISCUSSION QUESTIONS

1. Are managerial bounds always inappropriate? Under what conditions can a managerial bound on a channel design be justified?
2. Give an example of a purchase occasion when you chose *not* to buy a product at a particular outlet because the service output levels were not appropriate. Identify whether the demand gap was in the provision of too low a level or too high a level of service outputs. What did you do instead? Buy at another outlet with better service output provision? Do you know people who would be happy to buy from the outlet that you rejected? Why would they be happy to do so?
3. Use the concept of demand-side gaps to explain why it is frequently a bad idea to transplant a channel design from one country directly to another without any modification.
4. A manufacturer is in the habit of offering liberal payment terms to distributors: They can pay anytime within 45 days of receipt of the merchandise. The manufacturer currently has a bank line of credit to cover accounts receivable and pays an interest rate (prime + 1%) on the balance on loan from the bank. One of the manufacturer's key distributors offers to pay for shipments by immediate bank funds transfer upon receipt of merchandise if the manufacturer will reduce the price by 1%. Does this offer close a gap? If so, what sort (demand side, supply side, what flow)?
5. A retailer forms long-term supply relationships with several of its key manufacturers who supply it with product to sell in its stores. Part of the long-term agreement involves setting prices annually instead of on a transaction-by-transaction basis. Has a supply-side gap been closed here? What flow or flows have been involved in this change? Are there instances where this can increase (rather than decrease) the cost of running the channel?
6. When does a supply-side gap directly imply a demand-side gap, and when are they independent?
7. What are the disadvantages of closing channel gaps by incorporating into the channel a new channel member who is expert in performing one or more flows?

ENDNOTES

1. Adapted from Gebhardt, Gary (1992), "Achieving Maximum Marketing Efficiency," *Frank Lynn Associates, Inc. Client Communique* 4 (January), p. 3.
2. Stern, Louis W. and Frederick D. Sturdivant (1987), "Customer-Driven Distribution Systems," *Harvard Business Review* 65, no. 4 (July–August), pp. 34–41, originally discussed a process for confronting gaps in distribution systems as a part of the overall channel design process.

3. See, for example, Achrol, Ravi S., Torger Reve, and Louis W. Stern (1983), "The Environment of Marketing Channel Dyads: A Framework for Comparative Analysis," *Journal of Marketing* 47, no. 4 (Fall), pp. 55–67; Achrol, Ravi S. and Louis W. Stern (1988), "Environmental Determinants of Decision-Making Uncertainty in Marketing Channels," *Journal of Marketing Research* 25, no. 1 (February), pp. 36–50; Etgar, Michael (1977), "Channel Environment and Channel Leadership," *Journal of Marketing Research* 14, no. 1 (February), pp. 69–76; Dwyer, F. Robert and Sejo Oh (1987), "Output Sector Munificence Effects on the Internal Political Economy of Marketing Channels," *Journal of Marketing Research* 24, no. 4 (November), pp. 347–358; and Dwyer, F. Robert and M. Ann Welsh (1985), "Environmental Relationships of the Internal Political Economy of Marketing Channels," *Journal of Marketing Research* 22, no. 4 (November), pp. 397–414.

4. See Mateja, Jim (2003), "Electric GEM Sacrifices More than Fuel Tank," *Chicago Tribune*, July 17. One of this book's authors has been trying to buy and use an electric vehicle in Illinois but cannot due to these restrictions. The closest dealership that sells GEMs is almost 200 miles away in Indiana, making owning, driving, and especially postsale servicing of the vehicle a practical impossibility.

5. Achrol, Ravi S. and Louis W. Stern (1988), "Environmental Determinants of Decision-Making Uncertainty in Marketing Channels," *Journal of Marketing Research* 25, no. 1 (February), pp. 36–50, refer to the present and projected state of technology, the geographic dispersion of end-users, and the extent of turbulence and diversity in the marketplace as factors that can inhibit optimal channel design. All of these are examples of infrastructural dimensions of the market. Achrol and Stern also consider a set of competitive factors, such as industry concentration and competitors' behavior, which can be thought of as different dimensions of the infrastructure facing a firm seeking to manage its channel structure appropriately.

6. Information for this sidebar is drawn from: Campbell, Scott (2003), "CDW-G Calls on VARs," *Computer Reseller News*, November 17, p. 162; Campbell, Scott (2004), "CDW Snags Companywide Cisco Premier Status: Relationship Advances Reseller's Bid to Build Services Business," *Computer Reseller News*, April 12, p. 12; Gallagher, Kathleen (2002), "CDW Computer Remains Afloat Despite Market's Choppy Waters," *Milwaukee Journal Sentinel*, September 29, Business Section, p. 4D; Jones, Sandra (2004), "Challenges Ahead for CDW; Dell Deals Make Inroads in Already Difficult Market," *Crain's Chicago Business*, June 28, p. 4; Kaiser, Rob (2000), "Vernon Hills, Ill., Computer Products Reseller Has an Approach to Win Business," *Chicago Tribune*, August 16, online; McCafferty, Dennis (2002), "Growing Like Gangbusters: Sales at Chicago-Area CDW-Government Shot Up 63 percent from 2000 to 2001," *VAR Business*, July 8, online; Moltzen, Edward (2003), "Looking for SMB Traction, Gateway Inks Reseller Pact with CDW," *Computer Reseller News*, May 26, p. 55; O'Heir, Jeff (2003), "CDW Teams with Small VARs to Access Government Biz," *Computer Reseller News*, August 25, p. 6; O'Heir, Jeff (2003), "Time to Move On," *Computer Reseller News*, October 20, p. 98; Rose, Barbara and Mike Highlett (2005), "Balancing Success with High Stress," *Chicago Tribune*, June 5, online; Schmeltzer, John (2003), "CDW Pulls Out the Stops to Reach Small Business," *Chicago Tribune*, September 8, online; and Zarley, Craig and Jeff O'Heir (2003), "Seeking Solutions: CDW, Gateway and Dell Come Calling on Solution Providers for Services Expertise," *Computer Reseller News*, September 1, p. 16.

7. Trachtenberg, Jeffrey A. (2005), "Quest for Best Seller Creates a Pileup of Returned Books," *Wall Street Journal*, June 3, p. A1.

8. See the references for Sidebar 2.2 for more detail on online invoicing and payment systems, and particularly *Information Week* (2001), "Online Invoicing Ready for Business-to-Business Users," *InformationWeek*, November 12, p. 80;

Rosen, Cheryl (2001), "Seamless B-to-B Online Payment Systems Readied," *Information Week*, September 10, p. 54; Hoffman, Karen Epper (2002), "Electronic Bill Payment Comes of Age," *Community Banker* 11, no. 7 (July), pp. 16–21; Rombel, Adam (2002), "Electronic Billing Catches On," *Global Finance* 16, no. 3 (March), 49–50; Rombel, Adam (2002), "Businesses Tell Their Suppliers: Present Your Invoices Online," *Global Finance* 16, no. 8 (July/August), pp. 22–24; Varon, Elana (2002), "To Bill or Not to Bill (Online): Digital Invoicing Is the Next Big Step in E-Business Transactions," *CIO* 16, no. 3 (October 1), p. 1; Webster, John (2002), "Moving Beyond Just Paying the Bills," *Computerworld*, October 14, p. 40; Bernstel, Janet B. (2003), "Bill Pay: Where's the Payoff?" *ABA Bank Marketing* 35, no. 6 (July–August), pp. 12–17; Gonsalves, Antone (2003), "E-Bill Paying a Hit With Consumers," *Insurance and Technology* 28, no. 5 (May), p. 43; Scheier, Robert L. (2003), "The Price of E-Payment," *Computerworld*, May 26, pp. 25–26; Park, Andrew, Ben Elgin, and Timothy J. Mullaney (2004), "Checks Check Out: With Online Bill Payment and Processing, Use of Paper Checks Is Headed for a Steep Decline," *Business Week*, May 10, p. 83.

9. Background references for this sidebar include Andel, Tom (2004), "How to Advance in the Reverse Channel," *Material Handling Management* 59, no. 2 (February), pp. 24–30; Coia, Anthony (2003), "Channeling E-Tail Resources," *Apparel Magazine*, August, pp. 18–20; Cottrill, Ken (2003), "Dumping Debate," *TrafficWORLD*, March; Cottrill, Ken (2003), "Remedying Returns," *Commonwealth Business Media Joint Logistics Special Report, 2003*, p. L-19; Enright, Tony (2003), "Post-Holiday Logistics," *TrafficWORLD*, January 6, p. 20; Gooley, Toby B. (2003), "The Who, What, and Where of Reverse Logistics," *Logistics Management*, 42, no. 2 (February), pp. 38–44; Hughes, David (2003), "Reverse Thinking in the Supply Chain," *Logistics and Transport Focus* 5, no. 7 (September), pp. 30–36; Rogers, Dale S. and Ronald S. Tibben-Lembke (1998), *Going Backwards: Reverse Logistics Trends and Practices*, Reverse Logistics Executive Council, University of Nevada, Reno: Center for Logistics Management; Spencer, Jane (2002), "The Point of No Return: Stores from Gap to Target Tighten Refund Rules; a 15% 'Restocking Fee,'" *Wall Street Journal*, May 14, p. D1; Tibben-Lembke, Ronald S. and Dale S. Rogers (2002), "Differences Between Forward and Reverse Logistics in a Retail Environment," *Supply Chain Management* 7, no. 5, pp. 271–282; Trachtenberg, Jeffrey A. (2005), "Quest for Best Seller Creates a Pileup of Returned Books," *Wall Street Journal*, June 3, p. A1; and Zieger, Anne (2003), "Reverse Logistics: The New Priority?" *Frontline Solutions* 4, no. 11 (November), pp. 20–24.

10. Note that for this to be a strictly managerial bound, it must be that the small company's management could under some circumstances become larger. If some external reason prevents becoming large, one might instead categorize small size as an environmental bound (in relation to larger competitors' superior negotiation and promotional capabilities).

11. This sidebar is based on information from Desjardins, Doug (2004), "Music Industry Welcomes Back the Sweet Sound of Sales," *DSN Retailing Today* 43, no. 16 (August 16), pp. 11–12; Keegan, Paul (2004), "Is the Music Store Over?" *Business 2.0*, March, online; Smith, Ethan (2003a), "Universal Slashes Its CD Prices in Bid to Revive Music Industry," *Wall Street Journal*, September 4, p. B1; Smith, Ethan (2003b), "Universal's CD Price Slashes Will Squeeze Music Retailers," *Wall Street Journal*, September 18, p. B1; Smith, Ethan (2004), "Harsh Feedback: Why a Grand Plan to Cut CD Prices Went Off the Track," *Wall Street Journal*, June 4, p. A1; and "Upbeat: The Music Industry," *The Economist*, November 1, p. 76.

12. Louis P. Bucklin calls this phenomenon "functional substitutability." In Bucklin, Louis P. (1996), *A Theory of Distribution Channel Structure*, University of California, Berkeley, IBER Special Publications, pp. 14–15.

13. Bucklin, Louis P. (1966), calls the zero-based channel the "normative channel."

14. Bucklin, Louis P. (1967), "Postponement, Speculation, and the Structure of Distribution Channels," in Bruce E. Mallen, ed., *The Marketing Channel: A Conceptual Viewpoint* (New York: John Wiley & Sons, Inc.), pp. 67–74.

15. Jersild, Sarah (2004), "Small Specialty Stores Face Fresh Battle," *Chicago Tribune*, February 23, online at www.chicagotribune.com/ business/ chi-0402230116feb23,1,1513888.story? coll-chi-business-hed (accessed August 2005).

16. See Guth, Robert A., Nick Wingfield, and David Bank (2004), "As Microsoft Eyes Their Turf, Electronics Giants Play Defense," *Wall Street Journal*, February 23, p. A1; Mossberg, Walter S. (2004), "The Mossberg Report: Computer? TV? Stereo?" *SmartMoney Magazine*, February, p. 60; Saranow, Jennifer (2004), "Show, Don't Tell," *Wall Street Journal*, March 22, p. R9; and *Wall Street Journal*, "Gateway to Close Stores, Eliminate 2,500 Positions," *Wall Street Journal Online News Roundup*, April 1, 2004, and www.microsoft.com/ windowsxp/mediacenter/default.mspx (accessed August 2005) for background information on Microsoft's Windows Media Center operating system and competing systems.

17. See Stern, Louis W., Frederick D. Sturdivant, and Gary A Getz (1993), "Accomplishing Marketing Channel Change: Paths and Pitfalls," *European Management Journal* 11, no. 1 (March), pp. 1–8.

18. Lele, Milind (1986), "Matching Your Channels to Your Product's Life Cycle," *Business Marketing* 71, no. 12 (December), pp. 61–69, discusses at an aggregate level how the optimal channel form might change as a product moves from introduction through maturity to decline in its life cycle. While these insights are useful in the aggregate, each segment and each market's bounds and gaps may vary at different paces over time, with the need to respond individually to these different changes.

Channel Power: Getting It, Using It, Keeping It

Learning objectives

After reading this chapter, you should be able to do the following:

- View power as a tool without value connotations and explain why it is critical to marketing channels
- Explain the consequences of using power to appropriate the rewards earned by other channel members
- Understand the relation between power and dependence and explain when dependence exists
- Distinguish five sources of power and explain when each is effective and why
- Describe how to build power
- Explain how to use power as a tool to manage conflict and increase cooperation
- Understand the importance of the balance of dependence and whether the weaker party should exit the relationship or take countermeasures
- Distinguish six strategies for converting power into influence and project a channel member's reaction to each influence strategy
- Describe how the framing of an influence attempt drives the target's reaction

THE NATURE OF POWER

A good way to start an argument is to ask a roomful of people to define power. Several people will offer definitions with confidence, only to discover their ideas generate controversy. Other people will concede they are not sure how to define power but will insist that a definition is not really necessary because they can recognize power in any case ("I know it when I see it"). Experience shows, however, that many of us possess a false confidence: We really do not know how to recognize power, although we are quite sure we do. We see power when it does not exist. Conversely, we overlook power when it does exist. And we know that power has far-reaching consequences, whether or not we can define it neatly. It is not surprising that power is a subject of endless fascination, and rightly so.

In marketing channels, getting power, using it correctly, and keeping power are subjects of paramount importance. Considerations of power permeate virtually every element of marketing channels. This is because marketing channels are systems made up of players who depend on each other. Interdependence must be managed, and power is the way to manage it. The organizations who are players in a marketing channel must acquire power and use it wisely, first for the channel to work together to generate value ("grow the pie"), and second for each player to claim its fair share of that value ("divide the pie").

How the players gain and use their power today drives whether they can keep their power tomorrow. There are many sources and uses of power: They are *not* equivalent. Some ways of getting and using power are efficacious in the short term but disastrous in the long term. Other means have limited effectiveness in the short run but slowly gain in their effectiveness over time. Therefore, it behooves each member of a channel to understand where the power lies and to be able to weigh the best way to use it—and to react to the power of other channel members.

This chapter begins by considering the fundamental questions: What is the nature of power; is it good or bad; and why is it so important in marketing channels? We then turn to how to index power in a channel relationship. We cover two ways to estimate how much power is in a relationship. One way is to inventory five types of power. The other is to estimate how dependent each organization is on the other. We discuss how to deal with imbalances in power and explain the consequences of using one kind of power rather than another. Finally, we consider how to convert power (which is a latent ability) into day-to-day operating influence.

Over the last three decades, substantial resources have gone into studying the dynamics of power in actual distribution channels. This chapter focuses on presenting the major conclusions of this enormous body of research and examining their implications for the practicing manager. The generalizations presented here are field tested.

Power Defined

Power is the ability of one channel member (A) to get another channel member (B) to do something it otherwise would not have done. Simply put, power is a potential for influence.

Power is rather difficult to diagnose because false positives are common. That is, power seems to exist when one firm (the target of influence) follows the path that another firm (the influencer) desires. This is cooperation—but it is not power if the target would have followed the same path anyway, regardless of the other firm.

For example, the head of a large IT (information technology) distributor describes how one manufacturer behaves:

> It treats me like a slave . . . throws my business plan in a bin. It simply
> slices up its European target, divides it into countries and then allocates

an arbitrary figure to me. If I don't hit my target, they get on the phone and ask: "Why don't you buy more?" This company is not interested in my ideas. Anything we suggest is ignored or we are told to put it into next year's business plan.[1]

Ironically, such a manufacturer may believe it has more power than it really does. For example, suppose the supplier would like to see the distributor cut its prices on the manufacturer's brands. Next month, the distributor lowers those prices. Was the manufacturer's power at work? Perhaps not. The power could lie elsewhere: Customers could have provoked the price cut or the distributor's competitors or even the manufacturer's competitors. These are outside forces; perhaps the initiative came instead from inside the distributor organization. The distributor may be moving to a strategy of higher volume at lower margins, for example, or may be clearing out old inventory. What looks like an exercise of power by the manufacturer over the distributor may, in fact, be an act of free will, or a response to the power of the environment or of other players. Influence means altering *what would have been* the course of events. Exercising power means exerting influence.

Seeming acts of compliance that a player actually would have done anyway are common in channels. This sort of misdiagnosis of power (false positive) is hazardous. False positives lead the supposedly powerful channel member, A, to overestimate its ability to exert influence and, therefore, to make change happen. This optimism leads A to undertake channel initiatives that are doomed to fail. It is important to understand how a channel member has power in order to tell whether it has the potential for influence.

Power is the ability to change what would have happened. Therefore, power is hypothetical, speculative, impossible to verify precisely. Any ability that is unused is easy to overlook, and no one can be sure what would have happened in the normal course of events. This means false negatives are also common in channels. Channel member B can be acting under A's influence without knowing it, indeed, while denying it. For example, B may believe it is freely pursuing its economic self-interest—without realizing how much A has framed the cost-benefit trade-offs (exercising reward power) so that B's self-interest nicely coincides with A's desires.

Is Power Good or Bad?

Power is an emotionally charged term. It is laden with negative connotations: abuse, oppression, exploitation, inequity, brutality. And properly so. Power can be used to do great damage. In channels, power can be used to force a channel member to help generate value but not to receive compensation for it. Used in this way, power is (and should be) condemned.

But this critical view of power is one-sided. Because power is the potential for influence, its judicious use to drive a channel to operate in a coordinated way can achieve great benefits. For example, Hewlett-Packard is a pioneer in using the principle of postponement to achieve mass customization at low prices.[2] H-P designs printers to consist of standardized independent modules that can be combined and assembled easily to make many variations of the core product. At one time H-P made complete printers in a factory and then shipped them to the channel. Because customers demanded many versions of each printer, this policy resulted in high inventories of what turned out to be the wrong products.

In response, H-P used its considerable power to push light manufacturing and assembly out of the factory and down into the channel, a move that generated conflict. But the result is lower inventories and fewer stockouts, an ideal combination that is difficult to achieve (Chapter 14). The end-customer gains by having greater choice, even while paying a lower price. The downstream channel member gains by being able to offer its customers greater choice while holding lower inventory. H-P gains by expanding the market and taking a greater share, all the while building brand equity for the future. And H-P, desirous of preserving its sterling reputation for fair play, does not attempt to appropriate the downstream channel members' share of the wealth the channel has generated.

It is tempting to believe that H-P could have achieved this win-win result without wielding power, without pressuring its reluctant channel members. Indeed, H-P is also an exemplar of building strategic alliances with distributors (Chapter 8): Why, then, did it need to exercise power? Had the channel members seen how well it would work to assume some of the factory's functions, they surely would have adopted postponement of manufacturing of their own free will. But this clarity, this certainty, only exists with the benefit of hindsight. Mass customization via postponement of stages of assembly was a radical idea and even now is not widely used in most industries. Embracing the idea at that time would have required an act of faith. Absent faith, it actually required H-P's usage of power.

To be able to wield power is not always beneficial. An example is the newspaper industry in Northern Europe in the 1990s. Every newspaper had to choose whether to add an Internet channel to its existing routes to market, which, of course, objected to the competition. A number of newspapers were powerful enough to force their existing channels to accept competing with the Internet. For some firms, adding an Internet channel worked well, particularly if they differentiated the newspaper's Web content and waited to be an early follower (letting the pioneer make costly mistakes). But some 30 percent of newspapers lost market value (suffered lower stock prices) because they already had many routes to market and simply cannibalized their own sales. Their ability to oblige existing channels to accept the Web actually worked against the newspapers' interests.[3]

So is power good or bad? Like a hammer, power is a tool. A tool is neutral. We can judge how someone uses the tool, but then we are deciding whether the usage is good or bad. Power is merely an implement. It is value neutral. Throughout this book, power is treated as a term with no connotations, either positive or negative.

Why Marketing Channels Require Power

Marketing channel members must work with each other to serve end-users. But this interdependence does not mean that what is good for one is good for all. Each channel member is seeking its own profit. Maximizing the system's profits is not the same as maximizing each member's profits. All else being constant, each member of the system is better off to the extent that it can avoid costs (or push them onto someone else) while garnering revenues (perhaps by taking them from someone else). Further, one party's cost may generate disproportionate benefit to another party.

For example, consider the scenario of a manufacturer that would like to set a high price at wholesale to gain more revenue from its one and only (exclusive) retailer. The retailer, to preserve its margin, then will set a higher retail price (exclusivity will permit the retailer to uphold this price). As a result, retail demand will be lower than the level that would maximize the total channel's profits. (This is called the problem of double marginalization, as it involves an inefficiency resulting from the taking of two margins rather than one in the channel.) If the manufacturer were vertically integrated forward (or the retailer were vertically integrated backward), this single organization generating one income statement would set a lower retail price, following a strategy of lower overall margins but higher volumes.[4] Both the channel (higher profits) and the final customer (lower prices) would be better off. But because the retailer has one income statement and the manufacturer has another, retail prices will stay higher and unit sales will stay lower.

There is usually a better way to operate a marketing channel, a way that increases overall system profits, but the organizations comprising the channel are unwilling to adopt this approach. What is best for the system is not necessarily best for each member of it, and organizations are fearful—with good reason—that their sacrifices will be to someone else's gain.

Left alone, most channel members will not fully cooperate to achieve some system-level goal. Enter power as a way for one player to convince another player to change what it is inclined to do. This change can be for the good of the system or for the good of a single member. The tools of power can be used to create value or to destroy it, to appropriate value or to redistribute it. What to use power for is up to the decision maker. But whether the intent is malevolent or benevolent, channel members must be engaged in the exercise of building, using, and keeping power at all times. They must employ power both to defend themselves and to promote better ways for the channel to generate value.

Let us examine how this is done. We will begin with an elegantly simple conceptualization: Power is really the mirror image of dependence. Unfortunately, it turns out that this approach can be difficult to put into practice (diagnosing how much power each channel member has). To remedy this problem, we turn to the idea that there are five sources of power and firms can invest in creating each of the five.

POWER AS THE MIRROR IMAGE OF DEPENDENCE

How can we index the amount of power a channel member has? We need a concrete way of observing the potential for influence.

One way of conceptualizing power, drawn from sociology, is strikingly simple: A's power over B increases with B's dependence on A.[5] If dependent on party A, party B is more likely to change its normal behavior to fit A's desires. Party B's dependence gives party A the potential for influence.

Specifying Dependence

What determines dependence? B depends more heavily on A:

1. The greater the *utility* (value, benefits, satisfaction) B gets from A *and*
2. The fewer *alternative* sources of that utility B can find

Dependence is the utility provided, multiplied by scarcity of alternatives. Both elements are essential for dependence to occur. If B does not derive much value from what A provides (low benefits, or low utility), then whether there are alternative providers is irrelevant: B's dependence is low. Conversely, if A provides great value but

B can readily find other sources to provide just as much value, then it is irrelevant that A benefits B: dependence is still low. Either low utility or low scarcity of alternatives (that is, many alternatives) is like multiplying by zero: the product (dependence) is always zero.

Thinking of my power as your dependence is useful because it focuses the analyst on scarcity, which is the question of how readily B can replace A. This point is easy to overlook. Channel members often consider themselves powerful because they deliver value to their counterparts. But their counterparts do not need them if they are easy to replace, and this reduces their power.

It is easy to overestimate one's own scarcity. Sidebar 6.1 describes how a well-established capital equipment company fell into this trap.

A common channel scenario is that a manufacturer tries to change a downstream channel member's behavior only to be surprised to see the downstream organization refocus on competing brands. Also common is the scenario wherein a reseller thinks a manufacturer is dependent because end customers are loyal to the reseller. Manufacturers sometimes do change resellers without share loss, demonstrating their brands have equity that allows them to keep end customers. Both of these scenarios occur when a party generates benefits but underestimates how easily it can be replaced and, therefore, overestimates its power.

Measuring Dependence Directly

How can you form a reasonable estimate of how much a channel member depends on you? A direct method is to assess both elements (utility and scarcity) separately and then combine them.

To assess utility, you could tally the benefits you offer. To do this, it is important to understand the channel partner's goals, to understand how their organization values what you provide. You might estimate the utility you provide by inventorying the five bases of power to be discussed later. Or you might estimate roughly the profits you generate, directly and indirectly, as a summary indicator of the benefits you offer. Because you want to assess the worth they attach to what you provide, focus on what is important to them (it may be volume, rather than profits, for example).

To assess how easily you could be replaced, consider two factors. First, who could be (or become) your competitors? What other organizations exist (or might enter the market) that could supply what you provide, or an acceptable equivalent? If there are none, you can stop here.

But if there are alternatives, a second question arises: how easily can the channel member switch from your organization to one of these competitors? If switching is easy, your power is nil (in which case, it does not matter if you incorrectly estimated the utility you offer). But switching from your organization may be impractical or prohibitively expensive. In this case, you are scarce (even though alternatives to you do exist on paper). If you provide benefits, the other side needs you, and this makes you powerful.

Consider a manufacturer, P, of specialty steel, supplying distributors X and Y. How much power does P have over each of its distributors? For both X and Y, the manufacturer's brand opens the customer's door for the distributor's salespeople, who then sell other products in their portfolio. Benefits, therefore, are substantial. But manufacturer P has three competitors making equivalent products, so P appears to be easily replaceable. Therefore, Y does not depend on P, and P has little power over Y.

Sidebar 6.1

CNH group: Easier to replace than the manufacturer thinks it is

CNH Group is the holder of two venerable brands of farm and construction equipment, Case and New Holland. Management watched its market share erode by 30 percent in a key market, compact tractors, sold by 1,200 dealers to owners of homes and large properties. The share loss was puzzling. Due to heavy spending on engineering, the products offered high performance and reliability. Prices were competitive. Marketing was top flight: a superb Web site, heavy marketing communications, a customer relationship management (CRM) system to track leads and end-users. End-customer research showed nothing amiss. What was wrong?

CNH finally realized that the one element they had not studied was their channel. "Our traditional approach to the market didn't pay much attention to dealers. We just shipped product out and said, 'Mr. Dealer, just sell it,'" recounts the head of forecasting and global research. Elaborate market research on the channel members' perceptions of CNH and competition uncovered the problem. End-users care about their dealer relationships—and competitors were doing a much better job of meeting the dealers' needs. In spite of its considerable brand equity, the New Holland tractor was easy to replace. Dealers typically carry multiple brands and simply demoted New Holland to a far corner of their showroom. Chapter 8, "Strategic Alliances," describes how John Deere treats dealers as partners. A newer entrant, Kubota Tractor, also excelled at negotiating with and partnering with its dealers on both price and nonprice dimensions. In particular, Kubota was far ahead of New Holland in convincing dealers that the manufacturer treated them like valued partners and appreciated their business. In contrast, CNH received very low marks, summarized by the head of research like this:

If there was anything that could tick a dealer off, it seems as though we were doing it, and it was showing up in these scores. We had no idea we were doing so much damage to ourselves until we did this research.

Galvanized by this discovery, CNH is investing in making itself harder to replace by offering dealers a benefit that is hard to match. This benefit is sophisticated market research done by CNH for its dealers, to show them how they compare to other dealers in their markets and how they can best attack their competition. This investment in expert power is a way for CNH to reform itself to become a more responsive and helpful business partner.[6]

The situation is different for X, a small distributor, struggling to establish itself in its marketplace. The other three manufacturers will not supply X on the same terms as will P. So X has no real alternative to P (the other three manufacturers do not give the same benefits): X is, therefore, dependent on P.

Manufacturer P would also have power if X or Y had made investments in P that would be difficult to transfer to another manufacturer. This could include adopting P's proprietary ordering software, taking training in the unique features of P's products, joint advertising with P, and forging close relationships with P's personnel. Even though there are three other suppliers, a distributor would be reluctant to sacrifice these investments by switching suppliers (covered in depth in Chapter 8). The high costs of switching make P a de facto monopolist because the distributor has no ready alternative to P. Thus, the dependence of the distributor (in the face of apparent competition in supply) confers power on manufacturer P.

You now have assessed separately the benefits you provide and the difficulty a channel member would have in replacing you. You can combine these to get a sense of the channel member's dependence upon you. The conclusion is often sobering. Many parties come to realize through this exercise that they are replaceable in spite of the value of their offerings.

Measuring Dependence via Proxy Indicators

Several other ways, more direct and more simple, are often used to approximate dependence. The idea is to develop a rough proxy indicator in lieu of a thorough and detailed (i.e., slow and costly) assessment of utility and scarcity. Although each proxy indicator has its drawbacks, these methods are easier to implement and frequently offer a reasonable approximation.

One quick method of approximating the other party's dependence is to estimate what percentage of their sales or their profits you provide.[7] The assumption here is that the higher this percentage, the more important you are, and therefore, the more dependent they are. The premise of this approach is that to be important you must be providing benefits and switching costs are likely to exist whenever those benefits are a large fraction of business. Therefore, importance is thought to be a proxy for dependence. This argument has considerable merit. However, the sales-and-profit method is an approximation. It does not capture all the benefits you provide, nor does it directly assess your scarcity. For some situations, the method works poorly. For example, most franchisees derive 100 percent of their sales and profits from the franchisor, although some franchisees are more dependent than others.[8]

Another method of approximating the other party's dependence is to ask how well you perform your role in the channel compared to your competitors. The greater your superiority over them (your role performance), the fewer alternatives exist at your level of performance and, therefore, the greater their dependence on your organization.[9] This method is direct and comes closer to assessing scarcity. However, it does not address the importance of your role: Even if you perform it better than do competitors, your counterpart may not derive great utility from your organization. Further, if only one other organization performs the role as well as you do, the other party still has a meaningful alternative (and has even more alternatives if it is willing to accept some decline in role performance).

In some circumstances role performance does not index dependence well. For example, many emerging economies have sectors that are sellers' markets: Demand far outstrips supply; barriers to entry keep supply restricted; and there are many candidates to be resellers. In these sectors, every channel member is dependent on every supplier, regardless of their role performance.[10]

In spite of these potential shortcomings, role performance does appear to be a reasonable proxy for dependence in most circumstances outside of sellers' markets. Excellence in service provision confers uniqueness (scarcity), even if the product being sold is a commodity. Superb role performance creates dependence (hence, power) because excellence is scarce and valuable.

We now turn to another approach to indexing power, based on a different philosophy about how power grows. This is a bottom-up approach that takes an inventory of five ways to amass the potential to change a channel member's behavior. We will change the terminology to firms A and B, and focus on the firm (A) that wants to make change happen (the influencer) and the firm (B) whose behavior it wants to alter (the target).

THE GREATEST SOURCE: REWARD POWER

Power (the potential for influence) is an ability, and abilities are not easy to assess. An enormous body of research attempts to catalog all the facets, all the manifestations, of power and to ascertain who has power and what happens when they use it. Here, we will highlight how power is gathered, used, and maintained in marketing channels.

How do you take inventory of the extent of an organization's ability to change the behavior of another organization?[11] Numerous methods are available, and a considerable debate rages as to which is best.[12] Quite a number of methods work fairly well.[12] One way of thinking about indexing power has proven particularly fruitful in marketing channels. The French and Raven approach, borrowed from psychology, holds that the best way to index power is to count up to it from five power sources: rewards, coercion, expertise, reference, and legitimacy.[13] Each of these is reasonably observable (and some can be subdivided). So even though power is hidden, it can be approximated by compiling estimates of its sources. The most important of these is the ability to bestow rewards.

A reward is a benefit (or return) given in recompense to a channel member for altering its behavior. Distribution channels, of course, put great emphasis on the financial aspect of rewards. Financial returns need not always be immediate, nor precisely estimable, but the expectation of eventual payoffs, even indirectly, does pervade channel negotiations. Reward power is based on B's belief that A can grant rewards to B. The effective use of reward power rests on A's possession of some resource that B values and believes he or she can obtain by conforming to A's request.

Of course, the ability to grant rewards is not enough: B must also *perceive* that A *will* grant rewards. This means convincing B that (1) what A desires really will create benefits, and (2) B will get a fair share of those benefits.

The number of ways that exist to create reward power for channel members is bewildering. Sidebar 6.2 gives a comprehensive inventory and points out that rewards influence a channel member's behavior in many ways.

A very simple and fundamental message for producers is easily lost in the welter of reward initiatives: It all starts with the viability of the producer's own value proposition to the end-user. If the producer is seriously deficient on basic elements, no amount of rewards offered to the channel will compensate. Specifically, the producer must pass five thresholds:[14]

- ➤ A product/service that offers a quality level that meets the need of a segment of end-users
- ➤ At a price the end-user will consider paying
- ➤ That is saleable enough that the terms of trade offered to the channel member allow it to earn minimum acceptable financial returns given the price the end-user will pay
- ➤ Backed by a minimally acceptable producer reputation
- ➤ And delivered reliably, meaning the producer will honor the delays it has negotiated with channel members or their customers

Sidebar 6.2

Reward power in the IT industry

In high technology industries, the pace of competition is typically brutal. Producers habitually go to market through many resellers—and many different types of resellers. The result: Channel relationships typically exhibit very little loyalty, low levels of producer-reseller cooperation, high conflict, and poor communications. To heighten the tension, producers frequently have their own vertically integrated channels that compete with their independent resellers. To round out a highly competitive picture, customers are often saturated by excessive levels of marketing communication and fast product change. Further, suppliers tend to be less and less differentiated.

To cope, producers create standard packages of incentives and offer them to some categories of their resellers. What kinds of packaged channel programs do suppliers use in an effort to influence their channel members?[15]

High technology industries have been creative in inventing literally dozens of packaged programs to appeal to at least some categories of resellers. These channel programs fall into five broad categories. Examples of specific actions are given for each category.

Credible
channel policies

Credible channel policies. These are tangible, supportive operating principles that demonstrate a supplier's desire to maintain its intermediary channels rather than (as the reseller suspects) take their business in house or allow another independent party to take over.

Examples:

- Pledges are distinct actions taken by the supplier to show its support of the intermediary channel. Pledges create opportunities to reciprocate, as well as increase the supplier's reliance on the channel. Ways to pledge include:

- Relying 100 percent on indirect channels (no dual distribution)

- If using dual distribution, paying the employee channel the same, whether a customer buys from the direct channel or buys from a reseller supported by the direct channel

(continued)

Sidebar 6.2 (cont.)

Reward power in the IT industry

- Conflict resolution policies are designed to discourage the reseller from abandoning a sales effort if another authorized reseller competes. For example, channel member A might be compensated if B wins ("steals") a sale in which both parties participated.

Market development support policies

Market development support policies. These help resellers to build their business either on behalf of the producer or in general. Common examples include:

- Sales support information, such as training seminars for resellers

- Market development tools, such as trade show support
- Personal assistance of channel members, for example, joint sales calls
- Discretionary funds to channel members, to use as they see fit
- Certification programs

Supplemental contact programs

Supplemental contact programs. These programs raise the usual level of information exchanged. Examples include:

- Communication programs, for example, newsletters to resellers

- Automated information, for example, allowing channel members to track their earned rewards online
- Automated transactions, for example, online configuration and pricing

Sidebar 6.2 (cont.)

Reward power in the IT industry

High-powered
incentive programs

High-powered incentive programs. These are considered high-powered because they translate readily into money awarded for performing certain tasks. Such programs act as extensions of traditional gross or net margins. Examples include:

- Unique saleable solutions (Outside of high-tech, these would be labeled great products and services that are saleable because they offer an appealing proposition to the buyer.)
- Immediate cash incentives, such as cash bonuses for introducing new services to selected customers
- Financial programs for resellers that, in effect, serve to reduce their cost of purchase, such as discounts on small deals

End-user encouragement programs. These programs combine the producer's and the reseller's efforts to offer unique, value-enhancing solutions to end-users. As a side effect, they tend to bind resellers and suppliers to each other. Examples include:

- Reseller marketing programs in which the supplier promotes resellers to the end-user
- Comarketing (in which producers and resellers jointly pursue targets largely identified by the supplier)
- Risk reduction programs for the customer, offered through the reseller, such as trial usage programs

Many of these programs are particularly well suited to high tech industries, which tend to use information technology to track many elements of operations that would not necessarily be digitized or easily accessible in other industries.

(continued)

Sidebar 6.2 (cont.)

Reward power in the IT industry

End-user encouragement
programs

These programs help the supplier to meet four families of needs:

1. To achieve *results* that have a financial impact, directly or indirectly (that is, raise sales, lower costs, and lower the levels of investment needed to generate profit)

2. To respond to *changes* in the market environment

3. To induce channel members to *cooperate,* coordinate, and conform to the supplier's initiatives

4. To introduce *harmony* after a period of stress in the relationship

A supplier must address all four needs (results, change, cooperation, and harmony).

Some of these needs are of higher priority than others at different times. Therefore, suppliers calibrate how they use each of the five categories of incentives to address the four types of needs. In a typical cycle, after a period of conflict, suppliers resort to credible channel policies until the channel heals. Then they turn to high-powered incentives and supplemental contact to improve operating results. Focus then shifts to increasing market development support in order to increase the supplier's coordination with resellers. Then, as the market changes, suppliers may turn to end-user encouragements to help resellers adapt to new customer needs.

These five thresholds are fundamental because without them the downstream channel member has limited ability to create demand or limited reason to bother to try to do so.

In one way or another, many channel initiatives come back to create reward power. For example, efforts to boost a reseller's capabilities enable the reseller to grow its profits. Excelling in logistics in dealing with downstream channel members is another excellent way to indirectly increase their rewards for doing business with a producer—and has the added advantage of being difficult to imitate.[16] The examples in this chapter rely heavily on reward power because it is universally effective. These examples work both ways: Producers gain the ability to alter downstream behavior by increasing rewards for so doing; in turn, downstream channel members make markets and are the faces of their producers to those markets. Their ability to generate rewards for the producer—or to withhold rewards—gives them considerable leverage.

FOUR MORE SOURCES OF POWER

Although reward is the most important basis of power, it is not the only one. Four other sources are noteworthy: coercion, expertise, legitimate appeal, and reference. It is tempting to lump them in with reward power because many of them do trace back to generating rewards at some level. However, they are different and operate in different ways.

Coercive Power

Coercive power stems from B's expectation of punishment by A if B fails to conform to A's influence attempt. Coercion involves any negative sanction or punishment of which a firm is perceived to be capable. For example, in the United States, large supermarket chains extract substantial slotting allowances (fees) from branded producers in order to stock new products. While there is some economic rationale for this practice,[17] empirical evidence suggests that a considerable element of these fees is due simply to the retailer's ability to block market access to any manufacturer who refuses to pay.[18] Other examples of coercive power are reductions in margins, the withdrawal of rewards previously granted (e.g., an exclusive territorial right), and the slowing down of shipments.

Coercion is synonymous with the potential to threaten the other organization, implicitly and explicitly. The threat of being dropped from the approved vendor list is how Wal-Mart obliges many of its suppliers to adopt electronic data interchange (EDI) using Web-based systems that are not proprietary to any brand of IT or to any supplier. Similarly, Wal-Mart obliges many suppliers to absorb costs of bulk-breaking to its various stores. Sock manufacturers, for example, must mix different kinds of socks on a pallet to fit a store's requirements, rather than shipping complete pallets and thrusting the costs of recomposing the pallets onto Wal-Mart. This is not trivial: Mixing sock types on a pallet costs fifteen cents per pair—and the pair sells to Wal-Mart for $2.00.[19]

Coercive power is the reverse of reward power. Technically, it can be considered negative reward power (a reward that is withheld, that does not materialize). Why treat it as a separate category? Why not consider negative rewards as being just a step below giving a low level of rewards? The reason is because channel members do not see it this way. They do not view negative sanctions as being the absence of rewards or fewer rewards. They view coercion as an attack on themselves and their business. Coercion is synonymous with aggression and provokes self-defense. The threat and use of negative sanctions is often viewed as pathological. When channel members perceive low rewards, they react by indifference or withdrawal, but when they perceive coercion, they react by considering a counterattack. This defensive reaction means that using coercive power is usually less functional over the long run than other power bases, which usually produce more positive side effects.[20] Therefore, coercion should be employed only when all other avenues to evoke change have been traveled. Perceived aggression provokes retaliation (this theme is developed in Chapter 7 on conflict).

The user of coercive power may be surprised at the intensity of the target's reaction. This reaction may be delayed, as the target marshals its forces and composes its counterattack; nonetheless, often the target will, indeed, eventually react, which is itself an act of coercion. For example,[21] some department store chains, such as Saks Fifth Avenue and Bloomingdale's, see the opening of factory outlet stores as a manufacturer's efforts to coerce them into greater cooperation. Rather than cooperate, they have retaliated against these suppliers, both in the short run by canceling orders and in the long run by opening their own factory outlet stores, which they use to underprice their own suppliers' stores.

There are many ways to fight back. Many of them are not dramatic and may even pass unremarked. In general, when the target perceives that the influencer uses threats, the target will downgrade its estimation of the value of the influencer's business.[22] In the short term, the relationship will be damaged in three ways. First, the target will be less satisfied with the financial returns it derives from the influencer (this reaction is part perception and part reality). Second, the target will be less satisfied with the nonfinancial side of the relationship. It will view its partner as being less concerned, respectful, willing to exchange ideas, fulfilling, gratifying, and easy to work with. Third, the target will sense the relationship has become more conflictual.

Why should the influencer care about the target's disillusionment? The answer comes in the short run (target is less cooperative), in the medium run (target is less trusting), and in the long run (target feels less committed to its relationship).[23] What the influencer gains from its coercion may be lost later. There is an opportunity cost to alienating a channel member. Coercion erodes the relationship, sometimes so slowly that the influencer does not realize what it is losing.

This does not mean that channel members should never employ coercion. Sometimes the benefit is worth the cost. For example, electronic data interchange (EDI) is a way of automating the purchasing process between pairs of firms. Its potential to reduce costs has led many firms to adopt it in recent years, but that potential is more evident in hindsight than in foresight. Some evidence indicates that at least half of the early users of EDI were forced to do so by other members of the supply chain, who imposed deadlines for adoption by threatening to stop their orders.[24] If it becomes clear (and quickly) that EDI is beneficial, a channel member may forgive its partner for using coercion. Indeed, surviving the crisis that these threats provoke often strengthens channel relationships. But if the coerced channel member does not benefit or does not perceive a benefit, the relationship will be seriously damaged.[25]

Rather than focusing solely on reward and coercion, the manager should also invest in and use the remaining three power bases. Let us turn to these.

Expert Power

Expert (or expertise) power is based on the target's perception that the influencer has special knowledge, expertise that is useful and that the target does not possess itself. Cases of channel members assuming expert roles are widespread; indeed, such expertise is at the heart of the division of labor, specialization, and comparative advantage in channel function organization. Sidebar 6.3 gives an example of how a retailer pyramided its market access into expertise power that allowed the downstream channel member to bypass existing suppliers and bring new sources of supply to its market.

Sidebar 6.3

Retailers build expertise power over suppliers

A traditional way to view channels is that manu-facturers, being relatively narrow specialists, are the primary source of expertise in how their products are used. Downstream channel members, whose attention is spread over many product categories, are less well informed about end-user needs in any given product category.

The flaw in this thinking is that downstream channel members have the twin advantages of "customer touch" (closeness to the purchase process) and assortment, which gives them a superior view of the family of needs that buyers are meeting when they make a given purchase.[26] But translating that formidable advantage into action sometimes requires an extra investment. On occasion, resellers become frustrated with their suppliers' refusals to acknowledge their expertise and go so far as to create new sources of supply that reflect their own ideas of market needs.

An example is the sale of pharmaceutical drugs in Mexico. It is an empirical regularity that the poor often pay more than the well off for the same items. The reason is that poor neighborhoods are underserved by distribution, which is frequently badly developed and insufficiently competitive to offer value to poor consumers. For example, in Mumbai, India, price differentials between a shantytown and a prosperous neighborhood are substantial. In the shantytown, rice is 1.2 times more expensive; diarrhea medication is 20 times more expensive; safe water is 37 times more expensive; and credit is 53 times more expensive.[27]

Victor Gonzalez noticed these differentials in Mexico and determined to do something about them.[28] Gonzales owned a laboratory making generics, which are less expensive legal copies of branded pharmaceuticals. In 1997, although there was no legal barrier to selling generics, pharmacies chose to stock only expensive, patented foreign drugs, on which they enjoy a large margin. Thus, Gonzalez's sole customer was the Mexican government, which negotiated slender margins for generics to stock in public hospitals and clinics. This made generics available only to people covered by the public health system. That system excludes 50 million people, who, though usually very poor, were thus obliged to buy branded drugs at pharmacies. Says Gonzalez, "I realized I was in the wrong business. I had to sell my generics at the retail level and forget about the government."

In 1997, Gonzales founded Farmacias Similares, a drugstore chain that focuses on generics (mostly older drugs that are off patent). Today, the chain is highly successful, with over 2,000 stores. Next door to most of the stores is a clinic, founded and underwritten by Gonzalez and run by a nonprofit group that he set up. The clinics, which handle 800,000 visits a month, are much less expensive than private clinics. Doctors are independent (and are free to prescribe as they see fit): They keep the visit fees low.

In effect, Gonzalez has constructed an alternative health system. Farmacias Similares has created a boom in generics, raising their profile and bringing new suppliers into the market. Gonzalez's own generic laboratory now provides only one-fifth of the pharmacy chain's stock, with the rest made by local companies. Part of the pharmacy chain's expertise power rests on its knowledge of Mexico's drug market and regulations: The firm is expert at spotting gaps and convincing laboratories to create supply to fill them.

Typical is a customer who earns $4 a day: After spending $8 on the clinic visit *and* the drug for his sick child, he says, "This is the only place we can afford to buy our medicines." Says Gonzalez, "Before we appeared on the scene, poor people in Mexico used to pray to the Virgin to get better because they couldn't afford the medicines. Now they come to us."

Expertise, of course, does not exist automatically. It must be built via patient investment, as the discussion of mystery shoppers in Sidebar 6.4 illustrates.

The durability of expert power presents a problem in channel management.[29] If expert advice, once given, enables the recipient to operate without such assistance in the future, then the expertise has been transferred. The power of the original expert in the relationship is reduced considerably. A firm that wishes to retain expert power over the long run in a given channel has three options. First, it can dole out its expertise in small portions, always retaining enough vital data so that other channel members will remain dependent on it. But this would mean it would have to keep other channel members uninformed about some critical aspect of channel performance. Such a strategy can be self-defeating because it is important that all channel members work up to their capacities if the channel as a whole is to function successfully.

Second, the firm can continually invest in learning and thereby always have new and important information to offer its channel partners. This means the firm must accumulate knowledge about market trends, threats, and opportunities that other channel members would find difficult to generate on their own. The cost of this option is not trivial, but the benefits in terms of achieving channel goals are likely to be high.

A third option is to transmit only customized information. This means encouraging channel partners to invest in transaction-specific expertise because it is so specialized that they could not easily transfer it to other products or services. In other words, the specific nature of the expertise, along with the costs involved in acquiring it, would impede exit from the channel.

Some writers subdivide the expert power source, referring to expertise as the provision of good judgments (forecasts, analyses) and information as the provision of data (e.g., the news that a competitor has just dropped prices).[30] A good illustration that information is not identical to expertise comes from the supermarket industry in North America. Supermarkets receive huge amounts of consumer purchase data from their checkout scanners. To turn this information into insight, they give the data for each product category to selected suppliers (category captains), who use their knowledge of the type of product to see the patterns in millions of transactions. Supermarkets have information power over suppliers, who then invest in converting this to expertise power over supermarkets. This exercise is so important that both sides view it as an investment in building a strategic alliance.[31]

Using expert power is not as easy as it may sound, even for an organization that holds considerable knowledge that would be useful to the channel. There are three difficulties. First, to be able to exercise expert power, a channel member must be trusted. Otherwise, the expert advice is perceived as merely an attempt at manipulation and is discounted. Second, experts are usually accorded very high status; therefore, they are difficult people with whom to identify. This impedes building the necessary trust. Third, independent-minded, entrepreneurial businesspeople do not like to be told what to do. They believe that they are the experts (and they are often right). If the influencer is to employ expert power over the target, it is essential for the target to be willing to accept the influencer's information and judgments. This is easier to do if there is a good working relationship in which the target believes in the basic competence and trustworthiness of the influencer's personnel.[32] It is also easier when the target needs the influencer (dependence).[33]

Sidebar 6.4

The mystery shopper

Gathering marketplace expertise can be a challenge for any manager. In particular, it is not easy to gain expertise about the experience potential customers have at the point of sale. One method of doing so, the mystery shopper, started in the United States in the 1980s and has spread readily. Mystery shoppers, typically employees of specialty research firms, are trained to present themselves convincingly as though they are genuine customers, sample the service outputs provided, and score the point of sale on their experiences. Mystery shoppers provide data that the independent research firms compile into comprehensive reports.

Who are the clients? They can be producers wanting to know how their products fare in the hands of downstream channel members. But the clients are frequently the downstream channel members themselves. For example, retail chains regularly commission mystery shoppers to visit their own stores and report on adherence to company policy. Similarly, franchisors often use mystery shoppers to establish compliance with their business formats.

This means of gaining expertise power can be used by any firm to learn about the performance of outlet employees, outlet managers, entire stores, franchisees, even the competition. The information is customized to the company that commissions the study. Sometimes mystery shoppers enact an elaborate script, or they may simply check a list of up to 130 items per visit (how long did they wait in line, was the pizza hot, were the toilets clean). Shoppers are trained to memorize the information, then leave the premises and record it out of sight. Their employer then compiles a report.

The results are used in a number of ways. Specific stores (though seldom the employees the shopper encountered) may be complimented, sanctioned, tracked ("the report card"), or even paid (typically a bonus or a prize) according to the scores given by mystery shoppers. The reports also may feed into policy decisions. For example, Sharp paid mystery shoppers to see how electronics stores presented its liquid crystal flat screen televisions. The producer discovered that salespeople regularly advised shoppers to wait for price cuts. Sharp realized the reason for this was their own policy of frequently cutting wholesale prices. As a result, Sharp changed its pricing policy, constraining itself by announcing a policy of only two price cuts per year.

Why are mystery shoppers employees of third parties? Part of the answer is that this sort of research demands a specialized expertise in itself and, therefore, benefits from being aggregated across situations. The mystery shopper must be a good actor who fits the part and an accurate memorizer and note taker. Mystery shopper firms need a range of B2B customers. In this way, they can afford to keep on their payroll a variety of types of people who are believable in different situations—or who fit the special needs of specific roles. For example, Optic 2000, a large French eyeglasses chain, needs a large number of farsighted mystery shoppers to test, twice a year, how well the salesperson serves this segment.

Another major reason that mystery shoppers are third-party employees is that the firm provides sensitive and controversial information gained by "spying on people" and masking the true nature of the "customer." It is therefore critical that the grader be seen as neutral rather than as subordinate to the management that uses the information it provides. This is particularly true when the scenario could be seen as entrapment. For example, BMW sends mystery shoppers to test its motorcycle dealers' service bays. The motorcycles are rigged to

(continued)

Sidebar 6.4 (cont.)

The mystery shopper

have certain problems, and the service is scored on how well it finds and fixes them and on whether it charges fairly for the service. Similarly, a mystery shopper may be sent by a premium brand to visit upscale electronics stores with a script: The objective is to see if the salesperson can be induced to recommend less expensive brands. If so, the store is in violation of its partnership agreement with the brand. When confronted with this information, the store will be less combative if the mystery shopper is independent of the producer.

Legitimate Power

To be legitimate is to be seen as right and proper, as being in accordance with what is seen as normal or established standards. Legitimate power stems from the target company's sense that it is in some way *obligated* to comply with the requests of the influencer: The target thinks compliance is right and proper by normal or established standards. Thus, the influencer has legitimate power whenever the target feels a sense of duty, of being bound to carry out the influencer's request. The key feature of legitimate power is that the decision makers feel constrained morally, socially, or legally to go along with the influencer. This sense of responsibility, or duty, comes from two sources: the law (*legal legitimate power*), and norms or values (*traditional legitimate power*).

Legal legitimate power is conferred by governments, coming from the nation's law of contracts and the laws of commerce. For example, in many countries, patent and trademark laws give owners a certain amount of freedom and justification in supervising the distribution of their products. Similarly, commercial laws allow firms to maintain agreements, such as franchises and other contracts that confer legitimate power to demand behavior that is not required in conventional channel arrangements.

In principle, a major source of legitimate power is the contract channel members write with each other. In practice, contracts frequently do not carry the force one would expect them to have. In many cultures (particularly outside the Anglo-Saxon sphere of influence), contracts are difficult to enforce. Channel members often do not bother to write them (indeed, merely asking for a contract will signal distrust, which is self-perpetuating). Even in such litigious nations as the United States, channels frequently operate with sketchy, incomplete contracts—or no contract at all! Many channel members are unaware of the terms of their contracts ("the lawyer will look it up if we need it"), or pay little attention to contract clauses. Instead, they go by norms developed in the context of their relationship.[34] This is not peculiar to channels: Reliance on working understandings rather than norms is typical, even in societies with a strong tradition of legal structuring of commercial relationships.[35] This does not mean channel members do not invest in crafting thorough contracts: They often do, particularly in franchise arrangements.

A well-considered contract, however, is not necessarily all the power a channel member needs. For example, franchisees ("zees") sign contracts with franchisors ("zors") obliging the zees to maintain a certain appearance for their facilities, to honor standards and procedures set by the zors, to pay advertising fees or royalties, and to buy from sources approved by the zors. Zees regularly violate these terms, expecting the zors to tolerate their breach of contract. One might imagine that zors readily punish the offending zees. But enforcing a contract has its own costs, one of which is the zors' fear of angering other zees and provoking a backlash against their exercise of power. Therefore, even though they have the legitimate right to punish violators, zors use a cost-benefit analysis to determine whether punishing a violation is worth the costs. They frequently choose to tolerate a breach of contract.[36] Chapter 13, "Franchising," details how they decide on the trade-offs.

Legal legitimate authority exists objectively: The influencer can remind the target of its presence. In contrast, traditional legitimate authority is more ephemeral because it does not exist without the consent of the target. Traditional legitimate authority is based on values internalized by the target: The target believes that the influencer should or has a right to exert influence and that the target has an obligation to accept it.

The appearance of legitimate power is obvious inside a firm. When supervisors give directives to subordinates, the subordinates believe that the supervisors have a right to direct them in a certain manner and, therefore, will generally conform to the superiors' desires. Such legitimized power is synonymous with authority and is a major reason to vertically integrate forward or backward in a channel (see Chapter 9); however, there is no such hierarchical authority in most marketing channels.

Channel members sometimes forget this. A major source of friction between channel members is when one company is seen as trying to invoke authority, treating another as a subsidiary. This is often the case when those who interface (e.g., a district sales manager) with independent channel members (e.g., a sales agency) come from a background of dealing with employee channel members (e.g., a direct sales force). These boundary spanners often exhibit behavior patterns conditioned on the days when they really did have authority. Their normal, unconscious behavior can seem imperious and arrogant. Unintentionally, they threaten the channel member's autonomy as an independent business, creating needless resistance.

Legitimate power does exist in dealings between organizations, as in a marketing channel, but it does not stem from hierarchical authority. It stems from norms, values, and beliefs. One firm may believe that a channel member deserves to be accorded a certain deference, perhaps because of its successful track record or exemplary management. For example, the largest firm could be considered the leader (channel captain) by other channel members. If this is the case, then legitimate power is available to that firm.

Norms (expectations of normal behavior) that arise in a channel define roles and effectively confer legitimate power on certain channel members. For example, distributors in the information technology (IT) industry have a different norm than many other industries: They are far more likely to honor a supplier's request to name their customers and detail their shipments. Norms exist not only within industries but within certain channels, some of which manage to build such norms as:[37]

> *Solidarity:* Each side expects the other to focus on the relationship as a whole, rather than thinking transaction by transaction.

> *Role integrity:* Each side expects the other to perform complex roles that cover not just individual transactions but also cover a multitude of issues not related to any single transaction.

> *Mutuality:* Each side expects the other to divide their joint returns in a way that assures adequate returns to both.

These norms, once created, give one channel member the ability to exert legitimate power over the other by appealing to the norms as a reason to comply with a request.

Ultimately, the degree of traditional legitimate power is subjective. It exists in the eye of the beholder. Channel members build their legitimate power base by investing in partnership-building to increase a sense of common norms and values (see Chapter 8 on strategic alliances). Traditional legitimate power also can be built by selecting channel partners on the basis of compatibility in their attitudes, values, and operating methods. This is why some franchisors screen prospective franchisees on the basis of their attitudes toward legitimate authority. They favor candidates who express respect for the franchisor as an authority figure and for the franchise contract as a binding document. They screen out candidates who view a contract as "just a piece of paper," who take a skeptical approach to the franchisor ("try and convince me"), and who are too independent minded ("I'll do it my way, and if you don't like it, sue me"). Franchisors fear these candidates would become troublemakers if they joined the franchise system because they would not attribute legitimate authority to the franchisor.

Referent Power

Referent power exists when B views A as a standard of reference and, therefore, wishes to identify publicly with A. Between individuals, there are many personal, psychological reasons why person B would feel a oneness with person A and would wish to be associated (identified) with A. In a marketing channel, a prominent reason why one organization would want to be publicly identified with another is prestige. Downstream channel members would like to carry high-status brands to benefit their own image. Upstream channel members "rent the reputation" of prestigious downstream firms.[38]

The existence of referent power within many channels is undeniable. It is especially visible when wholesalers or retailers pride themselves on carrying certain brands (e.g., Harley-Davidson motorcycles, Ralph Lauren clothing, IBM hardware, or Intel semiconductors) and when manufacturers pride themselves on having their brands carried by certain outlets (e.g., Neiman-Marcus in the United States, Mitsukoshi in Japan, value-added resellers known for exceptional service to B2B clients). Creating and preserving referent power (the ability to confer prestige) is a major reason for manufacturers to restrict distribution coverage to selected outlets, as well as for downstream organizations to restrict representation to selected brands (Chapter 4).

A very effective strategy for a firm with proprietary know-how is to begin with patent protection (legitimate power), then use the patent lifetime to transition to other bases, especially referent power. Sidebar 6.5 illustrates this with the example of Gore-Tex.

Separating the Five Power Sources

When taking stock of the extent of power in a channel relationship, the five sources of power are a useful framework for generating ideas. It is important not to double count a power source when taking a power inventory. The separation between one source of power and another is not always clear. Many users of the five-sources framework do not even try. They rely on broader groupings. Two popular groupings are presented below.

Sidebar 6.5

Gore-Tex changes its power base

Gore-Tex is a family-owned firm built around an invention by William Gore, a former DuPont researcher who was involved in the invention of Teflon. Gore-Tex is an additive to textiles that uses a series of tiny pores to prevent wind and water from entering and a series of large pores to permit perspiration to exit. The product itself is technically complex and difficult to explain. The benefits are easy to name but somewhat difficult to present convincingly because most users find it hard to believe that the same product can keep them warm and dry without trapping sweat.

All Gore-Tex customers are manufacturers, usually of high-end outdoor clothing, who use Gore-Tex as an input to their production process. Gore-Tex does not see them as original equipment manufacturer OEM customers but rather as channels of distribution to the end-user (the clothing wearer). Hence, the producer seeks to control its channels. Initially, the producer did so by starting with the legitimate power of the Gore-Tex patent and the lack of comparable alternatives, branded or unbranded. This created dependence based on legitimate power. However, the company wisely viewed its patent period as a window of opportunity during which it could build referent power by practicing the art of making itself indispensable.[39]

Gore-Tex has built referent power by thirty years of heavy investments in marketing their trade name to outdoor-minded consumers. The result is high brand awareness in multiple countries (peaking at 70% in Sweden). This in turn creates pull, which makes closing a sale easier for retailers and producers. To reinforce the trade's perception that the Gore-Tex name translates into reward power, the firm also spends heavily on advertising to the trade. The firm further reinforces mass media with its own sales force, which works with vendor salespeople on the basis of expertise. Gore-Tex salespeople train the salespeople of its customers (clothing makers) and *their* customers (retailers) and provide kits to enable salespeople to demonstrate Gore-Tex's properties (for example, by spraying it on gloves).

These means of helping salespeople enable the firm to influence clothing makers. For example, Patagonia is a well-known name in outdoor clothing. For years, it resisted labeling its products as being made with Gore-Tex. Patagonia finally conceded because its own salespeople and its retailers' salespeople argued that it would be easier to invoke Gore-Tex than to keep explaining what Gore-Tex does.

Today, the company's legitimate power is gone because Gore-Tex has gone off patent. But the referent power built in the patented years has come to replace it. Further, the firm has been able to cut back on advertising because its name is established.

Of course, power is relationship-specific. Gore-Tex uses its power to oblige manufacturers of outdoor clothing to submit to rigid testing, to let the firm be involved in their design processes, and to bar certain choices (e.g., no Gore-Tex can be incorporated in private label merchandise). Producers accept this influence because, as a salesperson for a leading retailer puts it, "Hikers want first of all a Gore-Tex vest, and the brand comes before everything else."[40] Today, in a search for growth, Gore-Tex is moving into designer dress clothing, where its advantages are less well known and valued. As a result, the firm has discovered it cannot get the same level of cooperation from producers that it enjoys in the outdoor market. Seeking to partner with brands such as Boss, Prada, or Armani, the firm is forced to concede, "Our logo is not as decisive in the act of purchase. It is just a complement."[41]

One method is to separate out coercive power and lump all the others together as noncoercive power. This saves categorizing expert, referent, and legitimate power explicitly (they just go into the broad noncoercive inventory). Even this is a bit arbitrary: Is withholding a reward coercive or is it reward power? To circumvent the problem, this approach treats as coercion the removal of something a channel member already has. Everything else is noncoercive (no further distinction). For example, a sales agent has coercive power over a supplier if it can credibly threaten to reduce coverage or to drop some of the line. A credible offer to increase coverage or take on more of the line would be classed as noncoercive power. Similarly, an auto supplier's power base is coercive if it could slow down auto deliveries and noncoercive if it could speed them up. A variation on coercion that has been practiced is to slow the delivery of popular cars and speed the delivery of cars that turn slowly. This is coercive because it worsens the dealer's situation (more stockouts and more inventory).

Another way to minimize distinctions is to consider only mediated and unmediated power (no further categorization). Power is mediated (by the influencer) when it can be demonstrated to the target: The influencer can oblige the target to acknowledge these power bases. They are reward, coercion, and legal legitimate power bases. Unmediated (by the influencer) bases are those that would not exist without the perception of the target: These are expert, referent, and traditional legitimate power.

It is much easier for the influencer to create and wield mediated power. Unmediated power is more subtle and builds more slowly, through a process that is not easy to decipher. Because unmediated power rests on the target's implicit consent, the management of the influencer cannot simply put a program in place to guarantee an increase in unmediated power. This means that unmediated power, once acquired, is very difficult for a competitor to duplicate because even the influencer is not entirely sure how it acquired its unmediated power. Uncertain imitability is a feature of unmediated power—which makes it a potent competitive advantage.[42] Channel members that have expert, referent, and legitimate power (however they acquired it) should consider carefully before endangering this strategic intangible asset. This is the sort of asset that cannot enter a balance sheet yet is so valuable that it motivates mergers and acquisitions in marketing channels.

Putting It Together: What Is Power and How Do You Index It?

We have come full circle in our discussion of power. Power is not merely a descriptive concept summarizing the current power positions of the channel players. Power is also a choice of the firm, a strategic decision made over the medium to long term by investments (or lack thereof) in the power sources described above. Figure 6.1 shows how the nature and sources of channel power are related. Reading right to left, this figure shows that thinking of power as dependence harks back to asking how much utility one party gets from the other and how easy it would be to find this utility elsewhere. In turn, how much one party offers to another can be framed in terms of the five power bases (reward, coercion, legitimacy, expertise, and reference). The more a channel member invests over time to be able to provide these five sources, the greater its utility. Of course, its competitors' power bases determine just how scarce that utility is—as long as a channel member really has access to those competitors.

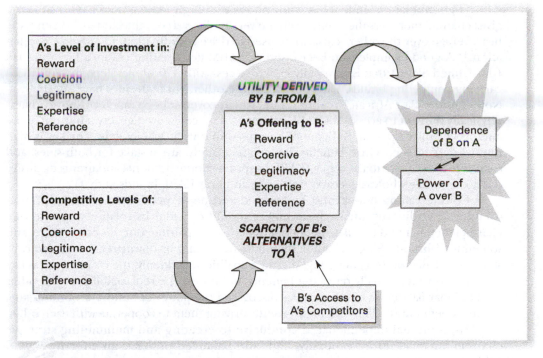

Figure 6.1   The nature and sources of channel power

THE BALANCE OF POWER

You may have noticed that this discussion so far is partial and one-sided. It is time to point out that power is not a property of an organization: It is a property of the relationship. In stating a power relationship, it is misleading to say, "A is powerful." A is powerful in relation to B but may be weak in relation to some other party. Also, in the A and B relationship, A has some sources of power of its own, but so does B. B has countervailing power, its own power bases, which it can use to offset the power sources of A. When taking an inventory of A's reward power, it is important to (a) focus on only *one relationship at a time,* rather than making general statements about power and (b) count up not only A's ability to reward B but B's countervailing power, its ability to bestow rewards upon A. Channel outcomes rest on the balance of power in a given relationship.

Net Dependence

Thus far, we have focused on A's power over B, conceptualizing it as B's dependence on A. Of course, dependence is never entirely one way. Just as B depends on A to provide utility, A depends on B for utility of a different type. A and B are interdependent. A's dependence on B creates countervailing power for B to use against A. This blunts A's ability to pressure B to alter its behavior. To get a complete picture of power, net dependence should be assessed in addition to each side's dependence. A complete discussion of how to balance net dependence to build strategic alliances is in Chapter 8.

High mutual dependence is synonymous with high mutual power. This situation gives channel members the ability to create very high levels of value added.[43] Each party has leverage over the other. This can be used to drive coordination, to enhance cooperation.[44] A good example is in beer brewers. SABMiller Brewing covers a large market (the United States) that is physically easy to access with 470 wholesalers, most of them carrying competing brands. Each side needs the other, but both sides have alternatives. Now consider East African Breweries, Ltd., which covers a large market (Kenya) that is physically difficult to access. Yet EABL achieves 98 percent coverage, even in rural areas, and drove Miller's parent, SAB, out of Kenya—with only 30 wholesalers. The key is high mutual dependence. Great benefits, hence great utility, are at stake for both sides, and each side is exclusive to the other (EABL keeps few house accounts and grants exclusive territories, while wholesalers carry only beer, and only EABL brands at that).

Countervailing power must be assessed and net dependence calculated. But at what level? Ordinarily, the decision maker should consider its relationship with one channel member and calculate net dependence in the pairing. But this can change, and sometimes abruptly. Single channel members (upstream or downstream) can radically shift the calculation by coming together in a coalition. Suddenly, the counterpart is facing a bloc—which usually raises the benefits and lowers the replaceability of the other side. Sidebar 6.6 details how Kmart has discovered the power of hundreds of miniscule, highly dependent resellers—by inadvertently driving them to cooperate with each other.

High mutual dependence is conducive to creating and maintaining strategic channel alliances. More generally, high and balanced power is an effective way to achieve coordination. A channel is coordinated when every channel member does what a single, vertically integrated firm would do: maximize overall channel profit. High and balanced power coordinates channels for two reasons. First, the two sides can drive each other to craft and implement creative, win-win solutions. Second, high and balanced (symmetric) dependence encourages cooperation by blocking exploitation. There is no weaker party in the relationship: both are giants. Each can force the other to share gains equitably. This fosters norms of fairness and solidarity, which makes coordination easier to achieve. Symmetric dependence promotes bilateral functioning by increasing each side's willingness to adapt in dealing with the other.[45]

Symmetry in dependence means that each side has countervailing power, which it can use for self-protection. Of course, symmetry also occurs when mutual dependence is low: Neither side has much need of the other. This low-low combination is very common in marketing channels. Mutually low dependence is, indeed, so common that it is the baseline for channel management. Channels with low-low dependence (each side is dispensable) tend to operate closely along the lines of classic economic relationships.[46]

Imbalanced Dependence: Is Exploitation Inevitable?

What happens when one channel member is much more dependent than the other? The balance of power favors the less dependent member. The more dependent member is open to exploitation.[47] All too often, that potential is realized. The more dependent party suffers in economic terms as well as in terms of noneconomic benefits.[48] This occurs even when the more powerful (less dependent) channel member is not attempting to appropriate the rewards due to the weaker (more dependent) member. This is because the weaker member suffers when the fortunes of the stronger member decline.

Sidebar 6.6

Kmart galvanizes micro outlets to offer macro resistance

Sears Roebuck & Co. is one of the oldest and most trusted names in U.S. retailing. In the nineteenth century, the firm was a catalog seller that revolutionized retailing by bringing mail order to rural areas and making it work so well that the format was rapidly copied by such firms as Spiegel and Montgomery Ward. But mail order proved to be profitable only in low-density areas and for products that are easy to describe.[49] In the 1990s, Sears closed its catalog operations creating a coverage problem for some highly saleable products.

Sears retails a popular line of private label appliances under brands such as Kenmore and Craftsman. Minus catalog sales, Sears needed an efficient way to reach small towns that could not support even a very small Sears department store. The solution was the "dealer store," a hybrid between an independent store and a franchise, selling only a limited line of washers, dryers, lawn mowers, tools, and electronics—but not clothing, home decoration, or other staples of a typical Sears store. These stores are owned by entrepreneurs but managed in a way that gives Sears considerable leverage: Sears owns the merchandise and sets the prices, but the dealers pay expenses and receive commissions. The stores are Sears branded and look like company-owned and operated stores to the shopper. Indeed, many of them were Sears catalog-sales outlets in the mail-order days.

But the entrepreneurs are local people, many of whom have mortgaged their homes, even cashed in their retirement savings, to open these limited-line stores. They accepted such dependence on a sole supplier because the Sears name was considered so trustworthy and the brands have referent power. Further, they were offered substantial protection. Sears handed micro dealers legitimate power by signing contracts giving them exclusive rights within their postal codes to sell the major Kenmore brand. Further, Sears agreed that if it wanted to open another store or sell the brand at a nearby location, it would buy out dealers at a price equivalent to 10 percent of the store's gross sales. Here is an example of dedicated capacity that is idiosyncratic to a usage and a user (Chapter 9): Sears was well aware that these small rural stores did not have an equivalent alternative use and, therefore, recognized the need to create a contractual safeguard to induce people to become dealers.

The system worked very well for both sides. In 2004, Sears had 818 of these stores, contributing some $1.5 billion in sales. Though per-store sales were low, the dealers were achieving returns that justified their investments (remember, these owners did not finance inventory). These many low-volume but low-cost stores gave Sears coverage, enhanced its reputation, and decreased its dependence on shopping malls, all while operating in the efficient, locally focused style that characterizes small entrepreneurs.

Sears had set its network so that no dealer stores were near any Sears stores. And then everything changed overnight. Kmart Holding Corporation acquired Sears and quickly began altering contracts as they came up for renewal. The new contracts left open the option for Kmart stores, which could be located near the dealers, to stock the Sears private labels consigned to the dealers. Further, these contract extensions seldom offered compensation for this unexpected competition. Sears (now a Kmart subsidiary) says publicly that it has not decided what to do when a micro dealer is near a Kmart. But management has sent letters to dealers stating that Sears will test market the dealers' brands in selected Kmart stores. A Sears spokesperson says the supplier will talk

(continued)

Sidebar 6.6 (cont.)

Kmart galvanizes micro outlets to offer macro resistance

to affected dealers to "explore whether we can find a mutually beneficial arrangement to keep operating the dealer stores. . . . We have a real positive relationship with our dealer-store owners, and we plan to continue that good relationship."[50]

Yet Sears' actions may suggest otherwise. Some 200 dealers are within 15 miles (24 kilometers) of a Kmart store or are in a Kmart zip code (postal zone). When their contracts have expired, they have been forced to sign contract extensions of only six months instead of the usual three years. These extensions offer no protection against their products being offered at the nearby Kmart. Dealers are alarmed: They fear being ruined by Kmart competition (and then being bought out at 10% of their collapsed gross sales) or being dropped after six months with only token compensation.

Viewed one way, Sears has 818 relationships, in each of which it has by far the greater power because its dependence on each dealer is low while each dealer's dependence is high. But now dealers are changing the calculation.

They are organizing into a dealer association that is contemplating legal action on behalf of all 818 micro dealers. Further, the association is embarrassing Sears by generating unfavorable front-page publicity in such prestigious newspapers as the *Wall Street Journal.* The coalition can coerce Sears by mounting actions no single member could afford and can get results no dealer could achieve alone.[51]

What do the dealers want? One organizer of the dealer group says the Kmart acquisition is good for Sears and for consumers and acknowledges that some dealer stores will probably have to close. "My desire is to have an excellent relationship with Sears and not contribute to their pain. But my belief is that if Sears is going to be the competition, they should buy the owners out at 10 percent so [the dealers will] at least have some money to reduce their damages."[52] But should Sears continue to use tough tactics, a spiral of conflict may ensue. Sears may come to consider today's dealer attitude exceptionally conciliatory and reasonable—hopefully before it hardens into bitterness and escalating demands.

Of course, the specter of exploitation is always present. The weaker (more dependent) party often feels its vulnerability and is quick to suspect the stronger party of bad faith. Asymmetric relationships tend to be more conflictual, less trusting, and less committed than interdependent relations.[53] What can channel members do when they are drawn into imbalanced relationships and find themselves the weaker party?

Imbalanced Dependence: Countermeasures for the Weaker Party

When B is dependent on A but A is not dependent on B, then B can cope with its hazardous situation by reducing its dependence on A. The weaker party can take three types of countermeasures:

1. Developing alternatives to A
2. Organizing a coalition to attack A
3. Exiting the situation, removing itself from danger by no longer seeking the benefits A provides

In channels, the first of these three countermeasures is the most common reaction. Fear of exploitation drives channel members to develop countervailing power as their dependence increases. For example, some sales agents (manufacturers' representatives, or reps) tailor their operations to some of the principals they represent. This creates potentially dangerous imbalances in dependence. To balance dependence and, therefore, power, some reps go to great lengths to cultivate the customers of these principals, building loyalty directly to the rep agency. This means the rep can induce the customer to change to another brand if necessary. The rep insures it could replace the principal by taking its customers elsewhere. Rep agencies that pursue this strategy fare better in profit terms than those that neglect to balance their dependence after tailoring their operations to a principal.[54]

This example preserves the ability to add a supplier if necessary. Many channel members deliberately keep a diversified portfolio of counterparts to allow them to react immediately if any one organization exploits the imbalance of power. For example, U.S. automobile dealers once represented only one brand of car. They were not legally obliged to do so but followed an industry norm of one dealer/one brand. This made them highly dependent on the manufacturer. The oil crisis of the early 1970s encouraged dealers to add other lines in order to offer fuel-efficient cars. From there, it was a short step to diversification. Now many auto dealers have multiple locations, each representing a different brand, or even a single location selling multiple brands. Having a diversified portfolio of brands reduces the dealer's dependence on any single make of car. This enables a dealer to resist a given auto maker's pressure. Diversification reduces the risk of being exploited.

Another countermeasure for B is to organize a coalition to counter A's power. More generally, this involves the strategy of bringing in third parties.[55] There are a number of ways to do this. A common method in Europe is to write contracts calling for mandatory arbitration of disputes. Arbitrators are usually private, but the third party also could be a government body.

Coalitions are sometimes created when channel members band into trade associations. Automobile dealers in the United States have used this tactic successfully. By organizing and then lobbying state legislatures, dealers have pushed through "dealers' day in court" laws in many states. These laws limit auto makers' ability to coerce or pressure their dealers by creating new grounds for lawsuits and new penalties for heavy-handed suppliers. Once organized, dealers are quick to coalesce again to face down new threats. For example, General Motors angered dealers by vertically integrating forward in selected markets.[56] Dealers organized and obliged GM to reverse its strategy. Said the CEO, "I learned a lot. Having your key constituents mad at you is not the way to be successful."

Developing alternatives to A is one strategy, while organizing a coalition to attack A is another. A third countermeasure is to withdraw from the business and, therefore, from the relationship. This is the strategy of ceasing to value what A can give. Exiting the business and putting the resources elsewhere (for example, selling off one's auto dealership) is a strategy many channel members consider unthinkable. But it is not. This is certainly the most conclusive way to escape dependence on A.

Instead of reducing its own dependence, a more creative strategy for the weaker party to rectify imbalanced dependence is to raise the other party's dependence. This can be done by offering greater utility and by making oneself more unusual, hence more rare. Chapters 4 on channel structure and 8 on channel alliances go into detail on these alternatives.

Tolerating Imbalanced Dependence: The Most Common Scenario

The most common reaction to being the weaker party in an imbalanced relationship is no reaction. More often than not, the more dependent party accepts the situation and tries to make the best of it. Frequently, the dependent party deliberately devotes a high proportion of its sales to the other party in the hope that it can become so important that the stronger party will value its contribution and not take advantage of its vulnerability. Alternatively, the weaker party relies on internal norms of joint decision making, and trusts the other party to takes its interests into account. Firms are (perhaps, surprisingly) willing to be vulnerable in this manner. For example, clothing suppliers often make investments tailored to a single powerful retailer and content themselves that the retailer will not abuse their position because they are an important supplier or have a tradition of joint decision making.[57]

What happens next? Are stronger parties always exploitative? Do weaker parties always suffer? Should imbalanced relationships be avoided at any cost? This question has become more pressing due to the global phenomenon of consolidation. In many industries and markets, mergers and acquisitions are leaving only a few giant players in the channels.[58]

Many relationships of imbalanced dependence actually work well. For example, department stores employ buyers to pick merchandise for each department.[59] Some manufacturers come to dominate these buyers: The buyers depend on them to supply appealing merchandise with a strong brand name, but the suppliers do not depend on the store as a major outlet. In spite of this imbalance of power, department stores in the United States have been demonstrated to benefit from a dominant-supplier relationship when the market environment is stable (predictable). Department stores are able to minimize price reductions by working closely with a dominant supplier when demand is predictable. This outcome is common because suppliers usually refrain from exploiting the vulnerability of their department stores' buyers.

In unpredictable settings, however, dominant suppliers become a liability. The store does not have the power to oblige a dominant supplier to react flexibly to fluctuating demand. In highly uncertain market environments, high mutual dependence is preferable: Both suppliers and buyers are motivated to find common solutions to the complex stocking problem. In general, when a market is diverse and unpredictable, one-sided dependence is dangerous. Stores are better off with either high balanced dependence (to oblige accommodation) or low dependence (to enable switching suppliers).

In short, imbalanced dependence is not always detrimental. It can work well, particularly in stable environments, which do not put much strain on the channel. In general, imbalanced power relationships work well when the less dependent party voluntarily refrains from abusing its position of power. The channel can function very effectively when the stronger party is careful to treat the more vulnerable party equitably.[60] Equitable treatment improves the quality of the relationship, hence, the functioning of the channel. Further, every channel member has a reputation at stake. Unfair treatment of one channel member reduces that reputation, making it difficult to attract, retain, and motivate other channel members in the future. See Sidebar 6.7 for an example of this in Spanish agriculture.

When does the more vulnerable (more dependent) channel member believe it is being treated fairly? Equitable treatment comes in two forms. One form of fairness

Sidebar 6.7

Imbalanced power benefits Spanish growers

A good example of how well an imbalanced relationship can work is in the Spanish market for fresh produce. Spanish growers are organized into small cooperatives. Time has proven them to be too small to offer the farmers much utility. For legal reasons, these first-order marketing cooperatives (1OMC) have stayed small rather than merging into a handful of large cooperatives. To gain economies of scale, they form channel relationships with cooperatives of cooperatives, or second-order marketing cooperatives (2OMC).

These 2OMCs, vastly larger and more sophisticated, treat the 1OMC in a formalized, direc-tive manner that comes surprisingly close to an authority relationship, or a channel captain. However, they also invite the 1OMC's participation in generating and evaluating ideas and treat the 1OMC with great procedural fairness. The result: The 1OMC credits the 2OMC with increasing its market orientation, making the 1OMC more able and willing to sense and react to the market. Since this generates rewards for the grower-members (distributive justice), the 1OMC accepts the surprising amount of formalization and direction the powerful 2OMC imposes.[61]

is distributive justice, which refers to how the rewards generated by the relationship are divided up (distributed) to the channel members. For example, many automobile dealers are dependent on manufacturers with strong brand names; the dealer invests heavily in these brands in ways that are difficult to salvage if the dealership switches brands or goes out of business. The dealer is dependent on the maker, but the maker often can find multiple candidates to become dealerships: The maker is less dependent on the dealer. The dealer, being the more vulnerable party, is quick to suspect manufacturer exploitation, which hurts the relationship. This deterioration can be avoided if the manufacturer shares profits with dealers in ways dealers consider fair.

In weighing distributive fairness, dealers do not merely consider absolute rewards. They compare the benefits they derive from the relationship against four baselines:

1. Their own inputs, what they put into the relationship
2. The benefits derived by their colleagues (comparable dealers)
3. The benefits they think they can get from their next best alternative[62] (which may be selling another make of car, or even investing their capital elsewhere)
4. The other party's inputs (what the car maker puts into the relationship)

Low rewards (in the absolute) seem fair if:

➤ The dealer invests little
➤ Other dealers do not gain much either
➤ The dealer sees no better use for the resources
➤ The car maker is investing heavily in the relationship (in which case, it is fair that the dealer would not earn much, even if the maker is highly profitable)

Conversely, dealers may not be satisfied with high rewards because their baseline of comparison can make them think they deserve even more. They will perceive even high absolute rewards as inequitable (not high enough) if

- The dealer invests heavily
- The maker invests little
- Other dealers are very profitable
- Other opportunities are appealing

The other facet of fairness is procedural justice, which is equity in the way the stronger party treats the weaker one on a day-to-day basis (its normal operating procedures). This issue is separate from the fairness of the rewards the weaker party derives. For example, auto dealers consider their supplier to be fairer procedurally when the auto maker

- Communicates both ways (listens as well as talks)
- Appears to be impartial
- Is open to argument and debate

The supplier's "boundary personnel," those who interact with the dealer, play an important role here. Dealers develop a strong sense that the supplier is procedurally fair when boundary personnel

- Explain themselves
- Are courteous
- Are knowledgeable about channel members' situations

This does a great deal to make the relationship work smoothly in spite of the inherent imbalance in dependence. Indeed, field evidence suggests that procedural justice actually has more impact than distributive justice on the vulnerable party's sense that the relationship is equitable. One reason is that distributive justice is not readily observable (who really knows all the factors that influence it?), whereas procedural justice is readily and regularly observable.[63]

EXERCISING POWER: INFLUENCE STRATEGIES

To this point, we have described circumstances in which power ought to be present (dependence, the five bases), and the consequences of the balance of dependence. Fundamentally, power is invisible: We can never be sure how much power one party has in a channel relationship. This leads to an intriguing question: What happens if a firm has power but does not exercise it? Will the other party realize that there is unused, or latent, power? What happens to power if no one uses it? Do the players alter their behavior anyway? Does unused power wither away? Can power be "banked," or stored, to be used when needed?

These questions are fascinating, but evidence from the field suggests that they are moot. The more that parties have power, the more they tend to use it. They do not leave it in a power bank or act in the same way they would without it. Latent power is rapidly converted to exercised power.[64]

Six Influence Strategies

How is latent power converted to exercised power? Converting the potential for influence into real changes in the other party's behavior requires communication.[65] The nature of that communication has an impact on channel relationships.[66] Boundary personnel use strategies to influence their channel counterparts. Extensive study of field interactions reveals that most of their channel communications can be grouped into six categories, or influence strategies:

1. *Promise Strategy:* If you do what we wish, we will reward you.
2. *Threat Strategy:* If you do not do what we wish, we will punish you.
3. *Legalistic Strategy:* You should do what we wish because in some way you agreed to do it. (The agreement could be a contract, or it could be the informal working understanding of how the parties do business.)
4. *Request Strategy:* Please do what we wish (no further specification).
5. *Information Exchange Strategy:* Without mentioning what we wish, pursuing a general discussion about the most profitable way for the counterpart to run its business. This strategy is oblique. The objective is to change the counterpart's perceptions of what is effective in a way that favors the objectives of the influencer. It is a subtle form of persuasion: The counterpart is left to draw its own conclusion as to what it should do.
6. *Recommendation Strategy:* This is the same as information exchange but the influencer states the conclusion. "You will be more profitable if you do what we wish." Compared to information exchange, the recommendation strategy is more overt, which makes this strategy more likely to generate skepticism and counterargument.

Each of these influence strategies rests on having certain sources of power. Figure 6.2 maps influence strategies to their corresponding power bases.

Channel members that have not invested in building the corresponding bases find their influence attempts futile. Of course, how much of each base a channel member has depends on the influencer and on the target. For example, Nestlé has far more reward power (and will use the promise strategy more effectively) with a small retailer rather than with a hypermarket.

As a general rule, boundary personnel eventually come to use all six strategies in each of their relationships. Each relationship has its own style, depending on which strategies are used most often. The predominant style (i.e., the influence strategy used

Figure 6.2   Using power to exert influence

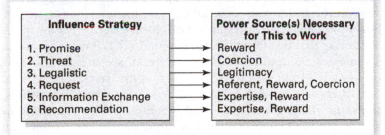

Influence Strategy	Power Source(s) Necessary for This to Work
1. Promise	Reward
2. Threat	Coercion
3. Legalistic	Legitimacy
4. Request	Referent, Reward, Coercion
5. Information Exchange	Expertise, Reward
6. Recommendation	Expertise, Reward

more often) influences how well the firm converts its power into actual behavior changes. This is because channel members interpret the six strategies differently.

The Consequences of Each Strategy

The first three styles (promise, threat, legalistic) often provoke a backlash. This is because they are perceived as heavy-handed, high-pressure techniques. Counterparts resent them and tend to respond by using the same strategies themselves. In particular, the use of threats provokes conflict and damages the counterpart's sense of satisfaction both economically and psychologically. In the short term, high-pressure techniques are effective, but they have damaging longer-term effects on the counterpart's trust and commitment.[67]

What about a promise strategy? Logically, this should be seen as a reward, which is altogether positive. But the object of this influence attempt often does not see a promise in such a cold-eyed manner. A promise can be perceived as a bribe, as insulting and unprofessional, something of a forcing technique. Or the promise may be seen as a veiled criticism of the counterpart's performance ("If they really thought I was doing a good job, they would have given me this already"). Promises beget more promises: Using this strategy encourages the counterpart to respond with its own promises. Using promises in marketing channels sets off a spiral of haggling.

Over the longer term, the promise strategy has mixed effects. From a process standpoint (psychological satisfaction based on interpersonal processes), channel members dislike the promise strategy, but from a strictly economic standpoint, they welcome promises. The counterpart usually delivers on these promises, and the channel member's financial indicators improve. This in turn does a great deal to dampen conflict.

The conclusion? The promise strategy, while self-perpetuating, is an effective way to change a channel member's behavior, even though it raises interpersonal tension.

The last three influence strategies (recommendation, request, information exchange) are more subtle and nuanced than the first three. Channel counterparts welcome these efforts and do not take offense at their use. These three strategies increase *all* facets of a counterpart's satisfaction economically and interpersonally. Recommendation and information exchange do not provoke the impression of high pressure or heavy-handedness, even when the influencer's objective is the same as with promises, threats, or legalism. Indeed, information exchange is so subtle that it is somewhat risky: It will not work if the counterpart does not even think of the desired behavior.

This risk does not occur with the recommendation strategy. Recommendation, while more overt (desired behavior is stated), does not threaten the counterpart's autonomy. This is because the desired action is presented as being in the counterpart's own overall business interests. It is difficult to imagine reacting to a pure request as being heavy-handed. A pure request, no reason given, is so low pressure that it is almost surprising that this strategy is common. There is some evidence that these light-handed strategies, recommendation and request, are the two most often used. The most heavy-handed strategies, threats and legalisms, are used least often.[68]

This pattern is somewhat different in close, long-term relationships. Here, recommendations, information exchange, and promises are the dominant influence strategies.[69] In these more committed relationships, the parties refrain from threatening each other and spend little time making requests without stating a reason. They are candid in their efforts to influence each other. Offering a reward for desired behavior is a frequently used strategy, along with leaving the other party to draw conclusions (information exchange) and arguing that the desired behavior benefits the counterpart (recommendations). In long-term relationships, both parties accept the importance of win-win solutions. This may be why the promises strategy is normal in these relationships and does not appear to generate resentment, backlash, or pressure, as it often does in more conventional channel relationships.

A caveat is in order here. Most of the available systematic evidence suggests that more subtle influence strategies improve the interpersonal quality of a relationship, while more overt influence strategies risk provoking resentment. However, most of this evidence is from Western business cultures. We should exercise caution in extrapolating to other settings. For example, overt efforts to influence distributors by employing threats and citing one's contract will damage relationships in North America. In Japan, there is some indication that these techniques may actually improve the interpersonal quality of working relationships between distributors and suppliers. This is not to say Japanese distributors welcome threats! But what may be perceived as menacing in a Western context may be perceived as an appropriate exercise of authority based on a supplier's prestige in the channel. This status may confer an inherent right to exact some degree of obedience.[70] In other words, what is considered coercive power in one culture may be considered legitimate power in another culture. It is likely that how a power base is perceived is to some degree culture specific. Unfortunately, evidence of these differences is sparse at present.

How to Frame an Influence Attempt

It is a truism that what you present is less important than how you frame it. There is considerable evidence that framing effects are powerful in channels.[71]

For example, take a distributor that is already carrying a supplier's line. The supplier is launching a major, risky, unproven new product and wants to influence the distributor to agree to carry it as well. How should the influencer frame the message to the target?

The *valence* of the frame is whether it is presented as a positive or a negative.

> *Positive Frame:* If you *do* take on our new product, you *will* get substantial additional marketing support.

> *Negative Frame:* If you *do not* take on our new product, you *will not* get substantial additional marketing support.

Both statements say the same thing: The new product is accompanied by its own support. But the positive frame is more effective. This is because the negative frame focuses the target on what sounds like a loss of something. Human beings feel threatened by losses (indeed, they dread loss more than they value gains). Negative framing makes decision makers feel pressured. Their satisfaction and trust are damaged, and they feel their autonomy threatened.

Valence is a matter of sheer presentation. In contrast, a more substantial issue is whether or not to frame an influence attempt as contingent.

> A contingent appeal hinges on compliance: If you take on our new product, we will give you the distributor-of-the-year award.

> A noncontingent appeal is unilaterally bestowed, whether or not compliance is forthcoming: "Congratulations, you've been named our distributor of the year! Oh, and we have a new product to propose to you. . . . "

It is no surprise that targets are more satisfied, more trusting, and feel their autonomy is more respected when the influencer uses noncontingent appeals. What is surprising is the way in which contingent framing undermines the force of the appeal. Often, the target can be persuaded without the contingency. If a contingency is presented and the target complies, the side effect is that the target believes it complied because of the contingency. At the extreme, targets feel bribed, pressured, purchased. Their intrinsic motivation (sense that they complied for their own reasons) declines. In contrast, without the contingency, the target has to explain compliance and is likely to do so by deciding, "This is what we wanted to do. This makes sense for us." This reasoning solidifies the relationship.

The implications are: Train boundary spanners to use positive frames and do not offer a contingent argument where a noncontingent argument will do.

It is worth noting that these framing effects work when the influencer initially approaches the target. Once the performance outcomes are known, however, they override the initial framing effects. For example, if five years later the distributor finds the new line performs well, negative frames and contingent appeals will be forgiven and forgotten. But if the line performs poorly, positive frames and noncontingent appeals will not stop the recrimination.

SUMMARY

Channel power is the ability to alter another organization's behavior. It is a tool, neither good nor bad, and it is a necessary tool. What is good for a marketing channel is not necessarily in the interests of every channel member. Power is needed to make channels realize their potential to add value. Like any tool, power should be used judiciously. In channels, this means sharing rewards equitably with channel members, even those in weak positions.

One way to think about power is to conceptualize the power of A as being equal to the dependence of B. The dependence of B on A is high when B derives great utility from dealing with A and cannot find that utility easily in one of A's competitors. Real alternatives to A are few when there are few competitors or when B faces very high switching costs if it leaves A. Thinking of power as dependence focuses the analyst on the issue of replaceability, which is an important aspect of power.

Power also can be conceptualized as coming from five sources. Reward power is the ability to deliver benefits in return for altering behavior. This is the most natural, and generally most effective, means of exerting power. One reason it works so well is that it is frequently unobtrusive. The players, in responding to economic incentives, are often unaware that they are altering their behavior to fit another's preferences.

Coercive power is the ability to impose punishment. It works well in the short run and is, therefore, addictive. It also escalates: Coercion tends to be reciprocated by the channel counterpart. In the long run, in Western business cultures, coercion is a corrosive influence. It either destroys relationships quickly or erodes them slowly. Occasionally, coercion is justified in the short term to force a major change that benefits all parties. Unless this benefit is apparent, however, coercive tactics will damage even successful relationships.

Expert power comes from possessing valuable information (including expert judgment) the channel member could use but does not have. It is an extremely effective mechanism in channels, although it is often difficult to implement. Legitimate power comes from laws, contracts, and agreements, as well as from industry norms and from norms and values specific to a channel relationship. Referent power comes from a channel member's desire to identify with another organization, often for reasons of borrowing prestige. These five bases of power can have synergistic effects when skillfully used together.

Of course, power is a two-sided affair. In particular, dependence operates in both directions. When B is dependent on A, the dependence often is mutual: A depends on B as well. These mutually dependent relationships often generate exceptional value added. Each side has leverage to drive the other to develop win-win solutions.

When dependence is imbalanced, the weaker party is the more dependent of the two. This is an uncomfortable position because the stronger party can readily exploit or ignore the weaker one. The more dependent party can take countermeasures, including diversifying (building in alternative suppliers of the channel member's services), forming a coalition to bring pressure on the powerful member, and exiting the business.

Nonetheless, imbalanced relationships are very common and can function quite well. The key is restraint on the part of the stronger party. It is important not only to act equitably but to be *perceived* to be a fair player. The stronger party can take steps to ensure it is seen as just, both in the distribution of rewards and the daily procedures it follows in its channel relationships.

Translating power, a latent ability, into influence involves communication. Six common ways to communicate are described. Three of them (promises, legalisms, and threats) are fairly obtrusive. In Western cultures, they often provoke resentment and conflict. These strategies may not be out of place in other business environments. Of these three obtrusive methods, making promises (offering rewards for desired behavior) is quite effective, on the whole, and is a staple of strong, long-term relationships. Three other common influence strategies are making requests for no stated reason, exchanging information (failing to suggest a conclusion while discussing the other party's business), and making recommendations (the explicit form of exchanging information). These strategies are more subtle (in some cases, they are too subtle). They do not explicitly invoke the influencer's desires and interests. This may be why they are perceived as low-pressure strategies. Their effectiveness is heightened by their unobtrusive nature.

In the short term, a negative, or contingent, framing is usually inferior to a positive, or noncontingent, framing. In the long run, performance outcomes substantially override these effects.

Power permeates all aspects of marketing channels. The interdependence of channel members makes power a critical feature of their functioning. Channel members must invest over time to build power. They must assess power accurately and use it wisely both to carry out their initiatives and to protect themselves. To ignore considerations of power is to sacrifice opportunities and to expose vulnerabilities.

Sidebar 6.8 reviews the major elements of channel power, illustrated in the astonishing success story of a highly respected African manufacturer.

Sidebar 6.8

East African Breweries Limited

East African Breweries, Ltd., (EABL) is the largest beer brewer and marketer in East Africa.[72] Its nine brands enjoy a virtual monopoly in the large Kenyan beer market. EABL's only major rival was South African Breweries (SAB), a multinational beer giant that owns, among other brands, Miller (well known in the North American market). SAB entered the Kenya market in 1995 and withdrew after seven years of intense competition with EABL. This is the story of how EABL radically altered its distribution network in response to SAB's competitive threat.

Chapter 9 on vertical integration notes that EABL dismantled its own vertically integrated distribution branch and turned to independent (third-party) wholesalers in response to SAB's entry. While potentially EABL stood to gain (thanks to the advantages of third parties), it also stood to lose by setting up a new system in the face of an aggressive competitive entry. What made EABL succeed was its skilled use of multiple sources of power. To begin with, EABL invested heavily in the improvement of its (now independent) distribution capabilities. This was a challenge for a company accustomed to exerting authority over employees. EABL adroitly replaced its legitimate authority as an employer with a myriad of ways to gain leverage as a supplier going to market through

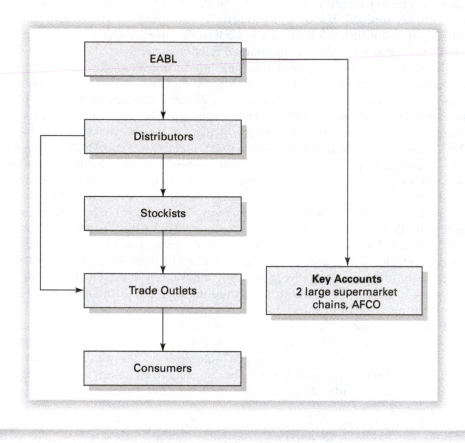

Sidebar 6.8 (cont.)

East African Breweries Limited

independent distributors. In so doing, EABL achieved nearly 98 percent coverage of the highly fragmented Kenyan market, both rural and urban. At the same time, the company retained firm control of its brands' images, blocked SAB's efforts to gain distribution and brand equity, fended off challenges from illegally brewed beers sold in unhygienic packages, *and* operated efficiently, growing sales and maintaining profits—all in the face of a declining economy and intense consumer price sensitivity. EABL has been rewarded in the stock market and in the East African business community, where it is highly respected.

Key to this astonishing performance is the nuanced usage of multiple sources of power coupled with the recognition that the objective is not to control the distribution network but to generate results. EABL knew when to seek control and when to give it up.

The Kenyan distribution network of EABL is shown below.

Distributors

EABL covers its very large and diverse market with a mere 30 distributors countrywide, with which it has strong relationships. Mutual dependence is high. Distributors deal exclusively in EABL products. In return, they enjoy territorial exclusivity and are largely free from competition by EABL itself (i.e., there are few house accounts). The distributors' role is to service retailers and stockists effectively on behalf of EABL while EABL invests substantial effort and resources in supporting them.

As a result of this mutual dependence, distributors work much more closely with their supplier than is typical in manufacturer-distributor relationships. They pay cash for inventories, which they hold in line with guidelines laid down by EABL (aimed at ensuring ready availability of

product in-market at all times). Distributors permit their supplier to closely monitor their financial well-being through business audits, and they price according to EABL's directives. In return, EABL not only offers exclusive territories and holds few house accounts but also supports distributors, for example, in developing their transport capacities. The company's sales force also works closely with distributors in monitoring sales trends, stock requirements, and the needs of retail outlets under their jurisdiction.

EABL uses a number of power sources in its dealings with its distributors. Legitimate power comes from contracts specifying an annual service level agreement with each distributor, in which performance standards required of the distributors are stipulated, as well as EABL's obligations. Reward power is high: Distributorships are very lucrative businesses and are in high demand. EABL has shown itself willing to be coercive. Although most distributors have represented its brand for many years and have fairly close-knit relationships with their supplier, EABL has a track record of terminating distributors and appointing replacements. Well-crafted contractual exit clauses protect EABL's legal right to do so.

As an example, one of EABL's main distributors began to carry SAB products. After an intense dispute, EABL terminated its agreement with this distributor, which then sued EABL. A lengthy, high-profile court case ensued in which a huge financial award was initially given to the distributor but then overturned upon EABL's appeal. This case led the company to comprehensively review all its existing distributorship agreements and territories. As a result, more distributors were recruited through open competitive bidding focused on the distributor's ability to raise capital, prior business experience, and familiarity with a given territory.

(continued)

Sidebar 6.8 (cont.)

East African Breweries Limited

In this way, EABL focused on competence rather than relationships or social status.

Key Accounts

The exception to EABL's policy of giving territory exclusives to distributors is a handful of key accounts. Two large supermarket chains centralize their procurement and operate their own distribution centers from which they supply their individual outlets. These chains insist on being serviced directly by EABL, and they use their bargaining power to negotiate better margins than those accorded to other retailers. Why does EABL concede? Management believes that a benefit is to be gained from the conspicuous display of its products in these supermarkets. The consumers who purchase from these supermarkets are the same as those who buy from bars, pubs, and restaurants (these are the principal beer outlets because beer drinking is a social activity in Kenyan culture). Thus, EABL believes these accounts are important for cultivating and sustaining demand in its main channels.

Another key account is AFCO, the Armed Forces Canteen Organization, which procures goods for use in Kenya's military installations. AFCO, a very large account, centrally sources products and distributes them to military bars, pubs, and restaurants. Because AFCO is exempt from paying any and all taxes on goods, it is supplied separately and directly by EABL with beer products. Products supplied to AFCO require unique packaging (have uniquely marked bottle tops) to identify them as duty-free, and hence prevent their resale in the open market.

All together, this is a modest level of house accounts at wholesale. All are large customers that centralize their purchasing and then distribute to their own sites. This enables EABL to

serve them directly but does not in itself justify doing so. It is important to have reasons that indirectly benefit the entire channel system. Ensuring merchandising in key supermarkets indirectly stimulates demand in the main channels, while serving AFCO puts the responsibility squarely on EABL to ensure that military products do not spill over in the civilian market.

Stockists

Only large urban areas can support a beer distributor. Stockists are independent traders dealing with unrelated FMCG (fast moving consumer goods) products in addition to beer. They tend to be located in smaller towns and urban centers, where they are closer to bars, pubs, restaurants, and other retail outlets than are the beer distributors. EABL needs stockists to reach these more remote markets but understands their need to carry a varied assortment and does not try to control them closely or influence them to concentrate on the beer category to the detriment of other products.

Retail and Trade Outlets

Kenya's retail sector for beer contains no fewer than 13 categories of formal outlets. These categories differ markedly in the service outputs they provide. Almost all beer sales are made through these formal channels, and of these, bars, pubs, cafes, and restaurants account for approximately 97 percent, with the remainder coming from hyper/supermarkets, grocery stores, and petrol stations.

Virtually all retailers of any type must go to distributors because EABL refuses to serve them directly. Unlike distributors, retailers are free to set their own prices. EABL does issue recommended retail prices, but these are no more than a guide and tend to be the minimum charged at any given outlet. It is at the retail level

Sidebar 6.8 (cont.)

East African Breweries Limited

that the beer market segments itself according to the social class of the outlet and its prices. For example, young upwardly mobile professionals tend to frequent a certain type and class of bar/restaurant where beer prices will be about double the EABL recommended prices. Nonetheless, they will generally drink the same brands as those found in bars perceived to cater to a lower social class: Here, the brands sell at or near EABL's recommended prices.

The company enjoys and has exploited to great effect tremendous goodwill from Kenyan beer consumers. It is a Kenyan-founded company with a long history in the market. During its contest with SAB, the theme of many of its marketing campaigns was the "Kenyan-ness" of its brands. The advertising slogan for its flagship brand, Tusker, is "My Country, My Beer." (Long wholly owned by Kenyans, today, EABL is 51 percent owned by multinational Diageo.) These factors combine to give EABL a high level of referent power. By building its brand equity, EABL gives downstream channel members a reason to associate. Further, EABL is widely respected for its management acumen, increasing its referent power beyond its brand pull.

During the beer war with SAB, EABL invested heavily in the development and maintenance of outlets at the retail level, thereby increasing its reward power one outlet at a time. For example, the supplier sponsored the painting of facades of bars, pubs, restaurants, and other outlets across the country with the logos and colors of its various brands. It also saturated outlets with merchandising materials such as table cloths, banners, shelf-strips, and neon signs, which it supplied to the outlets free. The highest impact came from supplying EABL-branded refrigerators free to outlets across the country, the only condition being that these could only be used to cool EABL

beverages. Cooled beer was rare because many bars and pubs in Kenya are small, undercapitalized sole proprietorships. EABL's cooler initiative made chilled beer available to even the smallest of outlets. Consumers quickly took to cold beer, which led to dramatic sales growth.

Another highly effective way in which EABL built reward power was its use of in-bar brand promotions on weekends, public holidays, and other days when human traffic to bars and pubs would be high. These promotions involved offers such as two-for-one or instant prizes of branded items such as shirts, umbrellas, and caps. The aim of these promotions was not only to encourage trials of new EABL product variants but also to keep consumers from trying SAB brands.

EABL targeted some strategically selected outlets, for example, popular nightspots in Nairobi and other major cities in Kenya. In return for an exclusivity agreement, EABL compensated the outlets with cash payments as well as support in the maintenance and upkeep of the outlets, including financing capital expansion. Here, the objective was to build brand equity, thereby increasing pull.

SAB tried to respond to and copy these initiatives but lacked the aggression and incumbency advantage of EABL and eventually lost out. One reason was that to prevent possible free-riding by retail outlets, EABL's support to them was on the strict understanding that it would be summarily withdrawn if they were caught promoting competitive products. To this end, the company aggressively policed the retail outlets. This use of coercive power was mainly carried out by a capability that EABL was late to acquire: its own sales force.

Sales Force

Before 1995, EABL had no established sales force. But SAB's entry awakened EABL to the

(continued)

Sidebar 6.8 (cont.)

East African Breweries Limited

necessity of providing service to its new network of independent distributors, as well as to their customers, the retail outlets. In the space of about three years, EABL grew its sales force from nil to over one hundred people. Sales people use branded sales vans to carry limited quantities of products that are used to top up inventories at retail outlets that may have run out of stock. However, there is no question that the distributor, not EABL, is the primary source. The sales force visits retail outlets, where it monitors inventory levels and either sells top-up stock to the outlet or secures replenishment orders (for larger quantities), which are then forwarded to the outlet's assigned distributor. The sales force operates on predefined call programs that specify a given number of outlets to be visited daily and weekly; this is done to ensure that each outlet is visited at least once every month. It is the salespeople who determine which retailers benefit from EABL's merchandising programs, in a direct demonstration of reward power.

EABL also relies on its wider staff for market intelligence and has an internal information collection mechanism by which employees report any pertinent observations to the marketing department for action. Together, the sales force and the market intelligence gathering create expertise power.

The sales team is also the primary point of contact between distributors and EABL. Notably, salespeople work with the distributors in determining weekly sales forecasts, on the basis of which the distributors place purchase orders with the company. The sales force also channels back distributor issues to management through weekly field activity reports.

Underlying all of these sources of power is reliable logistics. This, too, is outsourced. Tibbet and Britten (T&B) is a U.K.-founded multinational logistics company to which EABL has outsourced most of the logistical aspects of its distribution, including warehousing, inventory management, and transportation. Before its restructuring, EABL had a large fleet of beer-and-malt-distribution vehicles with their own fully fledged maintenance facilities. In outsourcing all of its noncore activities, the company sold its fleet to T&B, which was new to the market at the time and, hence, without a substantial fleet of vehicles. Chapter 8 on strategic alliances describes how EABL partnered with T&B to assure product availability. The performance of this partnership means that EABL can offer a high level of role performance to its channels, which further enhances EABL's power.

In short, EABL's remarkable success story rests on its conversion from a vertically integrated employer (theoretically in control of distribution flows) to a supplier able to draw on every power source to influence third parties while profiting from their dynamism and reach.

Take-Aways

- Channel power is the ability to alter another organization's behavior. It is a tool, neither good nor bad.
- Power permeates all aspects of marketing channels. The interdependence of channel members makes power a critical feature of their functioning.
- Channel members must invest over time to build power. They must assess power accurately and use it wisely, both to carry out their initiatives and to protect themselves.

- One way to think about power is to conceptualize the power of A as being equal to the dependence of B. The dependence of B on A is high when
  - B derives great utility from dealing with A *and* cannot find that utility easily in one of A's competitors.
  - Real alternatives to A are few when there are few competitors or when B faces very high switching costs if it leaves A.
- Power can also be conceptualized as coming from five sources, each of which influences how much one party depends on the other.
  - Reward
  - Coercive
  - Expert
  - Legitimate
  - Referent
- Power is a two-sided affair and applies to one relationship at a time. The analyst must consider the countervailing power of the other side. The best indicator of power is in the net dependence of the two sides on each other.
- Mutually dependent relationships often generate exceptional value added. Each side has leverage to drive the other to develop win-win solutions.
- When dependence is imbalanced, the stronger party can readily exploit or ignore the weaker one.
- The more dependent party can take countermeasures, including diversifying (building in alternative suppliers of the channel member's services), forming a coalition to bring pressure on the powerful member, and exiting the business.
- Imbalanced relationships are very common and can function quite well. The key is restraint on the part of the stronger party.
- It is important not only to act equitably but to be *perceived* to be a fair player, both in the distribution of rewards and the daily procedures the stronger player follows in its channel relationships.
- Translating power, a latent ability, into influence involves communication. In channels, there are six common ways to communicate.
  - Three ways of translating power (promises, legalisms, and threats) are fairly obtrusive. In Western cultures, they often provoke resentment and conflict. These strategies may not be out of place in other business environments.
  - Of these three obtrusive methods, the strategy of making promises (offering rewards for desired behavior) is quite effective, on the whole, and is a staple of strong, long-term relationships.
  - Three other common influence strategies are making requests for no stated reason, exchanging information (failing to draw a conclusion while discussing the other party's business), and making recommendations (the explicit form of exchanging information). Their effectiveness is heightened by their unobtrusive nature.
- In the short term, a negative framing (what one will lose) or a contingent framing (if you do this, then you get that) is usually inferior to a positive or noncontingent framing. In the long run, performance outcomes substantially override these effects.

DISCUSSION QUESTIONS

1. What is the relationship between coercive and reward power? Between reward power and referent, expert, and legitimate power? Give three examples to support your arguments.

2. Why is it unlikely that a marketing channel will be coordinated naturally? Why is power necessary to achieve coordination?

3. "Suppliers should not deal with intermediaries who are more powerful than they are." Debate this statement, which is often heard at trade association meetings.

4. "We should not deal with powerful suppliers. They are sure to abuse us—after they use us." Debate this statement, often heard in the meeting rooms of distributors and sales agents.

5. DuPont Agricultural Chemicals is an extremely large and diversified supplier of herbicides and pesticides to farmers. It has several competitors, also large and diversified (such as Monsanto and Dow). Imagine a dealer selling a full line of whatever a corporate or individual farmer would use, including agricultural chemicals. Is it possible to imagine a scenario in which the dealer is more powerful than DuPont? What factors might make this possible?

6. You are the owner/manager of an auto dealership in Germany selling the Audi line. Your dealership is exclusive to Audi; you have invested heavily to build the dealership; and your contract is such that, if you decide to sell your dealership, Audi has the right to approve or disapprove any buyer you might find. What is the balance of power in your relationship? What sort of working relationship are you likely to have with your supplier? What could your supplier do to ensure you do not become alienated?

7. Consider the Audi scenario above and put yourself in the role of the Audi liaison (the factory rep). What influence strategies would you use, and why? Now put yourself in the position of the factory rep's supervisor. What kind of person would you hire for this position? How would you supervise and compensate your rep?

8. "We give this supplier a lot of sales and a pretty good level of profit. We hold up their brand name, and we tend to follow their advice. This means we have very high leverage over them. We've got a lot of power, and we should use it." Debate this statement. Is it correct? What else do you need to know to assess whether it is true?

9. When is a channel member likely to overestimate its power? When will it underestimate its power?

10. What is the relationship between thinking of power as dependence and thinking of power as five sources? Which approach is simpler? Which is more useful to a manager?

11. "Coercion is just a negative reward. It's all reward power. Power all comes down to one question: Where's the money?" Debate this statement.

ENDNOTES

1. Hotopf, Max (2002), "Tackling the Real Issues," *Routes to Market* 2, no. 3 (Summer), p. 10.

2. Feitzinger, Edward and Hau L. Lee (1997), "Mass Customization at Hewlett-Packard: The Power of Postponement," *Harvard Business Review* 75, no. 1 (January–February), pp. 116–121.

3. Deleersnyder, Barbara, Inge Geyskens, Katrijn Gielens, and Marnik G. Dekimpe (2002), "How Cannibalistic Is the Internet Channel? A Study of the Newspaper Industry in the United Kingdom and the Netherlands," *International Journal of Research in Marketing* 19, no. 4 (December), pp. 337–348; and Geyskens,

Inge, Katrijn Gielens, and Marnik G. Dekimpe (2002), "The Market Value of Internet Channel Additions," *Journal of Marketing* 66, no. 2 (April), pp. 102–119.

4. Jeuland, Abel P. and Steven M. Shugan (1983), "Managing Channel Profits," *Marketing Science* 2, no. 3 (Summer), pp. 239–272.

5. Emerson, Richard M. (1962), "Power-Dependence Relations," *American Sociological Review* 27, no. 1 (February), pp. 31–41.

6. Donath, Bob (2002), "Value Studies Reveal Insufficient Attention to Dealers Plenty Costly," in *Marketing News*, October 28, pp. 8–9.

7. El-Ansary, Adel and Louis W. Stern (1972), "Power Measurement in the Distribution Channel," *Journal of Marketing Research* 9, no. 1 (February), pp. 47–52.

8. Kale, Sudhir H. (1986), "Dealer Perceptions of Manufacturer Power and Influence Strategies in a Developing Country," *Journal of Marketing Research* 23, no. 4 (November), pp. 387–393.

9. Frazier, Gary L. (1983), "On the Measurement of Interfirm Power in Channels of Distribution," *Journal of Marketing Research* 20, no. 2 (May), pp. 158–166.

10. Frazier, Gary L., James D. Gill, and Sudhir H. Kale. (1989), "Dealer Dependence Levels and Reciprocal Actions in a Channel of Distribution in a Developing Country," *Journal of Marketing* 53, no. 1 (January), pp. 50–69.

11. El-Ansary, Adel and Louis W. Stern (1972), previously cited.

12. Brown, James R., Jean L. Johnson, and Harold F. Koenig (1995), "Measuring the Sources of Marketing Channel Power: A Comparison of Alternative Approaches," *International Journal of Research in Marketing* 12, no. 4 (November), pp. 333–354.

13. French, John R. Jr. and Bertram Raven (1959), "The Bases of Social Power," in *Studies in Social Power*, Dorwin Cartwright, ed., (Ann Arbor, MI: University of Michigan), pp. 150–167.

14. Narus, James A. and James C. Anderson (1988), "Strengthen Distributor Performance Through Channel Positioning," *Sloan Management Review* 29, no. 4, pp. 31–40.

15. Gilliland, David I. (2003), "Toward a Business-to-Business Channel Incentives Classification Scheme," *Industrial Marketing Management* 32, no. 1 (January), pp. 55–67.

16. Mentzer, John T., Daniel J. Flint, and G. Tomas M. Hult (2001), "Logistics Service Quality as a Segment-Customized Process," *Journal of Marketing* 65, no. 4 (October), pp. 82–104.

17. Chu, Wujin (1992), "Demand Signalling and Screening in Channels of Distribution," *Marketing Science* 11, no. 4 (Fall), 327–347; and Bloom, Paul N., Gregory T. Gundlach, and Joseph P. Cannon (2000), "Slotting Allowances and Fees: School of Thought and the Views of Practicing Managers," *Journal of Marketing* 64, no. 2 (April), pp. 92–108.

18. Rao, Akshay R. and Humaira Mahi (2003), "The Price of Launching a New Product: Empirical Evidence on Factors Affecting the Relative Magnitude of Slotting Allowances," *Marketing Science* 22, no. 2 (Spring), pp. 246–268.

19. Zimmerman, Ann (2003), "To Sell Goods to Wal-Mart, Get on the Net," *Wall Street Journal*, November 21, pp. 1–2.

20. Gaski, John F. and John R. Nevin (1985), "The Differential Effects of Exercised and Unexercised Power Sources in a Marketing Channel," *Journal of Marketing Research* 22, no. 2 (May), pp. 130–142.

21. Munson, Charles L., Meir J. Rosenblatt, and Zehava Rosenblatt (1999), "The Use and Abuse of Power in Supply Chains," *Business Horizons* 30, no. 1 (January–February), pp. 55–65. This article gives many examples of channel power in operation.

22. Geyskens, Inge, Jan-Benedict E.M. Steenkamp, and Nirmalya Kumar (1999), "A Meta-Analysis of Satisfaction in Marketing Channel Relationships," *Journal of Marketing Research* 36 (May), pp. 223–238.

23. Geyskens, Inge, Jan-Benedict E.M. Steenkamp, and Nirmalya Kumar (1998), "Generalizations About Trust in Marketing Channel Relationships Using Meta

Analysis," *International Journal of Research in Marketing* 15, no. 3 (July), pp. 223–248.

24. Munson, Rosenblatt, and Rosenblatt (1999), previously cited.

25. Hart, Paul and Carol Saunders (1997), "Power and Trust: Critical Factors in the Adoption and Use of Electronic Data Interchange," *Organization Science* 8, no. 1 (January–February), pp. 23–42.

26. Anderson, Philip, and Erin Anderson (2002), "The New E-Commerce Intermediaries," *Sloan Management Review* 43, no. 4 (Summer), pp. 53–62.

27. Prahalad, C. K. and Allen Hammond (2002), "Serving the World's Poor *Profitably,*" *Harvard Business Review* 80, no. 9 (September), pp. 49–57.

28. Luhnow, David (2005), "In Mexico, Maker of Generics Adds Spice to Drug Business," *Wall Street Journal,* February 22, pp. A1, A6.

29. Rosencher, Anne (2004), "Le Client Mystère, Ou l'Art d'Espionner Ses Point de Vente," *Capital* 12, no. 11 (November), pp. 124–126.

30. Raven, Bertram H. and Arie W. Kruglanski (1970), "Conflict and Power," in *The Structure of Conflict,* P. Swingle, ed. (New York: Academic Press), pp. 69–99.

31. Dunne, David and Chakravarthi Narasimhan (1999), "The New Appeal of Private Labels," *Harvard Business Review* 53, no. 3 (May–June), pp. 41–52.

32. Anderson, Erin and Barton Weitz (1989), "Determinants of Continuity in Conventional Channel Dyads," *Marketing Science* 8 (Fall), pp. 310–323.

33. Keith, Janet E., Donald W. Jackson Jr., and Lawrence A. Crosby (1990), "Effects of Alternative Types of Influence Strategies Under Different Channel Dependence Structures," *Journal of Marketing* 54, no. 3, (July), pp. 30–41.

34. Anderson, Erin and Barton Weitz (1992), "The Use of Pledges to Build and Sustain Commitment in Distribution Channels," *Journal of Marketing Research* 29, no. 1 (February), pp. 18–34.

35. Macneil, Ian R. (1980), *The New Social Contract: An Inquiry into Modern Contractual Relations* (New Haven, CT: Yale University Press). Kaufmann, Patrick J. and Louis

W. Stern. (1988), "Relational Exchange Norms, Perceptions of Unfairness, and Retained Hostility in Commercial Litigation," *Journal of Conflict Resolution* 32 (September), pp. 534–552.

36. Antia, Kersi D. and Gary L. Frazier (2001), "The Severity of Contract Enforcement in Interfirm Channel Relationships," *Journal of Marketing* 65, no. 4 (October), pp. 67–81.

37. Heide, Jan B. and George John (1992), "Do Norms Matter in Marketing Relationships?" *Journal of Marketing* 56, no. 2 (April), pp. 32–44.

38. Chu, Wujin and Woosik Chu (1994), "Signaling Quality By Selling Through a Reputable Retailer: An Example of Renting the Reputation of Another Agent," *Marketing Science* 13, no. 2 (Spring), pp. 177–189.

39. Bouillin, Arnaud (2001), "Gore-Tex ou l'Art de se Rendre Indispensable," *Management* 12, no. 10 (October), pp. 30–32.

40. Bouillin, Arnaud (2001), "Gore-Tex ou l'Art de se Rendre Indispensable," *Management* 12, no. 10 (October), pp. 30–32.

41. Bouillin, Arnaud (2001), "Gore-Tex ou l'Art de se Rendre Indispensable," *Management* 12, no. 10 (October), pp. 30–32.

42. Lippman, Steven and Richard R. Rumelt (1982), "Uncertain Imitability: An Analysis of Interfirm Differences in Efficiency Under Competition," *Bell Journal of Economics* 13, no. 2 (Autumn), pp. 418–438.

43. Lusch, Robert F. and James R. Brown (1996), "Interdependency, Contracting, and Relational Behavior in Marketing Channels," *Journal of Marketing* 60, no. 4 (October), pp. 19–38.

44. Hallén, Lars, Jan Johanson, and Nazeem Seyed-Mohamed (1991), "Interfirm Adaptation in Business Relationships," *Journal of Marketing* 55, no. 2 (April), pp. 29–37.

45. Heide, Jan B. (1994), "Interorganizational Governance in Marketing Channels," *Journal of Marketing* 58, no. 1 (January), pp. 71–85.

46. Dwyer, F. Robert, Paul H. Schurr, and Sejo Oh (1987), "Developing Buyer-Seller

Relationships," *Journal of Marketing* 51, no. 2 (April), pp. 11–27.

47. Provan, Keith G. and Steven J. Skinner (1989), "Interorganizational Dependence and Control as Predictors of Opportunism in Dealer-Supplier Relations," *Academy of Management Journal* 32, no. 1 (March), pp. 202–212.

48. Ross, William T., Erin Anderson, and Barton Weitz (1997), "Performance in Principal-Agent Dyads: The Causes and Consequences of Perceived Asymmetry of Commitment to the Relationship," *Management Science* 43, no. 5 (May), pp. 680–704.

49. Michael, Steven C. (1994), "Competition in Organizational Form: Mail Order Versus Retail Stores, 1910–1940," *Journal of Economic Behavior and Organization* 23, no. 3 (May), pp. 269–286.

50. Merrick, Amy (2005), "Small Sears Dealers See Kmart as a Threat," *Wall Street Journal,* February 25, p. B1.

51. Merrick, "Small Sears Dealers See Kmart as a Threat."

52. Merrick, "Small Sears Dealers See Kmart as a Threat."

53. Kumar, Nirmalya, Lisa K. Scheer, and Jan-Benedict E. M. Steenkamp (1994), "The Effects of Perceived Interdependence on Dealer Attitudes," *Journal of Marketing Research* 32, no. 3 (August), pp. 348–356.

54. Heide, Jan B. and George John (1988), "The Role of Dependence Balancing in Safeguarding Transaction-Specific Assets in Conventional Channels," *Journal of Marketing* 52, no. 1 (January), pp. 20–35.

55. Skinner, Steven J. and Joseph P. Guiltinan (1985), "Perceptions of Channel Control," *Journal of Retailing* 61, no. 4 (Winter), pp. 65–88.

56. Taylor, Alex (2002), "Finally GM Is Looking Good," *Fortune*, April 1, pp. 42–46.

57. Subramani, Mani R. and N. Venkatraman (2003), "Safeguarding Investments in Asymmetric Interorganizational Relationships: Theory and Evidence," *Academy of Management Journal* 46, no. 1 (February), pp. 46–62.

58. An excellent discussion of this trend and its implications is Fein, Adam J. and Sandy D.

Jap (1999), "Manage Consolidation in the Distribution Channel," *Sloan Management Review* 41, no. 1 (Fall), pp. 61–72.

59. Buchanan, Lauranne (1992), "Vertical Trade Relationships: The Role of Dependence and Symmetry in Attaining Organizational Goals," *Journal of Marketing Research* 29, no. 1 (February), pp. 65–75.

60. Kumar, Nirmalya, Lisa K. Scheer, and Jan-Benedict E. M. Steenkamp (1995), "The Effects of Supplier Fairness on Vulnerable Resellers," *Journal of Marketing Research* 32, no. 1 (February), pp. 54–65.

61. Hernández-Espallardo, Miguel and Narciso Arcas-Lario (2003), "The Effects of Authoritative Mechanisms of Coordination on Market Orientation in Asymmetrical Channel Partnerships," *International Journal of Research in Marketing* 20, no. 2 (June), pp. 133–152.

62. Anderson, James C. and James A. Narus (1984), "A Model of the Distributor's Perspective of Distributor-Manufacturer Working Relationships," *Journal of Marketing* 48, no. 4 (Fall), pp. 62–74.

63. Kumar, Nirmalya (1996), "The Power of Trust in Manufacturer-Retailer Relationships," *Harvard Business Review* 76, no. 6 (November–December), pp. 92–106.

64. Gaski, John F. and John R. Nevin (1985), previously cited.

65. Angelmar, Reinhard and Louis W. Stern (1978), "Development of a Content Analytic System for Analysis of Bargaining Communication in Marketing," *Journal of Marketing Research* 15, no. 1 (February), pp. 93–102.

66. This discussion is based on Frazier, Gary L. and John O. Summers (1986), "Perceptions of Interfirm Power and Its Use Within a Franchise Channel of Distribution," *Journal of Marketing Research* 23, no. 2 (May), pp. 169–176.

67. Geyskens, Steenkamp, and Kumar (1999), previously cited.

68. Frazier, Gary L. and John O. Summers (1984), "Interfirm Influence Strategies and Their Application within Distribution Channels," *Journal of Marketing* 48, no. 3 (Summer), pp. 43–55.

69. Boyle, Brett, F. Robert Dwyer, Robert A. Robicheaux, and James T. Simpson (1992), "Influence Strategies in Marketing Channels: Measures and Use in Different Relationship Structures," *Journal of Marketing Research* 29, no. 4 (November), pp. 462–473.

70. Johnson, Jean L., Tomoaki Sakano, Joseph A. Cote, and Naoto Onzo (1993), "The Exercise of Interfirm Power and its Repercussions in U.S.-Japanese Channel Relationships," *Journal of Marketing* 57, no. 2 (April), pp. 1–10.

71. This discussion is based on Scheer, Lisa K. and Louis W. Stern (1992), "The Effect of Influence Type and Performance Outcomes on Attitude Toward the Influencer," *Journal of Marketing Research* 29, no. 1 (February), pp. 128–142.

72. The EABL story was developed in East Africa by Peter Kimurwa based on reports from Kenya-based market research firms, brokerage analysts, press reports, and EABL company reports.

Chapter 7

Managing Conflict to Increase Channel Coordination

Learning objectives

After reading this chapter you should be able to:

- Distinguish circumstances where conflict is not negative and is neutral or even positive
- Understand how to diagnose conflict in terms of issues, frequency, intensity, and importance
- Trace the negative effects of high conflict on channel performance
- Sketch the inherent sources of conflict in channel relationships
- Separate conflict into three main causes: goals, perceptions, and domains
- Understand why multiple channels have become the norm and describe ways to address the conflict they create
- Understand why many suppliers actually like gray markets (while protesting to the contrary)
- Trace the spiral of coercion and reciprocation
- Forecast the impact of a destructive act and suggest how to reduce it
- Describe the workings of institutionalized mechanisms management can use to dampen conflict and distinguish between those that management can decree and those that arise in a relationship (norms)
- Categorize conflict resolution styles and describe their effect on how well a channel functions
- Sketch the effect of economic incentives (especially hidden ones) on conflict

ASSESSING THE DEGREE AND NATURE OF CHANNEL CONFLICT

Channel conflict is a state of opposition, or discord, among the organizations comprising a marketing channel. Conflict is a normal state in a channel. Indeed, a certain amount of conflict is even a desirable state: For purposes of maximizing performance, a channel can be *too* harmonious. How can managers direct conflict to create functional channel outcomes?

This chapter examines how to recognize the many forms of conflict, including latent conflict (of which channel members may be unaware), perceived conflict, functional conflict, and overt conflict. The parties to a conflicting channel often diagnose their disagreements inaccurately. This chapter presents methods to help a third party discern the true nature and level of conflict in a channel relationship.

The chapter also covers questions such as:

> ➤ What are the effects of conflict, long and short term, on the functioning of the channel, its coordination, its ultimate performance, and its future?

> ➤ How does conflict arise and how can it be managed?

> ➤ What are the best strategies for containing destructive, excessive conflict, and redirecting the antagonists to achieve higher levels of channel coordination and performance?

Fortunately, a very substantial body of field research exists to offer answers to these questions based on the combined experience (much of it negative) of a variety of channels. This chapter covers the lessons to be drawn from the mistakes of existing channels—and from their successes. Background on how these lessons were drawn from field research is in the references cited in the endnotes.

What Is Channel Conflict?

The word *conflict* is derived from the Latin *confligere*, to collide. By the everyday meaning of the word, there is little that could be constructive in a conflict. *Conflict*, like *collision*, has negative connotations: contention, disunity, disharmony, argument, friction, hostility, antagonism, struggle, battle—the many synonyms are emotionally laden. In individual, personal relationships, conflict is almost invariably viewed as something to avoid, a sign of trouble.

For purposes of managing marketing channels, these everyday interpretations of conflict should be set aside because they are one-sided. Conflict between and among organizations comprising a channel should be considered in a more neutral light. Conflict per se is not a shortcoming in distribution channels. Rather than keeping channel members apart and damaging their relationship, some conflict (and in some forms) actually strengthens and improves a channel. To see why, let us reexamine what *conflict* means.

Channel conflict is behavior by a channel member that is in opposition *to its channel counterpart. It is opponent centered and direct, in which the goal or object sought is controlled by the counterpart.*

Channel conflict occurs when one member of a channel views its upstream or downstream partner as an adversary, as an opponent. The key is that interdependent parties at different levels of the same channel (upstream and downstream) attempt to block each other. In contrast, *competition* is behavior in which a channel member is working for a goal or object controlled by a third party (such as customers, regulators, or competitors). Competing parties struggle against obstacles in their environment. Conflicting parties struggle against each other.[1]

Conflict implies an incompatibility at some level. Conflict frequently exists at such a low level that channel members do not fully sense it. This latent conflict is due to conditions that set the interests of the parties at odds. Latent conflict is the norm in marketing channels. Inevitably, the interests of channel members collide as all parties pursue their separate goals, strive to retain their autonomy, and compete for limited resources. If each player could ignore the others, latent conflict would be nil. But companies linked as a channel are fundamentally interdependent.[2] Every member needs all the other members in order to meet the end-user's service output demands and to do so economically.

This fundamental interdependence is a given, taken for granted as a fact of life in marketing channels. Organizations (unlike most people) face more conflicts than they can deal with given the time and capacities available. To cope, organizations focus attention on only a few of their latent conflicts at a time.[3] Frequently, the conflicts they overlook involve their channel partners. Therefore, they fail to factor in latent conflict when they develop new channel initiatives and are surprised to meet active opposition to their suggestions for improvement.

Latent conflict exists when the conditions are right for contention but the organization is unaware of it. Perception is missing. In contrast, perceived conflict occurs when a channel member senses that opposition of some sort exists: opposition of viewpoints, of perceptions, of sentiments, of interests, or of intentions. Perceived conflict is cognitive, that is, emotionless and mental. It is a mere notation of a situation of contention.

Two organizations can perceive they are in disagreement, but their individual members experience little emotion as a result. They describe themselves as businesslike or professional and consider their differences to be "all in a day's work." This, too, is a normal state in marketing channels and gives little cause for alarm. Indeed, the members would not describe their dealings as conflictual, even though they oppose each other, perhaps, on important issues.

But when emotions (affect) do enter, the channel experiences *felt conflict,* or *affective conflict.* At this stage, the players describe their channel as conflictual because organization members experience detrimental emotions: tension, anxiety, anger, frustration, hostility. When conflict reaches this level, organization members begin to personalize their differences. Their descriptions of the interactions between their organizations begin to sound like disputes between people (i.e., they personify and then vilify the companies). Economic considerations fade into the background as the antagonists impute human features and personal motives to channel organizations. Often, emotions of outrage and unfairness reach a point that managers refuse economically sensible choices and hurt their own organizations in order to punish their channel counterparts.[4]

If not managed, felt conflict can escalate quickly into *manifest conflict.* This opposition is visible (manifest) because it is expressed in behavior. Between two organizations, manifest conflict usually appears as blocking each other's initiatives and withdrawing support. In the worst cases, one side tries to sabotage the other or take revenge. Fundamentally, one side tries to block the other from achieving its goals.

Conflict often is considered as a state: The level of conflict in a channel relationship is assessed, something like taking a photograph. But conflict is also a process, something like filming a movie: It consists of episodes, or incidents. How each episode is interpreted by the parties depends on the episodes the relationship already has experienced. When substantial felt and manifest conflict occurs frequently in a channel relationship, each new conflict incident will be seen in the worst light. Malevolent motives will be attributed to the channel counterpart; great weight will be attached to a single incident; and a channel member will become convinced its counterpart is incompetent, operates in bad faith, and has other faults. Conversely, a positive history creates a positive future: A new conflict incident will be downplayed or charitably interpreted.

Measuring Conflict

How should the observer go about diagnosing the true level of conflict that an organization faces in a channel relationship? The best way is to gather four kinds of information. The following example is from an assessment of how much conflict automobile dealers experience in their relationships with car manufacturers.[5]

Step 1: Counting Up the Issues

What are the major issues of relevance to two parties in their channel relationship? For car dealers, one study uncovers fifteen issues of relevance to dealers in their relationships with the manufacturer, including inventories (vehicles and parts), allocation and delivery of cars, the size of the dealer's staff, advertising, allowances for preparation of the car, and reimbursement for warranty work. Whether the issues are in dispute at the moment does not matter. What matters is that they are major aspects of the channel relationship.

Step 2: Importance

For each issue, ascertain how important the issue is to the dealer. This could be done judgmentally or could be done by asking dealers directly. For example, dealers may indicate on a scale of zero to ten (very unimportant to very important) how important each issue is to the dealership's profitability.

Step 3: Frequency of Disagreement

Ascertain (judgmentally or by collecting data) how often the two parties disagree over each particular issue. For example, dealers may be asked to recall discussion with the manufacturer over the issue during the last year and to indicate on a scale of zero to ten (never to always) how frequently those discussions involved disagreement.

Step 4: Intensity of Dispute

Ascertain (judgmentally or by collecting data) how intensely the two parties differ on each particular issue (how far apart the two parties are in their positions). For example, dealers may indicate on a scale of zero to ten (not very intense to very intense) how strongly they disagree during a typical discussion of the issue.

These four kinds of information should be combined to form an *index of manifest conflict*:

$$\text{Conflict} = \sum_{i=1}^{N} \text{Importance}_i \times \text{Frequency}_i \times \text{Intensity}_i$$

This formula suggests that, for each issue i, its importance, frequency, and intensity should be multiplied. Their product should be added over all the N issues (for the car dealers, $N = 15$) to form an index of conflict. These estimates can be compared across dealers to see where the most serious conflict occurs and why.

Behind this simple formula is an insight that channel combatants, overtaken by emotion, can easily overlook. There is no real argument over any issue if:

➤ The issue is petty (low importance)
➤ The difference of opinion rarely occurs (low frequency)
➤ The two parties are not very far apart on the issue (low intensity)

If any of these elements is low, the issue is not *a genuine source of conflict.* This principle is expressed by the fact that multiplying by zero creates a product of zero. So if an allowance for prepping a car is a minor issue, it is of no real import that disagreements over it are intense or frequent. Likewise, if the dealer and supplier are not far apart in their positions about car prep allowances, it is of little relevance if the issue is important or comes up regularly. Finally, if preparation allowances seldom present themselves as a topic of discussion, there is little need for concern, even if the preparation allowance is an important issue on which the parties hold quite different opinions.

This conflict formula has been shown in the field to do a good job of capturing the overall sense of frustration in a channel relationship. Its usefulness is that it allows the diagnostician to be specific, to pinpoint exactly where and why the parties are in opposition. The combatants themselves are frequently unable to disentangle the sources of their friction. Particularly in highly conflictual channels, the personalities involved become polarized and come to believe that they disagree more than they really do. Inflamed relationships lead people to double count issues, to overlook issues on which they do agree, and to exaggerate the importance, intensity, and frequency of their differences. A third party can help them see the true sources of their disagreements. This is the first step to finding a solution.

THE CONSEQUENCES OF CONFLICT

When Conflict Is Desirable

Conflict is usually thought to be dysfunctional, to hurt a relationship's coordination and performance. While this is generally true, there are occasions when opposition actually makes a relationship better. This is functional (useful) conflict. Functional conflict is common when channel members recognize each other's contribution and understand that each party's success depends on the other(s). In these channels, the parties can oppose each other without damaging their arrangement. Their opposition leads them to

➤ Communicate more frequently and effectively
➤ Establish outlets for expressing their grievances
➤ Critically review their past actions
➤ Devise and implement a more equitable split of system resources
➤ Develop a more balanced distribution of power in their relationship
➤ Develop standardized ways to deal with future conflict and keep it within bounds[6]

Net, conflict can be functional because channel members drive each other to improve their performance. By raising and working through their differences, they incite each other to do better and challenge each other to break old habits and assumptions. See Sidebar 7.1 for an example.

Sidebar 7.1

Functional conflict in plumbing
and heating supplies

The plumbing and heating supplies industry in the United States has a long history of conflict between suppliers and wholesalers over the use of co-op (cooperative) advertising money. Co-op advertising is a program whereby suppliers share the cost of downstream channel members' local advertising that features the supplier's products. In principle, co-op advertising is in the interest of both parties. It can be a powerful way to build supplier-wholesaler partnerships by bonding the two in a presentation to the market. In practice, however, co-op advertising in most industries is the source of much conflict. Resellers accuse suppliers of exercising too many bureaucratic controls over the ads, delaying payment of co-op funds once the campaign is over, and finding pretexts to refuse to pay at all. In turn, suppliers accuse downstream channel members of diverting co-op money to other purposes, running poor ad campaigns, and featuring their products with those of competitors.

Conflict over co-op in the plumbing and heating supplies industry has led some channel partners to devise creative new ways to do a better job of joint advertising. Some wholesalers have created their own internal advertising staff, greatly increasing their promotions competence. Some suppliers have revisited their own procedures and have devised streamlined approval and reimbursement policies, as well as upgrading their own co-op staffs. They have removed hurdles to reimbursement, eliminated bureaucratic rules, and shown a willingness to trust their channel partners and work with them to run joint ad campaigns.

Some suppliers have copied techniques from other industries. For example, they build a predefined co-op allowance into the wholesale price of some items. This sum (say, $2 for a $122 faucet) is tracked and set aside as co-op money. If the distributor runs a large-enough campaign by a fixed date, it collects the fund, which otherwise reverts to the manufacturer. This is a technique copied from Procter & Gamble in selling fast moving consumer goods. The existence of the fund puts pressure on the channel member to advertise (so as not to lose the money it has been advanced) and puts pressure on the supplier to be flexible (so as not to be seen as appropriating money of which it is the custodian).[7]

In principle, all channel conflict should be of this functional variety. In practice, it is not: Much conflict is destructive, not constructive. When is conflict functional?[8] From the downstream channel member's viewpoint, functional conflict is a natural outcome of close cooperation with a supplier. Working together to coordinate tightly inevitably generates disputes in ample measure. But when channel members are committed, these disputes serve to raise performance in the short term and do not damage the level of trust in the relationship.

Cooperative relationships are noisy and contentious, and this is inevitable. The resulting conflict should be tolerated, even welcomed as normal. This functional conflict is even more likely if the downstream channel member has considerable influence over the supplier. *An influential channel member is a disputatious one*—and is willing to give and take to push the channel to outperform its competitors. This should serve as a warning to suppliers that like to work with weaker channel members that they can dominate. The resulting relationship will appear harmonious but will not realize its full potential to perform.

Are peaceful channels better channels? Much depends on the reason why conflict is low. Often, when channel members are not in opposition (low conflict), their relationship is not one of peace and harmony. It is one of indifference. The two parties do not bother to disagree about anything. There is no issue between them about which they have an opinion, no issue that is important to them, no issue over which they care to invest the effort to argue. The two sides are not in agreement. They simply are not in disagreement—because they do not care.

This is readily observed when a distributor, sales agent, or downstream channel member has too many principals to pay attention to all of them. Similarly, many suppliers do not have the capacity to attend to all their channel members. Under these circumstances, one side neglects the other.

Frequently, neglect is mutual. These relationships exist on paper (and may even transact some business). Their lack of conflict disguises a lack of engagement. Thus, conflict is quite low—and so is the performance of the channel. These channels need to increase their activity levels and communication levels—which will increase conflict. This increase should be welcomed, not avoided.

To improve the performance of such a channel, its members need to care enough to communicate, to cooperate—and inevitably to discover their points of opposition. Their perception of conflict will grow, of course. Managed properly, their emerging disagreements can be channeled into constructive conflict. Even as perceived conflict becomes felt (emotions are aroused), channel members may prod each other into better results. This is functional conflict.

Eventually, however, conflict escalates into substantial manifest conflict accompanied by tension and frustration. *If not kept within bounds, manifest conflict becomes damaging, and ultimately destructive.*

How Intense Conflict Damages Channel Performance and Coordination

Given that some channel friction is mundane, should it be accepted as inevitable, dismissed as normal? No, because high channel friction creates costs. These are summarized in Figure 7.1. This figure represents a substantial amount of field research documenting literally thousands of channel relationships in developed economies, mostly Western.[9] The distillation of that experience is that high levels of manifest conflict affect an organization's satisfaction in a manner that damages the channel's long-term ability to function as a close partnership.

Consider a focal firm (the organization whose viewpoint we wish to understand) in a channel. Figure 7.1 takes the viewpoint of any organization in the channel (this can be either the supplier or a downstream channel member) and sketches what that organization will experience as it senses higher and higher levels of tension, frustration, and disagreement in a channel relationship. Perceived conflict will increase, as will felt (affective) conflict and manifest conflict (blocking behaviors).

As conflict increases, the focal firm will derive less from the channel. It will be less satisfied with the business rewards (financial and strategic) the relationship generates. This decrease in satisfaction is of mixed origin. Undoubtedly, there is an element that accountants can document: Profit indicators really do decline when conflict rises.

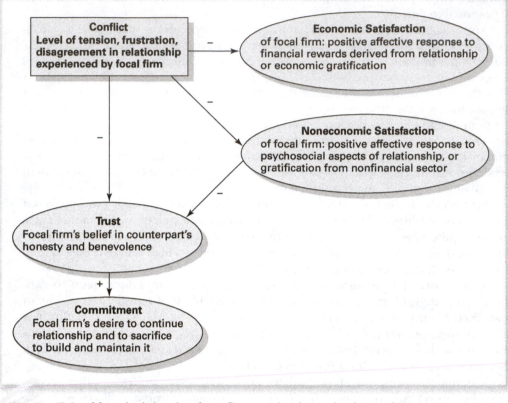

Figure 7.1   How high levels of conflict erode channel relationship

There is surely another element: In judging satisfaction, the focal firm weighs its assessment of what it could expect to gain from alternative uses of its resources. Conflict may increase a sense of disappointment by inflating the focal firm's sense that better alternatives are available.

Disappointing, unsatisfactory economic payoffs are bad enough in themselves. But the consequences of conflict do not end there. For the focal firm, the effects of conflict are not confined to financial aspects. Its satisfaction with the psychological and social side of the relationship declines as well.

It is tempting to disregard this unpleasant side effect of conflict simply because it does not translate easily into profit terms. To the focal firm, however, interpersonal dissatisfaction is a serious affair. It not only makes a workday less gratifying to the individuals involved (which is an important negative outcome in itself) but also damages the solidarity of the relationship. Unsatisfactory social relationships impede building or maintaining trust in a channel counterpart. Trust is a critical foundation for durable, well-coordinated relationships (see Chapter 8 on strategic alliances for more on developing trust). Trust—the belief that the other party will act with fairness, honesty, and concern for your well being—is essential to build committed relationships in which the parties make sacrifices in order to build and maintain their channel.

Conflict undermines channel commitment by damaging the focal party's trust in its counterpart. This effect is powerful and occurs in two ways. First, conflict directly and rapidly hurts the focal party's confidence in the counterpart's benevolence and honesty. Second, conflict reduces interpersonal satisfaction, and this, in turn, delivers another blow to trust.

When conflict between two parties becomes intense, it spills into other relationships and contaminates them as well. Repeated conflict encourages channel members to organize into a coalition, ready to take action swiftly when a new threat is perceived. An example is the U.S. automobile industry, which has a long history of conflictual channel relationships. As a result, many auto dealers have learned to come together quickly to oppose supplier actions. General Motors learned this when it bought up some of its dealers in the 1990s. GM dealers saw this move into dual distribution (GM-owned and independent channels serving the same market) as a threat and organized to pressure GM to withdraw. GM did exactly that. CEO Rick Wagoner reflects about his incident: "I learned a lot. Having your key constituents mad at you is not the way to be successful."[10]

Conflict *is* costly. But this does not mean that an organization always should avoid conflict. Any channel member will encounter conflict when it changes course or undertakes a new initiative. The benefits of change may be worth the costs of conflict. Figure 7.1 does not suggest that conflict should be minimized on all occasions, but it does suggest that conflict carries costs, some of which take time to materialize. Therefore, conflict should be managed, and organizations should choose to enter a conflict rather than discovering that their initiatives are not worth the consequences of the opposition they create.

MAJOR SOURCES OF CONFLICT IN MARKETING CHANNELS

Most conflict is rooted in differences in (a) channel members' goals, (b) their perceptions of reality, and (c) what they consider to be their domains, or areas where they should operate with autonomy. The most complex of these three sources of conflict is the last because domain conflict has many subdimensions. A critical one is product/markets: It is now ordinary for manufacturers to go to market by so many different routes that their channel members are bound to compete for some of the same business. Where channels are redundant, competition for the customer will turn into conflict with the supplier. Other subdimensions of domain conflict include clashes over what is each party's role and sphere of influence. Let us begin with one of the most intractable problems: competing goals.

Competing Goals

Each channel member has a set of goals and objectives that are very different from those of other channel members. This built-in difference in what firms seek to achieve is fundamental to all businesses, not just channels. A substantial literature on the theory of principals and their agents has been built around the clash between the desires of the principal (who creates work) and the agent (to whom the principal delegates the work). The inherent differences in what they are trying to achieve and what they value leads principals to devise ways to monitor and motivate their agents. Agency theory underscores how competing goals create conflict in any principal-agent relationship, regardless of the personalities and players involved and regardless of the history of their relationship. Too often, channel members personalize their conflicts and believe that a change of partner or of personnel will solve their problems. But fundamental goal conflict remains.[11]

The relationship between Nike, the maker of sport shoes, and retailer Foot Locker is a good example of a generic and perennial goal conflict between suppliers and resellers. Resellers carry a supplier's line in order to maximize their own profits. They can do so by several means: achieving higher gross margins per unit (paying the supplier less while charging the customer more), increasing unit sales, decreasing inventory, holding down expenses, and receiving higher allowances from the manufacturer. Of course, the manufacturer wishes to maximize its own profits. To this effect, the supplier prefers to see the reseller do almost exactly the reverse: accept lower gross margins (pay the supplier more while charging the customer less), hold more inventory (avoid stockouts, maximize selection), spend more to support the product line, and get by without allowances. The two parties' overall profit goals lead them to collide on every objective but one: raise unit sales. The Nike–Foot Locker relationship is profiled in Sidebar 7.2.

Figure 7.2 lists frequent reasons for conflict that are inherent in the upstream and downstream division of labor in a marketing channel.[12]

Surprisingly, a great deal of tension, anxiety, and frustration in a channel is due not so much to actual goal clashes as to the players' *perceptions* that their goals diverge.[13] The players in channels quite commonly believe that the incongruity in their goals is higher than it actually is. This misperception fuels conflict. The fundamental incompatibility of goals helps explain a curious finding: Salespeople and sales managers are willing to deceive distributors more than they will mislead customers or their own employer.[14]

Differing Perceptions of Reality

Differing perceptions of reality are important sources of conflict because they indicate that there will be differing bases of action in response to the same situation. As a general rule, channel members are often confident that they know the facts of the situation. Yet when their perceptions are compared, it frequently is difficult to believe they are members of the same channel because those perceptions are so different. Perceptions differ markedly,[15] even on such basic topics as:

➤ The attributes of the product/service
➤ The applications it serves and for which segments
➤ The competition

Given such a basic divergence of ideas about the situation, it is not surprising that channel members also disagree about more subjective, judgment-laden subjects, such as how readily the product or service is sold, the value added of each channel member, or how each side behaves. Indeed, channel members often have very inaccurate expectations of what the other will do. These expectations lead them to choose suboptimal strategies, which heightens conflict. Inaccurate expectations also lead to surprise, and frequently opposition, when the parties "fail" to react as expected.[16]

Why are misperceptions so common and so serious? A major reason is focus. The supplier is focused on its product and its processes and is typically at a remove from

Sidebar 7.2

Nike versus Foot Locker

When both sides need each other, a relationship is capable of superb performance. This is, indeed, what happened over three decades of partnership between Nike, the renowned maker of sport shoes, and Foot Locker, the world's largest retailer of sports shoes and apparel. Together, the two firms had helped create the enormous market for branded athletic shoes. Each had used its relationship to become dominant in its sector. Each was the other's biggest trading partner. Ordinarily, the players in such relationships see it in their mutual interest to come to an agreement. However, it can happen that one party decides to force the hand of the other in a high-stakes play for influence.

Nike placed rigid restrictions on all of its retailers in the name of protecting brand equity and promoting new products. These restrictions included taking only a 42 percent gross margin rather than 60 percent (thereby holding down the retail price) and taking an assortment of untested new shoes in order to get the current hot-selling shoes. Foot Locker, however, was a most-favored retailer. It received a preferential price as well as privileged access to best-selling shoes and first access to new shoes. In turn, Foot Locker gave Nike prominent display and, as a large retailer with several thousand locations, benefited from Nike's national advertising.

The rift between the two companies began in 2000, with the arrival of a new CEO, Mr. Matt Serra, who was concerned that Wal-Mart would destroy Foot Locker's business. Serra decided to extract better prices from Nike by increasing its order size. To liquidate the huge inventory needed to get these big quantity discounts, Foot Locker ran "buy one, get one half-price" sales. The intention was to ensure that customers stocked up at Foot Locker and did not go elsewhere to buy more shoes. Nike has always discouraged this tactic on grounds that it commodifies the market by starting price wars, and the company has withheld best-selling shoes from stores that run such promotions. But Foot Locker persisted and used this tactic even for premium models in the Nike line. Conflict between the two giants increased. "When your biggest partner, whose entire point of differentiation has been that they got your best, newest product first, decides it's a discounter," that changes the relationship, said a Nike spokesperson.[17]

In 2003, Nike introduced a line of expensive shoes that did not do well. This provoked Serra to cut Foot Locker's Nike orders by 15 percent to 25 percent and replace those shoes with rivals Puma and K-Swiss. His intent was to oblige Nike to lower its wholesale prices and to give Foot Locker even greater access to best sellers. He calculated that Nike would make these concessions, but Nike showed Foot Locker that the two firms are not equally dependent on each other. Instead of conceding, Nike retaliated by slashing its shipments to Foot Locker by 60 percent, designating the best-sellers and the newest shoes to be cut the most.

This punitive move had noticeable effects on Foot Locker's store traffic, sales, and profitability as customers driven by the Nike advertising budget looked for best sellers and popular new models of Nikes and could only find them elsewhere. As for Nike, its stock actually jumped at the announcement. Investors apparently saw it as a way to protect Nike's premium pricing, and they turned out to be right. Nike rapidly diversified to other retailers, giving them preferential treatment and cultivating them with a personal selling campaign by Nike executives. Further, Nike brought out a new line of shoes that proved to be hits.

Serra tried to personally mend the relationship but was rebuffed. Foot Locker is an international firm. Ultimately, Serra turned

(continued)

over the U.S. part of the Foot Locker business to the head of a division (Champs Sports) that focuses on high-end products and runs fewer promotions. Today, Foot Locker has improved its relationship with Nike and has recovered its profitability. However, the company's communications with investors include a statement of disclosure: Foot Locker is quite dependent on, and cannot guarantee the actions of, "a single supplier."[18]

customers. A downstream channel member, in contrast, is focused on its functions and its customers and is typically at a remove from manufacturing. These differences expose channel members to very different information and influences, giving them different pieces of the overall picture.

Seldom do channel members cooperate fully enough to assemble the entire picture from their separate pieces. When they do share information, the differences in perception that they uncover are dramatic. A lack of communication exacerbates conflict due to different perceptions of reality. Frequent, timely, and relevant communication assists in aligning perceptions and expectations.[19] This is an excellent investment in the prevention of conflict. For example, a top manager of Toyota regularly visited U.S. dealers and engaged them in conversation about problems that the district manager had failed to resolve. "I found out that out of ten complaints from each dealer, you could attribute about five or six to simple misunderstandings, another two or three could be solved on the spot, and only one or two needed further work."[20]

Even in domestic markets, channel members have conflicts over their different views of the situation. This is exacerbated when channel members come from different national business cultures. For example, a study of channels composed of U.S. suppliers and Mexican distributors demonstrates how cultures clash, which creates differences in perception and interpretation of the channel environment.[21] Regardless of the product or service sold, the channel members experience greater-than-usual friction, due in part to culturally divergent ideas of what is appropriate behavior. This, in turn, damages channel performance.

The solution to this problem is twofold. One is communication, which is made more difficult by cultural divergence. It is tempting to skimp on communication with a channel member from another culture. Nonetheless, more frequent, thorough, candid, and detailed communication involving more people in both organizations goes a long way toward rectifying the performance problems of cross-cultural channels.

The other solution is for each organization to develop greater sensitivity to the business culture of the other. Greater cultural sensitivity, in turn, is built on the foundations of respect for and understanding of the channel counterpart's language, customs, values, attitudes, and beliefs. Channel members that slight the importance of national culture or that economize on communication pay a price: excessive conflict, with decreased channel performance.

	Supplier Viewpoint	Reseller Viewpoint	Expression of Clash
Financial Goals	Maximize own profit by • Higher prices to reseller • Higher sales by reseller • Higher reseller expenses • Higher reseller inventory • Lower allowances to reseller	Maximize own profit by • Higher own-level margins (lower prices from our supplier and higher prices to our customer) • Lower expenses (less support) • Faster inventory turnover (lower reseller stocks) • Higher allowances from manufacturers	*Supplier:* You don't put enough effort behind my brand. Your prices are too high. *Reseller:* You don't support me enough. With your wholesale prices, we can't make money.
Desired Target Accounts	Focus on: • Multiple segments • Multiple markets • Many accounts (raise volume and share)	Focus on: • Segment corresponding to resellers' positioning (e.g., discounter) • Our markets only • Selected accounts (those that are profitable to serve)	*Supplier:* We need more coverage and more effort. Our reseller doesn't do enough for us. *Reseller:* You don't respect our marketing strategy. We need to make money too.
Desired Product and Accounts Policy	• Concentrate on our product category and our brand • Carry our full line (a variation for every conceivable need, plus our efforts to expand our line outside our traditional strengths)	• Achieve economies of scope over product categories • Serve customers by offering brand assortment • Do not carry inferior or slow-moving items (every supplier has some of these)	*Supplier:* You carry too many lines. You don't give us enough attention. You're disloyal. *Reseller:* Our customers come first. If we satisfy our customers, you will benefit. By the way, shouldn't you consider pruning your product line?

Figure 7.2 Natural sources of conflict: Inherent differences in viewpoints of suppliers and resellers

Source: Based on Magrath and Hardy (1989).

Clashes over Domains

Each channel member has its own domains, or spheres of function. Much conflict in channels occurs when one channel member perceives that the other is not taking proper care of its responsibilities in its appropriate domain. This can mean doing the job wrong, not doing the job at all, or trying to do the other channel member's job.

A classic example is market research. In many channels, each side (upstream or downstream) considers this the domain of the other. Another common case is pre- and postsales support: Suppliers and resellers clash regularly over who should do it, how it should be done, and how it should be compensated. Still another is inventory: Often, suppliers consider it the reseller's duty to carry quite a bit of inventory, while resellers consider it the supplier's duty to make sure they can be restocked quickly from a central location. Obviously these sorts of who-should-do-what-and-how-should-it-be-done disputes can carry into many domains.

Conflict is usually due to multiple causes. A fundamental issue in this example is clashing over markets, developed in the next section.

CLASH OF MARKET DOMAINS

One of the most serious sources of conflict occurs when channel members are potentially competing with each other for the same business. One solution to this problem—giving some degree of exclusivity to a channel partner—is covered in detail in Chapter 4 on channel structure and intensity.

Intrachannel Competition

From the upstream viewpoint, the problem of domain clash occurs when a supplier sees its downstream partners representing its competitors. Of course, this is common—downstream partners frequently position themselves as providers of an assortment and seek economies of scale by pooling demand for a class of products. Indeed, this is how many agents and resellers are able to provide high coverage and keep their prices down, but that does not prevent channel members from disputing with each other about it.

Representing competitors is usually an accepted fact of life as long as the downstream is not thought to be too eager about meeting its responsibilities in the competitors' domains. The more acrimonious disputes occur when the upstream party believes it has an understanding or agreement to limit competition and the downstream is reneging. Often, the understanding cannot be proven, but when it can be, the conflict can become quite expensive. For example, a California medical supply firm won almost $5 million in damages from a distributor for breach of contract. An arbitration panel found that its downstream channel partner, in violation of contract, promoted a competitor's products. Also at issue was the supplier's claim that the downstream channel member divulged its trade secrets to competition, enabling them to copy the products. This is a common allegation in disputes over channel domains.[22]

From the downstream viewpoint, domain clash occurs when a supplier sells through many of the firm's direct competitors in a market. This is intensive distribution, covered in Chapter 4.

Another source of domain conflict occurs when multiple types of channels represent the supplier's products to the same geographical market. This has many labels, including dual distribution (using both integrated and independent channels), plural distribution (using multiple types of channel members, such as discounters, sales ages, company salespeople, and value-added resellers—that may or may not be owned by the supplier), and hybrid distribution. Perhaps the best label is multiple channels, meaning using more than one route (*type* of channel member, whether integrated or independent) to get to the same market.[23] (Note that using multiple channels is not the same as distributing intensively—intensive distribution can be achieved by going through many channel entities, all of the same type.)

Multiple Channels: No Longer Unusual

Multiple channels have always been common. But at one time, many companies used one primary route to market: Their other routes were secondary and were often downplayed, even disguised, in order to avert channel conflict and avoid confusing customers. This was especially the case when suppliers owned sales/distribution organizations, thereby competing directly with their own channel customers for the end-user (dual distribution).

Now there has been an explosion in the use of multiple channels, to the point that it is the norm rather than the exception.[24] Why? Among other reasons, heightened competition drives suppliers to change their channels, while fragmented markets make it harder to serve customers efficiently through only one channel type. Channels once were kept simple to facilitate their administration. However, technological advances have made it feasible to manage a far more complex channel structure.

Suppliers like multiple channels because they may increase market penetration and raise entry barriers to potential competitors. Many different channel types afford the supplier a window on many markets. In addition, many channel types are bound to compete with each other. Suppliers are prone to consider this competition healthy, and sometimes they are right.

Of course, customers like multiple channels when it means they can find a channel that meets their service output demands. Multiple channel types make it easier for the customer to pit one channel against another in a search for more services at lower prices. Thus, multiple channels are a way to make markets: Suppliers and customers can find each other more easily and match their needs to channel types.[25]

The danger of multiple channels is the same as the danger of intensive distribution: Downstream channel members may lose motivation and can withhold support (a passive response), retaliate, or exit the supplier's channel structure (active responses). See Sidebar 7.3 for an example. This is particularly the case when the customer can free-ride, gaining services from one channel while placing its business with another. The ironic result is that by adding channel types the supplier may come to reduce, rather than increase, the breadth and vigor of its market representation.

A major reason why suppliers fail to anticipate that multiple channels will actually reduce their channels' motivation is that suppliers tend to think of their markets as distinct and well-behaved segments. They reason that one type of customer would like to buy in one manner (say, convenient and cheap, with few services), while another type prefers another manner (say, full support, with a willingness to spend time negotiating and to pay a higher price). Each segment calls for different service outputs, hence different channel types (say, a discount catalog and a value-added reseller, or VAR). Thus, suppliers expect that by offering multiple channels they can

Sidebar 7.3

Meccano and domain conflict

Meccano is an old and well-known brand of toys in Europe. Generations of children remember hours spent assembling intricate and elaborate metal constructions (buildings, vehicles, shapes) using the distinctive screws, disks, and bright pre-punched metal strips that Meccano sells in kits. Founded in 1898, Meccano dominated the European market for construction toys, a market it had essentially created. Meccano enjoyed the approval of parents, who saw its products as educational toys that occupied children for long periods and taught them mechanics, as well as patience and precision. The kit, once assembled, could become an object of display, but the point of the exercise was to build the kit more than to play with the completed construction.

A French firm, Meccano's troubles began in the 1960s with the entry of the Danish firm, Lego. Lego's colorful plastic snap-together blocks were potent competition to Meccano's screw-and-bolt metal pieces. As sales stagnated, Meccano was sold, first to General Mills, then to a French capitalist, and finally to a set of its own managers financed by a leveraged buyout.

What did these owners do? Facing mounting competition from video game consoles and computer games, Meccano responded with new products. Intending to leverage its brand equity, the firm enlarged its product line and engaged in expensive product launches. As part of this strategy, in the 1990s one of the series of owners decided to purchase the U.S. equivalent product brand, Erector. Meccano relaunched Erector sets with an ad campaign and by signing up traditional toy merchants, who offered sales and display support and who paid high wholesale prices. The strategy worked. Meccano saw its fortunes soar. The firm's turnaround appeared complete.

Then came the promise of an enormous order from the Toys "R" Us chain, a category killer (giant discount toy specialist). Meccano accepted the order, failing to anticipate retaliation from the traditional toy merchants that had resuscitated Erector sets. Furious, the traditional stores boycotted the brand. Meccano had the possibility of signing on other accounts (massive discount stores, such as Wal-Mart, Target, and Kmart), but was unable to do so. Why? To get the Toys "R" Us order, Meccano had granted the chain exclusivity in the mass-merchant channel. Rebuffed, these chains instead took on Steeltech, a less expensive Chinese-made copy of Meccano.

Thus weakened, Meccano experienced a series of other problems, some brought about by the failure of several new products. As of this writing, Meccano has been purchased for the sum of one franc by a Franco-American venture capitalist. The new owner plans a capital injection to enable Meccano to see the results of an extensive rework of its products, designed to adapt the line to the changing tastes of children. Meccano has made kits that break its own unspoken rules (e.g., no material but metal, no nontraditional colors, no human figures). In particular, management believes that children want to assemble the kits more quickly and easily (no more hours twisting screws and consulting blueprints) and to play with the kits once assembled. The new product line is thus a considerable departure from the company's past. To launch it, Meccano is counting on the support of newly recruited distribution channels, which appears to be forthcoming. Signs of channel support for the new line are a major reason why Meccano was able to find a buyer—even for one franc.[26] Today, the new owner is struggling to rebuild the firm and to launch new products that update the Meccano concept to meet the needs of a generation of children accustomed to plastic, color, fun, and fast results—none of which are part of the original product.

serve multiple segments. They genuinely believe their channels will not compete and dismiss those channels' complaints, warnings, or even threats.

On paper, a multiple channel strategy is always appealing: Buyers are neatly categorized and each segment of customers is served by one type of channel. The strategy collapses, however, when customers refuse to conform to their assigned categories, which happens quite often. Of course, customers free ride (getting advice from the VAR, then placing the order with the discount catalog). This is especially true for business-to-business customers, whose purchasing agents are paid to extract maximum value at the lowest delivered price. Increasingly, the same customers behave differently on different occasions when purchasing the same item. Wright Line learned this to its great cost: Segmentation schemes must consider the nature of the purchase, not just the nature of the buyer (Sidebar 7.4).

What kinds of markets are better able to support company-owned and independent channels without increasing conflict to ruinous levels? Four stand out:[27]

- ➤ Growing markets, which tend to offer opportunity for many players
- ➤ Markets in which customers perceive the product category as differentiated (allowing channel members to distinguish their offerings)
- ➤ Markets in which buyers have a consistent purchase style that involves one type of channel member (such customers are less likely to seek out competing channels and set them into competition for an order)
- ➤ Markets that are not dominated by buying groups (which actively arbitrage among channel types by setting them in competition)

Is It Really a Problem?

Multiple channels do not always compete. Often, channel members think they serve the same customer on the same occasion when, in fact, they do not. For example, Coca-Cola in Japan faced strong opposition from its retailers when it installed vending machines. Eventually, Coke was able to use market research to show that it was correct in its claims that vending machines were used for different occasions and offered a different value to the (same) customer.[28]

Multiple channels can even help each other by building primary demand for the product category or by building demand for each other. The classic example is the combination of a store and a direct marketing operation (such as a catalog or Web site). Potential customers are exposed to a brand both ways and then can purchase as they wish. Some retailers use this synergy to explore markets: Once catalog sales from an area reach a certain level, they take it as a sign that it is time to open a store.

Of course, the accounting for these combinations is approximate: The supplier cannot really know, for example, how many customers tried on clothing in the store, went home to think about it, then ordered from the Web site or catalog. Small wonder that many of these combinations have the same owner (such as Victoria's Secret for lingerie, Lands' End for clothing, Barnes & Noble for books). Conflict can be handled by a corporate accountant (to allocate costs and revenues) and a human resources manager to administer compensation.

When channels are independent, settling disputes is not so easy. To date, suppliers have not paid enough attention to mechanisms to compensate potential victims of excessive channel conflict. The growth of electronic commerce will make this a more pressing problem by elevating free riding to epidemic levels. To cope, suppliers and

Sidebar 7.4

Wright Line

Wright Line was a profitable supplier of products to help computer centers organize and file electronic information. The brand's marketing strategy was to sell at premium prices through its own sales force to large computer centers, offering high service and support for its large product line.

As the mainframe computer market waned, Wright Line sought to cover smaller customers. In an ambitious reorganization plan, Wright Line set up three internal divisions corresponding to different channels, each intended to serve a different customer segment. One division, direct sales, continued to seek and serve large customers. Another division sold via telemarketing, meant for medium customers. In addition, Wright Line built a third division to seek representation by furniture dealers and in catalogs offered by computer makers and office supply houses. This was intended to serve small customers.

The idea was a good one: to increase the variety and intensity of coverage in order to increase sales, while matching service levels (therefore, cost) to order sizes. This is prototypical reasoning in going to multiple channels. Unfortunately, nobody did what management thought they would do.

Large and medium customers shopped all the channels, sometimes pitting channel members against each other in price wars. Large accounts, in particular, proved willing to behave like small accounts on some occasions (fill-in orders, for example). To make matters worse, Wright Line had made a classic marketing error: It had segmented its accounts according to their current business with Wright Line, rather than their potential business in the product category. Consequently, in any given year, small customers would become large and large customers would become small, necessitating that they be reassigned. This disruption of the relationship was damaging to Wright Line morale and to customer loyalty.

Third parties freely competed with Wright Line's own divisions, often beating them on price. Management had not anticipated that they could do so because it viewed them as intermediaries and did not understand the services they rendered or the economies of scale they could reap by selling multiple lines.

Wright Line's own channels fought vigorously to protect their turf, even manipulating orders to prevent customer reassignment. Morale plummeted, causing turnover, which led to a spiral of declining sales performance and escalating sales costs.

Did all these new channels increase sales? Yes. Unfortunately, they increased costs even faster. Profits fell along with morale. Distracted by channel infighting, management failed to invest enough in new-product development. Eventually, Wright Line refocused on something closer to its original channel strategy. The supplier used a field sales force as its primary channel, treating a small in-house telemarketing and catalog unit as a supplement. The sales force received credit for all catalog sales and closed all sales generated by telemarketing, which only served to create leads.

Nonetheless, Wright Line was so weakened by the channel conflict that it fell to a hostile takeover.[29]

downstream channel members will be obliged to devise new ways of doing business, such as adding in flat payments (the equivalent of salary), fees for services (the equivalent of an expense account), or overrides, whereby one channel member is automatically compensated for sales made by another (the equivalent of a group bonus). Sidebar 7.5 suggests ways to introduce a Web channel without creating excessive channel conflict.

Sidebar 7.5

Domain conflict and Internet commerce

Channel conflict is a major issue for business-to-business (B2B) firms due to the introduction of online e-commerce. The Web threatens divisions within firms and threatens third-party vendors by competing with them to perform channel flows. Even if a Web site does not actually take orders but merely provides information, it is replacing, and potentially contradicting, another channel member. While this is an issue in business-to-consumer (B2C) marketing as well, it is particularly menacing in B2B because business customers are more motivated to put channel members in competition with each other. Further, B2B firms are rushing to embrace the Web as a way to improve their supply chain management, making the issues more urgent.[30]

How can suppliers minimize the conflict that e-commerce brings to B2B sectors? Eleven ways to do so are:

1. Do not offer a lower price on the supplier's Web site than the customer can find from channel members.

2. Divert the fulfillment of Web site orders to channel partners.

3. Provide information on products and services but do not take orders.

4. Use the supplier Web site to promote channel partners.

5. Encourage channel partners to advertise on the supplier's Web site.

6. Limit the online offering to a subset of products that particularly interest the online customer rather than the full line.

7. Use a unique brand name for products on the Web site.

8. Offer on the Web site products that are early in their product life cycle, when demand is growing rapidly and the Web site is, therefore, less likely to cannibalize partner efforts.

9. Communicate the firm's distribution strategy, internally and externally, so that constituents can see the role the Web site is expected to play.

10. Work to coordinate the elements of the distribution strategy (which is made easier by following suggestion no. 9). This includes such steps as paying overrides, creating rules of engagement, and assigning roles and responsibilities.

11. Appeal to superordinate goals, such as doing the best possible job of meeting customers' needs.

The most obvious benefit to a supplier of multiple channels is better coverage. Other motives, usually unspoken, are based on the idea that one channel can help a supplier to manage another. For example, many suppliers serve industrial customers by a manufacturers' representative (independent sales agency, or rep). In the same market, they also may reserve some customers (house accounts), serving them via company employees. This is dual distribution (vertically integrated and outsourced). This practice is so common that it is often grudgingly accepted, in which case it will not create enough conflict to harm a channel relationship. Suppliers use more house accounts:

➤ When the nature of the selling task is ambiguous, making it difficult to tell how well a rep is really doing (the performance ambiguity problem)

➤ When the selling task is complex and the salesperson is in position to learn so much about a particular sales task that he or she effectively becomes too valuable to replace (the lock-in problem)

These circumstances create a dependence of the supplier upon the rep and make it difficult to identify underperforming reps. The integrated channel is a partial solution to both problems (see Chapter 9 on vertical integration). By keeping a small sales force, the supplier learns more about the task, thereby gaining a performance benchmark. Further, the supplier can more credibly threaten to terminate a rep if it already has a sales presence in a market. In short, the second channel is useful for learning and for keeping options open.[31]

This theme reappears in Chapter 13, "Franchising": Having company outlets *and* franchised outlets helps the franchisor to run its entire distribution program (indeed, the entire business) better.

What Suppliers Can Do

An important issue is what responsibility suppliers have to protect their multiple channels from each other. Some suppliers, of course, often feel no regret, assume no responsibility, and take no action. Many suppliers question what action they could take even if they wanted to protect their channels. Actively trying to prevent one channel from competing with another (for example, by terminating discounters) can provoke legal action (see Chapter 10) and is often futile anyway. Suppliers can try to manage the problem by devising different pricing schemes for different channels (also legally dubious). This creates an opportunity for arbitrage (see the next section, on gray markets, to see how this can get out of control).

Suppliers can offer more support, more service, more product, and even different product to different channel types in order to help them differentiate themselves (see Chapter 8 on strategic alliances, and Chapter 4 on distribution intensity). In general, suppliers will gain more cooperation from multiple channels in terms of pricing, stocking, and display if they can supply what the buyer considers to be differentiated product lines to different groups of retailers.[32] This commonly means reserving the higher-end models for one channel and the rest of the line for another channel. It can also mean the use of branded variants, a strategy discussed in Chapter 4.

A variation on this theme is to offer essentially the same product under different brand names to different channels. This is a common strategy in automobiles and in appliances.[33] It is effective when buyers do not know that the products are virtually identical. But even if customers do not know, the channels do and will often let the customer know. Buying guides also point out that model X of brand Y is the same as model A of brand B. Hence, the same-product/different-name strategy can be futile.

Taken to the extreme, creating differentiation via different brands or products in different channels is a strategy of not really selling the same thing through multiple channels, that is, not using multiple channels. A common variation on this theme is to sell the primary or flagship part of the product line through one channel (usually an independent channel) and to sell secondary or peripheral products through another (usually a captive channel). For example, in the IT industry, some firms sell their major products through distributors and everything else over the Internet. Customers can access anything the supplier makes in this fashion, while the major business goes to independents. The supplier contents itself with product sales that might not interest the channel in any event.

An example of active intervention occurs in the marketing of durables, which are distinctive in that often they can be rented or sold and then resold. Auto makers practice a strategy of keeping factories running and battling for market share by selling huge volumes at ridiculously low prices to auto rental agencies. In the U.S. market in the 1990s, this virtual dumping of new cars was facilitated because many auto makers owned large shares of rental companies.

The result was that some rental agencies began reselling their fleet cars almost as soon as they purchased them. Suddenly, the sales lots of rental agencies were full of barely used cars—at very attractive retail prices. Invariably, this newly important channel hurt auto dealers, creating enough conflict to bring the issue to court. Several carmakers then intervened by buying used cars back from the rental agencies (thereby starving the agencies' car lots) and reselling them to dealers (thereby feeding the dealer's used car lots). This policy of intervention has allowed carmakers to have it both ways: keeping volume up while keeping two important channels from going to war, to the detriment of the channels, and eventually the suppliers.[34]

Conflict over domains is one of the most visible and least tractable forms of opposition in marketing channels. Over the long term, this conflict is an almost inevitable step as companies adjust to the advancing life cycle of the products and services they sell. Domain conflict often leads to a new channel strategy and a new equilibrium in which different channel forms come to coexist and to do business in new ways. This adjustment comes about when all parties can be made to realize that the environment has changed and that markets have split into new segments, each demanding a different level of service outputs.

Unwanted Channels: Gray Markets

One of the most pressing issues for channel managers, especially global marketers, is the existence and persistence of gray markets.[35]

Gray marketing is the sale of authorized, branded product through unauthorized distribution channels—usually bargain/discount outlets that provide less customer service than the authorized channels do. A great variety of products is sold through gray markets, including Swatch watches, designer clothing, and other chic apparel items. Gray marketing can be contrasted with black marketing, or counterfeiting, which involves selling fake goods as branded ones. Counterfeiting remains illegal in almost all world markets; in contrast, gray marketing is in many cases completely legal.[36]

Who is supplying these unauthorized outlets? The usual suppliers are:[37]

➤ Authorized distributors and dealers, often in other markets
➤ Professional arbitragers, which include
  ➤ Import/export houses
  ➤ Individuals, professional traders, who buy huge amounts at retail where prices are low and then transport them to where the prices are high. Often, these are people living near borders.
➤ And let us not forget the ultimate source—the protesting "victim," that is, the supplier itself, either through the home office or through its foreign divisions.

What motivates these more-or-less clandestine sources of supply and their customers, the gray marketers? Several factors create an environment ripe for the development of gray markets. One is differential pricing to different channel members: one channel often overorders to get a discount, then sells off the excess to unauthorized channels. Another factor is the practice of pricing differently to different geographic markets, whether because of taxation or exchange rate differences or simply because of differences in price sensitivity across regions. For example, foreign companies producing and selling in the People's Republic of China sometimes must compete for sales with smugglers who sell branded product that has been exported out of China and then reimported into China to avoid local taxes (in this case, while the product is authorized branded product, it is categorized as illegally smuggled product because of the avoidance of import taxes upon its reentry into the PRC).

Alternatively, it may be that domestic products are sold through high-service, high-price channels at home, opening an opportunity to introduce gray-marketed goods through discount retailers. For example, gray marketers regularly attempt to buy in Europe at designer outlets like Louis Vuitton and Chanel, bring the goods back to Japan (legally), and then put them on sale in Japanese stores at a price lower than the prevailing retail prices at authorized outlets in Japan. The unknowing shopper is surprised to see the elaborate security measures and limitations on purchase volume used by the Louis Vuitton flagship store in Paris: Blocking gray marketers is the motivation.

The development of emerging markets and the worldwide liberalization of trade also favor the growth of gray markets. These economic fundamentals create incentives for firms to capitalize on brand equity and volume potential by offering similar products across different countries. The problem with this strategy, however, is that optimal prices vary substantially across countries due to differences in exchange rates, purchasing power, and supply-side factors (e.g., distribution, servicing, and taxes).

Of course, the minute that price differences exist across boundaries or territories, substantial gains are available through arbitrage. This, in large part, explains the growth of gray markets. Gray markets need not involve cross-border trade: They are also common in domestic markets in which suppliers want to keep their products out of certain channels (e.g., discount chains).

While purchasers frequently gain from the availability of gray goods (due to their lower prices), other members of the channel often lose from them. Manufacturers complain that gray goods impair their ability to charge different prices in different markets. In addition, if service levels provided by gray market retailers are lower than those of authorized dealers, brand equity may suffer. Gray goods may be a concern for manufacturers, but frequently the strongest critics of the escalation in gray marketing are authorized dealers. Gray markets unequivocally erode potential volume for authorized dealers and may place severe pressure on after-sales service functions. All in all, this suggests that gray markets are generally bad: When it is feasible to intercept and monitor gray goods, it seems always to be in a producer's interest to do so.

Despite the many arguments against gray markets, it is curious that they not only continue to exist but are estimated to be growing quickly. Further, gray markets seem particularly active in countries such as the United States, Canada, and the European Union, where manufacturers have both the means and in some cases the legal framework to stop them.

Despite the evidence that some manufacturers do have legal recourse to limit the proliferation of gray goods, in most cases, evidence of their doing so is limited. It is not easy to block gray markets.[38] There is evidence[39] that suppliers make less effort to stop them (are more tolerant of gray markets) under certain circumstances:

> Violations are difficult to detect or document (especially in distant markets or when customers are geographically dispersed)
> When the potential for one channel to free ride on another channel member is low anyway (for example, when resellers do not provide much service, or are able to charge separately for services rendered)
> When the product is more mature
> When the violator (the distributor that is supplying the gray market) does not carry competing brands in the supplier's product category

The last item on this list is the most surprising: Such dealers are more vulnerable to the supplier's pressure. Suppliers may be more indulgent of these distributors because they are likely to be high performers and because they exhibit more loyalty than does a distributor that is diversified in the supplier's product category. Further, suppliers often grant a distributor some degree of market protection in return for the distributor's pledge of exclusive dealing in the category. The supplier may hesitate to alienate an important distributor in a relationship of mutual dependence.

Putting the evidence together, it appears that manufacturers weigh the costs (often high) and the benefits (sometimes low) of taking enforcement action and very frequently decide to look the other way. They are particularly forgiving of channel members that have made a powerful pledge to them (exclusive dealing), and they are philosophical about gray markets for maturing products, which are subject to greater price competition.

There are even indications that many manufacturers not only do little to stop gray markets but are actually positively disposed toward them. This suggests that other incentives may be at work. An obvious incentive is that the manufacturer increases its market coverage. Further, gray markets serve two purposes the supplier may favor when the product is more mature: They put pressure on authorized channels to compete harder, and they make the product available to a price-sensitive segment. The supplier may be better off in profit terms by tolerating gray markets (all the while claiming publicly to object)—as long as authorized channels do not cut back purchases or support in protest.

An intriguing possibility is that gray markets allow a supplier to serve two segments while appearing to serve only one. One segment cares a great deal about the shopping experience (including displays, atmosphere, sales help, the seller's reputation, and the like) and is less concerned about price. The other segment is the reverse and will buy anywhere, any way, from anyone to get a low price. The price-*in*sensitive segment is likely to be the supplier's target segment, for profit reasons. Gray markets allow a supplier to serve the price-sensitive segment (surreptitiously), while maintaining a more highbrow image.

In short, gray markets are a major cause of channel conflict, in part because both upstream and downstream channel members are of two minds about them. Suppliers have reason to bemoan them in public and encourage them in private. Downstream channel members protest about "unfair" competition even though they themselves are often the source of the goods. Even if channel members really do want to stop gray marketing, the many economic incentives to sell through unauthorized outlets mean that sought-after products will always be subject to some level of gray market activity. Enforcement is not so easy and carries its own cost. It is little wonder that gray markets are such a common cause of channel conflict.

FUELING CONFLICT

A recurring theme of this chapter is that channel conflict should be managed to make sure it is not excessive and is primarily functional. Channel players need to know what circumstances fuel conflict and what they can do to stay out of the high-conflict zone.

Conflict Begets More Conflict

An excellent predictor of how much channel members will dispute in the future is how much conflict they have experienced in the past. *Conflict creates more conflict.* A major reason why conflict proliferates is that once a relationship has experienced high levels of tension and frustration, the players find it very difficult to set their acrimonious history aside and move on. Each party questions whether the other is capable of becoming committed to the relationship.[40] Each party discounts the other's positive behaviors and accentuates its negative behaviors. The foundations of trust are thoroughly eroded by high levels of conflict.

Field experience indicates that high and sustained conflict, once experienced, is extremely difficult to overcome. Even when the individuals involved move on to other positions, the organization retains a memory of acrimony and withholds its full support from the channel. Withholding support in anticipation that the other party will not commit is a self-fulfilling prophecy: the other side reciprocates.

Threats

Abundant field research demonstrates that a highly effective and reliable way to increase channel conflict is to threaten a channel member.[41] To threaten means to imply that punishments, or negative sanctions, will be applied if desired behavior or performance is not provided (that is, if compliance is not forthcoming). The evidence is powerful that a strategy of repeated threats raises the temperature of a relationship by increasing conflict and by reducing the channel member's satisfaction with every aspect of the channel relationship. Threats are perceived as coercion. Repeated coercion eventually moves the threatened firm's sense of conflict into the zone of tension, frustration, and collision.

Coercive power is discussed in Chapter 6. It is worth repeating here that coercive power is a tool, like a hammer. It can be put to positive purpose if used properly. For example, channel members can (and do) pressure each other into taking actions that improve each party's performance. The coercion is mightily resented at the time but, if handled well, will be overlooked in the short term, forgiven in the medium term, and actually appreciated in the long term.

Any tool, however, can be overused. In general, heavy reliance on coercive tactics is dangerous to the functioning of a distribution channel. A major reason is that coercion escalates rapidly. Punishment (and the threat of it) provokes retaliation in kind. In relationships between automobile suppliers and their dealers, for example, the single best predictor of a dealer's punitive actions against a supplier (intentional efforts to hurt the auto maker) is the supplier's punitive actions against the dealer.[42] Car dealers and auto makers can find many ways to punish each other, including becoming difficult to work with, cutting service, and withholding information. This reciprocity of aggression rapidly comes to damage the channel's performance.

Contributing to the escalation of channel warfare is another factor: The better the weapon, the greater the likelihood of using it. The greater a party's punitive capability (ability to hurt the other channel member), the more coercive that party will be. When a supplier threatens a dealer that is capable of doing real damage, the supplier risks provoking coercion in kind. As coercion begets coercion, channel members rapidly begin to sanction each other. For example, auto makers punish dealers by failing to deliver cars on time. Auto dealers retaliate by withholding information from the manufacturer. Each reaction escalates their conflict, which encourages each side to try to contain the deteriorating situation by more coercion.

In short, using coercion is like striking a match. One match lights another. Under the right circumstances, a fire breaks out and will damage the channel.

Where the players have a short time horizon, conflict is often handled with aggressive or coercive strategies.[43] These strategies, in turn, accentuate conflict. Channel members also tend to employ punitive tactics when they have a power advantage over their counterpart.[44] This means that in one-sided channels, where one party dominates the other, the dominant party is more likely to threaten the dominated party. Therefore, it is not surprising that channel members count on a shorter time horizon in these imbalanced relationships. When power is lopsided, each channel member suspects the relationship will end sooner than when power is balanced.[45] (For further discussion of imbalanced relationships, see Chapter 6.)

This said, coercion is sometimes the best weapon, simply because it is the only weapon left in a critical situation. Sidebar 7.6 illustrates how Oakley, a sunglasses manufacturer, effectively used coercion when its largest retailer came into a conflict of interest by virtue of vertically integrating backward into production.

Industrial Marketing Channels in Developed Economies

Industrial marketing channels in developed economies are a good example of balanced power.[46] Frequently, each side is differentiated, and each side has many alternatives to the current channel partner. Thus, upstream and downstream channel members are powerful within their relationships. In these circumstances, both supplier and distributor tend to be intolerant of coercive tactics.

The dynamics of such balanced business-to-business relationships are revealing: They are anything but indifferent. Disagreements abound over a variety of issues, including inventory policies, new account development, participation in training and sales promotion programs, and representation of competing suppliers. Much of this difference of opinion is latent: It exists, but does not manifest itself in action.

Each side uses influence strategies in the relationship (see Chapter 8). Sometimes the influencer is seen as coercive, employing threats and high pressure. Otherwise, the influencer is seen as noncoercive: Discussion revolves around exchanging information, sharing points of view, discussing strategies, asking for cooperation (without threatening), and discussing possible payoffs. In business-to-business channels, both sides use coercive influence strategies to some degree. (Field evidence suggests suppliers are somewhat more fond of coercion than distributors.) But how much?

Sidebar 7.6

Oakley battles its biggest customer

Oakley is a California-based manufacturer of high-technology, high-design premium-priced sunglasses. Its biggest distribution channel customer is Sunglass Hut, a prominent retail chain whose specialty sunglasses stores offer excellent coverage of malls, airports, and business districts. Sunglass Hut's trained salespeople counsel browsers as they shop a deep assortment (many brands and models) in a narrow category (sunglasses). The chain excels at converting lookers into buyers and finding those prospects who are willing to pay a high price for technology, design, and innovation in a highly competitive product category.

In April 2001, Sunglass Hut was purchased by Luxottica Group, the world's largest maker of eyewear, profiled in Chapter 9, "Vertical Integration in Distribution." Luxottica makes many of Oakley's competitors, including Ray-Ban, Armani, Bulgari, and Chanel. In a matter of months, Luxottica drastically reduced its Oakley orders. By August 2001, Oakley was driven to issue an earnings warning, hurting its stock price. Oakley charged that Sunglass Hut engineered the sales decline by paying its floor salespeople higher commissions on Luxottica's products. Indeed, a Luxottica spokesperson informed the press, "Our idea is to increase the percentage of sales that will be Luxottica brands."

Oakley went to battle with its biggest customer, retaliating on multiple fronts.

- Oakley eyeglass wearers were contacted by mail and Web with a communication suggesting that Sunglass Hut salespeople were more interested in their commissions than in the customer's best interests and suggesting they shop elsewhere.

- Oakley launched a program to cultivate other retailers with rewards such as product exclusives, merchandise display fixtures, special point-of-sales materials, and marketing materials designed to drive traffic to these stores.

- Oakley convinced sport stores (such as Champs and Foot Locker), department stores (such as Nordstrom), and optical stores selling ordinary glasses to open or enlarge sunglass counters and even "Oakley corners" (boutiques). Effectively, Oakley created new retail competition for Sunglass Hut.

- Oakley accelerated its program to open its own stores, selling the brand's apparel, footwear, prescription glasses, and watches along with its sunglasses.

- In a direct attack on the parent company, Oakley sued Luxottica and its multiple manufacturing and retailing subsidiaries (such as Ray Ban, Lenscrafters, and Sunglass Hut itself) for patent infringement for making and selling selected lens colors. Oakley successfully secured a restraining order. This is particularly interesting because it is common practice for distribution channels to reverse engineer their suppliers' products, then incorporate the features into their own house brands. Suppliers often tolerate such behavior as a cost of doing business, and Oakley may have done so—until Sunglass Hut reduced the benefits that made tolerance worthwhile.

Sunglass Hut capitulated quickly. By November 2001, it had signed a new three-year agreement restoring its status as Oakley's biggest customer, and Oakley's stock price rebounded accordingly. But the damage to the relationship was done. Oakley settled its lawsuit but stated it would continue its diversification of its channels, determined not to be so dependent on one channel member.

This turned out to be easier said than done. In the three years following the battle, many of Oakley's new channels (such as Foot Locker) were badly hurt by the return of Sunglass Hut and withdrew their Oakley presence. Oakley management professed to be surprised: Like

Sidebar 7.6 (cont.)

Oakley battles its biggest customer

many suppliers, they may have overestimated their brand's appeal and may have believed that coverage, once gained, is stable (see Chapter 4 on intensity of coverage). Oakley's non-sunglass businesses have fluctuated. Further, Luxottica continues to pursue its interests. In 2003, it acquired OPSM, a prominent Australian-based sunglass retailer in Asia, and promptly reduced OPSM's business with Oakley, once again impacting earnings noticeably.

Finally, Sunglass Hut's business with Oakley, while strong, has fluctuated. Indeed, Oakley's communications to potential investors contain safe harbor disclaimers warning of its "dependence on eyewear sales to Luxottica Group S.p.A., which, as a major competitor, could materially alter or terminate its relationship" with Oakley. "A major competitor"—and at the same time, Oakley's largest distribution channel! Luxottica's position as a manufacturer vertically integrated forward into distribution creates a divergence of goals that suggests Oakley will always be in conflict with its largest channel member.

As a general rule, both sides rely more heavily on noncoercive strategies, particularly when dealing with powerful counterparts. Important relationships encourage noncoercive influence attempts: Channel members hesitate to jeopardize these relationships and realize that coercion can create a spiral of aggression and retaliation. In addition, powerful parties in balanced business-to-business relationships tend to refrain from coercion, even though they may be in the best position to use it.

This self-restraint is revealing. One of the best ways for a channel member to gain power is to perform its channel role exceptionally well. For example, suppliers gain power over distributors by doing a superior job of developing end-user preferences, insuring product availability, providing quality products, offering superior technical support, and performing other services. These suppliers are powerful because they offer benefits that are difficult for distributors to find elsewhere. Yet in spite of their power, these suppliers rely most heavily on noncoercive means of influencing their distributors. In turn, distributors are less likely to use coercion in dealing with such suppliers. Powerful parties rely on persuasion and communication rather than resorting readily to heavy-handed strategies.

Does this mean that channel members never should coerce each other? No—the message is not that coercion should be ruled out. On occasion, organizations do need to raise the temperature of their relationships to improve channel performance. Coercion in a channel is not comparable to coercion in a personal relationship: There is a place in business relationships for negotiating via withholding benefits or applying sanctions.

The message is not that threats should be disallowed entirely but that they are an extremely potent way to raise conflict. Therefore, threats should be used with caution, in the realization that coercion easily can be taken too far. This will provoke the other side to retaliate in kind, will reduce satisfaction, and will make the channel counterpart question whether it is worth discussing the issues to devise a solution. Coercion is particularly risky when used with a powerful channel member. In sum, in marketing channels, the use of coercion rapidly escapes the user's control.

Dealers are franchised retailers that carry a limited number of product lines supplied by a limited number of vendors (Chapter 1). Often they sell expensive items needing high after-sales service support, such as autos, garden equipment, or tires. Dealers are dependent on a narrow range of products and suppliers, which makes them vulnerable to destructive acts by the manufacturers whose lines they carry. Frequently these relationship-damaging actions threaten the dealer's domain (spheres of influence). Examples of actions that the dealer may perceive as destructive to the relationship include adding a mass merchandiser, adding a dealer in the existing dealer's territory, withdrawing a product line from the dealer, or imposing an outside credit agency to approve the dealer's applications for credit for new customers.

A major study of how dealers react to such destructive actions shows that five quite different reactions are common:[47]

- Passive acceptance; saying or doing very little about the issue
- Venting; complaining vigorously without taking action
- Neglecting the supplier; relegating the line to lower priority and cutting back on resources (which can mean the entrepreneur pulls back resources from the entire business, not just the supplier's brand!)
- Threatening to resign the line (even if it means closing down the business)
- Engaging the supplier in constructive discussion to try to work things out and improve the situation.

What will the dealer do? Much turns on why the dealer believes the supplier engaged in the destructive act. When dealers blame themselves, they tend to split into two camps: either constructive engagement (attempting to fix the situation going forward) or withdrawing from the relationship (apparently concluding the situation is not worth trying to salvage). When dealers blame the supplier, they are less likely to accept the situation passively and more likely to take any sort of action. The destructive act seems to serve as a wake-up call to drive dealers to movement. When dealers blame the environment ("the market is changing, so they had to do this"), there is more simple acceptance. All this suggests that if suppliers can convince dealers they had little choice, their actions will arouse less resistance.

Dependence also matters. In balanced relationships (supplier and dealer need each other), dealers are more likely to stay in the relationship. Nonetheless, they react actively. They are less likely to be passive or to merely complain and more likely to engage in constructive discussion. As for imbalanced relationships, dealers that are highly dependent on the supplier are more likely to simply accept the destructive act.

What happens to the relationship after the supplier's destructive act? Relationships that were strong before the act tend to survive rather well, particularly when both sides depend on each other. These relationships shrug off the disruption and move on. If the supplier's action meets with a good deal of passive acceptance, the relationship also continues along reasonably well. It is important, however, for the supplier to cushion the blow with high levels of communication in order to dampen venting and withdrawal. Even the better relationships deteriorate with repeated destructive acts.

One solution that appears to work well is the use of dealer councils, groups of carefully selected dealers who work with the supplier both to reduce the actions' destructive impact and to communicate both ways between dealers and suppliers. Chapter 8 on strategic alliances describes how John Deere used dealer councils to turn a destructive act—expanding distribution to a mass merchandiser—to its advantage. Sidebar 7.7 profiles Goodyear, a company whose move to mass merchandisers led to a decline in their dealer network.

CONFLICT RESOLUTION STRATEGIES: HOW THEY DRIVE CONFLICT AND SHAPE CHANNEL PERFORMANCE

How do channel members cope with conflict? We can distinguish two approaches. One is to try to keep conflict from escalating into the dysfunctional zone in the first place. This is done by developing institutionalized mechanisms, such as arbitration boards or norms of behavior in a channel, so as to diffuse disputes before they harden into hostile attitudes. The other is to use patterns of behavior to try to resolve conflict after it becomes manifest. These are discussed in the following sections.

Resolving Conflict: Institutionalized Mechanisms Designed to Contain Conflict Early

Channel members sometimes develop policies to address conflict in its early stages, even before it arises. These policies become institutionalized (part of the environment of the relationship, unquestioned, and taken for granted). These mechanisms serve many functions: Their conflict-management function is often overlooked by the participants themselves. These mechanisms include joint memberships in trade associations, distributor councils, and exchange-of-personnel programs. Some channels incorporate appeal to third parties, such as referral to boards of arbitration or mediation (a mechanism that is particularly popular in Europe).

Information-Intensive Mechanisms

Many of information-intensive mechanisms are designed to head off conflict by creating a way to share information. An information intensive mechanism is risky and expensive: Each side risks divulging sensitive information and must devote resources to communication. Trust and cooperation are helpful conditions: They keep conflict manageable.

Joint membership in trade associations (e.g., the committee jointly founded by the Grocery Manufacturers of America [GMA] and the Food Marketing Institute that was responsible for developing the Universal Product Code) is an example of devising and institutionalizing a mechanism to contain conflict. (This group also promotes progress on the Efficient Consumer Response [ECR] efforts discussed in Chapter 12, "Wholesaling").[48]

Some channels use an exchange of persons as an institutional vehicle to turn channel members to devising solutions rather than engaging in conflict. This may involve a unilateral or bilateral trade of personnel for a specified period. An example is the close connection between Wal-Mart and Procter & Gamble personnel. Although such exchanges require clear guidelines because of the possible disclosure

Sidebar 7.7

Goodyear and Firestone

Tire manufacturers in the United States traditionally sell through independent tire dealers, who sell three out of every five replacement tires. Some dealers are exclusive to one brand, though many carry multiple brands and can withdraw from a line by shifting resources to another brand already in the showroom. An issue for tire manufacturers is that many consumers have become willing to buy tires from mass merchandisers, such as Kmart or Sears. These consumers have high demands for spatial convenience and low demands for specialized tire service. Some mass merchandisers use their chain buying power to offer this combination at a price too low for tire dealers to match.

Firestone has expanded its distribution from a dealer-only network to include some mass merchandisers. Many dealers accepted this destructive act, often reasoning that the changing market gave Firestone little choice. But in 2000, Firestone was obliged to recall over six million tires implicated in fatal car accidents. This pushed some Firestone dealers to convert to rival Goodyear. But some have converted back, which is a symptom of Goodyear's problems with channel conflict.

Goodyear once had the premier tire reseller network in the United States. Aggressive pricing, timely deliveries, and effective advertising created reward power that made Goodyear dealers so loyal that many carried only this brand. But when Goodyear moved to mass merchandisers, its delivery rate to dealers declined dramatically. Further, the supplier gave such large quantity discounts to wholesalers and large retailers that some dealers paid more for their tires wholesale than the customer could buy them for at retail. Dealers were still expected to honor warranties and recalls, making them the victims of free riding.

Over time, Goodyear developed a reputation for poor role performance vis-à-vis dealers. This is why Firestone's misfortunes did not provoke dealer flight to Goodyear. Goodyear dealers complained of unfair and volatile pricing, poor product quality, frequent stockouts, and high-pressure tactics to keep unnecessarily high inventories (even terminating longstanding loyal dealers who did not order enough volume). On paper, coverage did not suffer: The number of dealers stayed constant over a decade. But those dealers were shifting their resources to other brands, increasingly offering Goodyear only nominal coverage (see Chapter 4 on intensity for more on nominal coverage). The result: The market for replacement tires grew 7 percent, but Goodyear's sales in this market declined 14 percent, a revenue loss of $500 million. Says an industry observer, "Goodyear took its eye off independent dealers. But independents are the company's greatest sales force."

Goodyear is taking steps to repair the damage. The supplier has centralized its dealer sales through a handful of wholesalers. The objective is to improve delivery and unify pricing. The firm is also improving its communication (for example, by running focus groups with dealers). It has brought out a very popular new tire (the Assurance), which it has reserved for dealer sales only, and has expanded production to avoid a repeat of Goodyear's many stockout problems. But the vice president for replacement tire sales admits, "We still have a long way to go," and adds, "We lost sight of the fact that it's in our interest that our dealers succeed."[49]

of proprietary information, the participants take back to their home organizations a view of their job in an interorganizational context and a personal and professional involvement in the channel network, as well as added training. Participants in such programs also have the opportunity to meet with channel counterparts who have the same specific tasks, professions, and interests.

Co-optation is a mechanism that is designed to absorb new elements into the leadership or policy-determining structure of an organization as a means of averting threats to its stability or existence. Effective co-optation may bring about ready accessibility among channel members because it requires the establishment of routine and reliable channels through which information, aid, and requests may be brought. Co-optation thus permits the sharing of responsibility so that a variety of channel members may become identified with and committed to the programs developed for a particular product or service. However, as with any information-intensive method of forestalling conflict, co-optation carries the risk of having one's perspective or decision-making process changed. It places an outsider in a position to participate in analyzing an existing situation, to suggest alternatives, and to take part in the deliberation of consequences. For example, firms that actively involve advisory councils in decision making find that the councils shape the decisions rather than merely acting as a communication vehicle between upstream and downstream. See John Deere (profiled in Chapter 8 on alliances) for an example.

Third-Party Mechanisms

Co-optation brings together representatives of channel members. In contrast, mediation and arbitration are ways to bring in third parties who are uninvolved with the channel. Third-party mechanisms are designed to prevent conflict from arising or to keep manifest conflict within bounds. They take two fundamental approaches that differ in how much control the disputing parties have over the outcome. Arbitration takes away a good deal of control, even complete control (binding arbitration), while mediation takes away only limited control (the parties can reject the mediator's idea).[50]

Mediation is the process whereby a third party attempts to secure settlement of a dispute by persuading the parties either to continue their negotiations or to consider procedural or substantive recommendations that the mediator may make. The mediator typically has a fresh view of the situation and may perceive opportunities that insiders overlook. Mediators allow the disputing parties to discover underlying points of agreement and promote integrative (win-win) solutions. Solutions might be given acceptability simply by being suggested by the mediator. Indeed, mediation in business in general has a very high settlement rate, typically 60–80 percent, in spite of the fact that no party is obliged to accept the recommendations. The mediator's solution is face saving, as each side can make concessions without appearing to be weak, and disputants tend to perceive the process as fair.

Mediators merely help the parties devise their own decision. An alternative to mediation is arbitration, wherein a third party actually makes a decision, which both parties have stated they will honor in advance. Arbitrators often begin with a formal fact-finding hearing that operates much like a judicial procedure with presentations, witness, and cross-examination. Arbitration can be compulsory or voluntary. Compulsory arbitration is a process wherein the parties are required by law to submit their dispute to a third party (whose decision is final and binding). Voluntary arbitration is a process wherein parties voluntarily submit their dispute to a third party (whose decision will be final and binding, and reneging on the decision will be viewed as a major breach of confidence). Arbitration has the advantages of mediation plus the advantage that the disputants can blame the arbitrator if constituents object to the settlement.

Sequencing is another possibility. For example, some firms practice mediation-arbitration. This means agreeing up front that if the mediator cannot settle the issue, it passes to an arbitrator—who is usually the same person who played the mediator's role. Another variation is arbitration-mediation, in which the arbitrator places a secret decision in a sealed envelope. Then the issue passes to mediation. If the parties cannot agree, the envelope is opened and the decision applied. The advantage of sequencing is that it threatens to reduce each party's decision control. This lowers each party's expectations (making them more reasonable) and motivates the parties to negotiate in a more cooperative way. If all else fails, the process is seen as more fair than simple arbitration, and the parties are more likely to comply with the ruling.

Institutionalizing the practice of taking disputes to third parties can actually forestall conflict. Facing the prospect of outside intervention, the disputants often will settle their differences internally rather than let them get to a point that a third party would be called. Of course, third parties are also a means to deal with conflict after it reaches high levels. There is some indication that using third parties once conflict is underway contributes to the success of channel relationships. Third-party intervention to settle open conflicts is associated with channel members' greater satisfaction with the financial rewards they derive from their relationship.[51]

Building Relational Norms

The mechanisms discussed so far are policies. They can be devised, put into place, and maintained by management. Their use represents a conscious choice of resources. These policies serve as a way for management to forestall conflict, as well as to manage conflict once it occurs.

Another important class of factors serves to forestall or direct conflict. These are norms that govern how channel members manage their relationship. Norms grow up over time as a relationship functions and management cannot simply decide to create them. A channel's norms are its expectations about behavior, expectations that are shared (at least partially) by the channel's members. In channels that are alliances, it is common to observe norms such as:

> *Flexibility:* Channel members expect each other to adapt readily to changing circumstances, with a minimum of obstruction and negotiation.
>
> *Information exchange:* Channel members expect each other to share any and all pertinent information, no matter how sensitive, freely, frequently, quickly, and thoroughly.
>
> *Solidarity:* Channel members expect each other to work for mutual benefit, not merely one-sided benefit.

These relational norms tend to come in a package: A relationship has a high level of all these norms if it has a high level of any one of them.[52] A channel with strong relational norms is particularly effective at forestalling conflict. It does so by discouraging the parties from pursuing their own interests at the expense of the channel. These norms also encourage the players to refrain from coercion and to make the effort to work through their differences, thus keeping conflict in the functional zone.[53]

Of course, management cannot decide to create relational norms and then "just do it." Norms (expectations of behavior) are created daily by the interactions of the people who constitute a marketing channel. These norms can be positive or negative. For example, a channel can have a norm of cutthroat competition, or of pure self-interest seeking. Unlike policies, managements do not decree norms, and unlike policies, norms are not easy to observe, announce, or publicize.

To this point, we have considered strategies that are intended to forestall excessive conflict. These mechanisms also keep conflict functional if it does occur. Below we turn to the behaviors and processes that organizations employ on a daily basis with the intention of coping with conflict once it is underway.

Styles of Conflict Resolution: How Channel Members Handle Disputes and Negotiate to Achieve Their Goals

Some conflict is a normal, even desirable, property of channels. How do channel members cope with manifest conflict? As a general rule, they seek not to eliminate it but to use it as a force for change. Sometimes these efforts are functional, but frequently they only make the situation worse. This section considers the conflict resolution strategies channel members use and examines the consequences in terms of how satisfied channel members are with their relationship. Note that the discussion is not about how channel members handle a particular issue or incident: It is about the general conflict resolution style they employ in their relationship.[54]

Figure 7.3 shows one way to conceptualize the way in which channel members deal with conflicts. This framework focuses on a channel member's approach to

Figure 7.3   Conflict resolution styles

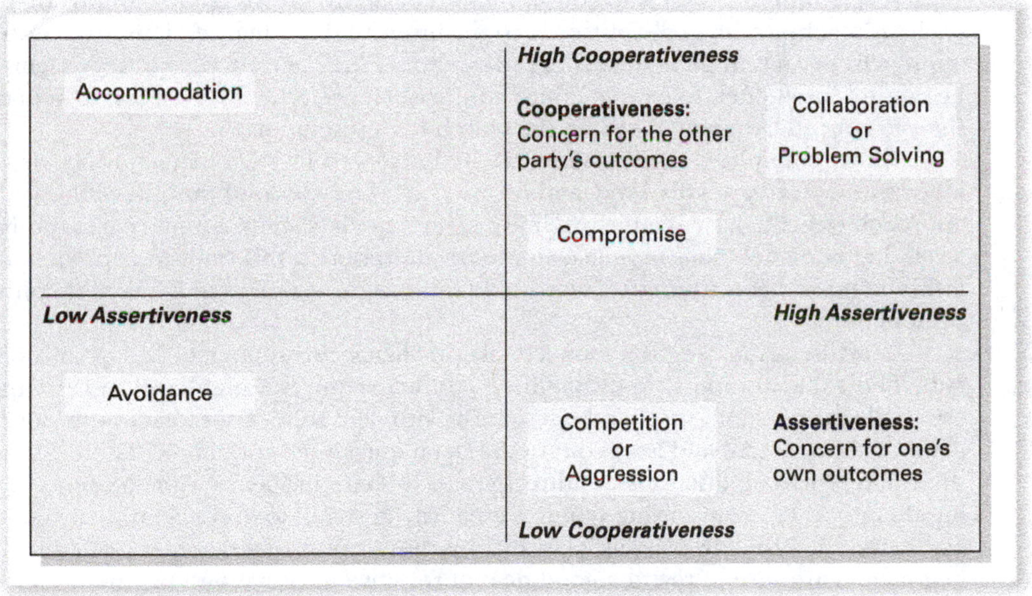

Source: Based on Kenneth W. Thomas (1976), "Conflict and Conflict Management," in M. D. Dunnette, ed., *Handbook of Industrial and Organizational Psychology* (Palo Alto, CA: Consulting Psychologists Press), pp. 889–935.

bargaining. For example, a retailer, in its dealings with a supplier, brings to the bargaining table a certain level of assertiveness (strength of emphasis on achieving its own goals, such as building store traffic, increasing the uniqueness of its assortment, or increasing margins) and a level of cooperativeness (concern for the other party's goals, such as the supplier's goals of building volume, creating a distinctive image, or taking share from a competitor).

A relatively passive channel member (perhaps one in a weak position or represented by a poor negotiator) has an avoidance style of dealing with conflict. The idea here is to prevent conflict from occurring by simply failing to press for much of anything. Typically, the avoider wants to save time and head off unpleasantness. Avoiders often do this by minimizing information exchange, thereby circumventing discussion. In most channels, avoidance is associated with relationships of convenience, where neither side feels much commitment to the other.

Another style of dealing with conflict is to be accommodating to the other party, meaning to be more focused on the other's goals than on one's own. Unlike avoidance (a passive strategy), this is more than just another way of keeping the peace. Accommodation is a proactive means of strengthening the relationship by cultivating the other channel member. Accommodation signals a genuine willingness to cooperate. This encourages reciprocation, which in turn should build trust and commitment over the longer term. But it also exposes the accommodator to being repeatedly exploited unless the other side reciprocates.

A strategy of competition (or aggression) involves playing a zero-sum game by pursuing one's own goals while ignoring the other party's goals. This approach focuses on pushing one's own position while conceding very little. Not surprisingly, this style aggravates conflict, fosters distrust, and shortens the time horizon of the channel members vis-à-vis their relationship. Channel members tend to limit their usage of the aggressive style, especially in long-term relationships.

A very different style is to compromise repeatedly, pressing for solutions that let each side achieve its goals but only to an intermediate degree. This is a centrist approach. Because it gives something to everyone, the compromise strategy seems to be fair. It is used often to handle minor conflicts: Here is where it is easiest to get both sides to concede, thereby speeding the search for a resolution.

Close, committed relationships are better served by a problem solving, or collaboration, strategy. This is an ambitious style. The channel member taking this approach wants to have it all—to achieve its own goals *and* the counterpart's, both to a very high degree! Many people claim to be interested in this win-win approach: It is fashionable and contributes to a favorable self-image, as well as to a favorable public presentation.

Our discussion here is about actually practicing the approach. Doing so is difficult. The collaboration style of handling conflict requires a high level of resources, especially information, time, and energy. The problem solver tries to get both sides to get all their concerns and issues out in the open quickly, to work immediately through their differences, to discuss issues directly, and to share problems with an eye to working them out. Problem solving requires creativity in trying to devise a mutually beneficial solution. Problem solving is an information-intensive strategy. In pursuing it, negotiators are sure to reveal a good deal of sensitive information that could then be used against them.

Resolving Conflict and Achieving Coordination via Incentives

To this point in our discussion of conflict resolution styles, we have focused on the negotiator's style. What are the best arguments to use to persuade the channel member? Considerable field evidence suggests that economic incentives work extremely well, regardless of the personalities, the players, and the history of their relationship. This is not surprising: Just as reward power is a highly effective way to influence a channel member (Chapter 6), appealing to economic self-interest is a highly effective way to settle a dispute. Thus, good negotiators pursuing a collaboration style of resolving conflict find ingenious ways to tie their arguments into economics. Further, economic arguments work extremely well when combined with a strong program of communications in a good interpersonal working relationship. Sidebar 7.8 profiles Sonic, a comprehensive example of the sources of conflict and the effective use of multiple ways to resolve it.

A good example occurs with manufacturer-sponsored promotion programs aimed at retailers. In fast moving consumer goods (FMCG) industries, suppliers spend enormous sums to create point-of-purchase (POP) advertising and displays for in-store use. These programs are a major issue of dispute. Manufacturers charge retailers with taking the promotion money without mounting the promised promotion. In turn, retailers charge manufacturers with not giving them their fair share of promotion allowances and with promising more than they actually deliver. The acrimony generated over this issue alone consumes pages of the grocery trade press.

Evidence indicates that much of the acrimony can be dissolved by combining appealing economic incentives to participate with a pay-for-performance system and presenting the proposal through a salesperson who has a good working relationship with the retailer. Economic incentives (such as a premium for participation) have an obvious appeal. The salesperson's good relationship helps him or her to direct the retailer's attention to the incentives. Further, the pay-for-performance system (for example, paying for items sold on promotion rather than merely items ordered) screens out retailers who are fundamentally uninterested in cooperating with the supplier.[55]

Economic incentives are not merely a matter of offering a better price or a higher allowance. They are quite visible and are easy for competitors to match in any case. Persuasive economic arguments are usually based on the package of factors that collectively create financial returns for a channel member.[56] For example, independent sales agencies have been shown to be highly sensitive to a product's ability to generate profits by:

➤ Compensating for lower volume by higher commission rate, and vice versa
➤ Compensating for lower commission rates by being easier to sell, thereby requiring less sales time (cutting costs)
➤ Establishing the sales agent in a growing product category (contributing to future profits)
➤ Increasing overall sales synergy, thereby spurring sales of other products in the agent's portfolio

In addition, independent agencies respond to indirect arguments about risk. A principal can settle disputes if it can convince the agent that sales are not unpredictable but instead can be accurately forecast. All of these arguments can be conveyed

Sidebar 7.8

Sonic is a masterpiece of conflict management

Sonic is a franchised chain of fast-food restaurants featuring high-calorie food in a distinctive, fun ambiance.[57] Everything is served in a 1950s retro décor designed to recall the United States' postwar period of the movie *Grease*. The chain had done well since its founding in 1953 and had grown to cover almost half the United States. By 1995, however, channel conflict had brought the firm's 1,483 franchisees to a state of near revolt. The results were apparent to the restaurant's customers. Franchisees bought ingredients on their own from different vendors, creating radical variations in menu and quality—even in the same city. A visible indicator of how little the franchisor could assure standardization was that renegade franchisees had signed up Pepsi to replace Coke. Internally as well, operations were poorly run. The franchisor was handicapped by its manual accounting system, which generated numbers that were four months late—and wrong.

Franchisees held strong negative perceptions about Sonic, believing that it took their money and did little for them. They criticized the ineffective advertising campaigns, which featured a long-forgotten singer from the 1950s, and considered them a poor use of the royalty (up to 4 percent) they were obliged to pay for advertising. They questioned what they saw as a lack of marketing and of training. In particular, franchisees felt their costs were too high and blamed the franchisor. They saw the franchisor itself in a negative light, considering that headquarters was ineffective, that Sonic management was secretive, and that Sonic competed with them, taking the best sites to use for company stores. Indeed, Sonic had 110 company stores, but like many of the franchisees, they were losing money. For its part, Sonic perceived the franchisees as uncooperative complainers.

Every source of conflict was present. Domain conflict occurred over the company stores, as well as disagreement over who was responsible for what. Perception conflict was rampant on many issues: Who was doing what for whom? Who was at fault for the poor results? What were Sonic's intentions (to "grab the best locations" or to be an effective coach to franchisees)? How open was Sonic? They even differed on the severity of the situation—franchisees were more worried than the typical manager. Goal conflict was built in because Sonic, as a franchisor, makes money from royalties and, therefore, is motivated to increase system volume by opening more stores. However, the franchisee wants profit (not volume) for its own stores, not for the system.

In 1995, Sonic got a new CEO, Cliff Hudson, a long-time company executive who had a good sense of the chain's problems. Hudson brought an ambitious list of goals: consistent menus and quality, truly cooperative purchasing and advertising, a huge increase in fees from $7,500 to $30,000, and an increase in royalties, going up to 5 percent for high-volume restaurants. Astonishingly, Hudson got what he wanted. How he did so is a masterpiece in conflict management.

Hudson began by deciding that in the battle of perceptions the franchisees were right—and said so publicly. He also fired most of his top management team and replaced them with accomplished executives raided from successful firms. Hudson went on a communications campaign, spending 13 months personally persuading hundreds of franchisees (many of whom then persuaded others).

Hudson focused his new management team on brand building, tripling the marketing budget and investing in market research. One result was superb new advertising campaigns on a large scale. The team developed new products, including a breakfast line (imagine fruit tacquitos) to help franchisors raise revenue

Sidebar 7.8 (cont.)

Sonic is a masterpiece of conflict management

and amortize fixed costs. Brand identity was improved by a campaign of remodeling based on a standard template whose costs were predictable. Sonic used its company stores as test sites to convince franchisees to adopt the new look. The result for franchisees was an average sales gain of 8 percent.

Internally, Sonic improved operations, carrying off purchasing coups and developing, then rolling out, lower-cost methods of operation. Using fast, accurate computerized information systems and point-of-sale terminals to examine purchase patterns, Sonic detected where costly menu variety could be reduced without hurting sales. These changes cut franchisee operating costs from 79 percent of sales to 73 percent. New data analysis processes helped to detect trends, such as types of sites that did well with odd items (chocolate cherry vanilla Cokes, for example). In this way, Sonic used franchisee ideas to develop new products, whereas prior management would harass franchisees for trying anything new. A new culture of two-way communication, listening as well as talking, took hold, pushed by an active franchisee advisory council. Said one influential franchisee of Hudson, "Cliff is very good at selling instead of forcing."

To gain cooperation, management made significant concessions to franchisees, including a guarantee of no new stores until the problems were fixed. Sonic also accepted limits on opening new stores where franchisees exist. Sonic conceded 20-year contracts with an option to renew for 10 more years, delighting the franchisees, who were negotiating to gain a mere 5 years. Master franchisees (holders of multiple locations) were guaranteed the first opportunity whenever new markets opened, as well as protection from company stores in their territories.

Five years later, the results were stunning. Morale was up, reflecting that franchisees were profitable and satisfied. And well they could be: Average unit sales were up 5 percent per year for five years running. A critical industry indicator, same-store sales were also up in a period when those at McDonald's were down. Cooperation was up and standardization largely achieved. As for the franchisor, Sonic enjoyed annual sales growth of 17 percent and profit growth of 28 percent over the same five years. Once the problems were solved, Sonic resumed system growth. By 2002 the chain had grown to over 2,400 stores, and it continues to grow today.

more effectively by principals that invest in vigorous programs of two-way communication within the channel.[58]

One drawback of economic incentives is that they can rapidly multiply and become difficult to administer. Complicating the matter is that channel networks come to have many points of contact and frequently are made up of many organizations. The sheer task of keeping track of one's channels is daunting. On the customer side, firms have moved to solve this problem by investing in customer relationship management (CRM). An emerging solution is the conceptual parallel for channel members, which has been dubbed partner relationship management (PRM), described in Sidebar 7.9.

Sidebar 7.9

Partner relationship management

Simply keeping track of channel members is a challenge. Some firms are responding by automating information systems to help them find and use information about their channel members, just as they do about their customers (customer relationship management, or CRM). Partner relationship management (PRM) is a software system that allows the user to communicate with channel members, manage marketing development funds, carry out profiling, and even automate some transactions. Channel automation tools, at their root, constitute electronic support for channel managers.[59]

These tools have been available since the 1990s, and have experienced varied market reception, some of it decidedly negative. Manufacturers have struggled to use these systems to get around a common problem: internal demarcations. Says one consultant, Olivier Choron of Noroch Consulting (a specialist in PRM application):

> Often the data about which partner sold what resides in finance, and channel-marketing people simply can't get their hands on it. Equally, leads are generated by a marketing department which is focused on end-user demand and which has little or no interest in allocation. At one division of a household name all leads were sent straight to the wholesalers for allocation to whomever they saw fit! A software company had no idea who its partners were. Until these processes are thought through properly, and until human behavior has changed, introducing a piece of clever software is about as likely to succeed as slapping Elastoplast onto a gangrenous wound. Before such a system can go live, a supplier has to change its behavior. It then also has to communicate this change of behavior to the channel.[60]

Not surprisingly, PRM has become a negative term in some companies, in part because they had overbuilt expectations about what the software would do and how quickly.

What do companies do with PRM systems? At a basic level, the system supports a producer Web site, which resembles a brochure dedicated to channel members. Often, these are prompted by the need to collect and pass on leads. But these systems are capable of much more. They can allow a user to see a channel member's transaction history. An extension is to input data about the channel member that is unconnected to its experience with this producer. A producer can see that a small partner that buys infrequently is really part of a large reseller, for example. With PRM, firms can introduce and track more subjective information, such as their assessments of a partner's strengths and weaknesses. This encourages thinking about segmenting channel members based on their behavior and profile.

Managing leads is a major motivation. "Closed loop" systems oblige a channel member to do something (such as provide feedback) in return for a lead. The most sophisticated systems are connected with a firm's e-commerce capability. These systems not only allocate and transmit leads to channel members (following decision rules set by the producer) but track whether the channel member followed up on the lead and whether business resulted. For example, Microsoft Europe processes 10,000 leads per day from small and medium businesses and knows the outcome of every one. Some systems even adjust the allocation rule to feed more leads to those channel members who make more use of them.

PRM systems also help manage marketing development funds. In general, systems help producers manage and change their rules of engagement with partners. For example, firms that practice dual distribution (independent and employee sales) can enforce rules such as "no employee salesperson gets a commission on any order less than a certain size."

Sidebar 7.9 (cont.)

Partner relationship management

PRM can help in tracking the firm's own order pipeline in various stages (development, bid, etc.). This capability can be used to improve production planning.

Just as CRM helps corporate gain control over marketing, PRM helps corporate gain control over channels. Some firms use PRM to combine profiles from different independently managed divisions to describe the total business that a given reseller does with the entire firm. Firms also use PRM to make it harder for field personnel to create exceptions to corporate rules (e.g., in pricing).

Once a system is in place, producers make new uses of it. For example, Cisco and Microsoft do extensive technical training of channel members via partner portals. Producers use the PRM system as a tactical communication platform (e.g., to download artwork approved for use in cooperative advertising campaigns).

The most advanced companies, such as Electrolux and Hewlett-Packard, have systems for tracking the profitability of each channel member. This is a very difficult task, in part because it is not evident what data to use and how to get it. Here, PRM systems have the advantage of tracking qualitative as well as quantitative inputs.

There is general agreement that technical challenges are present but are not insurmountable. For example, Oracle has been successful with its Partner Network portal (a project sponsored by Larry Elison, the firm's founder and CEO) in part because it consolidates no fewer than twenty-three sites into one. The portal offers different views to different users, depending on which of thirty-five job functions one fills and the status of the partner organization that is signing in. One benefit Oracle realizes from the system is that it frees salespeople from collecting partner data. This makes them more available to assist channel members (who themselves have taken over maintaining their profiles in return for such benefits as claiming ownership of new leads).

The biggest obstacle is implementation. As Olivier Choron notes, the behavior of people in an organization needs to change. Some firms have used this need proactively to moderate a culture driven by direct sales forces. Channel managers can be relegated to the sidelines in such firms. A well-functioning PRM system is a way for channel managers to enhance channel performance—and to document it for direct comparison to in-house sales force productivity. The result is that channel managers are better able to document the surprising effectiveness and efficiency of third parties in achieving affordable, high-performance coverage.

SUMMARY

Conflict, a negative in most human relationships is also a negative in many channel relationships. It is not uniformly undesirable, however. Indeed, a channel can be too peaceful; indifference and passivity often pass for harmony, masking great differences in motivation and intention. In contrast, a contentious channel is often engaged in functional conflict: The parties are raising their differences and working through them in search of a better understanding and a higher plane of performance. Channel conflict is often a necessary stage on the way to adapting to environmental changes. Thus, conflict in channels should not be judged automatically as a defect, as a state to be eliminated. Instead, conflict should be monitored and then managed. This can mean trying to increase conflict, as well as trying to reduce or redirect it.

Managing conflict first means assessing it. A good way to do so is to index, for each issue that is relevant to a channel, the level of frequency of disagreement, intensity of disagreement (how far apart are the parties), and the importance of the issue. If any of these is low, the issue is not a great source of conflict (the participants' opinions notwithstanding). The product of intensity, frequency, and importance of dispute over each issue, summed over the issues, gives a good rough approximation of actual conflict and suggests to the arbitrator how to convince parties to resolve their differences. This implies that more complex relationships are likely to experience more conflict.

Conflict is a staple in marketing channels because of built-in differences in viewpoint and goals. Goal differences are real enough: Curiously, perceived differences can actually outweigh them as causes of opposition. Different perceptions also spark much dispute, in part because channel members see different pieces of the channel environment. A perennial source of conflict is clash over domains, wherein suppliers perceive their channels represent competitors, and downstream channel members perceive their suppliers pit them against other channel members and other channel forms. This latter (multiple channels) has become quite normal as industries mature and customers become more demanding. Solutions involve communication, concession, creative compensation, compensating multiple parties, working together to devise win-win approaches, and selling differentiated products through different channels. Solutions also involve accepting conflict for the sake of serving customers better or more economically.

A major source of friction is gray markets, which are growing rapidly. These exist because both parties (especially suppliers) have reasons to permit them privately while bemoaning them publicly. For suppliers, reasons include higher sales, as well as the ability to prod authorized channels and to reach a different segment. Objectives aside, gray markets are not easy to eliminate, leading firms to tolerate them under certain circumstances.

Conflict is self-perpetuating, self-fueling. Once it is underway, parties develop long memories and interpret events negatively. The cycle is easily started by threats, which beget reaction in kind, especially the more capable the other party is of actually doing harm. Reciprocation of coercion can easily send the channel into a self-destructive spiral of aggression.

A number of ways to resolve disputes are effective. Institutionalized mechanisms to contain conflict early exist in abundance, including information intensive strategies and the use of third parties. Once conflict begins, the styles of the parties influence the course of their dispute. The most effective style is driving toward achieving the goals of both parties (collaboration, or problem solving). This requires the commitment of both parties, and it works well when both parties are powerful in the relationship. A good relationship recovers from destructive acts by suppliers, especially if it is one of balanced high dependence. Indeed, dealers, for example, may even passively accept a supplier's destructive act, especially if they believe the external environment pressures the supplier and explains its action. But destructive actions cannot go on indefinitely without provoking an angry, and perhaps damaging, counterreaction.

Of course, conflict can also be resolved via the use of economic incentives, which are quite effective when coupled with good communication. Particularly good incentives are less visible (therefore harder for competition to match) and encourage channel members to make an effort or investment and assume some risk in order to collect them.

Take-Aways

- Conflict is a negative in many channel relationships. However, indifference and passivity often pass for harmony, and a contentious channel may be raising differences and working through them in search of a better understanding and a higher plane of performance.

- Channel conflict is often a necessary stage on the way to adapting to environmental changes. Thus, conflict in channels should not be judged automatically as a defect, as a state to be eliminated. Instead, conflict should be monitored and then managed.

- A good way to assess the true degree of conflict is to index, for each issue that is relevant to a channel, the level of
  - Frequency of disagreement
  - Intensity of disagreement (how far apart are the parties)
  - Importance of the issue

    If any of these is low, the issue is not a great source of conflict (the participants' opinions notwithstanding).

- Conflict is a staple in marketing channels because of
  - Built-in differences in viewpoint and goals
  - Differing perceptions, in part because channel members see different pieces of the channel environment
  - Clash over domains (roles, responsibilities, territories)

- A major source of domain conflict is multiple channels. Solutions involve communication, concession, creative compensation, compensating multiple parties, working together to devise win-win approaches, and selling differentiated products through different channels. Solutions also involve accepting conflict for the sake of serving customers better or more economically.

- Gray markets are growing rapidly. These exist because both upstream and downstream channel members (especially suppliers) have reasons to permit them privately while bemoaning them publicly.

- Conflict is self-perpetuating, self-fueling. Reciprocation of coercion can easily send the channel into a self-destructive spiral of aggression.

- Institutionalized mechanisms to contain conflict early exist in abundance, including information intensive strategies and the use of third parties.

- The most effective style of resolving conflict is driving toward achieving the goals of both parties (collaboration, or problem solving). This requires commitment from both parties and works well when both parties are powerful in the relationship.

- A good relationship recovers from destructive acts by suppliers, especially if it is one of balanced high dependence.

- Destructive actions cannot go on indefinitely without provoking an angry, and perhaps damaging, counterreaction that can take years to erase.
- Conflict can be resolved via the use of economic incentives, which are quite effective when coupled with good communication. Particularly good incentives are less visible (therefore harder for competition to match) and encourage channel members to make an effort or investment and assume some risk in order to collect.

DISCUSSION QUESTIONS

1. A marketing channel is an interdependent set of entities: They need each other. Why, then, is conflict a normal state in channels? Why does vertical integration fail to eliminate conflict completely?

2. When do suppliers tolerate gray marketing, and why?

3. "As markets mature, it is essential to set up multiple channels (different types), and to let them compete head on." Debate this statement. What responsibility, if any, do suppliers have to manage conflict between multiple channels? How can they go about doing so?

4. Refer to the Meccano example. If you had been part of the management team when the Toys "R" Us deal was being negotiated, would you have opposed it? Was there a way to avert the catastrophic outcome? Was this outcome just bad luck? What would you have suggested doing instead? What channels would you approach today to launch the new product line, and how would you try to manage conflict as these channels grew?

5. When is coercion a good idea, and why? When is it most likely to be used, and by which channel members?

6. What can channel members do to prevent conflict from becoming dangerous? To what extent can management control conflict in its early stages?

7. "If you don't negotiate aggressively, you won't get anything. You have to push for what you want with channel members, and you have to negotiate hard." Debate this statement. What are the best conflict resolution styles, and when is each style likely to be used?

8. If economic incentives are effective ways to resolve conflict, why not simply offer better terms to the trade? What are the best ways to resolve conflict by making a resolution economically appealing? Why is it effective to couple incentives with communication?

9. What are the principal reasons why Cliff Hudson's strategy of resolving conflict at Sonic were successful?

10. Imagine you are a channel manager for Toro, a prestigious supplier of lawn mowers. You have relied on a dealer network but now wish to add a mass merchandiser chain. This means you are contemplating a destructive act. Imagine the reaction of one of your most important dealers. What would you need to know to forecast the dealer's reaction? What could you do to limit the negative consequences of this reaction, and would it be worthwhile to do so? Repeat the exercise for a minor dealer.

11. You are a B2B producer with a large and fragmented product line aimed at a large and fragmented market. Should you use multiple routes to reach this market? What are the trade-offs? How serious will channel conflict be, and what steps might you take to minimize conflict?

ENDNOTES

1. Stern, Louis W. (1996), "Relationships, Networks, and the Three Cs," in *Networks in Marketing*, D. Iacobucci, ed. (Thousand Oaks, CA: Sage Publications), pp. 3–7.

2. Stern, Louis W. and James L. Heskett (1969), "Conflict Management in Interorganizational Relations: A Conceptual Framework," in *Distribution Channels: Behavioral Dimensions*, Louis W. Stern, ed. (Boston: Houghton-Mifflin), pp. 156–175.

3. Pondy, Louis R. (1967), "Organizational Conflict: Concepts and Models," *Administrative Science Quarterly* 12, no. 2 (September), pp. 296–320.

4. Zwick, Rami and Xiao-Ping Chen (1999), "What Price Fairness? A Bargaining Study," *Management Science* 45, no. 6 (June), pp. 804–823.

5. Brown, James R. and Ralph L. Day (1981), "Measures of Manifest Conflict in Distribution Channels," *Journal of Marketing Research* 18, no. 3 (August), pp. 263–274. This article is the basis for the discussion and example of measuring channel conflict.

6. Dwyer, F. Robert, Paul H. Schurr, and Sejo Oh (1987), "Developing Buyer-Seller Relationships," *Journal of Marketing* 51, no. 2 (April), pp. 11–27.

7. Webster, Bruce (1998), "Uses and Abuses of Co-Op Advertising," *Supply House Times* 41, no. 1 (March), pp. 57–64.

8. Anderson, James C. and James A. Narus (1984), "A Model of the Distributor's Perspective of Distributor-Manufacturer Working Relationships," *Journal of Marketing* 48, no. 4 (Autumn), pp. 62–74.

9. Geyskens, Inge, Jan-Benedict E.M. Steenkamp, and Nirmalya Kumar (1999), "A Meta-Analysis of Satisfaction in Marketing Channel Relationships," *Journal of Marketing Research* 36, no. 2 (May), pp. 223–238.

10. Taylor, Alex (2002), "Finally GM Is Looking Good," *Fortune*, April 1, pp. 42–46.

11. Bergen, Mark, Shantanu Dutta, and Orville C. Walker Jr. (1992), "Agency Relationships in Marketing: A Review of the Implications and Applications of Agency and Related Theories," *Journal of Marketing* 56, no. 3 (July), pp. 1–24.

12. Magrath, Allan J. and Kenneth G. Hardy (1989), "A Strategic Paradigm for Predicting Manufacturer-Reseller Conflict," *European Journal of Marketing* 23, no. 2, pp. 94–108.

13. Eliashberg, Jehoshua and Donald A. Michie (1984), "Multiple Business Goals Sets as Determinants of Marketing Channel Conflict: An Empirical Study," *Journal of Marketing Research* 21, no. 1 (February), pp. 75–88.

14. Ross, William T. and Diana C. Robertson (2000), "Lying: The Impact of Decision Context," *Business Ethics Quarterly* 10, no. 2 (Summer), pp. 409–440.

15. John, George and Torger Reve (1982), "The Reliability and Validity of Key Informant Data from Dyadic Relationships in Marketing Channels," *Journal of Marketing Research* 19, no. 4 (November, Special Issue on Causal Modeling), pp. 517–524.

16. Brown, James R., Robert F. Lusch, and Laurie P. Smith (1991), "Conflict and Satisfaction in an Industrial Channel of Distribution," *International Journal of Physical Distribution and Logistics Management* 21, no. 6, pp. 15–26.

17. Tkacik, Maureen (2003), "In a Clash of Sneaker Titans, Nike Gets Leg Up on Foot Locker," *Wall Street Journal*, May 13, pp. A1, A6.

18. This sidebar is based on Tkacik, Maureen (2003), "In a Clash of Sneaker Titans, Nike Gets Leg Up on Foot Locker," *Wall Street Journal*, May 13, pp. A1, A6, complemented with information from Foot Locker's corporate Web site.

19. Morgan, Robert M. and Shelby D. Hunt (1994), "The Commitment-Trust Theory of Relationship Marketing," *Journal of Marketing* 58, no. 3 (July), pp. 20–38.

20. Johansson, Johnny K. and Ikujiro Nonaka (1987), "Market Research the Japanese Way," *Harvard Business Review* 65, no. 3 (May–June), pp. 1–5.

21. LaBahn, Douglas W. and Katrin R. Harich (1997), "Sensitivity to National Business Culture: Effects on U.S.-Mexican Channel Relationship Performance," *Journal of International Marketing* 5, no. 4 (December), pp. 29–51.

22. *Sales and Marketing Management* (1996), "Newsmakers: Acacia, Inc.," *Sales and Marketing Management* 148, no. 4 (April), p. 20.

23. The discussion in this section is based on communications with Alberto Sa Vinhas and Frazier, Gary L. (1999), "Organizing and Managing Channels of Distribution," *Journal of the Academy of Marketing Sciences* 27, no. 2 (Spring), pp. 226–240.

24. Frazier, Gary L. and Tasadduq A. Shervani (1992), "Multiple Channels of Distribution and Their Impact on Retailing," in *The Future of U.S. Retailing: An Agenda for the Twenty-First Century*, Robert A. Peterson, ed. (Westport, CT: Quorum Books), pp. 217–238.

25. Cespedes, Frank V. and Raymond Corey (1990), "Managing Multiple Channels," *Business Horizons* 33, no. 4 (July–August), pp. 67–77; and Moriarty, Rowland T. and Ursula Moran (1990), "Managing Hybrid Marketing Systems," *Harvard Business Review* no. 6 (November–December), pp. 146–150.

26. Bialobos, Chantal (1999), "Meccano en Pieces," *Capital* 10, no. 12 (December), pp. 53–54.

27. Sa Vinhas, Alberto, and Erin Anderson (2005), "How Potential Conflict Drives Channel Structure: Concurrent (Direct and Indirect) Channels," *Journal of Marketing Research* (forthcoming).

28. Bucklin, Christine B., Pamela A. Thomas-Graham, and Elizabeth A. Webster (1997), "Channel Conflict: When Is It Dangerous?" *McKinsey Quarterly* 7, no. 3, pp. 36–43.

29. Moriarty, Rowland T. and Ursula Moran (1990), "Managing Hybrid Marketing Systems," *Harvard Business Review* 44, no. 6 (November–December), pp. 146–150.

30. Webb, Kevin L. (2002), "Managing Channels of Distribution in the Age of Electronic Commerce," *Industrial Marketing Management* 31, no. 2 (February), pp. 95–102.

31. Dutta, Shantanu, Mark Bergen, Jan B. Heide, et al. (1995), "Understanding Dual Distribution: The Case of Reps and House Accounts," *Journal of Law, Economics, and Organization* 11, no. 1 (April), pp. 189–204.

32. Villas-Boas, Miguel (1997), "Product Line Design for a Distribution Channel," *Marketing Science* 17, no. 2, pp. 156–169.

33. Sullivan, Mary W. (1998), "How Brand Names Affect the Demand for Twin Automobiles," *Journal of Marketing Research* 35, no. 2 (May), pp. 154–65.

34. Purohit, Devavrat (1997), "Dual Distribution Channels: The Competition Between Rental Agencies and Dealers," *Marketing Science* 16, no. 3 (Summer), pp. 228–245; and Purohit, Devarat and Richard Staelin (1994), "Rentals, Sales, and Buybacks: Managing Secondary Distribution Channels," *Journal of Marketing Research* 31, no. 3 (August), pp. 325–338.

35. This section is adapted from Coughlan, Anne T. and David A. Soberman (2005), "Strategic Segmentation Using Outlet Malls," *International Journal of Research in Marketing*, 22, no. 1 (March), pp. 61–86; and Soberman, David A, and Anne T. Coughlan (1998), "When Is the Best Ship a Leaky One? Segmentation, Competition, and Gray Markets," INSEAD working paper 98/60/MKT, summarized in Champion, David (1998), "Marketing: The Bright Side of Gray Markets," *Harvard Business Review* 76, no. 5 (September–October), pp. 19–22.

36. Weigand, Robert E. (1991), "Parallel Import Channels: Options for Preserving Territorial Integrity," *Columbia Journal of World Business* 26, no. 1 (Spring), pp. 53–60; and Assmus, Gert and Carsten Wiese (1995), "How to Address the Gray Market Threat Using Price Coordination," *Sloan Management Review* 36, no. 3 (Spring), pp. 31–41.

37. Henricks, Mark (1997), "Harmful Diversions," *Apparel Industry Magazine* 58, no. 9 (September), pp. 72–78.

38. Cespedes, Frank V., E. Raymond Corey, and V. Kasturi Rangan (1988), "Gray Markets: Causes and Cures," *Harvard Business Review* 88, no. 4 (July–August), pp. 75–82; and Myers, Matthew B. and David A. Griffith (1999), "Strategies for Combating Gray

Market Activity," *Business Horizons*, 42, no. 6 (November–December), pp. 2–8.

39. Bergen, Mark, Jan B. Heide, and Shantanu Dutta (1998), "Managing Gray Markets Through Tolerance of Violations: A Transaction Cost Perspective," *Managerial and Decision Economics* 19, no. 8 (May), pp. 157–165.

40. Anderson, Erin and Barton Weitz (1992), "The Use of Pledges to Build and Sustain Commitment in Distribution Channels," *Journal of Marketing Research* 29, no. 1 (February), pp. 18–34.

41. Geyskens, Steenkamp, and Kumar (1999), previously cited.

42. Kumar, Nirmalya, Lisa K. Scheer, and Jan-Benedict E. M. Steenkamp (1998), "Interdependence, Punitive Capability, and the Reciprocation of Punitive Actions in Channel Relationships," *Journal of Marketing Research* 35, no. 2 (May), pp. 225–235.

43. Ganesan, Shankar (1993), "Negotiation Strategies and the Nature of Channel Relationships," *Journal of Marketing Research* 30, no. 2 (May), pp. 183–203.

44. Kumar, Scheer, and Steenkamp (1998), previously cited.

45. Anderson, Erin and Barton Weitz (1989), "Determinants of Continuity in Conventional Channel Dyads," *Marketing Science* 8, no. 4 (Fall), pp. 310–323.

46. This discussion is based on Frazier, Gary L. and Raymond C. Rody. (1991), "The Use of Influence Strategies in Interfirm Relationships in Industrial Product Channels," *Journal of Marketing* 55, no. 1 (January), pp. 52–69.

47. Hibbard, Jonathan D., Nirmalya Kumar, and Louis W. Stern (2001), "Examining the Impact of Destructive Acts in Marketing Channel Relationships," *Journal of Marketing Research* 38, no. 1 (February), pp. 45–61.

48. Stern, Louis W. and Patrick J. Kaufman (1985), "Electronic Data Interchange in Selected Consumer Goods Industries," in Robert D. Buzzell, ed., *Marketing in an Electronic Age* (Boston: Harvard Business School Press), pp. 52–73.

49. Kelleher, Kevin (2004), "Giving Dealers a Raw Deal," *Business 2.0* 5, no. 11 (December), pp. 5–6.

50. This section is based on Ross, William H. and Donald E. Conlon (2000), "Hybrid Forms of Third-Party Dispute Resolution: Theoretical Implications of Combining Mediation and Arbitration," *Academy of Management Review* 25, no. 2 (April), pp. 416–27.

51. Mohr, Jakki and Robert Spekman (1994), "Characteristics of Partnership Success: Partnership Attributes, Communication Behavior, and Conflict Resolution Techniques," *Strategic Management Journal* 15, no. 2 (February), pp. 135–152; and Mohr, Jakki, and Robert Spekman (1996), "Perfecting Partnerships," *Marketing Management* 4, no. 4 (Winter–Spring), pp. 34–43.

52. Heide, Jan B. and George John (1992), "Do Norms Matter in Marketing Relationships?" *Journal of Marketing* 56, no, 2 (April), pp. 32–44.

53. Heide, Jan B. (1994), "Interorganizational Governance in Marketing Channels," *Journal of Marketing* 58, no. 1 (January), pp. 71–85.

54. This material is based on Thomas, Kenneth W. (1976), "Conflict and Conflict Management," in *Handbook of Industrial and Organizational Psychology*, M. D. Dunnette, ed. (Palo Alto, CA: Consulting Psychologists Press), pp. 889–935; and Ganesan, Shankar (1993), "Negotiation Strategies and the Nature of Channel Relationships," *Journal of Marketing Research* 30, no. 2 (May), pp. 183–203.

55. Murray, John P. Jr., and Jan B. Heide (1998), "Managing Promotion Program Participation Within Manufacturer-Retailer Relationships," *Journal of Marketing* 62, no. 1 (January), pp. 58–68.

56. Anderson, Erin, Leonard M. Lodish, and Barton Weitz (1987), "Resource Allocation Behavior in Conventional Channels," *Journal of Marketing Research* 24, no. 1 (February), pp. 85–97.

57. Goldman, Lea (2002), "Greased Lightning," *Fortune*, October 28, pp. 24–26.

58. Mohr, Jakki and John R. Nevin (1990), "Communication Strategies in Marketing Channels: A Theoretical Perspective," *Journal of Marketing* 54, no. 4 (October), pp. 36–51.

59. Hotopf, Max (2004), "I Can See Clearly Now," *Routes to Market* (*The Channel Management Journal from VIA International*) 4, no. 1 (Spring), pp. 5–7; Hotopf, Max (2002), "Making Sense of PRM," *Routes to Market* (*The Channel Management Journal from VIA International*) 2, no. 3 (Autumn), pp. 2–4; Hotopf, Max (2004), "PRM + E-Commerce = Channel Automation," *Routes to Market* (*The Channel Management Journal from VIA International*) 4, no. 1 (Spring), pp. 13–14; and Hotopf, Max (2003), "What Numbers Should You Collect?" *Routes to Market* (*The Channel Management Journal from VIA International*) 3, no. 2 (Summer), pp. 7–8.

60. Hotopf, Max (2004), "PRM + E-Commerce = Channel Automation," *Routes to Market* (*The Channel Management Journal from VIA International*) 4, no. 1 (Spring), p. 13.

Chapter 8

Strategic Alliances in Distribution

Learning objectives

After reading this chapter, you should be able to do the following:

- ▧ Define and describe the hallmarks of committed relationships in marketing channels
- ▧ Distinguish upstream and downstream motivations to form an alliance
- ▧ Describe why many channel members do not want and do not have committed relationships
- ▧ Sketch the performance implications of channel alliances and explain why most firms should have a portfolio of relationships, many of which are *not* close
- ▧ Describe how to lengthen the time horizon of the relationship and why this is critical
- ▧ Explain why channel members deliberately increase their vulnerability and how they manage this exposure
- ▧ Detail the role of idiosyncratic investments and give examples for any channel member
- ▧ Sketch the bases of trust
- ▧ Describe how trust is built over time in a marketing channel
- ▧ Differentiate the five phases of a close marketing channel relationship

Marketing channels typically are composed of multiple companies, each pursuing its own interests. Because these interests are competing, channel members often fail to cooperate with each other and even work at cross-purposes. Strategic alliances in distribution are forged in order to solve this problem. In a well-functioning alliance, two parties in a marketing channel function as if they were one. They may even make end customers believe they are dealing with a single organization that is fully vertically integrated. Indeed, many alliances are better coordinated than are channels that really are vertically integrated.

Achieving such close coordination in a marketing channel is an almost utopian ideal. Yet, it can and does happen. Some strategic alliances perform marketing channel flows so well that the alliance members cooperate even better than do the divisions of a firm that really *is* a single vertically integrated market channel. This extraordinary achievement brings obvious benefits to the channel. But the costs are high and many are hidden. Although the channel as a whole functions effectively, to the benefit of the last buyer in the channel (the end-user), members of a distribution alliance may not share equitably in the rewards due to their coordinated efforts.

What is the difference between a strategic alliance and any other well-functioning marketing channel? What do the members of the alliance hope to get out of it? Do they actually gain the benefits they seek? At what cost? What characterizes an alliance in distribution? How can these alliances be built? In the end, is a distribution alliance worth its cost? A great deal of progress has been made in recent years to answer these questions and to illuminate the nature and value of strategic alliances in distribution. This chapter takes an inventory of the answers that have been developed to date.

STRATEGIC ALLIANCES: THEIR NATURE AND THE MOTIVES FOR CREATING THEM

What Is a Strategic Distribution Alliance?

In a strategic alliance, two or more organizations have connections (legal, economic, and/or interpersonal) that cause them to function according to a perception of a single interest shared by all the parties. An alliance is *strategic* when the connections that bind the organizations are enduring and substantial, cutting across numerous aspects of each business. Membership in an alliance causes each party to alter its behavior to fit the objectives of the alliance. Alliances go under many labels, including close relationships, partnerships, relational governance, hybrid governance, vertical quasi-integration, and committed relationships.

Strategic alliances are a subject of fascination, and not just in marketing channels. Ironically, in the 1970s, close, committed business partnerships were widely considered unnatural, unusual, and inferior forms of governance in Western business. An overcorrection resulted, such that some circles now tout alliances as a universal cure for any deficiency. Other ways of managing channels, such as the creative and equitable use of power (Chapter 6), have been inaccurately dismissed as ineffective or passé. This chapter presents a balanced view of what alliances can do, when they are appropriate, and how they are built and maintained.

The term *alliance* has become so popular that it is overused. Many so-called strategic alliances are really just tactical arrangements of convenience or are merely normal business relationships that run with little conflict. Sometimes an alliance is really a relationship of imbalanced power in which the more powerful organization exerts control over the weaker ones. The result is that the organizations do function as one but not because their enduring connections give them a single overriding interest. In an alliance, power is balanced and it is high: Each side exerts considerable influence over the other.[1]

A *distribution alliance exhibits* genuine commitment. Commitment exists when an organization desires the relationship to continue indefinitely. However, this in itself is not enough to make an alliance. The organization must also be willing to sacrifice to maintain and to grow the relationship. These sacrifices may take the form of giving up short-term profits or of not pursing other opportunities, preferring instead to devote the organization's resources to the alliance. Sacrifices also are made, for example, to accommodate the other side's needs, more so than would be done for an ordinary business transaction. In general, a committed party works hard to maintain and to grow the relationship, even though growth demands resources and puts a strain on the organization.

Commitment is difficult to observe. It is an attitude, an intention, and an expectation, all wrapped into one. *True alliances encumber the parties involved, imposing on them obligations that may be very costly.* Many organizations profess commitment to each and every one of their many business relations. This encourages pleasant interactions among people in upstream and downstream organizations but is seldom an accurate description of how their organizations really deal with each other. True commitment is often revealed rather than professed. In contrast, superficial commitment is disguised, presented as though it were real. Usually, the disguise is not effective. Figure 8.1 lists a cluster of behaviors and attitudes that have been demonstrated to accompany genuine commitment. While no single indicator is particularly informative, the set taken together gives a good index of the strength of commitment an organization has toward a member of a marketing channel.

Commitment, then, means a long time horizon *plus* an active desire to keep the relationship going *plus* a willingness to make sacrifices to maintain and grow the relationship. A committed distribution relationship is often likened to a marriage. The marriage analogy is misleading in one important respect: Channel organizations can

Figure 8.1   Symptoms of commitment in marketing channels

Symptoms of Commitment in Marketing Channels

A committed party to a relationship (a manufacturer, a distributor, or another channel member) views its arrangement as a long-term alliance. Some manifestations of this outlook show up in statements such as these, made by the committed party about its channel partner.

- We expect to be doing business with them for a long time.
- We defend them when others criticize them.
- We spend enough time with their people to work out problems and misunderstandings.
- We have a strong sense of loyalty to them.
- We are willing to grow the relationship.
- We are patient with their mistakes, even those that cause us trouble.
- We are willing to make long-term investments in them and to wait for the payoff.
- We will dedicate whatever people and resources it takes to grow the business we do with them.
- We are not continually looking for another organization as a business partner to replace or add to this one.
- If another organization offered us something better, we would not drop this organization, and we would hesitate to take on the new organization.

Clearly, this is not normal operating procedure for two organizations. Commitment is more than having an ongoing cordial relationship. It involves confidence in the future and a willingness to invest in the partner, at the expense of other opportunities, in order to maintain and grow the business relationship.

Source: Adapted from Anderson, Erin and Barton Weitz (1992), "The Use of Pledges to Build and Sustain Commitment in Distribution Channels," *Journal of Marketing Research* 29, no. 1 (February), pp. 18–34.

and do have multiple alliances simultaneously. A better analogy is to a deep friendship. These are difficult to build and costly to maintain, putting a natural limit on their number. Most people, like most organizations, should have a portfolio of relationships, many of which are ordinary friendships or acquaintances.

Of course, deep friendships (and marriages) exist in which one person is committed but the other is not. This is a situation of *asymmetric commitment*. It is not common in long-standing strategic alliances in distribution. Upstream and downstream channel members tend to commit in a symmetric way: Relationships persist if both are committed and, otherwise, neither is committed. The reasons for this symmetry are discussed later in this chapter.

Why Forge a Strategic Distribution Alliance? Upstream Motives

Why would an upstream channel member, such as a producer, desire to build a committed relationship with a downstream channel member, such as a distributor? Distribution alliances begin with the producer's recognition that it can profit from the many advantages a downstream channel member can offer, at least in principle. Chief among these, manufacturers tend to appreciate the ability to achieve better coverage and to do so at lower cost (including lower overhead).

At minimum, manufacturers must respect downstream channel members before building an alliance with them. Yet, it is surprising how often producers fail to appreciate the value that channel members provide them and how often producers overestimate their own ability to duplicate effectively and efficiently the third party's performance of these flows. It has been observed that "some manufacturers have a 'do it in house—technical' culture that prevents them from understanding, respecting, and trusting intermediaries to any degree."[2] Often, these organizations have an internal selling arm that views independent channel members as their competition. Alternatively, companies may be staffed by people who have never worked in channels and are distrustful of partners, people who "assume they will screw things up and they assume they will be very expensive."[3] In contrast, a channel-centric supplier is better able to understand and respect how an independent channel member undertakes flows and converts them into meaningful service outputs in order to generate results.

Given the building block of respect for the downstream organization, manufacturers desire an alliance in order to motivate distributors to represent them better in their current markets, in new markets, or with new products. Of course, there are ways to improve representation without going so far as to build an alliance. These include exerting power (particularly reward power) and encouraging functional conflict (disputes that move the parties toward aligning their viewpoints or agreeing on a course of action). Building commitment is, however, an effective and durable way to motivate downstream channel members. This is particularly true when the organization is being asked to assume the significant risks involved in performing channel flows for new products or in new markets. Sidebar 8.1 shows how John Deere motivated dealers to adapt to changing buyer behavior in the highly competitive market for lawn maintenance equipment while at the same time broadening their distribution and deepening their dealer relationships.

A producer may seek an alliance in order to coordinate its marketing efforts with distributors more tightly and thereby to do a better job of reaching the ultimate customer. Along these lines, the manufacturer may seek greater cooperation,

Sidebar 8.1

John Deere helps dealers reach out to women

John Deere is a venerable manufacturer of premium equipment for farmers and homeowners. Its trademark green tractors are a fixture both on the farm and in parks and larger private gardens. Cheryl Pletcher, director of channel marketing, and David Jeffers, manager of the retail brand experience, play important roles in Deere's Commercial and Consumer Division. Their jobs focus on helping the firm's 3,200 U.S. dealers adjust to radical changes in their markets.[4]

Deere invests heavily in consumer research, from which it learned that the firm enjoyed a high reputation but a low intention to buy. Sales were concentrated in the "pro-sumer" segment (consumers who want to buy products with a professional specification). People who simply wanted a lawn tractor (riding lawn mower) were not being persuaded. In particular, women influence some 80 percent of purchases (including making many purchases solo and mowing their own lawns). The Deere product, however, was not high in awareness or purchase intention among women.

A look at the dealer network helps explain why. Of the 3,200 dealers, 1,500 also sell agricultural products to farmers. Many channel relationships are very close and very old (up to a century). As American cities sprawl into the country, these dealers increasingly find their farmers being replaced by homeowners, a completely different market. Many dealers have difficulty adapting to a nontechnical, time-pressed customer. These prospects want solutions to their problems, but they are more interested in cup holders than in engine horsepower, which is not intuitive to farm equipment dealers. Many prospects have no idea where to find the dealers, who tend to be located outside of retail shopping districts. Says Jeffers, "We always joke that we have a great dealer network—cleverly hidden all over America!"[5]

Many a manufacturer would react by severing or downgrading relationships with such channel members. Deere, a channel-centric supplier that values continuity and trust, chooses to do the opposite. Deere works to help dealers make the transition, including helping to train dealer salespeople. Deere also helps stores redesign their store layout, working from a flexible format that can be adapted to the dealer's business mix—and to the other brands that Deere freely acknowledges the dealer needs to carry to generate sufficient sales volume. Says Pletcher,

Consumers are used to malls. They have told us that with some dealers, they just don't feel they have been invited in. You know the four Ps of marketing—price, place, product, and promotion? We know that even if you have the right products, at the right price, and with the right promotions, everything will come to naught unless the place is right. For consumers it really matters what the store looks like.[6]

Deere makes it a policy to pilot new programs on small groups of dealers and to garner their testimonials to use for rolling out the program after testing. In this way, it is encouraging dealers to try the new format. Notes Pletcher, "We have to convince them—they are not franchises."[7]

Deere made a decision not to abandon its dealer network and move to large retail after observing that Honda lost sales of outdoor power equipment in this way. How, then, to build sales to the average prospect? One solution is to offer a limited line of the firm's entry-level lawn tractors in Home Depot, a large building-supply firm that many dealers see as a prime competitor. Home Depot is interested in an exclusive (among building supply stores) and was disappointed with the high return rates of the brand it was carrying. Rather than going ahead unilaterally, Deere consulted its dealer

(continued)

Sidebar 8.1 (cont.)

John Deere helps dealers reach out to women

advisory council about this move. Dealers reluctantly accepted the idea and even asked to carry the same model line themselves on condition that Deere sell no other models to Home Depot.

The results have been beneficial to Deere, to its dealers, and even to Home Depot. Every machine sold through Home Depot is inspected first by a dealer mechanic, resulting in very low return levels to Home Depot. The dealer also services the machine and affixes its plate, even though Home Depot makes the sale. This is a source of income and gives the dealership an opportunity to contact the customer directly. Seeing the green machine in Home Depot has generated traffic to Deere dealers, much of it by pro-sumers who decide to find the dealer and see the full assortment once they have seen the entry-level model in a place they visit regularly.

Deere uses its resources to generate business for its dealers. For example, Deere products are available via a corporate Web site. All sales generated by the site go to the local dealers to "keep them in the loop." Similarly, Deere advertises to women and runs clinics for women via its dealers and has seen its sales to women soar as a result. The purpose is to drive prospects to find the dealers and to enable dealers to convert the lead into a pattern of repeat sales.

One side effect is that as dealers have consolidated into multiunit dealers owning three to five locations, they have scaled their Deere relationships to a higher level. Many suppliers are worried when consolidation forces them to deal with a smaller number of larger, more powerful channel members. But not Deere. Says Pletcher, "Frankly, we like it. You get a change of philosophy—they manage their dealership like a business and less like people who run a dealership because it is where they want to go to work everyday."

This story illustrates a crucial point. Because Deere has already created alliance-style relationships over decades of working with its dealer network, the company has been able to (a) convince dealers to accept distribution of the lower-end product through Home Depot and (b) build a win-win solution out of this situation, one that actually rewards the dealers for Home Depot sales. Augmenting specialty dealers with generalist mass-market competitors is usually a bitter issue of conflict with the dealers. It is not at all clear that Deere could have pushed through such an expansion of its distribution channels without this existing (very valuable) asset of the dealer alliance-quality relationships.

---

in particular, in the exchange of information. Via alliances, manufacturers hope to gain information about the marketplace. This is information that downstream channel members have economic motives to withhold. Distributors may withhold market information to prevent the manufacturer from using the information against them in negotiations (for example, over pricing). They may withhold information for a simpler reason: It takes time to brief a principal, and that time has other uses. Downstream channel members are often compared to a wall standing between the manufacturer and the final buyer, blocking the manufacturer's view and reducing its understanding of the final buyer. By gaining distributor commitment, the manufacturer hopes to increase information sharing, to look over the wall. An example is Hewlett-Packard's Imaging Division, which partners with selected European retailers. As a result of these selected alliances, H-P is singularly well informed about the retail side of the business: 40 percent of its retailers share weekly sales figures, information of immense value.[8]

An emerging motive to forge an alliance downstream is a wave of consolidation in wholesaling. Mergers and acquisitions in many industries are transforming the wholesaling level from many smaller players (fragmentation) to a handful of giant players (consolidation). Manufacturers seek alliances because they see the pool of potential partners drying up. They fear losing distribution not only due to the small number of players left standing but also because the survivors are themselves powerful organizations that often enter into more-or-less privileged relations with selected manufacturers. An alliance is a way to rebalance the power arrangement, as well as to retain access to markets.[9]

In the longer term, the manufacturer seeks to erect barriers to entry by future competitors. One of the best possible barriers is a good distribution network. This is because a channel, unlike a price cut or a product feature, is very hard to duplicate. A committed channel may refuse to carry or to actively promote an entrant's brands. Finding another channel that works as well as a distribution alliance is a challenging task for many manufacturers.

An example is the justly celebrated alliance between two old adversaries, Procter & Gamble (P&G) and Wal-Mart.[10] Both are noted for using their considerable power to sway the trade. P&G's brand appeal and market expertise in hundreds of fast moving consumer goods is so dominant it has been described as a "self-aggrandizing bully." Wal-Mart, the massive retailer, uses its volume and growth to oblige its suppliers to do business as it dictates: no intermediaries, extraordinarily low prices, extra service, preferred credit terms, investments in EDI (electronic data interchange) and RFID (radio frequency identification) technology, and similar demands.

These upstream and downstream giants built an alliance using the techniques described in this chapter, particularly making investments tailored to each other. For P&G, the payoffs have come in several forms. It receives continuous data by satellite from individual denoted Wal-Mart stores (*not* pooled over the entire store network). This microlevel data covers sales, inventory, and prices for each stock-keeping unit of each brand P&G sells. P&G is responsible for reordering from itself and automatically shipping, often directly to the stores (a practice called vendor managed inventory). The cycle is completed by electronic invoicing and electronic funds transfer.

This paperless system allows P&G to produce to demand, to cut inventories, *and* to reduce stockouts. Overall logistics costs have been reduced. P&G does an enormous business with Wal-Mart, protected from competition by the investments it has made and its intimate knowledge of Wal-Mart's needs. P&G further has an excellent source of market research in the store-level data it garners from Wal-Mart.

Why Forge a Strategic Distribution Alliance? Downstream Motives

The motives of downstream channel members to build alliances revolve around having an assured and stable supply of desirable products. Consolidation is a motive here: As mergers and acquisitions concentrate market share among a few manufacturers in many industries, downstream channel members commit to the survivors to maintain product supply. Channel members also build alliances to make their own marketing efforts more successful. By coordinating their efforts with a supplier, channel members

Sidebar 8.2

East African Breweries: Keeping beer in stock

East African Breweries Limited (EABL) is pro-filed in Chapter 9 for its decision to dismantle its wholly owned facilities, instead outsourcing distribution and in Chapter 6 for its decision to serve the large, fragmented, hard-to-reach Kenyan market with a mere 30 wholesalers. A critical challenge is to ensure that these whole-salers have enough stock without creating large inventories of a perishable, bulky product. The solution was to entrust all logistics, including warehousing, inventory management, and trans-portation, to a single provider and to govern that crucial relationship with an alliance.

Tibbet and Britten (T&B) is a U.K.-founded multinational logistics company. EABL had a large beer and malt distribution fleet of vehi-cles and fully fledged maintenance facilities for it. In outsourcing all of its noncore activities, EABL transferred (for a consideration) its fleet to T&B, which was new to the market at the time and, hence, without a substantial fleet of vehicles. The two companies entered into a long-term, open-book contract, under which T&B receives a fixed management fee and bonus calculated as a percentage of agreed cost savings annually. Under the open-book terms,

T&B bills EABL with all the costs it incurs in executing its obligations to the latter. These include the salaries of staff dedicated to the EABL account and all transport costs (includ-ing a capital charge for fleet depreciation).

T&B maintains storage and puts its transport personnel on all of EABL's factory premises. This staff works closely with EABL production and sales teams in inventory and distribution management and receives weekly sales forecasts from EABL for planning transport require-ments. Finished products leaving EABL's pro-duction lines are turned over to T&B, which moves the beer to its warehouses and assumes full responsibility for its delivery to the 30 dis-tributors who enjoy market exclusivity in Kenya on behalf of EABL brands.

For its part, EABL provides T&B with office facilities, including space and telephones, for staff based at EABL. The two parties have an annual service level agreement that forms the basis of performance and its measurement. For example, the agreement stipulates EABL's obligation to provide T&B with sales/demand forecasts of a specified accuracy in order for the latter to supply adequate transportation.

hope to work better together. This is not an objective in itself; it matters because it helps the channel member to serve its customer better. This, in turn, translates into higher volume and higher margins.

Channel members seek to cut costs via alliances. For example, by coordinating logistics, the channel member can increase inventory turnover, keep lower levels of stocks, and take fewer write-downs of obsolete stock. The best of all worlds is achieved when stock costs are cut *and* the channel member suffers fewer out-of-stock situations. Sidebar 8.2 sketches how East African Breweries Limited (EABL) did so by forging an alliance with a third-party logistics provider (3PL).

Downstream channel members, such as distributors, also build alliances to dif-ferentiate themselves from other distributors. By positioning themselves as the manufacturer's preferred outlets for desirable brands or for selected stock-keeping units (SKUs), distributors differentiate their assortment and related service. And by differentiating themselves, downstream channel members discourage new competitive entry into their markets.

Distributor differentiation is often based on a strategy of offering value-added services, such as preventive or corrective maintenance; application assistance; on-site product training; engineering and design; technical expertise on call; special packaging and handling; and expedited, free telephone assistance. Distributors pursuing this strategy are more likely to work closely with their suppliers, which helps the distributor set itself apart from fierce competition even while it helps the manufacturer build the market for its products.[11]

Returning to P&G's alliance with Wal-Mart, what benefits does the retailer gain? Inventories are lower, and the chain can offer its customers lower prices and greater availability of well-known brands. Wal-Mart is no longer responsible for managing its inventory (of course, this is only a benefit if the function is done well, which it is). And the paperless transaction system permits Wal-Mart to enjoy float: The retailer does not pay its supplier until after the consumer pays for the merchandise. This system, difficult to build and to duplicate, gives Wal-Mart a formidable competitive advantage in the saturated retail arena.

Upstream and downstream motives to forge a strategic alliance are much more similar than they appear at first glance. Figure 8.2 summarizes the preceding discussion and notes the parallels between the interests of both sides. As this figure shows, upstream and downstream channel members fundamentally pursue alliances for their same reasons: enduring competitive advantage, leading to profit. Both parties seek to improve their coordination within the channel in order to serve customers better and hold down accounting costs and opportunity costs. Both parties seek to build stable relationships that are difficult to duplicate. In this way, they aim to discourage entry into their respective businesses. Fundamentally, distribution alliances may resemble marriages, but the motives of both players are calculated strategically and economically.

Do Alliances Outperform Ordinary Channels?

Do the parties to an alliance do their calculations correctly? Do alliances really outperform ordinary channel relationships?

At first glance, the answer seems to be yes. Committed parties trust each other, and trust today enhances performance tomorrow.[12] Trusting parties will do more for each other, going so far out of their way to help each other that their actions resemble altruism rather than economic profit maximization. (As will be discussed, this appearance is deceiving.) Trusting parties find it easier to come to agreements, to work out conflicts, and to work with each other. In particular, trust helps the parties cope with unfavorable outcomes and turn them around.[13] Trust is social capital: Just like financial capital, organizations use it to increase their effectiveness. Later in this chapter, we cover the origins of trust.

Differentiation and commitment go together. Manufacturers whose marketing strategy is to differentiate their offerings (as opposed to a solely cost-oriented leadership strategy) are more likely to build closer relationships with channel members. These relationships enable producers to implement their strategy successfully in the marketplace. This is particularly important in many industrial markets, where the channel, rather than advertising, has a huge impact on the brand's image.[14]

Motives to Ally Strategically	The *Upstream* Channel Member	The *Downstream* Channel Member
Fundamentals	Motivating downstream channel members to represent them better • In current markets • With current products • In new markets • With new products	Avoiding stockouts while keeping costs under control • Lower costs of all flows performed, such as lower inventory holding costs
Generating customer preference	Coordinating marketing efforts more tightly with downstream channel members • Get closer to customers and prospects • Enhance understanding of the market	Coordinating marketing efforts more tightly with upstream channel members • Serve the customer better • Convert prospects into customers • Net effect: higher volume and margins
Preserving choice and flexibility of channel partners	Guaranteeing market access in the face of consolidation in wholesaling • Keep routes to market open • Rebalance power between the producer and surviving channels	Assuring a stable supply of desirable products, even as manufacturers consolidate • In current markets • Selling current products • Opening to new markets • With new products
Strategic preemption	Erecting barriers to entry to other brands • Induce channels to refuse access • Induce channels to offer low levels of support to entrants	Differentiating themselves from other downstream channel members • Supplier's preferred outlet • Value-added services, difficult to copy and of high value to their customers
Superordinate goal	Enduring competitive advantage leading to profit • Reduce accounting and opportunity costs	Enduring competitive advantage leading to profit • Reduce accounting and opportunity costs

Figure 8.2   Motives to create and maintain strategic alliances in channels

Manufacturers are not the only ones that benefit. Evidence suggests that some distributors have a pronounced market orientation. Even more than other distributors, they focus their organizations on collecting, spreading, and using information about customer needs to differentiate themselves. These distributors often ally with suppliers who are also market oriented. Together, the market-oriented pair tends to build an alliance from which the market-oriented distributors gain a notable improvement in their financial performance.[15] This links back to the message early in this book that the ultimate customer is the end-user, not the next channel member. The most successful channels are those in which all the channel members realize this and take actions to meet the end-users' demands.

In general, commitment today means cooperation tomorrow. The long time horizon that is part of an alliance creates better strategic and economic outcomes.[16] Because they know they will be there to reap the benefits, channel members are more willing to make investments that serve the end-user, reduce costs, and differentiate the channel system.

Indeed, concrete evidence indicates that channel partnerships generate higher profits together. Evidence also suggests that typically each side of a channel partnership collects more profit from its alliance than from ordinary relationships.[17] Channel partnerships generate higher profits and share them rather than degenerating into a situation whereby one side gets the lion's share of the benefits the partnership generates.

But this does not mean that all channel relationships should strive to become alliances. The reason is because alliances are very difficult and very costly to create. There is no guarantee that spending enough time and money will make commitment happen. Many circumstances do not lend themselves to the vertical quasi-integration represented by alliances.[18] Even in the right circumstances, building commitment is not easily done. Worst of all, we know how to recognize committed relationships when we see them, but it is very difficult to specify how to create some of their critical properties.

Most firms should have a portfolio of relationships, including some alliances. The rest of this chapter inventories what we know to date about the properties marketing channel alliances exhibit and how to build them. We conclude by returning to and closing the issue of when alliances are worth building.

BUILDING COMMITMENT BY CREATING MUTUAL VULNERABILITY

The Minimum Requirement: Expectations of Continuity

A channel member who wants to build commitment into a relationship must begin by building in the expectation that the prospective partners will be doing business with each other for a long time. The expectation of continuity is essential before any organization will cooperate and invest to build a future.[19] Continuity is not taken for granted. Channel members know that they will be replaced if their performance does not satisfy.

Worse yet, in environments where legal barriers to termination are low (such as the United States), channel members fear they will be replaced even if their performance *does* satisfy! For example, principals often engage agents or resellers to represent secondary products or to penetrate peripheral markets. If the downstream channel member makes a success of the business, it should (and does) fear that the producer will take the business away or will renegotiate the terms of the arrangement to appropriate some of the unexpected gains.[20]

What inspires a channel member's confidence that a business relationship will last?[21] Several key factors have been identified for downstream channel members. Their expectation of doing future business on behalf of a principal strengthens for producers whom they trust (more to come in a later section), and producers with whom they enjoy two-way communication, including active give and take of ideas. Communication plays a particularly powerful role. Trust and communication operate in a reinforcing cycle: the more trust, the more communication, which leads to more trust, which strengthens communication even more, and so forth. *Frequent, candid, detailed* mutual *communication is a must for a healthy channel partnership.*[22] This said, more than a few members of would-be channel alliances think they enjoy better communication and higher trust levels than they really do.

Downstream channel members also expect continuity of relationships with producers who enjoy a reputation for treating other channel members fairly, as well as producers with whom they have been doing business for some time already. But a problem lies hidden in old, seemingly stable channel relationships. Communication is often rather low in these older relationships, as though the two parties think they know each other so well that communication is superfluous. Older channel relationships frequently look stronger than they really are, because both sides take them for granted and permit communication to decline. Eventually, lack of communication will damage the trust that resides in old, stable relationships.

Continuity expectations are higher when power is balanced in a relationship. When power is imbalanced, the weaker party fears being exploited and is more likely to defect. Knowing this, the stronger party discounts the future of the relationship because it expects the weaker party to withdraw or to go out of business. Thus, even when one party has the upper hand, it has less confidence that its relationship will last than in a balanced-power scenario—in developed economies. Chapter 6 (on channel power) discusses why imbalanced relationships are more stable in emerging economies. As noted earlier, however, these relationships are not alliances, even though they have continuity.

The *combined stakes* of the two parties also play a role: The more the two sides get from the relationship, the more they expect it to continue. At least one party has too much to lose to let the relationship end without fighting to preserve it. Ideally, both parties have stakes (for example, both derive substantial revenues from the arrangement), so both parties have an interest in not capriciously letting the relationship end.

That the relationship has a future in the eyes of the players is a minimal condition for building commitment. To erect a true alliance, the next step is crucial: Each side must believe that the other is committed.

Why Commitment Is Nil Unless It Is Mutual

Given some expectation of continuity, the next step in alliance building is to earn the other party's commitment.[23] To do so, it is essential to be committed to the relationship.

Seriously asymmetric commitment is rare. This is because partners to an alliance do their calculations. They do not accept the obligations of being committed unless they believe their counterpart is also committed, also ready to assume obligations.

Channel members who doubt the commitment of another organization may proclaim themselves partners in the interest of preserving appearances, but they do not believe in, nor do they practice, commitment.

Is it not possible for a channel member to be deceived? Is it not possible to convince a channel partner that one's commitment is genuine when it is not? The evidence suggests this strategy does not work in most circumstances. Both upstream and downstream channel members are usually well informed about each other's true state of commitment, and they carefully condition their own attitude on what they believe (reasonably accurately) the other's commitment to be.

How do they know each other's true states? In part, they are aware because organizations, unlike some people, are not very good actors. Even if all points of contact are instructed to put up a façade, the counterpart sees through and discerns reality. This works both ways: Truly committed firms may project that they are not so committed because they want to conceal what they see as their dependence, their vulnerability, but the projection fails; their partners are not misled.

Wisely, organizations do not gauge each other's intentions so much by what the organization says as by what it does—and by what it has done. The past lingers in relationships. For example, while a certain level of conflict is to be expected in marketing channels, some parties have experienced an unusually high level of conflict. These relationships are very difficult to salvage. Sustained conflict operates like a feud, making it extremely difficult to move on to build commitment. Both upstream and downstream channel members discount the commitment of old adversaries, even if new management appears and assures its channel partners that their relationships will improve. The assurance is not convincing. Managements that permit conflict to go out of control for an extended period incur an opportunity cost: The relationship is unlikely ever to become a true partnership, even if peace is finally achieved.

The past lingers in a positive sense as well. For example, once trust is established between two organizations, it persists, even as individuals move on.[24] This surprises many people who believe that intangible relational states (such as trust, conflict, and agreement on goals) belong only to people and change when individuals leave their positions. However, relational states also belong to organizations and outlive personnel turnover. This organizational memory plays a large role in conditioning how each party gauges the commitment level of its channel counterpart.

What happens when the players come to suspect that commitment is not balanced? In the first stage, one party suspects—usually rightly—that it is more committed to the relationship than is the other party. This is an uncomfortable position, and the party that feels overcommitted does not like it. This party feels vulnerable, fears being exploited, perceives more conflict in the relationship, and derives lower profits than it would if the commitment levels were seen (and correctly so) to be more balanced. Conversely, the undercommitted party does like its position of feeling less tied to the relationship than does its counterpart. This party is more satisfied with what it gets from the partnership. This cannot go on indefinitely. Sooner or later, in stage two the overcommitted party scales back to bring the relationship into alignment. See Chapters 6 (on power) and 7 (on conflict) for more on the balance of commitment in relationships.

This situation involves a circle of perception followed by adjustment (Figure 8.3). Two parties, such as a supplier and a distributor, reveal their level of commitment to

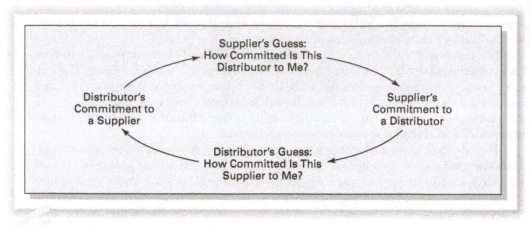

Figure 8.3   The circle of commitment

each other deliberately and, to a great extent, inadvertently. Thus, most perceptions of commitment are at least reasonably accurate. From these perceptions, organizations calibrate their own commitment as an act of reciprocation. This is how commitment tends to reach alignment, often at mutually low levels. To ratchet up commitment, one party must convince the other that its true commitment is higher, so that reciprocity will raise mutual commitment.

How the Other Side Gauges Your Commitment

Consider that you are a distributor dealing with a supplier. You will gauge the supplier's commitment to you based on their past behavior. You will focus on two critical aspects: (1) Have you had an acrimonious past with this supplier, and (2) what actions do you see the supplier taking to tie itself to doing business with you? Such actions convince you of the supplier's genuine commitment.

These actions take two forms. One is to give you some degree of protection from your competitors who also are selling the supplier's brand. The greater the degree of selectivity you see the supplier exercising in its coverage of your market, the more you believe the supplier is truly committed to a business partnership with you. At the limit, if you believe the supplier gives you territory exclusivity, you gauge this to be a highly committed supplier. Conversely, the more you see your competitors selling the same brand, the less commitment you believe your supplier feels toward you.

What if your supplier practices direct selling? This is the practice of keeping house accounts, which the supplier serves directly, thereby competing with its own downstream channel members. Should this not destroy your confidence in their commitment? Apparently, a manufacturer can practice direct selling to a rather substantial degree, yet still inspire confidence in its resellers. How does this happen?

To some extent, many manufacturers camouflage the full extent of their direct selling. But this is not the major factor. Downstream channel members have some private tolerance for direct selling (although many deny it publicly). They believe that some customers will only deal directly. If so, the business is already lost to downstream channel members. They also believe that some customers have needs the supplier is better able to fill. The key issue here is the perception that the manufacturer is handling direct business fairly, as opposed to "being greedy" (taking business capriciously or unnecessarily from the channel member).

As a distributor judging a supplier, selectivity is one indicator you would use to infer supplier commitment to you. Another major factor is the supplier's efforts to build assets that cannot be redeployed from you to another distributor. These assets are idiosyncratic (specialized, customized) to your supplier's relationship with you. Were the supplier to replace you, it would need to write off (or greatly write down) its investment in you. To duplicate the value created with you, the supplier would need to make a new investment in the competitor who replaces you. Examples of these difficult-to-redeploy investments (discussed further in Chapter 9 on vertical integration) are:

> Supplier personnel and facilities dedicated to you, the distributor
> The supplier's stock of learning about you—your methods, your people, your strengths and weaknesses
> Compatible reporting systems geared to the peculiarities of your system (especially if your system is proprietary)
> Investments designed to identify your business and their business in the mind of the customer
> Investments, such as general training programs, that help you run your business better
> A location near you, at a remove from your competitors

These investments vary in how easy they are to redeploy, but all of them are costly to move. Employees will be disrupted. Dedicated personnel can be reassigned if there is other work for them, but their relationships with you become worthless. Facilities may be retrofitted if they are still needed, but with effort. Learning about you can be discarded unless your competitors are essentially interchangeable, which is unlikely. The supplier could put on training programs for your replacement but cannot recoup the training invested in you. The supplier could serve your competitor from a location especially suited to you—but will incur extra cost. Worst of all for the supplier will be the job of explaining to customers that representation has changed. Sidebar 8.3 details an example of idiosyncratic investments made by clothing manufacturer Levi Strauss, investments that have radically shifted its customer base and market positioning and have tied the jeans maker closely to retailer Wal-Mart.

These idiosyncratic (to you) investments are otherwise known as credible commitments, pledges, or company-specific investments. When you see manufacturers invest in you in this fashion, your confidence in their commitment soars because they are erecting a barrier to their own exit from their relationship with you.

Consider the other side of the situation. You are now the supplier, gauging the distributor's commitment to its relationship with you. You, too, will discount the commitment of a formerly acrimonious relationship. You will believe in the commitment of a distributor that gives you some degree of selectivity in your product category. At the limit, you will be inspired by the apparent commitment of a distributor that gives you category exclusivity (in your category, carries only your brand).

Sidebar 8.3

Levi Strauss changes its routes to market

Levi Strauss, maker of Levi's blue jeans since 1853, was for decades a sought-after brand name that could use its referent power to dictate terms to retailers.[25] But the legendary firm has struggled for years with intensified competition in branded jeans. In the 1990s, the firm found that its traditional clientele was aging, and its customer base was not being renewed. Those customers young enough to prize jeans (and to fit into them) favored emerging brands, such as Diesel, or less expensive brands, such as Wrangler or private label jeans. Levi Strauss tried a multitude of approaches to improve its brand image and appeal, including suing some European retailers for selling gray-market Levis at a low price. Over time, in a bid to raise sales, Levi began selling to less prestigious retailers, such as J. C. Penney and Sears Roebuck. In retaliation, other retailers dropped the brand. A prime outlet, Gap, replaced Levis entirely with its private label.

As the situation worsened, Levi Strauss appointed a chief executive officer, Philip Marineau, who had no apparel experience at all. In fact, his background was in soft drinks, including selling to Wal-Mart, the mammoth retailer that accounts for 9 percent of all non-auto-related consumer sales in the United States.

To broaden appeal, a new jean line under a new brand name, Levi Strauss Signature, was created for mass merchants. In Europe, the company has a history of refusing to sell to mass merchants and then suing them for using gray marketers to supply Levis for these channels to sell at a low price. Not surprisingly, Signature has not been well accepted by most mass merchants in Europe. In the United States, the line has done much better. The reason is an alliance with Wal-Mart.

Within a week of his appointment, Wal-Mart called Marineau. Initially, Marineau rejected the chain's overtures, knowing that Levi had a history of late, incomplete deliveries and that Wal-Mart was known to make strict production demands. Wal-Mart agreed to wait. Levi opened an office in Bentonville, Arkansas (headquarters of Wal-Mart), and spent ten months completely remaking its distribution system—to Wal-Mart's specifications. The idea was that using feedback from Wal-Mart, Levi would learn how to forecast and manage its supply chain better. Other customers worried that Wal-Mart would undercut them on price. Marineau responded, "By learning to do business with Wal-Mart, you improve your supply chain and logistics in general. Our service to you will only get better as we service Wal-Mart."

Initially, the idea worked less well than expected, and Wal-Mart cut the price considerably to move the merchandise. But over time, with active adaptation of the product and the channel based on feedback from Wal-Mart, the Signature line has become established, albeit at a lower price than originally expected. Wal-Mart is satisfied because the line has brought in a new customer and has induced shoppers who only come to its stores for basic items to begin to shop for apparel. Levi's new supply chain capabilities have built a large mass merchant business, and its premium lines are starting to reenter higher-end stores.

The heritage of this wrenching change goes beyond the supply chain, extending to design, production, and pricing. Levi Strauss today considers itself better able to compete in a very different world. Says Marineau, "The balance of power has shifted. When I first started in this business, particularly in packaged goods, retailers were a way station to the consumer. Manufacturers had a tendency to tell retailers how to do business. We had to change people and practices. It's been somewhat of a 'D-Day invasion' approach."[26]

As of 2005, it is too soon to gauge whether Wal-Mart will reciprocate. Certainly, Levi Strauss

Sidebar 8.3 (cont.)

Levi Strauss changes its routes to market

hopes and expects that its idiosyncratic investments in Wal-Mart will send a credible signal of its commitment and will make Wal-Mart value the Signature brand highly. Levi's intention is clearly to duplicate the close relationship that Procter & Gamble enjoys with Wal-Mart. But will it work? The success of the strategy rests on just how Wal-Mart–specific these investments really are. Levi Strauss describes them as customized to Wal-Mart, but if they are, why does Marineau claim that Wal-Mart will teach Levi Strauss how to manage its supply chain? Marineau suggests that other retailers will benefit if, via the Wal-Mart adventure, Levi Strauss learns to forecast accurately and deliver on time. If so, Wal-Mart is teaching Levi Strauss skills that are generic, hence redeployable. This is the basis for business as usual, not a strategic alliance.

Ultimately, the relationship may be a way for Levi Strauss to transition its brand equity down market while Wal-Mart benefits for a limited time from a preferred supplier arrangement. The seeming alliance may be simply an arrangement of convenience for both sides.

You will believe in the commitment of a distributor that invests in you in an idiosyncratic manner, one that would be difficult to transplant whole to a competing supplier. You would welcome the distributor's:

- ➤ Dedication of people and facilities to your line
- ➤ Investment in upgrading and training the personnel serving your line
- ➤ Efforts to learn about you and build relations with your people
- ➤ Training of its customers on the use of your line
- ➤ Efforts to ally its name and yours in customers' eyes
- ➤ Investment in a reporting system particularly compatible with yours (especially if yours is proprietary)
- ➤ Location of a facility near you and far from your competitors

If your relationship with this distributor ends and if the distributor has another use for these assets (another supplier to take on), what happens to these assets? Some of them can be adapted but at substantial cost. Others must be recreated entirely, such as relationships or proprietary reporting systems. Seeing the distributor make these investments leads you to believe the organization really means to build a future with you and sacrifice on your behalf. If they do not, they impose a penalty on themselves.

Actions That Bind Distributors to Suppliers

So far, we have focused on the necessity of exhibiting commitment in order to inspire commitment. But what makes downstream channel members, such as distributors, commit to a supplier? Part of the story is calculation: The distributor enters relationships when it believes the payoffs will justify the cost. This means the downstream channel member expects results that it cannot get with a more conventional relationship.

To get these results, the distributor dedicates resources to a supplier. The supplier-specific investments mentioned above (dedicated personnel, joint marketing, and so forth) are made by the distributor to "expand the pie," that is, to generate exceptional results for the entire marketing channel.[27] If these investments are well considered, if the supplier works with the distributor, and if the distributor collects an equitable share of the pie, then the distributor is motivated to invest more. Over time, the distributor's accumulated investments become a motive to commit. The distributor works to keep an alliance going in order to protect these investments.

Other actions the distributor takes will build the distributor's commitment, particularly two-way communication. This means freely exchanging information (even though sensitive), getting involved in the supplier's marketing efforts, allowing the supplier to see weaknesses as well as strengths, and giving advice to the supplier. Of course, no distributor will do this if the supplier is not open to it: Two-way communication is a mutual effort.

Actions That Bind Suppliers to Distributors

Turning the lens around, what actions do suppliers take that commit them to a downstream channel member? Before making investments, many of them will rigorously verify the downstream channel member's ability and motivation.[28] They then make investments that are idiosyncratic to selected distributors in order to expand the channel pie. These investments (training, mingling the supplier's brand image with the distributor's image, etc.) serve not only to grow the pie but to strengthen the relationship. Suppliers that make distributor-specific investments increase their commitment because they know the assets will lose value if the distributor is replaced.

Two-way communication also plays a substantial role in assuring supplier commitment. Such communication allows the producer to look over the wall and see the market the distributor serves. Of course, this is dangerous for the distributor: The supplier could use the information against the downstream channel member.

It is worth underscoring that firms can create an alliance without creating a winning formula. The fact that two firms work together in a closely coordinated way does not ensure they will succeed. Indeed, the firms may reinforce each other's commitment to a poor strategy. For an example, see Sidebar 8.4 on the Smart car.

Creating Alliances via Ties That Bind

In a nutshell, the formula for building a channel alliance is: To get commitment, give commitment. But do not give commitment in a one-sided manner. Commit to those who commit to you. Observe their daily behavior and judge by the image they present every day, not the professed intentions of top management. Judge their commitment by their actions. Be wary of an acrimonious trading partner that claims to have positive intentions and to be ready to forget the past. Take seriously the commitment of those that limit dealings with your competitors, as well as those that make investments tailored to you—and difficult to redeploy to another organization.

Given the other party's commitment, do not hesitate to make these investments yourself. They generate value, inspire your counterpart, and oblige you to work to keep the alliance growing. Invest, as well, in two-way communication. Particularly if you are a supplier, manage the image of fair dealings you present to the channel. This reputation spreads quickly and influences the downstream channel member considerably.

Sidebar 8.4

Smart, the "Baby Benz"

Smart is a micro car conceived to be a solution to urban congestion and pollution. Originally a joint venture between Swatch (known for colorful, fun, fashionable, practical, inexpensive watches) and the Mercedes-Benz division of Daimler Benz (now DaimlerChrysler), the Smart was intended to be to automobiles what the Swatch is to watches. But Mercedes-Benz bought out Swatch and revamped the concept, making a car that was considerably more upscale, more highly engineered, and more expensive than the original vision.

The Smart (*Swatch Mercedes ART*) was launched in 1998 to great fanfare and high expectations. But the tiny, quirky car quickly ran into trouble. Mercedes made numerous adjustments to its marketing and production methods and injected large amounts of capital and management energy to make the Smart connect to a segment of buyers. Some of these measures worked briefly, and as the twenty-first century arrived, the micro car appeared to take off. But as of 2005, the Smart division is losing huge sums and does not appear to be close to a turnaround.

What went wrong? No single element can be named: Errors were made in pricing, advertising, positioning, the choice of models, and a range of other marketing and production decisions. But a decisive element is the strategy of distribution, which both contributes to and reflects the Smart's lack of market appeal.

Proud of its "Baby Benz," Mercedes believed that the car justified its own network of independent routes to market. Chapter 4 profiles the disastrous decision to cover all of Europe with only 110 points of sale. The result was that dealers were too far apart, particularly because service also had to be performed by those same dealers. As a result, the auto got off to a slow start, which made prospective buyers hesitate.

How could Mercedes have made such an obvious error as to give an enormous territory in exclusivity to one dealer? A possible explanation is that this concession was necessary to induce dealers not only to sell solely one car, then available solely in one model (an unusually risky and limited assortment) but also to invest in an extraordinary level of Smart-specific assets. Many of these are expensive gadgets, such as a multistory glass tower, 15 meters high (more than 45 feet). Inside the floodlit towers is a system of stands and elevators to stock and display the cars so as to make a colorful mosaic on all four sides, top to bottom. Although attractive and eye-catching, the glass towers are ruinously expensive and utterly unsuited to any other use. Further, they violate urban zoning laws. Mercedes insisted on the towers. Result: Dealers were located outside urban areas—yet, they were intended to sell and service a uniquely urban car.

In short, by insisting on Smart-specific investments in return for large exclusive territories, Mercedes convinced a handful of dealers to enter into an alliance. In spite of their best efforts, these dealers have been unable to overcome the fundamental flaws in the car's marketing and production strategy. Chapter 4 details the subsequent failure of placing the Smart with conventional Mercedes dealers, who hedged their investments, quickly concluded it does not fit their clientele, and rapidly redeployed the floor space back to conventional Mercedes cars.

Today, Smart is struggling to expand distribution, in part by dropping its idiosyncratic requirements of dealers (starting with the glass tower). A fundamental issue is that the car still exists in only a few models. Rectifying that problem is forcing Mercedes to escalate its commitment to a failing venture. It is hardly surprising that Mercedes has been obliged to expand distribution by creating "Smart centers" (essentially small, conventional showrooms) in

(continued)

cities. Smart management has decided that these sales outlets need not be so idiosyncratic after all. In the meantime, competitors have observed Smart's errors and are racing to enter the micro car niche or to expand efforts already devoted to their smallest cars.[29]

Sidebar 8.5 offers a comprehensive example of these principles. It details how Caterpillar, a leading maker of earthmoving equipment, has spent decades cultivating alliances with independent equipment dealers to create exceptional results through its marketing channels.

Fundamentally, this is a recipe for mutual vulnerability, that is, mutual exposure. The principle is that if both sides depend on each other, both sides will make the alliance strong. If one side tries to reduce its vulnerability, the other side will sense withdrawal and will match it. Indeed, it should—high and one-sided vulnerability is dangerous (Chapter 6 explores some ways of dealing with this). One entrepreneur describes an alliance like this:

> It's like a balance, a scale—in return for commitment on their part we say we are committed to you and we prove it. So it's a quid pro quo. It's a balanced relationship that says you make investments, we make investments; you take risks, we take risks; you perform, we perform. That's the basis on which you build trust and everything that I would consider to be a strong successful relationship.[30]

Management teams find this recipe unappealing. Commitment is costly. Alliances take time, risk, resources, and determination—from both sides. To justify these costs, alliances must generate exceptional returns. When they do, it is because they have made relationship-specific investments and have driven their organizations to communicate frequently, intensely, and thoroughly.

Another element also is essential to alliances. It is trust. To some extent, trust is created in the course of making relationship-specific investments and communicating. But trust is far more complex. It is a function of daily interactions, many of which are beyond top management's control. We turn next to the question of how to use trust to build stronger distribution alliances.

BUILDING COMMITMENT BY THE MANAGEMENT OF DAILY INTERACTIONS

What goes on "in the trenches" (i.e., in the conduct of daily business) has an enormous impact on relationship formation, far more than do pronouncements from corporate headquarters. Daily interactions between individuals in the channel drive the channel culture to improve, degrade, or stay stable. This creates a complex picture. The cumulative effect of daily interactions conditions the relationship heavily.

Sidebar 8.5

Caterpillar makes its dealers into partners

Caterpillar is a leading manufacturer of construction and mining equipment.[31] Its former CEO, Donald Fites, publicly proclaimed that the single biggest reason for Caterpillar's considerable success was its marketing channel. Fites' reasoning was tied to the nature of the product category ("the machines that make the world work"). Earthmoving equipment is highly expensive, so industry unit volume is low. Thus, there are few points of sale. The products are complex but fairly standard: The same machine, with minor customization, can be sold to mining operations, farms, and construction projects throughout the world. Though machines have a working life of up to thirty years, they break down frequently due to heavy use in difficult (often remote) environments. Breakdowns literally stop all operations. Minimizing the frequency and duration of breakdowns is, therefore, critical.

Caterpillar's strategy in this market was and is to charge a premium price, justified by differentiation on the basis of postsales service. Product service is critical to avoid breakdowns and to minimize downtime once they occur. To ensure superior service, Caterpillar sells most of its product worldwide through a close network of alliances with only 186 dealers, all of them independently owned, two thirds of them outside the company's North American home market.

Caterpillar sells through independent dealers because it believes no one else can provide the market intelligence and customer service that are essential to the company's marketing strategy. According to Fites, local dealers are long-standing members of their communities. They understand customers and can relate to them better than a global company can. For their customers, they serve as trusted sources of advice (which product, how to use it, when to trade it in), financing, insurance, operator training, maintenance, and repair. Repair is critical: Repairing or rebuilding a part must be done on the spot. Caterpillar commands a price premium by convincing customers they will have a higher percentage of uptime than they will with less expensive competing products.

To do this, Caterpillar forges alliances with dealers, who in turn are the face of the company to its customers. This may seem out of place for a company whose motto is "Buy the Iron, Get the Company." But Caterpillar believes that its dealers *are* a critical part of the company.

This does not mean dealers are solely responsible for all channel flows. Caterpillar maintains an extensive (and expensive) inventory of parts, with guaranteed delivery anywhere within 48 hours. And Caterpillar makes idiosyncratic investments in its dealers, including:

- Territory exclusivity
- Strong working relations between Caterpillar and dealer personnel, resulting in dealer-specific learning
- Assistance in inventory management, logistics, equipment management, and maintenance
- Generalized business training (forecasting, advertising, etc.)
- Joint marketing campaigns
- Technical training of dealer personnel

The accumulated value of these investments cannot be transferred to another dealer.

Dealers, in turn, make heavy Caterpillar-specific investments, including:

- Time put into their interactions with company personnel
- Exclusive dealing (no competing brands)
- Multimillion dollar inventories of parts
- Heavy fixed investments in Caterpillar-specific service equipment and information technology

(continued)

Sidebar 8.5 (cont.)

Caterpillar makes its dealers into partners

- Joint marketing
- Training their customers in the use of Caterpillar equipment

Of course, these are not the only investments dealers make. But they are the investments that would make it difficult to become a dealer for Komatsu, Hitachi, Kobelco, or Caterpillar's other competitors.

Caterpillar and dealers communicate frequently, giving them a common understanding of how to execute a strategy of superior customer service. Dealer input is used heavily in product design, and products are developed in consideration of what would fit the dealer network. Dealer and factory personnel work together to resolve product problems. Dealer and marketing personnel work together to keep massive data bases on customer experiences with the products. Virtually every Caterpillar employee has contact with dealer personnel. Perhaps most extraordinary, Caterpillar holds the financial statements of each dealer and even reviews them in annual meetings with dealer management. Caterpillar acts as a sort of benchmarking organization, using pooled data to tell dealers how their results fit with those of comparable dealers. The manufacturer is open as well: Virtually any of thousands of dealer personnel can access huge corporate databases.

Those 186 dealers combined are bigger than Caterpillar in employment and in financial worth. Like many strong relationships, Caterpillar and its dealers have many stories to tell of crises that were overcome by "sharing the pain and spreading the gain." In these stories, both sides take turns: The dealers save the situation on one occasion, Caterpillar steps in and loses money to protect dealers on another occasion. Caterpillar goes to lengths to project honesty, consistency, benevolence ("don't gouge your dealers"), and continuity.

In this regard, Caterpillar refuses to do direct selling around its dealers. Even when customers insist, Caterpillar refers the business to dealers (the Alaska Pipeline was one such project: The contract ultimately went to a partnership of two of the 186 Caterpillar dealers). Some markets in their entirety are served directly by the company: newly opened, formerly socialist countries, the United States government, and original equipment manufacturers (OEMs). Most of this business, however, gets its after-sales service and support from the dealer network.

Over time, a large stock of trust has accumulated. But there is also a reasonable level of conflict—functional conflict. Much of it is over perennial channel issues for any company: the limits of service territories, product and pricing policies, the dealer's desire to diversify into other product categories Caterpillar does not serve. While personal relationships are good and mutual respect is high, neither side misses an opportunity to criticize the other: Both are interventionist. Both sides are frankly interested in accumulating wealth, in making an attractive return on the very considerable investments that are required to manufacture and distribute earthmoving equipment.

Each dealer, with its stock of trust and idiosyncratic assets, is extremely valuable. Therefore, Caterpillar prefers to work with privately held companies, believing they have greater management continuity than publicly held companies. Indeed, Caterpillar is so interested in continuity that it runs programs for the teenage children of dealership owners to interest them in Caterpillar and in working in the family business.

What are the performance implications of these 186 alliances? Competitors have a substantial cost advantage, which Caterpillar counters by the premium pricing its dealers are able to uphold. Dealer input is essential in designing, manufacturing, and troubleshooting the

Sidebar 8.5 (cont.)

Caterpillar makes its dealers into partners

products, which benefits the supplier considerably. Caterpillar dealers pioneer new products for the company, enter new markets, and offer extraordinary cooperation, even helping the producer to sell products the dealers do not carry. For example, Caterpillar sells engines directly to original equipment manufacturers.

Dealers offer indirect assistance with these engine sales, and in return the dealers get the subsequent service contracts on the engines.

Ultimately, Caterpillar credits its dealers with its very survival and with its recovery from a very difficult period to restore its profitability and leading position as a global supplier.

In particular, the daily details of events and one-on-one interactions determine how much trust exists, which is essential for an alliance to function.

How Can Channel Members Manufacture Trust?

Trust, while easy to recognize, is difficult to define.[32] Your trust in a channel member is usefully conceptualized as your confidence that the other party is honest (stands by its word, fulfills obligations, is sincere). This is also associated with your assessment of the other party's benevolence, which is your confidence that the other party is genuinely interested in your welfare and your interests and will seek mutual gains rather than manipulate you to appropriate all the gains for itself. Overwhelming field evidence demonstrates that in channel relationships honesty and benevolence go together: Where one is missing, so is the other. To trust a channel member is to believe in that party's integrity and concern for mutual well being. To distrust is to fear deception and exploitation.

An alliance needs mutual commitment, and commitment cannot occur without a high level of trust. This is rational behavior: It is obviously a mistake to invest resources, sacrifice opportunities, and build a future with a party bent on exploitation and deception. A reasonable level of trust is necessary for any channel relationship to function. Distrust does not characterize channel relationships for long: It is either resolved or the channel dissolves. But committed relationships exhibit higher-than-usual trust levels.

If building commitment requires building trust, then how can channel members increase their stock of trust?

The Fundamental Role of Economic Satisfaction

Channel members commit in the rational expectation of financial rewards. They will not commit without the prospect of financial returns, and they will not wait indefinitely for those rewards to materialize. Economic satisfaction plays a fundamental role in building and maintaining the trust that is necessary for committed relationships.[33]

Economic satisfaction is a positive affective (emotional) response to the economic rewards generated by a channel relationship. Economic rewards are ultimately financial. Why cast this as an emotional state, rather than as, say, utility? Why not speak in terms of money rather than affect?

The reason is that the players do not count and compare money directly. It is difficult to put an accounting valuation with confidence on many of these outcomes (such as higher market share, or greater store traffic). Even if a valuation were to be made, it could not be compared directly across organizations. One hundred thousand euros worth of economic returns will satisfy one channel member but disappoint another.

Channel members do not react to results. They react to how the results *compare* with several baselines, such as what they had expected, what they consider possible, what they consider equitable, or what they expect to gain from their next best alternative use of the resources. The more the returns exceed the channel member's reference value, the higher is the likely level of satisfaction, and further, once an excess in returns is observed, the channel member has every reason to believe its partnership can continue to generate those high returns.[34] Therefore, economic satisfaction, rather than economic outcomes, is a major factor that increases trust.

Indeed, economic satisfaction is so important that many firms take the risk of making generic investments in channel members. These investments create vulnerability because they empower the recipient, who then can use the asset in the service of competitors. On the whole, firms that take this risk are rewarded by higher commitment, especially if they are industry leaders and if they mingle generic and idiosyncratic assets in a package.[35] See Sidebar 8.6 for an example from the tobacco industry.

This involves a circular logic. Organizations build alliances to produce outcomes and, therefore, to increase economic satisfaction. Economic satisfaction, in turn, increases trust and, therefore, builds alliances. Is economic performance a cause or an effect of committed relationships?

It is both. The better the alliance is doing financially, the more satisfied are the parties (at least, roughly), and the more they place their trust in the relationship. This builds commitment, which helps the parties increase their pie, which increases satisfaction (unless the baseline went up more than the results), which enhances trust, and so forth (as already presented in Figure 8.3).

Now we are in a difficult situation. We need results to build an alliance, but we need an alliance to generate results. This process must start somewhere. How do you build an alliance before having economic performance results to show?

Noneconomic Satisfaction Also Matters

A substantial body of evidence indicates that trust is associated with a set of other properties, many of which have to do with the psychological state of noneconomic satisfaction. Like economic satisfaction, this is a positive, affective (that is, emotional) response to the psychosocial aspects of the relationship.[36] A satisfied channel member finds interactions with the channel partner fulfilling, gratifying, and easy. Contacts with the other party are appreciated. A satisfied channel member likes working with its partner and perceives the partner to be concerned, respectful, and willing to exchange ideas (one foundation of two-way communication).

Noneconomic satisfaction can be purely interpersonal, but it can also be an interorganizational property that reproduces itself over and over at the level of daily interactions among people working for channel organizations. In some circles, these positive sentiments are dismissed as nice but not necessary. They are even ridiculed as being irrelevant, or not businesslike. Yet, study after study demonstrates that noneconomic satisfaction is tightly bound up with trust, which in turn is critical to building financially desirable alliances.

Sidebar 8.6

Philip Morris substitutes channels for advertising

An example of generic investment comes from Philip Morris in France, a country with a confused approach to limiting tobacco consumption.[37] On the one hand, cigarette advertising has become entirely forbidden, to be replaced by vigorous antismoking campaigns from the ministry of health. On the other hand, high tobacco taxes are a major source of revenue, which may be why government regulations oblige tobacco stores to accommodate smokers with long opening hours and a complete assortment of the 350 brands available in France. This creates a merchandising challenge for tobacconists, many of which are very small shops (because the government wishes to ensure that rural smokers have spatial convenience). Jeanne Polles is sales and marketing director for Philip Morris in France. She explains, "Tobacconist shops are cluttered, not always very clean, and yet, under the new laws, it is the only place we have left to talk to our consumers."

The supplier's solution is to give competency training in the form of a free half-day seminar on the importance of merchandising to any and all tobacco shops. Philip Morris sales reps provide the training, and the seminar is designed not to have the same feel as their once-a-month sales visit. This training is almost entirely generic and, therefore, benefits Philip Morris's competitors. The focus is merely to convince tobacconists of the seemingly obvious argument that better merchandising and shelf placement boosts sales. Anyone who has been in a typical French tobacco store can attest that the argument is not always obvious to the shopkeeper. But Philip Morris persists.

Philip Morris makes no special effort to protect this generic investment from free riding. However, in the process, the firm does try to create two idiosyncratic assets. One is an improved relationship between tobacconists and Philip Morris sales reps. The other idiosyncratic investment is the advice in one of the merchandising lessons: "More people will come in if they [the tobacconists] put Marlboro in the window." This is a credible statement that does not detract from the persuasive power of the training. This is an advantage of being a leading firm when making a largely generic investment upstream or downstream.

What produces noneconomic satisfaction? Two drivers stand out by their absence. One is the absence of dysfunctional conflict, which is lingering, unresolved intense disputes over major issues. The other is the absence of coercion by the other side. A party that sees its counterpart employing pressure, punishment, threats, and retribution experiences a rapid decline of positive sentiment even if the relationship moves in a direction that the channel member favors.

In contrast, liberal use of noncoercive influence strategies, such as exchanging information, offering high-quality assistance, and making requests, is an effective way to raise noneconomic satisfaction. These methods help to resolve conflict without appearing blunt or intrusive. By trying to influence partners in a noncoercive way, organizations create the impression of being accommodating, responsive problem solvers. Chapter 7 covers this issue in depth.

Noneconomic satisfaction is also bound up in perceptions of fairness on two fronts.[38] One is procedural fairness, the sense that one is treated equitably on a day-to-day basis regardless of the rewards derived from the relationship. The other is distributive fairness, the sense that one gains equitable rewards from the relationship regardless of daily interaction patterns. Distributive and procedural equity (discussed at length in Chapter 6) reinforce noneconomic satisfaction.

Picking the Partner and the Setting

At minimum, organizations are not good candidates for forging a committed relationship unless they possess complementary capabilities that they could exploit to create competitive advantage. Given complementarity, organizations can attempt to ally by declaration: Each corporate headquarters can issue instructions that bonding will commence, effective immediately. Of course, this does not work (as has been demonstrated by many channel members!). Trust is never awarded. It is earned. This takes time and effort (and may not work anyway).

This is why many organizations build on what they already have. When the parties have prior social and economic ties, they possess an asset (social capital). Frequently, they seek to leverage it by developing their ties further. In foreign markets, for example, firms that have a marketing arrangement with a distributor tend to add their new products to the existing arrangement even if it is not the best channel for the product in isolation. Familiarity causes termination if organizations do not like what they find. Otherwise, familiarity breeds trust. Firms do business with firms they know, and they extend their network by working with firms that are known by the firms they know (referral).[39] Personal relationships and reputations between people in the channel organizations play an important role in making existing relationships deeper, increasing the social capital that is already embedded in them.[40] These targeted firms may not be large or directly profitable in and of themselves. Sometimes the best partner is a smaller account that is critical to the firm's future (for example, by being an innovator that influences other firms).

Some firms use an elaborate strategy of "qualifying" a partner firm by attempting to find out a great deal about it before doing business with it. For example, some retailers qualify garment manufacturers by their actual garment quality, manufacturing capacity, price competitiveness, general business philosophy, reputation among other apparel companies and among other retailers, and reputation for garment quality and on-time delivery. This sort of investigation requires the cooperation of the resellers, which many of them will not give. Those who do cooperate in the qualification phase are already inclined to work with the prospective supplier. Hence, elaborate qualification efforts are a way to screen which channel members are most willing and able to partner in a trustworthy manner. The subsequent relationships are unusually flexible in the face of uncertainty.[41]

In contrast, some firms screen astonishingly little. They are content to go with impressions and assurances. For example, a channel manager of a motorcycle manufacturer was confident in his judgment based on his excellent track record in picking good distributors. He used his instincts to award exclusive distribution rights for Costa Rica to a seemingly impressive firm that promised a large initial order. The partner failed to deliver on the promised order. After some months, the manufacturer investigated, and only then learned that the owner of this exclusive distributor had a brother who was also a distributor—representing a directly competing line of motorcycles.[42]

Sidebar 8.7

Fujitsu and FedEx build a close relationship

This is a story of building an alliance from nothing in very little time.

In the 1990s, Fujitsu's PC division did 70 percent of its business in Japan. Fleeing fierce competition, Fujitsu entered the U.S. laptop market, only to discover the competitive situation was just as bad there. Disappointed with its performance, Fujitsu did a thorough review that pinpointed logistics as a major problem. Laptops were manufactured in Tokyo, then shipped by sea in large batches to two warehouses on the West Coast of the United States. The result was that channel partners were served too slowly.

In recognition that logistics is a channel competence, Fujitsu transferred all warehousing and distribution functions to a third party, FedEx. Fujitsu also made a FedEx-specific investment by opening a customer support center near Memphis, Tennessee. Memphis is the FedEx superhub but is poorly served by other carriers. Fujitsu further increased its reliance on FedEx by closing one of its West Coast warehouses.

Fujitsu's site-specific asset in Memphis created close physical proximity, which fueled communication. FedEx then came up with a radical idea: Why bring finished laptops from Tokyo? Why not instead expand the Memphis facility to create customized laptops? One hurdle was in determining how to do the final assembly: FedEx suggested CTI, a company that did such work for many other FedEx customers. (In turn, FedEx had gotten the entire idea by working with another of its customers, Dell Computer. This is an excellent example of channel members offering economies of scope.)

Fujitsu implemented the idea. Subassemblies are flown from Osaka to Memphis and turned over to FedEx and to CTI. FedEx takes operational responsibility for the entire subassembly and customization process and delivers the final product to the retailer or end-user.

Within a year, Fujitsu was no longer taking a month to supply mass-produced products to its channel. Instead, it transformed its business into customized production, with delivery guaranteed within four days of the placement of the order. The effect on Fujitsu's competitive advantage and profit is spectacular.

One analyst summarizes the alliance like this:

Fujitsu entered the relationship with a spirit of true strategic alliance. The company didn't choose FedEx because it was the cheapest provider. Nor did it reward its purchasing managers for jerking around and lying to FedEx to save a few yen. Nor did it enter the "partnership" with an arm's-length, quasi-adversarial, hyper-legalistic, supersecretive, no-trust, lowest-cost-at-all-cost, dump-them-tomorrow-if-we-get-a-better-deal mind-set.[43]

Instead, it enlisted FedEx as a full, active, intimate partner. Fujitsu and FedEx people tackled Fujitsu's operational problems together—openly and cooperatively—and developed a revamped logistics package.[44]

Of course, organizations do not always work with organizations they know. In building trust with another organization, it is useful to select one with similar goals. Goal congruence is effective in dampening conflict (see Chapter 7 for further discussion). Sidebar 8.7 explains out how a supplier, Fujitsu, swiftly built an alliance with a logistics provider, FedEx, from the ground up, beginning only with congruent business objectives.

Research has demonstrated that some people are trusting as a personality trait (similarly, some people are given to cynicism and unlikely to trust under any circumstances). Evidence suggests that the same is true for organizations. It is part of the culture of some companies to be trustworthy and to cultivate a reputation as such (others seek to disguise a culture of exploitation and dishonesty vis-à-vis trading partners). To some extent, an organization's trustworthiness is a part of its culture.[45]

Some environments are conducive to building trust. Trust goes up in generous (munificent) environments that offer resources, growth, and ample opportunity. These environments provide every incentive to work together, with rewards to be had by everyone. Conversely, trust goes down in volatile, complex, unpredictable environments. These environments are risky, treacherous, and difficult, requiring constant monitoring and fast adaptation. Conditions like this strain any relationship and create many opportunities for misunderstanding and dispute.

DECISION STRUCTURES THAT ENHANCE TRUST

The decision making that goes on inside a marketing channel has a structure. One very important element of that structure is the degree of its centralization in the upper reaches of an organization's hierarchy. This may be upstream or downstream. Whatever its source, centralization hurts trust.[46] Concentrating decision power in the upper echelons of one organization (as opposed to delegating decision making to the field level, preferably in both organizations) undermines the participation, cooperation, and daily interaction that help trust grow. Note, however, that centralization is a way for an organization to marshal its own resources to get things done. Centralized decision making should not be condemned, but its cost in terms of building trust must be acknowledged.

Another aspect of a channel's decision-making structure is formalization, the degree to which decision making is reduced to rules and explicit procedures. Formalization is widely considered to hurt trust. The reasoning is that this mechanistic approach to interactions robs the players of autonomy and thereby increases resentment. Formalization is also thought to be a signal that one party mistrusts the other, which invites reciprocal mistrust to develop. However, recent evidence suggests that it is the nature of the formalization that matters. Formalization can actually enhance positive attitudes and trust if it helps to clarify how tasks are to be done and who is responsible for doing them.[47] Formalization that focuses on clarifying roles can be helpful rather than constraining. In this vein, the more channel members agree about who is responsible for what (domain consensus), the higher their level of trust.

In general, the more channel members communicate, they more they also cooperate with each other on a daily basis. And the more they cooperate, the more they come to trust each other. Working together on issues of mutual relevance, such as on market plans, serves to build a basis for trust.

We are back to circular logic: Working together is both a cause (immediately) and an effect (later) of trust. This circularity—that actions that enhance trust and commitment create further trust and commitment—is why alliances take time to build.

How Do You Manufacture Trust in a Channel?

Consider that you are the top management of a downstream channel member desirous of building an upstream alliance with one of your suppliers. Your channel's trust level is low, and you intend to improve it. What should you do? Increase communication? Seek greater cooperation? Reduce conflict? Make conflict more functional? Align your organization's goals? Reduce your efforts to influence the other party coercively, substituting reasoned arguments and greater accommodation instead? Pay more attention to issues of fairness?

All of these actions are designed to create the properties of trusting relationships. Here is the paradox: Even though you, as top management, are dedicated to building trust, neither your employees nor the employees of your counterpart organization will be inclined to implement your plans. Why? Because they do not trust each other. Even if you can induce your own employees to make the effort, your channel counterpart may block their implementation and ignore your best efforts.

The top management of organizations can attempt to create a structure conducive to building trust and hope that employees will alter their everyday behavior accordingly. For example, organizations can balance each other's dependence by such actions as granting selectivity and creating idiosyncratic investments. Doing so in forgiving environments with little uncertainty or volatility makes it more likely that trust will take root. Further, organizations can eschew centralized decision making and can use their influence over their own personnel to elicit desired behavior, hoping for reciprocity.

Ultimately, however, structures and the policies to implement them only create a foundation for trust. From there, it is the daily interactions between people and the accumulation of experience that turn a structural opportunity into an operating reality. The bad news is that this is a slow, expensive, and uncertain process. The good news is that trust encourages the behaviors that maintain trust. Further, a marketing channel with high levels of trust is difficult for competition to imitate.

MOVING A TRANSACTION THROUGH STAGES OF DEVELOPMENT TO REACH ALLIANCE STATUS

From Cradle to Grave: The Life of a Marketing Channel Partnership

An appealing way to think about a close marketing channel relationship is to use the metaphor of a living creature, which moves through a life cycle marked by stages of development. An alliance represents the peak, the best and most intense part, of the close channel relationship's existence. Let us take a hypothetical supplier, Omega Industries, and a hypothetical distributor, Annecy, Ltd. These two organizations could form a marketing channel comprising a series of ongoing transactions, each evaluated on its own merits, with each side ready to terminate or reduce business dealings easily. This series of discrete transactions is a marketing channel but is not a close relationship. This channel could develop into an ongoing committed relationship by passing in order through up to five stages.[48]

Figure 8.4 gives additional details on these five stages.

Relationship Stage 1: Awareness	Relationship Stage 2: Exploration	Relationship Stage 3: Expansion	Relationship Stage 4: Commitment	Relationship Stage 5: Decline and Dissolution
• One organization sees another as a feasible exchange partner • Little interaction • Networks are critical: One player recommends another • Physical proximity matters: Parties more likely to be aware of each other • Experience with transactions in other domains (other products, markets, functions) can be used to identify parties	• Testing, probing by both sides • Investigation of each other's natures and motives • Interdependence grows • Bargaining is intensive • Selective revealing of information is initiated and must be reciprocated • Great sensitivity to issues of power and justice • Norms begin to emerge • Role definitions become more elaborated • Key feature: Each side draws inferences and tests them • This stage is easily terminated by either side	• Benefits expand for both sides • Interdependence expands • Risk taking increases • Satisfaction with results leads to greater motivation and deepening commitment • Goal congruence increases • Cooperation increases • Communication increases • Alternative partners look less attractive • Key feature: Momentum must be maintained. To progress, each party must seek new areas of activity and maintain consistent efforts to create mutual payoffs	• Each party invests to build and maintain the relationship • Long time horizon • Parties may be aware of alternatives but do not court them • High expectations on both sides • High mutual dependence • High trust • Partners resolve conflict and adapt to each other and to their changing environment • Shared values and/or contractual mechanisms (such as shared risk) reinforce mutual dependence • Key features: Loyalty, adaptability, continuity, high mutual dependence set these relationships apart	• One side tends to spark it • Mounting dissatisfaction leads one side to hold back investment • Lack of investment provokes the other side to reciprocate • Dissolution may be abrupt but is usually gradual • Key feature: It takes two to build but only one to undermine. Decline often sets in without the two parties' realization
1	2	3	4	5

Figure 8.4   Phases of relationships in marketing channels

Stage 1: Awareness   Omega is aware that Annecy is a feasible exchange partner but has not made contact to explore doing business or upgrading their one-by-one business dealings into a stronger, more continuous relationship. (We also could turn the scenario around, making Annecy the focal party, aware that Omega is a feasible supplier to upgrade to a preferred partnership level.) This stage can last a very long time with no real progress. Or it can disappear: Either firm could discard the other from its partnership consideration set. Or the arrangement can move forward.

Stage 2: Exploration   Omega and Annecy investigate forging a stable relationship. They may test each other during a trial and evaluation period (which can be lengthy, especially for important, risky, or complex channel flows). Each side forecasts and weighs the costs and benefits of creating a close marketing channel together. As Andrea Larson points out,

> You can't start out with a full-blown relationship. It's got to be incremental. You get closer as each side takes small steps.
> If it's going to be long-lasting, it doesn't happen overnight.[49]

If the players judge the calculation promising, they engage in communication and negotiation. Norms (expected patterns of behavior) may begin to form in the process. Mutual trust and joint satisfaction should start to grow. This delicate stage resembles two people in a dating relationship: These early behaviors have a great impact because each side is drawing inferences about the other but without a great deal of history to use as a basis. Such relationships accelerate sharply if the two sides make idiosyncratic investments in each other.[50] How each partner uses its power is important in determining whether both sides want to move on.

Stage 3: Expansion   Omega and Annecy grow their relationship considerably. Each is deriving greater benefits, developing greater motivation, and elaborating their relationship. Trust is spiraling. Interdependence is increasing. Annecy and Omega cooperate and feel they are pursuing common goals. Interaction becomes much greater than is strictly necessary, in part because each side's personnel like the communication. Larson notes,

> Over time, you build a history of situations, compromises, and solutions. You learn the unwritten rules and how they want to play the game, which makes it increasingly easier to do business.[51]

After this has gone on for some time, the relationship may move forward.

Stage 4: Commitment   This is when the alliance is easily recognizable by the stability both Annecy and Omega believe to exist in their relationship. Further, both sides invest heavily to maintain the strong partnership they have achieved. Neither side is very open to overtures by other firms: They prefer doing business with each other. Again quoting Larson,

> We are constantly changing things to try and improve the way we do business together. We will experiment with new ideas, test new processes, try

something different. Costs are incurred on both sides but we are willing to pay them. We have learned a lot from them. They have made us a better printing company because they are demanding, innovative, and willing to try things.[52]

But strains occur, even in committed relationships. Sometimes they deteriorate.

Stage 5: Decline and Dissolution   The Omega/Annecy relationship declines to the point that they cease to have a close partnership. They may resume their old one-deal-at-a-time transactions but are more likely to cease doing business at all. Dissolutions are usually accompanied by acrimony. Frequently, they are initiated by one side that has grown dissatisfied with the arrangement. This side begins to withdraw and to behave in a manner inconsistent with commitment. This annoys the other side, which often reciprocates with neglectful, damaging, even destructive behavior. Decline rapidly takes on a momentum of its own.

Decline and dissolution often happen because one party takes the relationship for granted, and does not work to keep it going. Sometimes, one party sabotages the relationship, perhaps to free itself to move on to other opportunities. Usually, decline is a lingering process. It may not be apparent that decline has set in until it is too far advanced to be repaired.

Managing the Stages

One implication of these stages of development is that relationships are difficult to build quickly and difficult to build from the ground up. Development takes time, particularly if the targeted partner firms do no business with each other as yet. Every existing channel member is a potential asset in this respect because extant business, even if minor, means the awareness and exploration phases can proceed much faster and the relationship can be upgraded more swiftly and surely.

The exploration phase is particularly sensitive. Intangible perceptions (such as goal congruence) play a major role, partly because the parties know each other poorly and have little shared history. Early interactions and outcomes are also crucial: They weigh heavily in each side's projections and calculations. The expectations developed during the exploration phase determine whether partnership becomes achievable.

In the expansion phase, management must ensure that each side perceives that the benefits are being shared equitably. This is an exciting stage when morale is high and sentiments are positive. Managements of both sides can use this stage to deepen the interdependence of the marketing channel members, setting the stage for commitment to stabilize.

In the commitment stage, the relationship has a substantial history marked by investments, interdependence, and strong norms. At this stage, intangible factors (such as the perception of goal congruence) are less important than they were in exploration, simply because the partnership has a rich infrastructure to make it robust. In the commitment stage, management must be attentive to maintaining the relationship, lest it slip into decline and dissolution. If the relationship moves to the last stage, it is not easy to salvage.

A caveat is in order here. The stages-of-development idea is an appealing way to think about creating an alliance and keeping it going. However, relationship development is frequently not as linear, orderly, and sequential as the five stages would seem.[53]

On a daily basis, relationships may be experienced as a series of episodes, or critical incidents. These events help the players define their common purpose, set boundaries to their relationship, create value (and claim their share of it), and evaluate what they are getting from the relationship. By repeated interaction, firms develop enough of these critical incidents to move their relationship from a series of transactions to a real partnership. When they go back over their history, managers may tend to remember their experiences as corresponding to stages that they can only recognize after considerable development has occurred.

In other words, many relationships do not develop in an orderly way. The bad news is that it is difficult to say with confidence what stage a relationship is in during much of its history. The good news is that if a relationship seems to be regressing (for example, moving backward from expansion to exploration), in all likelihood there is no real cause for alarm. This regression will appear in retrospect as a blip or a minor disturbance: The relationship is not doomed to deteriorate.[54]

Managing Troubled Relationships

Relationships, like automobiles, require maintenance and can wear out even if maintained properly. A common scenario is that one partner begins to suspect that the other partner is taking advantage of the spirit of their understanding and is failing to live up to its promises, actual or implied. This suspicion (that the other party is not exerting its best efforts or acting in good faith) can enter into even well-functioning relationships. It can then create a self-fulfilling prophecy, for the suspicious party may withhold effort, leading the suspected party to reciprocate. The relationship can then spiral downward as performance declines.

What kinds of relationships are best able to withstand the pressure of suspicion and keep performing? Research indicates that relationships that are bound by the ties of mutual idiosyncratic investments keep performing as suspicion increases.[55] Relationships that have a foundation of congruent goals also continue to perform. The parties often take their congruent goals for granted and forget about them when all is well but rediscover them and use them to enhance their joint results under the pressure of mounting suspicion. In contrast, performance declines as suspicion mounts in dyads that rely on interpersonal trust built up between a key person on each side. These two "custodians" come under scrutiny. Other people (accountants, sales managers, finance managers, etc.) question the relationship and intervene, offsetting the beneficial effects of trust between key individuals.

Indeed, some of the best, most trusting relationships have within them the seed of their own decline.[56] Trust has hidden costs. At very high levels of trust, people may not ask enough probing or difficult questions. Relationships may not have enough constructive conflict, may settle on an agreement too fast, and may become too homogeneous, thereby dampening creativity. Worst of all, trusted parties may exploit the trustee, using their bank of confidence to ensure that the trustee does not sense what is going on.[57]

The Virtues of a Portfolio of Relationships

We have come full circle: Even trusting relationships can fail, and alliances may not be worth their accounting and opportunity costs. It is not surprising that most firms have a portfolio of relationships, many of which are far from alliance status. Sidebar 8.8 profiles an innovative research effort by Xerox that revealed six segments among its thousands of European resellers.

Sidebar 8.8

Xerox profiles its resellers

Suppliers ordinarily divide their resellers by size, region, or profitability. In an innovative research project, Richard Gibbs, Director of European Distribution Operations for Xerox Europe, studied partner attitudes toward the supplier, using original survey data from 1,000 resellers themselves.[58] Statistical analysis revealed six clusters.

- Evangelists: Are highly positive about Xerox. Many have been working with the supplier for years.

- Possible Converts: Are positive about the supplier but have not invested much in the relationship. They enjoy a good return on the business and might consider making a serious investment to develop it.

- Problem Children: Have invested a great deal in their supplier and are somewhat dissatisfied with their returns. They would like Xerox to do more for them on all fronts. Typically, they believe they can rely only on the strength of the brand to sell it.

- Marginals: Have not invested very much and do not think much of the supplier's service or the product. They are unlikely to raise their investment.

- Potential Terrorists (also known as captive sharks): Heavy investors who feel the manufacturer has let them down in terms of service.

- Deserters: Have invested almost zero and hold a poor image of the manufacturer on all fronts.

Almost every large supplier has a number of problem children, but many do not realize that there may have been problems until the reseller turns into a shark or a deserter. The firm can be vulnerable: Potential terrorists, and even deserters, can hold large books of business. Gibbs cautions managers to identify and give priority focus to problem children (who are often dissatisfied large partners) and to develop turnaround strategies for potential terrorists. As for deserters, their attitudes are difficult to change: It is likely they do not merit management time. The same may be true of marginals. Possible converts are a target of opportunity, while evangelists need to be maintained in that positive state.

Ultimately, manufacturers need a portfolio of downstream relationships to cover the market and meet multiple service output demands. Downstream channel members need a portfolio of suppliers and brands to cover the assorted needs of their customers and prospects. It is unlikely that a larger firm can meet these needs without having relationships that are not so close as to be strategic alliances. Firms need some alliances to gather information and calibrate strategy and tactics, but more conventional relationships also work very well.[59] Firms can gain benefits even from weak ties. For example, when buying complex, information-intensive, high-risk products (such as information technology systems), customers prefer resellers that have strong ties to IT producers. Yet, they appreciate the virtue of a reseller that has weak ties but with a number of IT makers. The advantage of such resellers is the ability to scan varied sources of supply to get ideas and create new possibilities.[60]

PUTTING IT ALL TOGETHER: WHAT DOES IT TAKE AND WHEN DOES IT PAY TO CREATE A MARKETING CHANNEL ALLIANCE?

We have arrived at the point of taking stock. We know that marketing channel alliances, once achieved, function admirably. They generate competitive advantage with attendant financial rewards. When they work, they are capable of outperforming a channel owned by one organization. They function so well that the customer cannot see where one company stops and another begins. Should not every marketing channel aim to become an alliance?

We also know that an alliance is more akin to truffles than to wheat. A truffle is a type of mushroom prized by gourmet cooks. Wheat can be grown commercially to order, according to a known formula. Truffles cannot be produced to order. They cannot be produced at will. No one knows how to grow them. They appear randomly in nature, given certain conditions. This is why there are truffle hunters but not truffle farmers.

Similarly, the conditions that favor an alliance can be created, but an alliance may or may not grow up in them. Unlike wheat, alliances cannot be produced at will. Like truffles, alliances are often discovered by looking where the right conditions hold. Management's ability to create the right conditions is limited, and truffles do not always appear where they should be expected. In other words, many firms have tried unsuccessfully to build a channel alliance. The same firms often discover that they have an alliance that they may have failed to appreciate. These alliances occur seemingly spontaneously, without top management direction, due to the (often unsuspected) efforts of field personnel.

What are the right conditions? This depends on the firm's strategy, industry, and market. For most circumstances, an alliance may not be necessary. Building one may even be counterproductive because the costs of alliance building are so substantial that they may outweigh the benefits. A more typical marketing channel may not only be perfectly adequate but may generate better net results. In particular, an alliance bears a substantial opportunity cost because few firms have the resources to develop intense relationships with all the organizations necessary to cover their markets. A firm must select its alliances and invest in them. The risks are real that the firm has picked the wrong partner or that it would be better off with several more mundane but less demanding channel relationships.

This said, an alliance is appropriate when three conditions hold simultaneously.[61] Let us return to Omega (upstream) and Annecy (downstream). Their alliance is more likely to hold together and to meet their expectations when

1. One side has special needs
2. The other side has the capability to meet these needs
3. Each side faces barriers to exiting the relationship

Conditions one and two create the basis for distinctive value added, which is the foundation of a strategic alliance. Special needs means that most parties with these needs will not find satisfaction in the marketplace. They will be poorly served by using a mundane transaction and by using most of the available channel members. The channel member's ability to meet those out-of-the-ordinary needs is the basis for exchange between these two parties, to the exclusion of most other possible pairings.

Condition three (exit barriers) is necessary to prevent one side from exploiting the other. For example, if Omega has special needs (say, for product handling and customization) and Annecy can meet them, fruitful exchange goes on—but not indefinitely. Annecy may make investments specific to Omega, creating vulnerability. Or Annecy might train customers to value Omega's brands, only to have Omega appoint a new distributor to harvest this loyal customer base. Annecy can be exploited by Omega. If Omega builds barriers to exiting its relationship, however, the situation stabilizes because Omega now values Annecy more highly. Ideally, both Omega and Annecy will develop enduring reasons to stay in their relationship.

What kinds of barriers to exit exist? In general, relationships with strong norms or with mutual dependence are so difficult to disentangle that the parties prefer to invest to keep them going.

The Caterpillar situation illustrates these three conditions well. (1) Caterpillar has special needs for postsales support and market feedback. (2) Its small set of dealers is well able to meet these needs. They choose to do so, creating exceptional value. Neither side uses its valued position against the other, decade after decade. This situation seems utopian: How could it be duplicated 186 times and last so long? Put differently, why do the relationships not degenerate at some point due to perceived exploitation by one side or the other? It is because (3) strong relationship norms of solidarity and fairness, combined with heavy and nonredeployable investments by both sides, have created a relationship neither side wishes to leave—or can afford to abandon. These relationships are full of conflict—but the conflict stays functional and serves to motivate each partner to do better.

Take-Aways

- A strategic alliance exists when two or more organizations have enduring, substantial connections that cause them to function according to a perception of a single, shared interest. Committed parties
  - Desire a relationship to continue indefinitely
  - Are willing to sacrifice to maintain and grow the relationship
- Three conditions favor a strategic alliance:
  - The target has special needs
  - The potential partner is well able to meet these needs
  - The potential partner can erect barriers to exit
- Alliances serve upstream and downstream needs to create enduring competitive advantage, leading to profit.
- Alliances rest on an expectation of continuity, which grows with mutual communication, balanced power, and higher combined stakes of both parties.
- Older relationships may be more fragile than they appear because the parties may not communicate sufficiently, in the false belief they do not need to.
- While we do not know how to manufacture commitment with certainty, we do know that alliances need mutual dependence and the perception of mutual commitment.

- Firms rely more heavily on actions, particularly by people at the field level, than on what top management announces in forming their perceptions. In particular, they look for pledges, which are idiosyncratic investments in the partner firm.
  - Pledges make the giver more dependent on the target because they
    - Motivate the giver to support the relationship
    - Generate real productive value that is difficult to find elsewhere
    - Signal commitment intent to the counterpart
  - Firms pay attention to history, both their own and the history that underlies a firm's reputation for fair business dealings with channel members.
- The foundation of alliance is trust, a combination of confidence in the other party's honesty and in its genuine interest in your welfare.
- Trust, in turn, flourishes under conditions of satisfaction with noneconomic outcomes associated with the absence of coercion and of dysfunctional conflict. (Functional conflict and trust *do* coexist easily.)
- Perceptions of procedural and distributive fairness (equity in daily functioning and in the split of rewards) also support trust. They do so by enhancing noneconomic satisfaction.
- Economic satisfaction is both a driver of alliances and a result of an alliance. This is because as a party derives more financial rewards from the relationship, its trust increases. This strengthens the alliance, which then works together more effectively, generating even more rewards and accelerating an upward spiral of commitment.
- Who might be a good partner? The best place to look is in the set of channel members one already knows. There is usually some social capital in these arrangements, which can be enhanced. Particularly good candidates are firms with strengths and weaknesses that offset yours: Together, you have complementary capabilities.
- When is alliance building more likely to work?
  - Favorable settings are environments that offer resources, growth, and opportunity, while less favorable settings are complex, volatile, unpredictable.
  - Working with firms that decentralize decision making and that have a culture of cultivating trust raises the odds of success. So, too, does agreement about who is responsible for what.
  - Two factors are crucial to all efforts to build trust and create alliances: candid, mutual, frequent communication and the passage of time.
- Trust has a hidden downside. Trusting partners may not generate enough discussion to excel. One party may take advantage of the other's trust. The trust built up between two individuals will not suffice to keep the relationship performing if suspicions start to mount. In contrast, structural features of the relationship (goal congruence, mutual idiosyncratic investments) help keep the relationship performing when one party begins to suspect the other of failing to deliver on promises.
- A portfolio of relationships of varying degrees of closeness is desirable. Most firms need a mix of alliances and more conventional relationships if they are to cover their markets and meet customer needs effectively and efficiently.

DISCUSSION QUESTIONS

1. You are management of a manufacturer. You are highly committed to a distributor. You suspect your distributor is committed to you, but you are unsure. Should you try to project that you are not as highly committed as you are? Why or why not? How would you go about projecting lower commitment than is true? How well would you expect your efforts to work? Why?

2. A powerful idiosyncratic investment is mingling your identity with that of your channel member. Why? If you are the manufacturer, how could you do this mingling, and how could you induce your downstream channel member to cooperate? Now try the same exercise in reverse: How would you, the downstream channel member, mingle your identity with the upstream channel member's image, and how would you induce the upstream partner to cooperate?

3. What are upstream and downstream motives to ally? What are motives not to ally? Are upstream and downstream motives congruent?

4. What hostages does each side offer the other in the arrangement between EABL and T&B profiled in this chapter? Are these hostages adequate? What makes the relationship work so well? Answer the same questions regarding John Deere and its dealer network.

5. The Smart car has a unique design, eye catching and original. It is a tiny car, less than three meters (ten feet) long, with a very high roof. The car has been aimed at the market of upscale urban professionals as a primary car. It has also been positioned as a second car. Neither positioning has generated much volume. Mercedes has had difficulty finding a clientele willing to pay its premium price. Smart dealers are accustomed to curious visitors and have been unable to convert these browsers into buyers. Smart benefits from high brand awareness due in part to massive advertising featuring the car's high design and extreme suitability for densely populated cities (Smart is famously easy to park in a fraction of a normal parking space). However, the car is seldom seen outside of cities. It has the power to go on the freeway (where one does occasionally see Smarts passing Mercedes cars!) but is widely perceived as dangerously small for driving at high speed. Indeed, Smart has set up Avis rental counters inside some Smart centers to facilitate customers renting a weekend and vacation vehicle viewed to be more suitable in the country. Given all this, what would you suggest to Smart as its distribution strategy going forward:
   - In Europe, where the car has existed since 1998?
   - In North America, where it is scheduled to be launched?

   In framing your answer, keep in mind that the Smart is somewhat unconventional mechanically. It needs dedicated mechanics, its own parts, and even a specialty body shop (as Smart is made of snap-together fiberglass panels).

6. Marketing channel alliances are capable of extraordinary results. Should every management focus on alliances? If not, why not? Are there other ways of generating exceptional results?

7. As a supplier, what sort of program could you devise to build trust with a distributor? What distributor types would you target? How well would you expect your program to work? Now try the same exercise in reverse: What program can a distributor devise to build trust with a manufacturer, how well should it work, and what manufacturers would you target?

8. The idea of stages of a relationship has been described as being a good idea in theory but a difficult idea to put into practice. Do you agree? Why or why not? How would you know what stage you were in? How would you as a manager try to drive your firm to progress from an early stage to a later stage?

ENDNOTES

1. Frazier, Gary L. (1999), "Organizing and Managing Channels of Distribution," *Journal of the Academy of Marketing Sciences* 27, no. 2 (Spring), pp. 226–240.

2. Frazier (1999), previously cited, p. 238.

3. Hotopf, Max (2004), "The Beefs of Channel Managers," *Routes to Market* (*The Channel Management Journal from VIA International*) 4, no. 1 (Spring), pp. 3–4.

4. Hotopf, Max (2004), "Making a Multi-Channel Strategy Work," *Routes to Market* (*The Channel Management Journal from VIA International*) 4, no. 3 (Autumn), pp. 7–8.

5. Hotopf, "Making a Multi-Channel Strategy Work," p. 7.

6. Hotopf, "Making a Multi-Channel Strategy Work," p. 7.

7. Hotopf, "Making a Multi-Channel Strategy Work," p. 8.

8. Hotopf, Max (2003), "Snuggling Up to Big Retail," *Routes to Market* (*The Channel Management Journal from VIA International*) 3, no. 4 (Winter), pp. 13–14.

9. Fein, Adam J. and Sandy D. Jap (1999), "Manage Consolidation in the Distribution Channel," *Sloan Management Review* 41, no. 1 (Fall), pp. 61–72.

10. Kumar, Nirmalya (1996), "The Power of Trust in Manufacturer-Retailer Relationships," *Harvard Business Review* 60, no. 6 (November–December), pp. 92–106.

11. Kim, Keysuk (1999), "On Determinants of Joint Action in Industrial Distributor-Supplier Relationships: Beyond Economic Efficiency," *International Journal of Research in Marketing* 16, no. 3 (September), pp. 217–236.

12. Morgan, Robert M. and Shelby D. Hunt (1994), "The Commitment-Trust Theory of Relationship Marketing," *Journal of Marketing* 58, no. 3 (July), pp. 20–38.

13. Kramer, Roderick M. (1999), "Trust and Distrust in Organizations: Emerging Perspectives, Enduring Questions," *Annual Review of Psychology* 50, pp. 569–598.

14. Li, Zhan G. and Rajiv P. Dant (1999), "Effects of Manufacturers' Strategies on Channel Relationships," *Industrial Marketing Management* 28, no. 2 (March), pp. 131–143.

15. Siguaw, Judy A., Penny M. Simpson, and Thomas L. Baker (1998), "Effects of Supplier Market Orientation on Distributor Market Orientation and the Channel Relationship: The Distributor Perspective," *Journal of Marketing* 62 (no. 3, July), pp. 99–111; and Sethuraman, Rajagopalan, James C. Anderson, and James A. Narus (1988), "Partnership Advantage and Its Determinants in Distributor and Manufacturer Working Relationships," *Journal of Business Research* 17, no. 4 (December), pp. 327–347.

16. Iacobucci, Dawn and Jonathan D. Hibbard (1999), "Toward an Encompassing Theory of Business Marketing Relationships (BMRs) and Interpersonal Commercial Relationships (ICRs): An Empirical Examination," *Journal of Interactive Marketing* 13, no. 3 (Summer), pp. 13–33.

17. Anderson, Erin, William T. Ross, and Barton Weitz (1998), "Commitment and Its Consequences in the American Agency System of Selling Insurance," *Journal of Risk and Insurance* 65, no. 4 (December), pp. 637–669.

18. Jackson, Barbara Bund (1985), "Build Customer Relationships That Last," *Harvard Business Review* 63, no. 6 (November–December), pp. 120–128.

19. Heide, Jan B. and Anne S. Miner (1992), "The Shadow of the Future: Effects of Anticipated Interaction and Frequency of Contact on Buyer-Seller Cooperation," *Academy of Management Journal* 35, no. 2 (June), pp. 265–291.

20. Weiss, Allen M., Erin Anderson, and Deborah J. MacInnis (1999), "Reputation Management as a Motive for Sales Structure Decisions," *Journal of Marketing* 63, no. 4 (October), pp. 74–89.

21. Anderson, Erin and Barton Weitz (1989), "Determinants of Continuity in Conventional Channel Dyads," *Marketing Science* 8, no. 4 (Autumn), pp. 310–323.

22. Mohr, Jakki and John R. Nevin (1990), "Communication Strategies in Marketing Channels: A Theoretical Perspective," *Journal of Marketing* 54, no. 4 (October), pp. 36–51.

23. Much of this section draws on Anderson, Erin and Barton Weitz (1992), "The Use of Pledges to Build and Sustain Commitment in Distribution Channels," *Journal of Marketing Research* 29, no. 1 (February), pp. 18–34.

24. Zaheer, Akbar, Bill McEvily, and Vincenzo Perrone (1998), "Does Trust Matter? Exploring the Effects of Interorganizational and Interpersonal Trust on Performance," *Organization Science* 9, no. 2 (March), pp. 141–159.

25. *Wall Street Journal Europe* (2004), "Retailers' Growing Clout Forces Change on the Fly for Suppliers Like Levi," *Wall Street Journal Europe*, July 17, pp. A1, A6; and Garnier, Juliette (2003), "Les Hypers au Secours de Levi Strauss," *LSA*, November 6, pp. 22–24.

26. *Wall Street Journal Europe* (2004), "Retailers' Growing Clout Forces Change on the Fly for Suppliers Like Levi," *Wall Street Journal Europe*, July 17, p. A1.

27. Jap, Sandy D. (1999), "'Pie-Expansion' Efforts: Collaboration Processes in Buyer-Supplier Relationships," *Journal of Marketing Research* 36, no. 4 (November), pp. 461–75.

28. Stump, Rodney L., and Jan B. Heide (1996), "Controlling Supplier Opportunism in Industrial Relations," *Journal of Marketing Research* 33, no. 4 (November), pp. 431–441.

29. This sketch is based on research conducted by Aline Gatignon and includes as principal sources Chabert, Patrick (2005), "Smart, La Mauvaise Etoile de Mercedes," *Capital* 13, no. 3 (March), pp. 42–44;

Declairieux, Bruno (2001), "Les Recettes Miracles Qui Ont Sauvé la Smart," *Capital* 9, no. 3 (March), pp. 120–122; and Taylor, Alex (2003), "Mercedes Hits a Pothole," *Fortune*, October 27, pp. 42–49

30. Larson, Andrea (1992), "Network Dyads in Entrepreneurial Settings: A Study of the Governance of Exchange Relationships," *Administrative Science Quarterly* 37, no. 1 (March), pp. 76–104. Quotation from p. 89.

31. Fites, Donald V. (1996), "Make Your Dealers Your Partners," *Harvard Business Review* 74, no. 2 (March–April), pp. 84–95.

32. Geyskens, Inge, Jan-Benedict E. M. Steenkamp, and Nirmalya Kumar (1998), "Generalizations About Trust in Marketing Channel Relationships Using Meta Analysis," *International Journal of Research in Marketing* 15, no. 3 (July), pp. 223–248.

33. Ganesan, Shankar (1994), "Determinants of Long-Term Orientation in Buyer-Seller Relationships," *Journal of Marketing* 58, no. 2 (April), pp. 1–19.

34. The concept of a reference value for a monetary cost or profit is also seen in the pricing literature, where a consumer's reference price is the price the consumer expects to pay for an item; a price lower than that value has a positive impact on purchase intentions. See Kalyanaram, G. and R. S. Winer, "Empirical Generalizations from Reference Price Research," *Management Science* 14, no. 3 (Summer), pp. G 161–169; and Winer, R. S., "A Reference Price Model of Brand Choice for Frequently Purchased Products, *Journal of Consumer Research* 13, no. 2 (September 1986), pp. 250–256.

35. Galunic, Charles D. and Erin Anderson (2000), "From Security to Mobility: An Examination of Employee Commitment and an Emerging Psychological Contract," *Organization Science* 11, no. 1 (January–February), pp. 1–20.

36. Geyskens, Inge, Jan-Benedict E.M. Steenkamp, and Nirmalya Kumar (1999), "A Meta-Analysis of Satisfaction in Marketing Channel Relationships," *Journal of Marketing Research* 36, no. 2 (May), pp. 223–238.

37. Hotopf, Max (2002), "Skilling Your Channel," *Routes to Market* (*The Channel*

Management Journal from VIA International) 2, no. 3 (Autumn), pp. 4–7.

38. Kumar, Nirmalya, Lisa K. Scheer, and Jan-Benedict E.M. Steenkamp (1995), "The Effects of Supplier Fairness on Vulnerable Resellers," *Journal of Marketing Research* 32, no. 1 (February), pp. 54–65.

39. Gulati, Ranjay (1998), "Alliances and Networks," *Strategic Management Journal* 19, no. 4 (April), pp. 293–317.

40. Weitz, Barton A. and Sandy D. Jap (1995), "Relationship Marketing and Distribution Channels," *Journal of the Academy of Marketing Science* 23, no. 4 (Fall), pp. 305–320.

41. Wathne, Kenneth H. and Jan B. Heide (2004), "Relationship Governance in a Supply Chain Network," *Journal of Marketing* 68, no. 1 (January), pp. 73–89.

42. Thomas, Andrew R. and Timothy J. Wilkonson (2005), "It's the Distribution, Stupid!" *Business Horizons* 48, no. 2 (March–April), pp. 125–134.

43. Harari, Oren (1999), "The Logistics of Success," *Management Review* 88, no. 6 (June), p. 26.

44. Harari, "The Logistics of Success," pp. 24–26.

45. Dyer, Jeffery H. and Harbir Singh (1998), "The Relational View: Cooperative Strategy and Sources of Interorganizational Competitive Advantage," *Academy of Management Review* 23, no. 4 (October), pp. 660–679.

46. Frazier (1999), previously cited.

47. Dahlstrom, Robert and Arne Nygaard (1999), "An Empirical Investigation of Ex Post Transaction Costs in Franchised Distribution Channels," *Journal of Marketing Research* 36, no. 2 (May), pp. 160–170.

48. Dwyer, F. Robert, Paul H. Schurr, and Sejo Oh (1987), "Developing Buyer-Seller Relationships," *Journal of Marketing* 51, no. 2 (April), pp. 11–27.

49. Larson (1992), previously cited.

50. Jap, Sandy and Shankar Ganesan (2000), "Control Mechanisms and the Relationship Lifecycle: Implications for Safeguarding Specific Investments and Developing Commitment," *Journal of Marketing Research* 37, no. 2 (May), pp. 227–245.

51. Larson (1992), previously cited.

52. Larson (1992), previously cited.

53. Anderson, James C. (1995), "Relationships in Business Markets: Exchange Episodes, Value Creation, and Their Empirical Assessment," *Journal of the Academy of Marketing Science* 23, no. 4 (Fall), pp. 346–350.

54. Narayandas, Das and V. Kasturi Rangan (2004), "Building and Sustaining Buyer-Seller Relationships in Mature Industrial Markets," *Journal of Marketing* 68, no. 3 (July), pp. 63–77.

55. Jap, Sandy and Erin Anderson (2004), "Safeguarding Interorganizational Performance and Continuity Under *Ex Post* Opportunism," *Management Science* 49, no. 12 (December), pp. 1684–1701.

56. Anderson, Erin and Sandy D. Jap (2005), "The Dark Side of Close Relationships," *Sloan Management Review* 46, no. 3 (Spring), pp. 75–82.

57. Selnes, Fred and James Sallis (2003), "Promoting Relationship Learning," *Journal of Marketing* 67, no. 3 (July), p. 80.

58. Hotopf, Max (2003), "Building Channel Trust," *Routes to Market* (*The Channel Management Journal from VIA International*) 3, no. 4 (Winter), pp. 7–11.

59. Cannon, Joseph P. and William D. Perreault (1999), "Buyer-Seller Relationships in Business Markets," *Journal of Marketing Research* 36, no. 4 (November), pp. 439–460.

60. Wuyts, Stefan, Stefan Stremersch, Christophe Van Den Bulte, and Philip Hans Franses (2004), "Vertical Marketing Systems for Complex Products: A Triadic Perspective," *Journal of Marketing Research* 41, no. 4 (November), pp. 479–487.

61. Adapted from Jackson (1985), previously cited.

Vertical Integration in Distribution

Learning objectives

After reading this chapter, you will be able to:

- Understand vertical integration as a continuum from make to buy rather than as merely a binary choice

- Diagnose the reasons why channel players (such as manufacturers, wholesalers, or retailers) often integrate forward or backward with great expectations, only to divest within a few years

- Frame the vertical integration decision in terms of when owning the channel or some of its flows improves long-term return on investment

- Explain six reasons why outsourcing, *not* vertical integration, should be the starting point, the preferred choice, contrary to intuition

- Understand how three situations change this starting point so that vertical integration comes to dominate outsourcing in distribution

- Define and explain six categories of company-specific capabilities and distinguish specificity from rarity

- Trace how these categories become general purpose over time

- Trace the impact of a volatile environment on the returns from forward integration

- Explain the sources of performance ambiguity and relate them to the returns from forward or backward integration in distribution

- Recognize the role of vertical integration in learning and in creating strategic options—and understand when these are poor rationales

INTRODUCTION

This chapter concerns the most fundamental question to ask when structuring a delivery system: Should only one organization do the work, thereby vertically integrating into the distribution stage? In other words, who should perform a channel flow? Should it be a single organization (e.g., manufacturer, agent, distributor, retailer—all rolled into one company)? Or should distribution flows be outsourced (upstream looking down), or should production be outsourced (downstream looking up), thereby keeping separate the identities of manufacturers and downstream channel members?

Five Puzzles

➤ When retailers accept delivery of merchandise from Whirlpool, a large multinational producer of electrical appliances, the driver pulls up in a Whirlpool truck. When the appliance is unloaded, it sometimes has a blemish. The driver (delivery agent) immediately becomes a claims adjuster and commits Whirlpool to offer a markdown as an inducement to the retailer to keep the goods and repair them. It is invisible to the customer (and to Whirlpool's own sales force) that the negotiator actually works for a third-party logistics provider, Kenco, which manages every aspect of Whirlpool's inventory and owns all the trucks. Whirlpool appears to be vertically integrated into logistics but is not and has not been for decades.[1] Whirlpool can afford to do its own logistics in house and certainly has the scale of business to do so. Why let another company perform such a large and critical distribution function?

➤ Luxottica[2] is a little-known Italian company specializing in eyewear. Its many brands, however, are famous: Giorgio Armani, Chanel, Yves St. Laurent, Ray-Ban, and a host of others. Luxottica is the world's largest maker of branded eyewear and is highly profitable. This producer also owns the world's largest optical chain, LensCrafters, a U.S. firm, which it bought in 1995 from U.S. Shoe, a company eager to recoup its capital and reclaim its management attention from a highly competitive business. At the time, LensCrafters was bigger than Luxottica. Luxottica's brands have enormous power. Why take such a risk to purchase a retailer when there are plenty of other ways to take these brands to market? What is the reason to vertically integrate forward?

➤ Best Power makes uninterruptible power systems. To compete against larger producers in the U.S. market, Best Power owned its own distribution channel. Even though the company was gaining market share, it virtually dismantled its in-house operation and has turned to independent value-added resellers. This is a painful decision: Why take down a company-owned channel?[3]

➤ Jean Delatour is a large chain of discount jewelry retail stores in France. The chain has an unusual strategy: It locates large, warehouse-like stores near formidable competitors—hypermarkets—yet aims to compete not only with these enormous stores but also with smaller, focused jewelers offering a luxurious atmosphere in convenient urban locations. Jean Delatour is vertically integrated backward into the production of everything but clocks and watches. Why that exception? What role does integration backward into production play in the retailer's strategy?[4]

➤ The supermarket industry in North America is brutally competitive. Some retailers are investing heavily in creating their own brands, private labels. The limited distribution of these brands makes it uneconomical to match the national brands' massive promotional campaigns, and these brands have built formidable brand equity over the decades. It would seem a folly to enter their markets, not to mention the negative effect on trade relations of competing with one's own suppliers. Why integrate backward so late in the product life cycle?[5]

➤ Why do conglomerates that are vertically integrated forward into distribution prosper in Brazil and Chile but not elsewhere?[6]

To integrate is to become one, or singular. When the manufacturer integrates a distribution function (making sales, fulfilling orders, offering credit, etc.), the manufacturer's employees do the work and the manufacturer has integrated forward, or downstream, from the point of production. Vertical integration also occurs from the downstream direction: A downstream channel member, such as a distributor or retailer, can produce its own branded source of product, thereby integrating backward. Whether the manufacturer integrates forward or the downstream channel member integrates backward, the result is that one organization does all the work. The channel is said to be vertically integrated. In this chapter, we will cover the circumstances that make such a move economically viable, as well as some common rationales that are economically debatable.

Make or Buy: A Critical Determinant of Company Competencies

The vertical integration decision is not a channel structure decision per se, but rather, a decision that should be made channel flow by channel flow. The implication of thinking in this way is that a channel member, given sufficient power, can decide to vertically integrate some subset of all the channel flows in a way that creates a channel that looks decentralized (not vertically integrated), yet exhibits the best combination of make and buy together in one channel structure.

In marketing channels, make-or-buy decisions (vertically integrate or outsource) are critical strategic choices. This is because the firm's decision to own some or all of its marketing channel has an enduring influence on its ability not only to distribute but also to produce. The manufacturer becomes identified with its marketing channels, which influence its base of end customers and form their image of the manufacturer. In addition, the manufacturer gains much of its market intelligence from its channels: What the manufacturer knows (or can learn) about its markets is heavily conditioned by how it goes to market.

Hence, the decision whether or not to vertically integrate forward helps to determine what the manufacturer currently does and what it could learn to do. This decision, once made, is difficult to reverse because it involves making commitments that are not always easy to redeploy. Thus, a firm's vertical integration choices in distribution are enduring and important. These structural decisions should be made carefully, with emphasis on how they influence the firm's future performance path.[7]

As for downstream channel members, their decisions to integrate backward consume resources, put them into conflict with their other suppliers, and jeopardize their ability to offer unbiased advice to their customers. Moving up the value chain looks appealing (Why let the producer have the margins when it's the downstream channel member who understands demand?). But integrating backward can be hazardous, as we will see.

Chapter Organization

The issues involved in vertical integration of distribution are many and complex. Because the consequences are so great and the decisions so difficult to change, a company's internal discussions of vertical integration are heated, often dysfunctional.

Abstract presentations of the issue often take the form of long lists of pros, cons, examples, and admonitions. Major and minor issues are freely mingled without prioritization. What is fundamentally the same argument comes up many times under different labels. Some ideas are double and triple counted. More important arguments may be underweighted.

Managers need a structured way to work through the issues, frame a coherent, comprehensive rationale, and reach a decision (make or buy, flow by flow) that can be communicated convincingly. This chapter presents a structured framework for deciding whether the manufacturer should integrate a given flow or a subset of flows in going to market.[8] The premise is that more often than not the manufacturer should *not* vertically integrate a downstream flow because doing so is typically inefficient. However, the manufacturer should own the flows or set of flows (up to and including the entire channel to a market) if it has the resources to own and would increase its return on investment in the long run by so doing. Similarly, downstream channel members are typically worse off integrating backward but should do so if they have the resources and would increase their long-run return on investment. Our framework identifies the conditions under which vertical integration raises long-run return on investment. For ease of presentation, we start with the manufacturer going forward, then extend the arguments to downstream going backward. Before the end of this chapter, we will resolve each of the five opening puzzles.

The next section explains what vertical integration entails in terms of benefits and costs, long and short term. Then comes an economic framework for thinking through when a channel (or set of channel flows) should be owned by one party only. Finally, we leave aside what firms should do and consider why they integrate when the economic rationale for so doing is not overriding. Here, the chapter goes beyond the strictly normative financial viewpoint to introduce some of the complexities, constraints, errors, and organizational politics that influence whether a firm will make or buy a given distribution flow.[9] We focus on vertical integration to learn (the argument that the channel is an observatory on the market) or to create a strategic option. (Refer to Chapter 4 for a discussion of the strategy of concurrent, or dual distribution, in which the firm simultaneously goes to market by both integrated and independent channels.)

THE COSTS AND BENEFITS OF VERTICAL INTEGRATION IN MARKETING CHANNELS

To appreciate the hidden costs and benefits of vertical integration, imagine that you are a manufacturer looking downstream at the set of flows that your customer is willing to pay to have performed. The vertical integration decision, make or buy, do it yourself or outsource, should be made for each function or set of functions involved in distributing a product or service. The choice is not really binary. Make versus buy is a continuum that shows how the costs, benefits, and responsibilities of doing the work are split between two organizations. Figure 9.1 presents these options in the abstract terms of make (vertical integration) versus buy (outsourcing), with relational governance as a midrange option.

Degrees of Vertical Integration

When outsourcing under classical market contracts (the epitome of the buy mode), manufacturers and downstream channel members:

> Are interchangeable
> Deal with each other in a completely independent and impersonal fashion (arm's-length contracting)

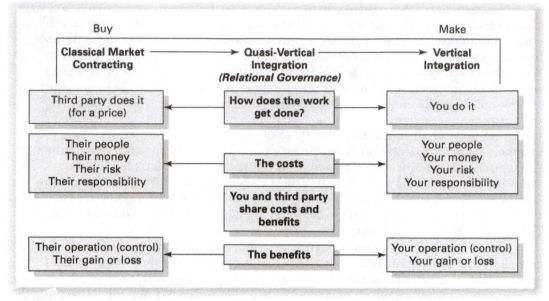

Figure 9.1   The continuum of degrees of vertical integration

> ➤ Negotiate each transaction as though it were the only one
> ➤ Begin and end their transactions based solely on the merits of the current set of offerings

At the extreme of buy, manufacturer-distributor arrangements involve no sharing (of risk, of expertise, of image, etc.), no distinction, and no continuity. This buy model (outsource each flow or bundle of flows) is a useful baseline in thinking about distribution. However, many, if not most, arrangements with third parties exhibit some degree of relationalism, meaning that the manufacturer has a greater share of the costs and benefits than is the case under strict delegation to a third party (classical market contracting).[10]

Relational governance means compromising between the make-buy extremes by creating channels that have some properties of both owned and independent channels.[11] Relational governance can be created many ways.[12] Building and maintaining close, committed relationships is covered in Chapter 8 on strategic alliances. One of the principal methods of building commitment is selective distribution, covered in Chapter 4. Another method, whereby two organizations attempt to coordinate as though they were only one, is franchising, covered in Chapter 13. Franchising and close relationships are channel strategies that simulate vertical integration (this is quasi-vertical integration, another term for relational governance).[13] Making these systems work requires power, the subject of Chapter 6.

Along the continuum of degree of integration, the fundamental issue is how the work of the channel is done. When your organization's employees carry out the flow, you have vertically integrated (the buy option).

In short, vertical integration is not a binary choice but a matter of degree. Degrees of integration form a continuum anchored by the extremes of classical marketing contracting and vertical integration. *Buy* is a large zone of outsourced relationships with third parties, and some of these relationships operate in a manner that resembles a single firm. Indeed, customers often believe they are dealing with the manufacturer when they are actually dealing with a committed third party in the marketing channel (such as Kenco in the Whirlpool puzzle).

Where the argument for integration is strong, but not entirely compelling, relational governance should be considered instead as a way to simulate vertical integration without assuming its burdens.

In principle, every distribution arrangement is unique and can be placed somewhere along the degree-of-vertical-integration continuum as a function of the relationship's operating methods and the nature of the contract (if any) between the parties. In practice, certain common institutional arrangements tend to correspond to regions within the continuum. Common examples are presented in Figure 9.2.

Costs and Benefits of the Choice to Make

What changes when you choose the make option over the buy option? If you are a manufacturer, your organization assumes all the accounting costs of distribution, which include all personnel costs as well as the costs of all other channel flows. Your organization also bears the risk of the distribution operation and is responsible for all actions. These costs (e.g., warehousing) are substantial and are frequently underestimated, particularly by firms that are accustomed to production but not to distribution. All too often, the result is that vertical integration forward not only fails to improve market share but actually reduces return on investment (ROI).[14]

Figure 9.2   Examples of institutions performing some channel functions

Function	Classical Market Contracting	Quasi-Vertical Integration	Vertical Integration
1) Selling (only)	Manufacturers' representatives	"Captive" or exclusive sales agency*	Producer sales force (direct sales force)
2) Wholesale distribution	Independent wholesaler	Distribution joint venture	Distribution arm of producer
3) Retail distribution	Independent (third party)	Franchise store	Company store

* Operationally, a sales agency deriving more than 50 percent of its revenue from one principal.

Many manufacturers find the heaviest of these costs to be the opportunity cost of the personnel. Manufacturers often have no one available to be diverted from the core activity of manufacturing, and as they do not know the market for expertise in distribution, these firms find it difficult to hire qualified personnel to meet service output demands economically. The top management of the vertically integrated firm is responsible for ensuring distribution and often finds that it does not have sufficient managerial resources to give attention to the distribution responsibility. (Of course, this and every other argument can be reversed for downstream channel members integrating upstream—this is a useful mental exercise.)

These costs can only be justified by substantial benefits. The fundamental reason firms give to integrate forward into distribution is to control the operation. However, from an economic standpoint, control per se has no value whatsoever. Control is beneficial only if the firm's managers can use it skillfully to improve overall economic results.[15] Manufacturers integrate forward (and resellers integrate backward) when they believe it will increase their profits. Control is psychologically appealing to managers (because they direct a larger enterprise) but goes against the interests of shareholders unless it improves profits.[16]

Sometimes this means merely appropriating the returns from the performance of marketing channel flows themselves to add to the returns from production. In this sense, vertical integration is a business opportunity like any other. A firm seeking to grow might consider taking on more of its current value chain if these other elements are attractive as a business proposition in and of themselves.

Some capital equipment manufacturers, such as IBM and General Electric, have moved into their downstream operations. For them, manufacturing is losing appeal as a business proposition. Competition has obliged producers to become efficient in production and more effective in marketing. The next logical place to find revenues and cut costs is the channel, not the factory. Further, much of the profit of capital equipment is not in its sale but in its maintenance. By integrating downstream, producers tap into a steady flow of maintenance contracts for the products they manufacture, many of which are very long lived.[17]

From this perspective, it is actually surprising that vertical integration is not even more common in channels than it really is. It is appealing to think that know-how from one part of the value chain could be amortized by applying it upstream or downstream. Downstream and upstream activities, however, are very different and conform to different financial models. These fundamental differences drive firms to grow and diversify into other (perhaps related) businesses but often at the same level of the value chain (e.g., production *or* wholesaling *or* logistics *or* retailing, but not all of them—wherever their expertise and expectations lie).

More often, appropriating returns from channel functions means directing the performance of channel flows for the purpose of improving sales and margins obtained at the integrator's level of the channel. The retailer integrating upstream is more interested in improving returns from retailing than in running a profitable production operation in and of itself. The manufacturer integrating downstream is more interested in using the channel to improve production results than in running a profitable marketing channel operation in and of itself. In other words, the integrator is prepared to sacrifice returns at one level of the value chain to improve returns at another level. In theory, the integrated entity is better off financially, weighing total returns against total assets employed, adjusting for the risk assumed. All too often, this scenario fails to materialize. The integrator underestimates the difficulty of assuming the new function and overestimates the benefits of control. See Sidebar 9.1 for examples.

The Choice to Buy Distribution: Terms of Payment to Third Parties

The manufacturer who wishes to focus solely on production, for whatever reason, will turn to the marketplace for distribution services. Here, it will seek a third party, an outside organization, and will contract with that organization to perform channel flows in return for some economic consideration, normally a price. The price is usually expressed as a margin (the difference between the price paid to the manufacturer [the reseller's cost of goods sold] and the price obtained by the reseller), as a commission (a fraction of the resale price), or as a percentage of the reseller's business (a royalty).

These are the most common ways to price the performance of channel flows. However, many variations are possible, such as paying the third party a flat fee or a lump sum or reimbursing some of the reseller's expenses (e.g., through a functional discount). The third party may also agree to work in return for some future consideration, such as the rights to future business or a percentage of equity in the manufacturer. Such arrangements are particularly common for entrepreneurial start-ups, new firms that are often poorly capitalized.

For example, fulfillment houses (which take orders generated by a seller, compose a package from warehoused goods, and ship the package) may agree to process the orders of a new mail-order firm without charge for a limited time in return for the rights to that firm's paying business after it becomes established. Here, the fulfillment house is not only carrying out the ordering flow for the manufacturer but is also performing the backward risking and financing flows (see Chapter 3).

These arrangements (that is, anything other than a commission or a gross margin, which are paid when the business is done) are not unusual. However, they are not the norm because they are risky. Paying a reseller a fee or reimbursing expenses subjects the manufacturer to the risk of moral hazard (i.e., being cheated after the arrangement has been put into place) because it is difficult to verify that the paid-for activities have been performed or that the expenses are not inflated. Hence, the manufacturer may be reluctant to pay in this manner.

As for the manufacturer's agreeing to pay in future business or in equity stakes, it is the downstream channel member who is assuming risk and who is likely to be reluctant to accept payment in this manner. The future business may never materialize, or the equity stakes may turn out to be worthless—or even a liability, if the manufacturer cannot cover its obligations. For every success story (for the supplier, getting in on the ground floor of what turns out to be a successful store, catalog, or Internet startup, and for the downstream channel member, getting in on the creation of the next successful producer), there are plenty of failures. Of course, everyone involved trumpets the successes and hides the failures, creating the impression that this deferred payment strategy is less risky than it really is.

This is not to say that channel members do not operate on deferred payment. For example, French *boulangers* (artisan bakers), having finished their apprenticeships, often start operations in a small town. As these artisans typically bring only their

Sidebar 9.1

Vertical integration forward: Harder than it looks

Allianz, a much admired German insurance giant, paid what is in retrospect a high price to acquire Dresdner, a prominent investment bank, in 2001. Allianz saw the move as a way to own a lucrative distribution channel to sell its insurance products. But the acquisition has proven financially disastrous for Allianz. Banking is a highly competitive industry and is managed quite differently from insurance. Some analysts argue that Allianz did not know enough about investment banking to judge whether Dresdner is well run and suggest that an investment bank fundamentally does not fit with an insurance company in the first place. Rather than enhance the Allianz core business, insurance, Dresdner has cost the integrated firm heavily.[18]

Manoukian, a French manufacturer of knitwear for women, also discovered that running a downstream channel is harder than it looks. Highly successful when selling knitwear through franchisees, the firm developed an ambitious growth strategy. It transformed itself into a full-line clothing maker, developing a men's collection and several women's collections at different price points and levels of style. Simultaneously, Manoukian became a clothing retailer by replacing franchisees with company-owned stores. The idea was to benefit from control. Rather than convince franchisees to go along with the new product strategy, the supplier could simply tell its own stores to do so.

The results have been catastrophic. As a manufacturer venturing outside women's knits, the firm has been unable to differentiate its clothes. As for distribution, management has proved singularly inept. Stock management and logistics are anarchic. Stores are too large to be profitable. The assortment is arranged such that all the Manoukian collections, from the top to the bottom of the price line, are easy to compare in the same store. Such an assortment (one brand, wide price points, all shown together) is unusual in fashion retailing. Management arranged the merchandise this way because it considered the collections, which vary considerably in price points, to be differentiated and expected each one to find its own clientele. Customers failed to appreciate the distinctions. The result: The least expensive line cannibalized the others.

This is an example of a common failing among manufacturers, whose managers are highly sensitive to differences in what they manufacture. Consequently, manufacturers tend to generate too many product variations in the belief that end customers are sensitive to fine distinctions. Independent downstream channel members correct the error by representing only the variations they judge the buyer will appreciate. In this case, Manoukian vertically integrated to ensure its stores would carry the full line (and no other brand). The result is a failure on a large scale.[19] This failure is a result of inadvertently giving up the expertise power of the independent retailer when Manoukian vertically integrated forward into retailing. The Manoukian example shows that vertical integration can fail not only because the vertical integrator misestimates the costs of replicating key channel flows performed by retailers but also because the vertical integrator fails to recognize the unique sources of power that its independent channel partners possess, and which are lost with vertical integration if the integrator does not explicitly seek to replicate them.

skills to the task, and as start-up capital is limited in Europe, the tiny new bakeries are frequently financed by producers of flour. Millers supply flour on extremely generous credit terms, on the understanding that they will be preferred suppliers if and when the *boulangerie* builds a clientele. There is no legal obligation to do so: The understanding is based on the norm of reciprocity in the industry.

Outsourcing shifts all the costs (accounting costs, including personnel, plus the risk of failure and the responsibility for action) to the third party. In return for assuming costs, the third party benefits by controlling the operation. This in itself is of no benefit in economic terms unless the third party can use that control to generate profits over and above the costs of distribution (both accounting and opportunity costs).

DECIDING WHEN TO VERTICALLY INTEGRATE FORWARD: AN ECONOMIC FRAMEWORK

It may seem that vertical integration is always desirable, for who would wish to be without control? Obviously, the decision must be more complex. This section presents a decision framework for determining when a greater degree of forward vertical integration is economically (as opposed to psychologically or politically) justifiable as a function of the characteristics of the decision maker and its choices. This framework is stylized, designed to cut through the confusion in systematic fashion by prioritizing the issues. Not every consideration is covered: The last section of this chapter covers justifications that are harder to defend economically but may be just as legitimate.

In the stylized approach outlined in this section, the decision maker begins by taking a preliminary decision *not* to vertically integrate forward. This starting-point decision is then examined. First, all the supporting arguments are marshaled. Then the preliminary outsource decision is challenged to see if the logic of outsourcing holds under the firm's circumstances and, if not, whether it should be overturned and replaced with vertical integration. The decision maker is asked to reason first as an advocate of the presumption of the superiority of outsourcing; then as a critic, who attacks the outsourcing argument; and finally as the arbitrator, who determines whether the advocate of outsourcing has been compellingly overturned. If not, the outsourcing decision carries the day.

The reader may find this exercise arbitrary, as the line of argument goes first all the way in favor of one side, then all the way in favor of the other. However, at the last (judging) phase, balance is (finally) achieved.

Return on Investment: The Usual Criterion

The premise of this section is that the organization's goal is to maximize the firm's overall return on investment in the long run. Overall return on investment does not refer to any single flow or product. In deciding whether to integrate forward into distribution (the manufacturer's choice) or backward into production (the downstream channel member's choice), the appropriate question is whether taking on this flow increases return on investment and does so more than some other use of the resources needed to provide the flow.

Why select this criterion? It is not always appropriate: Other criteria sometimes carry the day. (These will be discussed in the last section of this chapter.) But return on investment matters, and matters a very great deal. Why? Return on investment is the ratio of results obtained (roughly, operating performance: revenues minus direct costs) to the resources used to obtain them (roughly, overhead, reflecting the amortization of fixed investments). In the short term, the firm may be able to sustain losses or tolerate mediocre results (the numerator). Or the firm may be able to justify dedicating inordinate resources (the denominator) for the results achieved. Providers of resources (investors, corporate headquarters), however, will not permit this situation to last indefinitely. There comes a day of reckoning when the returns to resources will matter.

For our purposes, the relevant terms are the revenues, direct costs, and overhead incurred under vertical integration (make), compared to those incurred under outsourcing (buy). We use these terms in a conceptual sense only. The decision maker usually cannot create proper and precise accounting estimates for the situation. Fortunately, for purposes of channel decision making, this is not necessary. It is enough to focus on situational factors that drive revenue up and costs or overhead down.

Conceptually,

$$\frac{\text{Revenues} - \text{Direct Costs}}{\text{Overhead}} = \frac{\text{Net Effectiveness}}{\text{Overhead}} = \text{Efficiency}$$

Return on investment is the ratio of net effectiveness to overhead (results to resources). Net effectiveness is the revenues that accrue under vertical integration minus the direct (variable) costs incurred after integrating. For vertical integration to be efficient, it must somehow increase revenues more than it increases variable costs in order to improve net effectiveness. It is not enough merely to improve net effectiveness. Vertical integration is certain to encumber resources, thereby increasing overhead. The use of these resources must be justified by the increase in net effectiveness.

Two circumstances preclude vertical integration forward, even if it would add to return on investment. One is that the firm does not have and cannot obtain the resources to integrate forward. The other is that the firm has other priorities that contribute even more to return on investment and that exhaust the firm's capacities. The manufacturer should pursue these other actions instead, even if vertical integration has a positive payoff that earns a return on overhead exceeding the firm's hurdle rate returns on resources employed (e.g., capital).

Outsourcing as the Starting Point

A very substantial body of research suggests that any manufacturer should begin with the seemingly artificial premise that the distribution flow should be outsourced.[20] Why should outsourcing, that is, market contracting, be the default option for the distribution flow? The fundamental rationale is that under normal circumstances in a developed economy, markets for distribution services are efficient.

This does not mean that markets for distribution services function perfectly or even that they function well. It means that given current environmental conditions, technology, and know-how, it is difficult for a given manufacturer to get better operating results than can be delivered by the level of third-party services available to the manufacturer. It is noteworthy that the argument is strictly comparative, not absolute. And it does not mean that there is no room for improvement; however, improvement, under current environmental conditions, would require the manufacturer to introduce new technology or know-how that would change prevailing methods. Thus, the manufacturer would need to take on substantial risk.

This is happening now in China, which suffers from highly inefficient distribution, a heritage of decades of government regulation of the distribution sector. Change is happening fast, as exemplified in the auto industry, where leading Chinese (e.g., Legend) and foreign (e.g., Honda) firms partner with other Chinese firms to create new distribution entities. These new fusion companies bring the best attitudes, technology, and methods in channel management and adapt them to market conditions. Within a matter of years, Chinese distribution is likely to advance radically. In the meantime, manufacturers are indeed taking on very substantial risk. They must, because the caveat "under normal circumstances in a developed economy" does not yet apply.[21]

The efficient markets argument does not mean that all manufacturers will receive the same downstream services. Superior manufacturers offering superior rewards will attract better providers of marketing channel flows or will obtain the best level of service a given provider can offer. Other manufacturers will obtain what is left.

In sum, efficient markets for third-party marketing channel services means the manufacturer will be hard pressed to improve on the results it can obtain in the marketplace for marketing channel flows. Why should this be so?

Six Reasons to Outsource Distribution

A firm has six reasons to outsource the performance of a channel function to an outside party. Focusing on downstream functions for the moment, these are:

1. Motivation
2. Specialization
3. Survival of the economically fittest
4. Economies of scale
5. Heavier market coverage
6. Independence from any single manufacturer

Let us examine these one by one.

Motivation

Outside parties have high-powered incentives to do their jobs well because they are independent companies accepting risk in return for the prospect of rewards. Both positive motivation (profit) and negative motivation (fear of loss) spur the third party to perform. Sales agents, for example, are often more willing to prospect for customers, more persistent, and more inclined to ask for the sale (attempt to close a negotiation successfully) than are company salespeople (this is one reason why financial services, such as insurance, are often sold by third parties).[22] An outsider is attracted by entrepreneurial rewards and driven by fear of losses.

Part of motivation is the willingness to operate within a certain financial model. Downstream operations are frequently detail-oriented businesses that operate on narrow margins and focus on inventory turnover and cost management. For a producer, this mode of thinking is often alien, and the risk-adjusted returns may not appeal.

Key to the motivation advantage is that outside parties are replaceable, hence subject to market discipline by their principals. For example, if a distributor is underperforming, the manufacturer moves to another distributor. The mere threat of such a move is credible and, therefore, gives the distributor an incentive to attempt to meet the manufacturer's demands or to find an acceptable compromise. These demands include sharing distribution cost savings with the manufacturer, placing sales efforts on particular products, presenting products in a particular way, advertising, carrying more inventory—the possible requests to make of a third party are without limit.

Distributors are thus under constant pressure to improve operating results, which includes both increasing sales and decreasing costs. In contrast, a company distribution organization cannot be so readily terminated or restructured, and precedent makes it difficult to make substantial changes to incentive systems. Internal politics shields employees, making it more likely that an integrated distribution operation will become an unresponsive, inefficient bureaucracy. This is particularly the case where labor law makes it difficult to terminate employees, as is true in much of Europe. However, even in countries such is the United States, where employment is traditionally at the will of the employer, firing a single employee, let alone an entire division, is administratively difficult. Replaceability is the key to making the buy option work.

Specialization

Another advantage of outsiders is specialization. For wholesalers, distribution is all they do—they have no distractions. The reverse is true for manufacturers. Specialization engenders and deepens competence. This is why Whirlpool has been a pioneer for decades in the outsourcing of logistics. Kenco is a large logistics provider, deeply versed in the intricacies of storage, shipping, and delivery. Outsourcing allows each party (Whirlpool and Kenco) to stick to their specialties. This advantage has always existed. Increasing competition has made firms appreciate it more. A generalized move to identify and strip down to core competencies—and only those core competencies—is behind many decisions to outsource channel flows. See Sidebar 9.2 for an example in Kenya.

Survival of the Economic Fittest

If specialists fail to do their functions better than their competitors, they do not survive (which, of course, helps reinforce the above motivation factor). Distribution in most sectors has low mobility barriers: The business is easy to enter and easy to exit. Such businesses attract many entrants and readily eliminate the lesser performers among them because they can exit swiftly. This argument is connected with specialization, for an incompetent marketing channel member cannot stay in business by subsidizing its distribution losses with gains in other sectors, such as production. This is one reason why Whirlpool entrusts all its logistics to Kenco, a profitable survivor in a brutally competitive industry, and one that is unable to offset logistics losses with gains elsewhere.

Economies of Scale

Outside parties pool the demands of multiple manufacturers for marketing channel flows. This allows them to achieve economies of scale by doing a great deal of one thing (a set of distribution flows) for multiple parties. In turn, these economies of scale enable the outsider to perform flows that would otherwise be uneconomical to do at all. By offering many brands in a product category, a distributor can do enough business to amortize the fixed costs of distribution facilities, logistics software, and the

Sidebar 9.2

East African Breweries conquers the Kenyan beer market

East African Breweries Limited (EABL) is the largest beer brewer and marketer in East Africa. EABL's nine brands enjoy a virtual monopoly in the large Kenyan beer market, as its only rival, South African Breweries, withdrew from the market in 2002 after prolonged and intense competition between the two companies. South African Breweries (SAB), a multinational beer giant, entered the Kenyan market in 1995 by building a modern factory. Its efforts to win over a significant share were thwarted by an aggressive defense put up by EABL. This contest, referred to by industry observers as the Beer War, ended in July 2002 when SAB reached a market-sharing agreement with EABL. Under this agreement, EABL's Kenyan subsidiary now brews, markets, and distributes under license SAB brands in Kenya. In turn, EABL effectively withdrew from the Tanzanian market, and SAB now markets EABL brands there, also under license.

The situation EABL faced in Kenya was challenging. A long-running recession shrank the beer market in volume. Simultaneously, fierce competition with SAB encouraged consumers to be more price sensitive. Thus, EABL could not rely on price increases but, rather, had to focus on cost containment and demand stimulation. This led the company to undertake a major restructuring in 1994, whose principal aim was to refocus the company on its core business, beer manufacturing, and make it both leaner and more competitive.

A critical decision was to dismantle the company's distribution facilities. On the face of it, this is curious. Why give up control in order to win a market share battle? But EABL understood that beer distribution is not idiosyncratic and not subject to performance ambiguity. Hence, the company sold off noncore assets, including its transport fleet, and contracted distribution to third-party providers. Then, with a view to defending its market share, EABL focused on maximizing the effectiveness of its distribution network. In response to the market entry of SAB in 1995, EABL invested heavily in the improvement of its distribution capabilities. As a result, EABL achieved virtually 100 percent market coverage without ruinous levels of spending or investment.

The EABL success story has many elements, including dramatic improvements in manufacturing return on investment and an effective promotional campaign that created a strong pull effect on Kenya's thousands of outlets selling beer; however, most observers agree that EABL prevailed over SAB because of the strength of its distribution network. Not only did the company enhance its own coverage of a highly fragmented market but it successfully prevented SAB from doing the same through aggressive distribution initiatives focused on reward power. (Chapters 6 and 8 further develop the elements of EABL's winning strategy.) The fundamental decision, however, was to give up control and free resources by retreating from forward vertical integration.[23]

like. Similarly, a retailer that specializes in a single category of merchandise (such as appliances) pools the demand of many manufacturers for retailing services. The retailer's deep brand assortment, albeit in a narrow category of products, attracts customers. The customer base in turn justifies the existence of the specialty store or the category killer, which would otherwise be uneconomical.

Heavier Coverage

Heavier market coverage stems from the independent's ability to call on many customers, including small customers, and to call on them often. This advantage is based on providing more assortment to end-users. For example, a manufacturers' representative (rep, or independent sales agent) can create a portfolio of products and services meeting related needs. Via this portfolio, the rep can justify the activity of making a call on a prospect that is a small account—for any single brand of any single product. By meeting multiple needs for that customer, the rep can sell multiple brands and products on a single call, converting a small prospect (for a brand) into a large prospect (for the salesperson).

Further, by being able to meet many needs at once, the reps can induce time-pressed purchasers, who value one-stop shopping, to meet with them and to spend enough time for the reps to learn a good deal about the customers. The reps can then parlay this deep customer knowledge into more compelling sales presentations of a greater range of offerings. The sale of one item leads to the sale of another; that is, the rep creates selling synergy within the portfolio of offerings.[24]

Similarly, by meeting multiple needs, distributors are able to draw customers to their locations, Web sites, or catalogs. Once there, customers spend time making purchases, and one purchase often encourages another. For example, in office supplies, the prospect orders standard white paper for a printer, then remembers to order toner, then thinks of the need for nonstandard paper or colors, and so forth. The astute salesperson uses this interchange to learn about the customer's installation, information that is useful when it is time to replace the printer itself.

In short, sales mount in a pyramid if the intermediary has composed an appealing assortment of goods that represent related purchase occasions to the buyer. It is difficult for most manufacturers to duplicate the thorough coverage afforded by third parties, for few manufacturers can match the breadth of related products and services the third party can assemble. Some manufacturers do have very broad product lines, as broad as a distributor's; however, the distributor is free to select only the best products from a variety of manufacturers, bypassing the "weak links" in any manufacturer's offerings. Few broad-line manufacturers are uniformly strong in all elements of their product line.

Key here is that the independent can realize potential synergies that a vertically integrated manufacturer cannot reproduce. Why? Because the vertically integrated manufacturer may offer to carry the lines of its competitors in order to duplicate the independent's assortment, but competitors and sellers of complementary goods and services will hesitate to sell their products through the manufacturer's distribution arm. They fear the sales force will favor its own products at their expense.[25] This is why a manufacturer's acquisition of a distributor often provokes the distributor's other principals to terminate their contracts and seek representation elsewhere. It is also one reason why downstream channel members do not integrate backward into production more often. For examples see Sidebar 9.3.

The ability to amortize the cost of a call, then, creates a powerful advantage by allowing the independent to cover a market much more thoroughly (i.e., to make calls more often, to more influencers, in smaller accounts, even in pursuit of a low-probability sale) than can most vertically integrated manufacturers. The importance of this fundamental point is often understated. The sheer arithmetical advantage afforded by

> **Sidebar 9.3**
>
> ## Illusory benefits from vertical integration forward
>
> Pharmaceutical manufacturer Merck integrated forward in the 1990s by purchasing Medco Health Solutions, a pharmacy benefit manager that negotiates wholesale drug sales. The move was positioned as learning: Medco was to be Merck's observatory on the market. Competitors accused Medco of favoring Merck's products and withdrew their business, damaging Medco and ruining its ability to serve as an observatory. Merck finally sold Medco in 2003.[26]
>
> French luxury goods maker LVMH bought two retailing chains, Sephora and Duty Free Shoppers (DFS), for the purpose of controlling distribution of its perfume brands. But these are mass-market products, and consumers demand to see a deep brand assortment. Accordingly, LVMH is obliged to treat its retailing subsidiaries as though they are independent: Otherwise, the stores would lose their other suppliers—and thus their clientele. Says one LVMH brand manager, "The fact that LVMH owns DFS and Sephora is essentially neutral to my business. To be successful, they have to treat competitors as they treat me. There is no synergy from having these two businesses."[27]

superiority of coverage cannot be overlooked when reasonable estimates are incorporated in a spreadsheet analysis of the make-or-buy choice. This is an important reason why Best Power dismantled its direct sales force. Although they were effective, their narrow product line prevented them from calling on any but the largest customers. The value-added resellers who replaced them call on a huge range of customers and know how uninterruptible power supplies fit into the larger picture of the customer's needs.

Independence from a Single Manufacturer

For their customers, diversified outside providers of channel flows can serve as a sort of independent counsel, an impartial source of advice that does not come from a single manufacturer. A major drawback of Internet travel agents is that their independence from suppliers is dubious. For example, Travelocity is owned by airlines and hotels, and Orbitz is owned by a group of airlines. Though these services bill themselves as the best source for discounted tickets, seasoned travelers see the conflict of interest and do not assume they will get the best offer from these sources. Analysts were quick to point out that this issue—lack of independence from producers—was magnified in 2004 when Cendant purchased Orbitz. Cendant owns hotels and car rental agencies and is motivated by the ability to steer travelers to its own brands.[28]

Many outside specialists are local entities. Therefore, they are stable entities with the same personnel serving the same customer set year after year. They have the opportunity to know their customers well, forging strong customer loyalties.

Many manufacturers disagree that neutral status is an advantage. Indeed, they consider independence (i.e., obstinacy or conflict of interest) as one of the biggest drawbacks of outsourcing. They desire vertical integration so that they can resolve their differences of opinion by giving orders to subordinates; however, this represents a rather optimistic view of how things actually get done inside vertically integrated firms. The manufacturer's distribution arm, just like a third party, will seek to avoid carrying out orders it considers misguided.

It is worth considering why an independent would resist doing what the manufacturer desires. An independent acquires substantial information about the marketplace. If the independent has reservations about the manufacturer's ideas, it behooves the manufacturer to listen and to engage the channel member in a dialogue. The downstream channel member is analogous to a test market for a new product. If the test market results are poor, the appropriate reaction is to make modifications and test it again.

VERTICAL INTEGRATION FORWARD WHEN COMPETITION IS LOW

At this point, you may be thinking this sketch of independents is idealized and overly favorable. If so, you are right. It is time to change orientation and to become the critic of one's preliminary decision to outsource. It is not enough, however, merely to criticize third-party distribution. The critic must also make the case that a vertically integrated firm would do the job better (i.e., contribute enough to revenue or reduce direct cost enough to offset any other increases in direct cost and to justify the increase in overhead that will be necessary). This goes back to a foundation of marketing channels: You can eliminate the channel intermediary, but you cannot eliminate the functions it performs.

Two caveats open the discussion. First, vertical integration always involves substantial set-up costs and overhead; therefore, it is only worth considering if a substantial amount of business is potentially at stake. Second, it is only worth considering if the firm is prosperous enough to be able to muster the necessary resources—and does not have a better use for them.

The economic advantages of outsourcing distribution are variations on a familiar theme: Competitive markets of any kind are efficient. Finding situations that do not favor outsourcing distribution means finding situations in which markets for distribution services are not competitive.

Company-Specific Capabilities

The first and most frequent noncompetitive scenario is that of small-numbers bargaining arising from company-specific capabilities. Consider the following hypothetical and prototypical example.

> Atlas Electronics is a distributor of electronic components. Atlas is one of many distributors in its market area, for electronic components is a fiercely competitive industry. Atlas's salespeople are electrical engineers, well versed in their industry, its products, its customers, and the applications they make of the products.
>
> Jupiter Semiconductors is one of the many manufacturers that Atlas represents. Jupiter is a differentiated manufacturer whose products are unique. Over the years, Atlas salespeople have learned the myriad idiosyncrasies of the Jupiter product line, including how it functions in conjunction with other brands of electronic and electrical components. They have learned

how their customer base applies Jupiter products. Atlas management estimates that, even though Jupiter provides training at their factory, Atlas salespeople still require two years of on-the-job experience selling Jupiter to master this knowledge. These two years are necessary even though the salespeople are skilled and knowledgeable about the industry in general.

The key word here is *idiosyncrasies*. Because Jupiter products are quite different from competing semiconductors, even a salesperson who knows the industry requires substantial training and on-the-job experience to master them. That mastery, in turn, is an asset: It is of considerable value in selling Jupiter products—*only*. This knowledge is a company-specific capability, the company being Jupiter.

The greater the value of company-specific capabilities, the greater the economic rationale for the manufacturer to vertically integrate forward into distribution. This is because the holders of the capabilities (here, the salespeople, and by extension, their employer, Atlas) become so valuable that they are irreplaceable. If it takes two years to bring a salesperson to the mastery level, salespeople with at least two years of Jupiter experience are very expensive to replace. Not only must the replacement be trained, the less-effective sales effort during the recruiting and training period causes an opportunity cost. Thus, Jupiter is in small-numbers bargaining with Atlas. Jupiter cannot replace their sales quickly, even if it spends enough to hire very competent salespeople with generalized industry experience.

Small-numbers bargaining destroys the fundamental premise of competitive markets. It does so by destroying the presumption of market discipline. Because only small numbers of people possess company-specific capabilities, only small numbers of organizations are truly qualified to bid to perform the function (in this case, selling) in later periods. If the firm cannot readily find qualified bidders, it cannot credibly threaten to move its business (terminate the contract with Atlas) when it is dissatisfied. Notice that Jupiter does not start out (*ex ante*) with small-numbers bargaining— small-numbers bargaining emerges *ex post*. That is, the distribution relationship that was founded initially on a basis of large-numbers bargaining (choosing one from many available distributors) gradually becomes difficult to manage because the process of accumulating distribution relationship-specific investments will turn the initial large-numbers situation into a small-numbers situation.

Thus, Jupiter cannot count on *ex ante* competitive markets to ensure efficient outcomes *ex post*. Atlas salespeople may now engage in such behaviors as shirking, misrepresenting the product, unethical behavior, falsifying expense accounts, and demanding more compensation to do the same work. This is called opportunism, which is self-interest seeking in a deceitful or dishonest manner.[29]

In these circumstances, Jupiter needs to step in and replace the market mechanism in order to prevent opportunism.[30] The invisible hand of the market can be replaced by the visible hand of Jupiter management. By vertically integrating forward, the manufacturer creates an administrative mechanism (thereby increasing overhead). It can use that mechanism to direct activities for which the market would not otherwise provide the correct incentives.

How does this solve the problem? After all, it is really the salespeople who are irreplaceable. Whether they are employed by Atlas (outsourcing) or employed by Jupiter (vertical integration), they can still do great damage by leaving their jobs or by shirking or failing to cooperate.

The answer is that Jupiter gains more control over the salespeople directly. As Jupiter employees, salespeople have only Jupiter products to sell. They draw their income from a single principal rather than from a third party gathering revenue from multiple principals. Salespeople report to a Jupiter manager whose sole concern is their performance on behalf of Jupiter and no other principal and no other organization. After Jupiter-employee-salespeople make these idiosyncratic investments, they do not pose a strong threat to the company because those company-specific skills and assets have relatively little outside market value. Thus, salespeople are now highly dependent on Jupiter.

Jupiter also has the ability to employ negative sanctions against employees directly as well as to offer positive incentives, such as a salary, bonus, or commission. (This is why information collected by mystery shoppers, covered in Chapter 6 on power) is of more use to employers than it is to franchisors or third parties. Employers can do more with the data, including tying it to bonuses or penalties and performance evaluations.[31]

Jupiter not only controls monetary compensation but also controls nonmonetary compensation. Thus, it can build employee loyalty via its personnel practices. Finally, Jupiter has the right to demand detailed information on what the salespeople do (the right of audit, or monitoring). In contrast, Atlas management would act as a buffer, refusing to allow a single principal to direct its personnel.

In short, Jupiter gains much more power over the salespeople by eliminating a third party and employing the holders of the critical resources directly. This is not to say these irreplaceable salespeople will be easy to manage. They can still practice opportunism against Jupiter. Vertical integration will never eliminate shirking, dishonesty, and the like. However, opportunism will be lessened. In comparative return-on-investment terms, the manufacturer is better off. With less opportunism, revenues should increase (because salespeople are working more and performing more effectively) and direct costs should decline (e.g., lower costs due to lower expense account claims). Thus, net effectiveness should increase.

The value of company-specific capabilities, however, must be very high to justify vertical integration. Only when these idiosyncratic assets are very valuable is there much room for opportunism. By integrating, the firm greatly increases its overhead. Further, the manufacturer gives up some of the third party's coverage and economies of scale, which decreases net effectiveness. Therefore, vertical integration may actually decrease return on investment unless the potential for opportunism is so substantial as to constitute a greater threat than the cost of overhead and the lost benefits of dealing with an outsider.

You may wonder why Jupiter needs to intervene at all. If the problem is opportunism by salespeople, why not charge Atlas (their employer) with controlling opportunism rather than employing Atlas's salespeople directly? Jupiter cannot credibly threaten to terminate Atlas as its distributor, but does not Atlas itself have an interest in satisfying Jupiter, therefore, in controlling salesperson opportunism? After all, if Jupiter, the manufacturer, really does vertically integrate, Atlas, the distributor, will lose its own investment. Atlas cannot redeploy the know-how it has acquired about Jupiter products and customer applications to the service of another principal. This know-how has zero salvage value (i.e., it has no alternative use). Thus, Atlas loses its investment in knowledge, as well as in the customer relationships it has built serving

Jupiter customers. Because Jupiter products are unique, converting these customers to another principal's products will be difficult. Should not Atlas, contemplating the long-run prospect of losing Jupiter, undertake voluntarily to use its own influence as an employer to control the opportunism of its salespeople?

In rational terms, it would appear that the mere threat of vertical integration should allow Jupiter to pressure Atlas to simulate the outcome of market forces; however, there are two counterarguments. One is that it is not only the salespeople who can practice opportunism but Atlas itself. The irreplaceable nature of its salespeople puts Jupiter in small-numbers bargaining with Atlas itself after the onset of the distribution relationship. The distributor may then use Jupiter's vulnerability to demand more (e.g., better margins) while doing less to earn it (e.g., holding lower inventories). The second argument is that Jupiter cannot justify vertical integration until Atlas's opportunism becomes very substantial. If Atlas stays within a certain latitude of abuse, Jupiter will find it cheaper to be the victim of opportunism than to vertically integrate. (The same rationale explains why insurance companies tolerate a certain degree of claims fraud: To a point, it is cheaper to pay false claims than to pay the costs of detecting and fighting false claims.)[32]

Let us alter the scenario, taking it back in time. Jupiter is contemplating selling in Atlas's territory and has no representation. Should it sign up Atlas as its distributor or should it vertically integrate, setting up a distribution branch to serve Atlas's market? Knowing that its products are idiosyncratic, Jupiter may foresee the scenario of getting into small-numbers bargaining with Atlas or any other distributor that sells its products. If the idiosyncratic assets involved are sufficiently valuable, Jupiter is better off, in return-on-investment terms, by vertically integrating to begin with. A good deal of field research demonstrates that Jupiter is highly likely to do just that.

Vertically integrating in response to the mere prospect of company-specific assets has two major advantages. First, the producer can make sure its employees really do make the investments and acquire the needed capabilities. Second, the producer can show potential customers and other constituents (such as investors) that it is dedicated to the market and its products. Vertical integration is one way to establish credibility. By investing in its own operation, the firm makes a visible, credible commitment. This is particularly important when customers see the purchase as risky and fear the producer will abandon the market if problems arise.[33]

This is not to say that a manufacturer cannot work efficiently with a third party where idiosyncratic assets are at stake. To do so is very difficult, however, and requires careful structuring of the arrangement to achieve relational governance (Chapter 8).

In short, the prospect of accumulating company-specific assets creates an economic rationale to vertically integrate. These assets go by many labels.[34] Economists call them idiosyncratic assets or transaction-specific assets because they are customized (specific) to a business relationship (transaction). They are also called idiosyncratic or transaction-specific investments because effort, time, know-how, and other resources must be expended to create them.

Typically in marketing channels, these capabilities grow slowly over time, often without the realization of either party, until a crisis or an opportunity forces the parties to take stock of the assets they have accumulated. The key concepts here are (a) assets: tangible or intangible, they can be used to create economic value and

(b) specific: that is, made to specifications, customized, tailored, particular to, or idiosyncratic. Specific assets cannot be redeployed to another application without significant loss in value.

Six Types of Company-Specific Capabilities in Distribution

In distribution, most of the company-specific capabilities of great importance are intangible. (In contrast, vertical integration upstream from production turns on physical assets, such as customized parts and assemblies.) Six major forms of company-specific capabilities accrue in the distribution arena. These are:

1. Idiosyncratic knowledge
2. Relationships
3. Brand equity that derives from the channel partner's activities
4. Customized physical facilities
5. Dedicated capacity
6. Site specificity

Let us examine these in order.

Idiosyncratic knowledge is not merely knowledge of the manufacturer, its products, its operating methods, and the applications its customers make of these products. It is that *part* of this knowledge base that *cannot be readily redeployed to another principal.* There is a great deal to know about a company that makes standard products, uses operating procedures that are generic in its industry, and whose customers use the company's products as they would use those of another company in the same industry. Downstream channel members make investments to acquire this knowledge, which is indeed an asset. It is not an idiosyncratic asset, however. It is a general-purpose asset, meaning it can be put to the service of another principal without loss of productive value. Only when a principal makes unusual products or has its own unique methods of operation or has customers who make customized uses of the products does the downstream channel member acquire information that is idiosyncratic, hence a company-specific capability. Ordinary principals do not need to vertically integrate downstream: They can generate efficient distribution outcomes if they use the market for distribution services, given the market is competitive.[35] A principal that requires company-specific capabilities is at least moderately exotic. See Sidebar 9.4 for the example of Jean Delatour.

Relationships are connections between distributor personnel and the personnel of the manufacturer or the manufacturer's customers. The existence of a relationship implies the ability to get things done quickly and correctly and to make oneself understood swiftly. For some transactions, relationships are essential. For example, just-in-time supply arrangements involve exquisite coordination. For a manufacturer to replenish a downstream channel member's supplies just at the time it becomes necessary requires very close cooperation between the manufacturer and the channel member. This demands relationships, and the cost (accounting cost and opportunity cost) of a failed supply arrangement makes these relationships essential.[36]

Brand equity is a critical idiosyncratic investment in the manufacturer's brand name. Here we can distinguish two cases. In one case, the brand name enjoys substantial

Sidebar 9.4

Jean Delatour

Idiosyncratic knowledge is behind Jean Delatour's integration into the production of jewelry. The chain aims directly at hypermarkets, which have made great inroads into jewelry by using bulk purchase power to offer lower prices than most jewelers can match. Superficially, Jean Delatour mimics this strategy. Like hypermarkets, the stores are huge, unappealing boxlike structures made of corrugated metal and located on the peripheries of urban areas—indeed, near the hypermarkets themselves. Shoppers come expecting a price appeal, which they do find.

They also find unique merchandise because the chain manufactures the jewelry it sells. Backward integration also permits Jean Delatour to renew its collection twice a year, catering to the increasing fashion orientation of jewelry. The chain also practices the dying art of custom production on site. Every store has a workshop, permitting a customer not only to design a piece of jewelry but to see it realized within a week—at prices reflective of Delatour's expertise and presence in production.

To complete its uniqueness, the chain uses its production expertise to create a novel shopping experience. A computerized kiosk shows customers minute-by-minute activity on the Antwerp diamond exchange, creating merchandising excitement. Next to the kiosk, loose diamonds rated and certified by the chain are sold (under blister packs!). Customers often select them to fit into their own design of jewelry (aided by a lavishly staffed sales operation). This is not typical merchandising behavior: By projecting its production expertise, the retail chain creates an idiosyncratic experience that alters buyer behavior.

The only category Jean Delatour does not make is watches and clocks. This requires a different expertise, which the chain does not possess. Powerful brand names dominate this category, and few customers are interested in designing their own. Thus, Jean Delatour outsources production. Why carry the category at all? The reason is consumer expectation of assortment: A "real" jewelry store must carry fine clocks and watches.

brand equity with consumers independent of the downstream channel member's actions. In this case, vertical downstream is not only unnecessary but wasteful. The manufacturer can instead use brand equity as a source of referent power over channel members (Chapter 6). Here, the manufacturer does not need to integrate forward in order to exert considerable influence over the channel. In the second case, downstream channel members do have a critical impact on the firm's brand equity. Brand equity is not created in a manner largely independent of their actions. For example, channel members have a great influence on brand equity when:

> A sales force is required to create a credible image for the brand. This is often the case for industrial products.
> The brand's strategy demands it be stocked, displayed, and presented in a particular manner but allows for too low a downstream margin to invite the channel member to provide the support itself. This is why perfume makers sometimes rent dedicated space from department stores and pay the salespeople.[37]

➤ The brand's strategy demands a level of cooperation that completely overrides the decision-making discretion of a third party. Chapter 4 presents examples in the retailing of luxury goods.

➤ A brand-specific support service, before or after sales, is required to make sure the branded product is properly installed and used, so that the customer is satisfied and positive word-of-mouth is created. (Chapters 4 and 8 discuss how to get a similar result by building close relationships.)

In all these cases, brand equity is created and maintained via customer experiences, which are driven by marketing channel activities. If the brand name can be made truly valuable, it can be a substantial asset, one that is, of course, specific to the manufacturer. The more valuable this asset, the more the firm is better off if it vertically integrates. For assets that are somewhat valuable but not valuable enough to justify taking ownership of a flow or flows, the firm may protect its investment by forging close relationships downstream, by franchising, by imposing vertical restraints, or by seeking other means of influencing its channel members. Close relationships are a way to simulate vertical integration in circumstances that do not justify the make option but that are poorly suited to the classic buy option (arm's-length market contracts).

Brand equity derived from channel member activity is behind much of the increase in private label activity by North American supermarkets. They are not simply putting their name on what a manufacturer would be making anyway. The new style of private label is to use one's knowledge of the product category to design a new product and to work with manufacturers to figure out how to make it. A leader here is the Canadian chain Loblaws, which keeps an R&D facility for this purpose. Loblaws did market research to identify a demand for a much richer cookie than was currently available. The chain worked with a producer to devise a way to overcome substantial technical obstacles to manufacture. Then Loblaws branded the product (Decadent cookies) and invested heavily to promote it. The brand was so successful that even though Loblaws only holds 20 percent of the Canadian market, Decadent became the market share leader. Loblaws' investment backward (into product design and development) paid off handsomely. The chain has repeated this story in many categories.[38]

At a high enough level of value, the manufacturer is justified in trading influence for more control by vertically integrating forward. An example of this phenomenon is the ongoing rivalry between Coca-Cola and Pepsi Cola (see Sidebar 9.5).

Know-how, relationships, and brand equity (when driven by downstream activities) are the major categories of company-specific capabilities that justify vertical integration forward. They are all intangibles. Several categories of tangible assets also play a role.

Customized physical facilities can be an important transaction-specific asset. For example, Amazon, the online bookseller, outsourced its warehousing and shipping for years; however, book wholesalers operate on a model of sending many books at a time to one easy-to-find location (a bookstore). Picking one book to send to any private address was ruinously costly. Amazon did not become profitable until it invented a radically new way to stock and select books and built its own highly idiosyncratic warehousing and information system.[39]

The same scenario occurs in maritime shipping when the shipping vessel is specific to a narrow use for which there are very few users (such as shipping liquefied nitrogen). A ship may even be specific to a single user (some vessels are fitted to handle a particular brand of car). Redeploying these ships to appeal to a broader group of

Sidebar 9.5

Decades of rivalry between Coke and Pepsi in the United States

Both Coca-Cola and Pepsi Cola began U.S. operations in the early twentieth century by outsourcing distribution to third parties, one per market area. The producers also outsourced the assembly of the product to their channel members. These latter are known as bottlers because they formulate the product from ingredients supplied by the producer, according to the producer's instructions, and package the output (an operation called bottling, even though many containers other than bottles are now used). Initially, this decision was justified because transportation costs dominated the economics of the soft drink business. Weight was the driver: The product itself is heavy, and the empty glass bottles were returned to the store, where the bottler picked them up, and transported back to the plant to be cleaned and refilled. By producing and distributing locally, the independent bottler held down transportation costs. Brand building was a minor activity achieved largely by the producers via limited national advertising. The business, well suited to outsourcing assembly to completely independent bottlers, was stable, simple, and small.

By the 1960s the soft-drink business had changed dramatically. Coke and Pepsi were so well diffused in the United States that they had displaced conventional drinks on many purchase occasions (even for breakfast). Transportation became a lesser cost, in part because disposable containers replaced returnable bottles. Producers ran enormous national advertising campaigns requiring complex promotional tie-ins by all of their many regional bottlers simultaneously. The products and their packaging became more complex and volatile, while the product line expanded greatly. Building brand equity replaced holding down transportation costs as the most important aspect of the

business. The bottlers' participation was necessary to do this. Brand equity rested on their cooperation with the producer on terms of trade, delivery, promotions, advertisements, new products and packages, new product testing, custom promotion for key accounts, selling methods for key accounts, and similar concerns. These activities all were tightly synchronized with the producer, who in turn ensured that brand-equity building was consistent across market areas. The result was incessant and fruitless negotiation (haggling) between the producers (Pepsi, Coke) and their bottlers. Transaction costs between producers and their completely independent bottlers were getting out of control.

Coca-Cola ultimately vertically integrated forward into distribution, market by market, and is now largely the owner of its U.S. channels, a strategy it is in the process of repeating in Europe and continuing to expand in the United States. Pepsi is now following the same route. Both producers have done this by purchasing most of their bottlers (an acquisition strategy, versus a "greenfield" strategy, which is creating new operations). The economic value of this strategy is illustrated by one difference between the two producers. One segment of the business is fountain sales, in which institutions (such as restaurants) perform the final mixing step to create the product and dispense it in single servings without bottling it (serving from the fountain). For contractual reasons, Pepsi is unable to integrate distribution to the fountain segment. Coke has, however, integrated to serve this segment, and has much lower transaction costs than does Pepsi (due to Pepsi's continued haggling and poor coordination with bottlers). This transaction cost advantage has helped Coke achieve dominance in the segment. Coke is not the only beneficiary: The consumer has also

(continued)

Sidebar 9.5 (cont.)

Decades of rivalry between Coke and Pepsi in the United States

benefited from lower fountain prices, made possible by passing on transaction cost savings.[40]

In this case, vertical integration into distribution had been highly successful to achieve coordination between upstream and downstream channel members. However, it is notable that even these producers have had difficulty reconciling the differences, both financial and operating, between manufacturing and distribution. As a result, Coke moved to relational governance (quasi-vertical integration) in an effort to stay coordinated without assuming the responsibilities of full ownership. In 1986, Coca-Cola divested its distribution arm and sold it off as a separate company. This change in structure separates bottling (which requires substantial cash and operates on high volumes at low margins) from the production of concentrate (which exhibits the opposite properties). This is a classic difference between production and distribution: Management felt that mixing these businesses discouraged investors and lowered the company's stock price.

How well did the strategy work? Initial results for the newly independent bottler, Coca-Cola Enterprises (CCE), were disappointing. In retrospect, Coca-Cola now considers that it tried to exert too much control, taking advantage of its large equity stake (49%) in CCE. The result was that management lost touch with the considerable differences between markets that occur at the field level. After five years of disappointing results, Coca-Cola turned CCE over to management recruited from an acquired bottler, then granted autonomy to CCE to enable it to respond locally to each unique marketplace and to focus on the myriad details that are usually more critical in distribution than in production. Seeing CCE's autonomy has reassured independent bottlers that Coca-Cola is sincere when it assures them that it respects their acumen and independence.

The results of decentralization in terms of growth and profits have been exceptional, so much so that CCE's share price has actually grown faster than that of Coca-Cola itself. One result is that Pepsi has imitated Coke's strategy of spinning off bottling as a separate company.[41]

In short, producers changed their vertical integration strategy to follow changes in the market. Starting with fully independent bottlers was appropriate until brand building became a critical value driver. Then vertical integration successfully created coordination, allowing Pepsi and Coke to build their brands. Once brand equity was firmly established, Coke, and later Pepsi, realized they no longer needed to closely control what is fundamentally a very different business. Hence, Coke gave bottlers operating autonomy in two steps, greatly improving long-run return on investment. Today, Pepsi and Coke can use referent power to influence their bottlers and no longer need to own their downstream channel members to achieve coordinated results.

users requires extensive retrofitting (the brand of car) or may be impossible (liquefied nitrogen). The key factor is that the assets (the ships) are difficult to redeploy to the service of multiple users, thereby creating contracting hazards. The carrier hesitates in fear of the manufacturer's opportunism, while the manufacturer also fears the carrier's opportunism. Although rationally it may appear that the "balance of fear" should make all parties act reasonably, the reality is that neither side is eager to enter into small-numbers bargaining with the other. Vertical integration is a viable solution.

Dedicated capacity is distribution capability (warehousing, transportation, selling, billing, and so forth) that is not customized but has been created to serve a manufacturer and which, by itself, represents overcapacity. Thus, if the manufacturer terminates the business, the downstream channel member has excess capacity that it cannot redeploy without sacrifice of productive value (i.e., losses). Unlike customized physical facilities, this capacity could be put to use in serving another manufacturer—if there were demand for it, which there is not.

A forward-looking channel member will hesitate to incur these obligations, fearing the opportunism of the manufacturer once the capacity has been put in place. Channel members may refuse to add the capacity or may require very high compensation to do so. It may be worthwhile in return-on-investment terms for the manufacturer to integrate forward. Conversely, once the capacity is in place, the downstream channel member is vulnerable and may be economically justified in protecting its investment in dedicated capacity. It can do so by vertically integrating backward—acquiring the manufacturer—in order to hold the business.

A manufacturer may need site-specific marketing channel flows performed in a location that is well suited to its needs but ill suited to the needs of other manufacturers. A channel member that creates a facility (for example, a warehouse) near the manufacturer has created a general-purpose asset if the manufacturer is near other manufacturers whom the warehouse could serve. If the manufacturer is in a location remote from other suppliers, the warehouse will be difficult to redeploy. Its value is specific to the manufacturer (it is worth little or nothing to other manufacturers).

An example occurs in maritime shipping of cargo.[42] For many products, raw materials are mined in remote parts of the world and shipped from one obscure port to another obscure port for processing in a refinery that is specially built to handle the output of the originating mine. Cargo carriers may refuse to offer service on such routes because few other customers desire to ship in either direction. Thus, manufacturers are sometimes obliged to integrate forward into shipping. Alternatively, they may form alliances with shippers.

The common thread uniting all of these factors—idiosyncratic knowledge, relationships, brand equity, customized physical facilities, dedicated capacity, and site specificity—is their production of firm-specific assets that have very low value in any alternative outside use. The ensuing difficulties (and/or cost) a manufacturer may have in convincing a high-quality channel partner to take on these investments, therefore, often lead the manufacturer to integrate vertically forward (or backward) to perform those functions and flows itself.

Specific Assets Can Change to General-Purpose Assets

Many specific assets gradually lose their customized nature and become general purpose assets. Usually this happens when the reason for specificity is innovation. Whenever a manufacturer brings an innovative product, process, or practice to a market, that innovation is, by definition, unique. No bidders will be qualified to distribute the new product or capable of carrying out the new process or practice. The manufacturer will have to train an organization. Assuming the manufacturer can find an organization willing to make the investment, the manufacturer will of necessity enter into small-numbers bargaining. Foreseeing this situation, the manufacturer may choose to integrate vertically. For example, when entering foreign markets, manufacturers tend to set up their own distribution arms to sell unusual products in spite of the expense and uncertainty involved.

But the novelty of the arrangement often disappears over time. Practices diffuse. Products and processes are copied. Competitors enter with similar methods. The market for providing these once-specific services expands as more providers acquire the requisite know-how, relationships, sites, and physical facilities. The day may come when the manufacturer no longer needs to be vertically integrated. An example occurred in the nineteenth-century United States (see Sidebar 9.6).

What was once specific becomes general. Small-numbers bargaining then gives way to large-numbers bargaining, and the competitiveness of the marketplace is restored. A manufacturer entering the market at that point would do well to outsource; however, it may not follow that the vertically integrated manufacturer would do well to dismantle its vertically integrated distribution operation.

Switching Costs

Changing from a vertically integrated distribution operation to outsourcing involves switching costs. Switching costs are the one-time losses incurred in taking down the current operation and setting up a new operation (here, from vertical integration to outsourcing, though switching costs are incurred in either direction of the switch). These include accounting costs, opportunity costs, and psychological costs associated with terminating or displacing the operation that is being dismantled, as well as recruiting, relocating, and training personnel and setting up infrastructure associated with the new operation. Note that these are one-time costs of set-up and take-down. Switching costs should not be confused with the operating costs of the new system once it is in place.

The switching costs of going from a company operation to a third party are particularly painful because they involve terminating the positions of employees. Terminating positions, however, need not mean terminating the employees or their relationships. Some manufacturers shift these employees to other positions in their firm. Indeed, innovative firms often have pressing needs for experienced personnel and welcome the opportunity to free them from distributing what have become standardized products through standardized processes. Failing transfer of personnel, progressive employers realize that former personnel possess company-specific knowledge and relationships of value and, if handled correctly, retain a loyalty to their former employer. Thus, manufacturers often arrange for their new third party to hire their former personnel (this is particularly the case under European labor laws, which frequently encourage, even demand, this practice).

A creative solution involves actually setting up former employees in business as third-party providers of distribution services (sales agencies, franchisees, dealers, distributors, export agents, etc.). For many manufacturers, this is a way to ensure exclusive representation of their products and services. For example, Rank Xerox in Europe sets up exclusive office-equipment dealers on high streets (urban commercial districts) owned by former employees. However, exclusivity is not essential. Some firms set up truly independent agencies, supporting them by training, secured bank loans, and promises of representation for a guaranteed number of years. Indeed, rather than viewing this practice in altruistic terms as a humane way to dispose of excess personnel, some firms view it as a proactive solution to the problem of finding good representation in markets where the capable third parties already are locked in with their competitors.

Sidebar 9.6

Gustavus Swift revolutionizes meat packing

In the 1870s, cattle were raised in the West and shipped live to the East by rail car.[49] Many animals died on the trip; the survivors arrived in an emaciated state. Upon arrival, they were slaughtered, and 60 percent of the animal was discarded. The remaining meat was dressed locally and sold fresh. Gustavus Swift saw the production economies of gathering the animals, slaughtering them, and dressing the meat in western cities in massive slaughterhouses, then shipping the meat by refrigerated rail car to the East. This was a novel way to distribute fresh meat. The critical aspect was a refrigerated rail car whose invention Swift commissioned in 1878.

Three years later, the designs were ready. Swift then discovered that the railroads, fearing the loss of the lucrative business of shipping live cattle, refused to build his refrigerated rail cars. So Swift integrated into railroad car construction. Then the main railroad association refused to carry his cars. Fortunately, Swift did not have to build his own railroad, as a competitor existed and agreed to use his highly idiosyncratic refrigerated cars. To meet the cars upon arrival, Swift built an elaborate network of branch houses and delivery routes. Swift's vision was correct: He was able to offer high quality at low prices, thereby overcoming opposition to the idea of eating "fresh" meat slaughtered many days before in a distant location. It was not only the idiosyncratic rail car that made this possible but the entire idiosyncratic system of wholesaling the meat. As demand expanded, Swift continually refined his model, keeping it idiosyncratic.

The speed with which Swift's model was imitated is instructive. Within a year, Philip Armour was imitating Swift (even today, Swift and Armour are valuable brand names in packaged meats, demonstrating the enduring value of their pioneering advantage). By the mid-1880s, several other meat-packing firms had imitated Swift. The local, fragmented meat packing industry was soon dominated by a handful of giants, all imitating Swift's distribution. By the 1890s, his model had been imitated in other industries, notably beer, and later, dairy products and bananas, spreading finally to frozen foods. Eventually, Swift's model was no longer Swift's model, but simply the know-how of transporting chilled perishables. A highly idiosyncratic asset passed into rare but general know-how, then passed into simple know-how.

These are means of minimizing switching costs. The switching-costs concept itself is easy to discuss in theory but difficult to estimate in practice. Research shows that firms contemplating switching are often conscious of those costs that accountants can track (such as recruiting costs). This is particularly the case in the United States, where surveys of such costs incurred by firms are regularly conducted and easily available. Other costs, such as the opportunity cost of lost business during the disruption of the transition or the psychological cost of the change, are often overlooked or misstated.

Indeed, the nature of switching costs is so fluid that managers manipulate their estimates, often unconsciously, to justify decisions they have made on other grounds. For example, manufacturers who are satisfied with the performance of their manufacturers' representatives become desirous of retaining them and estimate the one-time costs of switching to a company sales force to be very high.[44] In otherwise similar circumstances, however, if they have reasons to go direct (including dissatisfaction with performance), they will estimate the switching cost to be low.

The presence of switching costs in distribution is a major reason why late movers in a market or an industry often have an advantage over established firms. Late movers can enter directly with outsourced distribution in industries or markets that have lost their specificity (have become ordinary). Incumbents are left to struggle with the obstacles to switching and may find them so great that they must either carry excessive overhead (by staying vertically integrated) or exit the business due to inability to distribute effectively and efficiently.

Rarity versus Specificity: The Effects of Thin Markets

The key to asset specificity is that a resource, tangible or intangible, not only creates substantial value (making it an important asset) but that this asset loses value if redeployed to a different usage or user. These assets are customized, making them highly unusual. In contrast, some assets are rare (in short supply), but are not specific. For example, the conjunction of selling ability and technical knowledge that makes a good salesperson for semiconductors is uncommon, while demand for their services is enormous: These salespeople are rare. Hence, they are expensive. A semiconductor manufacturer may be tempted to reduce selling costs by employing salespeople directly rather than going through a manufacturers' representative. Unless the manufacturer's products are unlike other semiconductors or its methods are highly unusual, this strategy will not work. The manufacturer will discover that in lieu of paying high commissions to the manufacturers' representative, it is meeting a high payroll. Indeed, the manufacturer's costs will actually increase, as it is giving up the rep's economies.

Another case of rarity (not due to specificity) results from industry consolidation.[45] Consolidations among manufacturers due to mergers and acquisitions command headlines, but consolidation is also a substantial phenomenon downstream. For example, wholesale distribution was the second most active industry for mergers and acquisitions in the United States in 1997. Consolidation (the concentration of market share in the hands of a few players) prunes markets so much that they become thin. The effect is that suppliers cannot find resellers or agents, and downstream channel members cannot find suppliers. In fear of having little real choice, organizations scramble to form alliances with those players they estimate will be left standing as a level of an industry consolidates. Since alliances often serve to exclude other parties, this thins the market even further. To foreclose the prospect of dealing with a monopolist, many firms integrate backward or forward as consolidation occurs. However, this is no panacea if the integrating firm does not have a competitive competence level in performing these functions (see Sidebar 9.7 for an example).

Turning the Lens Around: Should the Channel Member Integrate Backward?

For purposes of exposition, the principles here have been presented from the standpoint of the manufacturer looking downstream. However, the principles are perfectly general and can be applied to the downstream channel member contemplating backward integration into production. Several of the issues already discussed have been

Sidebar 9.7

Fleming integrates forward from wholesaling

Fleming Companies was the largest wholesaler of food in the United States in the 1980s and 1990s, when consolidation was taking place downstream in the retail grocery industry. To improve profitability in the low-margin, high-volume retail business, some retail chains, such as Wal-Mart, developed their own wholesale distribution facilities, thereby making wholesalers such as Fleming redundant. As a reaction to its changing environment, Fleming decided to vertically integrate downstream by a series of acquisitions; that is, to get into the business of retail grocery stores. Management saw retail stores as attractive as a separate business and appealing as a captive market for Fleming's wholesale business.

The strategy did not work well, and sales per store declined. Thus, Fleming maintained its interest in retailing but decided to focus its efforts on developing Price Impact supermarkets. These supermarkets targeted highly price sensitive consumers, offering large discounts and everyday low prices in a warehouse-style format. Fleming believed it could use its unique position of being a wholesaler as well as a retailer to make money with this low-price formula. Fleming also believed it would be able to keep prices low compared to other stores thanks to the low-cost features of the new format, such as a narrow range of products, and its focus on popular brands. Other initiatives included low product storage and handling expenses by the implementation of flow-through distribution. The stores would have basic physical features such as cement floors, cinder block walls, and exposed ceilings to keep the costs low and would also have walk-in freezers, thereby combining the storage and display area. Fleming management believed the success of Price Impact stores would be based on an underserved trade area and would not require a significant market share. Thus advertising and marketing expenditures lower than the grocery norm would suffice.

By 2002, Fleming had run into serious financial difficulties. In addition to such factors as Kmart, a major customer, going bankrupt, Fleming's financial troubles were driven by the high capital expenditure associated with the retail business and the difficulty of holding market share in the hypercompetitive retail grocery industry. In 2003, Fleming exited the retail business, freeing up much-needed capital to return to wholesaling, its core competence.

presented in this fashion, for if the manufacturer is at risk of being held up by the channel member who owns a unique asset, the channel member is also at risk of being held up by the manufacturer. The manufacturer that is willing to abandon the channel member inflicts a loss on that party, who is left with an asset that is suddenly worthless. This prospect tempts the channel member to integrate backward, just as it tempts the manufacturer to integrate forward.

The symmetry of this situation is often overlooked. Many readers will find it more "natural" to consider the prospect of a manufacturer integrating forward than the prospect of, say, a distributor integrating backward. Backward integration, however, is not at all unusual. Indeed, it is often invited by manufacturers themselves, who welcome the infusion of capital and know-how, particularly market knowledge.

How, then, should a downstream channel member consider the issue? It should consider it in the same fashion as we have already discussed for forward integration. In general, vertical integration is a poor idea. In making an exception, the key issue is this: Does the ongoing transaction involve specificities in assets that are of great value? These may be in any form: know-how, relationships, the creation of brand equity, dedicated capacity, site, and physical facilities. Where these specificities are of value, a contracting hazard exists. The higher the value of these company-specific capabilities, the more it is worthwhile to provide protection, first in the form of relational contracting and eventually in the form of vertical integration (backward).

Sidebar 9.8 examines how downstream channel members can falter when they vertically integrate for the purpose of assuring themselves sources of supply or lock in outlets. Absent specificities, downstream firms risk foundering in a business they do not know or that conflicts with their core business.

VERTICAL INTEGRATION TO COPE WITH ENVIRONMENTAL UNCERTAINTY

An uncertain environment is one that is difficult to forecast. This may be because the environment is very dynamic (fast changing) or very complex (therefore, difficult to grasp). Such volatile environments pose special challenges.[46] Should the manufacturer integrate forward to meet them?

This is a controversial issue, and the evidence is mixed. One school of thought holds that a manufacturer needs to take control in order to cope with this environment. The manufacturer can use its control to learn more about the environment and to carry out a coherent strategy for dealing with it. Accordingly, it is argued that uncertainty demands integration. The opposing school of thought likens managing under uncertainty to betting on the winner of a race among many comparable horses: One bet is as good as another, and most bets will lose anyway. From this viewpoint, the firm is urged not to bet until the race is far enough along that it can improve the odds by guessing who is winning (or at least avoiding those who are losing). Accordingly, the manufacturer is advised not to commit to any distribution system, including its own system, unless and until the uncertainty is reduced to a level that makes it easier to ascertain the best way to distribute in the environment. This means outsourcing. The argument is that uncertainty demands distributing through third parties, changing third parties as the situation demands (committing to no one).

Proponents of vertical integration retort that it is defeatist to wait until the race is well along to place a bet: By integrating, the firm can alter the course of the race. Critics respond that it is arrogant of the manufacturer to imagine that it possesses such wisdom. Better to switch from one third party to another and finally settle on the best option (the best third party, or one's own means of going to market) when the best option actually can be ascertained.

The proponents retort that the best option may be closed by the time the manufacturer is ready to pursue it. A key feature of this argument concerns how easy it will be to change the marketing channel as the environment changes. Proponents of vertical integration often underestimate the difficulty of making real organizational change happen once in-house distribution is in place.

Sidebar 9.8

A retailer loses focus by integrating backward

Intermarché is a large French grocery retailer organized as a membership of independent grocery store owners. Although the members ("adherents" under French law) are technically independent businesses, Intermarché is tightly managed. The adherents are obliged to follow the initiatives of headquarters and face restrictive contracts that make it difficult to exit the Intermarché network. The chain is fraught with internal frictions. A prime reason is that many of its adherents feel that management is sacrificing their interests as retailers to a higher priority—production.

Intermarché was among the first French grocers to integrate backward into food production and has done so aggressively. One third of the average store's sales are of house brands, a fraction that has grown steadily. Some observers (and some adherents) question whether consumers abandon Intermarché stores because they cannot find their preferred brands. Some adherents also feel that management has diverted resources into production that should be going into matters more immediately relevant to a store owner, such as marketing, merchandising, and store renovation. For example, Intermarché has the largest fishing fleet in Europe and proudly trumpets that distinction to its members. This is precisely what many adherents resent. One adherent comments that the decision to backward integrate into fishing

> gave us a real independence vis-à-vis the multinationals. It also permits us to have our own brands that are comparable to national brands. It's a fabulous tool; we don't want to break it, but rather to put it at the service of stores. We want to move from a situation where the points of sale are outlets for the factories to a situation where they are really at our service. Who cares if we are the #1 European fish producer? What we want to be is the #1 European fish market.

As of this writing, Intermarché continues to suffer steady declines in share and profits. Vertical integration backward continues to consume management attention at a time when the core business—retailing—clamors for a return to the basics.[47]

Both sides of the debate have valid arguments. How to incorporate them into one approach? A useful frame to resolve this issue is to complicate it slightly (see Figure 9.3). One begins by asking whether the distribution involves (or will involve) substantial company-specific capabilities. If not, the firm can easily change third parties. This flexibility is of great value in volatile environments. Absent significant specificity, uncertainty favors outsourcing.

But if specificities are substantial, flexibility is already lost. The firm will become locked into its third parties, and there can be no changing one's bet. Then the manufacturer faces the worst of all worlds: small-numbers bargaining in an environment that requires constant adaptation. The result will be endless bargaining, high levels of opportunism, and high transaction costs. In the presence of significant specificity, uncertainty favors vertical integration forward.

There is, of course, a third argument: In the presence of significant specificities, do not go into the business at all. To justify the overhead of vertically integrating, the business must be very promising, and yet by nature the uncertainty makes it

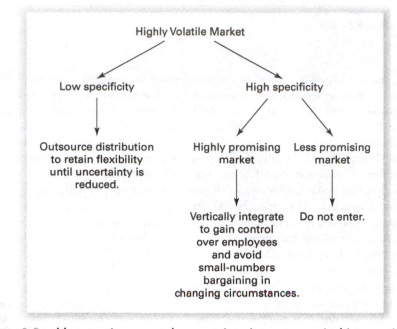

Figure 9.3   How environmental uncertainty impacts vertical integration

difficult to tell how promising the business really is. This conundrum can be solved by avoiding the business altogether. Perhaps the most common approach to distributing in uncertain environments when specificities are high is not to enter the market at all. Because those activities that firms decide not to pursue are difficult to observe, it is not known how often such business activities are never undertaken. Yet, non-market-entry, while difficult to notice, is always present—and is frequently attributed to other factors.

For example, multinational business activity occurs at very low levels in sub-Saharan Africa, even though there are rich potential markets in a region of more than 700 million people. This often is attributed to high political risk and lack of economic development; however, multinationals operate in other risky, underdeveloped markets, many of which were largely ignored only a decade earlier. Why continue to overlook Africa? One explanation is that (a) many African markets are little known and potentially highly volatile and (b) the lack of distribution infrastructure implies that much of what the manufacturer does to distribute will be idiosyncratic in that market. The combination of uncertainty and specificity, as opposed to uncertainty alone, may help explain low investment in Africa (of course, many other factors contribute to the phenomenon as well). In contrast, some politically risky Asian countries have better distribution infrastructures, permitting multinationals to find qualified third parties already operating in the market. With specificity removed, uncertainty can be handled by outsourcing, encouraging more market entry.

It is noteworthy that market entry by some firms encourages more entry and that it does so by reducing specificity. Once a number of multinational corporations (MNCs) have entered a market, they create a pool of local personnel who know the procedures of MNCs. This makes it easier to find third parties that qualified to work in a manner that is nonstandard in the market but standard in MNCs. India, for example, has seen growth in the number of qualified joint-venture partners and distributors as a cumulative result of decades of multinational investment. This process is now underway in China.[48]

VERTICAL INTEGRATION TO REDUCE PERFORMANCE AMBIGUITY

Thus far we have covered scenarios (specificity, rarity, and uncertainty) in which competition in the market for distribution services fails to yield efficient outcomes. These scenarios turn on one idea: Few bidders are available to replace a firm that is performing poorly. This, of course, presumes that the manufacturer can tell that outsourcing is not working.

Another scenario favoring vertical integration is not a failure of the market to provide bidders. It is a failure of information. In a normal market, the contracting firm (the principal or, in our exposition, the manufacturer) offers to pay an organization (in the language of contracting, an agent) for distribution services to be provided. If the services are not performed satisfactorily, the principal either negotiates for better outcomes with the agent or finds another agent. In normal markets, many other agents are qualified, and their bidding for the business improves the return on investment of the principal's outcomes. This process (bid, monitor the results, reconsider the arrangement, rebid) works well—assuming the principal can tell what it is getting.

Herein lies a fundamental problem with market contracting. When there is performance ambiguity, the manufacturer cannot discern what level of performance it is getting. Therefore, the process by which market contracting improves outcomes cannot function.[49]

The Baseline Problem

To illustrate the problem of performance ambiguity, let us take the selling function, which combines the promotion and negotiation flows.[50] This can be outsourced to a manufacturers' representative. The manufacturer knows the rep's performance in terms of sales. If sales levels are a good indicator of performance, the manufacturer has little performance ambiguity. Most of the time this is the case, for most sales forces are charged primarily with selling, and most of the time the manufacturer has some idea what level of sales to reasonably expect.

If the product is radically new, say, a discontinuous innovation (unlike anything that currently exists), current sales may not be a good indicator of performance. This is because radically new products usually diffuse slowly. In addition, no one knows any reasonable sales level for such a product. The result is that if the manufacturer's representative goes for long periods with low or no sales, the manufacturer does not know whether or not it should be dissatisfied and search for a new rep. Fundamentally, it is impossible to tell how well the rep is doing. There are no baselines and many excuses for failure. Hence, performance ambiguity is high.

In general, one class of circumstances creating performance ambiguity occurs when the sorts of measures that would indicate performance are unknown, as is the case for the discontinuous innovation. In this case, the principal may vertically integrate forward not to circumvent small-numbers bargaining but to gain information and control. Monitoring what salespeople are doing in detail, the principal can differentiate excuses from genuine reasons for low sales. From its salespeople, the principal also can acquire market research that helps establish the baseline of performance. Further, and this is perhaps the most powerful advantage, the principal can control the salespeople's behavior. Failing good indicators of achievement, the principal can fall back on the ability to direct salespeople to do what it considers best to develop the market. Instead of rewarding for outputs (achievements), the principal can reward for inputs (activities). In the absence of good information about what outputs are and what they should be, inputs are the next best substitute.

In general, market contracting yields indicators of current results. Where current results are not good indicators of performance, there is performance ambiguity. The principal may raise long-term return on investment by vertically integrating forward to gain information and to gain the ability to direct behavior.

Results Indicators That Are Inaccurate, Late, or Nonexistent

When are current results poor indicators of performance? There are two classes of circumstances. We have already described the situation where performance indicators exist but are difficult to evaluate because there are no baselines. Another circumstance is when measures of performance output do exist but are of poor quality. For example, pharmaceutical firms are unable to tell how much their salespeople are selling in many markets. Salespeople (detailers) call on specifiers (such as doctors) and describe (detail) the drugs, the firm hopes in a persuasive fashion. Specifiers in turn prescribe the drugs, which leads the patient to ask the pharmacist for the drug, which leads the pharmacist to purchase the drug, often from a wholesaler.

Pharmaceutical firms do have measures of performance (sales): They know how much they sell and ship to wholesalers and pharmacy chains. To bring this information down to the selling level involves (1) approximating the movement of stock over time from wholesalers and chains to the individual pharmacy, and (2) at the pharmacy level, matching the drug to the specifier. These approximations can be done, but they are so arbitrary that it is difficult to consider them accurate, timely indicators of the relationship between detailing and sales. Thus, the path from sales activity to orders is so convoluted that drug companies cannot tell if their salespeople are effective. How, then, to compensate a contract sales force?

In general, measures are poor when they are untimely or inaccurate. Late or inaccurate information, or no information, creates performance ambiguity. This performance ambiguity induces pharmaceutical firms to employ a sales force and to use the power of the employer to monitor and direct activity (calling on defined specifiers at a certain frequency, detailing particular drugs on a call, reporting back to the firm the reaction of the specifier). In this way, the firm satisfies itself that salespeople are doing the right thing (detailing correctly and providing market research). Of course, these activities are thought to create performance (sales). If this belief is incorrect, the pharmaceutical firm will be unknowingly wasting resources. This is the risk and responsibility cost of vertically integrating. (Note: In some markets, particularly the United States, specialty research firms have arisen that purchase detailed prescription information from pharmacists, consolidate it into reports at the level of the specifier [the doctor], and sell the information to pharmaceutical firms. This is reducing performance ambiguity in this sector in many markets.)

The fundamental issue is that the outputs, or achievements, of a third party do not serve as good indicators of performance, either because there is no real baseline against which to compare results or because the obtainable data are of poor quality. The solution, in either case, is to vertically integrate in order to direct employees to perform what are believed to be appropriate behaviors, in lieu of tallying their results and compensating them for results obtained.

If the solution to performance ambiguity is to monitor and direct activities rather than to tally achieved results, how does vertical integration really solve the problem? Would it not be adequate to write a contract with another organization specifying the desired activities and then let that organization do the monitoring and directing? After all, the essence of outsourcing is delegating to another organization. Why not delegate the execution of activities, as opposed to the achievement of results?

Technically, this is, indeed, possible. The problem is that it is impossible to verify that the activities are actually being performed. It is not difficult to claim that activities are being carried out when they are not. To verify the claim, it is necessary to monitor (or audit) activity, and this violates the independent status of the third party.

Why not bypass auditing, instead placing one's trust in the third party's promise that it will execute the desired activities? This, too, is possible, and it is sometimes done. However, it is very difficult to know when a party can be trusted. Many a firm has come to regret having placed its trust in a third party. While trustworthy parties exist, it is exceedingly difficult to know who they are. It is also difficult, though not impossible, to create incentive structures such that the agent has no desire to betray the principal's trust—and the principal has no desire to take advantage of the agent's promise, once given. The solution of mutual trust is covered in Chapter 8.

SUMMARY OF THE DECISION FRAMEWORK

The logic of the economic argument for greater degrees of vertical integration is summarized in Figure 9.4. This shows the nature and direction of the effects of market features on each element of return on investment (revenues, direct costs, and overhead).

Let us map from return on investment to the vertical integration decision in the typical case, in which markets do not suffer from thin supply. One begins with the presumption of the superiority of outsourcing. But even when markets are well populated, vertical integration improves return on investment in two scenarios. The critic of the initial outsourcing decision has made a good case for vertical integration (given that substantial business is at stake and the firm has the resources), if either of these two circumstances prevails:

1. Company-specific capabilities are likely to become substantial. These can be intangible (know-how, relationships, downstream activities creating brand equity) or tangible (dedicated capacity, site specificity, physical customization). The effect of idiosyncratic assets is magnified by environmental uncertainty.

2. Performance ambiguity, due to no measures of results or poor measures of results, forces the firm to monitor and direct activity rather than tally up and pay for performance.

Where markets work poorly but vertical integration is too drastic a solution, relational contracting is an efficient solution. The logic of vertical integration is summarized graphically in Figure 9.5.

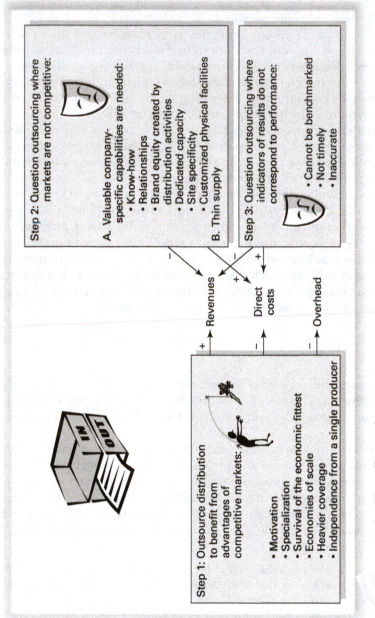

Step 1: Outsource distribution to benefit from advantages of competitive markets:

- Motivation
- Specialization
- Survival of the economic fittest
- Economies of scale
- Heavier coverage
- Independence from a single producer

Step 2: Question outsourcing where markets are not competitive:

A. Valuable company-specific capabilities are needed:
- Know-how
- Relationships
- Brand equity created by distribution activities
- Dedicated capacity
- Site specificity
- Customized physical facilities

B. Thin supply

Step 3: Question outsourcing where indicators of results do not correspond to performance:

- Cannot be benchmarked
- Not timely
- Inaccurate

Revenues

Direct costs

Overhead

Figure 9.4 The effects of outsourcing

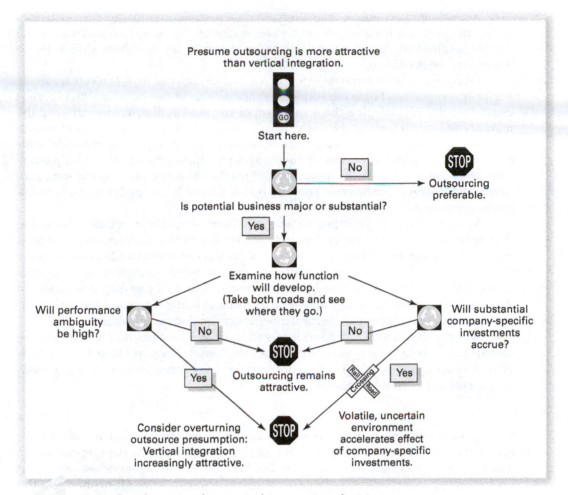

Figure 9.5   Road map to the vertical integration decision

VERTICAL INTEGRATION AS AN OBSERVATORY ON THE MARKET OR AS AN OPTION: ECONOMIC RATIONALITY OR RATIONALIZATION?

Thus far, the argument has been strictly normative: What should the firm do to maximize long-term return on investment? While the firm can never calculate the numbers (at least not to an accountant's satisfaction), the direction of the arguments is clear, given the premise that, when in doubt, outsourcing is best. But do managers really follow these guidelines? In competitive industries, the evidence indicates that they do, eventually, and roughly; however, firms do deviate from these return-on-investment-maximizing normative prescriptions. Let us consider three major reasons to integrate vertically when our long-term efficiency-maximizing framework indicates outsourcing is better.

According to economic theory, return on investment is a paramount criterion. Firms that overlook it should be swiftly eliminated by the relentless workings of the market mechanism. Assuming the normative theory is correct, there should be no divergence between theory and practice.[51]

Of course, there is some divergence, for a variety of reasons.[52] Markets are never perfectly competitive. Firms can subsidize shortcomings in one domain with successes in another domain, keeping the erring firm in the market. Barriers to exit keep the market from swiftly forcing the departure of inefficient firms. Noneconomic considerations also enter in, such as a government, employee group, or investor desirous of keeping a firm in business or of encouraging business practices for multiple reasons. Decision makers may be more focused on the short run than on the long run. Above all, managers are human: They are not machines at the service of a return-on-investment-maximizing investor.

Many managers, if given their choice, would choose vertical integration, reasoning that more control is always better than less. This leads to optimism: Managers frequently underestimate the direct costs and overhead of vertical integration while overstating the likely increase in revenues. This is particularly the case when managers have little experience with the functions they propose to integrate. Taken all together, it is inevitable that the long-run return on investment of performing a single function is not the only factor at work when firms make vertical integration decisions in distribution.

When a firm makes a vertical integration choice that has no clear return-on-investment rationale, two reasons are frequently offered. These are long-run effectiveness rationales. Vertical integration is presented as an observatory from which to study the market or as a strategic option.

The Channel as an Observatory

Having operations in another part of the value chain may be justified as a window on the market and, therefore, a way to learn. An example is Luxottica, the eyeglass maker. The firm is majority owned by Leonardo Del Vecchio, whose rags-to-riches story turns on becoming a worker in an eyeglass factory as a way to leave an orphanage. Del Vecchio became a highly skilled artisan, founding Luxottica in 1961. Today, his self-description anchors him firmly in production: "I am a technician, a producer. It is thanks to our products, our quality, and our productivity that we have made our way."[53] Luxottica's Italian factory is noted for extreme productivity, which enables the firm to compete with lower-cost Asian production.

LensCrafters offers an enormous selection of frames, offers eye examinations, and manufactures prescription glasses on the premises in one hour. It has a substantial presence in the U.S. market, which is the largest and most representative in the world. Del Vecchio justifies his purchase of LensCrafters by saying, "It's an ideal observatory to know what the market wants."[54] He has other "observatories" as well in a web of exclusive wholesalers serving the European channel of individual opticians. Thus, Del Vecchio uses both intermediate and extreme degrees of vertical integration as a way to understand end-user demand for eyeglasses.

Luxottica uses this market knowledge in its dealings with designers. Even powerful names, such as Sergio Tacchini, are obliged to submit their designs for consideration, modification, and approval by Luxottica's house technicians. Designers tolerate this control because Luxottica is a proven performer and the world's largest eyeglass producer. The producer also uses its market knowledge to forecast eyewear fashions 18 months in advance of making 500 new models a year. In short, relational governance and vertical integration give Luxottica expertise power (Chapter 6) upstream.

In short, integration forward or backward is often justified as a way to learn, a sort of classroom/laboratory/observation post. The decision to integrate is not made on the basis of the stand-alone return-on-investment gains of integrating the flow. It is made on grounds that integration increases effectiveness (profits) for the operation as a whole.

Is this a sensible economic rationale, or is it a rationalization? It is difficult to know. Certainly, learning is a lofty objective, easy to invoke to explain any act of vertical integration no matter how ill advised it might be on operating grounds. In a world of omniscient accountants, the inefficiencies that accrue would be calculated and charged to budgets for R&D or market research. This would throw a spotlight on this resource allocation decision and spark debate as to its merits.

This is not to say that learning is not a worthwhile investment. It is no accident that the most large-scale integrations in our examples (Jean Delatour and Luxottica) occur in fashion-sensitive industries where massive and frequent change is certain but its direction is unknown. In many cases, however, it is difficult to know whether learning is an economically justifiable reason to vertically integrate.

Vertical integration as an option is a related argument. In finance, purchasing an option means paying for the right to write a contract now, to be exercised (or not exercised, at the buyer's option) at a specified future date. If not exercised, the option expires. Options are justified as a form of insurance: You pay a relatively small amount now in case of catastrophe later. In options theory, the catastrophe is often of the opportunity cost variety (I could have made a profit if I could buy now at yesterday's price).

The idea has been generalized to marketing strategy.[55] A strategic option is a relatively limited investment now, made to hold open the door to making a greater investment late should developments prove it to be a good idea. Many joint ventures are justified on this basis. Like a financial option, a strategic option can be exercised (converted to a substantial investment) or allowed to expire (dismantled or downsized). The key is not to hold an option indefinitely (this is mere indecisiveness rather than purposeful hedging against risk). An options strategist decides whether to exercise or dispose of an opportunity as soon as it becomes clear which way to go.

Superficially, this looks like the learning rationale. The difference is that an investment in learning is constant: Jean Delatour and Luxottica know fashions change constantly, so they keep a permanent classroom on a large scale. An investment in an option is meant to be temporary. It is a wedge, designed to preserve an opportunity until management can determine whether to pursue it.

This means that using vertical integration as an option can be sensible only when shifts occur unpredictably. This is the case in high-velocity environments, such as sectors of the information technology industry.[56] This is one reason why firms such as Sun Microsystems, IBM, and Hewlett-Packard regularly keep a large staff on payroll to handle some channel flows in some sectors.

These options are something like paying for insurance coverage: They drain resources steadily but can pay off handsomely when you most need the protection. Like learning, option thinking is a rationale that can be invoked to justify any vertical integration decision in channels. And like learning, it is a rationale that sometimes makes sense but often masks a rationalization.

SUMMARY

Who should do the work of distribution, in whole or in part? Should the same party do manufacturing and distribution? Should two parties split the work? If so, how? Splitting the work means sharing the costs (resources, risk, responsibility) and the benefits (or lack of them). Vertical integration in distribution is not an all-or-nothing decision but can pertain to the decision of whether to make or buy any individual channel flow or set of flows. Thus, a manufacturer can totally vertically integrate just a subset of channel functions but still use independent intermediaries to perform other functions. It is common that both vertical integration and decentralization (outsourcing to a third party) characterize the channel system.

The fundamental idea behind this analysis is that any player should respect the fact that the work of any other player requires competencies. Therefore, no party should merely assume that it can take over another party's functions and perform them better and/or more cheaply. In short, arrogance has no place in a vertical integration decision, which should be undertaken with respect for the competence of another type of organization.

Being committed to a system (such as outsourcing) is not the same thing as being committed to a given member of the system. Vertical integration is too often used as a way to go around unsatisfactory results from or relationships with another organization. If this is the rationale, the firm should first ask whether the current relationship can be made to work better (using the techniques in this book, for example), or whether another third party would be more effective. Vertical integration is a drastic step that invariably raises overhead and that often fails to reduce direct costs or increase revenue. The step should not be undertaken lightly.

Many readers will be surprised at the assertion that markets for distribution services are frequently efficient. This does not mean that a firm cannot do better by vertically integrating, but it does mean that to get better results the firm must be prepared to make a very substantial commitment and often to operate in a manner that is unusual for its industry or market. For vertical integration to improve on outsourcing, the firm must take large risks and make substantial commitments.

It is never possible to estimate transaction costs, production costs, and return on investment precisely under any scenario, vertically integrated or otherwise; however, the framework presented here allows the decision maker to forecast the direction in which these costs will go and to arrive at a rough approximation of which system works best in the longer term.

This chapter presents the decision path in steps, beginning with the assumption that outsourcing distribution is superior because it profits from six advantages of the outsider: motivation, specialization, survival of the fittest, economies of scale, coverage, and independence. Step 2 involves questioning this assumption under these circumstances: company-specific capabilities (especially when combined with environmental uncertainty), thin markets (rare, rather than idiosyncratic), and performance ambiguity.

Some readers find themselves uncomfortable with opportunism, one of the fundamental ideas underlying this analysis. They find self-interest seeking in a deceitful or dishonest manner to be negative, discouraging, perhaps unrepresentative of human nature (or perhaps representative of the worst of human nature). However, it is important not to personalize the discussion. Opportunistic behavior is a characteristic of organizations interacting with each other in conducting business. This is not to say that it is the nature of two people interacting with each other in their private lives. Further, to focus on opportunism does not mean that all organizations are opportunistic at all times. It is merely to say that some organizations are opportunistic in some circumstances, and it is difficult to forecast in advance which will be opportunistic. The make-or-buy decision rests on pragmatically anticipating and forestalling opportunism.

An important reason to undertake vertical integration is to gain market research or to create an option to be evaluated in the future. Thus, in some circumstances it is justified to integrate distribution, not to do a better job of distributing but do a better job of learning or to hold open a door to a future investment. Integration forward or backward is often a means of improving overall performance, not improving the performance per se.

The vertical integration decision is fundamental, for it drives the firm's capabilities for the long term and is difficult to reverse. The chapters that follow cover other methods of improving the performance of marketing channel flows. "Owning it all" is a solution of last resort to the problems of distributing effectively and efficiently.

Take-Aways

- The vertical integration decision, make or buy, do it yourself or outsource, should be made for each function or set of functions involved in distributing a product or service. The choice is not really binary. Make versus buy is a continuum that shows how the costs, benefits, and responsibilities of doing the work are split between two organizations.

- Creating a relationship is a way to compromise between make and buy. The closer that relationship, the more it approximates vertical integration. The more distant the relationship, the more it approximates the epitome of outsourcing, the arm's-length market contract.

- Integrating forward or backward is harder than it looks. The firm should not simply assume it can outperform a specialist by taking control of its functions.

- The key question to ask is: Will integrating a function improve my long-run economic return on investment? That is, will I improve my revenues or reduce my costs, and will these gains justify the resources I will need to commit?

- The analysis should stop here, and the firm should outsource, if:

  - Little money is at stake (for example, this is a minor function)

  - The firm cannot afford the resources needed to create an internal operation

  - The firm has better uses for these resources

- Deciding whether to outsource requires a two-step process. In step 1, the decision maker asks whether the market for distribution services is competitive. If so, outsourcing is the right starting point to benefit from the six fundamental advantages of an outside specialist:

- Superior motivation
- Specialization
- Survival of the economic fittest
- Economies of scale
- Heavier market coverage
- Independence from any single supplier
- In step 2, the decision maker asks whether conditions exist that mean the firm will not benefit from these six advantages. In that case, vertical integration is called for, or a close relationship (as a substitute for full ownership). These conditions include company-specific capabilities (especially when the environment is volatile), performance ambiguity, and thin markets.
- The potential for substantial company-specific capabilities to arise puts the firm into small-numbers bargaining with a third party, which traps the firm. Unable to switch to a better supplier, the firm risks being the victim of opportunism (deceitful pursuit of self-interest).
- Six company-specific capabilities critical in distribution are:
  - Intangible capabilities
    - Idiosyncratic (company-specific) knowledge
    - Relationships among personnel
    - Brand equity that rests on the downstream channel member's actions
  - Tangible capabilities
    - Customized physical facilities
    - Dedicated capacity
    - Site specificity
- The greater the potential for company-specific capabilities to grow and become valuable, the more likely vertical integration will be more efficient than outsourcing.
  - This is particularly the case in volatile, uncertain environments.
  - This combination (uncertainty and specific capabilities) is so difficult to manage that firms should demand a very high return to enter such a business.
- Over time, specific assets tend to become general purpose. At this point, vertical integration is no longer efficient. Incumbents may be trapped by high switching costs, unable to change to outsourcing. This creates an opportunity for late entrants to come in using outsourced distribution and gain a late-mover advantage.
- The necessary capabilities may be rare (low supply relative to demand) but not specific (customized). Securing these capabilities will always be costly, even if the firm vertically integrates. As the market for these capabilities becomes very thin, the firm may vertically integrate simply to assure a source of supply but should still expect the function to be expensive to perform.
- Performance ambiguity occurs when it is very difficult to ascertain by observing results alone whether a third party is doing a job well. It arises under two circumstances.
  - The market is so unfamiliar that the firm has no baseline to judge whether results are good or bad. This is particularly common for radical innovations.
  - It is difficult or impossible to gather relevant, timely, accurate results indicators.

- The higher the performance ambiguity, the more likely vertical integration is more efficient than outsourcing.
- These arguments apply to a producer considering integrating forward, as well as to a downstream channel member considering integrating backward.
- Vertical integration forward may be a strategic decision undertaken to enhance effectiveness in a somewhat speculative manner. Two major rationales are:
  - The function serves as a market testing and feedback mechanism (an observatory, or classroom). If so, the channel is a cost center, and the firm should forgive its distribution division for operating inefficiently relative to outsourced competition.
  - The function is an option. The firm may exercise this option later as a way to get into distribution faster and better should it turn out to be a good idea. If so, the return-on-investment losses should be viewed as akin to an insurance premium.

DISCUSSION QUESTIONS

1. Assume you are the manufacturer of a broad line of moderately priced furniture. When would you seriously consider owning your own retail outlets? What factors would you take into account in making your decision?
2. Is it likely that vertical disintegration is typical of growing industries while vertical integration is typical of declining industries? Explain your answer.
3. Debate the pros and cons of forward vertical integration of wholesaling functions by manufacturers and by retailers.
4. According to Bucklin, the issue of channel performance focuses on the conflict between two major dimensions of channel performance. On the one hand, consumers and users are concerned primarily with lowering the costs of the goods and services sold and, therefore, with reducing the costs of distribution. On the other hand, buyers want to benefit from and receive some marketing services in conjunction with the good or service they purchase. However, provision of these services increases the cost of distribution. Compare and contrast vertical integration and outsourcing relative to the performance dimensions mentioned by Bucklin. Which would tend to be superior overall?
5. A theme that appears in advertisements for stores owned by manufacturers is, "Buy factory direct at our store. You'll save money. We can offer you low prices because we cut out the middleman." Evaluate this argument. Is it valid? Would you expect a factory store to offer lower prices? Why or why not? Are there other differences you would expect to find between a manufacturer-owned store and an independent retailer?
6. The Fleming failure profiled in this chapter surprised many industry observers. In particular, many analysts like the logic that a combined wholesaler and retailer ought to be able to make more money on an ultra-low-price format than the usual retailer-wholesaler supply arrangement. Was the Fleming case unusual? Is the logic sound?
7. A number of companies seem to cycle in and out of vertical integration. For example, Apple Computers moves in and out of having its own store network versus relying on third parties. What might be behind cyclical vertical integration?

ENDNOTES

1. *Material Handling Engineering* (1997), "A First-Party Perspective," *Material Handling Engineering* 52, no. 6 (June), pp. 51–52.

2. Villard, Nathalie (1999), "Cet Italien Fabrique Toutes les Lunettes du Monde," *Capital* 10, no. 6 (June), pp. 63–64.

3. Lyons, Daniel (1997), "Turning to the Channel to Stay Afloat," *Computer Reseller News*, December 15, p. 124.

4. Sellerin, Raphael (1999) "Jean Delatour: le Category Killer," *LSA* 10, no. 35 (September 9), pp. 62–63.

5. Dunne, David and Chakravarthi Narasimhan (1999), "The New Appeal of Private Labels," *Harvard Business Review* 53, no. 3 (May–June), pp. 41–52.

6. Economist (1998), "When Eight Arms Are Better Than One," *Economist* 348, no. 8085 (September 12), pp. 67–68.

7. Corey, E. Raymond, Frank V. Cespedes, and V. Kasturi Rangan (1989), *Going to Market: Distribution Systems for Industrial Products* (Boston: Harvard Business School Press).

8. Anderson, Erin and Barton A. Weitz (1986), "Make or Buy Decisions: Vertical Integration and Marketing Productivity," *Sloan Management Review* 27, no. 3 (Spring), pp. 3–20.

9. Stern, Louis W. and Torger Reve (1980), "Distribution Channels as Political Economies: A Framework for Comparative Analysis," *Journal of Marketing* 44, no. 3 (Summer), pp. 52–64.

10. Hennart, Jean-Francois (1993), "Explaining the Swollen Middle: Why Most Transactions Are a Mix of 'Market' and 'Hierarchy,'" *Organization Science* 4, no. 4 (November), pp. 529–547.

11. Heide, Jan B. (1994), "Interorganizational Governance in Marketing Channels," *Journal of Marketing* 58, no. 1 (January), pp. 71–85.

12. Williamson, Oliver E. (1991), "Comparative Economic Organization: The Analysis of Discrete Structural Alternatives," *Administrative Science Quarterly* 36, no. 2 (June), pp. 269–296.

13. Dwyer, F. Robert and Sejo Oh (1988), "A Transaction Cost Perspective on Vertical Contractual Structure and Interchannel Competitive Strategies," *Journal of Marketing* 52, no. 2 (April), pp. 21–34.

14. Szymanski, David M., Sundar G. Bharadwaj, and P. Rajan Varadarajan (1993), "Standardization versus Adaptation of International Marketing Strategy: An Empirical Investigation," *Journal of Marketing* 57, no. 4 (October), pp. 1–17.

15. Williamson, Oliver E. (1996), *The Mechanisms of Governance* (New York: Oxford University Press).

16. Bergen, Mark, Shantanu Dutta, and Orville C. Walker Jr. (1992), "Agency Relationships in Marketing: A Review of the Implications and Applications of Agency and Related Theories," *Journal of Marketing* 56, no. 3 (July), pp. 1–24.

17. Wise, Richard and Peter Baumgartner (1999), "Go Downstream: The New Profit Imperative in Manufacturing," *Harvard Business Review* 77, no. 5 (September–October), pp. 133–160.

18. Tomlinson, Richard (2003), "Insurance for Dummies," *Fortune*, May 26, pp. 31–36.

19. Michel, Caroline (2004), "Manoukian S'Emmêle Dans Sa Maille," *Capital* 12, no. 7 (July), pp. 36–38.

20. Rindfleisch, Aric and Jan B. Heide (1997), "Transaction Cost Analysis: Present, Past, and Future," *Journal of Marketing* 61, no. 4 (October), pp. 30–54.

21. Bolton, Jamie M., and Yan Wei (2003), "The Supply Chain: Distribution and Logistics in Today's China," *The China Business Review* 10, no. 5 (September–October), pp. 8–17.

22. Anderson, Erin and Richard L. Oliver (1987), "Perspectives on Behavior-Based versus Outcome-Based Sales Force Control Systems," *Journal of Marketing* 51, no. 4 (October), pp. 76–88.

23. The EABL story was developed in East Africa by Peter Kimurwa based on reports from Kenya-based market research firms, brokerage analysts, press reports, and EABL company reports.

24. Anderson, Erin and Bob Trinkle (2005), *Outsourcing the Sales Function: The Real Costs*

of Field Sales (Cincinnati, OH: Thomson Texere Publishing).

25. Terpstra, Vern and Bernard L. Simonin (1993), "Strategic Alliances in the Triad: An Exploratory Study," *Journal of International Marketing* 1, no. 1, pp. 4–26.

26. *Economist* (2003), "The World This Week," *Economist*, August 23, p. 9.

27. Johnson, Jo (2001), "A Veteran Dealmaker Chews Over His Core," *Financial Times*, November 21, p. 13.

28. Economist (2004), "Bon Voyage," *Economist*, October 2, pp. 62–63.

29. John, George (1984), "An Empirical Investigation of Some Antecedents of Opportunism in a Marketing Channel," *Journal of Marketing Research* 21, no. 3 (August), pp. 278–289.

30. Anderson, Erin (1988), "Determinants of Opportunistic Behavior: An Empirical Comparison of Integrated and Independent Channels," *Journal of Economic Behavior and Organization* 9, no. 3 (April), pp. 247–264.

31. Rosencher, Anne (2004), "Le Client Mystère, Ou l'Art d'Espionner Ses Points de Vente," *Capital* 12, no. 11 (November), pp. 124–126.

32. Klein, Benjamin (1996), "Why Hold-Ups Occur: The Self-Enforcing Range of Contractual Relationships," *Economic Inquiry* 34, no. 3 (July), pp. 444–463.

33. Osegowitsch, Thomas and Anoop Madhok (2003), "Vertical Integration Is Dead, Or Is It?" *Business Horizons* 46, no. 2 (March–April), pp. 25–34.

34. Masten, Scott E., James W. Meehan Jr., and Edward A. Snyder (1991), "The Costs of Organization," *The Journal of Law, Economics, and Organization* 7, no. 1 (Spring), pp. 1–25.

35. Coughlan, Anne T. (1985), "Competition and Cooperation in Marketing Channel Choice: Theory and Application," *Marketing Science* 4, no. 2 (Spring), pp. 110–129; and McGuire, Timothy W. and Richard Staelin (1983), "An Industry Equilibrium Analysis of Downstream Vertical Integration," *Marketing Science* 2, no. 2 (Spring), pp. 161–191.

36. Frazier, Gary L., Robert E. Spekman, and Charles R. O'Neal (1988), "Just-In-Time Exchange Relationships in Industrial Markets," *Journal of Marketing* 52, no. 4 (October), pp. 52–67.

37. Klein, Benjamin and Kevin M. Murphy (1988), "Vertical Restraints as Contract Enforcement Mechanisms," *Journal of Law and Economics* 31, no. 2 (October), pp. 265–297.

38. Dunne and Narasimhan (1999), previously cited.

39. Vogelstein, Fred (2003), "Mighty Amazon," *Fortune*, May 26, pp. 20–28.

40. Muris, Timothy J., David T. Scheffman, and Pablo T. Spiller (1992), "Strategy and Transaction Costs: The Organization of Distribution in the Carbonated Soft Drink Industry," *Journal of Economics and Management Strategy* 1, no. 1 (Spring), pp. 83–128.

41. Holleran, Joan (1999), "Strength Through Sense: 1999 Company of the Year, Coca-Cola Enterprises, Inc.," *Beverage Industry* 90, no. 1 (January), pp. 16–20; Machan, Dyan (1998), "There's Something About Henry," *Forbes* 162, no. 7 (October 5), pp. 82–84; and Rublin, Lauren R. (1999), "Offerings in the Offing: Pepsi Play," *Barron's* 79, no. 9 (March 1), pp. 34–35.

42. Pirrong, Stephen Craig (1993), "Contracting Practices in Bulk Shipping Markets: A Transactions Cost Explanation," *Journal of Law, Economics, and Organization* 36, no. 2 (October), pp. 937–976.

43. This example is from Chandler, Alfred D. (1977), *The Visible Hand: The Managerial Revolution in American Business* (Cambridge, MA: Belknap Press).

44. Weiss, Allen and Erin Anderson (1992), "Converting from Independent to Employee Sales Forces: The Role of Perceived Switching Costs," *Journal of Marketing Research* 29, no. 1 (February), pp. 101–115.

45. This discussion is based on Fein, Adam J. and Sandy D. Jap (1999), "Manage Consolidation in the Distribution Channel," *Sloan Management Review* 41, no. 1 (Fall), pp. 61–72.

46. Dwyer, F. Robert and M. Ann Walsh (1985), "Environmental Relationships of the Internal Political Economy of Marketing Channels," *Journal of Marketing Research* 22, no. 4 (November), 397–414.

47. Parigi, Jerôme and Marc Reidboym (2002), "Vent de Contestation Chez Intermarché," *LSA* 19, no. 14 (April), pp. 26–29.

48. Bolton and Wei (2003), previously cited.

49. Bergen, Mark, Shantanu Dutta, and Orville C. Walker Jr. (1992), "Agency Relationships in Marketing: A Review of the Implications and Applications of Agency and Related Theories," *Journal of Marketing* 56, no. 3 (July), pp. 1–24.

50. Anderson, Erin (1985), "The Salesperson as Outside Agent or Employee: A Transaction-Cost Analysis," *Marketing Science* 4, no. 3 (Summer), pp. 234–254.

51. Anderson, Erin (1988), "Strategic Implications of Darwinian Economics for Selling Efficiency and Choice of Integrated or Independent Salesforces," *Management Science* 34, no. 5 (May), pp. 599–618.

52. Grewal, Rajdeep and Ravi Dharwadkar (2002), "The Role of the Institutional Environment in Marketing Channels," *Journal of Marketing* 66, no. 3 (July), pp. 82–97.

53. Bonazza, Patrick (1999), "Le 'Signore' des Lunettes, "*Le Point*, May 14, pp. 107–111. Quotation from p. 109.

54. Bonazza, Patrick, previously cited, p. 111.

55. Kogut, Bruce and Nalin Kulatilaka (1994), "Options Thinking and Platform Investments: Investing in Opportunity," *California Management Review* 36, no. 2 (Winter), pp. 52–71.

56. Barney, Jay B. (1999), "How a Firm's Capabilities Affect Boundary Decisions," *Sloan Management Review* 40, no. 3 (Spring), pp. 137–145.

Chapter 10

Legal Constraints on Marketing Channel Policies

After reading this chapter, you will:

■ Understand the array of channel policies available for channel management

■ Know the types of channel activities subject to governmental scrutiny

■ Understand the difference between per se criteria and rule of reason criteria

■ Be familiar with the major U.S. legal cases that shape channel practices

Channel managers can use many different policies to administer distribution systems. Some of these policies restrain or redirect the activities of the various members of channels and may affect the competitiveness of the overall market. As such, they can fall under legal antitrust scrutiny.

The purpose of this chapter is twofold. Its main purpose is to catalog a variety of the policies available for managing channels and explain the reasons why they might be adopted. Second, it lays out when and how such policies might run afoul of U.S. federal antitrust laws. The chapter focuses primarily on legal stances on these policies in the United States, although the discussion of each policy's *business* purpose is useful regardless of the market in which the channel manager operates.

The policies addressed are:

➤ Market coverage policies
➤ Customer coverage policies

> ➤ Pricing policies
> ➤ Product line policies
> ➤ Selection and termination policies
> ➤ Ownership policies

The principal federal antitrust laws affecting the setting of these policies are listed in Figure 10.1.

MARKET COVERAGE POLICIES

One of the key elements of channel management is deciding how many sales outlets should be established in a given geographic area and what kind of participation in the marketing flows should be required from each of the outlets so that the needs of existing and potential customers may be adequately served. Chapter 4 discusses in depth the channel design and management issues concerning channel intensity. From a legal perspective, channel intensity is linked to the concept of market coverage, about which there is significant legal concern.

Implicit in the term *market coverage* are issues concerned with geography or territory. The more a channel structure moves away from intensive to selective coverage, the fewer resellers of a particular brand will be in any given area. Selective and exclusive coverage policies have been called territorial restrictions by antitrust enforcement agencies because they are used by suppliers to limit the number of resellers in a defined territory. In reality, territorial assignments are rewards or spatial allocations given by suppliers adopting selective or exclusive market coverage policies in return for distributors' promises to cultivate the geography they have been given.

The supplier's objective in instituting territorial restrictions and a number of other kinds of so-called vertical restraints is to limit the extent of intrabrand competition. A critical issue that has evolved in antitrust cases is whether such policies actually promote (or at least do not substantially lessen) *interbrand competition*. Intrabrand competition is defined as competition among wholesalers or retailers of the same brand (e.g., Coca-Cola or Chevrolet). Interbrand competition is defined as competition among all the suppliers of different brands of the same generic product (e.g., brands of soft drinks or automobiles). The rationale behind restricting intrabrand competition is that by protecting resellers of its brand from competition among themselves a supplier will supposedly improve their effectiveness against resellers of other brands. From an interorganizational management perspective, the attempt to dampen intrabrand competition in order to strengthen interbrand competition is very sensible. A manufacturer often would rather have the channel members handling its brand compete with those who handle other brands than compete among themselves.

In the language of antitrust enforcement, territorial restrictions range from *absolute confinement of reseller sales*, which is intended to completely foreclose or eliminate intrabrand competition, to lesser territorial restrictions designed to inhibit such competition. These lesser restrictions include areas of primary responsibility, profit pass-over arrangements, and location clauses. For example, a manufacturer may prohibit its bricks-and-mortar resellers from engaging in Internet selling, which is essentially without geographic boundaries.

Act	Key Provisions
Sherman Antitrust Act, 1890	1. Prohibits contracts, combinations, or conspiracies in restraint of interstate or foreign commerce.
Clayton Antitrust Act, 1914	Where competition is, or may be, substantially lessened, it prohibits: 1. Price discrimination in sales or leasing of goods 2. Exclusive dealing 3. Tying contracts 4. Interlocking directorates among competitors 5. Mergers and acquisitions
Federal Trade Comission (FTC) Act, 1914	1. Prohibits unfair or deceptive trade practices injurious to competition or a competitor. 2. Sets up FTC to determine unfairness.
Robinson-Patman Act, 1936	1. Discriminatory prices for goods are prohibited if they reduce competition at any point in the channel. 2. Discriminatory prices can be given in good faith to meet competition. 3. Brokerage allowances are allowed only if earned by an independent broker. 4. Sellers must give all services and promotional allowances to all buyers on a proportionately equal basis if the buyers are in competition. The offering of alternatives may be necessary. 5. Buyers are prohibited from knowingly inducing price or promotional discrimination. 6. Price discrimination can be legal if it results from real cost differences in serving different customers.
FTC Trade Practice Rules	1. Enforced by FTC. Define unfair competition for individual industries. These practices are prohibited by the FTC. 2. Defines rules of sound practice. These rules are not enforced by the FTC but are recommended.

Figure 10.1 Principal U.S. federal laws affecting marketing channel management

Absolute confinement involves a promise by a channel member that it will not sell outside its assigned territory. Often combined with such a promise is a pledge by the supplier not to sell to anyone else in that territory, an arrangement known as an exclusive distributorship. A territory is described as airtight when absolute confinement is combined with an exclusive distributorship. On the other hand, an area of primary responsibility requires the channel member to use its best efforts, or to attain a quantified performance level, to maintain effective distribution of the supplier's goods in the territory specifically assigned to it. Failure to meet performance targets may result in termination, but the channel member is free to sell outside its area, and other wholesalers or retailers may sell in its territory.

Profit pass-over arrangements require that a channel member who sells to a customer located outside its assigned territory compensate the distributor in whose territory the customer is located. Such compensation is ostensibly to reimburse the distributor for its efforts to stimulate demand in its territory and for the cost of providing services on which the channel member might have capitalized.

Finally, a location clause specifies the site of a channel member's place of business. Such clauses are used to deploy resellers in a given territory so that each has a "natural" market comprising those customers who are closest to the reseller's location. However, the reseller may sell to any customer walking through its door. Furthermore, the customers located closest to the reseller may decide to purchase at more distant locations.

Any attempt to confine wholesalers' or retailers' selling activities to one area may be viewed as either a restraint of trade or as an unfair method of competition and, therefore, may be challenged under the Sherman Act or Section 5 of the FTC Act. The dominant antitrust perspective relative to territorial restrictions (market coverage policies) was established on June 23, 1977, when the U.S. Supreme Court handed down the decision in the *Sylvania* case profiled in Sidebar 10.1.[1]

For definitions of the various legal rules applied in vertical restraint antitrust cases, see Figure 10.2.

Empirical research suggests that manufacturers in fact do use a wide array of efficiency-related reasons to justify territorial restrictions in their channels.[2] Free-riding concerns, such as those operative in Sylvania's decision to impose restrictions, have been shown to be important. But beyond this, vertical restrictions have been shown to be more likely when (a) distributors have superior market information to that of the manufacturer; (b) detecting distributor violations of the restrictions is easier; (c) distributors invest more in manufacturer-specific assets; (d) competition at the manufacturer level is more intense; and (e) distributors are willing to limit their sales to this manufacturer's product. Of these reasons, the last two could be anticompetitive, but the first three are efficiency-motivated and support a rule-of-reason legal stance.

Although the use of territorial restrictions in the United States is widespread and, for the most part, legal, treatment of territorial restrictions varies elsewhere in the world. For example, until 2000, European Union Law (first established in the Treaty of Rome), held to the premise that all territorial restriction agreements were distortions of free trade, whether vertical (i.e., between channel members at different levels of distribution) or horizontal (i.e., among competitors). The EC

Sidebar 10.1

Sylvania case[3]

Prior to 1962, Sylvania, a manufacturer of television sets, sold its sets through both independent and company-owned distributors to a large number of independent retailers. RCA dominated the market at the time, holding 60 to 70 percent of national sales, with Zenith and Magnavox as major rivals. Sylvania had only 1 to 2 percent of the market. In 1962, Sylvania decided to abandon efforts at saturation distribution and chose instead to phase out its wholesalers and sell directly to a smaller group of franchised retailers. Sylvania retained sole discretion to determine how many retailers would operate in any geographic area, and in fact, at least two retailers were franchised in every metropolitan center of more than 100,000 people. Dealers were free to sell anywhere and to any class of customers but agreed to operate only from locations approved by Sylvania. A critical factor in the decision was Sylvania's desire to decrease the likelihood of one retailer free-riding on the efforts of another retailer's marketing activities in the area.

Continental TV was one of Sylvania's most successful retailers in northern California. After a series of disagreements arising from Sylvania's authorizing a new outlet near one of Continental's best locations, Continental opened a new outlet in Sacramento, although its earlier request for approval for that location had been denied. Sylvania then terminated Continental's franchise. In resulting litigation, Continental counterclaimed against Sylvania. The Court sided with Sylvania, which had argued that the use of its territorial allocation policy permitted its marketing channels to compete more successfully against those established by its large competitors.

In its decision, the Court favored the promotion of interbrand competition even if intrabrand competition were restricted. It indicated that territorial restrictions encourage interbrand competition by allowing the manufacturer to achieve certain efficiencies in the distribution of its products. In a footnote, the Court recognized that the imposition of such restrictions is consistent with increased societal demands that manufacturers directly assume responsibility for the safety and quality of their products. As a result of the Court's decision, territorial restrictions, when challenged, are to be evaluated under a rule of reason doctrine in which proof must be established that the restrictions substantially lessen interbrand competition. Furthermore, the burden is on the plaintiff to prove that the restraints are unreasonable.

competition rules essentially required manufacturers to supply goods to anyone who wanted to sell them. The only way in which manufacturers could employ policies like selective distribution was for them to secure exemption from the rules from the EC headquarters in Brussels.[4] Three industries in which exemptions were granted were cars, consumer electronics, and perfume. In the case of cars and electronics, selective distribution was permitted on the grounds that the products were complex and needed after-sales service. For perfume, the justification was that the products were luxury goods that depended for their appeal on an aura of exclusivity maintained by high price, large investments in marketing, and a sophisticated sales environment.[5]

Per se illegality:	The marketing policy is automatically unlawful regardless of the reasons for the practice and without extended inquiry into its effects. It is only necessary for the complainant to prove the occurrence of the conduct and antitrust injury.
Modified rule of reason:	(also called "quick look") The marketing policy is presumed to be anticompetitive if evidence of the existence and use of significant market power is found, subject to rebuttal by the defendant.
Rule of reason:	Before a decision is made about the legality of a marketing policy, it is necessary to undertake a broad inquiry into the nature, purpose, and effect of the policy. This requires an examination of the facts peculiar to the contested policy, its history, the reasons why it was implemented, and its competitive significance.
Per se legality:	The marketing policy is presumed legal.

Figure 10.2 Legal rules used in antitrust enforcement

In 1999, the European Commission worked on relaxing the rules on vertical restraints so as to impose instead a single block exemption rule, to take effect in early 2000. Under this exemption, in any case where the firm in question has less than 30 percent market share, it can engage in distribution agreements with its distributors or retailers without explicit permission. Any restrictive business agreement involving firms with more than 30 percent market share is still prohibited without an individual exemption from the Commission.[6] Clearly, it is wise to check carefully into specific regulations pertaining in each region of the world in which one's products are sold because regulations vary.

CUSTOMER COVERAGE POLICIES

Suppliers may wish to set policies regarding customers to whom wholesalers or retailers may resell their goods and services. For a variety of reasons, suppliers may wish to reserve certain customers as house accounts. These include the desire to maintain close relationships with highly valuable customers, their requirements for technical assistance, the efficiency associated with serving accounts directly, the expected profits on the sale, the need for price concessions to win certain accounts, and in the case of some retailers like Home Depot and Wal-Mart, the insistence of accounts to be sold on a direct basis. In other cases, suppliers may set customer coverage policies that have the goal of assuring their goods and services will be sold by intermediaries capable of providing specific service outputs to their customers. This way, suppliers can be confident that their products are handled only by competent resellers.

Many manufacturers have used such policies in their attempts to prevent the emergence of gray markets, which appear when their brands are sold by unauthorized resellers. Clauses in contracts written by manufacturers often stipulate that authorized dealers are prohibited from selling their brands to anyone but bona fide end-users. Authorized dealers often are tempted to sell off their excess inventories to unauthorized dealers, such as 47th Street Photo, Kmart, Syms, and other well-known discounters.

In addition, suppliers might wish to allocate different accounts to different intermediaries.[7] This policy is one way to limit intrabrand competition; the customer sees only one seller of the firm's product. It can also facilitate segmented pricing, charging higher prices to segments of buyers with a higher willingness to pay for the firm's product. Or the different service output demands of different segments may suggest that they be served by different intermediaries, each with the necessary skills to provide the demanded service outputs. Customer coverage policies could also be used for safety reasons; certain specialized dealers may be willing to screen potential customers or provide information required in a product's use (e.g., herbicides).

Such policies have an economic rationale as well as a service rationale. As already mentioned in the context of market coverage policies, if multiple channels are permitted to compete for the same customer, it is possible that one channel will bear the cost of providing valued service outputs to the customer while another channel closes the sale. The free-riding channel does not bear the costs of channel flows necessary to provide the demanded service outputs but does get the sale and the profit from the customer. In the long run, profits and economic viability will suffer in the cost-bearing channel. This is not in the manufacturer's best interest because the failure of the cost-bearing channel will hurt the manufacturer as well as the free-riding channel.[8]

Indeed, many of the reasons for adopting customer coverage policies are the same as those for adopting market coverage policies. Customer coverage restrictions are basically exercises of coercive power (e.g., prohibitions on distributors reselling to discount houses) whereas territorial restrictions are basically exercises of reward power (e.g., the granting of a monopoly on the sale of a brand within a defined territory). For this reason, the antitrust concerns are handled similarly. The antitrust enforcement agencies and the courts refer to customer coverage policies as customer or resale restrictions. Policies of this type become illegal when their effects can be shown to reduce competition substantially.

Despite their different characters, territorial and resale restrictions are treated identically under the law. Both are viewed as restraints of trade and, therefore, can be directly challenged under the Sherman Act. But, given the *Sylvania* decision, their legality is to be judged under a rule-of-reason approach. That is, they will be considered legal if they have not substantially lessened interbrand competition.

Although gray markets are not necessarily an antitrust concern, it may be useful for channel managers to note that in 1988 the U.S. Supreme Court upheld a Customs Service regulation permitting gray market imports (although it did not endorse the entire concept of gray markets under all conditions). Gray markets into the United States are specifically permitted when the U.S. trademark is owned by a U.S. company with its own manufacturing facility abroad or when the U.S. trademark owner has established a subsidiary or affiliate abroad that is under the U.S. company's common control.[9] Duracell batteries fit this description, for example, because they are manufactured abroad in plants owned by Duracell, as well as in U.S. plants under Duracell's control. Gray market importers in the United States generally obtain their goods from foreign distributors who buy the products overseas.[10] As a result of the lack of protection against gray market imports from the U.S. Customs Service, some manufacturers have used other laws to challenge gray market imports to the United States, such as the Lanham Act, which governs trademark use. Chapter 7 further discusses gray marketing as a source of channel conflict and explains how manufacturers seek to manage gray markets.

PRICING POLICIES

Prices and price levels can be influenced in many ways throughout marketing channels. In fact, we have just finished discussing two of them—market coverage and customer coverage. Because both of these policies are aimed at reducing or restraining the amount of intrabrand competition, the indirect effect of the reduction is, in theory, supposed to be an increase in the price of the brand from its level in the absence of the policies. If the price is at a reasonable level, gross margins available to resellers may be sufficient to pay for the provision of service outputs desired by end-users (as assessed by the supplier setting the policy). In other words, restrictions on intrabrand competition are indirectly supposed to result in higher prices and, thus, higher gross margins. Obviously, price competition induced by interbrand competitors can upset this arrangement.

Here we describe two policies that have a direct effect on price—price maintenance and price discrimination. We discuss the two separately because their motivation, implementation, and antitrust concerns are very different.

Price Maintenance

Price maintenance in marketing channels is the specification by suppliers, typically manufacturers, of the prices below or above which other channel members, typically wholesalers and retailers, may not resell their products. Because of this, the policy is frequently called resale price maintenance (RPM). Minimum RPM designates the manufacturer's specification of a downstream price below which the product cannot be sold. Maximum RPM designates the manufacturer's specification of a downstream price above which the product cannot be sold. It is also possible to specify an exact price at which the product should be sold downstream, as is done with Saturn automobiles.

The main argument in favor of maximum RPM is related to the use of selective or exclusive distribution. Manufacturers who grant exclusivity to their dealers endow them with a local monopoly for the sale of their products. With local monopoly power, dealers have a strong incentive to raise prices above competitive levels, contrary to the interests of manufacturers and consumers. But through the use of maximum RPM, price can be maintained at a competitive level even if limited numbers of intermediaries are used.

Several arguments favor minimum RPM. The main thrust of the arguments follows from an understanding of the service outputs consumers get from a channel, in addition to the products they buy. Shoppers can choose to gain information and services at full-price dealers and then purchase through price discounters who do not offer service but do offer lower prices. By not offering the same level of presale and postsale service as full-price dealers, such as extensive product information and demonstrations, and postsale installation, maintenance, and repair, discounters free ride on the services offered elsewhere. Full-service dealers will then have provided costly service without the compensating revenue from the sale of the product. Their natural reaction will be to reduce service levels. But if service really is a necessary extension of buying the product, reducing service will lead in turn to a reduction in demand, to the detriment of all parties. Minimum resale price maintenance prevents discounting, reducing the extent of rival-dealer free riding on services. In these types of markets, then, it can be argued that minimum resale price maintenance is actually a procompetitive policy.

Variants on the argument in favor of minimum RPM include the following:

➤ Manufacturers must gain entry to dealers faced with limited shelf and floor space. For many goods, dealer networks compatible with a product's quality and image are required. Manufacturers purchase such access through higher markups, advertising and brand name drawing power, advertising allowances to dealers, and other expenditures in competition with rival brands. Minimum RPM provides a means for new manufacturers to gain dealer access by assuring dealers a given retail markup and ensuring against loss-leader pricing.[11]

> If dealers can earn a reasonable retail markup through minimum RPM, channel intermediaries may engage in quality certification for end-users so that the normal risks associated with purchasing a good or service are minimized.

> Minimum RPM may provide a high enough margin to the intermediary to induce it to push the firm's product over others carried by the intermediary, thus increasing the brand's visibility in the market.

> For products for which spatial convenience demands are high, minimum RPM helps assure widespread and immediate availability of the brand.

> Because minimum RPM guarantees a reasonably high profit margin to the intermediary, termination (causing the loss of these profits) would be very costly to the intermediary. Such powerful incentives are likely to discourage price maintainers from becoming price discounters.[12]

Despite all of these reasons supporting an RPM policy, the legal status of minimum and maximum RPM has been varied over time. Minimum RPM has been considered per se illegal since the *Dr. Miles Medical Co. v. John D. Park & Sons Co.* decision in 1911. The illegality of minimum RPM was weakened, however, by two legal decisions, one in 1984 (in *Monsanto Company v. Spray-Rite Service Corporation*) and the other in 1988 (in *Business Electronics, Corp. v. Sharp Electronics*), profiled in Sidebars 10.2 and 10.3.

The *Monsanto* and *Business Electronics* decisions appear to have stimulated a number of manufacturers of upscale consumer goods, such as Prince Manufacturing, Inc. (makers of Prince tennis racquets), and Specialized Bicycle Components (makers of mountain bikes), to use unilaterally implemented minimum resale price maintenance as one of their major distribution policies.[13] In fact, it is claimed that resale prices have been set for certain brands of televisions, athletic shoes, cameras, china, furniture, cosmetics, golf clubs, VCRs, women's sportswear, men's suits, stereos, toys, ceiling fans, watches, appliances, skis, cookware, perfume, chocolates, luggage, and video games, among others.

Some of the arguments that have been raised in opposition to the increasing minimum price maintenance activity are:

> Minimum RPM does not ensure that retailers will use their larger gross margins to provide service; they may simply pocket the extra money.

> Although interbrand competition may be fostered, minimum RPM inhibits competition between stores carrying the same brand.

> If a manufacturer deems service to be essential, it can be required of all retailers through dealership contracts rather than through minimum RPM.

> Higher prices deny goods to consumers with less money.[14]

Despite these arguments, setting minimum resale prices remains legal as long as it is not done as part of a concerted effort among multiple parties.

The status of maximum RPM has followed a somewhat different route, as exemplified by the *Albrecht* and *State Oil Co. v. Khan* cases, summarized in Sidebar 10.4.[15] These cases established that minimum, maximum, or exact RPM can be implemented if not done so in the context of an agreement to restrain trade. That is, if RPM is a policy of the manufacturer, enacted unilaterally, there is by definition no agreement that could be construed as an antitrust violation. Maximum RPM agreements can be used

Sidebar 10.2

Monsanto v. Spray-Rite case

In the *Monsanto Company v. Spray-Rite Service Corporation* case,[16] Spray-Rite (now defunct) sued Monsanto after Monsanto cut off Spray-Rite's distributorship of herbicides in northern Illinois in 1968. Spray-Rite claimed that Monsanto did this because Spray-Rite would not join in an effort to fix prices at which herbicides were sold. Spray-Rite alleged a conspiracy between Monsanto and some of its distributors to set resale prices. The U.S. Supreme Court found in Spray-Rite's favor but made it clear that the presence of concerted action between Monsanto and its distributors was critical to its per se ruling. In fact, the court explicitly stated that "a manufacturer . . . generally has a right to deal, or refuse to deal, with whomever it likes, as long as it does so independently." Citing the Colgate doctrine (discussed later in this chapter), the court went on to say that "the manufacturer can announce its resale prices in advance and refuse to deal with those who fail to comply." In other words, manufacturers may stipulate resale prices to their distributors as long as the stipulations are made on a unilateral basis. Where concerted conspiratorial action is found, a per se illegal ruling can be expected.

The *Monsanto* decision may be viewed as a chink in the armor of the per se illegal status of resale price maintenance. The problem that Monsanto has created is how the term *agreement* ought to be defined and what evidence is sufficient to support a jury verdict that there was a price-fixing conspiracy. The Supreme Court said that evidence must be presented both that the distributor communicated its acquiescence regarding the manufacturer's resale pricing policy and that the acquiescence was sought by the manufacturer. It added that the mere fact that other distributors complained about a price cutter prior to termination was not sufficient to support a finding of agreement.

as long as they do not harm competition. But minimum or exact RPM arrangements, when arrived at through a legal contract or agreement, are per se illegal. These criteria suggest that legal control over resale prices by manufacturers is possible under various conditions:[17]

> ➤ Act unilaterally, that is, statements and actions should come only from the manufacturer.
> ➤ Avoid coercion, that is, do not use annually renewable contracts conditioned on dealer adherence to manufacturer's specified resale price.
> ➤ Vertically integrate, that is, form a corporate vertical marketing system.
> ➤ Avoid known discounters, that is, establish screening and performance criteria difficult for discounters to meet.
> ➤ Announce resale price policy up front, that is, the policy should be established when arrangements are first made with channel members and should specify that the manufacturer will refuse to deal with any dealer not willing to adhere to the announced terms.

The Supreme Court noted in *Business Electronics*, however, that the per se prohibitions on resale price maintenance do not apply "to restrictions on price to be

Sidebar 10.3

Business Electronics Corp. v. Sharp Electronics case

The second major case weakening the per se illegality of maximum RPM was *Business Electronics Corp. v. Sharp Electronics*, decided in 1988. In this case, the Supreme Court ruled in a vote of six to two that a manufacturer's agreement with one dealer to stop supplying a price-cutting dealer would not necessarily violate the Sherman Act.[18] The plaintiff, Business Electronics, was the exclusive retailer of Sharp calculators in Houston from 1968 to 1972. During that period, Sharp became dissatisfied with Business Electronics' policy of selling calculators at prices lower than those suggested by Sharp. In 1972 Sharp appointed Hartwell's Office World as a second retailer of its calculators in Houston. Subsequently, Hartwell's told Sharp that it would quit distributing its products unless Sharp ended its relationship with Business Electronics, and in 1973, Sharp terminated Business Electronics' dealership. Business Electronics then sued Sharp.

The U.S. Supreme Court upheld an appeals court ruling that the agreement to terminate Business Electronics was not a per se violation of antitrust law. It stated that such an agreement would be illegal per se only if it had been part of an agreement by the manufacturer and one or more retailers to fix prices at some level. There was no proof in the case of such a specific price-fixing agreement between Sharp and Hartwell's. Writing for the Court, Justice Antonin Scalia observed that it is sometimes legitimate and competitively useful for manufacturers to curb price competition among their dealers, and he referred to the free rider problem as a reason for manufacturers' actions. Thus, if there is no specific agreement as to price between the complaining dealers and the manufacturer, the reasonableness of an agreement to terminate will be determined by the rule of reason, that is, by balancing the anticompetitive intrabrand effects against any procompetitive interbrand effects.[19]

charged by one who is in reality an agent of, not a buyer from, the manufacturer."[20] For example, where the restrictions would apply in the case of a distributor, who takes title to the goods it sells for a manufacturer, they would not apply in the case of an independent sales representative, who does not take title to the manufacturer's goods. The Court was quoting from *U.S. v. General Electric Co.* where it was stated that "The owner of an article . . . is not violating the common law, or the Anti-Trust Law, by seeking to dispose of his article directly to the consumer and fixing the price by which his agents transfer the title from him directly to the consumer."[21] This stance is echoed in the words of a lower court in a more recent case: "where the manufacturer bears the financial risks of transactions with the customers and continues to retain 'title, dominion and control over its goods,' then it is likely that the distributor is merely an agent for the manufacturer."[22]

Price Discrimination

When a seller offers or grants one buyer a lower price than another buyer on the exact same product, the seller is discriminating between the buyers by giving one of them a monetary reward. In actuality, discriminating among buyers, whether via prices, service

Sidebar 10.4

Albrecht and State Oil Co. v. Khan cases

The *Albrecht* decision in 1968 was a major case establishing the per se illegality of maximum resale price maintenance.[23] Albrecht was a newspaper carrier for the Herald Company, which granted exclusive territories to its carriers. The Herald Company advertised a subscription price for home newspaper delivery and required its carriers to charge that price. Albrecht charged a higher price to his customers, leading to his termination by the Herald Company. Albrecht sued and won in the U.S. Supreme Court, which argued that when maximum RPM sets prices too low, it prevents a dealer from offering services that customers need and value. While this argument was challenged in the academic literature, the per se illegality of maximum RPM was maintained until 1997.

The *State Oil Co. v. Khan* (1997) decision by the U.S. Supreme Court overturned the *Albrecht* decision, ruling that henceforth maximum RPM agreements would be decided on a rule of reason basis (i.e., being viewed as legal unless they

harm competition) rather than being viewed as per se illegal.[24] In this case, Khan was a dealer of Union 76 gasoline. The supply contract he had with State Oil in essence was a maximum RPM contract, although this was somewhat veiled by the specific pricing stipulations in the agreement. Khan sued, seeking to be able to charge higher prices for his gasoline and pocket the increased revenue from doing so.

In a unanimous ruling, the U.S. Supreme Court found in favor of State Oil. It found that the benefit to consumers in the form of lower prices outweighed the possible harm that could be caused by the practices and pointed out that in the previous 30 years firms had found many ways around the *Albrecht* ruling against maximum RPM in any event. These actions, they argued, had not had a serious negative impact on competitiveness or welfare and, hence, suggested the appropriateness of returning to a rule of reason criterion for determining the legality of maximum RPM when engaged in through concerted action.

outputs, or product features, makes abundant sense. From a managerial perspective, it would be foolish not to approach buyers typified by high demand elasticities differently from those with low demand elasticities. At the core of well-conceived market segmentation schemes are discriminatory tactics because segments are supposed to be solicited dissimilarly. In fact, optimal profits can only be achieved if sellers discriminate among buyers. Not only price sensitivity but also cost to serve and intensity of competition vary across market segments. Charging different, or segmented, prices is the right economic decision.[25]

Although channel members can discriminate among their customers and suppliers in many ways, the focus here is mainly on price. The major segmented pricing policies enacted by channel managers tend to revolve around reductions from list price, promotional allowances and services, and functional discounts. The rationale for each of these is straightforward—the object is to increase demand, fight off competitors, reward customers, and compensate channel partners for services rendered. While price discrimination can certainly be profitable, it can also be illegal. Instances of illegal price discrimination are covered under the Robinson-Patman Act. In what follows, we summarize the legal stance on price discrimination by sellers and by buyers, as well as promotional allowances and functional discounts.

Price Discrimination by Sellers

When sellers offer different prices to different buyers, the most directly relevant part of the Robinson-Patman Act is Section 2(a), which states:

> It shall be unlawful for any person engaged in commerce, . . . either directly or indirectly, to discriminate in price between different purchasers of commodities of like grade and quality, where either or any of the purchases involved in such discrimination are in commerce, where such commodities are sold for use, consumption, or resale within [any area] under the jurisdiction of the United States, and where the effect of such discrimination may be to substantially lessen competition or tend to create a monopoly in any line of commerce, or to injure, destroy or prevent competition with any person who either grants or knowingly receives the benefit of such discrimination, or with customers of either of them.

We can clarify three of the more significant phrases as follows:

➤ *Commodities.* The Robinson-Patman Act applies to goods and to goods bundled with services where the value of the goods predominates. It does not cover the sale of services. Some excluded categories therefore are printing, advertising space, and even real estate.

➤ *Like grade and quality.* Where products are of different materials or workmanship level, they are not ordinarily considered to be of like grade and quality, but where differences are small and do not affect the basic use of the goods, then selling at price differentials has been attacked. For example, price differences involving private label versus branded goods have been challenged where the product was identical in both instances (i.e., evaporated milk made by Borden).[26]

➤ *Substantially lessen competition.* This factor is a critical issue in all antitrust cases (including those filed under Section 2(a) of the Robinson-Patman Act), which are tried under the rule of reason doctrine. It has become increasingly difficult for plaintiffs to prove, because there is an important difference between injury to competitors and injury to competition. A loss of sales by one firm and their gain by another is the essence of competition, and the object of each competitor is to outsell rivals. Evidence of intent to destroy a competitor, however, may indicate an injury to competition.

Price discrimination between customers who are not competing is not illegal. This means it is perfectly legal for retailers to charge consumers different prices for identical goods and services (e.g., airline tickets or automobiles)—consumers are not in competition with one another. Also, if one retailer does business only on the East Coast of the United States and another does business only on the West Coast, a vendor may charge them different prices as long as they do not compete for the same end-users.

Price discrimination that injures any of three levels of competition may end up being prohibited by the Robinson-Patman Act:

➤ *Primary Level.* Competition between two sellers may be injured when one of them gives discriminatory prices to some customers.

➤ *Secondary Level.* Competition between two customers of a seller may be affected if the seller differentiates between them in price. In effect the seller is aiding one customer and harming the other in their mutual competition, and this is illegal if it is sufficient to cause substantial lessening of competition.

➤ *Tertiary Level.* If a manufacturer discriminates in prices between two wholesalers such that the customers of one wholesaler are favored over those of the other, competition is being injured by the price discrimination.

Perhaps one of the most important Robinson-Patman Act cases in decades was decided in 1993 (see Sidebar 10.5). It involved primary level discrimination in which Liggett & Myers, formerly the Brooke Group, charged Brown & Williamson (B&W) with predatory pricing. Defendant Brown & Williamson won the case, which established that predatory pricing could only be proven if the predator could actually recover the costs of lowering prices to predatory levels, as well as reaffirming the positive consumer welfare implications of lower prices under these competitive moves. In particular, successful predatory pricing requires that the predator lower prices to force the victim out of the market, but the predator is also harmed thereby (at least in the short term). In the case of Brown & Williamson, the court found that even if it did force Liggett & Myers out of the market, it could not force all the other competitors out of the market, and therefore, predatory pricing could not be proven.

Defenses to Price Discrimination Charges

Price discrimination is not a per se violation of the antitrust laws. There are three potential escape routes beyond the fact that the discrimination may have an insignificant impact on competition. Discrimination may be justified through proof that (a) it was carried out to dispose of perishable or obsolete goods or under a close-out or bankruptcy sale; (b) it merely made due allowance for differences in "the cost of manufacture, sale, or delivery resulting from the differing methods or quantities" in which the commodity was sold or delivered; or (c) it was effected "in good faith to meet an equally low price of a competitor."[27] The first defense poses few problems, but the second and third are more complex.

Cost Justification Defense Companies attempting to sustain a Robinson-Patman Act cost justification defense have seldom been successful because of the stringent standards set by the U.S. Federal Trade Commission and the courts, that is, requiring detailed documentation of full (not marginal) costs and causing the defense to fail if less than 100 percent of the price differential is shown to result from cost differences.[28] The burden of proof is on the seller, as quantity discounts are permitted under Section 2(a) only to the extent that they are justified by cost savings.

For example, the U.S. Supreme Court has ruled that quantity discounts must reflect cost savings in deliveries made to one place at one time. This places limitations on the use of cumulative quantity discounts. In 1988 the Federal Trade Commission charged six of the nation's largest book publishers with illegally discriminating against independent bookstores by selling books at lower prices to major bookstore chains, such as Waldenbooks, B. Dalton, and Crown Books. The FTC said the publishers treated orders placed by the chains as a single order, even if the books were separately packed, itemized, and shipped to individual chain outlets.

Sidebar 10.5

Liggett & Myers v. Brown & Williamson Tobacco case

In 1980, Liggett & Myers, which had a 2.3 percent market share, introduced a generic, unadvertised cigarette that sold for 30 percent less than the branded price. Eventually, Brown & Williamson entered with a generic product packaged in an identical box to Liggett's and began to undercut Liggett's price. B&W had a market share of around 12 percent at the time. During the 18-month price war that ensued, B&W allegedly cut its prices substantially below average variable cost. Liggett could not sustain the below-cost pricing, and the price of generic cigarettes rose.

Liggett sued under the Robinson-Patman Act[29] because B&W's predatory price cuts were implemented via discounts that were given to different distributors in varying degrees—hence, the price discrimination. Although many aspects of this case that make for interesting reading and analysis from a marketing-management perspective, the most important is the decision itself. The Court's decision rested on its assessment of whether B&W could earn back, via monopoly pricing, the costs of its predatory

actions after Liggett was quieted. The Court stated that, in addition to showing below-cost prices, the plaintiff (Liggett) must also demonstrate "that the competitor had a reasonable prospect . . . of recouping its investment in below-cost prices."[30] As the Court noted, "Recoupment is the ultimate object of an unlawful predatory scheme; it is the means by which a predator profits from predation."[31]

Through an analysis of competition in the cigarette industry, the Court came to the conclusion that B&W, despite the fact that it had quieted Liggett, did not have the power to quiet R. J. Reynolds, Philip Morris, and the rest of its competitors and, therefore, would not be able to retrieve its investment. It found in favor of B&W, stating that, without recoupment, predatory pricing produces lower aggregate prices in the market, and consumer welfare is enhanced. A federal court in Texas followed the same line of reasoning shortly after the Brooke Group decision when it cleared American Airlines of predatory pricing against Northwest and Continental Airlines.[32]

As a result, the chain stores were able to pay lower prices than independent bookstores "that receive shipments as large as or larger than shipments to individual chain outlets."[33]

Pricing policies in the health care industry have attracted considerable litigious attention over the past decade. Late in 1994, 1,346 independent pharmacies in 15 states sued the largest drug manufacturers and mail-order distributors, charging them with price discrimination. Early in 1994, four major grocery chains (Kroger, Albertson's, Safeway, and Vons) filed a suit in Cincinnati federal court charging 16 pharmaceutical firms and a mail-order prescription company with discriminatory and pernicious pricing. The suit claims the firms' pricing policies favor institutional pharmacies, health-maintenance organizations, and mail-order prescription (pharmacy benefit management) companies with lower prices, while charging supermarket chains more. Late in 1993, similar charges were levied by 20 chain and independent drugstores in yet another suit.[34] The suits were settled in 1996 and in mid-1998, with pharmaceutical companies paying about $350 million in each settlement to independent pharmacies and agreeing not to charge two-tier prices to the market.[35] However, the nonsettling defendants succeeded in having the case dismissed when it went to trial, and this ruling was upheld on appeal.

Meeting Competition Defense   The meeting competition defense (which is found in Section 2[b] of the act) has proven as difficult to apply as the cost justification defense but is even more complex. The defense is valid even if there is substantial injury to competition, but the burden of proving good faith falls on the defendant:[36]

> ➤ The price being met must be lawful and not a price produced by collusion. A seller does not have to prove the price that it is meeting is lawful, but it must make some effort to find out if it is.

> ➤ The price being met must really exist,[37] and the price must be met and not under-cut. Price reductions on a premium product to the level of standard products can be a form of illegal price discrimination. If the public is willing to pay a higher price for the premium product, the equal prices may be considered beating and not meeting competition.

> ➤ The competition being met may have to be at the primary level. Granting a discrimi-natory price to some customers to enable them to meet their own competition may not be protected.[38]

According to a 1983 Supreme Court ruling, the good faith defense is applicable to gaining new customers as well as retaining old ones. But firms practicing discrimi-nation are only permitted to match rival prices exactly; they cannot undercut, or beat, them.[39]

Availability Defense   Pricing differences for different customers can be defended if the reason for the actual price differences was the offering of a pricing policy available equally to all customers but not chosen by all customers. For example, a manufacturer may offer a discount for early payment of invoices. Even though all customers do not take advantage of the discount, all have equal opportunity to do so, and there is no violation.

Price Discrimination by Buyers

Price discrimination by a seller between two competing channel members can be viewed as an attempt to exercise reward power relative to the channel member receiv-ing the lower price. However, forcing a discriminatory price from an upstream seller in a channel may be viewed as coercion by the buyer.

Section 2(f) of the Robinson-Patman Act makes it unlawful for a person in com-merce knowingly to induce or receive a discriminatory price. To violate this section, buyers must be reasonably aware of the illegality of the prices they have received. This section prevents large, powerful channel members from compelling sellers to give them discriminatory lower prices. It is enforced by means of Section 5 of the Federal Trade Commission Act on the grounds that this use of coercive power is an unfair method of competition.

It is also illegal for buyers to coerce favors from suppliers in the form of special promotional allowances and services. This stipulation has led to government interest in the use of slotting allowances, although they are not specifically viewed as illegal.

Slotting allowances are fixed payments made by a manufacturer to a retailer for access to the retailer's shelf space: One definition specifies that they are "a family of marketing practices that involve payments and other incentives . . . given by manufacturers to persuade downstream channel members to stock, display, and support their products."[40] They are used predominantly in grocery retailing but have also been observed in the software, music, pharmaceutical, and book selling industries.[41] Retailers claim that slotting allowances are necessary to defray the costs of stocking a new product in the store, including one-time costs of incorporating the new product in the store's computer system, warehouse management, and shelf placement. They argue that these costs have risen with the increase in new product introductions in recent years.[42] This argument is consistent with the fact that a standard supermarket can stock about 40,000 products, but there are about 100,000 grocery products available to the market, with thousands of new product introductions per year and as high as an 80 percent failure rate for new products.[43] Slotting allowances also have been argued to perform a beneficial signaling role. Only if its product has high market potential would a manufacturer be willing to offer an up-front fixed payment to the retailer to stock the product, so retailers could use slotting allowances to screen potentially poor products from the store shelf.[44]

Slotting allowances are very commonly used and can involve very substantial fees, particularly in grocery retailing. In a study done by ACNielsen in 1997, manufacturers reported on the slotting allowance costs of their most recent national product introduction. One-third of respondents in the food category spent between $500,000 and $1 million on slotting allowances alone, and 14 percent spent more than $3 million. Only 6 percent of respondents reported paying no slotting allowances.[45]

Manufacturers complain that slotting allowances are nothing more than price discrimination or even extortion. Particular complaints have been raised by small manufacturers, who say that slotting allowances prevent their very access to store shelves. Indeed, in the 1997 Nielsen study, 83 percent of manufacturers selling through retailers paid some slotting allowances, but the percentage was higher for companies with sales under $1 billion (86 percent) than for larger ones (75 percent).[46]

Slotting allowances are not illegal in and of themselves. However, they could be construed as illegal under certain conditions. A panel session on slotting allowances at an annual meeting of the American Bar Association Section of Antitrust Law in 1997 noted that slotting allowances could be challenged under the Sherman Act and the FTC Act if competing retailers agreed on the amount of slotting allowances or the allocation of shelf space to manufacturers. The practice also could be challenged if used as part of a conspiracy to monopolize trade or if used to exclude certain manufacturers from retail shelf space. In a merger of two retailers, slotting allowances could be prohibited if they could prevent some manufacturers' market entry. Finally, slotting allowances could violate the Robinson-Patman Act if it were possible to prove their use as price discrimination mechanisms.[47]

Despite all of these possibilities, the use of slotting allowances continues and has yet to be ruled illegal. The assistant director of the FTC's Bureau of Competition noted that while manufacturers commonly "grumble" about slotting allowances, none had made a formal complaint in recent history. It is also hard to prove that retailers' increased power gives them the ability to extract profits from manufacturers through slotting allowances because retailers' profits have not risen appreciably as a result of slotting allowances.[48] In one case, *Augusta News Co. v. Hudson News Co.*, the plaintiffs were wholesale magazine distributors who refused to pay chain store retailers slotting fees that amounted to as much as $15,000 per store. As a result, they lost distribution through the chain stores and sued, arguing that the slotting fees violated the Sherman Act and the Robinson-Patman Act. They lost the case, with the judge ruling that slotting fees were not illegal broker-age payments but simply "price reduction offers to buyers for the exclusive rights to supply a set of stores under multi-year contracts" and further stating that the payments were competitively healthy.[49] Both the academic research evidence and real-world examples suggest that a successful lawsuit involving slotting allowance violations is unlikely.[50]

In a different context, large buyers, such as A&P, have been known to set up dummy brokerage firms as part of their businesses in order to obtain a brokerage allowance from sellers, which in effect permits them to receive lower prices than their competitors. This form of coercive power is deemed illegal under Section 2(c) of the Robinson-Patman Act, which makes it unlawful to pay brokerage fees or discounts or to accept them except for services rendered in connection with sales or purchases. It also prohibits brokerage fees or discounts paid to any broker who is not indepen-dent of both buyer and seller.

As is the case with slotting allowances, however, the reality is that buyer-induced price discrimination is extremely difficult to prove and, therefore, seems to be widely practiced. For example, in 1991, Coca-Cola allegedly lost a major con-tract to PepsiCo to provide soda-fountain service to Marriott Corporation after Coke refused to lend Marriott $50 million to $100 million at less than prevailing interest rates. Marriott is a hotel and food service chain that provides food services for its own 600 hotels and about 2,300 restaurants and kitchens at schools, busi-nesses, hospitals, and other institutions. Apparently, Pepsi was willing to lend Marriott the money. The Marriott business meant about $2 million in annual profit to Coke.[51]

Promotional Allowances and Services

To entice channel members to advertise, display, promote, or demonstrate their wares, suppliers use all sorts of monetary inducements. These rewards are circum-scribed by Sections 2(d) and 2(e) of the Robinson-Patman Act, which prohibit a seller from granting advertising allowances, offering other types of promotional assis-tance, or providing services, display facilities, or equipment to any buyer unless simi-lar allowances and assistance are made available to all purchasers. Section 2(d) applies to payments by a seller to a buyer for the performance of promotional ser-vices; Section 2(e) applies to the actual provision of such services (e.g., display racks or signs). Because buyers differ in size of physical establishment and volume of sales, allowances obviously cannot be made available to all customers on the same absolute basis. Therefore, the law stipulates that the allowances be made available to buyers on proportionately equal terms.

The prohibitions of these sections of the Robinson-Patman Act are absolute and are not dependent on injury to competition. Although meeting competition is a defense, cost justification of the discrimination is not. If it can be shown that discriminatory allowances exist and that the victims of the discrimination are firms in competition with each other, then the violation is deemed illegal per se unless the pricing action was taken to meet the competition. However, for firms to be in competition, they must be in sufficient geographical proximity to compete for the same customer groups. For example, if retailers are involved, only those retailers in a limited market territory need be included when granting allowances. Conversely, the market might be construed as national if mail-order or e-commerce companies are involved. In the latter situation, a manufacturer (or wholesaler) would have to grant allowances or services to all national sellers if it were to grant them to one, unless the meeting competition defense is available. In addition, a time dimension is important in defining the domain of the allowance. For example, if advertising allowances are granted in one month, they do not have to be granted to another buyer five months later. Otherwise, the initial allowance would determine all future allowances.[52]

According to the U.S. Federal Trade Commission's guidelines, certain stipulations have been made regarding adherence to Sections 2(d) and 2(e).[53] Among them are the following:

> Allowances may be made only for services actually rendered, and they must not substantially exceed the cost of these services to the buyer or their value to the seller.

> The seller must design a promotional program in such a way that all competing buyers can realistically implement it.

> The seller should take action designed to inform all competing customers of the existence and essential features of the promotional program in ample time for them to take full advantage of it.

> If a program is not functionally available to (i.e., suitable for and usable by) some of the seller's competing customers, the seller must make certain that suitable alternatives are offered to such customers.

> The seller should provide its customers with sufficient information to permit a clear understanding of the exact terms of the offer, including all alternatives, and the conditions on which payment will be made or services furnished.

The FTC has stipulated that, when promotional allowances or merchandising services are provided, they should be furnished in accordance with a written plan that meets the listed requirements.[54] In the case of sellers who market their products directly to retailers as well as sell through wholesalers, any promotional allowance offered to the retailers must also be offered to the wholesalers on a proportionately equal basis. The wholesalers would then be expected to pass along the allowance to their retail customers, who are in competition with the direct-buying retailers.[55]

In a 1990 revision of the Guides for Advertising Allowances and other Merchandising Payments and Services, the FTC recognized two ways of measuring proportional equality: either purchase-based, or based on the customer's cost. Offering an equal amount of allowances or services per unit of sales is a permissible example of the purchase-based measurement method. Placing newspaper advertisements in connection with the resale of products for which advertising allowances are provided is an example of the customer cost basis. In addition, the FTC reiterated its previous position that a company that grants a discriminatory promotional allowance may argue that the allowance was given in good faith to meet the promotional program of a competitor.[56]

Functional Discounts

In the discussion of channel flows in Chapter 3, the equity principle was introduced. That principle involves the use of reward power in granting discounts to individual channel members based on the functions (or marketing flows) they perform as they divide distribution labor. A functional discount is a means of implementing the equity principle directly. It provides for a set of list prices at which products are transferred from the manufacturer to a downstream channel member plus a list of discounts off list price to be offered in return for the performance of certain channel flows or functions.

Functional discounts are tied directly to the performance of actual channel flows, and therefore, payment is made differentially to channel members who perform valued channel flows to different degrees. For example, a discount of 3 percent off list price might be offered for payment in 10 days after purchase rather than the usual 30 days. The discount is directly tied to the distributor's bearing of the financing flow through early payment. Or a discount of 2 percent might be offered to the distributor in return for a promise to maintain a certain level of safety stocks of inventory in the distributor's warehouses, including permission for the manufacturer to periodically inspect the warehouses. In this case, compensation is given directly for bearing the physical possession and ownership flows.

In theory, functional discounts should be allotted to each channel member on the basis of the degree of its participation in the marketing flows (e.g., physical possession, ownership, promotion, etc.) associated with making a product or service available to end-users. In reality, the legality of functional discounts (which are a form of price discrimination) has been shrouded in controversy and confusion for decades. One of the major reasons for the confusion is that, historically, the discounts were primarily based on the level of distribution (e.g., wholesale vs. retail) in which a recipient resided and not strictly on the functions the company performed. For this reason, they are frequently called trade, as opposed to functional, discounts.

When independent wholesalers sold to numerous, relatively small retail outlets, each level in the channel was distinct and could be rewarded differently (e.g., the wholesaler got a larger price discount from the manufacturer than the retailer). In addition, each level in the channel dealt with a specific class of customer (e.g., the wholesaler sold only to retailers, and retailers only to consumers). Wholesalers and retailers normally performed different functions in different markets and, thus, did not compete against each other.

Now, however, the commercial world is much more complex. Distinctions in distribution systems have blurred as wholesalers have formed voluntary chains and as retailers have vertically integrated backward, assuming numerous wholesaling functions. Major mass merchandisers like Wal-Mart perform many of their own wholesaling operations. Wal-Mart receives merchandise in large lots from manufacturers, breaks bulk, assorts merchandise, and reships merchandise from its warehouses to its

Sidebar 10.6

Texaco v. Hasbrouck case

In *Texaco Inc. v. Hasbrouck*,[57] Texaco had sold gasoline directly to a number of independent retailers in Spokane, Washington, at its "retail tank wagon" prices, while it granted more substantial discounts to two distributors. Those two distributors sold the gasoline to service stations that the distributors owned and operated, passing on nearly the whole discount from Texaco. The distributor-controlled retailers thereby were able to sell well below the price charged by the competing independent retailers. Between 1972 and 1981, sales at the stations supplied by the two wholesaler-distributors increased dramatically, whereas sales at the competing independents declined.

Texaco argued that its discriminatory pricing was justified by cost savings, by a good faith attempt to meet competition, and as lawful functional discounts. The Ninth Circuit Court of Appeals and the Supreme Court did not accept Texaco's arguments in defense of its actions, even though they validated the use of the cost-based and good faith defenses in lawsuits challenging functional discounts.

The Supreme Court's affirmation of the cost justification defense is very significant for channel management, because this means that functional discounts are no longer merely tied to classification schemes. The Court stated that:

> In general, a supplier's functional discount is said to be a discount given to a purchaser based on the purchaser's role in the supplier's distributive system, reflecting, at least in a generalized sense, the services performed by the purchaser for the supplier.
> . . . a legitimate functional discount constituting a reasonable reimbursement for a purchaser's actual marketing functions does not violate Section 2(a).[58]

retail stores. However, it is generally classified as a retailer and, therefore, is supposedly entitled only to the functional (trade) discounts given to retailers. (It can, of course, avail itself of whatever quantity discounts are offered by its suppliers.)

The problem underlying this whole controversy is one of classification. Because of it, the Food Marketing Institute (whose members are primarily supermarket chains), the Grocery Manufacturers of America, the National Association of Chain Drug Stores, and a number of other wholesale and retail trade associations issued a statement in 1989 urging manufacturers not to make distinctions among competing distributor customers in a market area based on their class of trade. Manufacturers were instead urged to offer equally to all downstream members all prices and terms of sale that were offered to one. Such exhortations are of course only necessary when the manufacturer uses dual distribution to reach the market (see Chapter 4 for a discussion of dual distribution) and when functional discounts are offered differentially to the different channels used.

Functional discounts are not specifically referred to in the Robinson-Patman Act, but via a number of court decisions, it has been established that the stipulations of the act (including the defenses mentioned above) apply to them. A 1990 Supreme Court decision relevant in this regard is described in Sidebar 10.6, *Texaco Inc. v. Hasbrouck*.[59] This case leaves the door open to manufacturers to use functional discounts to compensate channel members for their participation in specific marketing flows. It further suggests that functional discounts bearing a reasonable relationship to the supplier's savings or the channel member's costs are legal, refuting the need for precise measurement. Which cost-base to use, the supplier's or the reseller's, remains a problem. In the latter case, setting discounts based on the reseller's costs may grant different discounts to competing resellers and possibly larger discounts to less efficient buyers, a strange outcome indeed. In the former case, the discounts based on the seller's savings would not necessarily be adequate or fair compensation to the reseller for performing the function.[60] The sentiment seems to favor using seller's savings, although both approaches have imperfections.

PRODUCT LINE POLICIES

For a wide variety of logical reasons, channel managers may wish to restrict the breadth or depth of the product lines that their channel partners sell. Here, we look at the rationale for four policies—exclusive dealing, tying, full-line forcing, and designated product policies—as well as the antitrust concerns surrounding them.

Exclusive Dealing

Exclusive dealing is the requirement by a seller or lessor that its channel intermediaries sell or lease only its products or brands, or at least no products or brands in direct competition with the seller's products. If intermediaries do not comply, the seller may invoke negative sanctions by refusing to deal with them. Such arrangements clearly reduce the freedom of choice of the intermediaries (resellers). Some of the managerial benefits of exclusive dealing are:

> Resellers become more dependent on the supplier, enabling the supplier to secure exclusive benefit of the reseller's energies. If the supplier has devoted considerable effort to develop a brand image, it may fear that the resellers will use the brand as a loss leader and that suppliers of other, directly competing brands stocked by the reseller will free ride on the demand stimulated by the supplier's heavily promoted, well-known brand. The supplier may be concerned about free riding with regard to other services as well, such as the use of specialized display cases, the provision of technical training or financing, and assistance in the operations of the business.

> Competitors are foreclosed from selling through valuable resellers.

> With a long-term exclusive relationship, sales forecasting may be easier, permitting the supplier to achieve more precise and efficient production and logistics.

> Resellers may obtain more stable prices and may gain more regular and frequent deliveries of the supplier's products.

> Transactions between resellers and the supplier may be fewer in number and larger in volume.

> Resellers and the supplier may be able to reduce administrative costs.

> Both resellers and the supplier may be able to secure specialized assets and long-term financing from each other.

> Resellers generally receive added promotional and other support, as well as avoiding the added inventory costs that go with carrying multiple brands.[61]

The example of Kodak and Fuji in the photofinishing business is illustrative. From 1954 until 1995, Kodak was prevented from linking sales of film to photofinishing (for example, by offering coupons in photofinishing envelopes good for Kodak film). When the consent decree was lifted, Kodak started making deals with U.S. retailers to be their exclusive provider of photofinishing services. By the end of 1996, Kodak had deals in place giving it exclusive rights at Kmart, Walgreen (a nationwide pharmacy chain), CVS (another national pharmacy chain), Eckerd (also a pharmacy chain), Price/Costco, and American Stores (the parent company of several U.S. grocery retailers). Meanwhile, Kodak's main rival, Fuji, signed a contract to be Wal-Mart's exclusive supplier of photofinishing services. Despite Fuji's signing with a retail giant like Wal-Mart, Kodak still controlled about 75 percent of the wholesale photofinishing market by the end of 1996. Retailers supported the exclusive agreements, citing the expense of upgrading photofinishing equipment and training staff.[62]

Requirements contracts are variants of exclusive dealing. Under requirements contracts, buyers agree to purchase all or a part of their requirements of a product from one seller, usually for a specified period and price. Such arrangements clearly reduce the freedom of choice of the buyer but guarantee the buyer a source of supply at a known cost, often over a very long period of time (e.g., 10 years).

Exclusive dealing lessens interbrand competition directly because competing brands available from other suppliers are excluded from outlets. Exclusive dealing and requirements contracts are circumscribed mainly by Section 3 of the Clayton Act, which stipulates that

> it shall be unlawful for any person . . . to lease or make a sale or contract for sale of goods, wares, merchandise, machinery, supplies or other commodities, whether patented or unpatented, . . . on the condition, agreement, or understanding that the lessee or purchaser thereof shall not use or deal in the goods, . . . of a competitor or competitors of the lessor or seller, where the effect of such lease, sale, or contract for sale or such condition, agreement or understanding may be to substantially lessen competition or tend to create a monopoly in any line of commerce.

However, these policies may also violate Section 1 of the Sherman Act and Section 5 of the FTC Act. Under the Sherman Act, various types of exclusive contracts may be deemed unlawful restraints of trade when a dominant firm is involved and when the contracts go so far beyond reasonable business needs as to have the necessary effect, or disclose a clear intention, of suppressing competition.[63]

The *Tampa Electric Co. v. Nashville Coal Co.* case, decided in 1961, established the modern guidelines for assessing exclusive dealing policies from an antitrust perspective (see Sidebar 10.7). The decision in this case indicates that the type of goods or merchandise, the geographic area of effective competition, and the substantiality of the competition foreclosed must all be assessed in determining illegality or legality. It also indicates that exclusive dealing arrangements or requirements contracts that are negotiated by sellers possessing a very small share of the relevant market have a good chance of standing up in court.[64] The critical issue may involve

Sidebar 10.7

Tampa Electric Co. v. Nashville Coal Co. case

The *Tampa Electric Co. v. Nashville Coal Co.* case[65] involved a contract between Nashville Coal and Tampa Electric, a Florida public utility producing electricity, covering Tampa's expected requirements of coal (i.e., not less than 500,000 tons per year) for a period of 20 years. Before any coal was delivered, Nashville declined to perform the contract on the ground that it was illegal under the antitrust laws because it amounted to an exclusive dealing arrangement, which foreclosed other suppliers from serving Tampa Electric. (In actuality, the price of coal had jumped, making the arrangement less profitable for the Nashville Coal Co.) Tampa brought suit, arguing that the contract was both valid and enforceable.

To be illegal, the court explained, such arrangements must have a tendency to work a substantial, not merely remote, lessening of competition in the relevant competitive market. Justice Clark, speaking for the majority, indicated that substantiality was to be determined by taking into account the following factors:

- The relative strength of the parties involved
- The proportionate volume of commerce involved in relation to the total volume of commerce in the relevant market area

- The probable immediate and future effects that preemption of that share of the market might have on effective competition within it

The district court and the court of appeals had accepted the argument that the contract foreclosed a substantial share of the market, because Tampa's requirements equaled the total volume of coal purchased in the state of Florida before the contract's inception. The Supreme Court, in an interesting piece of economic reasoning, defined the relevant market as the *supply* market in an eight-state area, noting that mines in that coal-producing region were eager to sell more coal in Florida. When the market was defined as the entire multistate Appalachian coal region, the foreclosure amounted to less than 1 percent of the tonnage produced each year. The Court concluded that given the nature of the market (i.e., the needs of a utility for a stable supply at reasonable prices over a long period as well as the level of concentration), the small percentage of foreclosure did not actually or potentially cause a substantial reduction of competition, nor did it tend toward a monopoly.

the definition of the relevant market; firms with large shares may still be circumscribed. When shares are sufficiently high (e.g., 30 to 40%), the so-called modified rule of reason standard established in *Tampa Electric* requires courts to examine the following factors:

- The duration of the contracts
- The likelihood of collusion in the industry and the degree to which other firms in the market also employ exclusive dealing
- The height of entry barriers
- The nature of the distribution system and distribution alternatives remaining available after exclusive dealing is taken into account
- Other obvious anti- or procompetitive effects, such as the prevention of free-riding and the encouragement of the reseller to promote the supplier's product more heavily[66]

Sidebar 10.8

R. J. Reynolds Tobacco Co. v. Philip Morris case

The U.S. cigarette maker Philip Morris, which had a 53 percent market share for cigarettes, initiated a "Retail Leaders" program in the fall of 1998. This was an incentive program for retailers that granted them significant benefits (including rebates of $5.50 or more per cigarette carton, as well as merchandising aid) in return for 100 percent of the visible display rights in the retail outlet and the exclusive right to offer consumer discounts for three months of each year. The company placed about 80,000 cigarette displays in retail outlets as a result of the program.

In March 1999, competitor R. J. Reynolds filed a lawsuit against Philip Morris (later joined by two other major competitors, Loew's Corporation's Lorillard unit and Brown & Williamson Tobacco Corp.), charging that Philip Morris was attempting to monopolize the U.S. cigarette market by making exclusive dealing arrangements with retailers.[67] The plaintiffs showed evidence that 14 percent of the smoking population (6 million adult smokers) had switched brands in the prior two years and that store displays are important tools in competing for these sales. Hence, they argued, Philip Morris's campaign would prevent them from fair competition for these sales and could increase Philip Morris's market share significantly. On June 29, 1999, a federal judge granted the plaintiffs' request for a preliminary injunction against Philip Morris, requiring Philip Morris to dismantle the program completely pending the conclusion of the lawsuit filed by the three rivals. The judge found that the program irreparably damaged Philip Morris's competitors and further, that Philip Morris would suffer no substantial hardship due to the injunction. This interim ruling illustrates how exclusive dealing by a dominant-market-share firm, when combined with a harm to competition, is looked upon dimly by the courts.[68]

Even though the *Tampa Electric* case was decided almost 40 years ago, legal battles surrounding exclusive dealing are very much alive, as exemplified in the case of *R. J. Reynolds v. Philip Morris,* charging that Philip Morris was attempting to monopolize the U.S. cigarette market by making exclusive dealing arrangements with retailers (see Sidebar 10.8). Although the case was dismissed on summary judgment in 2003, the court previously enjoined the defendants from practicing parts of their Retail Leaders program.[69]

Like the *R. J. Reynolds v. Philip Morris* case, the *Conwood Co. v. United States Tobacco Co.* case dealt with exclusive dealing issues in the context of category management by category captains. Category management, widely practiced in retail marketing channels today, involves a collaborative agreement between a retailer and one of its major suppliers (designated the category captain) in a particular product category. The category captain (supplier) is given detailed information on *all* the products in the category by the retailer (that is, on competitors' products as well as its own), and is expected to analyze the data and generate recommendations about how to better manage the entire category in the store. Recommendations can concern shelf space allocations for various products, pricing, and targeting of new products to the market.

The obvious risks of engaging in this behavior are (a) that the category captain's recommendations could lead to competitive exclusion, and (b) that the category captain will act to facilitate competitive collusion in the category rather than enhancing competition.[70]

In this context, the *Conwood* case centered on the alleged use of category management to exclude a small competitor. Sales in the U.S. market for moist snuff were $1.7 billion, and the United States Tobacco Company's (USTC) products accounted for 77 percent of market share, while Conwood had 13 percent of market share. Conwood sued USTC, claiming that its actions as a category manager constituted unlawful monopolization of the market and led to the exclusion of competition. Conwood won the case, with a $1.05 billion award against USTC. The court found that USTC urged retailers to carry fewer products, especially competitive ones; tried to control how many lower-priced brands were allowed into the market; and suggested that retailers carry USTC's slower-moving brands rather than better-selling competitive products, all deemed to be abuses of the category captain role. Further, the court ruled that because of these actions, retail prices for moist snuff rose in the market, harming consumer welfare as well.[71] The message in the case was that abuse of the category management process by a category captain can constitute clear violation of the antitrust laws.

Tying

Tying exists when a seller of a product or service that buyers want (the "tying product") refuses to sell it unless a second ("tied") product or service is also purchased, or at least is not purchased from anyone other than the seller of the tying product. Thus, a manufacturer of motion picture projectors (the tying product) might insist that only its film (the tied product) be used with the projectors, or a manufacturer of shoe machinery (the tying product) might insist that lessees of the machinery purchase service contracts (tied service) from it for the proper maintenance of the machinery.

Many of the business reasons for using tying policies are similar to those for using exclusive dealing; their immediate aim is to lock in the purchase of a supplier-specific brand and lock out the purchase of directly competing brands. Additional reasons for tying, beyond those that apply from the discussion of exclusive dealing, are:

> Transferring the market demand already established for the tying product (e.g., can closing machines) to the tied product (e.g., cans)

> Using the tied product (e.g., paper) to meter usage of the tying product (e.g., copying machines)

> Using a low-margin tying product (e.g., razors) to sell a high-margin tied product (e.g., blades)

> Achieving cost savings via package sales (e.g., the costs of supplying and servicing channel members might be lower, the greater the number of products included in the "package")

> Assuring the successful operation of the tying product (e.g., an automobile) by obliging dealers to purchase tied products (e.g., repair parts) from the supplier[72]

A tying agreement in effect forecloses competing sellers from the opportunity of selling the tied commodity or service to the purchaser. Indeed, like exclusive dealing policies, the critical issue in the condemnation of tying is the foreclosing of interbrand competition from a marketplace. But tying contracts are viewed much more negatively by the courts than exclusive dealing arrangements or requirements contracts. For example, in distinguishing between a requirements contract and a tying contract in the *Standard Stations* case, Justice Frankfurter stated that tying arrangements "serve hardly any purpose beyond the suppression of competition."[73] Like exclusive dealing, tying is circumscribed by the Sherman Act, the Clayton Act, and the FTC Act. Given the overwhelmingly negative attitude of the courts toward tying, it is little wonder that its use would rarely be approved.

However, certain types of tying contracts are legal. The courts have ruled that if two products are made to be used jointly and one will not function properly without the other, a tying agreement is within the law. (Shoes are sold in pairs, and automobiles are sold with tires.) In other cases, if a company's goodwill depends on proper operation of equipment, a service contract may be tied to the sale or lease of the machine.[74] The practicality of alternatives to the tying arrangement appears to be crucial. If a firm will suffer injury unless it can protect its product, and there is no feasible alternative, the courts permit tying agreements. Despite these exceptions, the general rule is that tying agreements are presumptively anticompetitive, although defenses are still available.

Serious legal questions regarding tying agreements have been raised relative to the franchising of restaurants and other eating places, motels, and movie theaters, among others. As detailed in Chapter 13, an individual or group of individuals (franchisees) are usually permitted to set up outlets of a national chain in return for a capital investment and a periodic fee to the parent company (the franchisor). In some cases, the parent company also requires the franchise holders to buy various supplies, such as meat, baked goods, and paper cups in the case of restaurants, either from the corporation or an approved supplier.

In franchising, the tying product is the franchise itself and the tied products are the supplies that the franchisee must purchase to operate his business. Companies with such requirements have argued that they are necessary in order to maintain the quality of their services and reputation. However, critics of such agreements assert that franchisors often require franchisees to purchase supplies and raw materials at prices far above those of the competitive market. The potential for a conflict of interest on the part of the franchisors is high.

In franchising, the primary tying product is the trademark itself (e.g., McDonald's, Budget car rentals, Sheraton hotels). Therefore, tying agreements that link the trademark to supplies have been sustained by the courts only when franchisors have been able to prove that their trademarks are inseparable from their supplies and that the tied product (the supplies) are, in fact, essential to the maintenance of quality control. For example, in a lawsuit involving Baskin-Robbins, a chain of franchised ice cream stores, certain franchisees contended the Baskin-Robbins ice cream products were unlawfully tied to the license of the Baskin-Robbins trademark.[75] However, the tie-in claim was disallowed because the franchisees did not establish that the trademark was a product separate from the ice cream; in tying cases, two distinct products must be involved in order for tying to be present.

In a decision involving the Chock full o'Nuts Corporation, it was held that the franchisor "successfully proved its affirmative defense (to tying charges) of maintaining quality control with regard to its coffee and baked goods."[76] On the other hand, Chock full o'Nuts was unsuccessful in defending its tying practices with respect to a number of other products (e.g., french fries, soft drink syrups, napkins, and glasses). These products were viewed as illegally tied to the franchise because they were easily reproducible.

Full-Line Forcing

One special form of product policy is called full-line forcing. Here a seller's leverage with a product is used to force a buyer to purchase its whole line of goods. This policy is illegal if competitive sellers are unreasonably prevented from market access. In the case of a farm machinery manufacturer, a court held that the practice was within the law but implied that full-line forcing that caused the exclusion of competitors from this part of the market might be illegal if a substantial share of business was affected.[77]

Block booking imposed by motion picture distributors and producers on independent theater owners can also be viewed as full-line forcing or tying. This practice compels theaters to take many pictures they do not want in order to obtain the ones they do. Independent producers have consequently been unable to rent their films to theaters whose programs were thus crowded with the products of the major firms. Similar arrangements have been found in the sale of motion picture packages to television. Such practices have typically been held to be illegal, especially when copyrighted films have been used as tying mechanisms.[78]

Other instances of prohibition of full-line forcing have occurred. For example, E&J Gallo Winery, the largest seller of wine in the United States, consented to a Federal Trade Commission order prohibiting it, among other things, from requiring its wholesalers to distribute any Gallo wines in order to obtain other kinds.[79] Similarly, Union Carbide Corporation agreed to a consent order prohibiting the company from requiring its dealers to purchase from it their total requirements of six industrial gases (acetylene, argon, helium, hydrogen, nitrogen, and oxygen) and from making the purchase of the six gases a prerequisite for dealers' buying other gases or welding products.[80]

Even though tying has been labeled per se illegal, courts have sought answers to a number of critical questions before condemning these policies. For example, it is necessary to determine when conditions of economic power exist. In theory, where no leverage exists in a product, there can be no tying arrangement by coercion; the buyer can always go elsewhere to purchase. Thus, plaintiffs must prove more than the existence of a tie. As Sullivan points out, they must also show that the tying product is successfully differentiated and that the commerce affected by the tie is significant.[81] Therefore, the presumption against tying arrangements is not quite as strong as the per se rule against horizontal price-fixing conspiracies. Evidence of this comes from a 1984 U.S. Supreme Court case involving hospital services (see Sidebar 10.9). The *Jefferson Parish* case provides the foundation on which other tying cases are to be analyzed.

The issues on which courts are most likely to focus are whether (a) there are two distinct products, (b) the seller has required the buyer to purchase the tied product in

Sidebar 10.9

Jefferson Parish Hospital District No. 2 v. Hyde case

In the *Jefferson Parish* case,[82] anesthesiologist Edwin Hyde, who had been denied admission to the staff of East Jefferson Hospital, sued the governance board of the hospital because the hospital had an exclusive contract with a firm of anesthesiologists requiring that all anesthesiological services for the hospital's patients be performed by that firm. The Supreme Court agreed with the district court that the relevant geographic market was Jefferson Parish (i.e., metropolitan New Orleans) and not the neighborhood immediately surrounding East Jefferson Hospital. The Court reasoned that "Seventy percent of the patients residing in Jefferson Parish enter hospitals other than East Jefferson. . . . Thus, East Jefferson's 'dominance' over persons residing in Jefferson Parish is far from overwhelming."

The Court further explained that "the fact that the exclusive contract requires purchase of two services that would otherwise be purchased separately does not make the contract illegal. Only if patients are forced to purchase the contracting firm's services as a result of the hospital's market power would the arrangement have anticompetitive consequences." East Jefferson's market power was not significant enough to make the contract illegal.

The most important dictum in the *Jefferson Parish* decision was the following sentence, which provides the foundation on which other tying cases are to be analyzed:

The essential characteristic of an invalid tying arrangement lies in the seller's exploitation of its control over the tying product to force the buyer into the purchase of a tied product that the buyer either did not want at all, or might have preferred to purchase elsewhere on different terms.[83]

order to obtain the tying product, (c) the seller has sufficient market power to force a tie-in, (d) the tying arrangement affects a substantial amount of commerce in the market for the tied product, and (e) whether the tie is necessary to fulfill a legitimate business purpose. However, these structural per se criteria are not likely to be satisfied for sellers with relatively small market shares, especially when the tying product is unpatented.[84] The Eastman Kodak case profiled in Sidebar 10.10 illustrates a successful prosecution on these criteria.

The criteria are more likely to be satisfied in situations typified by the FTC's 1991 investigation of Sandoz Pharmaceuticals Corp., which was accused of violating antitrust laws by requiring buyers of Clozaril, a drug for schizophrenia, to also purchase a weekly blood test from a company under contract with Sandoz.[85] Sandoz's dominant position relative to the specific drug category under investigation was obvious at the time. The company agreed to settle the charges by promising not to require Clozaril purchasers to buy the blood monitoring service from Sandoz or anyone designated by Sandoz.[86]

In Europe, reactions similar to those in the Sandoz situation are evident. For example, in 1994, Tetra Pak, the Swedish packaging group, lost an appeal case. The European Commission Court found, among other things, that customer contracts that

Sidebar 10.10

Eastman Kodak Co. v. Image Technical Service, Inc., case

One of the most remarkable and significant cases involving tying was decided by the U.S. Supreme Court on June 8, 1992. At that time, the Court ruled that Eastman Kodak Company would have to stand trial on a tying claim brought against it by 18 independent service organizations (ISOs).[87] The case arose out of Kodak's efforts to keep to itself the business of servicing Kodak-brand copiers. Kodak had refused to sell replacement parts to the ISOs that wanted to service Kodak copiers. They alleged that Kodak's conduct amounted to an illegal monopolization of the business of servicing Kodak-brand copiers and an illegal tying of the sale of servicing copiers to the sale of replacement parts.

To succeed on the tying claim, the ISOs had to prove that Kodak had "appreciable market power" in the business of selling replacement parts for Kodak-brand copiers. To succeed on the monopolization claim, the ISOs had to prove that Kodak had "monopoly power" in the sale of the replacement parts. Kodak argued that sales of its copiers represented, at most,

23 percent of the sale of copiers for all manufacturers, and the Supreme Court agreed that the 23 percent share did not amount to appreciable power in the copier sales business. Nonetheless, the Court found that Kodak controlled nearly 100 percent of the market for its replacement parts—which are not interchangeable with the parts of other manufacturer's machines—and between 80 percent and 95 percent of the service market.

The Court reasoned that the relevant market for antitrust purposes is determined by the choices available to Kodak equipment owners who must use Kodak parts. Thus, Kodak's motion for summary judgment (i.e., it wanted the Supreme Court to dismiss the case because of its lack of market power in the copier market) was rejected by a 6 to 3 vote, and the case was sent back to the federal district court in San Francisco for trial. Kodak lost verdicts both in that trial and in an appeal to the Ninth U.S. Circuit Court of Appeals in August 1997, and was ordered to pay $35 million to the eleven plaintiffs in the case.[88]

tied Tetra Pak machine users to using Tetra Pak cartons were not objectively justified and were intended to strengthen the company's dominant position in such packaging by reinforcing its customers' economic dependence on it.[89]

Designated Product Policies

A manufacturer may want to sell some portion of its product line only through a limited number of resellers, while its other resellers may sell a different subset of the company's products. For instance, very sophisticated Toro brand lawnmowers may sell only through authorized service-providing Toro dealers, while less exclusive products (such as lawn edging tools) can sell through mass merchandisers as well. Such a policy can help preserve the manufacturer's exclusive brand name and prevent its erosion through overly broad distribution through outlets with an insufficiently high quality image or service provision capabilities. Further, this is an effective way to give resellers reasonable profit-making opportunities. If the reseller has at least some products for which there is little or no competition, it can confidently invest in customer service and promotional activities, secure in the knowledge that its efforts will not fall victim to free riding by other resellers.

In the United States, a manufacturer has no legal obligation to sell all of its products to all resellers who wish to do so, under most circumstances. Two exceptions apply. One is the situation where the manufacturer is a monopolist with excess capacity. Then, because there is no other source for the product, the manufacturer is required to supply it to requesting resellers. This was the case when AT&T was forced to open its exchanges to the independent long-distance phone companies MCI and Sprint in the United States; AT&T was the only holder of these exchanges and thus was required to grant access to its competitors.

The other exception is the case where the manufacturer has signed a contract with its reseller promising to supply all of its products. In this case, the manufacturer is required to honor the contract. Beyond these two exceptions, however, there is still the usual antitrust restriction that a refusal to deal with a reseller is not the result of a conspiracy or other agreement in restraint of trade. An interesting instance of a case in this area involved the toy retailer Toys "R" Us, summarized in Sidebar 10.11. The situation is somewhat unusual because it was Toys "R" Us, the retailer, rather than a manufacturer, that was accused of instigating limited access to various manufacturers' products at competing retailers. In a ruling against Toys "R" Us, FTC chairman Robert Pitofsky wrote that it had "used its dominant position as toy distributor to extract agreements from and among toy manufacturers to stop selling to warehouse clubs the same toys that they had sold to other toy distributors." Although the ultimate case was settled by all parties, payments made by Toys "R" Us and the toy manufacturers who were also defendants indicates that the degree of harm to competition and the concerted effort made to influence multiple manufacturers, who all agreed to the restrictive dealing practices, were key factors in the outcome.

SELECTION AND TERMINATION POLICIES

A central theme throughout this text is that organizations must devote a great deal of time, attention, effort, and monetary resources to the design and management of their distribution systems. To achieve success with their marketing channels, channel managers must set selection criteria with regard to potential channel partners and must monitor the performance of anyone admitted to the distribution system. Even with intensive distribution systems, selection procedures are necessary because it is unlikely that every conceivable outlet will be asked to sell every intensively distributed product. (Department stores are not typically asked to sell milk, for example.) Anytime anyone establishes selection criteria, the likelihood is extremely high that someone will not make the cut-off, no matter how low the standards for admission are set. Therefore, refusing to deal with certain channel members is a key element of channel policy. The same rationale applies to performance criteria, which means that another key element of channel policy is termination.

Sellers can select their own distributors according to their own criteria and judgment. They may also announce in advance the circumstances under which they would

Sidebar 10.11

U.S. Federal Trade Commission v. Toys "R" Us case

This case is somewhat unusual because it was Toys "R" Us, the *retailer*, rather than a manufacturer, who was accused of instigating limited access to various manufacturers' products at competing retailers.[90] In May 1996, the Federal Trade Commission filed charges against Toys "R" Us, alleging that the retailer threatened not to buy any toy whose manufacturer also sold the toy through a warehouse club store chain. It thus effectively forced the suppliers into exclusive dealing with Toys "R" Us for the most popular toys in the market. In particular, the charges alleged that Toys "R" Us did this to prevent warehouse clubs like Sam's Club, Price Club, and Costco from competing with Toys "R" Us. The threat to Toys "R" Us was real, because the warehouse clubs had a much lower cost structure than Toys "R" Us and, therefore, could effectively price compete, given product supply. For example, Mattel's Hollywood Hair Barbie was offered at a retail price of $10.99 at Toys "R" Us, but was only sold to warehouse clubs packaged with an extra dress, forcing the retail price up to $15.99 and preventing direct price comparisons between Toys "R" Us and other retailers. Hasbro, another toy manufacturer, refused to supply "Hall of Fame G.I. Joe" dolls directly to warehouse clubs; Mattel also declined to offer Fisher-Price brand pool tables to warehouse clubs; and Toys "R" Us allegedly blocked sales of Disney's "Toy Story" movie figures to the discount chains as well. The FTC argued that the anticompetitive threat was great because Toys "R" Us had an approximate 20 percent market share of all U.S. retail toy sales. While this figure was seen as somewhat low overall, the relevant manufacturers sold as much as 30 percent of their total volume through Toys "R" Us, thus creating a significant degree of dependence on the retailer and allowing Toys "R" Us to force them into anticompetitive actions. Further, after Toys "R" Us

started this enforced boycott in 1993, Costco Co.'s toy sales dropped by 1.6 percent, even while its overall sales grew by 19.5 percent. Mattel's sales to warehouse clubs fell from over $23 million in 1991 to only $7.5 million in 1993.

On October 1, 1997, an FTC administrative judge ruled against Toys "R" Us, and while awaiting review by the full commission, New York's attorney general filed a lawsuit against Toys "R" Us and three of its largest suppliers (Mattel, Hasbro, and Rubbermaid, Inc.'s, Little Tikes Co.), alleging an illegal conspiracy to raise prices and stifle competition. On November 17, the suit was amended to add 37 additional states, Puerto Rico, and Washington, D.C., to the lawsuit. Eventually 44 of the 50 states joined the lawsuit. On October 15, 1998, the FTC upheld the administrative law judge's 1997 ruling, issuing a cease and desist order to Toys "R" Us. FTC chairman Robert Pitofsky wrote that Toys "R" Us had "used its dominant position as toy distributor to extract agreements from and among toy manufacturers to stop selling to warehouse clubs the same toys that they had sold to other toy distributors." The retailer appealed this decision to the U.S. Circuit Court of Appeals.

In December 1998, Hasbro settled in the suit filed by the states, agreeing to pay $6 million in donations and other payments to the states and charities. In May 1999, Toys "R" Us and the other suppliers also settled in that lawsuit. Toys "R" Us agreed to pay a total of $40.5 million in cash and toy donations in the settlement. Mattel agreed to pay $8.2 million in cash and toy donations, and Little Tikes agreed to pay $1.3 million in cash and toys. None of the parties admitted wrongdoing in agreeing to the settlement. The key to the case was both the degree of harm to competition and the concerted effort made to influence multiple manufacturers, all of whom agreed to the restrictive dealing practices.

refuse to sell to certain intermediaries. These two commercial freedoms were granted in *U.S. v. Colgate & Co.* in 1919 and are referred to as the Colgate doctrine.[91] The doctrine was formally recognized by Congress in Section 2(a) of the Robinson-Patman Act, which reads that "nothing herein contained shall prevent persons engaged in selling goods, wares, or merchandise in commerce from selecting their own customers in bona fide transactions and not in restraint of trade." Implicit in a seller's general right to select its preferred distribution system is the right to deal with certain channel members on a limited basis. General Motors, for example, is not obligated to sell Chevrolets to a Buick dealer.

The Colgate doctrine contains two explicit exceptions. First, the decision not to deal must be independent, or unilateral (i.e., it cannot be part of a concerted action). This was one of the problems faced by the toy manufacturers named in the *Toys "R" Us* case: It would not have been illegal for any of the manufacturers named in the case to unilaterally refuse to sell a particular product to warehouse club stores. It was rather the concerted effort led by Toys "R" Us that made the action illegal. Second, the refusal must occur in the absence of any intent to create or maintain a monopoly. If a unilateral refusal to deal is ever illegal, it is when the refusal is undertaken by a monopolist or by someone who hopes by the refusal to become one.[92]

Clearly, refusal to deal is a major punishment underlying a channel member's coercive power. After a number of court decisions dealing with the right of refusal to deal, that right has been narrowly confined. Suppliers may formally cut off dealers for valid business reasons, such as failure to pay or poor performance in sales or service. But where the suppliers have set up restrictive, regulated, or programmed distribution systems and there are complaints that the dealers who are being cut off have somehow stepped out of line with the edicts of the programmed system, refusal to deal becomes harder to defend. Losing such a lawsuit imposes treble damages on the defendant, so the stakes are high. The courts generally ask two important questions in determining whether a refusal to deal violates the law:

> ➤ Was the decision to delete certain channel members a unilateral decision on the part of the manufacturer?
> ➤ Was there a legitimate business reason for the change in channel membership?[93]

Many cases continue to be brought under Sections 1 and 2 of the Sherman Act involving decisions by suppliers or franchisors to terminate an existing dealer, to substitute a new for an old dealer, or to vertically integrate. Although it appears the original selection of distributors or dealers for a new product poses no legal problems, it is increasingly clear that the termination of existing distributors and dealers can cause difficulties, even in the absence of group boycotts or conspiracies. It is risky to drop a distributor or dealer who refuses to do as the manufacturer asks.[94] Thus, when a supplier has applied exclusive dealing, customer or territorial restrictions, or other types of vertical restraints within its distribution network and when a dealer is cut off from that network, the dealer may take the supplier to court, charging that the refusal to deal was based on the supplier's desire to maintain an unlawful practice.

The orientation toward litigation in these cases has been furthered by particularistic legislation, such as the Automobile Dealers Franchise Act of 1956, which entitles a car dealer to sue any car manufacturer who fails to act in good faith in connection with the termination, cancellation, or nonrenewal of the dealer's franchise. It is open to the manufacturer, however, to produce evidence that the dealer has not acted in good faith and that its own action was thereby justified. In nearly all the cases to date, this defense has been successful.[95] Nevertheless, many lawsuits are filed every year by franchisees who claim to be wrongly terminated by franchisors. Most of these cases are fought over contract and property rights; few of them involve antitrust.

Outside the United States, a manufacturer's right to terminate resellers varies widely from country to country. In many countries, it is very difficult to terminate a distributor, particularly if the distributor has been the exclusive representative of the manufacturer's product. Given the wide variation in the laws on termination in various areas, a manufacturer seeking to expand distribution transnationally must check local regulations carefully.

OWNERSHIP POLICIES

The make versus buy (vertical integration) question is another central concern in this text (see Chapter 9). Here, we focus on the antitrust concerns surrounding vertical integration. Frequently, the decision to vertically integrate puts a company in competition with independent channel intermediaries that are already carrying or being asked to carry the company's brands. We have already argued that most suppliers, for example, will have a number of different channels so that the needs of various market segments can be addressed. In most cases, one of those channels is a direct channel comprised of salespeople employed by the company. Clearly, dual distribution is the rule rather than the exception.

Vertical integration may come about through forward integration by a producer, backward integration by a retailer, or integration in either direction by a wholesaler or a logistics firm, such as a common carrier. Integration may be brought about by the creation of a new business function by existing firms (internal expansion) or by acquisition of the stock or the assets of other firms (mergers).

The two methods of creating integration are fundamentally different in their relationship to the law. Internal expansion is regulated by Section 2 of the Sherman Act, which prohibits monopoly or attempts to monopolize any part of the interstate or foreign commerce of the United States. External expansion is regulated by Section 7 of the Clayton Act, which prohibits the purchase of stock or assets of other firms if the effects may be to substantially lessen competition or tend to create a monopoly in any line of commerce in any part of the country.[96] Internal expansion is given favored treatment under the law, according to the theory that internal expansion expands investment and production and thus increases competition, whereas growth by merger removes an entity from the market.

Integration, whether by merger or internal expansion, may result in the lowering of costs and make possible more effective interorganizational management of the channel. It may also be a means of avoiding many of the legal problems previously discussed because an integrated firm is free to control prices and allocate products to its integrated outlets without conflict with the laws governing restrictive distribution policies.

Vertical Integration by Merger

The danger posed by vertical mergers from an antitrust perspective is the same as that posed by many of the policies already discussed in this chapter—the possibility that vertical integration will foreclose competitors by limiting their access to sources of supply or to customers. Thus, prior to the purchase of McCaw Cellular by AT&T in 1994, the U.S. Justice Department focused attention on the fact that AT&T makes equipment, such as radio towers, that some of McCaw's competitors, including several regional Bell operating companies, use in their cellular-phone operations. Officials were concerned that the merger would give AT&T an incentive to charge McCaw's competitors more while providing poor service.[97]

Similarly, in 1993, when Merck (the world's largest drug company), bought Medco Containment Services (the largest distributor of discount prescription medicines in the United States) for $6.6 billion, competitors raised antitrust concerns about foreclosure from Medco. Indeed, when Eli Lilly, another major pharmaceutical manufacturer, indicated in 1994 that it wanted to purchase PCS Health Systems, another enormous managed care drug distributor, for $4 billion, it agreed to restrictions imposed by the Federal Trade Commission preventing it from unfairly pushing sales of its own brands through PCS or gaining information about prices at which competing drugs sell.[98] In a statement announcing its decision to reexamine the Merck/Medco merger and another one involving SmithKline Beechham (SKB) and Diversified Pharmaceutical Services (DPS), the FTC said, "We remain concerned about the overall competitive impact of vertical integration by drug companies into the pharmacy benefits management market."[99] Although all of these mergers (including AT&T–McCaw) eventually were approved, the questions that were raised indicate that from time to time vertical mergers will draw the attention of the antitrust enforcement agencies.

The most significant vertical merger case in the United States over the last 45 years was decided in 1962 when the U.S. Supreme Court declared the merger of the Brown Shoe Company and the G. R. Kinney Company, the largest independent chain of shoe stores, illegal because the Court believed the merger would foreclose other manufacturers from selling through Kinney.[100] However, since the 1970s, the government has refrained from challenging vertical mergers by and large. In its 1982 Merger Guidelines, the Justice Department announced that it would challenge vertical mergers only when they facilitated collusion or significantly raised barriers to new entry.[101] Nevertheless, this should not be interpreted to mean that the issue is dead and gone. In addition to the drug mergers mentioned above, the Federal Trade Commission became active in 1994 when TCI and Comcast, the largest and third-largest cable-TV companies in the United States, agreed to form a joint venture to take ownership of QVC. At the time, QVC was one of two cable-shopping ventures that controlled 98 percent of sales made via TV. The other was Home Shopping Network, which was 79 percent controlled by TCI. The vertical issue investigated by the Federal Trade Commission was whether existing and potential competitors to QVC and Home Shopping Network would have trouble selling on cable TV because TCI and Comcast together controlled access to about 30 percent of cable-wired homes.[102] The merger was finally approved because the relevant market was defined as all of retailing, not just home shopping via television.

Vertical mergers also have attracted attention outside the United States. For example, in 1990, Grand Metropolitan, the United Kingdom food, beverage, and retailing conglomerate, and Elders IXL, the Australian brewer, agreed to a $5 billion pubs-for-breweries swap. Grand Met was to transfer its four breweries and the Ruddles, Watneys, Truman, and Webster's beer brands to Courage, owned by Elder, whereas Courage was to combine its 4,900 pubs with GrandMet's 3,570 pubs. A major challenge to the merger arose when the United Kingdom's Monopolies and Mergers Commission issued a 500-page report concluding that the United Kingdom's large breweries were operating a "complex monopoly"—a series of practices that restrict competition. These were said to be centered on the long-established tied-house system, which ensures that most of Britain's 80,000 pubs stock the products of only one supplier—the company that owns them.[103] The merger was allowed but only after the British government put into effect "guest beer orders" allowing pubs to stock beers from suppliers other than the ones that own them.[104]

Vertical Integration by Internal Expansion

This form of integration is limited only by the laws preventing monopoly or attempts to monopolize. A firm is ordinarily free to set up its own supply, distribution, and/or retailing system unless doing so would overconcentrate the market for its product.[105] Section 7 of the Clayton Act specifically permits a firm to set up subsidiary corporations to carry on business or extensions thereof if competition is not substantially reduced.

Dual Distribution

The term *dual distribution* describes a wide variety of marketing arrangements in which a manufacturer or a wholesaler reaches its final markets by employing two or more different types of channels for the same basic product. However, the dual arrangement (whereby manufacturers market their products through competing vertically integrated and independently owned outlets on either the wholesale or retail level) often creates controversy. This practice is customary in many lines of trade, such as the automotive passenger tire, personal computer, paint, and petroleum industries. Dual distribution also takes place when a manufacturer sells similar products under different brand names for distribution through different channels. This latter kind of dual distribution comes about because of market segmentation, or because of sales to distributors under private labels.

In all dual distribution situations, conflict among channel members is likely to be relatively high. Serious legal questions arise mainly in two situations: (1) when price squeezing is suspected or (2) when horizontal combinations or conspiracies are possible among competitors. The first situation brings about issues comparable to those found when examining the use of functional discounts. The second relates to potential restraints of trade arrived at in concert by vertically integrated firms and their customers.

Price Squeezes

A seller operating at only one market level in competition with a powerful vertically integrated firm might be subject to a price squeeze at its particular level. For example, a manufacturer of fabricated aluminum might be under pressure from its raw material (ingot) supplier to increase prices. If the supplier were also a fabricator, it could take its gain from the price increase (which represents higher costs to the customer-competitor) and use all or a portion of the increased returns for marketing activities at the fabricating level. This was exactly the scenario in the *Alcoa* case.[106] A number of lower court decisions have declared unlawful an integrated supplier's attempt to eliminate a customer as a competitor by undercutting the customer's prices and placing the customer in a price squeeze.[107]

The same kind of competitive inequality arises from granting functional discounts when different functional categories may be represented by buyers that, at least in part of their trade, are in competition with each other. As was the situation in the previously mentioned *Hasbrouck* case, oil jobbers, for example, sometimes sell at retail, and they may use their functional discounts received as jobbers to advantage in competition with retailers. Such pricing raises the possibility of Robinson-Patman Act as well as Sherman Act violations.

Horizontal Combinations or Conspiracies

In dual distribution situations, the distinction between purely vertical restraints and horizontal restraints may be critical in determining the legality of a marketing activity. Section 1 of the Sherman Act is not violated by the purely unilateral action of a supplier; there must be at least one additional party present that the court may find contracted, combined, or conspired with the supplier. Dominant manufacturers may replace distributors, but they may not enter into competition with them and destroy them.

In sum, each challenge to dual distribution is generally appraised in terms of its special circumstance. Whenever a supplier competes directly with its customers, however, any of its actions that threaten the customers are likely to be subject to antitrust scrutiny. The question of intent will be crucial. The decision may rest on the issues raised in the *Sylvania* case discussed earlier in this chapter. There, the Supreme Court mandated a balancing of the effects of a marketing policy on intrabrand and interbrand competition in situations involving vertical restraints.

SUMMARY AND CONCLUSIONS

The setting of channel policies is at the center of distribution strategy. Policies are rules to guide the functioning of channels. They are the means by which channel managers can achieve effective integration, coordination, and role performance throughout the channel in the absence of outright ownership. However, whenever policies are set, the potential for conflict arises because policies tend to be exclusionary, elitist, or restrictive. That is, policies are used to focus or redirect efforts of channel members and to assure that behavior within channels is not random. These limits on behavior have evoked a series of antitrust concerns.

Six different but frequently interrelated channel policy areas have been addressed in this chapter. They deal with market coverage, customer coverage, pricing, product lines, selection and termination, and ownership. Regarding market coverage, the major focus is on the geographic spacing of channel members. It is in this policy area where attention is given to intensive versus selective versus exclusive distribution. The more intensive distribution becomes, the greater the sales a company can expect in the short run. However, over time, channel members will be less and less willing to provide costly service outputs because of the price competition that is likely to ensue from the presence of many intrabrand competitors in the same territory. This fact compels suppliers to consider selective and exclusive distribution policies, thereby dampening the amount of intrabrand competition. Following the *Sylvania* case, the legality of these policies is determined under the rule of reason doctrine.

Marketing managers may also wish to assure that only the right channel members service specific kinds of customers. They may want company-employed salespeople to call on technically sophisticated heavy users and distributor salespeople to call on other kinds of accounts. Or they may want authorized dealers to sell the company's brand only to end-users and to prevent them from acting like master distributors making sales to other, unauthorized dealers. Antitrust enforcement agencies often categorize these and other customer coverage policies as customer or resale restrictions. They are governed by the same line of reasoning applied to market coverage policies.

Both market and customer coverage policies have an indirect effect on prices. Direct effects are achieved via price setting procedures. Although a host of pricing policies can be adopted in marketing channels, two of particular interest here are price maintenance and price discrimination. The former deals with the setting of specific resale prices throughout a marketing channel. The latter deals with setting different prices to different buyers. Minimum resale price maintenance is per se illegal if there is some form of agreement or concerted action between or among channel members involved in setting or policing the policy. Otherwise, it can be adopted unilaterally. Maximum resale price maintenance (when arrived at by agreement) is now subject to a rule of reason and hence may be implemented as long as there are no anticompetitive effects. Price discrimination is at the heart of market segmentation strategies but can run afoul of the law if it substantially lessens competition. It covers such significant activities as the granting of promotional allowances and services and the offering of quantity and functional discounts.

The product line policies addressed in this chapter—exclusive dealing, tying, and full-line forcing—are all adopted with the aim of gaining the undivided attention of channel members on suppliers' products. They restrict interbrand competition directly, whereas market and customer coverage policies restrict intrabrand competition. Because of this potential for foreclosing competitors, antitrust agencies sometimes show more concern about them than about the coverage policies. Exclusive dealing is the requirement by a supplier that its distributor sell or lease only its products or at least no products in direct competition with the supplier's products. Tying is the requirement that customers purchase other products in order to obtain a product they desire. Full-line forcing is a variant of tying, under which the buyer must buy the entire line of items to obtain one item.

Finally, the vertical integration question is addressed by ownership policies. If the decision has been made to make (own one's own distribution system or source of supply) rather than to buy (deal with independently owned channel intermediaries or suppliers), then the choice remaining is either acquisition (or merger) or internal expansion. Internal expansion seems to pose little problem from an antitrust perspective. Until recently, the same was true for vertical mergers, but in the wake of acquisition and merger activity in the pharmaceutical and entertainment distribution channels, the issue has been brought back to life. In any case, when vertical integration takes place and the company continues to employ other, nonintegrated channels as well, conflicts often arise with regard to the common dual distribution problem.

This chapter has addressed only federal antitrust law, with a predominantly U.S. focus. The states of the United States have become much more active in the antitrust arena, and therefore, marketing executives would make a serious mistake to ignore the vast outpouring of legislation and court case precedents regulating distribution practices in each of the states in which the products of their companies are sold. In addition, antitrust and competitive laws vary widely throughout different countries of the world. It behooves the international channel manager to become familiar with local variations.

Take-Aways

- Many channel policies and decisions potentially fall under the scrutiny of antitrust authorities, including:
  - Market coverage policies
  - Customer coverage policies
  - Pricing policies
  - Product line policies
  - Selection and termination policies
  - Ownership policies
- The main laws in the United States affecting these activities are the Sherman Antitrust Act of 1890, the Clayton Antitrust Act of 1914, the Federal Trade Commission (FTC) Act of 1914, the Robinson-Patman Act of 1936, and FTC Trade Practice Rules.
- Key elements of these laws include:
  - The prohibition of conspiracies in restraint of interstate or foreign trade
  - The prohibition of price discrimination, exclusive dealing, tying contracts, interlocking directorates among competitors, and mergers and acquisitions, when any of these substantially lessens competition
  - The prohibition of unfair or deceptive trade practices
  - The identification of defenses for price discrimination:
    - Used in good faith to meet the competition
    - Backed by real differences in cost to serve different customers

- • The lower price was available to all customers but not chosen by them
  - • When price discrimination does not harm competition (e.g., when used to set different prices to different segments of final end-users, who by definition do not compete)

- • One of the guiding principles of antitrust law enforcement is the impact of the business practice on *intrabrand* versus *interbrand* competition. The courts sometimes allow the restriction of intrabrand competition when it serves to enhance interbrand competition.

- • An action that is deemed *per se illegal* is illegal under all circumstances, regardless of the reason for the action or of any other implications of the action. An action that is illegal only under a rule of reason is one for which mitigating circumstances can permit its use.

- • The legality of certain business practices, like resale price maintenance, has changed over time; minimum RPM was deemed per se illegal until the mid-1980s, and maximum RPM until the late 1980s. Now, however, both are considered under a rule of reason. To be considered legal, the following should be true of the RPM practice:
  - • It is not undertaken as part of an agreement to restrain trade.
  - • It is therefore undertaken unilaterally.
  - • It does not use coercion.
  - • It is announced up front rather than being imposed after the fact.

- • Functional discounts are a useful channel tool to align the incentives of manufacturers and their channel partners, and under antitrust law, they are legal as long as they obey the laws governing price discrimination.

- • Exclusive dealing is illegal when a dominant firm is involved and when the agreement serves to suppress competition in the market.

- • Tying contracts, involving requirements that the buyer purchase a second product (the tied product) when a first product (the tying product) is bought, are generally illegal unless it can be shown that the two products are made to be used jointly and one will not function properly without the other.

- • U.S. antitrust law defends the right of a seller to choose which resellers have access to its product and to choose *not* to sell to certain intermediaries, under the 1919 Colgate doctrine. The exception to this rule occurs when the seller is a monopolist (and therefore denying access to the product to any particular intermediary would be denying that firm access to the market at large).

- • Channel alteration through vertical integration (the purchase of an upstream or downstream channel partner) is generally allowed unless by doing so the combined firm would monopolize the market or otherwise stifle competition. The law treats vertical integration by internal expansion more favorably than vertical integration by merger or acquisition of another preexisting firm.

- • The focus of this chapter is primarily on U.S. law affecting channel management policies. The manager is urged to learn the details of antitrust law in other countries in which the company operates channels because they can differ widely from U.S. laws.

DISCUSSION QUESTIONS

1. Debate the pros and cons of the following policies for the products listed below. (Do not be concerned about the antitrust issues; just ask yourself whether you would adopt them from a managerial point of view.)

Policies	Products/Brands
Exclusive distribution	Ping brand golf clubs
Price maintenance	General Electric washing machines
Tying	DeWalt power tools
Exclusive dealing	Copeland compressors
Price discrimination	Wrigley chewing gum
	Mead notepads
	Liz Claiborne pants

2. Which is preferable, intrabrand or interbrand competition? Can there be one without the other? Where do you stand on the issue of intrabrand competition: Is it necessary in order for there to be viable general competition from a macro perspective? Discuss these questions in the context of resale restrictions and the granting of exclusive territories.

3. Which of the policies discussed in this chapter are governed by the following legal rules and why: (a) rule of reason, (b) per se illegal, (c) modified rule of reason, and (d) per se legal?

4. Do you believe that the Robinson-Patman Act should be stricken from the laws of the United States? Debate the pros and cons of this question and come out with a position on it.

5. The president of an automobile accessory manufacturing business wants to purchase a chain of automotive retail stores. What managerial questions might you raise about the decision? What legal issues might this raise?

6. Name five uses of coercive power that would be legal in interorganizational management. Name five uses of reward power that would be legal.

7. From a strictly managerial perspective, what are the differences between market coverage and customer coverage policies? Do they accomplish the same or different ends in the same or different ways? If different, why do you think they were coupled together in the *Sylvania* case by the Supreme Court justices? Was this a mistake?

8. Which conflict management strategies suggested in Chapter 7 might be questionable from a legal perspective? Why?

ENDNOTES

1. *Continental T.V., Inc., v. GTE Sylvania, Inc.,* 433 U.S. 36 (1977).

2. Dutta, Shantanu, Jan B. Heide, and Mark Bergen (1999), "Vertical Territorial Restrictions and Public Policy: Theories and Industry Evidence," *Journal of Marketing* 63, no. 4 (October), pp. 121–134.

3. *Continental T.V., Inc., v. GTE Sylvania, Inc.,* 433 U.S. 36 (1977).

4. Thunder, David (1991), "Key Considerations in European Distribution," client communique 3 (April), p. 1.

5. See Griffiths, John (1994), "Commission Plans Will Loosen Carmakers' Grip on Dealers," *Financial Times*, October 6,

p. 6; *Economist* (1992) "Carved Up," *Economist*, October 31, p. 73; de Jonquieres, Guy (1992), "Electric Suppliers Blamed for EC Price Variations," *Financial Times*, August 3, p. 1; Rice, Robert (1993), "Whiff of Controversy Hangs in the Air," *Financial Times*, November 16, p. 10; and Tucker, Emma and Haig Simonian (1995), "Brussels Plans to Give More Freedom to Car Dealers," *Financial Times*, May 26, p. 1.

6. Tucker, Emma (1997), "Easing the Pain of 'Vertical Restraints,'" *Financial Times*, January 22, p. 2; *Financial Times* (1998) "'Vertical Restraints' Eased," *Financial Times*, October 1, p. 2; *European Report* (1999), "Competition: Industry Council Gives Green Light for Changes to Vertical Restraints Rules," *European Report*, no. 2404, May 1 (no page); *European Report* (1999), "Council Formally Adopts Two Competition Regulations," *European Report*, no. 2416, June 16; and *European Report* (1999), "Competition: Commission Firms Up Single Block Exemption Rule," *European Report*, no. 2425, July 17.

7. Areeda, Phillip and Louis Kaplow (1998), *Antitrust Analysis: Problems, Text, Cases*, 4th ed. (Boston: Little, Brown and Company), p. 659.

8. Posner, Richard A. (1976), *Antitrust Law: An Economic Perspective* (Chicago: University of Chicago Press), p. 162.

9. *K Mart Corporation v. Cartier, Inc.*, 56 LW 4480 (1988).

10. *K Mart Corporation v. Cartier, Inc.*, 56 LW 4480 (1988). See also, Wermiel, Stephen (1988), "Justices Uphold Customs Rules on Gray Market," *Wall Street Journal*, June 1, 1988, p. 2; and *Business Week* (1988), "A Red-Letter Day for Gray Marketeers," *Business Week*, June 13, p. 30.

11. These and other reasons can be found in Ornstein, Stanley I. (1989), "Exclusive Dealing and Antitrust," *The Antitrust Bulletin* (Spring), pp. 71–74.

12. See Areeda and Kaplow, previously cited, pp. 630–635; and Rubin, Paul H., *Managing Business Transactions* (New

York: The Free Press, 1990), pp. 126–127.

13. Barrett, Paul M. (1991), "Anti-Discount Policies of Manufacturers Are Penalizing Certain Cut-Price Stores," *Wall Street Journal*, February 27, p. B1.

14. Arndt, Michael (1991), "Consumers Pay More as Price-Fixing Spreads," *Chicago Tribune*, August 18, Section 7, p. 5.

15. See, for example, Blair, Roger D. and Francine Lafontaine (1999), "Will *Khan* Foster or Hinder Franchising? An Economic Analysis of Maximum Resale Price Maintenance," *Journal of Public Policy & Marketing* 18, no. 1 (Spring), pp. 25–36.

16. *Monsanto Co. v. Spray-Rite Service Corp.*, 104 U.S. 1464 (1984).

17. Sheffet, Mary Jane and Debra L. Scammon (1985), "Resale Price Maintenance: Is It Safe to Suggest Retail Prices?" *Journal of Marketing* 49, no. 4 (Fall), pp. 82–91.

18. *Business Electronics Corp. v. Sharp Electronics Corp.*, 99 S. Ct. 808 (1988).

19. Kaufmann, Patrick J. (1988), "Dealer Termination Agreements and Resale Price Maintenance: Implications of the Business Electronics Case and the Proposed Amendment to the Sherman Act," *Journal of Retailing* 64, no. 2 (Summer), p. 120.

20. *Business Electronics Corp.*, 485 U.S. at 733.

21. 272 U.S. 476, 486–488 (1926).

22. *Ryko Manufacturing Co. v. Eden Services*, 823 F.2d 1215 at 1223 (8th Cir. 1987).

23. *Albrecht v. Herald Co.*, 390 U.S. 145 (1968).

24. Blair and Lafontaine, previously cited; Felsenthal, Edward (1997), "Manufacturers Allowed to Cap Retail Prices," *Wall Street Journal*, November 5, p. A3; and Garland, Susan B. and Mike France (1997), "You'll Charge What I Tell You to Charge," *Business Week*, October 6, pp. 118–120.

25. See Nagle, Thomas T. and Reed K. Holden (2002), *The Strategy and Tactics of Pricing*, 3rd ed. (Englewood Cliffs, NJ: Prentice Hall), Chapter 9, for a discussion of segmented pricing.

26. *U.S. v. Borden Co.*, 383 U.S. 637 (1966).

27. Quotations are from the Robinson-Patman Act of 1936.

28. Scherer, F. M. and David Ross (1990), *Industrial Market Structure and Economic Performance*, 3rd ed. (Boston, MA: Houghton Mifflin Co.), p. 514.

29. *Brooke Group Ltd. v. Brown & Williamson Tobacco Corp.*, U.S. 114 S.Ct. 13 (1993).

30. *Brooke Group Ltd. v. Brown & Williamson Tobacco Corp.*, U.S. 114 S.Ct. 13 (1993) at 25.

31. *Brooke Group Ltd. v. Brown & Williamson Tobacco Corp.*, U.S. 114 S.Ct. 13 (1993) at 25.

32. See O'Brian, Bridget (1993), "Verdict Clears AMR on Illegal Pricing Charges," *Wall Street Journal*, August 11, p. A3.

33. Federal Trade Commission (1988), *FTC News Notes* 89 (December 26), p. 1.

34. Sharpe, Anita (1994), "Pharmacies Sue Drug Manufacturers and Distributors Over Pricing Policies," *Wall Street Journal*, October 18, p. B9; Kansas, Dave (1994), "Four Grocery Chains Sue 16 Drug Firms, Mail-Order Concern in Pricing Debate," *Wall Street Journal*, March 7, p. B5; and Morris, Steven (1994), "Independent Pharmacies Face Bitter Pill," *Chicago Tribune*, November 6, Business Section, p. 1.

35. Langreth, Robert (1996), "Settlement Cleared in Pharmacies' Suit Over Price Fixing, but Debate Lingers," *Wall Street Journal*, June 24, p. B5; Tanouye, Elyse and Thomas M. Burton (1998), "Drug Makers Agree to Offer Discounts for Pharmacies," *Wall Street Journal*, July 15, p. B4.

36. See *Fall City Industries, Inc. v. Vanco Beverage, Inc.*, 460 U.S. 428 (1983).

37. *Standard Oil Co. v. FTC*, 340 U.S. 231 (1951).

38. *Federal Trade Commission v. Sun Oil Co.*, 371 U.S. 505 (1963).

39. *Fall City Industries v. Vanco Beverage*, 460 U.S. 428, 446 (1983).

40. Bloom, Paul N., Gregory T. Gundlach, and Joseph P. Cannon (2000), "Slotting Allowances and Fees: Schools of Thought and the Views of Practicing Managers," *Journal of Marketing* 64 (April), pp. 92–108;

and quoted in Wilkie, William L., Debra M. Desrochers, and Gregory T. Gundlach (2002), "Marketing Research and Public Policy: The Case of Slotting Fees," *Journal of Public Policy and Marketing* 21, no. 2 (Fall), pp. 275–288.

41. Grundlach, Gregory T. and Paul N. Bloom (1998), "Slotting Allowances and the Retail Sale of Alcohol Beverages," *Journal of Public Policy & Marketing* 17, no. 2 (Fall), pp. 173–184.

42. Sullivan, Mary W. (1997), "Slotting Allowances and the Market for New Products," *Journal of Law and Economics* 40, no. 2 (October), pp. 461–493.

43. Food Marketing Institute (2002), "Slotting Allowances in the Supermarket Industry," available at www.fmi.org/ media/bg/ slottingfees2002.pdf (accessed 9/9/2005).

44. Chu, Wujin (1992), "Demand Signalling and Screening in Channels of Distribution," *Marketing Science* 11, no. 4 (Autumn), pp. 327–347; and Lariviere, Martin A. and V. Padmanabhan (1997), "Slotting Allowances and New Product Introductions," *Marketing Science* 16, no. 2 (Spring), pp. 112–28.

45. *Supermarket Business* (1997), "More Facts and Figures on Slotting," *Supermarket Business*, July, p. 19. The percentages were lower for health and beauty products and for general merchandise/ nonfood products, with 14 and 15 percent, respectively, paying between $500,000 and $1 million, and close to 30 percent of respondents reporting no payment of slotting allowances.

46. *Supermarket Business* (1997), previously cited.

47. Stoll, Neal R. and Shepard Goldfein (1997), "The Spring Trade Show: Explaining the Guidelines," *New York Law Journal*, May 20, Antitrust and Trade Practice Section, p. 3, available from Lexis/Nexis (accessed September 9, 2005).

48. Kim, Sang-Yong and Richard Staelin (1999), "Manufacturer Allowances and Retailer Pass-Through Rates in a Competitive Environment," *Marketing Science* 18, no. 1, pp. 59–76.

49. *Augusta News Co. v. Hudson News Co.* (2001), 269 Fed. 41 (1st Circuit), described in Balto, David (2002), "Recent Legal and Regulatory Developments in Slotting Allowances and Category Management," *Journal of Public Policy & Marketing* 21, no. 2 (Fall), pp. 289–294.

50. Harps, Leslie Hansen and Warren Thayer (1997), "FTC Is Investigating 'Exclusive Dealing,'" *Frozen Food Age,* May, p. 78; Sullivan, previously cited; Cannon, Joseph P. and Paul N. Bloom (1991), "Are Slotting Allowances Legal Under the Antitrust Laws?" *Journal of Public Policy & Marketing* 10, no. 1 (Spring), pp. 167–186. Note, however, that slotting allowances are prohibited for alcoholic beverages, as discussed by Gundlach and Bloom, previously cited. Nevertheless, Gundlach and Bloom also stress that the logic for slotting allowances varies from market to market and, thus, a general rule for its use should not be inferred.

51. Brannigan, Martha (1991), "Coke Is Victim of Hardball on Soft Drinks," *Wall Street Journal,* March 15, p. B1.

52. See *Atlantic Trading Corp. v. FTC,* 258 F.2d 375 (2d Cir. 1958).

53. Federal Trade Commission (1983), Guides for Advertising Allowances and Other Merchandising Payments and Services, 16 C.F.R. part 240.

54. Federal Trade Commission (1983), Guides for Advertising Allowances and Other Merchandising Payments and Services, 16 C.F.R. part 240.6.

55. *FTC v. Fred Meyer Company, Inc.,* 390 U.S. 341 (1968).

56. Federal Trade Commission (1990), "Federal Trade Commission Adopts Changes in Robinson-Patman Act Guides," *FTC News,* August 7, pp. 1–2.

57. 496 U.S. 492 (1990).

58. 496 U.S. 492 at 493 (1990).

59. 496 U.S. 492 (1990).

60. For an excellent discussion of this problem, see Spriggs, Mark T. and John R. Nevin (1994), "The Legal Status of Trade and Functional Price Discounts," *Journal of Public Policy and Marketing* 13, no. 1 (Spring), p. 63.

61. See Ornstein, Stanley I. (1989), "Exclusive Dealing and Antitrust," *The Antitrust Bulletin* 34, no. 1 (Spring), pp. 71–79; and Areeda and Kaplow, previously cited, pp. 773–776.

62. Bounds, Wendy (1996), "Kodak Signs Pact to Take Control of Eckerd's Regional Photo Labs," *Wall Street Journal,* February 6, p. B4; Bounds, Wendy (1996), "Kodak Rebuilds Photofinishing Empire, Quietly Buying Labs, Wooing Retailers," *Wall Street Journal,* June 4, p. B1; Bounds, Wendy (1996), "Fuji Will Buy Wal-Mart's Photo Business," *Wall Street Journal,* July 9, p. A3; Yates, Ronald E. (1996), "Fuji Knocks Kodak out of Focus," *Chicago Tribune,* July 12, Section 3, p. 1; Nelson, Emily (1996), "Kodak to Supply Photofinishing to American Stores," *Wall Street Journal,* July 30, p. A10; Nelson, Emily (1996), "Kodak Signs Pact with Price/Costco, Dealing Fuji Blow," *Wall Street Journal,* December 5, p. B13.

63. Neale, A. D. and D. G. Goyder (1980), *The Antitrust Laws of the U.S.A.,* 3rd ed. (New York: Cambridge University Press, 1980), p. 266.

64. Scherer and Ross, previously cited, p. 563.

65. 365 U.S. 320 (1961).

66. Hovenkamp, Herbert (1994), *Federal Antitrust Policy* (St. Paul, MN: West Publishing Company), p. 390.

67. *R.J. Reynolds Tobacco Co. v. Philip Morris,* No. 1:99cv00185; the lawsuits by the two other competitors that were merged into this case were *Lorillard Tobacco Co. v. Philip Morris Inc.,* No. 1:99cv00207, and *Brown & Williamson v. Philip Morris Inc.,* No. 1:99cv00232, M.D. N.C.). See *Mealey's Litigation Report: Tobacco* (1999), "Court Tells Philip Morris to Halt Contracts for Prime Retail Space," *Mealey's Litigation Report: Tobacco,* 13, no. 5 (July 1).

68. See Hwang, Suein L. (1997), "Philip Morris Is Investigated On Marketing," *Wall Street Journal,* May 15, p. A3; Ono, Yumiko (1998), "For Philip Morris, Every Store Is a Battlefield," *Wall Street Journal,*

June 29, p. B1; Turcsik, Richard (1999), "Philip Morris Fires Up New Program," *Brandmarketing* 7, no. 2 (February), p. 50; Nowell, Paul (1999), "Philip Morris Exec Says Program Wasn't Intended to Coerce Retailers," The Associated Press State & Local Wire, June 10; Nowell, Paul (1999), "Judge Issues Preliminary Injunction in Cigarette Display Case," The Associated Press State & Local Wire, June 30; *New York Times* (1999), "Philip Morris Enjoined on Store Displays," *The New York Times*, June 30, 1999, Section C, p. 2; Bloomberg News (1999), "Rivals Win Temporary Ban on Philip Morris Ad Strategy," *The Plain Dealer*, Business Section, p. 2C; *Mealey's Litigation Report: Tobacco* (1999), "Court Tells Philip Morris to Halt Contracts for Prime Retail Space," *Mealey's Litigation Report: Tobacco* 13, no. 5 (July 1); and Willman, John and Emma Tucker (1999), "Space Invaders," *Financial Times*, October 21, p. 16.

69. Desrochers, Debra M., Gregory T. Gundlach, and Albert A Foer (2003), "Analysis of Antitrust Challenges to Category Captain Arrangements," *Journal of Public Policy & Marketing* 22, no. 2 (Fall), pp. 201–215.

70. For a detailed discussion of the issues surrounding category management and category captains, see Desrochers, Debra M., Gregory T. Gundlach, and Albert A. Foer (2003), "Analysis of Antitrust Challenges to Category Captain Arrangements," *Journal of Public Policy & Marketing* 22, no. 2 (Fall), pp. 201–215.

71. This case is summarized in both Desrochers, Gundlach, and Foer (2003), previously cited, and Balto, David (2002), "Recent Legal and Regulatory Developments in Slotting Allowances and Category Management," *Journal of Public Policy & Marketing* 21, no. 2 (Fall), pp. 289–294.

72. See Areeda and Kaplow, previously cited, pp. 705–710.

73. *Standard Oil Company of California v. U.S.*, 337 U.S. 293 (1949) at 305.

74. *U.S. v. Jerrold Electronics Corp.*, 187 F. Supp. 545 (1960), affirmed per curian at 363 U.S. 567 (1961).

75. *Norman E. Krehl, et al. v. Baskin-Robbins Ice Cream Company, et al.*, 42 F. 2d 115 (8th Cir. 1982).

76. *In re: Chock Full O'Nuts Corp. Inc.*, 3 Trade Reg. Rep. 20, 441 (Oct. 1973).

77. *U.S. v. J. I. Case Co.*, 101 F. Supp. 856 (1951).

78. *U.S. v. Paramount Pictures*, 334 U.S. 131 (1948); *U.S. v. Loew's Inc.*, 371 U.S. 45 (1962).

79. Federal Trade Commission (1976), "Consent Agreement Cites E&J Gallo Winery," *FTC News Summary* (May 21), p. 1. See also *Wall Street Journal* (1976), "Gallo Winery Consents to FTC Rule Covering Wholesaler Dealings," *Wall Street Journal*, May 20, p. 15.

80. *Wall Street Journal* (1977), "Union Carbide Settles Complaint by FTC on Industrial-Gas Sales; Airco to Fight," *Wall Street Journal*, May 20, p. 8.

81. Sullivan, previously cited, p. 439.

82. *Jefferson Parish Hospital District No. 2 v. Hyde*, 104 LW 1551 (1984). See also Taylor, Robert E. and Stephen Wermiel (1984), "High Court Eases Antitrust Restrictions on Accords Linking Sales of Goods, Services," *Wall Street Journal*, March 28, p. 6.

83. *Jefferson Parish Hospital District No. 2 v. Hyde*, 466 U.S. 12 (1984).

84. Scherer and Ross, previously cited, p. 568.

85. See Barrett, Paul M. (1991), "FTC's Hard Line on Price Fixing May Foster Discounts," *Wall Street Journal*, January 11, p. B1.

86. *FTC News Notes* (1991), 91 (June 17), p. 1; and Barrett, Paul M. (1991), "Sandoz Settles FTC Charges Over Clozaril," *Wall Street Journal*, June 21, p. B3.

87. *Eastman Kodak Co. v. Image Technical Service Inc.*, U.S. 112 S.Ct. 2072 (1992).

88. Bounds, Wendy (1995), "Jury Finds Kodak Monopolized Markets in Services and Parts for Its Machines," *Wall Street Journal*, September 19, 1995, p. A4; and *The Buffalo News* (1997), "Court Upholds

Jury Verdict Against Kodak, Cuts Damages," *The Buffalo News*, August 27, 1997, Business Section, p. 6B.

89. *The Financial Times* (1994), "Tetra Pak Appeal," *The Financial Times*, October 18, p. 10.

90. See Gruley, Bryan and Joseph Pereira (1996), "FTC Is to Vote Soon on Staff's Request for Antitrust Action Against Toys 'R' Us," *Wall Street Journal*, May 21, p. A3; Pereira, Joseph and Bryan Gruley (1996), "Toys 'R' Us Vows It Will Challenge Any Antitrust Charges Brought by FTC," *Wall Street Journal*, May 22, p. A3; Pereira, Joseph and Bryan Gruley (1996), "Relative Power of Toys 'R' Us Is Central to Suit," *Wall Street Journal*, May 24, p. B1; Bulkeley, William M. and John R. Wilke (1997), "Toys Loses a Warehouse-Club Ruling with Broad Marketing Implications," *Wall Street Journal*, October 1, p. A10; *International Herald Tribune* (1997), "Judge Faults Toys 'R' Us," *International Herald Tribune*, October 1, p. 13; Broder, John M. (1997), "Toys 'R' Us Led Price Collusion, U.S. Judge Says," *The New York Times*, October 1, Section A, p. 1; Segal, David (1997), "Judge Rules Toys R Us Wasn't Playing Fair; Product Agreements Found Anti-Competitive," *The Washington Post*, October 1, Financial Section, p. D10; *The Arizona Republic* (1997), "Action Against Toymakers Grows," *The Arizona Republic*, November 18, Business Section, p. E4; Stroud, Jerri (1997), "Missouri and Illinois Join Suit Over Toys; The FCC Concluded the Retailer Bullied Toymakers," *St. Louis Post-Dispatch*, November 19, Business Section, p. C1; Williams, Norman D. (1997), "California, 37 Other States Claim Toys 'R' Us Fixed Prices," *Sacramento Bee*, November 19; Segal, David (1998), "Toys R Us Told to Change Its Tactics; FTC Says Methods Limited Manufacturers' Sales to Discounters," *The Washington Post*, October 15, Financial Section, p. C12; Brinkley, Joel (1998), "F.T.C. Tells Toys 'R' Us to End Anticompetitive

Measures," *The New York Times*, October 15, Section C, p. 22; Chon, Gina (1998), "Hasbro Agrees to Pay $6 Million in Antitrust Settlement," The Associated Press State & Local Wire, December 11; Segal, David, "Toys R Us to Settle Suit for $40.5 Million; Discount Clubs Squeezed Out, States Allege," *The Washington Post*, Financial Section, May 26, 1999, p. E03; and Westfeldt, Amy (1999), "Toy Makers to Pay $50 Million in Cash and Toys to Settle Antitrust Suit," The Associated Press State & Local Wire, May 26.

91. *U.S. v. Colgate & Co.*, 250 U.S. 300 (1919).

92. See Hovenkamp, previously cited, p. 263.

93. Scammon, Debra L. and Mary Jane Sheffet (1986), "Legal Issues in Channels Modification Decisions: The Question of Refusals to Deal," *Journal of Public Policy & Marketing* 5, no. 1 (Spring), p. 82.

94. Neale and Goyder, previously cited, p. 282.

95. Neale and Goyder, previously cited, p. 282.

96. Under the wording of Section 7 of the Clayton Act, it is unnecessary to prove that the restraint involved has actually restrained competition. It is enough that it "may" tend to substantially lessen competition.

97. Felsenthal, Edward and Joe Davidson (1993), "Two Big Deals Spur Concerns About Antitrust," *Wall Street Journal*, December 9, p. B1.

98. Burton Thomas M. (1994), "Eli Lilly Agrees to Restrictions on Buying PCS," *Wall Street Journal*, October 26, p. A3.

99. Novak, Viveca and Elyse Tanouye (1994), "FTC Restudies 2 Acquisitions by Drug Firms," *Wall Street Journal*, November 15, p. A16.

100. *Brown Shoe Co. v. U.S.*, 370 U.S. 294, Vertical Aspects, 370 U.S. 323 (1962).

101. U.S. Department of Justice (1982), Merger Guidelines (Washington, DC: June 14), pp. 22–26.

102. Novak, Viveca (1994), "TCI-Comcast Agreement to Buy QVC May Face an FTC Antitrust Challenge," *Wall Street Journal*, September 15, p. B3.

103. Maddocks, Tom (1990), "Brewers Play the Tie-Break," *Business*, August, p. 76;

Rawstorne, Philip (1990), "A Change of Pace to Restructuring," *Financial Times*, September 19, p. 17; and Rawstorne, Philip (1990), "GrandMet Backed on $2.6bn Deal," *Financial Times*, November 21, p. 34.

104. Rawstorne, Philip (1991), "Reduced Importance of the Brewer's Tie," *Financial Times*, February 25, p. 20.

105. *FTC v. Consolidated Foods Corp.*, 380 U.S. 592 (1965).

106. *U.S. v. Aluminum Co. of America*, 148 F. 2d 416 (2nd Cir. 1945).

107. See, for example, *Columbia, Metal Culvert Co., Inc. v. Kaiser Aluminum & Chemical Corp.*, 579 F. 2d 20 (3rd Cir. 1978); *Coleman Motor Co. v. Chrysler Corp.*, 525 F. 2d 1338 (3d Cir. 1975); and *Industrial Building Materials, Inc. v. Inter-Chemical Corp.* 437 F. 2d 1336 (19th Cir. 1970).

Retailing

Learning objectives

After reading this chapter, you will:

- Be familiar with the types of retail structures that exist worldwide
- Understand how a retail positioning strategy flows from both cost-side and demand-side factors
- Understand that the retailer's positioning strategy implies a set of service outputs delivered to the market, and helps differentiate a retailer from its competitors, even if the products sold are identical
- Be aware of important trends and developments on the consumer and channel side that affect retail management
- Understand the power and coordination issues facing retailers and their suppliers and how suppliers respond to retailers' use of power to influence channel behavior
- Be aware of the increasing globalization of retailing and how it affects not just the retailers who themselves are selling outside their national borders but also their suppliers and local competitors

Modern retailing is fiercely competitive and innovation oriented. It is populated by an ever-growing variety of institutions and constantly buffeted by a highly fluid environment. The purpose of this chapter is to describe how retailers position themselves in this environment and to discuss some of the more significant competitive developments that have made retailing so volatile. An understanding of the chapter's material will help channel managers more fully account for "bottom-up" pressures when forming strategies and designing distribution systems.[1]

The chapter proceeds by first defining the distinction between retail sales and wholesale sales. Then, it explains the operational characteristics that define retail position and the nature of retailing competition. Finally, it considers some of the strategic issues currently facing retailers.

RETAILING DEFINED

> *Retailing consists of the activities involved in selling* goods *and* services *to* ultimate consumers *for* personal consumption.

Thus, a retail sale is one in which the buyer is an ultimate consumer, as opposed to a business or institutional purchaser. In contrast to wholesale sales (i.e., purchases for resale or for business, industrial, or institutional use), the buying motive for a retail sale is always personal or family satisfaction stemming from the final consumption of the item being purchased.[2]

Although the distinction between retail and wholesale sales may seem trite, it is really very important because buying motives are critical in segmenting markets. Companies that sell personal computers to high-school students for doing their homework (or playing computer games) are engaged in retail sales. Companies that sell personal computers to their parents for use in a family business run out of a home office are engaged in wholesale sales. CompUSA or Office Depot in the United States make both retail and wholesale sales. It is important for them to understand the differences in serving these different market segments even though they are served out of the same retail establishments.

Table 11.1 profiles the world's 100 leading retailers in 2003 sales. The table shows wide varieties of retail types (supermarkets, hypermarkets, department stores, automobile sellers, etc.) and countries of origin, suggesting that retail success comes in many shapes, sizes, and cultural origins.

United States retailers account for 47.7 percent—almost half—of the sales of the world's top 250 retailers, so it is still the world's biggest retail marketplace. The United States hosts the greatest number of large retailers as well, with 43 of the top 100 headquartered there. European countries and Japan follow, with 12 of the top 100 retailers in the U.K., and 9 each in Japan, France, and Germany. Increasing globalization, however, is clear in the data. In an analogous table in the sixth edition of this book, the top 10 world retailers operated in 9.3 countries on average. In the data presented here, that figure has climbed to 12.8 countries on average for the top 10 retailers. Only two of the top 10 are single-country retailers (Kroger and Target), both in the United States. These top retailers also account for about 9.5 percent of world retail sales; this is far from a completely concentrated marketplace but still a very large percentage, given the inherently local and fragmented nature of much of the world's retailing.

The data further show that food retailing plays a role in the biggest of the big retailers, with 9 of the top 10 selling food as some or all of their products. One cannot ignore the huge and growing dominance of Wal-Mart on the world retailing stage. Wal-Mart's sales are more than three times as large as those of the next largest retailer (Carrefour), and its sales account for about 3.25 percent of all global retail sales.[3]

Chapter 12 focuses on wholesale sales. More and more businesses sell to other businesses out of what look and feel like retail stores. Here, though, the focus is on businesses engaged in making retail sales. The discussion includes both store and nonstore (e.g., mail order, online, or direct selling) retailing.

CHOOSING A RETAIL POSITIONING STRATEGY

How a retailer chooses to position itself in the marketplace has a significant effect on its competitiveness and performance. Retailers make choices about cost-side and demand-side characteristics of their businesses. On the cost side, retailers commonly focus on margin and inventory turnover goals. On the demand side, the retailer chooses what service outputs to provide to its shoppers. Here, we discuss each of these issues in turn and then summarize by showing how choices on each of these dimensions help shape the overall strategy of the retailer.

Table 11.1 The world's top 100 retailers (2003)

Retailer by Rank, (home country and rank in 1998)	Retail Formats	2003 Retail Sales (US$ million)	5-Year Retail Sales Compound Annual Growth Rate	Number of Countries (on which continents[i])
1. Wal-Mart Stores, Inc. (USA) (1)	Discount, hypermarket, supermarket, superstore, warehouse	256,329	13.2%	10 (N.Am., S.Am., Asia, Eur.)
2. Carrefour (France) (8)	Cash and carry, convenience, discount, hypermarket, specialty, supermarket	79,796	20.8%	30 (Af., S.Am., Asia, Eur.)
3. Home Depot (USA) (16)	DIY	64,816	16.5%	4 (N.Am.)
4. Metro (Germany) (2)	Cash and carry, department, DIY, food service, hypermarket, specialty, superstore	60,503	3.1%	28 (Af., Asia, Eur.)
5. Kroger (USA) (3)	Convenience, discount, specialty, supercenter, supermarket, warehouse	53,791	14.4%	1 (N.Am.)
6. Tesco (UK) (18)	Convenience, department, hypermarket, supermarket, superstore	51,535	12.5%	12 (Asia, Eur.)
7. Target[ii] (USA)	Department, discount, supercenter	46,781	8.9%	1 (N.Am.)
8. Ahold (Netherlands) (5)	Cash and carry, drug, convenience, discount, hypermarket, specialty, supermarket	44,584	10.7%	21 (N.Am., C.Am., S.Am., Asia, Eur.)
9. Costco (USA) (24)	Warehouse	41,693	11.8%	9 (N.Am., S.Am., Asia, Eur.)
10. Aldi Einkauf (Germany) (17)	Discount, supermarket	40,060[e]	14.4%	12 (N.Am., Eur., Pac.)
11. Rewe (Germany) (12)	Cash and carry, discount, DIY, drug, hypermarket, specialty, supermarket, superstore	38,931[e]	1.5%	13 (Eur.)
12. Intermarche (France) (4)	Cash and carry, convenience, discount, DIY, food service, specialty, supermarket, superstore	37,472[e]	204%	7 (Eur.)

(continued)

Table 11.1 (cont.)

Retailer by Rank, (home country and rank in 1998)	Retail Formats	2003 Retail Sales (US$ million)	5-Year Retail Sales Compound Annual Growth Rate	Number of Countries (on which continents)
13. Sears (USA) (6)	Department, mail order, specialty	36,372	-2.5%	3 (N.Am.)
14. Safeway, Inc. (USA) (19)	Supermarket	35,553	7.7%	3 (N.Am.)
15. Albertson's (USA) (9)	Convenience, drug, supermarket	35,436	17.2%	1 (N.Am.)
16. Schwarz Group (Germany) (36)	Discount, hypermarket, superstore	33,435e	22.4%	17 (Eur.)
17. Walgreens (USA) (31)	Drug	32,505	16.3%	1 (N.Am.)
18. Auchan (France) (21)	Department, DIY, hypermarket, specialty, supermarket, superstore	32,497	1.4%	12 (Af., S.Am., Asia, Eur.)
19. Lowe's (USA) (40)	DIY	30,838	20.3%	1 (N.Am.)
20. Ito-Yokado (Japan) (23)	Convenience, department, food service, specialty, supermarket, superstore	30,819	4.4%	4 (N.Am., Asia)
21. Tengelmann (Germany) (13)	Cash and carry, discount, DIY, drug, hypermarket, specialty, supermarket, superstore	29,091e	-2.0%	15 (N.Am., Asia, Eur.)
22. AEON (Japan) (n.l.)	Convenience, drug, department, discount, DIY, food service, specialty, supermarket, superstore	28,697	6.9%	11 (N.Am., Asia, Eur.)
23. J. Sainsbury (UK) (20)	Convenience, hypermarket, supermarket, superstore	28,630	1.0%	2 (N.Am., Eur.)
24. Edeka (Germany) (11)	Cash and carry, convenience, discount, DIY, specialty, supermarket, hypermarket, superstore	28,330e	-3.1%	5 (Asia, Eur.)
25. E. Leclerc (France) (22)	Convenience, hypermarket, supermarket	27,396e	5.7%	6 (Eur.)

Table 11.1 (cont.)

Retailer by Rank, (home country and rank in 1998)	Retail Formats	2003 Retail Sales (US$ million)	5-Year Retail Sales Compound Annual Growth Rate	Number of Countries (on which continents[1])
26. CVS (USA) (32)	Drug	26,588	11.7%	1 (N.Am.)
27. Casino (France) (33)	Cash and carry, convenience, department, discount, food service, hypermarket, specialty, supermarket, warehouse	26,018	10.6%	19 (N.Am., S.Am., Asia, Eur.)
28. Best Buy (USA) (51)	Specialty	24,547	19.5%	2 (N.Am.)
29. Kmart (USA) (10)	Discount, superstore	23,253	−7.1%	1 (N.Am.)
30. Delhaize Group (Belgium) (34)	Cash and carry, convenience, drug, specialty	21,306	7.8%	10 (N.Am., Asia, Eur.)
31. Woolworths (Australia) (48)	Convenience, department, specialty, supermarket	19,941	10.6%	2 (Pac.)
32. J. C. Penney (USA) (15)	Department, mail order	17,786	−9.7%	3 (N.Am., S. Am.)
33. KarstadtQuelle (Germany) (47)	Department, food service, mail order, specialty	16,976	−2.3%	23 (N.Am., Eur.)
34. AutoNation (USA) (n.l.)	Auto	16,867	5.9%	1 (N.Am.)
35. Publix (USA) (46)	Convenience, supermarket	16,848	6.9%	1 (N.Am.)
36. Rite Aid (USA) (44)	Drug	16,600	5.6%	1 (N.Am.)
37. Coles Myer (Australia) (43)	Convenience, department, specialty, supermarket	16,045	5.6%	2 (Pac.)
38. Gap (USA) (57)	Specialty	15,854	11.9%	6 (N.Am., Asia, Eur.)
39. Pinault-Printemps-Redoute (France) (52)	Auto, department, mail order, specialty	15,739e	10.2%	46 (Af., N.Am., S.Am., Asia, Eur.)
40. Federated Department Stores (USA) (29)	Department, specialty	15,264	−0.7%	1 (N.Am.)

(continued)

Table 11.1 (cont.)

Retailer by Rank, (home country and rank in 1998)	Retail Formats	2003 Retail Sales (US$ million)	5-Year Retail Sales Compound Annual Growth Rate	Number of Countries (on which continents[i])
41. Safeway (UK) (45)	Convenience, hypermarket, supermarket, superstore	15,129[e]	3.5%	1 (Eur.)
42. Daiei (Japan) (25)	Department, discount, specialty, supermarket, superstore	14,562	–10.3%	3 (N.Am., Asia)
43. Kingfisher (UK) (30)	DIY	14,522	3.5%	11 (Asia, Eur.)
44. El Corte Ingles (Spain) (70)	Convenience, department, hypermarket, specialty, supermarket	13,686	17.1%	2 (Eur.)
45. Marks & Spencer (UK) (38)	Department, specialty, supermarket	13,498	0.2%	27 (N.Am., Asia, Eur.)
46. Loblaws (Canada) (63)	Cash and carry, convenience, hypermarket, supermarket, superstore, warehouse	13,441	8.5%	1 (N.Am.)
47. May Department Stores (USA) (41)	Department, specialty	13,343	0.4%	1 (N.Am.)
48. TJX Cos. (USA) (68)	Discount	13,328	10.9%	4 (N.Am., Eur.)
49. McDonald's (USA) (n.l.)	Food service	12,795	0.6%	More than 100 (Af., N.Am., C.Am., S. Am., Asia, Eur., Pac.)
50. IKEA (Sweden) (75)	Specialty	12,118	12.5%	32 (N.Am., Asia, Eur., Pac.)
51. Coop Italia (Italy) (64)	Discount, DIY, hypermarket, supermarket	11,784[e]	6.7%	2 (Eur.)
52. Toys "R" Us (USA) (49)	Specialty	11,566	0.7%	31 (Af., N.Am., Asia, Eur., Pac.)

Table 11.1 (cont.)

Retailer by Rank, (home country and rank in 1998)	Retail Formats	2003 Retail Sales (US$ million)	5-Year Retail Sales Compound Annual Growth Rate	Number of Countries (on which continents[i])
53. Otto Versand (Germany) (26)	Cash and carry, mail order; specialty	11,419	-10.3%	18 (N.Am., Asia, Eur.)
54. Meijer (USA) (60)	Superstore	11,100[e]	7.9%	1 (N.Am.)
55. Migros Genossenschaft (Switzerland) (50)	Convenience, department, hypermarket, specialty, supermarket, superstore	10,704	-0.1%	3 (Eur.)
56. Dixons (UK) (98)	Specialty	10,702[e]	15.1%	13 (Eur.)
57. H. E. Butt (USA) (77)	Supermarket	10,700[e]	11.4%	2 (N.Am.)
58. Coop Norden (Sweden) (n.l.)	Convenience, discount, DIY, supermarket, superstore	10,683	ne	3 (Eur.)
59. Winn-Dixie (USA) (37)	Supermarket	10,633	-5.5%	2 (N.Am.)
60. SuperValu (USA) (89)	Discount, supermarket, superstore	10,551	15.7%	1 (N.Am.)
61. Kohl's (USA) (n.l.)	Department	10,282	22.8%	1 (N.Am.)
62. Louis Delhaize (France) (n.l.)	Cash and carry, convenience, discount, hypermarket, specialty, supermarket	10,189[e]	5.1%	8 (S.Am., Eur.)
63. Uny (Japan) (62)	Convenience, department, DIY, drug, specialty, supermarket, superstore	10,141	1.0%	2 (Asia)
64. Circuit City (USA) (53)	Specialty	9,745	0.9%	1 (N.Am.)
65. Dell (USA) (n.l.)	E-commerce	9,700[e]	n/a	Global (e-commerce)
66. Coop Switzerland (Switzerland) (61)	Convenience, department, drug, DIY, food service, hypermarket, mail order, specialty, supermarket	9,454	2.6%	1 (N.Am.)
67. Great Universal Stores, PLC (GUS) (UK) (73)	Department, DIY, specialty	9,447	6.2%	26 (Af., N.Am., Asia, Eur., Pac.)

(continued)

431

Table 11.1 (cont.)

Retailer by Rank, (home country and rank in 1998)	Retail Formats	2003 Retail Sales (US$ million)	5-Year Retail Sales Compound Annual Growth Rate	Number of Countries (on which continents[i]
68. Staples (USA) (74)	E-commerce, mail order, specialty	9,440e	5.8%	10 (N.Am., Eur.)
69. Limited Brands (USA) (55)	Specialty	8,934	-0.9%	1 (N.Am.)
70. Millennium Retailing Group (Japan) (n.l.)	Department	8,546	ne	1 (Asia)
71. Office Depot (USA) (58)	E-commerce, mail order, specialty	8,397e	-1.4%	23 (N.Am., C. Am., Asia, Eur.)
72. Takashimaya (Japan) (56)	Department, specialty	8,360	-1.2%	6 (N.Am., Asia, Eur.)
73. Yamada Denki (Japan) (n.l.)	Specialty	8,330	31.1%	1 (Asia)
74. Systeme U Centrale Nationale SA (France) (54)	Hypermarket, supermarket, superstore	8,264e	-2.7%	4 (Eur.)
75. Empire/Sobey's (Canada) (72)	Convenience, discount, drug, supermarket, superstore	8,234	12.1%	1 (N.Am.)
76. Wm. Morrison (UK) (n.l.)	Supermarket, superstore	8,171	14.3%	1 (Eur.)
77. Seiyu (Japan) (n.l.)	Department, DIY, specialty, supermarket, superstore	7,876	-3.1%	4 (Asia)
78. Somerfield (UK) (65)	Convenience, discount, supermarket	7,742	-5.2%	1 (Eur.)
79. Boots (UK) (71)	Drug	7,649	-0.5%	8 (N.Am., Asia, Eur.)
80. Lotte (S. Korea) (n.l.)	Convenience, department, food service, hypermarket, supermarket	7,633	12.7%	2 (Asia)
81. Dillard's (USA) (59)	Department	7,599	-0.5%	1 (N.Am.)
82. Mercadona (Spain) (n.l.)	Supermarket	7,592	25.2%	1 (Eur.)

Table 11.1 (cont.)

Retailer by Rank, (home country and rank in 1998)	Retail Formats	2003 Retail Sales (US$ million)	5-Year Retail Sales Compound Annual Growth Rate	Number of Countries (on which continents)[1]
83. Army & Air Force (USA) (79)	Specialty, exchange services	7,585	1.3%	Global
84. Yum! Brands (USA) (n.l.)	Food service	7,441	–1.1%	Global
85. John Lewis (UK) (88)	Department, hypermarket, supermarket	7,437	5.0%	1 (Eur.)
86. United Auto Group (USA) (n.l.)	Auto	7,400[e]	20.8%	3 (N.Am., S. Am., Eur.)
87. CCA Global (USA) (n.l.)	Specialty	7,000[e]	23.9%	5 (N.Am., Eur., Pac.)
88. Mitsukoshi (Japan) (67)	Department	6,943	–3.5%	10 (N.Am., Asia, Eur.)
89. Dollar General (USA) (n.l.)	Discount	6,872	16.4%	1 (N.Am.)
90. Kesko (Finland) (100)	Auto, department, DIY, discount, food service, hypermarket, supermarket, specialty	6,812	10.7%	5 (Eur.)
91. Avon (USA) (n.l.)	Direct selling cosmetics	6,805	5.5%	Global
92. S. Group (Finland) (84)	Auto, convenience, department, discount, food service, hypermarket, specialty, supermarket	6,728	10.1%	3 (Eur.)
93. Metcash (South Africa) (n.l.)	Cash and carry, convenience, specialty, supermarket	6,698[e]	10.4%	14 (Af., Asia, Pac.)
94. Hutchison Whampoa/AS Watson (Hong Kong SAR) (n.l.)	Drug, specialty, supermarket	6,631[e]	31.9%	15 (Asia, Eur.)
95. GJ's Wholesale Club (USA) (n.l.)	Warehouse	6,585	13.6%	1 (N.Am.)

(continued)

Table 11.1 (cont.)

Retailer by Rank, (home country and rank in 1998)	Retail Formats	2003 Retail Sales (US$ million)	5-Year Retail Sales Compound Annual Growth Rate	Number of Countries (on which continents[i])
96. Nordstrom (USA) (90)	Department, specialty	6,492	5.2%	5 (N.Am., Eur.)
97. Schlecker (Germany) (96)	Drug, DIY, hypermarket	6,453e	6.6%	8 (Eur.)
98. Galeries Lafayette (France) (83)	Department, hypermarket	6,261	3.7%	1 (Eur.)
99. CompUSA (USA) (82)	Specialty	4,700e	-2.3%	1 (N.Am.)
100. KESA Electricals (UK) (n.l.)	Specialty	6,233	ne	6 (Eur.)

Source. "2005 Global Powers of Retailing," *Stores*, January 2005, downloaded from www.stores.org (accessed July 1, 2005).

[i] *Continents are abbreviated as follows: Af. = Africa; N. Am. = North America; C. Am. = Central America; S. Am. = South America; Asia = Asia; Eur. = Europe; Pac. = Pacific (Australia, New Zealand).*

[ii] *Target was part of Dayton-Hudson Corporation in 1998. Dayton-Hudson itself was ranked 14th in 1998 sales, and if Target's 1998 sales are taken alone, it would have ranked 25th in sales in 1998 among global retailers.*

"n.l." = not listed in top 100 retailers in 1998.

"e" = estimated.

"ne" = not in existence (created by merger or divestment since 1998).

Financial and Cost-Side Positioning: Margin and Inventory Turnover Goals

"High-service" retailing systems have been categorized as high-margin, low-turnover operations offering numerous personal services (turnover refers to the number of times per year inventory turns on the retail shelf). These can be contrasted with "low-price" retailing systems, which are characterized by low margins, high inventory turnover, and minimal service levels. Both sets of institutions continue to exist, but in recent years, the spotlight has focused on the revolutionary volume efficiencies flowing out of low-price retailing systems. The most advanced retailers, such as Wal-Mart or Home Depot, are able to combine low margin and high turnover with excellent personal service. These retailers are able to generate high rates of return on the capital employed in their businesses through continuous improvements in asset management made possible by sophisticated information systems. Service attracts consumers, but it can only be provided if it can be paid for.

Historically, the low-margin/high-turnover model has been oriented toward generating high operational efficiency with the savings generated passed on to the customer. However, many of those savings passed on to the customer must be seen as involving a transfer of cost (opportunity cost as well as actual effort cost) rather than a clear elimination of cost. The consumer who shops at Costco, Sam's Club, or Carrefour, for example, does get a lower price, but "pays" for it through large-volume buying, travel to inconvenient store locations, and toleration of poor customer service. Thus, reductions in service output levels, such as those associated with product selection opportunity, convenience in location, atmosphere of the retail environment, personal services, financial and delivery accommodations, and the like, accompany the typical retail package offered by the low-margin/high-turnover operation. The operational philosophy trading off margin and turnover is thus based on a recognition of the costs (represented by marketing flows) that certain segments of consumers are willing to absorb in certain classes of purchasing behavior. Only if consumers are willing to trade lower service levels for the lower price that can accompany low-margin retail operations should the retailer pursue this strategy.

Lowering the costs of operating a retail company need not always mean lower levels of all consumer service outputs. Two fashion-forward clothing retailers, Zara and H&M, are able to offer their target consumers up-to-date assortments (i.e., excellent assortment and variety) and quick delivery of the hottest new styles while holding costs down and, therefore, being able to offer competitive prices to the market. Sidebars 11.1 and 11.2 highlight the different ways in which these two retailers have built their channel systems to meet these seemingly contradictory goals: Zara, through a highly vertically integrated path, and H&M, through a much more highly outsourced path. Each method has its strengths, and it is possible for both to succeed in the future if the companies continue their discipline in holding down costs.

Of critical importance in determining which path to follow—low-margin/high-turnover or high-margin/low-turnover—are management's perceptions of the organization's best chance for achieving its financial target. The appropriate pathway can be highlighted using the strategic profit model (SPM). A brief description of the SPM is introduced here so that the reader can gain some appreciation of its

Sidebar 11.1

Zara: A European retailer using the low-margin, high-turnover model of retailing

Zara was founded in Spain in 1975 and in the three decades of its existence has built and fine-tuned a particular model of retailing that appears to balance extremely well the need to control costs with the need to meet demands of the target shopper for fashion-forward, trendy merchandise.

Zara's target consumer in Europe is a fashion-conscious young female buyer of clothing who values novelty and exclusivity but is also quite price sensitive. The most important service output demands of this consumer are, therefore, assortment and variety (which should be extensive and novel) and quick delivery (i.e., extremely fashion-forward and available to buy). Providing a quickly changing, market-responsive assortment of reasonably-priced, fashion-forward clothing has long been one of the thorniest challenges for retailers. Zara has met this challenge through a combination of the following strategies:

- It makes 40 percent of its own fabric and owns its own dyeing company, which permits it to buy undyed fabric from outsiders and postpone coloring fabric until it knows what colors are really popular in a given season.

- It owns its own production for over 50 percent of its clothes, thus retaining control over production from start to finish.

- It concentrates all of its owned production and warehousing in one area, in Galicia in northern Spain.

- It purposely makes small amounts of product at a time, rather than large batch volumes.

- It owns its own logistics and trucking operations, even though this can mean sending a half-empty truck through Europe.

- It has invested in significant communications capabilities from the store manager level back to the designers, from designers to production, from production to warehousing, and from the warehouse back to retail stores.

- It sticks to a rigid reordering, production, and shipping schedule that makes restocking stores extremely predictable to everyone in the system, including consumers.

- It favors introducing new styles over restocking styles it has already shipped once, and has invested in an extremely flexible manufacturing operation to enable this to happen.

These policies are actually contradictory to much of what is practiced throughout retailing today—from the highly vertically integrated set of operations Zara pursues, to the rigid controls it exerts throughout its logistics and ordering systems, to its small-batch production practices, to the constant revamping of product lines in the stores. How can Zara make money with such a topsy-turvy retailing system?

The answer lies in the fact that, through its apparently high-cost methods of operation, it is really *maximizing turnover and saving costs* in other parts of its business. Because Zara has invested in significant amounts of communication at all levels of its business (which is also possible because of its investments in vertical integration through the system), it is possible for designers at headquarters to learn about new "hot" styles in midseason, before any of Zara's competitors are able to see the trends and respond to them. Because Zara is vertically integrated and has invested in flexible manufacturing operations, with clothing designers well integrated into the headquarters design/manufacturing operations, it is possible to quickly use that market-level information to create new designs and to feed them to manufacturing with no delay. It is also feasible to respond to this information because Zara has

Sidebar 11.1 (cont.)

Zara: A European retailer using the low-margin, high-turnover model of retailing

chosen *not* to make large batch volumes of any styles it innovates; thus, it has the space in the stores to accommodate new styles. Further, it does not suffer from large overstocks and, hence, does not need to mark down merchandise as heavily as its competitors do, again because it never produces large volumes of any style to begin with and only produces styles for which it has market-level indication of demand.

Because Zara actually cultivates slack (i.e., unused) capacity in its factories and warehouse, it can accommodate rush jobs that would cause bottlenecks in standard retail systems. And because Zara's consumers *know* that Zara is constantly coming out with new styles (as well as knowing *exactly when* the stores are restocked!), they shop at the store more often (particularly right after a new shipment comes in) in order to keep up with the new styles. For example, a shopper in London visits a standard clothing store (where she shops routinely) about four times per year; but the same shopper visits a Zara store 17 times per year. The Zara shopper feels a certain urgency to buy a garment when she sees it at the store because she may not be able to find it again if she waits to get it. This increases sales rates and merchandise turnover.

What are the results of Zara's retailing strategy?

- Zara has almost no inventories in its system:
  - An item sits in its warehouse only a few *hours* on average (not days or weeks).
  - Store deliveries occur (on schedule) twice per week to each store in the system, worldwide.
  - Most items turn over in less than one week (significantly less than its competitors' inventory turn rates).
- Zara can create a new design, manufacture it, and have it on its stores' racks or shelves in just *two weeks.* This compares to 9 to 12 *months* for other retailers (for

example, Gap and VF Corporation take 9 months to bring a new design collection to market, while J. Jill, another clothing maker, takes up to 12 months).

- Zara's shipments are 98.9 percent accurate, and it enjoys a very low shrinkage rate of 0.5 percent (shrinkage is loss of inventory due to theft or damage).
- Zara's designers bring over 10,000 new designs to the market each year (versus 2,000 to 4,000 items introduced by Gap or H&M annually).
- Zara maintains net profit margins of about 10 percent annually, as good as the best retailers in the business, even though its prices are fairly low.
- Zara does little advertising, spending only 0.3 percent of sales on ads, versus the more typical 3 to 4 percent of sales for its competitors. It does not need to spend on advertising, because its shoppers are in the stores so many times a year that there is no need for advertising to remind them to come.
- On average, Zara collects 85 percent of list price on its clothing items, versus an industry average of only 60 to 70 percent (including markdowns). This leads to higher net margins; in 2001, Zara's net margin was 10.5 percent; H&M's was 9.5 percent; Benetton's was 7 percent; and Gap's was zero percent.

In short, Zara's formula for success rests upon highly centralized control all the way through from its input sourcing (dyes, fabrics), to design, to logistics and shipping, and finally to retailing. Given the high cost of owning all of these resources, Zara has to maximize the value created from them—which it does very well by excelling at meeting the core service output demands of its target market, namely, providing novel and extensive variety and assortment, quickly.

Sidebar 11.2

H&M: Another low-margin, high-turnover European retailer with a different channel strategy

In contrast to the example of Zara in Sidebar 11.1, consider the strategy of H&M, an international retailer founded in 1947 in Sweden. Like Zara, it sells "cheap chic" clothing, and its core consumer is similar to Zara's (although in Europe, its stores also offer men's, teens', and children's clothing). The average price of an item in H&M in 2002 was just $18.00, and shoppers look there for current-season fashions at bargain prices.

H&M's formula for offering this assortment to its consumers at aggressively low prices is somewhat different than Zara's, however. H&M does not own any manufacturing capacity, relying on relationships with a network of 900 suppliers located in low-wage countries like Bangladesh, China, and Turkey. It frequently shifts production from one supplier to another, depending on demand in the market for various fabrics, styles, and fashions. All of H&M's merchandise is designed in-house by a cadre of 95 designers in Stockholm (Zara has about 300 designers, all at its headquarters in Spain). The management style is extremely frugal; not only does the company control manufacturing costs, but its managers do not fly business class, try not to take cabs when traveling, and (for the most part) do not have company-supplied cell phones.

H&M focuses on minimizing inventory everywhere in its system, as does Zara. It has the ability to create a new design and get it into stores in as little as three weeks (a bit longer than Zara, but still extremely impressive, given industry norms). It restocks stores daily, although even that is not always frequent enough (when it opened its flagship store in New York City in the spring of 2002, it had to restock on an *hourly* basis). Because its merchandise turns very quickly (like Zara's), it can charge very low prices for it yet maintain good profitability; in 2002, H&M's pretax profit was $833 million on sales of $5.8 billion (or 14.4 percent), while Gap's pretax profit was $554 million on sales of $13.8 billion (or 4.0 percent).

H&M has chosen a more aggressive store growth strategy than Zara, which has caused it some problems in recent years. Its entry into the United States was plagued by poor location choices and signing leases for stores that were too big. It has worked on these problems, and reached breakeven in the United States in 2004. Whether the H&M-style model—farming out production to third parties and slavishly cutting costs everywhere in the system—or the Zara model—purposely cultivating slack capacity and investing in highly flexible but vertically integrated facilities—is a dominant strategy is not at all clear. It is entirely possible that both will flourish in the future, as both have a well-integrated system in place that meets the needs of the market, albeit in different ways.

influence on the margin and turnover dimensions of retail strategy.[4] The SPM can be stated as follows:

$$\frac{\text{net profit}}{\text{net sales}} \times \frac{\text{net sales}}{\text{total assets}} = \frac{\text{net profit}}{\text{total assets}}, \text{ and}$$

$$\frac{\text{net profit}}{\text{total assets}} \times \frac{\text{total assets}}{\text{net worth}} = \frac{\text{net profit}}{\text{net worth}}. \text{ Thus:}$$

$$\frac{\text{net profit}}{\text{net sales}} \times \frac{\text{net sales}}{\text{total assets}} \times \frac{\text{total assets}}{\text{net worth}} = \frac{\text{net profit}}{\text{net worth}}.$$

Management can pursue margin management (net profit/net sales), asset turnover (net sales/total assets), and/or financial management via financial leverage (total assets/net worth) in order to secure a target return on net worth (net profit/net worth). (Net sales are gross sales less customer returns and allowances.) If there is strong downward pressure on margins because of competitive forces and economic conditions, then a likely path for management to pursue is asset turnover. These sets of conditions have led management to emphasize such criteria as sales per square foot (which reflects space and location productivity), sales per employee (which reflects labor productivity), and sales per transaction (which reflects merchandising program productivity).

More specific to the retail context are three interrelated measures of performance that help retailers improve profitability (see also Appendix 11A)[5]:

> *Gross margin return on inventory investment (GMROI).* GMROI is equal to the gross margin percentage times the ratio of sales to inventory (at cost). It combines margin management and inventory management and can be calculated for companies, markets, stores, departments, classes of products, and stock-keeping units (SKUs). GMROI allows the retailer to evaluate inventory on the return on investment it produces and not just on the gross margin percentage. Efficient consumer response (ECR) initiatives in the grocery industry have been aimed at reducing average inventory levels while maintaining sales through the use of just-in-time shipments, electronic data interchange (EDI) linkages between manufacturers and retailers, and like measures. Such actions reduce the denominator of GMROI without reducing the numerator, thus increasing retailing returns. GMROI often considers items with widely varying gross margin percentages as equally profitable, as in the following example.

	Gross Margin	×	Sales to Inventory Ratio	= GMROI
A	50%	×	3	= 150%
B	30%	×	5	= 150%
C	25%	×	6	= 150%

> *Gross margin per full-time equivalent employee (GMROL).* Retailers should optimize, not maximize, GMROL. As sales rise per square foot, not all fixed costs (e.g., rent, utilities, and advertising) rise in proportion. In fact, they decline as a percentage of sales as sales increase. Having more salespersons may actually lower average sales per full-time equivalent (FTE) employee but nevertheless increase profitability because they leverage the other fixed assets in the store. That said, within a particular retailing category, comparisons between companies may be meaningful: for example, Wal-Mart's sales per employee were about $178,000 in 2005, compared to $136,000 for Kmart.[6] Knowing Wal-Mart's superior cost control systems, the additional higher sales per employee suggest very efficient use of personnel and thus good control of labor costs.

> *Gross margin per square foot (GMROS).* Such a measure permits an assessment of how well retailers are using their unique asset—the shelf or floor space they can allocate to suppliers' products.

A problem with GMROI, however, is that gross margin only accounts for the cost of goods sold and fails to account for differences in variable costs associated with selling different kinds of merchandise. Other measures, such as contribution dollars per square foot of selling space or direct product profit (DPP), are more comprehensive but more difficult to derive. In any case, retailers' use of measures such as GMROI or DPP places pressure on suppliers. They must attend to the gross margins their brands permit retailers to earn, the sales volume (in units) their brands generate, the amount of shelf or floor space consumed by their brands, and the costs incurred in storing, handling, and selling their brands. There is increasing emphasis on systems designed by suppliers to speed the replenishment of inventory (e.g., vendor-managed inventory initiatives), because faster replenishment rates mean less need for shelf space and less inventory replenishment and, therefore, a reduction in the denominators of these formulae.

Large fixed-cost investments that bear fruit by reducing later marginal costs can be difficult to bring into the channel, especially when those fixed costs must be borne by multiple channel partners. For example, innovative retailers that lead in their categories can face challenges in instituting state-of-the-art inventory management systems when their suppliers are reluctant to incur the necessary up-front costs to put the systems in place. Michaels Craft Stores, the leading arts and crafts retailer in the world, started out by educating its suppliers about the benefits of incorporating bar coding, common stock-keeping numbers, computerized labeling, and electronic invoicing, but many suppliers were reluctant to bear the initial fixed costs of incorporating these technologies into their relatively small, largely noncomputerized businesses.[7] This sort of problem arises for two reasons. First, the channel partner may not understand the later marginal cost savings that fixed-cost investments in improved retailing technologies can bring. Second, the channel partner may not trust the channel captain, believing instead that the high up-front costs will generate benefits in the future, but only for the captain, not for other channel members. The understanding problem requires the channel captain to use its expertise power to educate channel partners about the cost-reduction benefits; the trust problem requires investments in conflict reduction to make the channel partner willing to incur a cost before seeing the ultimate benefit.

One significant element of retailing cost, the rent paid to landlords for bricks-and-mortar stores, ideally should be charged based on the return the specific retailer generates for the mall developer (who is the retailer's landlord). In shopping malls in particular, the largest stores, or anchor stores as they are known, generate disproportionate benefits for the developer because they attract shoppers who then also patronize other stores in the mall—that is, they generate positive externalities. One research study documented differences in rents charged to various retailers at shopping malls and, consistent with this notion, found that anchor stores pay a significantly lower rental rate (72 percent lower per square foot) than nonanchor stores. One could conjecture that bargaining power on the part of large desirable retailers is the sole reason for this, but the research also found that anchor stores pay a lower rent per square foot in larger superregional malls than in smaller regional malls, suggesting that the mall developers recognize the differentially larger positive externality endowed upon the larger mall. These subsidies persist despite the generally lower sales per square foot that anchor stores generate versus specialty and other smaller stores. Thus, the economics of the retail store depend not just on internal cost factors but also on cost factors determined by the retail environment in which the store is found.[8]

More generally, the product-by-product profitability calculations mentioned above are done not just by grocery retailers but also by department and specialty stores. Table 11.2 details the product categories, their floor locations, and the percentage of

Table 11.2 Profit percentages at Saks Fifth Avenue's flagship store (1996)

Floor	Department	Percent of Total Store Profit Generated by This Department
Main floor (39% of total profit)	Cosmetics	18%
	Accessories (belts, handbags, sunglasses)	10%
	Costume jewelry	3%
	Fine jewelry	4%
	Hosiery	0.5%
	Men's shirts, ties, accessories	3%
	Penhaligon's (British shop)	0.5%
Second floor (12% of total profit)	Designer sportswear	8%
	Men's sportswear	4%
Third floor (6% of total profit)	High-end designer collections	4.5%
	Furs	1%
	Bridal boutique	0.5%
Fourth floor (9% of total profit)	Career wear	8%
	Designer shoes	1%
Fifth floor (7% of total profit)	Women's contemporary designers	6%
	Shoes	1%
Sixth floor (10% of total profit)	Men's suits	8%
	Men's designer clothing	2%
Seventh floor (9% of total profit)	Women's coats	3%
	Women's petite sizes	4%
	Women's dresses	2%
Eighth floor (5.5% of total profit)	Lingerie	3%
	Children's clothes	2%
	Restaurant & candy shop	0.5%
Ninth floor (2.5% of total profit)	Salon Z (large sizes)	2%
	Beauty salon	0.5%

Source: Adapted from Steinhauer, Jennifer (1997), "The Money Department," *New York Times*, Magazine Section 6, April 6, pp. 62–64.

total store profits earned by each at Saks Fifth Avenue's flagship store on Fifth Avenue in New York City in 1996. Total revenue for the store was $420 million, and operating profits for this store alone were about $36 million, one-third of the company's total operating profit. The table shows a standard retailing strategy of a multifloor department store or specialty store: to put the highest profit-margin items on the easily accessible main floor, while locating more specialized merchandise or merchandise that the shopper is willing to search for on higher floors. Each of the lower floors has at least one important department to attract shoppers. The image of a high-end department store is that of a retailer that makes high profits from the sale of designer clothing. But the profitability data suggest otherwise. Saks compensates for the low-volume designer label business with its own attractive (and profitable) private-label clothes and seeks to target a younger customer than its traditional target.

Demand-Side Positioning

Clearly, higher retail profits through higher margins, higher merchandise turnover, and lower retailing costs are desirable. It should be clear that the same financial outcome is possible with many combinations of these variables. Thus, the stance the retailer chooses on the supply side constitutes part of its positioning strategy in the retail landscape. The demand side, too, is important. The retailer's choice of service outputs to provide makes any given product purchase more or less attractive to the chosen target market.

Bulk-Breaking

One of the classic functions of a retail intermediary is the breaking of bulk. Manufacturers make their products in large batch lot sizes, but consumers may want to consume just one unit of the product. Higher-service retailers may buy in large quantities from their suppliers, but offer the consumer the opportunity to purchase in small quantities.

Some retailers, such as warehouse stores (e.g., Sam's Club or Costco), offer consumers a lower price but require them to buy in larger lot sizes (i.e., they break bulk less) than at traditional grocery retailers. Consumers who do not have a high cost of transportation or storage and who have adequate disposable income can choose to buy a case of paper towels or 10-pound bags of frozen vegetables at lower unit prices. Clearly, only those consumers who can afford to buy in such quantities, transport their purchases home, and store unused product until it is needed choose to buy from these retailers. More traditional grocery retailers may encourage, but not force, large-lot-size purchases through special pricing, such as buy one get one free (BOGO) deals or pricing products in multiple units (e.g., three for $1.00).

In an interesting countertrend, so-called dollar stores are enjoying success in the United States. These are stores where everything is for sale for $1.00 (or, in the case of 99-cent stores, for $0.99).[9] The retailer achieves this by offering small quantities of product rather than large ones. The consumer might be able to buy a small bottle of dishwashing detergent, for example, for just a dollar, or a small package of cookies. The unit price on these items (price per quart or per pound) is higher than one would pay at a hypermarket where volume purchasing is the order of the day, but the consumer gets the benefit of bulk breaking at the dollar store, which is valuable either when disposable income is scarce or when the consumer simply does not want to stock up.

Spatial Convenience

In a general sense, products can be classified as convenience, shopping, or specialty goods. Implicit in this understanding is the extent of search-shopping activity the consumer is willing to undertake. For example, convenience goods should require little effort to obtain, whereas considerable effort may be required to secure highly regarded, relatively scarce specialty goods. More generally, retail locations should be chosen to be convenient to the target market, so that consumers do not have to travel far to get to the store. This was one of the problems plaguing H&M's entry into the United States (see Sidebar 11.2); it chose suburban locations in New Jersey and in Syracuse, New York, where consumers were not as attuned to its urban fashions as in its European locations. Because location decisions are costly and somewhat hard to reverse, the retail location decision can and does receive a great deal of attention.

Consumer search-shopping behavior varies between consumer segments as well as between product categories. It also varies over time as demographic and lifestyle changes occur across market segments. As women enter the labor force in increasing numbers and the opportunity cost of time increases, the effective costs of search and shopping increase. For these consumers, time saved is becoming as important as money saved. Consider one shopper, impressed with the food offerings and samples available at the SuperTarget store in her area (a format for Target stores that includes food as well as nonfood items); even though she likes the food and service there, SuperTarget's distance from her home leads her to say, "It won't replace my weekly grocery store trip."[10] Recognizing the importance of spatial convenience (as well as quick service) in its target market, Walgreens, a major drug and convenience store chain, has purposefully chosen locations to be convenient to consumers' usual shopping paths, choosing sites near major grocery stores; it has also decreased the average transaction time in the store to 14 minutes, increasing the chance that a shopper will get a parking space close to the store.[11]

Waiting and Delivery Time

Consumers differ in their willingness to tolerate out-of-stock products when they shop. This variation occurs not just between different consumers but for the same consumer across different purchase occasions. An intense demand for this service output translates to a demand that the product be in stock at all times and be quick to find, buy, and take home. Retailers can respond to a demand for low waiting time by holding extra safety stocks in their stores, but this is expensive. As with the other consumer service output demands, the retailer must gauge how damaging to its business an out-of-stock occurrence would be. For example, most grocery retailers make it a high priority to avoid out-of-stocks on basic products like milk or bread, which are frequently purchased and important items in many families' shopping baskets. A family purchasing a piece of furniture like a sofa, however, is typically willing to wait a long time (e.g., 8 to 12 weeks) to get delivery of the product and virtually never expects the product to be in-stock in the store. The classic (and perhaps somewhat parodied) profile of the consumer with a high demand for quick delivery is the male shopper "Larry," profiled in Sidebar 11.3.

How important it is to have product in stock also depends on competitive norms, which can change through time. Sears, once dubbed "America's retailer," has always had a strong market following in appliances, tools, and other hard goods. Consumers

Sidebar 11.3

Larry, the speed shopper[12]

One journalist chronicles the shopping behavior of her editor at the *Washington Post*, a man named Larry. Larry views shopping as a hit-and-run operation, where speed is of the utmost importance. The ideal clothes shopping experience for Larry involves visiting a department store accessible immediately from the parking lot, without the need to navigate either other stores or even other departments (such as fragrances) of the one store he visits. He shops once or, perhaps, twice a year and looks for all of his clothing—suits, jackets, shirts, pants, socks, ties, and shoes—at once. Other than tailoring, he has no interest in interacting with sales staff, saying, "It just prolongs the experience when someone helps you."

In contrast, another colleague, Steve, genuinely enjoys shopping and takes more time at it, consulting with the salesman about what styles, colors, and fits are best. Larry remarks that Steve's shopping style is "fussy" and that "there's too much other stuff to do in life." Steve responds that Larry's shopping habits produce a fashion statement that is "not encouraging."

The journalist concludes that while there may be some Steves in the world, most men seem to be more like Larry. While a Steve might shop when he sees that a new style is available, Larry only shops when the shirts in his closet are worn and need replacing. Retailers serving the Larry segment have learned to provide a quick retail experience in several ways: by locating the men's department on the ground floor of the department store, by making clothes easy to find, by having on-site tailoring, and by having sufficient floor staff to speed the shopping process for their customers.

routinely shopped at Sears and waited for delivery of their new washing machines, clothes dryers, and dishwashers to their homes. In today's market, however, Sears faces competition from the likes of Lowe's and Home Depot, two strong home products retailers that carry inventory in the stores that consumers can carry home the day they shop, as well as providing strong price competition and, in some cases, better customer service. Lowe's offers next-day delivery of any product not in the store at the time of purchase, a speed matched by Sears in only about two-thirds of its stores.[13] When the competition improves its provision of a key service output like quick delivery, the old norms of performance may no longer be enough to keep consumers loyal—requiring a constant updating of retail strategy.

This drive to ever quicker delivery times has also reached the furniture business. Midlevel U.S. furniture makers face stiff competition from imported furniture companies that produce narrower product lines (i.e., less assortment and variety) but stock them for immediate sale in price-competitive retailers like Wal-Mart. One manufacturer, England, Inc., has refigured its manufacturing operation to build about 11,000 upholstered sofas and chairs per week, each made to order, for delivery to the consumer within three weeks of order. This speed greatly exceeds the usual eight to twelve weeks a consumer can expect to wait for custom furniture and contributes to England's strong sales performance (for example, its sales grew 8.3 percent from 2001 to 2002, while the rest of the U.S. upholstered furniture industry's sales dropped by 9.3 percent during the same period).[14] The speed of delivery, combined with a broad choice of fabrics and styles, beats both domestic and imported competition.

Despite these norms of consumer expectation, retailers do create positions in the market by deviating from standard practice on the waiting-delivery time dimension. Zara's purposeful stock-out policies (see Sidebar 11.1) are used both to minimize inventory holding costs and to create consumer excitement and urgency to purchase when the product is seen in the store. Discount grocery retailers do not routinely stock a given brand of product, and therefore, the shopper visiting a hypermarket might or might not find a favorite brand of laundry detergent. The consumer could wait a long (and more importantly, an *unpredictable*) amount of time before finding the product in the store again. A very brand-loyal consumer would find this intolerable because it might involve purchasing a nonfavored brand until the favorite brand once again appears on the store shelf, and it also would involve revisiting the store (possibly multiple times) until the brand is once again on the shelf.

Product Variety

In the retailing world, the service output of product variety is represented by two dimensions. On the one hand, variety describes generically different classes of goods making up the product offering, that is, the breadth of product lines. Assortment, on the other hand, refers to the depth of product brands or models offered within each generic product category. Discounters like Target and Wal-Mart have limited assortments of fast-moving, low-priced items across a wide variety of household goods, ready-to-wear, cosmetics, sporting goods, electric appliances, auto accessories, and the like. In contrast, a specialty store dealing only, or primarily, in home audiovisual electronic goods, such as Tweeter, would have a very large and complete line of radios, tape recorders, and high-fidelity equipment, offering the deepest assortment of models, styles, sizes, prices, and so on.

One retailer whose positioning depends inherently on depth of assortment is Book Baron, a used-book store in Anaheim, California. Book Baron was listed as one of the best used-book stores in the United States in 2002; it has an inventory of some 500,000 volumes, which makes it the largest used and rare book store in Southern California.[15] Bob Weinstein, owner of Book Baron, specializes in selling rare books in particular and has deep expertise in the value of used and rare books, which lets him choose the right assortment to offer at the right prices. Table 11.3 shows a selection of the 55 books by Sue Grafton, a popular mystery writer, available on Book Baron's Web site on one particular day. A Sue Grafton aficionado would be able to choose between a $30.00 copy or a $15.00 copy of her *M Is for Malice*, depending on whether it was important to have a copy signed by the author. A collector would be able to find a first edition of one of Grafton's earlier books, *E Is for Evidence*, in fine condition for $125.00. Other copies would be available in the physical store itself. Book Baron is one of the suppliers of used and out-of-print books to Amazon.com, indicating that its depth of assortment is a competitive asset of interest to that huge online bookseller.

Sometimes a retailer's variety and assortment choice is purposely narrow in order to appeal to a particular niche, but eventually the retail concept saturates the market, stifling any further attempts at growth. Such was the conundrum facing Gymboree, a chain of more than 500 stores selling upscale children's clothes in mall stores. To continue growth, the company has expanded into different store concepts rather than trying to extend the assortment or variety within the Gymboree store itself.

Table 11.3   Example of assortment available at Book Baron (www.bookbaron.com)

Author: Sue Grafton, a popular mystery writer; book titles each start with a letter of the alphabet, beginning with *A Is for Alibi*, published in 1982. *R Is for Ricochet* was published in 2004.

Some of the Sue Grafton books available at www.bookbaron.com on July 5, 2005:

Title	Pub. date	Price	Condition
E Is for Evidence	1988	$125.00	1st edition; near fine in near fine dust jacket (DJ). Light browning to edges of DJ.
H Is for Homicide	1991	$50.00	1st edition; near fine in DJ. Signed by author, review copy.
F Is for Fugitive	1989	$35.00	1st edition; fine in near fine DJ; slight yellowing along edge of flaps.
I Is for Innocent	1992	$35.00	1st edition; near fine in DJ. Inscribed by the author. Light shelfwear, spine lean.
M Is for Malice	1996	$30.00	1st edition; fine in DJ. Signed.
N Is for Noose	1998	$30.00	1st edition; fine in DJ. Signed.
P Is for Peril	2001	$30.00	1st edition; fine in DJ. Signed by author.
I Is for Innocent	1992	$25.00	1st edition; fine in DJ.
M Is for Malice	1996	$15.00	1st edition; near fine in DJ. Light shelfwear.

The new store is called Janie and Jack and sells upscale baby gifts. The company's strategy calls for an array of different retail concepts of this sort over the years. Other retailers following this strategy include Chico's (an apparel store for baby-boomer women), which has opened Pazo, aimed at yuppie women in their thirties; and Bebe, a fashion store for women in their teens and twenties, which has opened Bebe Sport, selling sportswear to the same target market.[16] This approach to expanding assortment and variety has pitfalls, however; retailers must be careful to avoid cannibalization of the core retail concept, on the one hand, while sticking close to the retailing concepts in which it has expertise, on the other hand.

The variety and assortment dimension of retailing operations is clearly a matter that demands the attention of top management, for decisions in this area color the entire character of the enterprise. Once the basic strategy is established for the organization, however, the task of choosing specific products or brands usually falls to functionaries called buyers. Buyers play a central role in retailing; unlike their counterparts in manufacturing concerns, their status within their home organizations is very high. Some retailers generate more profits via negotiations for trade deals and allowances than they do through merchandising efforts. Because buying is such a critical aspect of retailing, it is important to understand the evaluative processes and procedures that take place in merchandise and supplier selection. The appendices to this chapter are geared to that end. Appendix 11A is a glossary of pricing and buying terms commonly used by retailers, and Appendix 11B briefly describes some of their merchandise planning and control procedures.

Customer Service Possibilities

Virtually all recent major retail innovations have relied on manipulating the customer service variable to greater or lesser degrees. The principle is easy to appreciate when we consider such services as in-store sales help. When retailers drop the friendly behind-the-counter sales assistant who helps customers locate and compare merchandise and is available for expert advice, the whole locate-compare-select process is shifted to the consumer. For suppliers, the change from in-store assistance to self-service on the part of retailers is a major reason for shifting from a push strategy to a pull strategy.

Retailing is one of the few remaining industries that is highly labor intensive, even though it is becoming less so. Sales, general, and administrative (SG&A) expenses for retailers include the cost of having salespeople on the floor of the stores to help shoppers. SG&A as a percentage of net sales is higher in general for specialty stores (like Ann Taylor or Gap) and department stores (like Nordstrom or J. C. Penney) than for office supply or drug stores (like Best Buy or Walgreens), while the lowest SG&A percentage retailers are the general merchandise and hypermarket retailers (like Costco or Wal-Mart). Table 11.4 summarizes net sales, SG&A expenses, and the SG&A-to-net sales percentages for several stores in each of these categories. The data are certainly consistent with the idea that providing better service in the store is a very costly endeavor for retailers. Looking at the lower-service retailers like Wal-Mart or Costco, it appears that the savings that can be passed on to the consumer by eliminating certain kinds of in-store assistance and/or improving the productivity of a down-sized workforce are usually substantial. A higher SG&A percentage (e.g., at Ann Taylor or Chico's) may be entirely consistent with a very high level of in-store service offered if the retailer is able to charge commensurately high prices; it is more disconcerting when a retailer's SG&A percentage is very high in a typically low-customer-service category, as is true for J. C. Penney, for example. It is also interesting to note that Nordstrom's annual report specifically remarks on the decline in SG&A expenses from 31.2% in 2000 to 28.3% in 2004, showing a concern even among high-service retailers over controlling in-store costs while maintaining appropriate service levels.

It is true that customer service is a costly benefit to provide. But retailers continue to invest in customer service because it can bring substantial benefits, particularly when it is well targeted. Lowe's is a good example in the home improvement retail marketplace. It has focused on providing customer service and education to women consumers, who may need more information and help than their male counterparts and who find Home Depot formidable and unhelpful. One female shopper who tried to buy a refrigerator at Home Depot unsuccessfully and ended up buying at Lowe's remarked, "I have to sing their [Lowe's] praises, because they were very nice. At Home Depot, you can't find anybody to help—and if you do, they just point." Lowe's stores offer wider aisles, where two shopping carts can pass each other easily, as well as focusing its product lines on high-end, high-fashion goods like Laura Ashley paints. As a result of these efforts, the proportion of women in Lowe's total customer base has risen from 13 percent in the late 1980s to half in 2002, and its percent earnings growth outpaced that of Home Depot in 2000, 2001, and 2002.[17]

Another example of targeted investments in customer service comes from the retail operations of the banking firm Washington Mutual. WaMu, as it is called,[18] targets dense urban markets with high banking dissatisfaction rates, offering quick

Table 11.4   Sales, general, and administrative (SG&A) costs as a percentage of net sales for selected retailers

	Net Sales ($million)	SG&A Expenses ($million)	SG&A as % of Net Sales
General merchandise, hypermarkets, category killers:			
Wal-Mart	285,222	51,105	17.9%
Home Depot	73,094	16,504	22.6%
Costco	47,146	4,598	9.7%
Target	45,682	9,797	21.4%
Lowe's	36,464	7,562	20.7%
Office supplies, electronics, drugs:			
Walgreens	37,508	8,072	21.5%
Best Buy	27,433	5,053	18.4%
Office Depot	13,565	3,703	27.3%
Circuit City	10,018	2,308	23.0%
Department stores:			
J. C. Penney	18,424	5,827	31.6%
May	14,441	3,021	20.9%
Kohl's	11,701	2,540	21.7%
Dillard's	7,529	2,099	27.9%
Nordstrom	7,131	2,020	28.3%
Specialty stores:			
Gap	16,267	4,296	26.4%
Limited	9,408	1,872	19.9%
Ann Taylor	1,854	843	45.5%
Chico's	1,067	398	37.3%

Source: Annual reports for 2004/2005 for each company. Depending on the company's fiscal year end, 2004 or 2005 figures are used. The actual fiscal years overlap in all cases.

mortgage underwriting and fast closing services on mortgages, free checking and free ATM use, bank tellers who are out in the open in the bank rather than behind glass, children's play corners in the banks, and promotions when WaMu enters a new market (such as cash giveaways from the bank's "Wa-Moola" machine). This strategy attracts younger, lower-income customers, whom WaMu hopes to retain as their incomes rise over time; the company hired Earvin "Magic" Johnson's consulting firm to advise it on better ways to sell mortgages to low- and moderate-income urban households. As a result, WaMu's deposits grew an average of 38 percent annually over the 10-year period from 1993 to 2003 (versus 14 percent for its peer group of banks), and it became the biggest provider of mortgage servicing and the second largest in mortgage originations in the nation in 2003.[19]

Another somewhat humble example of profitable customer service is the provision of shopping carts in retail stores. Carts are of course common in grocery stores, as well as in mass merchandisers or hypermarkets like Carrefour, Costco, or Wal-Mart, but soft goods (apparel) retailers have resisted them as inconsistent with the stores' images. It is hard to imagine a shopper at a department store like Nordstrom or Macy's using a shopping cart. Nevertheless, shoppers in mass-market retail outlets have been shown to buy 7.2 items when using a cart, but only 6.1 items without a cart. One relieved Montgomery Ward department store shopper with one child in the cart's seat, one child at her side, and several items of children's clothing remarked that she would be likely to shop at the store more often since it started offering carts. It is easy to see why such a relatively small investment (each cart costs about $100) generates such large consumer service benefits to certain segments of shoppers.[20] This investment, like others that can be made in customer service, implies an expenditure on channel functions that takes a cost from the consumer's shoulders. As with the other demand-based dimensions of retailing strategy, a successful operation is dependent on being able to identify the functions that consumers are (or are not) willing to assume and the cost in time, money, effort, and convenience at which taking them on becomes attractive.

Implications for a Taxonomy of Retail Types

Given the cost-side and demand-side dimensions just discussed, retailers have a wide variety of possibilities for positioning their retail operation in the marketplace. The positioning strategy chosen should always be driven by the demands of the target market segment for service outputs. Thus, a high-cost, high-service retail strategy (which might work perfectly well in an affluent neighborhood) is a mistake in an area populated by less wealthy consumers who cannot afford to consume high service levels at high prices. Further, the decision is not just to offer generically high service output levels. Within a certain intensity of demand for service outputs, there are almost always variations in the importance given to one or another specific service output. Thus, in furniture purchasing, there is room for retailers that offer broader variety and assortment but at the cost of longer waiting and delivery times, alongside retailers that offer a somewhat curtailed product line but can deliver to the consumer in a shorter time. Finally, price clearly is the arbiter of the system. Higher service output levels can only be offered at higher price levels when all is said and done because of the cost to produce these service outputs. Thus, retailers are always constrained by the target consumer's total willingness to pay in deciding which services to offer and which to drop.

Table 11.5 shows how different classes of retailers can be characterized by their cost-side and demand-side positioning strategies. It is the differences across these different retailer types that permit the survival of multiple types of retail outlets selling the same physical merchandise. For example, consider two electronics stores, Tweeter and Best Buy. Tweeter is an electronics specialty store, while Best Buy is a category killer. While both break bulk, offer a low waiting time to consumers (i.e., few out-of-stocks), and carry a narrow variety (electronics) along with a deep assortment (many makes and types of products), few consumers would confuse the two stores. Tweeter differs from Best Buy in its focus on high margin rather than high turnover as a key to retail profitability, along with slightly lower spatial convenience on average (due to

Table 11.5 A taxonomy of retailer types

Retailer Type	Main Focus (Margin or Turnover)	Bulk-Breaking	Spatial Convenience	Waiting and Delivery Time	Variety (Breadth)	Assortment (Depth)
Department store (e.g., May Co.)	Margin	Yes	Moderate	Low wait time	Broad	Moderate/ shallow
Specialty store (e.g., Gap)	Margin	Yes	Moderate	Low wait time	Narrow	Deep
Mail Order/ Catalog (e.g., Lands' End)	Margin	Yes	Extremely high	Moderate/high wait time	Narrow	Moderate
Convenience store (e.g., 7-Eleven)	Both	Yes	Very high	Low wait time	Broad	Shallow
Category killer (e.g., Best Buy)	Turnover	Yes	Moderate	Low wait time	Narrow	Deep
Mass merchandiser (e.g., Wal-Mart)	Turnover	Yes	Low	Moderate wait time (may be out of stock)	Broad	Shallow
Hypermarket (e.g., Carrefour)	Turnover	Yes	Low	Moderate wait time	Broad	Moderate
Warehouse club (e.g., Sam's Club)	Turnover	No	Low	Moderate/high wait time (may be out of stock)	Broad	Shallow

Tweeter's smaller number of stores than Best Buy's). Similar comparisons among the rows of the table suggest that it is through its choices on these dimensions that a store creates its position in the marketplace and can survive even in the face of competition offering a seemingly similar set of products to consumers.

STRATEGIC ISSUES IN RETAILING

From a marketing channel design and management perspective, suppliers attempting to sell their products to ultimate consumers for personal consumption must think strategically about their retailing policies. We focus on three issues of importance in today's retail marketplace:

- ➤ The management of a multichannel shopping experience, including hybrid shopping behavior and a combination of "bricks and clicks" buying strategies
- ➤ How to recognize and respond to the continued strong power position of major retailers
- ➤ The continued globalization of retailing

Managing the Multichannel Shopping Experience

Consumers are increasingly comfortable with retail buying through multiple channels and types of outlets, and their purchase behavior varies by segment and by purchase occasion. For example, some consumers only like to buy books in a bricks-and-mortar bookstore because they like to browse and actually see the book before they buy it. Other consumers rarely if ever visit a bookstore, buying all of their books online. Yet other consumers practice hybrid shopping, meaning that they use both online and bricks-and-mortar outlets to complete the shopping process. Even among hybrid shoppers, some do their prepurchase research online, finding information about books at sources like Amazon.com before going to a bricks-and-mortar bookstore to actually purchase the book. Others browse in retail bookstores but then look online to buy their books—often because they believe they will get a better price by doing so.

This broad array of shopping behaviors, combined with the use of yet other channels for other purchases, means that a manufacturer seeking to put together a retail strategy has to think carefully about the entire process the consumer engages in that eventually culminates in product purchase—and to make sure to be present in all of the channel entities that touch that process. In this section, we provide some information on current Internet use as a retail outlet and retail facilitator; on direct selling, an alternative mode of reaching the consumer; and on hybrid shopping behavior.

The Internet as a Retail Outlet

Although where to physically locate a store remains a critical decision for any bricks-and-mortar retailer, the dominant locational consideration in many consumers' choices is convenience, usually defined in terms of ease and speed of access (thus, correlating in many situations with a demand for quick delivery of product in the shopping experience). The tremendous increase in the use of various home shopping technologies (catalogs or online retailing) is a testimony to the importance of spatial convenience in this expanded dimension because shopping from home essentially makes physical outlet location a nonissue. U.S. retail e-commerce sales were $19.8 billion in the first quarter of 2005, a 6.4 percent increase over fourth-quarter sales for 2004 and a 23.8 percent increase over first-quarter 2004 sales. E-commerce sales accounted for 2.2 percent of total U.S. retail sales, showing a steady increase in importance in the economy since late 1999, when data were first collected. Figure 11.1 shows the increase in e-commerce sales, and the importance of e-commerce sales as a percentage of total U.S. retail sales, over the 1999–2005 period. Not only have e-commerce sales steadily increased, but they have increased at a rate greater than the rate of total U.S. retail sales growth, so that the proportion of all retail sales that are consummated through e-commerce channels has increased as well. Figure 11.2 shows the percentage growth of e-commerce (and total retail) sales in any quarter, as compared to sales in the same quarter a year earlier. This way of depicting the data keeps seasonal effects constant. The data show that, while total U.S. retail sales have a rather steady (and, in some periods, low) growth rate, e-commerce sales have grown at a much higher (although erratic) rate over the time period. Both figures suggest that the convenience of electronic buying is high and of increasing value over time.

Figure 11.1   U.S. e-commerce sales, in $ million and as a percentage of total U.S. retail sales

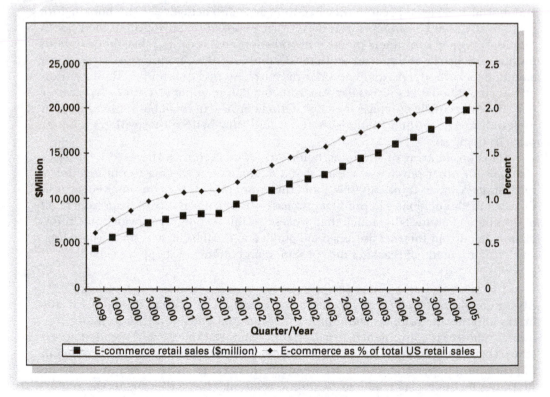

Source: U.S. Census Bureau, released May 20, 2005, available at www.census.gov/mrts/www.ecomm.html.

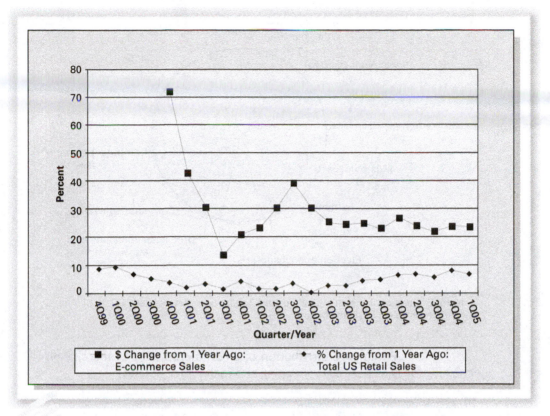

Figure 11.2   **Percentage change from one year ago, in total U.S. retail sales and U.S. e-commerce sales**

Source: U.S. Census Bureau, released May 20, 2005, available at www.census.gov/mrts/www.ecomm.html.

Electronic channels are more important for certain product lines than for others. Figure 11.3 shows the percentage breakdown of e-commerce sales across various physical merchandise lines in a census of firms that sell electronically for some or all of their business. The chart shows that computer hardware and software account for one fifth of e-commerce sales; clothing and books/magazines account for another one fifth. Other important e-commerce product categories include electronics/appliances, furniture, and office equipment/supplies. Among the companies in this U.S. Census sample (all of which sell at least some product through e-commerce), 30 percent of sales are made electronically, suggesting first that e-commerce is a significant part of the multichannel commitment made by many firms, and second that e-commerce is not a total commitment.

Using the same database, Figure 11.4 shows the percentage of e-commerce sales within each category of products. For example, among firms that sell at least some of their product through electronic channels, 49.9 percent of office equipment and supplies are sold online but only 7.2 percent of drug/health and beauty aids products. No category achieves significantly more than half its sales from e-commerce,

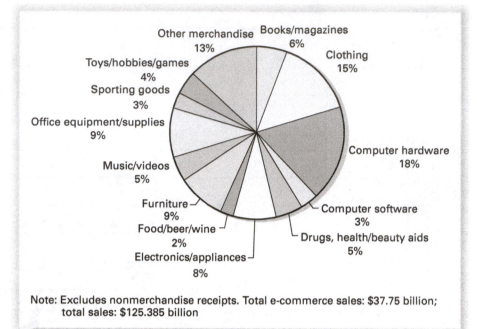

Note: Excludes nonmerchandise receipts. Total e-commerce sales: $37.75 billion; total sales: $125.385 billion

Figure 11.3   Percentage distribution of e-commerce sales by merchandise line, 2003 (for U.S. electronic shopping and mail-order houses)

suggesting that electronic buying is popular but unlikely to completely supplant bricks-and-mortar retailing.

The indications from these aggregate statistics are borne out in individual companies' experiences. For example, Active Endeavors, a Chicago-area retailer selling urban and outdoor gear, started Web sales in 2000, but its Web sales have ramped up very slowly (to just 2 percent of total revenue by 2002). Nevertheless, it sees a Web presence as part of its overall strategy, providing information to consumers who then make purchases in its bricks-and-mortar stores. A study by Jupiter Research reinforces this, finding that 45 percent of surveyed consumers have used a retailer's Web site to get product information before buying at the company's store.[21]

Direct Selling: Retailing Through Network Connections

Direct selling is defined as "the sale of a consumer product or service in a face to face manner away from a fixed retail location."[22] Direct selling organizations, or DSOs, are companies that use direct selling techniques to reach final consumers. They are distinguished from catalog sales operations by their reliance on personal selling, which is the key to both the DSO's channel structure and its positioning as a retail option. Some of the best-known DSOs worldwide include Amway (household cleaning products, personal care products, appliances, etc.), Mary Kay (cosmetics), Herbalife (nutritional supplements and vitamins), Avon (cosmetics), and Tupperware (household storage containers). There were 187 companies listed as members of the U.S. Direct Selling Organization as of July 2005.

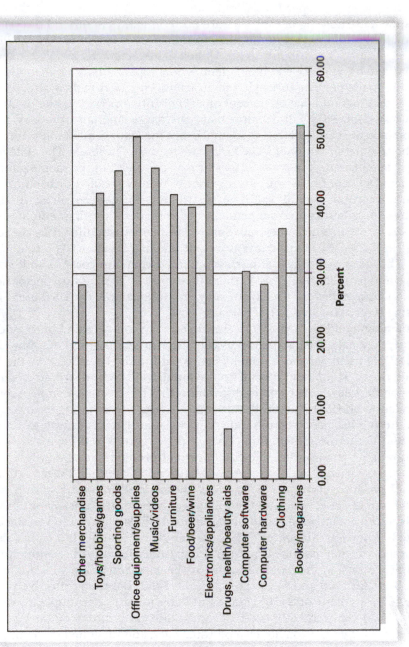

Figure 11.4 E-commerce as a percent of sales, 2003 (for U.S. electronic shopping and mail-order houses)

Global retail sales through direct selling organizations were almost $93 billion in 2005, employing over 53 million salespeople worldwide. The top 25 countries by DSO retail sales are listed in Table 11.6, along with the number of salespeople in each country and the average sales per DSO salesperson.

As the data show, significant sales are made in many countries; however, in most countries, the typical DSO distributor does not make his or her living through direct selling. The typical DSO distributor in the United States is female, married, between the ages of 35 and 54, and likely to have a high school diploma but not a graduate school degree. Eighty-five percent worked less than 30 hours per week at their direct selling job. A 1992 study also found that 56 percent of DSO distributors work at one or more other jobs.[23] Clearly, some DSO distributors make very large amounts of money, but much more common are earning levels that supplement the family's main source of income.

The channel structure of a DSO can have many or few levels. The DSO company itself may manufacture the goods it sells or may contract out the manufacture of the goods. The DSO contracts with intermediaries, variously called distributors, consultants, or salespeople (we will call them distributors for convenience). In almost all cases, these distributors are independent contractors rather than employees of the companies whose products they sell. Further, in many cases, they truly do act as distributors in the sense of buying inventory and reselling it at a markup to downstream buyers. They thus bear physical possession and ownership costs, as well as risking, ordering, and payment flow costs. Perhaps their most important flow performed is the promotion flow, as they are usually the only promotional tool the DSO uses (standard advertising is very rare among DSOs).

In a multilevel DSO (MLDSO), distributors are compensated in three different ways. First, they make the distributor-to-retail markup on the goods they buy wholesale from the DSO itself. Second, a commission is paid to the distributor by the DSO on every sale made. Third (and specific to the multilevel DSO), distributors make commissions on the sales made by other distributors that they recruit. Compensation plans differ widely in MLDSOs, but for illustration, consider the following example.[24]

Catherine has been recruited directly by Janet. Janet is known as Catherine's upline, and Catherine, Susan, Kent, and all their recruits collectively are known as Janet's downline. Janet herself sells $200 worth of product in the month in question, while Catherine, Susan, and Kent each sell $100, and Catherine's three recruits each sell $50 of product. Thus, Janet's personal volume is $200, but her group volume is $650 (the sum of her volume and the volumes of every distributor in her downline).

Given the commission schedule in Figure 11.5, Janet's group volume commission rate is 7 percent. She earns $45.50 on her group volume. But from this $45.50 is deducted the net commissions earned by her downlines. Susan, Kent, and Catherine are each in the 5 percent category because the group volume for each of them is between $100 and $275. Thus, on the $450 that they collectively sell, they get $22.50 (5 percent of $450). Janet's net commission earnings are, therefore, $23.00 ($45.50 minus $22.50). Janet, of course, also earns money on the wholesale-to-retail markup she garners on her own personal sales, and suggested markups generally range from 40 to 50 percent. The commission earnings of the other distributors in Janet's downline can be calculated similarly (for instance, Catherine does not keep all of the gross commissions her group volume earns; she gives some of it up to her downline distributors).

Table 11.6   Direct sales by country

Country	Year	Retail Sales (in U.S. $)	Number of Salespeople	Average Sales per Salesperson	Per Capita Income (1998)
1. United States	2003	$29.5 billion	13,300,000	$2,218	$41,400
2. Japan	2003	$27.0 billion	2,000,000	$13,500	$37,180
3. Brazil	2004	$3.92 billion	1,538,945	$2,547	$3,090
4. United Kingdom	2004	$3.03 billion	520,000	$5,827	$33,940
5. Italy	2004	$2.98 billion	272,000	$10,956	$26,120
6. Mexico	2003	$2.89 billion	1,850,000	$1,562	$6,770
7. Germany	2004	$2.88 billion	206,346	$13,957	$30,120
8. Korea	2003	$2.73 billion	3,208,000	$851	$13,980
9. France	2004	$1.72 billion	170,000	$10,117	$30,090
10. Taiwan	2003	$1.56 billion	3,818,000	$409	$25,300*
11. Malaysia	2003	$1.26 billion	4,000,000	$315	$4,650
12. Australia	2004	$1.07 billion	690,000	$1,550	$26,900
13. Canada	2004	$1 billion	898,120	$1,113	$28,390
13. Russia	2004	$1 billion	2,305,318	$434	$3,410
15. Thailand	2004	$880 million	4,100,000	$215	$2,540
16. Venezuela	2000	$681 million	502,000	$1,357	$4,020
17. Argentina	2004	$662 million	683,214	$969	$3,720
18. Poland	2004	$644 million	585,200	$1,100	$6,090
19. Colombia	2004	$583 million	650,000	$897	$2,000
20. Turkey	2004	$539 million	571,799	$943	$3,750
21. India	2004	$533 million	1,300,000	$410	$620
22. Indonesia	2002	$522 million	4,765,353	$110	$1,140
23. Spain	2002	$497 million	132,000	$3,765	$21,210
24. Switzerland	2003	$355 million	6,885	$51,561	$48,230
25. Chile	2004	$338 million	223,000	$1,516	$4,910

(continued)

Table 11.6   Top 10 direct selling countries by ratio of (Average sales/salesperson) to (Per capita income) (cont.)

Country	Ratio of (Avg. Sales per Salesperson) to (Per Capita Income)
1. Switzerland	1.07
2. Brazil	.82
3. India	.66
4. Germany	.46
5. Colombia	.45
6. Italy	.42
7. Japan	.36
8. France	.34
9. Venezuela	.34
10. Chile	.31

Source: Adapted from World Federation of Direct Selling Associations Web site, www.wfdsa.org, December 1999. Average sales per salesperson are calculated. Per capita income is from the World Development Indicators database of the World Bank, available at www.worldbank.org.

Note: The upper table lists the top 20 countries by level of direct sales. The lower table lists the top 10 countries ranked by the ratio of sales per direct selling salesperson to per capita income (a value of .66, for example, means that the average direct salesperson makes 66 percent of the average per capita income in that country).

*Taiwan per capita income is reported as gross domestic product (GDP) per capita, purchasing power parity (PPP), for 1998, in The World Factbook 1999, published by the U.S. Central Intelligence Agency, downloaded from www.odci.gov/cia/publications/factbook/index.html (accessed July 6, 2005).

Clearly, depending on the structure of the compensation system (the relative rewards from personal selling versus those from override commissions on the sales of downline distributors), different incentives are created for direct selling of product versus building of the direct selling network. There is a delicate balance here. On the one hand, the more time one's current distributors spend in recruiting new distributors, the bigger the DSO's network gets. On the other hand, recruiting new distributors without spending sufficient time selling product does not generate revenues and profits for the DSO.[25] Indeed, a clear distinction is drawn between legitimate direct selling organizations and illegitimate pyramid schemes.[26] A pyramid scheme is a fraudulent mechanism whereby new recruits are required to pay a nonrefundable fee for becoming a distributor. Furthermore, distributors are rewarded simply for getting new recruits to sign on and pay this fee. Thus, both the company and the distributor earn money without selling a product or service. Because companies can succeed only to the extent that they provide value and benefits in exchange for customer payments, this reward system is economically unstable. Many pyramid-scheme victims do not appreciate the risk of this instability, although even those who do appreciate it will participate in the hope that the system will not collapse before they benefit from it.

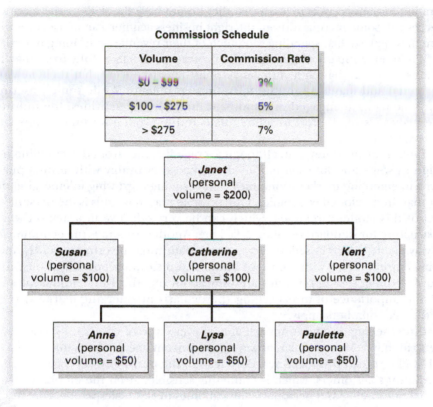

Commission Schedule

Volume	Commission Rate
$0 – $99	3%
$100 – $275	5%
> $275	7%

Janet
(personal
volume = $200)

Susan
(personal
volume = $100)

Catherine
(personal
volume = $100)

Kent
(personal
volume = $100)

Anne
(personal
volume = $50)

Lysa
(personal
volume = $50)

Paulette
(personal
volume = $50)

Figure 11.5   A sample multilevel direct selling organization: Structure and compensation

Source: Coughlan, Anne T. and Kent Grayson (1998), "Network Marketing Organizations: Compensation Plans, Retail Network Growth, and Profitability," *International Journal of Research in Marketing*, 15, p. 403.

To guard against illegal pyramid schemes, legitimate DSOs have created a code of ethics that every member must follow. Legitimate DSOs are characterized by the low expense of joining the organization (e.g., a reasonable fee for a starter kit may be charged); by the ability to return unsold merchandise for a 90 percent or better refund; and by the provision of rewards based on product sales rather than on the recruiting of downline members of the network. The sample compensation scheme described above fits these criteria, since Janet's commissions are all based on someone's actual product sales, not on the mere fact that Janet recruited Catherine, Susan, and Kent into her downline.

The distinction between a legitimate DSO and an illegal pyramid scheme, however, is not usually obvious to the casual observer. This means that legitimate DSOs can sometimes be blamed for the excesses of their illegal cousins. DSOs have also historically come under fire from time to time for other reasons. For example, DSO distributors often are encouraged to use their existing social network as a potential customer base, and some view this as an inappropriate use of friends and relatives for commercial gain.

Furthermore, because it is relatively easy to sign on as a distributor, many do so without serious consideration for what it takes to run a part-time sales business. It can be frustrating for new recruits to learn that they do not have the skills or the motivation to be successful. Some recruits without the right business acumen can make costly mistakes before they quit, such as spending too much of their revenue on training materials.

While no company of any kind can protect its associates fully from making bad decisions, DSOs do have a legitimate responsibility to ensure that their new recruits are selected and managed to minimize these problems. While some unscrupulous entrepreneurs have engaged in fraudulent direct selling activities, the industry as a whole makes a strong effort to self-regulate and to avoid government imposition of DSO restrictions.

Table 11.6 illustrates that, although average incomes from direct selling may not be high in some absolute sense, they do compare favorably with annual per capita income in emerging market economies. Direct selling is growing in emerging markets faster than in developed economies. One possible reason for this is the personal-selling aspect of this mode of retailing, which can be very effective in a market where the infrastructure for standard retailing is lacking. Another reason is the economic opportunity available to direct sellers: For a very small initial investment, individuals can become entrepreneurs with their own business and earning capability. Thus, although worldwide direct selling revenues arc only about one-third the annual sales of Wal-Mart, the importance of direct selling (particularly in emerging markets) is greater than the sales numbers imply.[27]

Direct selling organizations sell almost every type of good and service that consumers can buy.[28] Most popular, however, are consumable products that can be repeat-purchased or broad product lines. Both lead to the possibility of repeat purchases by a distributor's customers, which is eminently sensible, given the emphasis placed on personal networking and personal selling abilities of DSO salespeople. Direct selling is a very old method of distribution. It remains a viable channel because of consumers' interest in personal interactions in the selling process and because of the low cost of forming and running these channels.

Hybrid Shopping: Multiple Channels Complete the Consumer's Shopping Experience

Figures 11.3 and 11.4, previously considered in our discussion of online retailing, carry an important implicit message: No single retail form is necessarily sufficient to reach the market or to satisfy a particular target consumer's set of service output demands. Among the companies the U.S. Census sampled that have at least some online sales, 30 percent of sales were electronic in 2003. This indicates that, although online selling is significant in these firms' retailing efforts, it is not a total commitment for all. Clearly, some firms in the sample are pure-play online sellers (such as Amazon.com), but many others purposely pair up bricks-and-mortar with online selling strategies (in books, for example, Barnes & Noble or Borders). Similarly, the message from Figure 11.4 is that no category focuses entirely (or even in the majority) on online selling; rather, there is a mixture of retail solutions in each of the product categories considered. The persistent survival of multiple types of outlets suggests that on the demand side consumers value having more than one way to get a desired product. This value placed on a multiplicity of outlets, interestingly, may be merely a segmentation indication (i.e., some consumers prefer always to shop online while others prefer always to shop in bricks-and-mortar stores—so in order to be able to cater to both segments, a manufacturer or retailer must use both retail outlets), or it may be instead an indication that any single consumer routinely can and does use multiple retail outlets to complete a single purchase.

This latter explanation is clearly at work in today's retail marketplace. Consumers routinely remark on using Amazon.com as a sort of online *Books in Print*, a reference source to find information on what books or music are available in a particular area; consumers may or may not end up actually consummating the purchase on Amazon.com but may instead go to their favorite bookstore or music store and find the desired item. Conversely, consumers may browse in a retail shop (such as an apparel store), find which styles and sizes fit and appeal to them, and then eventually buy those items online. Sometimes the goal in ultimately buying online is to price shop when the consumer believes the lowest price is available online, but sometimes it is merely for convenience; in this case, the retail store serves as a "touch-and-feel" location, not necessarily as a purchase location.

The implications of insights like these are many. First of all, it may well be a very bad idea to close a particular retail outlet type when it is observed that sales through that type are falling; the role of that outlet type may not be to consummate the sale but rather to provide the valued service outputs of information provision or customer service. This makes the task of determining the true economic value added of this retail outlet harder, but it is still clear that economic value is being added through preservation of multiple retail routes to market. The channel manager's task becomes yet more difficult when the role of information provider and customer service representative is played by an independent channel member, one that may not be compensated for the costly service outputs it is providing to the market. In short, when free riding is a by-product of hybrid retail channel usage, the channel manager must decide how to maintain the willingness of each channel member to play its designated role in the overall channel design.

It may seem merely a semantic detail to ask whether hybrid shopping by consumers means they are using just one channel or, in fact, more than one—but it is not a trivial question. Suppose that a manufacturer uses both independent bricks-and-mortar retailers and also Internet retail outlets (which might or might not be owned by the bricks-and-mortar retailer as part of its own hybrid retailing strategy) to reach consumers. Further suppose that some consumers buy solely through the bricks-and-mortar route, while others might browse in the bricks-and-mortar store but ultimately buy online. Others might want to buy online but pick up their purchase at the store (perhaps to avoid delivery charges; this service is offered by several sellers, including Sears, Best Buy, and Ace Hardware).[29] Still other consumers are loyal online shoppers and rarely visit a physical store. Clearly, in this case, both the bricks-and-mortar outlet and the online outlet are retail outlets because both of them can (and do) actually sell to the consumer. However, the bricks-and-mortar store serves as more than just a retail outlet; in effect, for the hybrid shopping segment, it serves not as a retail purchasing point but as an "infomediary"—an intermediary whose role is to provide information. In this type of situation, which is increasingly common in many retail product categories, there are really three routes to market or channels in operation: (1) the bricks-and-mortar channel (with no use of the online channel); (2) the online channel (with no use of the bricks-and-mortar channel); and (3) the hybrid channel, in which the consumer consumes some service outputs online and others in the physical store. It is only by recognizing the three-part channel structure that the channel manager can try to accurately measure the incremental effectiveness of either the bricks-and-mortar outlet or the online outlet. This way of looking at the channel structure also can be useful when the channel captain is negotiating with disgruntled channel partners who feel that their markets are being stolen or that they are not being fairly compensated for the services they render. This logic is borne out in the experiences of companies like Active Endeavors, described previously.

Manufacturers or retailers may use multiple retail routes to market in order to create broader brand awareness and market reach but seek to control channel conflict by giving sales credit to dealers. Such a strategy was used by Harley-Davidson, the motorcycle manufacturer. Customers who go online to buy Harley clothing or accessories must select a participating Harley dealer who then fulfills the order and thus gets credit for the sale. Participating dealers must agree to maintain certain online business standards, such as checking orders at least twice per day and shipping product promptly. Dealers were consulted in setting up the system and suggested adding dealer-specific items to the Web sites to promote not just the Harley brand name but the dealer relationship as well. As a result of the collaboration, monthly visits to the Harley-Davidson Web site topped 1 million in 2003, with very high overall customer satisfaction.[30]

Even bricks-and-mortar retailers open their own catalog and online outlets in order to increase their reach; Neiman Marcus, the upscale retailer based in Dallas, Texas, has published a Christmas catalog since 1926; it now sends out ninety different catalogs annually, with more than 100 million copies distributed overall. Other department store retailers have done the same, including Marshall Fields, Nordstrom, and Bloomingdale's, in a bid to reach more consumers and to reinforce relationships with their current consumers.[31] In this case, adding a route to market does not create conflict because the retailer owns both the bricks-and-mortar stores and the online or catalog effort.

Even direct sellers have faced the hybrid-channel challenge. The direct selling model, which inherently rests on the importance of person-to-person selling and relationships, would seem to be immune to the pressure to sell online, but as women have flocked back to work over the last few decades, the stay-at-home-mom model that supported so many companies' direct selling operations has been challenged. This demographic shift, along with the rise of the Internet as a selling outlet, tempted many direct selling organizations to add online selling to their channel mix. Avon, the cosmetics company, yielded to the temptation, only to find that its "Avon ladies" (its independent direct-selling distributor force) were very irritated at the new competition from online. Avon had chosen to simply sell online directly to end-users, bypassing the Avon ladies entirely and not giving them sales credit when online sales were made. After a period of some disarray and the loss of many distributors, Avon moved to a modified model where individual Avon ladies themselves could have Web sites and thus get sales credit for online sales. The issue in the end was not whether to go online but how to do so in such a way as to gain the benefits from access to another route to market without incurring the costs of increased channel conflict and cannibalization.[32]

Managing multiple retail routes to market is a challenge for manufacturers and their retail partners in many industries. Hybrid shopping behavior penetrates all combinations of multiple channels and can result in free riding on one channel member while another gets credit for the sale. The successful response to these problems is not to shut down the offending channel because that would cause provision of valued service outputs to fall. Rather, the solution involves offering the right rewards for performance of valued channel flows, so that all members of all retail routes to market retain their incentives to perform according to the channel design.

Recognizing and Responding to the Continued Strong Power Position of Major Retailers

Packaged-goods manufacturers (makers of branded health and beauty aids and of packaged foods and beverages) are arguably the smartest marketing people in the world. At one time, companies like Procter & Gamble, Colgate, Kraft, and Clorox dominated retailers; now the retailers tend to dominate them. How could such a thing happen?

The reasons for this reversal are many and diverse. First, the sales of most items normally sold through grocery, drug, and mass-merchandising chains have not been increasing at rapid rates in the aggregate. This means that if these retailers are to grow, they must take sales away from their competitors rather than waiting for overall demand to expand. Competition has, therefore, evolved into a market share game. This has created enormous pressure on retailers to perform, and given that most chains tend to carry the same products, the type of competition that has consumed them has tended to be price oriented. In other words, better prices (coupled with excellent locations, appealing stores, and reasonable service) have been the major routes to survival and success in this arena. It is little wonder, then, that the chain retailers have increasingly begun to pressure suppliers for price concessions.

Food stores, in particular supermarket chains, still remain the major outlets for packaged goods. Over the recent past, however, warehouse clubs, deep-discount drugstores, and mass merchandisers have been growing more rapidly than food stores. Although none of these so-called alternative formats to the supermarket can match the supermarket in terms of variety and assortment of grocery items, they have been able to expand at the expense of the supermarket. Each of them offers a unique combination of benefits that appeals to a particular niche market of consumers, including not only a value price but also a selected set of valued services.[33]

Given the fact that supermarket profit ratios (net profits-to-sales) are only about 1 percent, any loss of sales to alternative formats, especially from heavy buyers (such as household heads of large families), could be disastrous. The investments made by retailers like Wal-Mart and Target in supercenter retailing outlets pressures standard retailers even further. Although the power of these traditional retailers has been diminished by the new entrants, the pressure they feel is being immediately transmitted back up the channel to suppliers. Of course, the long-term solution for supermarkets does not come via squeezing suppliers but from meeting the needs of consumers.

Second, retailers are continuously concerned with improving their productivity. Given the competitive environment, it is virtually impossible for grocery retailers to raise prices, but it is not impossible to find ways to lower costs. Retailers are always trying to achieve economies of scale while simultaneously providing consumers with the convenience of one-stop shopping. Consequently, they have built larger and larger stores, thereby elevating their fixed costs. This has created higher breakeven points, forcing supermarket and mass merchandisers (such as discount stores) to place even greater emphasis on the need to generate enormous sales volumes.

The resulting competition for store traffic has led to consolidation. For example, in a 1993 study, the three leading grocery chains in 26 out of 50 major markets controlled at least 50 percent of all commodity volume (ACV).[34] Loblaw's, Canada's largest grocer, purchased Provigo, the dominant grocery chain in Quebec, in December 1998, increasing its national market share from 19 percent to 26.2 percent. In the Atlantic provinces of Canada, Loblaw's commands a 32.9 percent market share. But Loblaw's is not alone: One report details eleven major grocery acquisitions in the United States and Canada in the 1996–98 period alone. This list does not include acquisitions elsewhere in the world, which have also been progressing (see the discussion of international retailing below). To put these changes in perspective, consider that Kroger's purchase of Fred Meyer gives it annual sales of $43 billion, which is five times the sales of Nestlé USA. Such statistics indicate that the nature of supplier/retailer relations in the grocery arena have changed significantly.[35]

Third, there is more and more pressure on retail buyers as a result of the increased pressures on the companies in which they are employed. At one time, buyers focused primarily on purchasing and maintaining balanced inventories. Now, they are profit centers that are also responsible for capital management, service levels, turnover, retail margins and pricing, quality control, competitiveness and variety, operating costs, shelf space and position, and vendor float and terms.[36] In order to help their companies make money, they look for suppliers to give them price breaks and merchandising support, and they become very upset when those price breaks and support are not forthcoming.[37]

Fourth, retailers have many new products from which to choose when deciding what to stock on their shelves. About 100,000 grocery products exist in the U.S. market, with thousands introduced every year; meanwhile, the typical supermarket carries just 40,000 products. Retailers are therefore likely to choose which products to stock on their shelves with a goal of making themselves (not the manufacturers) better off. The manufacturers' bargaining position is weakened further when one recognizes that most new products do not succeed, with estimated failure rates ranging from 25 percent to 80 percent.[38] To be fair, it should be noted that not all consumer product categories are like groceries. Apparel markets, for example, are characterized by a strong preference for new products each season, leading to virtual total turnover of SKUs from season to season. However, the fundamental issue of number of products chasing after a fixed amount of shelf space persists in any bricks-and-mortar retail context.

Although other events have contributed to the influence of retail buyers, suppliers themselves are partly to blame. We have already mentioned the thousands of new products introduced every year. In addition, manufacturers have engaged in many new product price and promotional allowances as a way of "bribing" their way onto retailers' shelves. These activities play into the hands of already powerful buyers. Figure 11.6 and Table 11.7 describe the types and objectives of various trade deals.

In 2002, about $234 billion was spent in the United States on consumer promotions, with an additional $92 billion spent on trade promotions (promotions to retailers rather than to final consumers). By comparison, consumer advertising was only about $212 billion, so that of total spending for both advertising and promotions, promotions (consumer plus trade) accounted for well over 60 percent. In 2003, just 24 percent of marketing dollars went into consumer advertising, with 46 percent going to consumer promotion and about 19 percent to trade promotion.[39] These numbers

1. *Off invoice.* The purpose of an off-invoice promotion is to discount the product to the dealer for a fixed period of time. It consists of a temporary price cut, and when the time period elapses, the price goes back to its normal level. The specific terms of the discount usually require performance, and the discount lasts for a specified period (e.g., month). Sometimes the trade can buy multiple times and sometimes only once.

2. *Bill-back.* Bill-backs are similar to off-invoice except that the retailer computes the discount per unit for all units bought during the promotional period and then bills the manufacturer for the units sold and any other promotional allowances that are owed after the promotional period is complete. The advantage from the manufacturer's position is the control it gives and guarantees that the retailer performs as the contract indicates before payment is issued. Generally, retailers do not like bill-backs because of the time and effort required.

3. *Free goods.* Usually free goods take the form of extra cases at the same price. For example, buy 3 get 1 free is a free-goods offer.

4. *Cooperative advertising allowances.* Paying for part of the dealers' advertising is called cooperative advertising, which is often abbreviated as co-op advertising. The manufacturer either offers the dealer a fixed dollar amount per unit sold or offers to pay a percentage of the advertising costs. The percentage varies depending on the type of advertising run. If the dealer is prominent in the advertisement, then the manufacturer often pays less, but if the manufacturer is prominent, then he pays more.

5. *Display allowances.* A display allowance is similar to cooperative advertising allowances. The manufacturer wants the retailer to display a given item when a price promotion is being run. To induce the retailer to do this and to help defray the costs, a display allowance is offered. Display allowances are usually a fixed amount per case, such as 50 cents per case.

6. *Sales drives.* For manufacturers selling through brokers or wholesalers, it is necessary to offer incentives. Sales drives are intended to offer the brokers and wholesalers incentives to push the trade deal to the retailer. For every unit sold during the promotional period, the broker and wholesaler receive a percentage or fixed payment per case sold to the retailer. It works as an additional commission for an independent sales organization or additional margin for a wholesaler.

7. *Terms or inventory financing.* The manufacturer may not require payment for 90 days, thus increasing the profitability to the retailer who does not need to borrow to finance inventories.

8. *Count-recount.* Rather than paying retailers on the number of units ordered, the manufacturer does it on the number of units sold. This is accomplished by determining the number of units on hand at the beginning of the promotional period (count) and then determining the number of units on hand at the end of the period (recount). Then, by tracking orders, the manufacturers know the quantity sold during the promotional period. (This differs from a bill-back because the manufacturer verifies the actual sales in count-recount.)

9. *Slotting allowances.* Manufacturers have been paying retailers funds known as slotting allowances to receive space for new products. When a new product is introduced the manufacturer pays the retailer X dollars for a "slot" for the new product. Slotting allowances offer a fixed payment to the retailer for accepting and testing a new product.

10. *Street money.* Manufacturers have begun to pay retailers lump sums to run promotions. The lump sum, not per case sold, is based on the amount of support (feature advertising, price reduction, and display space) offered by the retailer. The name comes from the manufacturer's need to offer independent retailers a fixed fund to promote the product because the trade deal goes to the wholesaler.

Figure 11.6   Trade deals for consumer nondurable goods

Source: Robert C. Blattberg and Scott A. Neslin (1990), *Sales Promotion: Concepts, Methods, and Strategies* (Englewood Cliffs, NJ: Prentice Hall), pp. 318-319.

Table 11.7   Objectives of trade deals for nondurable goods

TACTICS	OBJECTIVES*					
	1	2	3	4	5	6
Off invoice	x	x	x	x	x	
Bill-back	x	x	x	x	x	
Free goods	x		x			
Cooperative advertising	x				x	x
Display allowances	x				x	
Sales drives	x	x				
Slotting allowances		x	x			
Street money	x				x	

Source: Blattberg, Robert C. and Scott A. Neslin (1990), *Sales Promotion: Concepts, Methods, and Strategies* (Englewood Cliffs, NJ: Prentice Hall), p. 321.

Objectives:

1. Retailer merchandising activities
2. Loading the retailer
3. Gaining or maintaining distribution
4. Obtaining price reduction
5. Competitive tool
6. Retailer goodwill

reflect an enduring shift in marketing spending away from advertising and toward promotions in retailing. Buyers who receive these deals grow to expect and insist on them as a price of doing business. Further, manufacturers and retailers have discrepant perceptions of the value and sufficiency of spending in the promotional area; a study by ACNielsen[40] reported less than one fourth of manufacturers perceiving the spending value of their trade promotions as excellent or good (where the choices were excellent, good, fair, and poor). Meanwhile, retailers were asked their perception of whether the share of manufacturer trade promotion dollars received was "more than enough," "sufficient," or "less than enough." Most (83 percent) reported that their share was not enough, with less than 20 percent saying the share was sufficient. Further differences in assessment of trade promotion effects were evident in manufacturers' and retailers' responses to questions about the effect of trade promotions on brand loyalty: 21 percent of retailers said trade promotion spending "definitely helps" brand loyalty, but only 12 percent of manufacturers said the same.

With these types of attitudes and responses, it seems clear that manufacturers are spending more and more on promotion although perceiving their value to be low. Retailer negotiating power forces them to continue spending increases on promotions, however. More specifically, some of the types of deals offered by manufacturers to retailers include:

➤ Forward buying on deals
➤ Slotting allowances
➤ Failure fees

➤ Payment for participation in newspaper inserts
➤ Deepest case allowances possible
➤ Highest possible payments for displays and even shelf placements
➤ No-cost new item introductions
➤ Guaranteed returns at full retail
➤ Invoice deductions for late coupon redemption reimbursements
➤ Manufacturer-supplied labor for shelf sets.[41]

To illustrate the array of offers, we describe the first three deal types in more detail in the following sections.

Forward Buying on Deals

Consumer packaged goods manufacturers can experience wide swings in demand for their products from retailers when they use trade promotions heavily. Temporary wholesale price cuts of one sort or another cause the retailer to engage in forward buying—buying significantly more product than the retailer needs, and stockpiling it until stocks run down again. In the past, companies like Campbell Soup Co. sometimes sold as much as 40 percent of annual chicken noodle soup production to wholesalers and retailers in just 6 weeks because of trade dealing practices. While this strategy clearly increases quantity sold to the retail trade (particularly during the promotional period), it plays havoc with the manufacturers' costs and marketing plans. When a manufacturer marks down a product by 10 percent, for example, it has become common practice for the trade to stock up with a 10- to 12-week supply. That means fewer products are purchased at list price after the promotion ends, and manufacturer profitability is not guaranteed to increase.

The increasing use of EDI technologies in the grocery channel has decreased the forward buying problem somewhat. Continuous replenishment programs (CRP) have been particularly helpful in changing buying practices. Under CRP, a manufacturer and retailer maintain an electronic linkage that informs the manufacturer when the retailer's stocks are running low, triggering a reorder. If manufacturers and retailers have this level of cooperation, forward buying is much less likely to be a problem. However, the pricing practices of manufacturers are the clear drivers of forward buying behavior. These pricing practices induce periodic heavy buying by retailers, and as long as they remain in vogue, forward buying is likely to result.[42]

A related problem is *diverting*. When manufacturers offer a regional trade promotion, for example on the West Coast of the United States, some retailers and wholesalers will buy large volumes and then distribute some cases to stores in the Midwest where the discount is not available. This practice upsets manufacturers' efforts to tailor marketing efforts to regions or neighborhoods. It is the domestic counterpart to gray marketing, the distribution of authorized, branded goods through unauthorized channels overseas. Gray marketing is discussed in more detail in Chapter 7 as a channel conflict problem.

Slotting Allowances

Slotting allowances originated in the 1970s as a way to compensate the grocery trade for all the costs of working a new product into their systems: creating a space, or slot, in the warehouse; revising computerized inventory systems; resetting the shelves to make a place in the store; and helping to defray the cost of stocking and restocking the item. (See Chapter 10 for a discussion of the legal status of slotting allowances.) Because of the scarcity of shelf space, slotting allowances have grown significantly. Suppliers paid $300 to $1,500 per new item in 1982 in slotting allowances. In a study done by ACNielsen in 1997, one third of respondents in the food category spent between $500,000 and $1 million on slotting allowances, and 14 percent spent more than $3 million. Only 6 percent of respondents reported paying no slotting allowances.[43] Slotting allowances reportedly cost manufacturers up to $9 billion in 1999,[44] but the total amount spent on slotting allowances is not known for certain.

In October 1999, the United States Congress held hearings on slotting allowances and began an investigation of them. Some manufacturers even testified anonymously for fear of retailer reprisals. While small manufacturers argue that slotting allowances are so high as to prevent their access to store shelf space, retailers counter that manufacturers should share in the risk of failure of new products. Up to that point, the Federal Trade Commission had reviewed the practice and failed to find it a violation of antitrust law, but the persisting complaints from manufacturers illustrate the continued use of retail power.[45] An FTC report in February 2001, summarizing a workshop in May–June 2000 on slotting allowances and other grocery industry practices, found little consensus between manufacturers and retailers on the amount or effect of slotting allowances, although one speaker estimated it would cost $16.8 million to introduce a small, four-product line in all supermarkets in the United States (suggesting that small manufacturers would have a hard time penetrating national grocery markets with their new products). The report called for more research on the issues and failed to make any recommendations about the legality of slotting.[46] Since that time, there have been some studies on slotting allowances (for a summary, see the discussion in Chapter 10 on legal constraints in channels), but no clear consensus on the net effect of these fees on retail performance or prices has emerged.

Failure Fees

Starting in April 1989, J. M. Jones Co., a wholesaling unit of Super Valu Stores, Inc., began imposing a fee when it had to pull a failing product from its warehouses. If a new product failed to reach a minimum sales target within three months, Jones withdrew it and charged $2,000 for the effort.[47] Failure fees, like slotting allowances, were a focus of the 2000 U.S. Federal Trade Commission conference on grocery retailing practices. Some argue in favor of failure fees because they represent a credible commitment on the part of a manufacturer that its product is good enough to sell well in the retail store. Further, unlike slotting fees, failure fees do not have to be paid up front and, therefore, could be offered even by small manufacturers seeking product placement in grocery stores. But others question how effective failure fees are because a product may fail not due to its inferiority or lack of appeal but due to a lack of retailer support (creating a so-called moral hazard problem). Collecting failure fees after a product has had poor sales may also be much more difficult than collecting slotting allowances up front, making failure fees problematic as a product-signaling tool.[48] Regardless of their efficacy, the continued use of failure fees is another indication of the degree of retailer control in the channel for consumer packaged goods.

Broadened Role and Impact of Private Branding

There is some debate as to whether private branding by retailers is increasing or decreasing. Private labels (also known as store brands) have been, and continue to be, very popular in the United Kingdom. Their sales account for about 36 percent of all grocery sales in Britain. Sainsbury, a leading British grocery chain, launches 1,400 to 1,500 new private-label items per year; private labels account for about half of the products in its stores and 54 percent of its sales.[49] Marks & Spencer, a British retailing legend, has always relied upon its own St. Michael's brand label to carry its product lines.

Years ago, some American retailers—notably Sears, J. C. Penney, Montgomery Ward, and A&P—also committed themselves to private labels as a way of generating loyalty to their stores (rather than to the manufacturers' brands they carried) and of earning extra profits because private-label merchandise generally affords retailers higher gross margins than comparable branded merchandise. Private labels have always been used to provide consumers with extra value, but at these retailers, they have also usually come in generic wrappings and varieties. In other words, they were money-saving but unexciting alternatives relative to national, heavily advertised brands.

Now, however, a number of retailers are upgrading their private-label programs in order to offer an even closer substitute to branded products. A private brand (or private label) is one that is owned or controlled through contract rights by a retailing company, an affiliated group of retailers, or a buying organization. There are five basic categories of private brands: (1) store-name identification programs (products bear the retailer's store name or logo, e.g., The Gap, Ace, NAPA, Benetton); (2) retailer's own brand name identity programs (a brand image independent of the store name that is available in only that company's stores, e.g. Kenmore and Craftsman [Sears], True-Value and Tru-Test [Cotter & Co.]); (3) designer-exclusive programs (merchandise designed and sold under a designer's name in an exclusive arrangement with the retailer, e.g. Martha Stewart [Kmart]); (4) other exclusive licensed name programs (celebrity-endorsed lines or other signature or character label lines developed under exclusive arrangements with the retailer, e.g. Michael Graves [Target]); and (5) generic programs (goods that are essentially unbranded, e.g., Yellow pack no name [Loblaw], Cost Cutter [Kroger]).[50]

Increasingly, private brands of large retailing companies are being positioned as the leading brand in their assortment. Loblaw's, the Canadian grocery chain, pioneered the store brand President's Choice, an upscale offering in everything from chocolate chip cookies to olive oil. The brand has been so successful that Loblaw's sells it through several chains in the United States as well, where it is also positioned as a very credible alternative to the national brands.

On first glance, supermarkets and discount stores have a clear incentive for pushing their own offerings: Private label goods typically cost consumers 10 to 20 percent less than other brands, but their gross margins are as much as twice as high as those for nonstore brands.[51] United States supermarkets get 15 percent of their sales from private labels and make an average pretax profit of 2 percent on sales. In contrast, European grocery chains, which focus much more heavily on store brands, average 7 percent pretax profits. Clearly, private labels are not the only reason for higher profits in European grocery chains; the industry is also much more concentrated in Europe than in the United States, leading to less price competition (the top five supermarket chains in the United States in 1996 accounted for 21 percent of grocery sales, while the top five in the United Kingdom accounted for 62 percent of national grocery sales). Nevertheless, European chains' success with private labels makes their competitors in the United States consider them more seriously.[52]

Although a great deal of media attention has been given to the use of private brands by supermarkets, in fact they have accounted for an average of only 14 percent of total dollar supermarket sales in the United States in the 1980s and 1990s. In comparison, approximately 20 percent of United States apparel purchases are private-label clothes. For specific product classes, however, there are large deviations from the mean. Research shows that private labels tend to do well in grocery categories where they offer quality comparable to national brands. Surprisingly, high quality is much more important than lower price. They also perform better in large dollar-volume categories offering high margins (e.g., paper goods, bleach). They do much worse in categories in which there are multiple national manufacturers investing heavily in national advertising.[53]

The use of private branding has resulted in even greater power for the retailer in the channel of distribution. It has changed the character of manufacturer-retailer relationships in that there is more (1) retailer initiative or responsibility for fashion direction, trend setting, innovation, etc.; (2) retailer responsibility for marketing to consumers, as opposed to an orientation as a distributing agent for suppliers; and (3) strategic concern on the part of many suppliers with marketing to important retailers as opposed to direct concern with the consumer market.[54]

In addition, a private-label program can go too far. Private-label programs often must rely on a strong national-brand program in order for the value comparison to come alive to consumers.[55] When store brands soared to 35 percent of A&P's sales mix in the 1960s, shoppers perceiving a lack of choice defected to competitors. In the late 1980s, Sears began to add more brand-name goods so that it could begin to appeal to a broader base of customers. Competition from competent and stylish specialty retailers has weakened the position of some formerly strong private-goods retailers such as Marks & Spencer in the late 1990s, whose management admits that it "lost touch with our customers."[56]

On balance, the retailer can clearly use private-label products to effectively target its consumers who seek value for the money they spend in the store. When done well, these private labels are formidable competitors to national (or international) brands. However, if not executed properly, or if the environment changes to make the private label program obsolete in its product design, the retailer may suffer. Thus, the threat to branded-goods manufacturers lies not in private labels in general, but in the more upscale private labels that are well managed by their retailers.

The Continued Globalization of Retailing

Retailing has lagged behind other industries in the race to globalize. In 1996, for example, the top five retailers in the world had only 12 percent of their sales outside their home markets. This percentage was far higher for other industries at the time (e.g., entertainment, 34 percent; aerospace, 35 percent; banking, 48 percent; and petroleum refining, 66 percent).[57] While Table 11.1 at the beginning of this chapter makes clear that internationalization of retailing is much broader today than in 1996, there remain several sources of difficulty in expanding a retail operation across national boundaries:

> The need for quality real estate locations on which to site stores
> The need to develop physical logistics operations comparable to those in the home country to source and distribute product
> The need to develop supplier relationships in new markets or to internationalize one's home market suppliers
> The differences in zoning, pricing, taxation, hours-of-operation, labor and hiring, and other regulations in each market
> The need to offer locally attractive products, packaged and positioned in a culturally sensitive manner

As a result of these difficulties, even well-known retailers like Marks & Spencer, Tiffany's, and Price/Costco failed to generate a return on invested capital in international retail operations exceeding their average corporate cost of capital.[58] The difficulties are particularly troublesome in emerging market economies, where in addition to the above problems, the necessary infrastructure to support a retail effort may be lacking.

Despite these difficulties, retailers increasingly are choosing to globalize (or at least internationalize) their operations. They are driven by many factors, including slowing growth in their home markets and the overwhelming attractiveness of overseas markets that offer less intense competition and weakening barriers to foreign market entry. Developing markets offer quickly improving environments. By 1994, free currency convertibility was offered in Indonesia, Poland, Argentina, Mexico, Hungary, Russia, India, China, and Brazil; free majority ownership by a foreign business was permitted in Indonesia, Poland, Argentina, Mexico, Russia, India, and Brazil; and free repatriation of capital and earnings was permitted from Poland, Argentina, Mexico, Hungary, India, China, and Brazil.[59] Such liberalizations have made expansion into developing as well as developed nations much more attractive.

The result has been a flurry of expansionary activity by major world retailers, some of it greenfield investment and some of it fueled by acquisitions. Of the top 20 world retailers listed in Table 11.1, only five operate in just one country (and for all five, that country is the United States). Carrefour operates stores in 20 countries across Europe, Asia, South America, and Africa. Wal-Mart operates stores in South America, Asia, and Europe in addition to North America.

What makes for a successful entry into a foreign retail market? There have certainly been failures (the French department store Galeries Lafayette was forced to withdraw from the U.S. market after an abortive attempt at operating a store in Manhattan; Carrefour pulled out of the United States after attempting to enter; and Wal-Mart sold out to its Hong Kong partner after trying to set up a warehouse club there). The key is a sensible balance between exporting the distinctive retail competencies that make the retailer strong in the home market and being sensitive to local preferences for products and retail services. Wal-Mart's initial entry into Argentina in 1995 showed a lack on these dimensions; at first it tried to import its American style of retailing with no adaptations. The merchandise mix included appliances wired for 110-volt electric power (Argentina operates on 220 volts) and American cuts of beef, and the stores themselves had too-narrow aisles and carpeting that quickly looked faded and dirty. Meanwhile, French competitor Carrefour had been operating hyper-markets in Argentina for some time, very successfully. Not surprisingly, Wal-Mart made large losses in its first two years in Argentina, which it only began to turn around in 1998 when it revised its local strategy to be more in keeping with local norms.[60]

The retailers that successfully expand outside their local borders can benefit from what is known as a virtuous cycle. As they grow in scale, they benefit ever more from economies of scale in purchasing and sourcing as well as in advertising and infor-mation technology management. Successful products from one market can be easily exported into another. Large scale also permits efficient investment in common assets such as marketing research expertise and financing. With successful expansion, profits can be funneled into the enhancement of brand equity in worldwide markets. Thus, the big can get bigger, and this is part of what motivates the worldwide expansion char-acterizing retailing today.[61]

Faced with stronger and stronger transnational competitors, what can a local incumbent retailer do? Some have found the ability to sell to niche segments in their home markets, offering superior service, products, and location, tailored to local tastes. Brazil's grocery chain Pao de Azucar followed this strategy following the entry of Carrefour and then Wal-Mart into the country. Rather than try to beat these retail behe-moths at their own game, Pao de Azucar instead refocused its business to emphasize the convenient locations its stores enjoyed and to provide credit to its customers, a popular local service that the entrants did not provide. Since the entrants could not match the locations of the incumbent retailer, Pao de Azucar had a basis for viable competition even in the face of higher costs.[62] A market for high-service, conveniently located retail outlets is likely to remain in these markets, just as in Wal-Mart's or Carrefour's home markets. But only those local competitors who excel at providing the extra service that these segments demand will survive the onslaught of multinational retailers like these.

An important insight to take away from this description of the globalization of retailing is that international competition is now a given rather than an exception, as it was until recently. This is not just an item of curiosity, even for local retailers who themselves do not cross national borders to do business. Given the entry of multina-tional retailers into many markets, and not just the major developed ones, even local retailers are well advised to consider how international retail competition is likely to affect them and how to protect their businesses (or profitably harvest them) in the face of potential and actual competition from outside entrants.

SUMMARY AND CONCLUSIONS

Retailing is an enormously complex and varied enterprise the world over. As the key channel member in direct contact with the consumer end-user, the retailer's actions are critical to the success of the marketing channel. A retailer's position is defined by the demand-side and cost-side characteristics of its operation. These characteristics map into the service outputs provided to consumers who shop with the retailer. Because markets are made up of distinct consumer seg-ments, each of which demands different levels of service outputs, a retailer can successfully differentiate itself from the competition on the demand and cost sides, even if it sells comparable or identical products to those of its competitors. Indeed, without a distinct offering on the service output side or a distinct cost advantage, a retailer of competitive products risks failure in the marketplace. Different types of retailers can be categorized by the levels of service outputs they provide and by their cost positions.

One of the most important developments on the consumer side has been the increasing importance of convenience in retail shopping. Consumers in many countries suffer from time poverty, and when this is combined with growing purchasing power, consumers demand a broader array of channel services that lower their time cost of shopping. Conversely, if they choose to buy at a lower-service retail outlet, they demand a lower price to compensate for the full cost of shopping there. This places increasing pressure on retailers both to control costs and to enhance the value they add to the products sold in their stores.

Power and coordination issues still affect retail channel management. Retailers use their leverage to engage in forward buying on deals, and to demand concessions from their suppliers such as slotting allowances and failure fees. Retailers in grocery and apparel industries have also developed strong private branding programs that pose a competitive threat to the nationally branded goods supplied by manufacturers. Manufacturers respond by building and maintaining strong brands and by bearing the cost of more channel flows. They also seek to change the basis for pricing to their retailers and use multiple channel strategies to limit their dependence on any one retailer.

The globalization of retailing is an emerging phenomenon that will affect consumers and competing retailers very significantly. Hypermarkets have been very active in global expansion, although some specialty retailers also have moved overseas. Globalization and consolidation have been facilitated by the formalization of regional blocs, such as the European Union. The increasing level of concentration on a transnational level suggests that suppliers will sell to fewer retail corporations in the future and that these global retailers in turn will seek more and more favorable terms from their suppliers, who will be expected to serve them on a worldwide basis. International product sourcing of the most popular products, combined with greater cost controls, is likely to mean greater choice at lower prices for many consumers. Even local retailers who themselves do not intend to sell in overseas markets cannot escape the competitive effects of global retailers entering their home markets.

Take-Aways

- Retailing is defined as the set of activities involved in selling goods and services to ultimate consumers for personal consumption.
- A retail positioning strategy involves both cost-side and demand-side decisions:
  - On the cost side, the retailer must decide in general whether to emphasize *high margin* or *high merchandise turnover*, while both are financially good, it is extremely difficult to achieve them together.
  - On the demand side, the retailer must choose which service outputs to focus on providing for the target consumer segment(s).
  - Together, the cost-side and demand-side decisions the retailer makes constitute its *retail position*.

- Retailing strategically involves:
  - Managing a multichannel shopping experience that is increasingly demanded by consumers
    - The Internet is now a well-established retail outlet, as well as an enabler of shopping through other outlets.
    - Direct selling provides an alternative method of going to market when close interpersonal ties are crucial to building and maintaining consumer relationships.
    - Hybrid shopping, where consumers use more than one retail outlet to complete the shopping experience, requires special skill to avoid channel conflict.
  - Recognition at the manufacturer level of the continued strong power position of the biggest retailers in one's market. These retailers use many tools to further their interests, including:
    - Forward buying on deals
    - Slotting allowances
    - Failure fees
    - Private branding
  - Understanding and leveraging the increased international and even global reach of retailing today. Even if you as a retailer are not present in multiple national markets, it is likely that one of your competitors is, and therefore, in all situations it is important to understand the effect of globalization in retailing.

DISCUSSION QUESTIONS

1. Think of a product you have recently purchased at retail. Evaluate (a) what service outputs you expected to get from the retail experience, (b) how you chose the retailer to visit based on your service output demands, and (c) how well the retailer met those service output demands. Would you buy the same product at a different type of retailer on a different purchase occasion (e.g., when shopping for home use versus at work; when shopping at home versus on vacation)?

2. Why are a low average retail margin and a high turnover rate in a retail outlet a viable combination for retail financial success? What would happen if margin and turnover were both low? Both high? Can you think of retailer examples that fit (a) a low margin and high turnover strategy; (b) a high margin and low turnover strategy; or (c) a high margin and high turnover strategy?

3. What type(s) of power are represented by retailers demanding slotting allowances or failure fees from their suppliers? Why do suppliers comply? Is conflict generated by the use of this power and, if so, of what sort?

4. You are an apparel manufacturer, selling to major department stores in the United States. Each retailer makes different demands of you. One requires that you ship garments to each store rather than to one central warehouse and that each garment already be tagged and ready to hang on the retailer's store racks. Another requires you to adopt its electronic data interchange (EDI) system to implement continuous replenishment, meaning that you will have to ship frequent replacements for garments that sell throughout the season. Your cost structure is increasing significantly as a result. What can you do to protect your profit margins?

5. Why do retailers sometimes choose to acquire overseas retailers or build their own overseas retail outlets and sometimes choose to partner with a local licensee or retailer (without completely acquiring them)? Benetton, for example, chooses to license its retailers and not control their activities, but it controls the creation of the merchandise and how it is promoted. Wal-Mart chooses to acquire and/or build outlets rather than franchise or license them. In your answer, consider the strategic competencies of a retailer, the local market conditions, and costs.

ENDNOTES

1. For a more comprehensive discussion of retailing structure, competition, and management than space allows here, the reader is urged to consult Levy, Michael and Barton A. Weitz (2003), *Retailing Management*, 5th ed. (Boston, MA: Irwin/McGraw-Hill), and Berman, Barry and Joel R. Evans (2000), *Retail Management: A Strategic Approach*, 8th ed. (Englewood Cliffs, NJ: Pearson Education).

2. Davidson, William R., Daniel J. Sweeney, and Ronald W. Stampfl (1984), *Retailing Management*, 5th ed. (New York: John Wiley & Sons), p. 14.

3. Specifically, global retail sales in 2003 were about $8 trillion. Wal-Mart's 2003 sales were $259 billion. The ratio of Wal-Mart's sales to global sales is therefore 3.24 percent, or roughly three and one-fourth percent of all world retail sales.

4. For a detailed discussion of financial strategies adopted by retailers, including the strategic profit model, see Levy and Weitz, previously cited.

5. Lusch, Robert F., Patrick Dunne, and Randall Gebhardt (1993), *Retail Marketing*, 2nd ed. (Cincinnati, OH: South-Western Publishing Co.).

6. Information on Wal-Mart comes from the Wal-Mart Web site and its annual report. Information on Kmart comes from the Kmart Web site and the financial reports of Sears Holding Corporation, which now owns Kmart (accessed July 1, 2005).

7. See Coughlan, Anne T. (2004), *Michaels Craft Stores: Integrated Channel Management and Vendor-Retailer Relations* Case, Kellogg Case Clearing House Number 5-104-010.

8. Pashigian, B. Peter and Eric D. Gould (1998), "Internalizing Externalities: The Pricing of Space in Shopping Malls," *Journal of Law and Economics* 41, no. 1 (April), pp. 115–142.

9. *Economist* (2001), "Face Value: The Physics of Shopping," *Economist*, August 18, p. 52, describes the case of 99¢ Only Stores.

10. Berner, Robert (2002), "Has Target's Food Foray Missed the Mark?" *Business Week*, November 25, p. 76.

11. Spurgeon, Devon (2000), "Walgreen Takes Aim at Discount Chains, Supermarkets," *Wall Street Journal*, June 29, p. B4.

12. Pressler, Margaret Webb (2002), "Male Shoppers Adopt Speed Over Style," *Chicago Tribune*, September 26, Section 5, p. 8.

13. Berner, Robert (2003), "Dark Days in White Goods for Sears," *Business Week*, March 10, pp. 78–79.

14. Morse, Dan (2002), "Tennessee Producer Tries New Tactic in Sofas: Speed," *Wall Street Journal*, November 19, p. A1.

15. Norman, Jan (2003), "Used Book Seller Exploits Good Read on Niche Market," *Chicago Tribune*, June 23, Section 4, p. 6.

16. Lee, Louise (2003), "Thinking Small at the Mall," *BusinessWeek*, May 26, pp. 94–95.

17. Pascual, Aixa M. (2002), "Lowe's Is Sprucing Up Its House," *BusinessWeek*, June 3, pp. 56–58.

18. And its employees call themselves "WaMulians"!

19. Allers, Kimberly (2003), "A New Banking Model," *Fortune*, March 31, pp. 102–104, and personal communication with a Washington Mutual manager.

20. Cahill, Joseph B. (1999), "The Secret Weapon of Big Discounters: Lowly Shopping Cart," *Wall Street Journal*, November 24, pp. A1, A10.

21. Song, Lisa (2002), "Retailers Find Way on the Web," *Chicago Tribune*, November 25, Section 4, pp. 3, 5.

22. This definition is taken from the Direct Selling Association's Web site, www.dsa.org, and is very similar to a definition provided in Robert A. Peterson and Thomas R. Wotruba (1996), "What Is Direct Selling? Definition, Perspectives, and Research Agenda," *Journal of Personal Selling & Sales Management* 16, no. 4 (Fall), pp. 1–16. The Direct Selling Association (DSA) is a United States trade association of direct selling organizations, including such well-known multilevel marketing organizations as Amway (soaps, detergents, and many other home products) and Mary Kay (cosmetics), and party-plan organizations such as Tupperware (home storage) and Discovery Toys (children's educational toys). The DSA serves as the Secretariat for the World Federation of Direct Selling Organizations (WFDSA, www.wfdsa.org), which is the superorganization of all national DSAs around the world. The WFDSA has over 50 national DSAs as members.

23. Peterson and Wotruba, previously cited.

24. The example is drawn from Coughlan, Anne T. and Kent Grayson (1998), "Network Marketing Organizations: Compensation Plans, Retail Network Growth, and Profitability," *International Journal of Research in Marketing* 15, no. 5 (December), pp. 401–426.

25. See Coughlan and Grayson, previously cited, for a model showing these effects.

26. Other names for pyramid schemes include Ponzi schemes, chain letters, chain selling, money games, referral selling, and investment lotteries. See, for example, the World Federation of Direct Selling Associations Web site, www.wfdsa.org, and a consumer alert on the U.S. Federal Trade Commission's Web site entitled "Profits in Pyramid Schemes? Don't Bank on It!" downloaded from www.ftc.gov (accessed July 1, 2005). Also see Vander Nat, Peter J. and William W. Keep (2002), "Marketing Fraud: An Approach for Differentiating Multilevel Marketing from Pyramid Schemes," *Journal of Public Policy & Marketing* 21, no. 1 (Spring), pp. 139–151.

27. Personal communication with Richard Bartlett, Vice Chairman, Mary Kay Corporation, December 1999. See also Bartlett, Richard C. (1994), *The Direct Option* (College Station, Texas: Texas A&M University Press), Chapter 12.

28. For a fascinating set of profiles of successful direct selling companies, see Richard C. Bartlett (1994), *The Direct Option* (College Station, TX: Texas A&M University Press).

29. Yue, Lorene (2003), "Retailers Let Web Shoppers Pick Up the Goods at Stores," *Chicago Tribune*, July 8, Section 3, p. 3.

30. Tedeschi, Bob (2002/2003), "How Harley Revved Online Sales," *Business 2.0*, December 2002/January 2003, p. 44.

31. Chandler, Susan (2002), "Retailers Heed Call of Catalogs," *Chicago Tribune*, September 21, Section 2, pp. 1–2.

32. See Godes, David B. (2002), *Avon.com* Case, Harvard Case Clearing House, Case number N9-503-016. For another company's challenge in this realm, see Coughlan, Anne T. (2004), *Mary Kay Corporation: Direct Selling and the Challenge of Online Channels* Case, Kellogg Case Clearing House, Case number 5-104-009.

33. McKinsey & Company, Inc. (1992), *Evaluating the Impact of Alternative Store Formats, Final Report* (Chicago: McKinsey & Company, Inc., May), p. 2.

34. ACNielsen Company (1993), *1992/1993 Profiles of Nielsen SCANTRACK Marketing*, ACNielsen Company, December.

35. Aufreiter, Nora and Tim McGuire (1999), "Walking Down the Aisles," *Ivey Business Journal* 63, no. 3 (March–April), pp. 49–54; Peltz, James F. (1998), "Food Companies' Fight Spills into Aisles," *Los Angeles Times*, October 28, Business Section, p. 1; *MMR/Business and Industry* (1999), "Loblaw's Continues to Strengthen Position," *MMR/Business and Industry* 16, no. 21 (October 18), p. 20.

36. Hoyt, Christopher W. (1987), "Key Account Manager Fills Hot Seat in Food Business," *Marketing News*, November 6, 1987, p. 22.

37. See Duff, Christina (1993), "Nation's Retailers Ask Vendors to Help Share Expenses," *Wall Street Journal*, August 4, 1993, p. B3.

38. *Food Marketing Institute Backgrounder* (2002), "Slotting Allowances in the Supermarket Industry," *Food Marketing Institute Backgrounder,* downloaded from www.fmi.org (accessed July 1, 2005).

39. Data for 2002 and 2003 are from the Promotion Marketing Association and *Promo* Magazine's annual survey of promotion and advertising activity, published online on March 26, 2003, and April 1, 2004, respectively. Summaries were downloaded from www.promomagazine.com (accessed July 1, 2005).

40. *Consumer Insight* (2003) ACNielsen 2002 Trade Promotion Practices Study, *Consumer Insight,* Summer, downloaded from www2.acnielsen.com/pubs/2003_q2_ci_tpp.shtml (accessed July 6, 2005).

41. Hoyt, Christopher W., previously cited, p. 22.

42. See, for example, *Supermarket News* (1996), "Distribution Discourse," *Supermarket News,* October 14, pp. 17, 20, 22.

43. *Supermarket Business* (1997), "More Facts and Figures on Slotting," *Supermarket Business,* July 1997, p. 19. The percentages were lower for health and beauty products and for general merchandise/nonfood products, with 14 and 15 percent, respectively, paying between $500,000 and $1 million and close to 30 percent of respondents reporting no payment of slotting allowances.

44. Toosi, Nahal (1999), "Congress Looks at the Selling of Shelf Space," *St. Louis Post-Dispatch,* September 15, Business Section, p. C1; Superville, Darlene (1999), "Are 'Slotting Fees' Fair? Senate Panel Investigates; Practice Involves Paying Grocers for Shelf Space," *The San Diego Union-Tribune,* September 15, Business Section, p. C-1.

45. Toosi, Nahal (1999), "Congress Looks at the Selling of Shelf Space," *St. Louis Post-Dispatch,* September 15, Business Section, p. C1; Superville, Darlene (1999), "Are 'Slotting Fees' Fair? Senate Panel Investigates; Practice Involves Paying Grocers for Shelf Space," *The San Diego Union-Tribune,* September 15, Business Section, p. C-1.

46. Federal Trade Commission (2001), "Report on the Federal Trade Commission Workshop on Slotting Allowances and Other Marketing Practices in the Grocery Industry," February, available at www.ftc.gov.

47. Zwiebach, Elliott (1989), "Super Value Division Imposes Failure Fee," *Supermarket News,* May 8, p. 1.

48. Federal Trade Commission (2001), "Report on the Federal Trade Commission Workshop on Slotting Allowances and Other Marketing Practices in the Grocery Industry," February, available at www.ftc.gov.

49. deLisser, Eleena and Kevin Helliker (1994), "Private Labels Reign in British Groceries," *Wall Street Journal,* March 3, pp. B1, B9; Quelch, John A. and David Harding (1996), "Brands Versus Private Labels: Fighting to Win," *Harvard Business Review* 74, no. 1 (January–February), pp. 99–109.

50. Sweeney, Daniel J. (1987), *Product Development and Branding* (Dublin, OH: Management Horizons).

51. deLisser, Eleena and Kevin Helliker (1994), previously cited.

52. Quelch, John A. and David Harding (1996), previously cited.

53. Sethuraman, Raj (1991), "The Effect of Marketplace Factors on Private Label Penetration in Grocery Products," University of Iowa Working Paper, December; Hoch, Stephan J. and Shumeet Banerji (1993), "When Do Private Labels Succeed?" *Sloan Management Review,* Summer pp. 57–67.

54. Sweeney, Daniel J., previously cited.

55. For example, Perrigo Company supplies no less than 857 imitations of major health and beauty aid brands to chains like Wal-Mart, Kmart, and Rite Aid. See Stern, Gabriella (1993), "Perrigo's Knockoffs of Name-Brand Drugs Turn into Big Sellers," *Wall Street Journal,* July 15, p. A1.

56. Beck, Ernest (1999), "Britain's Marks & Spencer Struggles to Revive Its Old Luster in Retailing," *Wall Street Journal,* November 8, p. A34.

57. Incandela, Denise, Kathleen L. McLaughlin, and Christiana Smith Shi (1999), "Retailers to the World," *McKinsey Quarterly*, no. 3, pp. 84–97.

58. Barth, Karen, Nancy J. Karch, Kathleen McLaughlin, and Christiana Smith Shi (1996), "Global Retailing: Tempting Trouble?" *McKinsey Quarterly*, no. 1, pp. 116–125.

59. Barth et. al. 1996, previously cited.

60. Krauss, Clifford (1999), "Selling to Argentina (as Translated from the French)," *The New York Times on the Web*, December 5, Business World Section.

61. Incandela et al. (1999), previously cited.

62. *Economist* (1997), "Retailing in South America: Survival Skills," *Economist*, July 12, pp. 57–58.

A Glossary of Pricing and Buying Terms Commonly Used by Retailers

Cash Datings: Cash datings include C.O.D. (cash on delivery), C.W.O. (cash with order), R.O.G. (receipt of goods), S.D.–B.L. (sight draft–bill of lading). S.D.–B.L. means that a sight draft is attached to the bill of lading and must be honored before the buyer takes possession of the shipment.

Cash Discount: Vendors selling on credit offer a cash discount for payment within a specified period. The cash discount is usually expressed in the following format: "2/10, net 30." This means that the seller extends credit for 30 days. If payment is made within 10 days, a 2% discount is offered to the buyer. The 2% interest rate for 10 days is equivalent to a 36% effective interest rate per year. Therefore, passing up cash discounts can be very costly. Some intermediaries who operate on slim margins simply cannot realize a profit on a merchandise shipment unless they take advantage of the cash discount. Channel intermediaries usually maintain a line of credit at low interest rates to pay their bills within the cash discount period.

Delivered Sale: The seller pays all freight charges to the buyer's destination and retains title to the goods until they are received by the buyer.

F.O.B.: The seller places the merchandise "free on board" the carrier at the point of shipment or other predesignated place. The buyer assumes title to the merchandise and pays all freight charges from this point.

Freight Allowances: F.O.B. terms can be used with freight allowances to transfer the title to the buyer at the point of shipping, whereas the seller absorbs the transportation cost. The seller ships F.O.B. and the buyer deducts freight costs from the invoice payment.

Future Datings: Future datings include:

1. Ordinary dating, such as "2/10, net 30."
2. End-of-month dating, such as "2/10, net 30, E.O.M.," where the cash discount and the net credit periods begin on the first day of the following month rather than on the invoice date.
3. Proximo dating, such as "2%, 10th proximo, net 60," which specifies a date in the following month on which payment must be made in order to take the cash discount.
4. Extra dating, such as "2/10—30 days extra," which means that the buyer has 70 days from the invoice date to pay his bill and benefit from the discount.
5. Advance or season dating, such as "2/10, net 30 as of May 1," which means that the discount and net periods are calculated from May 1. Sometimes extra dating is accompanied by an anticipation allowance. For example, if the buyer is quoted "2/10, 60 days extra," and he pays in 10 days, or 60 days ahead, an additional discount is made available to him.

Gross Margin of Profit: The dollar difference between the *total* cost of goods and net sales.

Gross Margin Return on Inventory (GMROI): Total gross margin dollars divided by average inventory (at cost). GMROI is used most appropriately in measuring the performance of products within a single merchandise category. The measure permits the buyer to look at products with different gross margin percentages and different rates of inventory turnover and make a relatively quick evaluation as to which are the best performers. The components of GMROI are:

Gross Margin Percentage
(gross margin)/(net sales)

Sales-to-Inventory Ratio
× (net sales)/(average inventory) (at cost)

GMROI
= (gross margin)/(average inventory) (at cost)

Initial Markup or Mark-On: The difference between merchandise cost and the original retail value.

Maintained Markup or Margin: The difference between the *gross* cost of goods sold and net sales.

Markdown: A reduction in the original or previous retail price of merchandise. The *markdown percentage* is the ratio of the dollar markdown during a period to the net sales for the same period.

Markup: The difference between merchandise cost and the retail price.

Merchandise Cost: The billed cost of merchandise less any applicable trade or quantity discounts plus inbound transportation costs, if paid by the buyer. Cash discounts are not deducted to arrive at merchandise cost. Usually, they are either deducted from "aggregate cost of goods sold" at the end of an accounting period or added to net operating profits. If cash discounts are added to net operating profit, the amount added is treated as financial income with no effect on gross margins.

Off-Retail: Designates specific reductions off the original retail price. Retailers can express markup in terms of retail price or cost. Large retailers and progressive small retailers express markups in terms of retail for several reasons. First, other operating ratios are expressed in terms of percentage net sales. Second, net sales figures are available more often than cost figures. Finally, most trade statistics are expressed in terms of sales.

Markup on retail can be converted to cost base by using the following formula:

markup % on cost = (markup % on retail)/(100% − markup % on retail).

Conversely,

markup % on retail = (markup % on cost)/(100% + markup % on cost).

Original Retail: The first price at which the merchandise is offered for sale.

Quantity Discounts: Vendors offer two types of quantity discounts: noncumulative and cumulative. Although noncumulative discounts are offered on volume of each order, cumulative discounts are offered on total volume for a specified period. Quantity discounts are offered to encourage volume buying. Legally, they should not exceed production and distribution cost savings to the seller because of volume buying.

Sale Retail: The final selling price.

Seasonal Discounts: Discounts offered to buyers of seasonal products who place their order before the season's buying period. This enables the manufacturer to use his equipment more efficiently by spreading production throughout the year.

Total Cost: Total cost of goods sold = gross cost of goods sold + workroom costs − cash discounts.

Trade Discount: Vendors usually quote a list price and offer a trade discount to provide the purchaser a reasonable margin to cover his operating expenses and provide for net profit margin. Trade discounts are sometimes labeled *functional discounts*. They are usually quoted in a series of percentages, such as list price less 33%, 15%, 5%, for different channel functions performed by different intermediaries. Therefore, if a list price of $100 is assumed, the discount applies as follows for the different channel members:

List Price	$100.00	
Less 33%	$ 33.00	(retailer-performed flow)
	$ 67.00	
Less 15%	$ 10.05	(wholesaler-performed flow)
	$ 56.95	
Less 5%	$ 2.85	(manufacturers' representative-performed flow)
	$ 54.10	

Merchandise Planning
and Control

Merchandise planning and control start with decisions about merchandise variety and assortment. Variety decisions involve determining the different kinds of goods to be carried or services offered. For example, a department store carries a wide variety of merchandise ranging from men's clothing and women's fashions to sports equipment and appliances. On the other hand, assortment decisions involve determination of the range of choice (e.g., brands, styles or models, colors, sizes, prices) offered to the customer within a variety classification. The more carefully and wisely decisions on variety and assortment are made, the more likely the retailer is to achieve a satisfactory rate of stockturn (stock turnover).

The rate of stockturn is the number of times during a given period in which the average amount of stock on hand is sold. It is most commonly determined by dividing the average inventory at cost into the cost of the merchandise sold. It is also computed by dividing average inventory at retail into the net sales figure or by dividing average inventory in physical units into sales in physical units. To achieve a high rate of stockturn, retailers frequently attempt to limit their investment in inventory, which in turn reduces storage space as well as such expenses as interest, taxes, and insurance on merchandise. Fresher merchandise will be on hand, thereby generating more sales. Thus, a rapid stockturn can lead to greater returns on invested capital.[1]

Although the retailing firms with the highest rates of turnover tend to realize the greatest profit-to-sales ratios,[2] significant problems may be encountered by adopting high-turnover goals. For example, higher sales volume can be generated through lower margins, which in turn reduce profitability; lower inventory levels may result in additional ordering (clerical) costs and the loss of quantity discounts; and greater expense may be involved in receiving, checking, and marking merchandise. Merchandise budget planning provides the means by which the appropriate balance can be achieved between retail stock and sales volume.

Merchandise Budgeting

The merchandise budget plan is a forecast of specified merchandise-related activities for a definite period. Although the usual period is one season of 6 months, in practice it is often broken down into monthly or even shorter periods. Merchandise budgeting requires the retail decision maker to make forecasts and plans relative to five basic variables: sales, stock levels, reductions, purchases, and gross margin and operating profit.[3] Each of these variables will be addressed briefly.

Planned Sales and Stock Levels

The first step in budget determination is the preparation of the sales forecast for the season and for each month in the season for which the budget is being prepared. The second step involves the determination of the beginning-of-the-month (B.O.M.) inventory (stock on hand), which necessitates specification of a desired rate of stockturn for each month of the season. If, for example, the desired stock-sales ratio for the month of June is 4 and forecasted (planned) sales during June are $10,000, then the planned B.O.M. stock would be $40,000.[4] It is also important for budgeting purposes to calculate stock available at the end of the month (E.O.M. stock). This figure is identical to the B.O.M. stock for the following month. Thus, in our example, May's E.O.M. stock is $40,000 (or June's B.O.M. stock).

Planned Reductions

This third step in budget preparation involves accounting for markdowns, shortages, and employee discounts. Reduction planning is critical because any amount of reductions has exactly the same effect on the value of stock as an equal amount of sales. Markdowns vary from month to month, depending on special and sales events. In addition, shortages are becoming an increasing problem for retailers. Shortages result from shoplifting, employee pilferage, miscounting, and pricing and checkout mistakes. Generally, merchandise managers can rely on past data in forecasting both shortages and employee discounts.

Planned Purchases

When figures for sales, opening (B.O.M.) and closing (E.O.M.) stocks, and reductions have been forecast, the fourth step, the planning of purchases in dollars, becomes merely a mechanical mathematical operation. Thus, planned purchases are equal to planned stock at the end of the month (E.O.M.) + planned sales + planned reductions − stock at the beginning of the month (B.O.M.). Suppose, for example, that the planned E.O.M. stock for June was $67,500[5] and that reductions for June were forecasted to be $2,500. Then,

Planned E.O.M. stock (June 30)	$67,500
Planned sales (June 1–June 30)	10,000
Planned reductions	2,500
Total:	$80,000
Less	
Planned B.O.M. stock (June 1)	40,000
Planned purchases	$40,000

The planned-purchases figure is, however, based on retail prices. To determine the financial resources needed to acquire the merchandise, it is necessary to determine planned purchases at cost. The difference between planned purchases at retail and at cost represents the initial markup goal for the merchandise in question. This goal is established by determining the amount of operating expenses necessary to achieve the forecasted sales volume, as well as the profits desired from the specific operation, and combining this information with the data on reductions. Thus,

$$\text{Initial markup goal} = (\text{expenses} + \text{profit} + \text{reductions}) / (\text{net sales} + \text{reductions})$$

A term frequently used in retailing is *open-to-buy*. It refers to the amount, in terms of retail prices or at cost, that a buyer can receive into stock during a certain period on the basis of the plans formulated.[6] Thus, planned purchases and open-to-buy may be synonymous where forecasts coincide with actual results. However, adjustments in inventories, fluctuations in sales volume, unplanned markdowns, and goods ordered but not received all serve to complicate the determination of the amount that a buyer may spend.[7]

Planned Gross Margin and Operating Profit

The *gross margin* is the initial markup adjusted for price changes, stock shortages, and other reductions. The difference between gross margin and expenses required to generate sales will yield either a contribution to profit or a net operating profit (before taxes), depending, of course, on the sophistication of a retailer's accounting system and the narrowness of his merchandise budgeting.

ENDNOTES

1. Duncan, Delbert J., Stanley C. Hollander, and Ronald Savitt (1983), *Modern Retailing Management*, 10th ed. (Homewood, IL: Richard D. Irwin), p. 266.

2. Duncan, Delbert J., Stanley C. Hollander, and Ronald Savitt, previously cited, pp. 266–267.

3. All of these variables have been treated more completely elsewhere, should the reader desire more detail. See Duncan, Hollander, and Savitt, previously cited. See also Levy, Michael and Barton A. Weitz (1995), *Retailing Management*, 2nd ed.

    (Chicago: Richard D. Irwin, Inc., 1995), pp. 303–324.

4. Numerous variations are used to determine B.O.M. stock. See Duncan, Hollander, and Savitt, previously cited, p. 229.

5. Derived from a desired stock-sales ratio for July of 4.5 and projected sales for July of $15,000. Remember, June's E.O.M. is the same as July's B.O.M.

6. Duncan, Hollander, and Savitt, previously cited, p. 234.

7. Duncan, Hollander, and Savitt, previously cited, p. 234.

Wholesaling

After reading this chapter you will be able to:

- Distinguish three broad categories of institutions that constitute the wholesaling sector
- Describe the nature of an independent wholesaler-distributor's value added and explain why this sector is growing
- Sketch mechanisms by which channel members become a federation to offer exceptional services while cutting their costs
- Pinpoint the major distinctions between a wholesaler voluntary group and a dealer cooperative and relate this to the value they provide their members
- Explain why consolidation is common in wholesaling and sketch the manufacturer's possible responses to a consolidation wave
- Sketch the ways in which wholesaling is being altered by electronic commerce
- Contrast sales agents and wholesaler-distributors in the ways that matter to a manufacturer
- Explain why the future for the wholesaler-distributor is optimistic

INTRODUCTION

Wholesaling (wholesale trade, wholesale distribution) refers to business establishments that do not sell products to a significant degree to ultimate household consumers. Instead, these businesses sell products primarily to other businesses: retailers, merchants, contractors, industrial users, institutional users, and commercial users. *Wholesale businesses sell physical inputs and products to other businesses.* Wholesaling is closely associated with tangible goods; however, these entities create their value added through providing services, that is, channel flows. Although that value added is quite real, very little about wholesaling is tangible: It is the epitome of a service industry. In a channel stretching from the manufacturer to the final household user, wholesaling is an intermediate step.

This chapter is about the institutions that wholesale, that is, provide physical goods as inputs to other businesses. The rest of this chapter covers in depth what wholesalers do and how to deal with them. This chapter is about the *nature of these institutions* and the unique challenges they face.[1] What is behind such an important sector of the world's largest economy?

This chapter focuses on wholesaler-distributors, the largest and most prevalent companies in business-to-business channels. It first explores the nature of the wholesaler-distributor sector and describes how they create value added. Then it describes innovative ways of banding together to provide exceptional services and lower channel costs. While these methods (called adaptive channels) are novel, there is every reason to believe they will become more widespread. Next, it examines contractual arrangements to achieve economies of scale (voluntary groups and cooperatives). This leads to a discussion of the wave of consolidation that is altering wholesaling in many industries. It explores causes and effects of wholesale consolidation and examines the possible responses of manufacturers. Next, it presents special issues concerning export distribution channels. Then the chapter turns to informed speculation on the future of the wholesaling sector (including e-commerce and reverse auctions) and closes by returning to that part of the wholesaling sector that is not covered by independent wholesaler distributors. These are the options of vertical integration and outside sales agents.

This chapter will refer heavily to statistics from the United States. These are not unrepresentative of other developed economies. In emerging economies, the size and activity of the wholesale sector is more difficult to document, but it is surely substantial and varied.

AN OVERVIEW OF THE WHOLESALING SECTOR

Wholesaler-Distributors

Many different institutions perform the channel flows in business-to-business (B2B) marketing channels. Wholesaler-distributors are the largest and most significant participants.

Wholesaler-distributors are independently owned and operated firms that buy and sell products to which they have taken ownership. Generally, wholesaler-distributors operate one or more warehouses in which they receive and inventory goods for later reshipping. In the United States, the industry plays a large and influential role in the economy.[2] Consider these figures.

- ➤ In aggregate, wholesale distribution contributed 7 percent of U.S. private gross domestic product income in 2003. To put this figure into perspective, retailing contributes 8 percent, manufacturing contributes 15 percent, and services contribute 52 percent.

- ➤ Wholesale distribution contributes disproportionately to economic growth, accounting for 25 percent of total productivity gains in the U.S. economy in the last decade.

- ➤ One reason for wholesale distribution's disproportionate contribution to economic growth is that distributors account for one out of every five dollars spent on computer hardware and software. Wholesale distribution spends more on IT on a per-employee basis than almost any industry in the United States.

- ➤ Independent wholesaler-distributors have consistently accounted for roughly one in every 20 jobs in the United States throughout the past century.

The U.S. wholesale distribution industry is represented by the National Association of Wholesaler-Distributors (NAW), a federation of 97 national wholesale distribution line-of-trade associations and individual firms totaling more than 400,000 companies. Table 12.1 lists some sources of information on wholesaler-distributors and on the wholesaling industry in general.

Table 12.1   Some sources of information about the wholesaling sector

Internet Resources	There are many sources of information about wholesale distribution on the Internet.
General Industry Information	• The National Association of Wholesaler-Distributors operates two Web sites: www.NAWpubs.org—Online bookstore of NAW reports www.NAWmeetings.org—Upcoming NAW-sponsored events • www.PembrokeConsulting.com (A source of forecasts, data, and analyses exclusively on wholesale distribution)

Total U.S. sales of wholesaler-distributors in 2003 were approximately $2.9 trillion. As a result, wholesaler-distributors are the largest and most important of the organizations counted in wholesale trade. As this is the largest and best-documented category, it is the focus of this chapter.

There is a distinction between wholesalers and distributors, which we shall ignore. It is worth noting, however, that the terms have different roots and at one time represented distinct sectors in themselves. Typically, the term *wholesaler* refers to a company that resells products to another intermediary, while the term *distributor* refers to a company that resells product to the customer that will use the product. Thus, a pharmaceutical wholesaler resells prescription drugs to a retail pharmacy, which then resells the product to a household consumer. An industrial MRO distributor sells products such as cutting tools to an industrial customer that may use the tools in its manufacturing facilities.

Terminology varies from industry to industry. For example, distributors of printing paper are called merchants, and distributors of automotive aftermarket products are called jobbers. Further, the terminology can vary from market to market within an industry. Regardless of terminology, the critical point is that wholesaler-distributors have the title to the goods they resell. This means they have the authority to set price. It also means they know the identity of the next buyer in the channel, which they may or may not share with the manufacturer. Wholesaler-distributors are defined by their performance of the channel flow of ownership.[3]

The Wholesaler-Distributor's Role in the Supply Chain

Supply chains can be complex, involving many participants, intermediaries, and service providers to facilitate the movement of goods and services from sourcing to consumption. Thus, the channel functions and activities of wholesaler-distributors can be, and often are, performed by other supply chain participants. For example, manufacturers' sales branches are captive wholesaling operations that are owned and operated by manufacturers. Many manufacturers also have sales offices to perform certain selling and marketing functions. These locations do not take physical possession of inventory and may work with independent wholesaler-distributors. Customers, particularly larger multi-establishment retail firms, often perform the functions of wholesale distribution. These represent the vertical integration mode of governing the channel, either forward integration by the manufacturer or backward integration by the end customer in the B2B sector. Unfortunately, limited comparable data exist about the overall magnitude or importance of these activities.

Agents, brokers, and commission agents buy or sell products for commissions or fees but do not take ownership to the products they represent. These are important channels, particularly for service industries, where there is nothing to inventory and, therefore, nothing to own. By convention, agents in service industries are not considered part of the wholesale trade because no goods are involved. Wholesaling is historically related to tangibles.

Many other types of companies perform supply chain activities in a B2B marketing channel. For example, the transportation and warehousing industry provides some logistics functions. Increasingly, third-party logistics providers and value-added warehousing companies are also vying to perform some of the functions of wholesaler-distributors. Unlike wholesaler-distributors, third-party logistics providers (3PL) do not take title (legal possession) for the products that they handle. These supply-chain companies charge their customers on an activity-based, fee for service basis in place of the traditional sell-side mark-up pricing model of wholesaler-distributor. Indeed, the emergence of large, sophisticated, end-to-end logistics providers is a major challenge for wholesaler-distributors (more to come on this subject). In the last decade, the number of manufacturer-owned distribution centers has declined sharply, in part as manufacturers have outsourced their work to 3PLs.[4]

The Importance of Wholesaler-Distributors

The importance of wholesaler-distributors is striking, partly in and of itself and partly because it is not apparent from the business press. It is common to pick up reports that offer pessimistic predictions of the sector's future based on a gloomy reading of the sector's past. To some extent, this pessimism prevails because the sector in the United States is well organized into active trade associations. These bodies commission regular reports focusing the membership on how it can improve operations and cautioning against complacency.

But a more fundamental reason for misplaced pessimism is that the wholesale sector has been subject to a massive wave of consolidation, industry by industry, for several decades. The reasons for this are examined in a later section. For now, suffice it to say that the rapid disappearance of two thirds of the companies in an industry (which has happened in some sectors) creates an atmosphere of panic and dread. This is unfounded. The reality is that most firms in a consolidation wave in the wholesale sector exit by being acquired, not by going bankrupt or being shut down. The acquirers are large and healthy businesses that help account for the steady progression of the wholesale sector's share of business over the decades. Consolidation strengthens wholesaler-distributors even while reducing their number.

A major reason for consolidation is the central role of information technology. Distribution is subject to intense pressure to invest in IT. Customer-facing parts of the business are increasingly expected to be Internet-enabled in a sophisticated way. Concurrently, operations benefit from IT systems investments that allow distributors to participate in the supply chain management revolution (Chapter 14). All of these new systems need to interface seamlessly. These competitive demands encourage wholesaler-distributors to consolidate to achieve the scale economies that justify such massive investments in automation.

Despite these consolidation trends, traditional measures of industry concentration are low relative to most manufacturing sectors. To some extent, this low level of concentration reflects the fact that competition among wholesaler-distributors traditionally occurs in geographically distinct markets. A wholesaler-distributor can dominate one region of a country yet account for a very small proportion of national sales. Thus, the apparent fragmentation of wholesale distribution may not accurately reflect the true nature of concentration in any single region.[5]

This sets up an issue discussed in Chapter 6: Power is a property of a relationship, not of a business. Paradoxically, this means a very large and reputable manufacturer, such as Monsanto or DuPont, may not be more powerful than a single wholesaler-distributor in a given market. Indeed, such a supplier may be less powerful: Customer loyalty may mean that the supplier cannot go around a downstream channel member to reach a territory effectively. For example, some distributors of pesticides, herbicides, and farm equipment enjoy excellent relations with the farmers in their markets, many of whom who will not do business without going through the distributor.

WHAT THE INDEPENDENT WHOLESALE SECTOR OFFERS: THE ESSENTIAL TASKS

What exactly is this value added by the wholesale sector? Wholesalers perform each of the eight generic channel flows (Chapter 3). They take physical possession of the goods, take title (ownership), promote the product to prospective customers, negotiate transactions, finance their operations, risk their capital (often in giving credit to both suppliers and customers), process orders, and handle payments. In general, they manage the flow of information in both directions: upstream to the supplier and downstream to other channel members and to prospective customers. In so doing, they provide utility upstream and downstream in a variety of ways. Wholesaler-distributors survive and thrive only when they can perform these functions more effectively and efficiently than either manufacturers or customers.

This generalization, of course, varies from one economy to another. Japan is noted for very long channels with multiple wholesalers passing goods several times between manufacturers and the final point of consumption. Many of these wholesalers add margin but little value. Beginning in the 1990s, the wholesale sector in Japan has been steadily shrinking. Channels are getting shorter, and it is wholesalers that are being cut out. The first to go are secondary and tertiary wholesalers, but even primary wholesalers are giving way as more retailers purchase directly from manufacturers. Shortening channels—and the subsequent squeeze on wholesalers—are a response to the increasing price consciousness of Japanese consumers.[6]

Three Great Challenges of Wholesaling: 200 Years of Pharmaceuticals

The size and economic vitality of the wholesale sector belies the fact that many of these functions are invisible to the buyer, who takes them for granted. Both manufacturer and customer often understate three great challenges of wholesaling: doing the job correctly (no errors), doing the job effectively (a maximum of service), and doing the job efficiently (low costs).

The history of the pharmaceutical wholesaling industry in the United States offers a good example of these three points.[7] The wholesale drug trade can be traced back to the mid-1700s. Europe already had retail pharmacies, but the colonies did not. Medical practitioners both prescribed and dispensed medicine. Wholesalers arose to meet their demand for medicines imported from Europe. These wholesalers were also integrated forward (some of them held a few retail apothecaries) and backward (manufacturing drugs from indigenous plants).

In the nineteenth century, pharmacies arose that were independent of physicians. These, in turn, grew with an increase in hospitals. The wholesaling industry grew in turn to serve this burgeoning retail industry. Drug wholesalers were local, and there were many of them. They stayed in the wholesale sector, no longer integrating forward or backward.

From 1929 to 1977, the industry entered a phase in which larger wholesalers arose to offer regional, even national coverage, not only of pharmaceuticals but also of health and beauty aids. Apart from two large national firms, most were smaller, regional firms operated by the original founding family out of one location.

From 1978 to 1996, this established industry went through a period of dramatic consolidation. The number of drug wholesalers fell from 147 firms to 53, mostly by acquisition. At the end of this period, six firms held 77 percent of the national market.

Why did it take so long to discover such enormous economies of scale in this industry? The answer is the difficulty of doing the simple job of wholesaling drugs correctly, effectively, and efficiently. The heart of drug wholesaling (and much of wholesaling in general) is the banal task of picking. Picking means taking from a shelf the items the customer needs and assembling them for shipment. Pharmacies typically order frequently, in a pattern of a few units of many different items. The variety of the units is substantial, with many stock-keeping units (SKUs). As the products are medical, doing the job correctly (picking exactly the right item in the right quantity) is critical. For generations, this job was done by people picking from warehouse shelves. Few economies of scale are to be had in picking millions of items to move from a pallet to a warehouse loading dock to a storage shelf (taking inventory from the supplier), then picking those items from the shelves to put into a box for an individual customer.

Beginning in the 1950s, firms experimented with different ways to do the picking better, and they did find some. The potential of massively restructuring the task via information technology and automation, however, is what really changed the fundamentals of the industry. In the period from 1978 to 1996, firms experimented furiously with IT and automation. Which approach was best was not at all clear (to this day, multiple methods are in use—there is no standard). A number of firms bet all their resources on one approach or another and went out of business when their bets turned out to be wrong.

The winners changed so many aspects of their operations that they became unrecognizable. On the operations side, they changed not only their picking technology but order processing, billing, inventory control, delivery route scheduling, and tracking inventory movement through warehouses that had became enormous. They developed electronic links with suppliers, replacing hundreds of clerks with their ordering innovations.

On the demand side, wholesalers also made massive changes, profiting from IT. For their customers, they developed bar coding, scanning, and electronic order systems with direct data entry (replacing the salesperson who wrote down the pharmacist's order and the clerk who entered it). Wholesalers created systems that allowed their customers, the pharmacies, to offer computerized accounts receivable and credit (charge accounts) to their own customers, services the pharmacies could never have been able to afford otherwise. Using the information thus obtained, wholesalers also offered detailed advice about what inventory to hold and how to display it (planograms) and updated prices quickly.

In short, technology made it possible to change everything, and it did so very rapidly. Acquiring firms were rushing to achieve the size needed to amortize their huge investments. Firms that sold out were seeking to avoid making those same investments. The freedom of action that mergers and acquisitions create allowed a few big firms to achieve an astonishing degree of organizational change. The winners used technology to do the job right (fewer errors in picking, the key task), do it effectively (with swift and complete service to pharmacies), and do it efficiently (at lower cost). This is how one industry took two hundred years to grow large—and then only twenty years to consolidate.

In a later section of this chapter, we profile wholesalers that dominate after the shakeout phase is over. We also suggest strategies for manufacturers to cope as their first level of downstream channels (wholesalers) shrinks to a small number of viable players.

Wholesaling in an Emerging Economy

Earlier we noted that customers tend to take for granted the services provided by a wholesaler and to be unaware of the costs the wholesaler incurs to provide them. While this holds in developed economies, it may be even more the case in emerging economies. Effective and efficient wholesaling is a vital prerequisite to allow any other industry to flourish. In developing economies, the need for good distribution is particularly acute and is often badly met.[8] Even so, societal attitudes may work against the wholesale sector.

An example is in Niger, a desperately poor nation in West Africa.[9] A harsh natural environment means that few high-value-added agricultural commodities grow well in the Niger Republic, but one success story is onions. Violet de Galmi, a superior variety of onion, has such a competitive advantage that it could even be a viable export crop. Since the 1960s, onion growing has taken off well in Niger. Curiously, onions have not been nearly as successful as they should be, given the features of the agricultural situation and market demand. A team of aid agency analysts discovered what is holding onions back: not the farmer and not the consumer, but the wholesaling sector.

This wholesaling sector has two major players: brokers and wholesalers. Brokers get the crop from the field to the wholesaler, a considerable physical operation of sorting, sacking, and moving. From there, wholesalers get onions to distributors, who sell to retailers (street merchants or fixed stores). Some 50 to 75 percent of the retail price of the onion goes to the wholesaler (and this even after farmer cooperatives use their countervailing power to hold that number down). On the surface, this appears to be exploitation, and that is indeed what farmers, retailers, and government officials think it is. Wholesalers are reviled, even hated, by other members of the distribution channel and by ordinary citizens who feel the price they pay is too high.

Wholesalers, however, are not getting rich, either. As one put it, "It's a lot like playing the national lottery." Few people know the wholesalers' costs or how much of the onion's final market value they consume:

- Locating, assembling, and sorting varied produce from farmers in many locations. Sorting is particularly important because it is a way to break bulk. Many consumers can afford only one onion. Bulk breaking means buying a smaller onion.

- Assume credit risk to any and all actors in the channel, including farmers and retailers. These actors regularly pay late if at all, or in another currency, or in goods or future considerations (offsets) rather than currency.

- Absorb opportunism by retailers, who systematically make false claims after taking delivery that 10 percent of the merchandise arrived spoiled and change wholesalers if their claim is challenged.

- Build and maintain expensive storage facilities, impossible to disguise, that expose wholesalers to jealousy.

- Absorb the risk of wrong pricing, which is considerable. Information about prices, supply, and demand is difficult to obtain in a timely way, due to poor national infrastructure.

- Transportation. The greatest element of this cost is not the truck, even though Niger suffers from poor roads that drive up shipping costs. The greatest expense is illicit rent seeking by government officials (customs officers, police). These officials erect multiple unnecessary check points, even inside Niger's borders, extorting bribes and handing out fictitious traffic tickets at each one. Wholesalers who protest find their trucks held up until the onions spoil. Wholesalers who take their grievance to the government find their truck fleet vandalized in the night.

- Absorb risk of losing the crop (not only the onion crop but the merchandise they take as payment in lieu of cash).

- Absorb costs involved in meeting regulations and in observing informal arrangements of all kinds.

These costs are difficult to estimate. The analysts did estimate them and were unpleasantly surprised by their magnitude. By far the greatest cost was illicit rent seeking. This adds to costs directly and indirectly. For example, onion production is subject to sharp seasonal swings, which can be smoothed by holding onions in storage facilities. Wholesalers hesitate to build those facilities because, like trucks, they are easy to see and vandalize. Further, the vandals are likely to be disgruntled government employees who feel entitled to more bribe money than they are getting.

Why do officials behave this way, and why does public pressure not stop them? The single greatest reason is that wholesalers are reviled everywhere in Niger. They are viewed as greedy parasites who exploit hapless farmers and consumers without adding value. The public believes wholesalers are getting rich by speculative hoarding and by oligopolistic and collusive behavior. Hence, extorting the wholesalers and vandalizing their property is viewed as fair treatment. Officials even put a positive face on it by arguing that bribe money saves the taxpayer higher civil-servant wages.

A look at who is in the wholesaling sector helps explain the charge of collusion. Risk is everywhere in wholesaling onions, both in credit risks and in the risks of commitments not being honored. Contracts are not a solution, given the institutional infrastructure of Niger. To circumvent these problems, wholesalers tend to work with relatives, friends, even members of the same political party in order to coordinate responses and mobilize unsecured credit on short notice. (Relying on informal ties is a standard way to hedge high risks in any economy, including highly developed ones.[10]) Further, women, who have a lesser role in most sectors, flourish in wholesaling. Many owners are illiterate and employ literate people to read and write for them. Illiterates, women, relatives, members of one affinity group—superficially, this looks like connections, nepotism, and favoritism rather than merit (particularly given that the costs the wholesalers are covering go unnoticed in the first place). Consumers take for granted the time and place utility these wholesalers create and believe they are making supernormal profits. It is not so surprising that few people sympathize when wholesalers are poorly treated.

Net, wholesalers are not well compensated for their risks. Aid agency analysts concluded that they do a fairly good job under onerous conditions. But they could do more, particularly if they were willing to invest more. A saddening example is that Niger onions would be perfect for a Nestlé factory *in Niger* that makes dried onions but it does not source locally. Why? The multinational requires its onions to be certified to meet strict standards. Certification requires wholesaler investment.

Analysts concluded that the best way to help the Niger farmer would be to help the Niger wholesaler. Among other steps, they recommended a program of public education to change attitudes and create social pressure to stop illicit rent seeking. This is not an isolated situation. For example, a sidebar in Chapter 1 describes Taiwanese tea wholesalers from 1865 to 1945. Unfavorable public attitudes (again based on the impression that exploitative middlemen added no value) encouraged the Japanese colonial administrators to back farmers' cooperatives to compete with wholesalers. Yet even with a tax subsidy, cooperatives could not match the wholesalers' efficiency in providing services most consumers take for granted.[11]

This is not to say that wholesalers are never exploitative: Indeed, they can be. Like any other channel member, they will pursue their own interests to a dysfunctional level unless checked by countervailing forces. In Niger, those countervailing forces include farmers' co-ops and the fact that there are many wholesalers, though they are small. In Taiwan, many wholesalers also competed vigorously among themselves. This is as it should be.

Lest you imagine that emerging economies are unusual, let us consider attitudes toward wholesalers in the United States. Here, too, there is widespread skepticism about whether wholesaling adds any genuine value, whether it covers significant costs, and whether it operates efficiently. We will return to this theme when we discuss how wholesalers generate revenue.

Surprising Ways for Wholesalers to Add Value

How many people can readily list what wholesalers do?[12] Most are quick to note that they gather, process, use information about buyers, suppliers, and products to encourage transactions. This function has traditionally been well compensated. Today's methods of communication, particularly the Internet, will erode that advantage for all but the most complex, idiosyncratic transactions, which involve a great deal of tacit knowledge (difficult to codify and transmit).

Wholesalers also add value by creating an efficient infrastructure to exploit economies of scope (operating across brands and product categories) and scale (high volume). Effectively, wholesalers share that infrastructure with suppliers (upstream) and customers downstream. This advantage, due to specialization in channel flows, is why wholesalers can compete with manufacturers on price, even though their cost structure includes the wholesale price to the supplier. Manufacturers frequently underestimate the magnitude of the wholesaler's efficiencies in providing market coverage.

Many customers value the wholesaler's role of absorbing risk for them by standing behind everything they sell, pre- and postsales. Of course, wholesalers provide time and place utility (putting the right product in the right place when the customer wants it). Wholesalers filter the product offering, suggesting appropriate choices and reducing the customer's information overload. Some observers believe the future for wholesalers lies in collaborative filtering software, which uses information about the preferences and choices of the wholesaler's other customers (invisible, unknowing collaborators) to suggest, on line, only the best solutions to the prospect's needs. Superb collaborative filtering is a key reason why customers shop Amazon. Amazon was early to develop collaborative filtering systems to steer customers to books and music favored by other people who bought what the prospect is about to buy. This software gives different suggestions to different shoppers, based on their shopping clickstream behavior.

B2B buyers know that wholesalers also engage in many functions that properly fall under manufacturing. That is, wholesalers transform the goods they sell. They may receive components and subassemblies and put them together at the last minute (assemble to order). In general, they allow customization by permitting postponement of the final step of manufacture. They create kits of components (Kitting means making them into sets with instructions). They add on proprietary complements, such as hardware and software. Wholesalers even design new products from components, as well as program semiconductors and other actions that treat what comes from the factor as an input. Here, wholesalers have an advantage in adding value because they can unite their knowledge of the supplier base and the customer base with their knowledge of the customer's needs.

For example, Wesco is a distributor of electrical equipment and supplies. Distributing these products takes Wesco throughout a B2B customer's facility because electricity touches all functions. Wesco uses this knowledge to help key accounts do a better job of managing their facilities. This can come into play in unexpected ways. For example, when a hurricane destroyed a customer's oil refinery, Wesco's knowledge of how the electricity flowed through the facility helped the owner to reconstruct it in only six months.[13]

Master Distributors

A phenomenon that puzzles many observers is the master distributor, a type of super-wholesaler.[14] Figure 12.1 shows a representative structure.

An example is RCI, a master distributor of electrical motors for the refrigeration industry.[15] (Here, and throughout this chapter, we use the terms *wholesaler* and *distributor* interchangeably.) The end-user (e.g., an air conditioning contractor) buys from one of 4,000 conveniently located branches of 1,250 independent wholesalers (distributors to

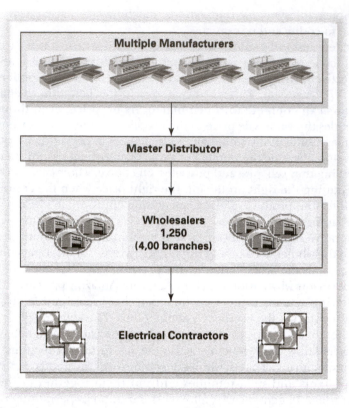

Figure 12.1   A representative master distributor channel

Source: Based on Narayandas, Das and V. Kasturi Rangan (2004), "Building and Sustaining Buyer-Seller Relationships in Mature Industrial Markets," *Journal of Marketing* 68 no.3, pp. 63–77.

B2B customers). These in turn do not deal with the manufacturer but with one point of contact: the master distributor. This is a distributor only to other distributors. Put differently, Figure 12.1 shows not 1,250 but 1,251 wholesalers (because the master distributor and its 1,250 wholesaler customers all sell to other businesses, not to consumers). But for a given manufacturer's products, one wholesaler (the master distributor) is the only contact point for all the others—and does not compete with them for contractors' business. Although this system looks on paper like an extra layer, it is stable and prosperous and suits all parties. What functions would be pushed onto some other player in the channel if the master distributor were eliminated?

Distributors need many services from manufacturers. Master distributors provide those services and thrive when they can do so more effectively and/or more efficiently than the manufacturer.[16] Contractors, the end of the B2B channel, need enormous assortment (a particular replacement motor) and need fast delivery (refrigerated goods spoil quickly). Hence, the 4,000 branches of 1,250 wholesalers need to rush one of thousands of parts. It is not feasible to keep adequate stock close to the customer. Distributors can buy product as needed, using the master distributor as their "invisible warehouse." (Not surprisingly, the master distributor spends large sums on express delivery services.)

Master distributors consolidate orders from all their manufacturers, allowing their customers to avoid a manufacturer's minimum order requirements for any given item.

Distributors can buy a variety of products from a multitude of vendors and get a quantity discount and lower transportation costs than any single manufacturer could give them.

Master distributors also assume a role not unlike that of a franchisor. That is, they help their customers (other distributors) to improve their business processes and carry out their functions. For example, they often help with advertising.

Essentially, master distributors give their distributors economies of scope and scale and help them solve their problems. Competitive pressure has driven their customers to rediscover these benefits, while driving manufacturers to rediscover that it does not pay to service all their distributors directly. In the United States, master distributors have gained ground.[17] One reason is that manufacturers are more likely to use a balanced scorecard when evaluating their performance. Rather than merely looking at volume, manufacturers are increasingly looking at other performance criteria, such as marketing support given, service levels, and next-day delivery. Master distributors fare well on a balanced scorecard. One reason is that they can help manufacturers expand into new channels. For example, Georgia-Pacific sells paper products and dispensing systems. Many distributors view these bulky, inexpensive products as minor and will not carry them. Master distributors solve that problem, allowing distributors to meet their customers' needs without devoting warehouse space to products that offer low value per cubic meter.

Many manufacturers are becoming more sophisticated in how they price to distributors. They are increasingly willing to offer functional discounts for:

- No minimum order size
- Willingness to break case quantities down to small lots
- Same-day shipping
- Marketing support (such as customized catalogs, flyers, and Internet ordering)
- Holding inventory
- Taking on logistics

This fine-grained approach favors master distributors because it offers more ways they can be paid for what they do. What creates this new flexibility? It is manufacturers' increasing focus on supply chain management (Chapter 14) and their resulting interest in anything that will increase coordination with downstream channel members.

FEDERATIONS OF WHOLESALERS

Wholesaler-distributors keep goods on hand that customers need and have them accessible instantly. That availability very often makes the wholesaler-distributor a backup for, and an extension of, the customer's own inventory system. In breakdown emergencies and other unplanned repairs or maintenance, distributors are an invaluable resource for supplying products that minimize downtime. As noted above, master distributors are one way to do this. A trend in wholesaling is to find other, innovative ways to respond to emergencies *while cutting costs*. This section covers some ways to accomplish this extraordinary feat.

The key is for one business to take the lead to organize federations of businesses. These federations are based on making progressive, cooperative arrangements with other channel members, with all elements—the nature of assistance, the procedures for providing it, and the appropriate compensation—defined in advance.[18] Such arrangements have the potential to cut costs, often by 15 percent to 20 percent, while improving service and opening new business opportunities. The common feature of these arrangements is that by cooperating the players pare redundant pools of inventory and duplicate service operations. These adaptive practices are being developed by Japanese, European, and U.S. corporations, among others. They are not common (as yet). Below, we describe some of the prototypes, led by wholesalers or by manufacturers.

Wholesaler-Led Initiatives

An example of these new adaptive channels is the growth of alliance (or consortium) relationships—wholesaler-distributors pooling resources to create a new, separate organization for joint action.[19] These alliances now exist in almost every industry and can become very large. For example, Affiliated Distributors is one of the largest distribution alliances in North America, comprised of over 350 independent wholesaler-distributors with over $18 billion in aggregate sales.

One alliance is led by four wholesalers. The consortium, Intercore Resources, Inc., sells machine tools. Each of the four distributors who formed it has difficulty providing timely, high-quality service to large customers on large contracts. It is these customers who are most likely to have an emergency and to demand exceptional service. Each distributor in the consortium refers business it has trouble handling to Intercore Resources, which is largely an administrative operation staffed by personnel sent by each distributor. Intercore Resources draws on the resources of all four distributors (including their inventories, engineers, and other service personnel) to service these customers, and it can call on each distributor to demand the help it needs. Intercore Resources sends invoices and collects payments in its own name. Its profits are then distributed to the owners (the four distributors) via dividends.

Another way for downstream channel members to create their organizer is through a holding company. For example, Otra N.V. is a Dutch company holding 70 wholesalers of electrical products. One of these firms, BLE, excels in service and training. Otra N.V. uses BLE to provide training programs and materials for all the other wholesalers in the group. (BLE has become so proficient that it also offers training to some of the group's suppliers!) Due to BLE's focus on the market, not on the producer, these programs are more thorough and less biased than the programs suppliers themselves present.

Integrated Supply

Integrated supply, a more sophisticated type of customer-distributor relationship, is changing wholesale distribution in industrial markets.[20] In an integrated supply arrangement, a customer gives a single wholesaler-distributor (or a selected group of wholesaler-distributors) all of its business in a particular product category or categories. In exchange, the distributor agrees to provide a high level of service on the entire product mix at set prices. Alternatively, the distributor may agree to cost-plus product pricing in combination with a service management fee.[21]

Manufacturer-Led Initiatives

Adaptive channels need one party to take the initiative, to act as organizer. We have focused so far on wholesalers, who create such mechanisms as a consortium, a holding company, or a division. Manufacturers also take the initiative to organize distributors to pool their abilities.

An example is Volvo Trucks North America, Inc., which sells commercial trucks and repair parts in the United States via truck dealers and its own regional warehouses. Dealers reported they were losing lucrative repair business because they could not provide consistent, timely repairs. The problem was stockouts of needed parts, although the channel collectively carried huge inventories. Via market research, Volvo GM learned that dealers could not predict the nature of demand for emergency roadside repairs and did not know what to stock. Truck downtime is so expensive that truck owners would shop competing dealers to find substitute parts rather than wait for an authorized Volvo GM dealer to get the right part.

Volvo GM addressed the problem by assuming more of the inventory flow itself and by setting up a delivery service, for which it bills its dealers. The supplier closed three warehouses and then built a massive new warehouse stocking every part. The warehouse is near the FedEx hub in Memphis, Tennessee. This is a rather obscure airport: Volvo GM made a FedEx-specific investment, thereby taking on risk. The supplier set up a mechanism for dealers to call for the precise part they need and get it by FedEx the same day. Dealers are billed for the service but pass it on to customers, who are price insensitive in the face of roadside emergencies. The result is more business for the supplier and its dealers and a sharp drop in inventory costs, more than offsetting the sharp rise in express delivery charges.

This solution is centralized: It all passes through Volvo GM. A decentralized solution is demonstrated by Okuma, a Japanese machine tool manufacturer. Okuma operates two of its own warehouses, electronically linked to 46 distributors. In addition, Okuma links the distributors to each other and facilitates drawing on each other's inventories. The Okuma electronic system creates 48 sources (2 warehouses, 46 distributors) for any tool.

The Requirements for Innovative Wholesale Service

The above success stories, whether led by wholesalers or manufacturers, all draw on the idea of pooling resources to improve service and cut costs simultaneously. This is done by eliminating redundancies, particularly in inventory and in expertise (technical support). These federations simulate the advantages of one firm (coordination, scale) while preserving the advantages of separate firms (manageable size, entrepreneurial motivation, specialization, independence). This is a very difficult feat to achieve. The players are required to make considerable changes in their operating methods and to reveal a good deal of privileged information (such as opening electronic access to their inventories). Most of all, they are required to rely on each other. How is this achieved?

The leaders of this initiative must build trust and gain commitment. To do this, they must make pledges of essential resources and make guarantees of performance (see Chapter 8 on building strategic alliances). This means assuming considerable risk. Okuma, for example, backs its distributors by guaranteeing 24-hour delivery of parts ordered by the distributor to the customer's site from its warehouse. The part is free if the deadline is missed. This encourages the 46 distributors to rely on Okuma rather than duplicating its inventories.

Another critical property of these federations is equitable compensation, specified in advance. This requires channel members to experiment with more complex pay mechanisms than the traditional trade discount. Typically, the investments each party must make are the basis for setting compensation, some of which is fixed.

For example, LeBlond, Ltd., a machine-tool maker, has a limited presence in Europe, too small to justify a full-scale service facility. The supplier has an arrangement with its distributors to call on them for service engineers. Distributors invest in the supplier by training their own engineers to support the brand and then guaranteeing a number of hours of availability. The supplier compensates them for this investment by paying for the hours whether or not they are used, as well as paying for any additional hours. This is effectively a fee (retainer, salary, fixed pay). Such take-or-pay contracts (either take the services at the agreed price or do not take them—but pay for them anyway) are not unusual in manufacturing. They are excellent ways to induce the other party in a wholesale arrangement to make specialized investments.[22]

Despite these control mechanisms, alliances have important limitations. Many channels are filled with small, independent wholesaler-distributors. Alliances attempt to maintain this density, often at the expense of creating a low-cost distribution channel. By sharing resources, hard decisions are postponed into the future, even when proactive channel change is required.[23]

Thus, the consolidation trend that we discuss below is another manifestation of wholesaler-distributors creating structures for joint action. However, there are crucial differences between consolidations and alliances. Most importantly, wholesaler-distributors that come together through a consolidation formally and legally combine their ownership structure. The newly created company has the authority to eliminate redundant activities and assets among its member companies. This can be a crucial source of competitive advantage in the face of margin pressure and other challenges. Alliance relationships rarely involve rationalization or reduction of assets among the members.

VOLUNTARY AND COOPERATIVE GROUPS

Often organizations want to formalize the division of marketing labor within their channels in order to assure themselves that the responsibility for performing specific distribution tasks is clearly placed. In these situations, vertical coordination is frequently accomplished through the use of contractual agreements. We concentrate here on one way to do this: wholesaler-sponsored voluntary and cooperative groups.

Wholesaler Voluntary Groups

A wholesaler, by banding together a number of independently owned retailers in a voluntary group, can provide goods and support services far more economically than these same retailers could secure solely as individuals. A well-known wholesaler-sponsored voluntary is the Independent Grocers Alliance (IGA). Wholesaler voluntary groups are particularly popular in the hardware industry. The principal services provided by a number of major hardware voluntaries are listed in Table 12.2. Underlying this list is the principle of economies of scale. This is important in the hardware industry, where a huge assortment of low-value items makes stock keeping particularly difficult and where the presence of large chains makes retailing very competitive.

Wholesaler voluntary groups enlist a number of independently owned dealers. The wholesaler acts as a leader, and the members agree to purchase a substantial portion of their merchandise from the organization. They also agree to standardize some operating procedures and present a common logo to consumers via signage and promotion. The wholesaler is a locus of expertise and a source of leadership.

Table 12.2 Principal services provided by major hardware wholesaler-sponsored voluntary groups and wholesaler buying groups in the United States

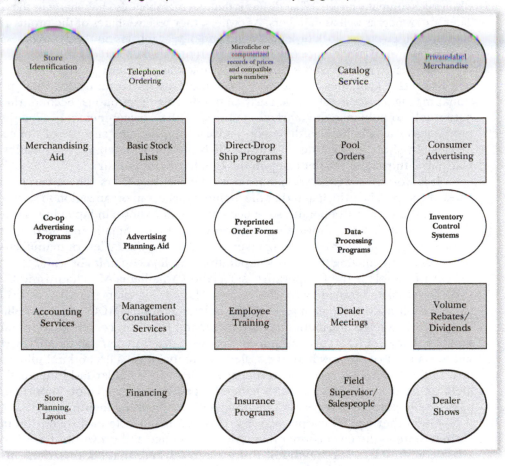

Member retailers give up some of their autonomy to the wholesaler. Net, wholesaler voluntary groups are intended to simulate vertical integration to some degree.

In practice, the simulation turns out to be a poor one. The wholesaler cannot and does not exercise the authority of a chain organization because the dealers can and will walk away from the voluntary group. Although the voluntary group does offer cost savings to its members (due to bulk purchasing), the dealers themselves compete via niche strategies in their neighborhoods: They leave price competition to the chains. Wholesaler voluntary groups function rather loosely.[24] As such, they do not achieve the same operating efficiencies as a well-run vertically integrated firm.[25]

Alternative Federations of Downstream Channel Members

A fascinating alternative to wholesaler voluntary groups is superficially similar. This alternative is the retailer-sponsored cooperative (often simply called co-op). On paper, it is the same idea but initiated by the retailers, not by a wholesaler. In practice, there is a substantial difference.

In order to coordinate among themselves, dealers are obliged to create an organization like a consortium. They then join this organization and agree to do a certain amount of business with it and to follow some of its procedures. So far, this looks like a wholesaler voluntary group. What differs is that the members also buy shares in the co-op: They are owners as well as members. As owners, they receive shares of the profits generated by their co-op (as stock dividends) and end-of-year rebates on their purchases. This creates a powerful congruence between the goals of the co-op and of its members.

As a result, retailer co-ops differ from wholesaler voluntary groups in two important respects.[26] First, they have a more formalized structure, run by dedicated professional managers whose jobs have fairly elaborate role descriptions. Second, they are better able to influence the marketing efforts of their owner-members. The dealers more aggressively adhere to the co-op's advertising, signage, and use of the co-op's brands. In short, marketing coordination is stronger. Sidebar 12.1 profiles Ace Hardware, the largest retailer co-op in the U.S. hardware industry.

It is worth noting that *co-op* does not refer just to dealers. There can be many types of co-ops. The principal is that the members set up an organization to serve them and own shares in it. Cooperatives are becoming better known in Japan in response to the pressures that are shortening marketing channels. Small- and medium-sized wholesalers, seeing their roles being taken over by large wholesalers or manufacturers, have reacted by creating their own cooperatives to gain economies of scale.

An example is the Cooperative Association Yokohama Merchandising Center (MDC), set up and owned by 75 wholesalers. These wholesalers use MDC as a vehicle to pool their activities to gain scale. The wholesalers supply MDC, which warehouses the goods in a huge distribution center. By serving from this center, MDC minimizes separate deliveries. This cuts transportation costs, a major item in Japan. MDC's wholesalers, via their co-op, now have the scale to serve major retailers and to build a modern, online information center to manage orders. In a similar fashion, small- and medium-sized wholesalers have also banded together to create co-op import companies, for the purpose of increasing their flexibility and cutting their inventories.

One other type of cooperative has played a major role in distribution in the United States—the farm cooperative. The emergence and growth of farm cooperatives could fill an entire textbook. Suffice it to say here that organizations such as Sunkist, Ocean Spray, and Land O'Lakes have become extremely powerful forces on behalf of their memberships in organizing both the farm equipment and supply markets, as well as the markets into which farmers sell their produce. Although some farm co-ops have vertically integrated both backward and forward within their marketing channels, they are primarily wholesalers of goods and services, and they administer the channels that they control with the approval of the farmers who own them.

Another type of cooperative—the consumer cooperative—has also had an impact on distribution. In the United States, consumer coops are not common, and tend to flourish in small, homogeneous, closed communities, such as college towns or rural communities.[27] But they do better in some countries. For example, Sidebar 12.2 profiles the direct selling movement in France.

Consumer cooperatives, their properties, and the reasons for their success (or lack of it) are not well understood at this time. They deserve further study because they have great potential to improve consumer welfare.[28]

Sidebar 12.1

Ace Hardware Corporation

The roots of Ace Hardware go back to 1924, when Richard Hesse, owner of a Chicago hardware store, decided to circumvent wholesalers to reduce costs. Hesse formed a partnership with other small retailers to buy in bulk. The idea worked so well that in 1928 Ace Hardware Stores incorporated. Today, Ace is a very profitable *Fortune* 500 firm (in size), counting its sales in billions of dollars. Yet, its stock is not traded: It is owned by its network of more than 4,800 retailers.

To become an Ace dealer requires an initial membership fee of $5,000, an initial purchase of $5,000 in voting stock, and substantial sums to remodel the store and convert operations to the Ace standard. Then there is the real commitment—a minimum annual commitment of merchandise purchased from Ace. Much of this is private label merchandise, brightly trademarked in red and difficult to sell if one is no longer an Ace dealer. These sums are a substantial commitment because most members are small family-owned operations (mom-and-pop stores). At the end of each year, dealer/owners receive a cash rebate and more stock, based on how much they bought from Ace. This incentive draws members farther into the profitable Ace system and gives them a reason not to leave it. Should they decide to leave, Ace will buy back their stock immediately—unless they join a competing co-op. If a dealer leaves Ace for another co-op, Ace will still buy back its stock—very slowly. Defection is one thing, but joining the enemy is another.

The real enemy, however, has ceased to be other dealer cooperatives but has become the vertically integrated retail chain store, such as Home Depot. The business of independent hardware stores is growing, but the chains' business is growing faster. These chain retailers operate enormous, impersonal stores ("big boxes") featuring selection and price. Their soaring popularity has driven more small hardware independents to join co-ops such as Ace.

Over time, Ace has changed its focus from signing up new outlets (for purposes of blocking other co-ops) to helping its existing members compete against the big boxes. How does Ace do it?[29] In the sketch that follows (benefits to the dealer are italicized), you will be reminded of another way to help independents compete: franchising.

By managing the wholesale side of its business carefully, Ace uses its buying power to get low prices from suppliers. It achieves high inventory turns, even though there are many thousands of SKUs. This keeps *procurement costs down* for its members while providing them with an appealing *assortment*.

A major problem for independent hardware dealers is consumer perception. Shoppers tend to view Ace stores as "little corner stores with great service" but without competitive pricing. To counter this view, Ace mounts advertising campaigns to project the *image* that the local "helpful hardware people" are part of a larger organization with buying power and expertise.

Another problem is that Ace's members are heterogeneous. They serve local communities, adapting to local tastes. The result is that their offerings vary so much that it is difficult to figure out how to help them. To overcome this problem, Ace has studied its members' businesses intensively, using point-of-sale (POS) data from those dealers with scanners in order to search for the best assortments. Ace also sends more than 100 retail consultants to work closely with dealers to develop and implement new business plans, store by store.

Through this learning, Ace has come to categorize its members' businesses in five ways: (1) home center, (2) lumber, (3) farm, (4) general store, and (5) hardware. Hardware is further subdivided into three formats: convenience, neighborhood focus, and superstore. By studying its members, Ace has been able to distinguish

(continued)

Sidebar 12.1 (cont.)

Ace Hardware Corporation

best practices and to turn that knowledge into elaborate format manuals for different store types. Thus, Ace offers *detailed, proven operational recommendations* for each category of its membership. The retail consultants *customize* these recommendations to each of the members and help them in *implementation.*

To further its learning, Ace operates some of its own stores. This helps Ace to appreciate the dealers' *daily management problems* and to devise solutions by experimenting at its own risk. This covers issues much beyond the traditional inventory questions—issues such as how to recruit, motivate, and retain good retail personnel. The stores also provide a good place for Ace to experiment with items its dealers usually will not carry, such as water heaters and lawn tractors (Ace dealers tend to specialize in small, inexpensive items). Ace is able to *demonstrate* that certain of its owner/member's stores could step up to these complex, high-margin items.

In short, Ace binds its members to the system but delivers value to them in return for their compliance and participation. Members make commitments to the system, erecting barriers to their own exit. Thus motivated, they are more willing to work with Ace, to accept Ace's suggestions, and to funnel their purchases through Ace. The system is surprisingly close to a franchise, whereby Ace acts as a franchisor. The difference is that the profits go not to the franchisor (since Ace is the "franchisor" in role) but to the dealers (as *they* are the owners of Ace). Should Ace be called a model of self-franchising?

CONSOLIDATION

The popular image of wholesaling as small business contrasts with today's reality in many industries of a wholesaler as a large, sophisticated, capital-intensive corporation. This transformation is due to consolidation, a phenomenon that has swept through many industries along with improvements in information technology and changes in the wholesaler's customer base. In the United States, wholesaling is a very active area for merger and acquisition, often funded by private buyout capital.

Consolidation Pressures in Wholesaling

In wholesaling, the pressure to consolidate[30] often comes from a wholesaler-distributor's larger downstream customers, including large manufacturers, multiunit retailers, and sizable purchasing groups. Such buyers value being able to access multiple suppliers over a large geography, all the while passing through a single source. This creates a demand for huge wholesalers.

Typically, distribution consolidators grow rapidly by acquisition, as noted earlier. They use their newfound scale to form partnerships with customers. This cuts down the ability of manufacturers to access these same customers. Indeed, newly large wholesalers often prune their supplier list, using their bargaining leverage to wring concessions from their shorter list of vendors. This, in turn, sets off a wave of consolidation upstream.

Sidebar 12.2

Direct selling in France

A large and growing phenomenon in France is direct selling from producers to consumers, entirely bypassing any and all intermediaries. Several French models are emerging, inspired by Japanese models established in the 1960s. These models vary in what service outputs they create and how they carry out channel flows. The constraints and obligations accepted by both sides also vary.

The major success stories of this movement are in food. In a representative model, consumers organized as a cooperative that contracts directly with a group of farmers. Farmers and consumers work together to decide what the farmer will plant and how it will be distributed (the negotiation flow). Then consumers subscribe in advance, taking on risk and advancing money to the farmer (credit). They pay a price and in return must take whatever the farmer succeeds in growing. Thus, buyers limit their assortments and assume the risk of crop failure. They must come to get their food in a fixed way (for example, pick up a prepacked basket at the town social hall, from 4:00 to 5:00 on Friday afternoons). Then they bring their purchases home, discover what they have bought, and figure out how to cook it. Fruits and vegetables are commonly bought this way, but even meat and oysters are often distributed directly from farmer or fisher to consumer. In the process, consumers forgo third-party certification, taking it on faith that the meat is organic and freshly slaughtered, for example.

What is in it for buyers? Many French shoppers prize regional foods and artisan-like variations in food, but the French distribution system for food is heavily concentrated, standardized, closed, and rule driven. The startling success of direct selling can be interpreted as an expression of protest against this national one-size-fits-all system. In some regions, up to 50 percent of volume of oysters or wine moves directly. Up to two thirds of people who regularly eat biological (organic) food meet some of their needs by direct-to-farmer co-ops. One grocery chain, System U, has taken heed. It views the success of direct selling as a signal of frustration and has relaxed its own rules as a result, in part by greatly increasing its sourcing of regional foods that do not meet national standards and can vary considerably from one day to the next.

Consumers who buy directly do not do so for the prices (which are no lower and can be higher). Instead, some are militantly opposed to intensive farming, with its herbicides, pesticides, and crowding of animals. These consumers believe they are getting more authentic organic merchandise. As one consumer put it, holding an apple full of insect marks and holes, "I know what the worm is eating." For many consumers, the motive is political. They are suspicious of intermediaries, viewing them with the same disdain as onion consumers in Niger and tea farmers in nineteenth-century Taiwan. These consumers buy directly in the belief that farmers do not receive a fair share of channel revenues: By cutting out intermediaries, they want more of their retail euro to go straight to the farmer.

Farmers, for their part, agree to deal directly to find markets, to gain financing, to avoid certification procedures, and to bypass intermediaries. Many of them share the consumers' political convictions and feel they are beating what they consider an oppressive system. There is an aura of like-mindedness and solidarity around many of the consumer-farmer encounters. Selling directly, however, has given many farmers a newfound appreciation of the flows that intermediaries take on. In particular, many of them discover that

(continued)

Sidebar 12.2 (cont.)

Direct selling in France

- Dealing with the public can be quite frustrating, and many farmers discover they prefer rural solitude to the ambiance of a market or town hall.
- Consumers in the co-op get first priority at a semifixed price. When demand turns out to be high, this can be frustrating. For example, fish producers dock with their catch and must carry it past motivated prospects who are ready to pay a higher price than the co-op. The prospects often become angry, creating dockside scenes at high season.
- They are often expected to provide credit or take checks.

- They need to engage in promotion to build clientele.
- They need to locate where the customer wants to buy and open when the customer wants to shop. For wine, this means locating on well-traveled roads and opening on weekends.
- It is difficult to find a match between what their soil can grow and the assortment the consumer wants.

As a result, some farmers diversify, dealing both with co-ops and the much-reviled intermediaries. Some have renounced direct selling to the public altogether.

Net, large customers provoke wholesaler consolidation, which stimulates manufacturer consolidation. The pace of consolidation can be startlingly fast. For example, periodical and magazine wholesalers in the United States dropped from over 180 firms to under 50 firms in only nine years: The five largest wholesalers controlled 65 percent of the national market by the end of the 1990s.

The Manufacturer's Response to Wholesale Consolidation

What can manufacturers do when a wholesale consolidation wave starts? There are four solutions. The first is to predict winning wholesalers and build a partnership with them. This has been going on in Europe at a feverish pace because economic union makes national boundaries become less relevant.

Who are likely to be winners? There are four basic types:

1. Catalyst firms. These firms trigger consolidation by moving rapidly to acquire.
2. Wholesalers that enter late, after consolidation is well along: These firms do not enter unless they have found defensible niches.
3. Extreme specialists. These are already attuned to the conditions that are likely to prevail after consolidation.
4. Extreme generalists. These are large full-line firms that can serve many environments well. Their versatility is valuable once the market has consolidated.

The second strategy for manufacturers facing wholesale consolidation is to invest in fragmentation. This is a strategy of betting on and working with smaller independents trying to survive the wave of consolidation. This is the opposite of the strategy of betting on a few winners. One way to invest in fragmentation is to capitalize on a wholesaling trend: Smaller wholesaler-distributors are banding together into alliances. Members can bid for national or multiregional contracts, offering the same geographic reach as a larger multi-establishment company. The groups can also take advantage of volume purchasing opportunities from suppliers. At the same time, the alliance members retain operational autonomy, enabling them to maintain high levels of service for local customers.

The manufacturer can deal with these alliances, or it can help independents to create an alliance that is a credible alternative to consolidators. For example, Old Mutual is a diversified provider of financial services in South Africa. Traditionally, financial services are sold through independent brokers. A wave of consolidation threatened to decimate the ranks of brokers and shift the distribution of financial services to banks and to vertically integrated competitors. To keep a broker network alive and thriving, Old Mutual launched Masthead Broker Association, a division that sells distribution support services to brokers on highly favorable terms. The program has been highly successful and has given Old Mutual (and its competitors) multiple routes to market that otherwise would have disappeared.

The third strategy for the manufacturer facing wholesale consolidation is to build an alternative route to market by vertically integrating forward. This is the topic of Chapter 9.

The fourth strategy for a manufacturer is to increase its own attractiveness to the channels that are left. In general, this involves increasing the manufacturer's ability to offer benefits to the channel (for example, the benefit of a strong brand name). This fourth strategy of becoming more attractive to channel members is a theme that permeates this book.

Once wholesale consolidation has occurred, the balance of power in the channel changes. The majority of industry sales at wholesale now goes through a handful of large, publicly traded, professionally managed companies. Entry barriers are high, and entrants must seek niche markets. These large wholesalers have lower gross margins than in the days when the industry's wholesalers were fragmented, local, and privately held. However, the large firms have a higher total business and operate so efficiently that their net margins are healthy, even though their gross margins are lower. These wholesalers put great pressures on their suppliers, particularly in terms of pricing. They also offer increased service to their customers. The large surviving wholesalers redesign supply chain management processes in their industry, often revolutionizing current operating methods.

Wholesaler consolidation is a significant change in an industry. Once it begins, it tends to progress quite rapidly. Manufacturers must react rapidly and be ready to change their marketing channels and methods. Wholesale consolidation is a force that cannot be overlooked.

EXPORT DISTRIBUTION CHANNELS

When a manufacturer exports to a foreign market, new complications can easily arise. The manufacturer is likely to be poorly versed in the market situation. The product may be badly suited to the market, or the proper marketing strategy to make it fit might not be evident. The strategy that worked in the home market could be a disastrous misfit if exported to the foreign country right along with the product. Moreover, there are the inevitable issues of foreign currency, customs regulations, and language. Faced with these complexities, many manufacturers enter foreign markets with little ambition—and little investment. Particularly among the small and medium manufacturers that make up the bulk of exporting firms, exporting is almost seen as a throw away. If it works, the incremental business is welcome. If it does not, little is lost. Sidebar 12.3 profiles a type of intermediary that can be very helpful to a manufacturer considering entering into export.

Studies of the drivers of export performance[31] demonstrate the folly of seeing exporting as a throw away. Profitable sales and strategic advantage emerge from a strategy of supporting the channel members responsible for the exported good. In this way, manufacturers enable their channel members to make arguments other than sheer price competition and help them achieve a sustainable differentiated position.[32]

Exporters need to be ready to adapt their distribution strategy to the market situation they face. A strategy of "this is our global distribution policy" dampens export performance. On the whole, it matters little what type of intermediary the manufacturer uses (merchants, agents, distributors, direct buying offices), as long as the producer's choice reflects local conditions and supports whatever channel member it uses. A critical issue here is one element of the manufacturer's role performance, which is delivering the exported goods to the channel member in a timely, reliable way. This has a very substantial impact on the export performance of the good. Quite rightly, channel intermediaries screen suppliers on the basis of their ability to meet delivery commitments.

Relationships between manufacturers and their export distribution channels pay off in particularly high performance when the two parties are able to forge solid working relationships.[33] Such relationships are flexible, with both parties willing to make modifications as the need arises. They are open: the parties exchange information freely, frequently, and informally. And they are cooperative, with each party interested in sharing gains and seeing the relationship pay off for both sides. Such relationships have strong internal working norms. These, in turn, are the direct result of the time, effort, and resources the manufacturer devotes to its export efforts. Firms that view export as a side activity create a self-fulfilling prophecy that they will do poorly.

THE FUTURE OF WHOLESALER-DISTRIBUTORS

International Expansion

A striking feature of wholesaler-distributors is that, although they can become quite large, they seldom become global. Is this a historical artifact of the days of family-owned businesses? Will the large firms that survive an industry consolidation go global?

Many domestic wholesaler-distributors are expanding internationally (often by acquiring foreign wholesaler-distributors) in order to meet the needs of both customers and suppliers. Global manufacturers and customers are asking that their distribution partners have a presence in all major markets. The reduced costs of crossborder shipping and falling trade barriers also encourage expansion. For the same reasons, foreign wholesaler-distributors are making inroads into domestic markets. This trend of crossborder growth and acquisitions is particularly strong in Europe.

Nonetheless, the nature of wholesaling suggests that most wholesalers will never be truly global. Fundamentally, wholesaling means meeting the needs of a local market, and these needs are so varied that it is exceedingly difficult to standardize marketing channels. This makes it very difficult for suppliers, customers, or wholesaler-distributors

---

Sidebar 12.3

Export trading companies

One type of channel member for exports is the export intermediary.[34] This is an independent firm located in the exporter's country, not the host country. These export intermediaries perform channel flows (and forge marketing strategy) for multiple manufacturers in non-competing product categories. In effect, they function as outsourced export departments for multiple manufacturers. As such, they search for markets, negotiate contracts, and monitor contracts for performance. In the United States, they are known as export management companies or as export trading companies. While many manufacturers bypass them, these intermediaries can help a manufacturer make a quantum leap in its level of international sophistication—and therefore its export performance.

The best performers in this category have two characteristics. First, they master the products they sell by taking training from manufacturers and then training foreign customers and giving them after-sales service. Second, they are deeply knowledgeable about foreign markets and export processes. A number of visible indicators flag these firms, including multilingual personnel and foreign-born personnel. Because these are usually small firms, another good indicator of their knowledge level is the makeup of the top three managers. In more knowledgeable firms, the top three individuals

- Travel frequently
- Have long export experience
- Have considerable industry experience

On an overall basis, the firm as a whole has extensive foreign connections, as well as strong industry experience.

---

to pursue a truly global supply-chain strategy. The few successful examples come from industries in which many participants in the channel are global, such as the electronic components and computer industries.

Electronic Commerce

Debate rages about the impact of electronic commerce on wholesalers. On the one hand, doomsday predictions abound to the effect that intermediaries will be eliminated by the ruthless efficiency of an Internet search engine. On the other hand, wholesaling has genuine value added. Eliminating wholesalers will not eliminate their functions, and the Internet cannot provide all channel flows.

A more likely scenario is that e-commerce will change but not replace wholesalers. Wholesalers, indeed all channel intermediaries, thrive by gaining customer knowledge and marrying it with knowledge of producers to solve problems of both customer and producers.[35] The Internet creates new problems (such as heightened risk of defective goods, fraudulent merchants, credit card theft, and release of private information). At the same time, the Internet creates new ways to solve problems (such as collaborative filtering to help the customer spend less time yet make better choices). Consequently, the Internet should not eliminate intermediaries—but it does oblige a reconsideration of all the fundamentals of how they create value and capture a fair share of it.

There are early indications that wholesalers are actually benefiting from e-commerce. They are co-opting the Internet, finding ways to use it to bring in new business and to improve how they go about their work. Indeed, many distributors are racing to find ways to use the Internet as a tool to create even more value. In the process, they are using artificial intelligence to replace the service role of their salespeople. As a result, growth in hiring of salespeople by wholesalers has slowed dramatically. Concurrently, salespeople are increasingly expected to provide higher levels of service, including consultative selling—a role for which many employees are not fully prepared.[36]

B2B E-Online Exchanges

Independent electronic exchanges operate as online brokers within a given industry. A large number of these exchanges have been formed, particularly in the late 1990s. These companies aggregate supplier catalogs on the Internet, enabling buyers of like products to source and purchase items from multiple suppliers in a single location. To the surprise of many, these exchanges, which were expected to have a devastating impact on wholesalers, have failed at a very high rate. Where they have made inroads, it has often been in industries that are already commoditized, such as personal computers.

This has sparked examination of why, and a rediscovery of the basic value added of wholesalers. For example, Arrow Electronics is a large wholesaler of electronic components. In the 1990s, more than fifty Internet exchanges were formed to challenge Arrow's business model.[37] These exchanges proposed to cut out the intermediary by handling the information flows and letting the producer handle the product flows. Arrow beat back these exchanges by bundling. Arrow does three classes of business:

➤ Book and ship: Commodity, standardized products that constitute 25 percent of the business and are subject to competition from gray markets. This is the business the exchanges expected to win.

➤ Value-added orders: The idea here is to rationalize the supply chain and lower total ordering costs by services such as kitting, programming, managing the customer's inventory on the customer's own site, and guaranteeing to hold inventory buffers. The customer benefits from the wholesaler's knowledge of the needs of this customer and similar customers.

➤ Design wins: These are complex sells to customers who are unsure of their requirements. The customer wants the brand-neutral advice it cannot get from the supplier itself.

In retrospect, the failure of the exchanges is predictable. The book-and-ship business had already been competed down to miniscule margins. The costs the exchanges proposed to reduce (for a 6% fee) were 4 percent of the purchase price! Further, the exchanges were unknown, whereas Arrow is known and trusted. As for design wins and value-added orders, the distributor has large advantages here. Finally, because customers benefit from one-stop shopping, the distributor could resist unbundling the book and ship business.

The Arrow story has been repeated in a number of sectors. Wholesaling is a brutally competitive sector. Entrants have had difficulty unseating incumbent wholesalers, who benefit from established and well-working routines and lean operations.[38] The exchanges have had difficulty creating new values that are not readily matched by incumbents, many of which have co-opted the Web as a tool.

Nonetheless, exchanges should not be written off. They are gaining ground in sectors where commodities can be separated from other parts of the business. The major obstacle appears to be codification of parameters that are difficult to estimate (such as the quality of customer service). Exchanges often founder when customers discover they need something that they failed to consider, such as emergency or rush service, or design know-how. Another obstacle is that establishing a reliable relationship is itself costly. Expertise, credit worthiness, and general qualification to bid must be factored in, and this is not easily done.[39]

Online Reverse Auctions

Perhaps a greater threat to wholesalers than online exchanges is online bidding by reverse auction.[40] This is a real-time price competition between prequalified suppliers to win a customer's business. Specialized software is needed to run them over the Internet. Bidders (distributors or producers or both) submit progressively declining bids, and the winner submits the lowest bid before time runs out. Although still a small part of overall transactions, reverse auctions are gaining rapidly. Many buyers perceive them as a fast, easy way to set aside irrational considerations (such as relationships or soft, or subjective, qualifications) and get straight to a low price.

Wholesalers tend to be suspicious of reverse auctions, viewing them as a way for buyers to reduce their procurement prices without letting the wholesalers show their capabilities (many of which come from having made supplier-specific investments). This is particularly the case when bids are open (revealed to all bidders) versus sealed (so that only winning bids are known). Wholesalers feel that open bidding is a way to trick them into revealing their positions.

Reverse auctions have their dangers. They may destroy excellent relationships that generate performance breakthroughs and new ideas. Wholesalers (and other suppliers) hesitate to make investments specific to suppliers that run reverse auctions. Furthermore, reverse auctions focus simply on lowest product price rather than lowest procurement cost or lowest cost of ownership over product lifetime. These broader cost concepts involve many intangible factors. In general, consideration of warranties, delivery time, switching costs, and capabilities are quickly lost in the bidding. Efforts to incorporate such factors into the auction have foundered because they are difficult to codify.

Ultimately, the long-run danger of reverse auctions is that suppliers will use them to extract excessive concessions, thereby driving suppliers (both wholesalers and manufacturers) out of business. This forced consolidation of supply will put buyers into negotiations with a small number of large wholesalers and producers. Over the long run, this may not be the route to sustainable competitive advantage for the buyers.

Capturing Value After Creating Value: Wholesaler Profitability

It has always been difficult for wholesalers to calculate the profitability of a given product line or customer. Product lines compose a portfolio, and customers come for the assortment. Dropping a line that is unprofitable in and of itself can hurt the appeal of the package. As for dropping a customer that is unprofitable in itself, this goes against the culture of spreading costs over a large customer base.

Consequently, wholesalers carry many customers that actually cost more than they bring in. The reason, typically, is that these customers take a great deal of service along with their products. Traditionally, wholesalers charge for the product and include the service for free. This bundling is based on the idea that customers will pay more for products from distributors that give them more service.

Over time, however, many customers have come to violate this convention by relentlessly wearing down distributors on price while training the distributors' personnel not to withhold service. Why do wholesalers tolerate such money-losing customers? Frequently, it is because they cannot tell who they are. It is no simple matter to assign costs to customers in a nonarbitrary way. However, it can be done using activity based costing (ABC), which assigns costs based on approximations of the activities needed to support each customer. ABC analysis suggests that the typical distributor's portfolio of customers follows the 80/20 rule: 80 percent of profits are generated by only 20 percent of customers, while many of the remaining 80 percent of customers actually drain profits away.[41]

A solution to this problem is rapidly gaining ground: fee for service.[42] The idea is to break the traditional connection between the pricing model (gross margin on product) and the value model (providing superior service, which may be worth far more than the product and which is more difficult to find elsewhere). Wholesalers are moving toward a product price coupled with a fee for each service the customer uses. Unbundling product and services makes it visible that the customer is paying for each and every service, a value proposition that is invisible when gross margin on product is the only way to compensate a distributor. For example, TMI is a cutting tools distributor that has introduced fees for inspecting, kitting, and tracking services associated with cutting tools. These services save the customer time and money in a demonstrable way, which is why TMI is able to collect the fees rather than (trying to) charge more for the tools.

Indeed, at the limit, distributors can and do offer services for a fee without supplying the product (which is sourced elsewhere). Fee for service is a revolution in wholesaling. It is not easy to introduce, particularly because customers are used to thinking of services as included in gross margins. Wholesalers will need to demonstrate that their services are valuable. They may need to do so by accepting risk, for example, agreeing to be paid only if targets are met (such as cost savings, labor savings, or performance improvements).

A SKETCH OF VERTICAL INTEGRATION AND OF AGENTS IN WHOLESALING

This chapter has focused heavily on wholesaler-distributors because they are the largest and best-documented sector of wholesaling. Let us return to the other two broad categories of wholesale activity and sketch them briefly.

Vertical Integration Forward into Wholesaling by Manufacturers

When manufacturers perform wholesaling activities themselves, they are operating manufacturer's sales branches and offices. The merits and demerits of this approach are analyzed in Chapter 9 on vertical integration. Here we address a trend at the retail level for huge "power retailers" to bypass independent wholesaler-distributors by setting up their own branches to perform channel flows. This trend is gathering momentum in Europe (fueled by economic union) and in Japan (fueled by rising price elasticity among consumers and a trend in industry to question the length and operating methods of Japanese channels). Let us examine the U.S. case, where the trend is already well advanced.

Wholesaler-distributors are a small part of many traditional (physical) retail channels in the United States due the influence of power retailers[43] that dominate many sectors of retail activity. Power retailers typically buy in large quantities in select product categories (e.g., toys), giving them a very prominent position in the channel. This purchase volume has caused many power retailers to adopt a buy direct approach. Retailers such as Wal-Mart have squeezed costs out of the channel by creating in-house distribution systems in which wholesaler-distributors play a small role. Manufacturers have been forced to respond to the demands of dominant buyers, often at the expense of wholesaler-distributors. In addition, power retailers have triggered industry consolidation among the small- and medium-sized retailers that were traditional wholesale distribution customers.

These retailers have reduced or eliminated the role of wholesaler-distributors in retail channels during the past twenty years, leaving fewer, but larger, wholesaler-distributors among the survivors. This is one reason why e-commerce should not have a devastating effect on independent wholesalers in many retail sectors. The devastation has already occurred. Due to power retailers, there are few wholesaler-distributors for the Internet to effect.

At the same time, the hyperefficient retail distribution systems used by power retailers are ill-suited for the unit-of-one shipping required for online buying and shipping to a consumer's home. Currently, many retailers are partnering with either wholesaler-distributors or third-party fulfillment companies such as Fingerhut as they enter e-commerce. The Internet, curiously, may prove to be a way to bring independent wholesalers back into retail channels.

Set the Price and See the Buyer: Agents, Brokers, and Commission Agents

Agents, brokers, and commission agents buy or sell products for commissions or fees. They focus on the flows of promotion and negotiation and are critical players in the transmission of information up and down the marketing channel. They do not take ownership to the products they represent.

This distinction has critical ramifications. Essentially, agents are pure specialists in selling. They leave the ownership, handling, and financing of the goods to other players. Manufacturers using agents are free to unbundle other channel flows and to assign them to other channel members. Using agents gives manufacturers freedom to fashion channels with multiple players.

Further, the manufacturer has much greater control over the channel in going through an agent than in going through a wholesaler-distributor. The agent sells but does not set the price (unless the manufacturer delegates pricing authority). Thus, the manufacturer has more pricing discretion. The manufacturer also has much better information. Via the agent, the manufacturer knows who bought what and at what price. Thus, the supplier can see the customer. In contrast, wholesaler-distributors own the goods and can do with them as they see fit. The manufacturer knows as much (or as little) as the wholesaler divulges.

Sales agents are typically called manufacturers' representatives.[44] Conceptually, they are outsourced sales professionals: OSP is the terminology we shall adopt here. Like wholesalers, OSPs (often known simply as reps) go by different names in different sectors and vary in their properties. Their defining characteristic is that they are an independent firm acting as an agent for a manufacturer (the principal) to sell products. They are almost always paid by a commission on their sales. OSPs can also sell services: For example, much radio advertising time is sold by radio reps in the United States. As this chapter focuses on wholesaling, we set aside services OSPs to concentrate on OSPs selling tangibles.

The fundamental issues around OSPs are the domain of sales force management, a topic separate from the management of marketing channels. For our purposes, a key question is what role an OSP fills. An outsourced sales professional is a downstream channel member, functioning as an equivalent to a company sales force. Like the direct sales force (that is, employed directly and solely by the manufacturer), an OSP sells to other channel members, such as wholesalers-distributors, OEMs, and retailers.

Conventions for OSPs vary widely. In the United States, they traditionally (but not always) sell a portfolio of complementary products but give each manufacturer exclusive representation in its own product class. In this manner, an OSP offers assortment to the customer while offering exclusive dealing to (each) manufacturer. This is an appealing combination for the customer, who enjoys one-stop shopping, and the manufacturer, who faces no interbrand competition. In Europe, OSPs are not used as extensively, perhaps due to more restrictive labor laws. In Asia, OSPs have traditionally been captive agencies, serving one manufacturer on an exclusive basis. This is changing, with more manufacturers experimenting with allowing their reps more autonomy.[45]

Whether to use a rep or a company sales force is a vertical integration issue (Chapter 9). For many companies, the question is not whether to go "rep or direct" but *how* to go rep *and* direct. This is because the decision to use an OSP depends on the nature of the market and the brand/product class. For many brand/markets, an OSP is a compelling choice. For others, a direct sales force is preferable. Net, it is common for a manufacturer, especially a large one (with a broad product line and multiple markets to cover) to use an OSP to take some products to market and to use a direct sales force (or forces) to take other products to other markets.

How much are OSPs used? It is somewhat difficult to say, given the variety of forms and titles that fit this channel institution. In the United States, OSP usage has been increasing since the 1970s, particularly in business-to-business transactions. Estimates of the OSP's share of industrial selling in the United States go as high as 50 percent, although some observers put the figure closer to one third. The OSP's share of sales varies considerably by industry and by market. For example, they may account for greater than half the sales in the electrical products and food service industries, while accounting for much less than half in health and beauty items (dominated by chain stores).

A manufacturers' representative or OSP can be difficult to recognize. To their customers, they may appear to be employees of the manufacturers they represent (much as a franchisee may be indistinguishable from a company-owned outlet). To their manufacturers, they are capable of forming a strategic partnership so close that the lines between firms are not sharp. To the observer, the only indicator of their status may be the many product lines listed on their business cards.

An OSP provides professional services on an outsourced basis. In this respect, the institution resembles a law office, an accounting firm, or an advertising agency.

Like these service providers, a rep can be quite large, employing hundreds of people and supporting heavy fixed investments in buildings, IT facilities, even private airplanes. (Reps are often used in large geographies with low density of customers.) However, the economies of scale in this business are not great, with the result that most OSPs cover a restricted territory.

The same issues that arise with any downstream channel member arise with an OSP. The principles described in this book (such as how to gain and use power) apply to this channel institution as to any other.

SUMMARY

The wholesaling sector covers the sale of product between businesses, as opposed to ultimate household consumers. The sector creates value added by providing channel flows. Just as the value of these flows is often underappreciated, so too the value added and economic importance of the wholesaling sector is frequently overlooked. The essential tasks the industry performs are mundane, but it is no simple matter to carry them out with few errors, bundled with valued services, and at low cost.

Players in the wholesale sector are experimenting with innovative ways to deliver value to the customer base while simultaneously cutting costs. This is done by assembling federations of channel members to share resources, thereby cutting down redundancies in inventories and in processes. These efforts may be led by wholesalers or by manufacturers and can be organized in multiple ways. Channel members farther downstream, such as dealers, can also organize to capitalize on economies of scale. The cooperative is an effective vehicle for so doing.

One way to achieve economies of scale is consolidation. In wholesaling, consolidation is endemic and is usually achieved by a wave of mergers and acquisitions by a handful of players. The causes and consequences of consolidation are explored in this chapter, and four generic manufacturer responses are outlined.

The future of wholesaler-distributors will be one of changes. This is due to the pressures and opportunities of international expansion, as well as the new possibilities opened up by electronic commerce. The idea that electronic commerce will eliminate wholesaler-distributors is simplistic: Indeed, these institutions are finding ways to benefit from the Internet. But change is certain and will affect various wholesaling sectors in different ways.

No discussion of wholesaling is complete without examining the role of manufacturers' representatives (more generally, sales agents and brokers). These institutions are professional services firms. They do not take title and do not offer inventory. By specializing in a subset of channel flows, they offer the manufacturer the ability to fashion a variety of channels. Via agents, suppliers have a better view of the market and more control over price than they typically do when title changes hands.

Wholesaling is a vibrant, economically important sector of most economies. The players continually reinvent themselves to provide new value added. More on the functions they provide is available in Chapter 14, on logistics.

Take-Aways

- **Wholesale businesses sell physical inputs and products to other businesses:** retailers, merchants, contractors, industrial users, institutional users, and commercial users. Wholesaling is closely associated with tangible goods. However, these entities create their **value added through providing services**, that is, channel flows.
- Buyers typically understate the difficulty of the three critical challenges of wholesaling:
  - Doing the job without errors
  - Doing the job effectively (i.e., with a maximum of service)
  - Doing the job efficiently (i.e., at low costs)
    - This is particularly true in developing economies, in which a healthy wholesaling sector could spur considerable development
- The challenges of wholesaling spur firms to create economies of scope and scale up and down the channel of distribution. The objective is to offer exceptional service at acceptable costs. A number of ways to do so exist.
  - Master distributors, a type of super wholesaler
  - Federations of wholesalers
    - Manufacturers can also lead initiatives to unite wholesalers
  - Voluntary and cooperative groups
    - Of wholesalers, retailers, consumers, or producers
- Consolidation is a common phenomenon in wholesaling, due in part to the economies of scale available through IT (information technology). Nonetheless, the wholesaling sector is typically less concentrated than the manufacturing sector.
- Four types of winners emerge when a wholesaling sector consolidates:
  - Catalyst firms (serial acquirers)
  - Late entrants that find defensible niches
  - Extreme specialists attuned to post-consolidation conditions
  - Extreme generalists that trade depth for breadth
- Manufacturers can react to consolidation in wholesaling by:
  - Partnering with one of the four winner profiles
  - Investing in fragmentation (supporting small independents)
  - Vertically integrating forward
  - Investing in becoming more attractive to survivors of the consolidation
- Export distribution channels present special challenges that require the manufacturer to develop cultural sensitivity and alter its normal working arrangements.
- Electronic commerce promises to change the wholesaling sector in many ways—some of which will benefit the sector enormously. Online exchanges and reverse auctions are among these developments. In response, wholesalers are experimenting with new ways to add value and capture a fair share of it.
- Agents are important players in the wholesaling sector, and are an alternative to the manufacturer's employee sales force.

DISCUSSION QUESTIONS

1. What are the essential distinctions among the three categories of wholesale trade?
2. Consider the following statement: "A wholesaling operation can be eliminated as an entity, but someone must perform the wholesaling tasks and absorb the costs sustained by the wholesaler if it is assumed that those tasks are necessary." Take a position on this statement, pro or con, and offer support for your reasoning.
3. Inventories and accounts receivable represent 65 percent to 85 percent of the total assets of a wholesaler. Many bankers consider that these are the only assets worth considering when deciding whether to lend to a wholesaler. What are the bankers overlooking? What determines the true value of a wholesaler?
4. Wholesaling is often thought of as a less glamorous intermediary venture when compared with other channel intermediary operations, such as retailing. In your opinion, which of these two would be the more difficult to manage—a wholesaling or a retailing operation? Which would seem to have the best chance, on the average, of achieving a high ROI (return on investment) today? Which would you say has had to face more challenges to its survival in the last 50 years?
5. When facing consolidation at the wholesale level, what is the manufacturer's best reaction?
6. Farmers' co-ops often start off well, then find themselves unable to compete with private wholesalers. What would you suggest are the major issues? What are steps a farmers' co-op can take to increase its chances of success?

ENDNOTES

1. Fein, Adam J. (2000), "Wholesaling," in *U.S. Industry and Trade Outlook 1999* McGraw-Hill and U.S. Department of Commerce, eds., (New York: DRI/McGraw-Hill), pages 41-1–41-8.
2. NAW/DREF and Pembroke Consulting (2004), *Facing the Forces of Change: The Road to Opportunity* (Washington, DC: NAW Publications). This comprehensive publication underlies many of the trends described in this chapter. See also Fein, Adam J. (2004), "The Road to Opportunity in Wholesale Distribution," *Progressive Distributor*, May, pp. 6–10, and www.PembrokeConsulting.com.
3. Lusch, R. L. and D. Zizzo (1996), *Foundations of Wholesaling: A Strategic and Financial Chart Book* (Washington, DC: Distribution Research and Education Foundation).
4. NAW/DREF and Pembroke Consulting (2004), previously cited.
5. Fein, Adam J. (2000), previously cited.
6. Focus Japan (1997), "Ever-Shorter Channels: Wholesale Industry Restructures," *Focus Japan* 24 , no. 7–8 (July–August), pp. 3–4.
7. Fein, Adam J. (1998), "Understanding Evolutionary Processes in Non-Manufacturing Industries: Empirical Insights from the Shakeout in Pharmaceutical Wholesaling," *Journal of Evolutionary Economics* 8, no. 1 (Spring), pp. 231–270.
8. Prahalad, C. K. and Allen Hammond (2002), "Serving the World's Poor Profitably," *Harvard Business Review* 80, no. 9 (September), pp. 49–57.
9. Arnould, Eric J. (2001), "Ethnography, Export Marketing Policy, and Economic Development in Niger," *Journal of Public Policy & Marketing* 20, no. 2 (Fall), pp. 151–169.
10. Lyons, Bruce R. (1996), "Empirical Relevance of Efficient Contract Theory: Inter-Firm Contracts," *Oxford Review of*

Economic Policy 12, no. 4 (Winter), pp. 27–52.

11. Koo, Hui-wen, and Pei-yu Lo (2004), "Sorting: The Function of Tea Middlemen in Taiwan During the Japanese Colonial Era," *Journal of Institutional and Theoretical Economics* 160, no. 4 (December), pp. 607–626.

12. Anderson, Philip, and Erin Anderson (2002), "The New E-Commerce Intermediaries," *Sloan Management Review* 43, no. 4 (Summer), pp. 53–62. This reference is the basis for this section.

13. These services are described on the Wesco corporate Web site and in Harvard Business School case #9-598-021, Wesco Distribution.

14. Anderson, Erin, George S. Day, and Kasturi V. Rangan (1997), "A Strategic Perspective on Distribution Channels," *Sloan Management Review* 38 (Summer), pp. 59–70.

15. Narayandas, Das and V. Kasturi Rangan (2004), "Building and Sustaining Buyer-Seller Relationships in Mature Industrial Markets," *Journal of Marketing* 68, no. 3 (July), pp. 63–77; and Rangan, Kasturi, RCI Master Distributor, HBS case #59500.

16. This discussion is based on Vurva, Richard (2002), "Wholesale Change," *Progressive Distributor*, March–April, pp. 1–4.

17. Keough, Jack (2003), "It Was the Worst of Times," *Industrial Distribution*, August 1, pp. 2–6.

18. Narus, James A. and James C. Anderson (1996), "Rethinking Distribution," *Harvard Business Review* 96, no. 4 (July–August), pp. 112–120. The section on adaptive contracts and the examples are drawn from this article, which goes into much greater depth on the specifics of such arrangements.

19. Fein, Adam J. (1998), "The Future of Distributor Alliances," *Modern Distribution Management*, September, pp. 17-21.

20. Lynn, F. and J. Baden (1998), *Integrated Supply 2: Shaping the Future of the Industrial Marketplace* (Chicago, IL: Frank Lynn & Associates).

21. Fein, Adam J. and Sandy D. Jap (1999), "Manage Consolidation in the Distribution

Channel," *Sloan Management Review* 41, no. 1 (Fall), pp. 61–72.

22. Williamson, Oliver E. (1996), *The Mechanisms of Governance* (New York: Oxford University Press).

23. Fein, Adam J. (1997), "How Good Is Your Consolidation Survival Strategy?" *Modern Distribution Management*, November.

24. Dwyer, F. Robert and Sejo Oh (1988), "A Transaction Cost Perspective on Vertical Contractual Structure and Interchannel Competitive Strategies," *Journal of Marketing* 52, no. 2 (April), pp. 21–34.

25. Porter, Philip K. and Gerald W. Scully (1987), "Economic Efficiency in Cooperatives," *Journal of Law & Economics* 30, no. 2 (October), pp. 489–512.

26. Dwyer and Oh (1988), previously cited.

27. Weinstein, Steven (1996), "A Consuming Interest," *Progressive Grocer* 75, no. 5 (May), pp. 161–163.

28. Sexton, Richard J. and Terri A. Sexton (1987), "Cooperatives as Entrants," *Rand Journal of Economics* 18, no. 4 (Winter), pp. 581–595.

29. This sidebar is based on research carried out (using public sources and Ace Hardware press releases) by William Weil, Edward Stumpf, Stuart Quin, and Ahmed Nasirwarraich.

30. For a more complete discussion of the forces triggering consolidation, see Fein, Adam J. (1997), *Consolidation in Wholesale Distribution: Understanding Industry Change* (Washington, DC: Distribution Research and Education Foundation).

31. Leonidou, Leonidas C., Constantine S. Katsikeas, and Saeed Samiee (2002), "Marketing Strategy Determinants of Export Performance: A Meta Analysis," *Journal of Business Research* 55, no. 1 (January), pp. 51–67.

32. Cavusgil, S. Tamer and Shaoming Zou (1994), "Marketing Strategy-Performance Relationship: An Investigation of the Empirical Link in Export Market Ventures," *Journal of Marketing* 58, no. 1 (January), pp. 1–21.

33. Bello, Daniel C., Cristian Chelariu, and Li Zhang (2003), "The Antecedents and Performance Consequences of

Relationalism in Export Distribution Channels," *Journal of Business Research* 56, no. 1 (January), pp. 1–16.

34. Peng, Mike W. and Anne S. York (2001), "Behind Intermediary Performance in Export Trade: Transactions, Agents, and Resources," *Journal of International Business Studies* 32, no. 2 (Second Quarter), pp. 327–346.

35. Anderson and Anderson (2002), previously cited.

36. NAW/DREF and Pembroke Consulting (2004), previously cited.

37. Narayandas, Das, Mary Caravella, and John Deighton (2002), "The Impact of Internet Exchanges on Business-to-Business Distribution," *Journal of the Academy of Marketing Sciences* 30, no. 4 (Fall), pp. 500–505.

38. Day, George S., Adam J. Fein, and Gregg Ruppersberger (2003), "Shakeouts in Digital Markets: Lessons from B2B Exchanges," *California Management Review* 45, no. 2 (Winter), pp. 131–150.

39. Kleindorfer, Paul R. and D. J. Wu (2003), "Integrating Long- and Short-Term Contracting via Business-to-Business Exchanges for Capital-Intensive Products," *Management Science* 49, no. 11 (November), pp. 1,597–1,615.

40. This discussion is based on NAW/DREF and Pembroke Consulting (2004), previously cited; and on Jap, Sandy D. (2003), "An Exploratory Study of the Introduction of Online Reverse Auctions," *Journal of Marketing* 67, no. 3 (July), p, 96.

41. Niraj, Rakesh, Mahendra Gupta, and Chakravarthi Narasimhan (2001), "Customer Profitability in a Supply Chain," *Journal of Marketing* 65, no. 3 (July), p. 1.

42. This discussion is based on NAW/DREF and Pembroke Consulting (2004), previously cited.

43. Lusch, R. F., and D. Zizzo (1995), *Competing for Customers: How Wholesaler-Distributors Can Meet the Power Retailer Challenge* (Washington, DC: Distribution Research and Education Foundation).

44. This discussion is based on Anderson, Erin and Bob Trinkle (2005), *Outsourcing the Sales Function: The Real Costs of Field Sales* (Cincinnati, OH: Thomson Texere Publishing).

45. Frazier, Gary L. (1999), "Organizing and Managing Channels of Distribution," *Journal of the Academy of Marketing Sciences* 27, no. 2 (Spring), pp. 226–240.

Franchising

After reading this chapter you will be able to:

- Define franchising and distinguish the two major forms, business format franchising and the authorized franchise system

- Describe why an entrepreneurial individual would become a franchisee rather than founding a new business—and what would make a candidate hesitate to join a franchise system

- Explain why a firm with a business model would opt for franchising rather than expanding by setting up its own branches run by employee managers

- Sketch the features of businesses that are *not* well suited to franchising

- Describe the essential elements of a franchise contract—and why contracts are so important when franchising

- Weigh the positive and negative features of a business that mixes some franchisees with company-owned outlets—and describe why most franchising systems evolve to this mixed form

- Appreciate that multiunit franchising, a curious phenomenon, has much to do with scarcity of good management

- Evaluate the biggest problems the franchisor faces once the business becomes clearly viable—*if* it survives the founding stage

WHAT IS FRANCHISING?

Franchising is a marketing channel structure intended to convince end-users that they are buying from a vertically integrated manufacturer when, in fact, they may be buying from a separately owned company. As such, franchise systems masquerade as company subsidiaries. In reality, they are a category within the classic marketing channel structure of two firms, one supplying, the other performing downstream marketing channel flows.[1] Franchisors[2] are upstream manufacturers of a product or originators of a service. They write contracts with franchisees, separate companies that are downstream providers of marketing channel flows. There are, however, several crucial distinctions to a franchise system.

End-users (customers of the franchisee) should believe they are dealing with the franchisor's subsidiary. Therefore, the franchisee assumes the identity of the franchisor, projecting itself as though it were the franchisor's operation. This *deliberate loss of separate identity is a hallmark of franchising*. To accomplish this loss of identity, the franchisee awards the franchisor category exclusivity (no competing brands in the product category). Usually, the masquerade is completed by carrying no other product categories, either. Thus, franchising goes beyond granting a producer favored status in one of the reseller's product categories.

To further the projection of the franchisor's identity, the franchisee purchases, via contract and by the payment of fees, the right to market the franchisor's brand, using the methods, trademarks, names, products, know-how, production techniques, and marketing techniques developed by the franchisor. Effectively, the franchisor develops an entire business system, a business format, and licenses it to the franchisee to use in a given market area.

By paying fees and signing a contract, the franchisee assumes more than the right to exploit a broad license. It also assumes the obligation to follow the franchisor's methods. By contract, the franchisee cedes a great deal of legitimate power to the franchisor. Nonetheless, the franchisee is a separate business with its own balance sheet and income statement. From the standpoint of an accountant or a tax authority, a franchise is a business like any other. Franchisees invest their own capital, run the business, and keep the profits or assume the losses. They own the business: It is theirs to alter, sell, or terminate (although even this fundamental property right can be circumscribed by the franchise contract).

Franchising is an inherently contradictory marketing channel, yet it functions surprisingly well in many circumstances. It is technically two independent businesses joining forces to perform marketing flows to their mutual benefit; however, it is actually an attempt to project something else entirely: One company, owned and operated by the owner of the brand name. In order to convince the final customer that the channel and the brand name have only one owner, franchisees compromise their independence. They voluntarily cede an almost astonishing degree of power to the franchisor—and pay the franchisor for the privilege of doing so.

Why would any downstream entrepreneur accept (indeed, seek out and pay for) a franchise? For that matter, why would any manufacturer go to market through independent companies when its real intention is to control the channel so tightly that the final customer does not know the difference? Why not give customers what they think they are getting: company-owned and managed outlets?

On the face of it, franchising might seem like such a flawed concept that it should be rare. On the contrary, franchising is the fastest-growing form of retailing and has been for some time. Chain organizations using franchising, in whole or in part, account for over 40 percent of retail sales in the United States.[3] Franchising, broadly construed, in the U.S. retailing sector, accounts for one out of twelve retail establishments[4] and generates $1 trillion in sales in 75 industries, thereby employing over 300,000 people.[5] In Europe, franchising was once dismissed in some circles as an aberrant form of organization, suitable only in North America. This viewpoint has been discredited: Franchising has taken off in Europe, having appeared in the 1970s.[6] Further, although franchising is perceived as a retail institution, it is also growing in the B2B sector, particularly in services to businesses.

Indeed, franchising has become a global phenomenon. As an institution, franchising is so well established globally that it has come full circle. Countries that first experienced franchising as a U.S. import have spawned their own firms, which have developed a business format and exported franchising to other countries—including back to the United States.[7] Franchising has become an institution so stable and so pervasive that it is the single most common way to become an entrepreneur in North America, in Europe, and in Asia.[8]

Clearly, franchising has advantages that are not evident at first glance. Its meteoric rise has attracted considerable research attention in many fields, provoking a great deal of recent theorizing and empirical study. This chapter brings the principal arguments together, frames them in a common terminology, and organizes them around the managerial issue of whether, when, and how to enter a franchise agreement as either the franchisor or the franchisee. The references in the footnotes delve farther into the rich and puzzling institution that is franchising.[9]

This chapter begins by asking why either side, franchisee or franchisor, would enter into such an arrangement. Business format franchising is then contrasted with an earlier-generation form, product or trade name franchising. Next, the broad outlines of the contract are discussed. This is critical because the contract determines who will enter the agreement and why, as well as setting the balance of power. The chapter then turns to a curious fact: Most franchisors also own some outlets. The motives for this and how it is implemented are discussed at length. Finally, the daily issues of surviving and gaining cooperation from established franchisees are examined. The chapter explores a curious phenomenon, multiunit franchising, and closes with a brief discussion of other ways for franchisors to gain cooperation from their franchisees. Sidebar 13.1 describes the world's most admired franchisor, McDonald's, whose operations touch on every aspect of the franchising system.

WHY BECOME A FRANCHISEE?

You are a private individual with a certain amount of capital, perhaps due to an inheritance, severance pay, accumulated savings, or liquidating your equity in a previous business. You could invest the money and collect the earnings, but you are more interested in starting a business, say, a fast-food restaurant. You find the idea of owning your own business attractive. You may find ownership intrinsically appealing for psychological reasons. You feel that other opportunities in society are closed to you, perhaps because of your gender, race, or background. Or perhaps you simply value independence from an employer, and you are willing to assume some risk to get it. You are confident that you can get better returns in the long run from your own company than from investing in someone else's. You see a variety of advantages in being the owner of a business: For example, you may be a recent immigrant looking to bring family members to join you by offering them employment.

What would divert you from starting a fast-food restaurant from the ground up? Failure rates for new businesses are high. It takes time and resources to build a clientele. Literally thousands of decisions, big and small, must be made: Where should the restaurant be located? Should it have a theme? What size should it be? What kind of food should it serve, and how should that food be prepared—economically? So many legal, financial, marketing, managerial, and operating decisions must be made that any entrepreneur can be overwhelmed. Setting up a business takes months, even years. After all that, it may well fail, wiping out your capital.

Sidebar 13.1

McDonald's

McDonald's is the world's largest and most admired franchisor. It is also the world's largest retail chain organization in number of outlets (over 25,000 units in 115 countries representing 95% of the world's wealth). Franchising is the backbone of this highly profitable system, the scale of which is difficult to grasp. Here are a few indicators.

- On average, a new outlet opens somewhere in the world every five hours.
- With 1.5 million employees, McDonald's is the world's largest private employer.
- McDonald's is the world's largest holder of real estate.

Of the 25,000 outlets, McDonald's owns 5,500, generating a quarter of its worldwide sales. Four thousand outlets (mostly in Asia and the Middle East) are joint ventures with local shareholders. The remaining 15,500 outlets are owned by 5,300 franchisees. These franchisees invest heavily to build an outlet, often selling all their possessions to raise the capital. Then they pay McDonald's up to 25 percent of their revenue in fees and in rent because McDonald's is usually their landlord. In return, they share in the system. Let us examine the critical elements.

Method. The operating manual weighs two kilograms (over four pounds) and specifies how operations are to be performed down to tiny details. For example, all servers wear a uniform that has no pockets. This is thought to discourage both accepting tips and putting one's hands in the pockets. Free hands in turn encourage constant action ("If you've got time to lean, you've got time to clean"). Other details include cooking and serving specifications down to the second, as well as detailed role descriptions for personnel.

Set-up assistance. Months of on-site training terminate at Hamburger University, which teaches 7,000 people a year how to run the business. McDonald's also undertakes to secure the site and build the restaurant, which it then rents back.

Enforcement of norms. Once in operation, a franchisee is assisted by an army of regional consultants who run frequent and detailed checks on operations. McDonald's insists that franchisees abide by its intricate system: The first franchisee in France lost his twelve units when he was terminated in 1982 for noncompliance.

Worldwide supply. McDonald's has a network of favored suppliers who function almost as subsidiaries. When entering a new market, McDonald's begins with local suppliers, then asks them to adapt to its methods. Often, the franchisor finds them inadequate and induces its own suppliers to enter the market as replacements. These key suppliers process astonishing quantities of food and supplies to McDonald's exacting specifications. The result is uniformity of product, as well as economies of scale that allow the franchisor to operate profitably yet charge low prices.

Marketing strategy. McDonald's positions itself to families (the target segment) as fast and inexpensive. To draw in the family, the strategy focuses on pleasing children by in-store events (birthday parties, for example), Happy Meals, and the Ronald McDonald clown mascot. The menu is extremely similar worldwide with limited adaptation to local tastes. This standardization enhances the capture of economies of scale, and not just in food: McDonald's is one of the world's leading distributors of toys (via the Happy Meal).

Marketing communication. Massive advertising budgets go to campaigns, particularly the backing of sporting events. For example, McDonald's spends millions of dollars on advertising world soccer events. Unlike the rest of the strategy, advertising is not standardized: Countries and regions have their own slogans and campaigns. Communication is partly

(continued)

Sidebar 13.1 (cont.)

McDonald's

financed by franchisees, who pay 4.5 percent of revenue as an advertising fee. They may also run their own local campaigns: For this, they are aided by ready-to-use kits provided by the franchisor.

To enter this system, a prospective franchisee must pass a number of tests of motivation and capability. Doctors, lawyers, and executives are among the applicants. They are frequently screened out for inadequate motivation and lack of a customer service orientation. In France, successful candidates invest substantial sums in up-front fees and costs of outfitting the interior and the kitchen (although the franchisor pays the bulk of the costs of building the restaurant and is the landlord).

In spite of these costs, McDonald's locations break even after several years (often sooner) and become quite profitable. In France, for example, a franchisee draws a salary comparable to an executive paycheck, as well as collecting substantial dividends and building wealth through the location (resale values typically run upward of several million French francs). Satisfactory performance means a franchisee can open more stores. However, McDonald's discourages building large operations, fearing the owner will become too removed from operations.

Of course, McDonald's draws criticism as well as admiration. Social critics charge the franchisor is heavy-handed and antiunion in its personnel practices. Some suppliers feel exploited. The chain is often accused of being secretive and portrayed as a heartless multinational. Many a critic charges that McDonald's creates an unhealthy fast-food culture wherever it goes, suppressing local businesses and displacing local customs. On the other hand, McDonald's is praised for offering employment (and ultimately franchising opportunities) to young people and to people who face discrimination in their job market (for example, Latinos and African Americans in the United States, youths of North African descent in France). McDonald's franchisees operate in blighted neighborhoods, creating jobs and businesses that benefit residents. The popularity of the product suggests that fast-food culture is not unwelcome.

McDonald's acknowledges it has made errors along the way. The format was developed by a family business in California after the Second World War. Ray Kroc, a salesman of milk-shake machines, realized its potential and licensed the concept from its developers. In 1955, Kroc opened his own McDonald's and began to build his empire. Growth was steady until 1996, when franchisee profitability began to fall. A major reason was that the U.S. market was becoming saturated, yet McDonald's continued to add units at a pace that cannibalized existing franchises. This led to an in-house revolt and a change of management. Subsequently, the chain slowed its growth (in part by closing one unit for every two it opened) and invested heavily to modernize kitchens in order to improve both product and profitability. This back-to-basics approach, focused on growing same-store sales to the benefit of franchisees, has led the firm back to growth.[10]

Contemplating this prospect may extinguish your entrepreneurial ambition and send you to the job market. If you remain interested in owning your own business, it is little wonder that you would be attracted to a franchising arrangement. In effect, you sell a piece of your independence to the franchisor. In return, you purchase the services of a corporate backer, a coach, a problem solver—and, curiously, another role, to be discussed in a later section. Franchisor personnel step in to assist you. They train you, work with you, share with you the franchisor's formula, its business format. The business format should be a prepackaged solution to all your start-up problems. By paying a fee (usually in several parts, fixed and variable—further discussed later in this chapter), you buy a license to exploit the format in a market area.

The Start-Up Package

When you buy the license for a business format, that is, a franchise, you acquire a brand name and an explanation from the franchisor of all the marketing decisions that have been made for the business. You also acquire all the decisions you need to make initially, and you acquire training and assistance to implement them. This includes:

- Market survey and site selection
- Facility design and layout (architectural and building services)
- Lease negotiation advice
- Financing advice
- Operating manuals
- Management training programs
- Training the franchisee's employees

All of these initial services are valuable, but site selection is particularly important to a retail operation because market potential is a critical determinant of a store's sales and productivity.[11] Exactly how much help the franchisor will give you will vary. For example, McDonald's typically does all site analysis and most land acquisition and development. In contrast, Budget Rent-A-Car merely assigns a territory and allows the franchisee to build where he/she pleases, subject to franchisor review and advice.

Another critical piece of the start-up is usually the brand name itself. The franchisee uses the brand equity of the name to build a clientele, and quickly.

These initial services are all subject to economies of scale, which the franchisor can capture and share with the franchisee. By providing these services over and over, the franchisor acquires a deep knowledge of the nuances of each activity. The franchisor also pools demand for these services. This makes it economical to dedicate personnel to the set-up job (e.g., statistical specialists to do site analyses; company lawyers to help deal with zoning authorities and draft documents; architects to draw plans and supervise construction; technicians to train, install, and test equipment). The franchisor's scale also makes it possible to have preferred-customer status with service providers (such as contractors and bankers). All of this means better results and at lower cost.

Ongoing Benefits

Were this the end of the story, franchising would only be a system for launching a business. But it is primarily a system for running a business. Once you have started your franchised fast-food restaurant, what services could you expect your franchisor to provide continuously? These include:

- Field supervision of your operation, including quality inspection
- Management reports
- Merchandising and promotional materials
- Management and employee retraining
- National advertising

➤ Centralized planning
➤ Market data and guidance
➤ Auditing and record keeping
➤ Group insurance plans

Of this list, the first two items stand out for their potential for conflict. Almost all franchisors have a continuous program of field supervision, including monitoring and correcting quality problems. Field representatives (with titles such as franchise consultant) visit the franchise outlet. Their purpose is to aid the franchisee in everyday operation, check the quality of product and service, and monitor performance. They should play the roles of coach and consultant. They also play the roles of inspector, evaluator, and reporter to the franchisor. The policing role conflicts with the coach and consultant roles. Balancing them requires diplomacy and skill.

Many franchisees are required to submit to the franchisor monthly or semimonthly management reports on key elements of their operations—weekly sales, local advertising, employee turnover, profits, and other financial and marketing information. This regular reporting reflects the almost-a-subsidiary nature of franchising and is highly unusual in other contractual channels. Reporting on operations is intended to facilitate the various financial, operating, and marketing control procedures. It is the basis of franchisor feedback intended to assist the franchisee. This is confidential information that goes to the heart of the business. To oblige feedback, many systems require franchisees to buy special electronic invoicing and reporting systems. The franchisor's review of the books can create resentment. After all, is not part of the idea of franchising to run your own business so as to escape having a boss?

Why Ask a Franchisor to Provide These Services?

We now have a list of services that you are willing to use your capital to pay someone to provide. Now the question is: Who should be the provider? Put another way, *why should the provider be a franchisor?* These services are available from others. One could contract with an architect, an accountant, a consultant, and other professionals. What advantage does a franchisor have?

First, franchisors act as consolidators: They bring all the necessary services, no more, no less, together under one roof and consolidate them, achieving economies of scale (size) and of scope (synergy). But others could do that, too.

Second, franchisors focus on one product line (fast food restaurants, car repair, etc.). They develop benefits from this specialization. But others could do that, too.

The critical and distinguishing benefit of a franchisor is to bring everything together to focus it on a *branded concept.* Everything is dedicated to the needs of the brand and to the implementation of the concept. The franchisor develops specialization benefits that are tied to brand equity. This, in turn, cannot be built unless there are many units. A major reason to go to a franchisor is to *rent brand equity, to become part of a large network*, not just to contract for business services.

This brings us to a crucial and often misunderstood reason why you would pay for a franchise. *You are hiring an enforcement agency.* The franchisor acts as a police officer, judge, and jury. The business format is a system, and the franchisor makes sure that all players (franchisees) observe its rules. You, the franchisee, hire the franchisor to police the system, to make sure that *everyone else* implements the concept. It is in your interest to have a police officer to protect brand equity—and brand equity is the basis of the franchising concept.

This idea is often labeled the prevention of free riding. Free riding is when one party reaps benefits (gets a ride) while another party bears the costs. Thus, the ride is free to the one who benefits. For example, Dunkin' Donuts positions itself as a producer of premium fresh bakery goods. To sustain this positioning, franchisees agree to throw out unsold product after a few hours and to replace it with freshly produced goods. This is costly. It is tempting to keep selling the donuts for a few more hours, hoping that no one will notice they are a bit stale. The franchisee that sells stale donuts benefits from the Dunkin' Donuts image, but this practice hurts the brand's image, which hurts all franchisees.

If franchisees did not have a franchisor, they would invent one for the purpose of policing each other. This is because brand equity is so critical to the franchising proposition. Safeguarding brand equity is one reason why franchising has become associated with the production of services of all kinds: document handling, building, business aids and services, child care, hospitality, tourism, travel, weight control—even the conduct of autopsies! One of the most important problems of a services business is ensuring consistency of the result. By branding a service business, a producer guarantees consistency, which attracts customers. By franchising, the producer of a service implements the guarantee it gives its customers, thereby enhancing its brand equity.

WHY BECOME A FRANCHISOR?

Let us turn the lens around, changing your perspective. Now you head a company with a concept and a brand. You have a business format. You desire tight control over the implementation of your concept. You want that control to uphold the brand's image and to ensure the proper sale and servicing of your product. Given your focus on directing how your brand is presented, sold, and serviced, the logical thing for you to do is to set up a network of outlets, owned and operated by you. This means hiring managers, who in turn will hire a staff for each outlet. The outlet needs to be set up and the manager and staff hired and trained. Once past these initial actions, your company will run the outlet. With this, you have control.

Why would you instead rent your brand name and format to a person who has a fierce drive for independence, a desire to be an entrepreneur? Why would you reveal your business secrets to someone else and then entrust the business to this entrepreneur? Why would you encumber yourself with a contract and take on the responsibility of coaching, consulting, and policing a group of entrepreneurs? Inexperienced franchisors imagine that guiding a group of entrepreneurs is like herding a flock of sheep. It is more like herding cats. If you really want control, why not own the channel?

Raising Financial and Managerial Capital to Grow Fast

You want to grow fast. You are not just motivated by entrepreneurial ego and impatience. Perhaps you have a unique idea, and you want to exploit it as fast as possible to gain a first-mover advantage before others copy you. Or you are entering a business where competition is fragmented, with no strong brands, and you want to build a brand name before someone else does. Conversely, there may be a strong competitor, and you wish to grow large before the competitor notices you and tries to block you. You may wish to reach minimum efficient scale quickly, so that you can amortize costs over a large operation. Minimum efficient scale may be very large: To justify national advertising in the United States, for example, requires national coverage of a market of several hundred million people. Or you might want to exploit a developing trend (e.g., American-style fast food in Southeast Asia) rapidly before the market becomes saturated.

Immediately, you will need a high level of financial capital. You could go public, selling shares in your company. Early explanations of franchising focused on the idea that franchisees are a cheaper source of capital (or even the only source of capital). Franchisees would invest for a lower rate of return than would a passive investor because franchisees understand the business in their location better. This idea, while appealing, was discredited for some time because it appears to run counter to financial portfolio theory. Investors should prefer less risk. The risk of any single location is likely to be greater than the risk of the entire chain. Therefore, prospective franchisees should prefer to buy a share of the entire chain rather than the rights to one location.

The idea that entrepreneurs franchise to get access to capital has come back, in part because evidence suggests that it is true in practice.[12] Perhaps capital markets are not so efficient that a prospective franchisor can access them readily. Or perhaps franchisees are *not* just financial investors, indifferent between owning their own business and owning a piece of a company.[13] Let us explore this idea further.

A franchisee is the manager of her outlet and so influences the risk/return ratio of her operation. She will not invest unless she is confident that she herself can run the outlet well. She reasons that if she buys the franchise rights to a location of her choice, she can drive her unit to high profit at low risk. But if she buys a piece of a company, her influence on operations will be miniscule. Further, if her expectation is correct, she may become wealthy because she is the residual claimant (after paying suppliers and the franchisor, she owns all the profits). She would not expect the returns to her share of a company run by other people over many locations to be as great. Thus, she is not indifferent between owning a franchise and owning a piece of the franchisor.

This idea—that entrepreneurs value the return from their own wholly controlled operation more than they value the return from a piece of a larger organization—rests on more than conventional measures of profit. *Entrepreneurs have other motives.*[14] They gain substantial "psychic income" from owning their own business. They may assign to their businesses elements of their lifestyle, such as luxury cars, substantial personal salaries, and relatives on the payroll, thereby reducing taxable income (up to the limit of the tolerance of tax authorities). Perhaps most importantly, exploiting one's own business is a way to maximize the return on knowledge and relationships that are tied to the business. This sort of human capital is often so specific that it helps entrepreneurs perform inside their own ventures—but does not increase their performance outside the venture. This idea—maximizing the return to specialized human capital— will return in our later discussion of multiunit franchisees.

The key to this argument is that anyone who can find franchisees has passed a screen, a sort of examination of their investment idea. (Many would-be franchisors never find any franchisees—and cannot find buyers for their stock, either.) With their investment, franchisees endorse their own operation. They may not value the entire chain as highly as they value their location. This makes it easier for you, the franchisor, to persuade the franchisee to invest. You do not need to present the entire operation as being as interesting as any single location.

By finding franchisees, you have done more than alleviate your financial problem. You have also addressed another pressing issue, which is a shortage of good managers. Once you have capital, you need to find managers for your outlets. Once you have enough managers, you need to build layers of management to manage your managers. Having solved the capital scarcity problem, you, the entrepreneur, will quickly find yourself spending inordinate time trying to solve your managerial scarcity problem.[15]

Because you are racing to grow your business and have plenty of other issues to occupy your attention, you will want to build your management team fast. You could spend your resources looking at employment applications from people whose motivation and qualifications are very difficult to assess. Are they misrepresenting themselves? Are they adept at projecting capability and drive, or are they really what they say they are? One way to tell is to screen applicants *by asking them to become franchisees.* The unmotivated, uninterested, or incapable are less likely to pay your lump-sum entry fee and put up the initial investment. Nor will they agree to pay an ongoing royalty and live off what profits are left.

These arguments for starting up by franchising are defensible on rational grounds. Do franchisors reason this way? Some do. But the reality is not always so rational. Many founders of franchise organizations take the franchising route because their overriding objective is to control the enterprise as it grows. They believe that it is easier to influence (really, dominate) each franchisee (hence, the entire operation) than it is to influence a board of directors. Their decision is driven by fear of losing control if they sell shares, rather than by the desire to raise financial capital or solve a shortage of human capital. Ironically, these founders often find they underestimated the independent spirit of their franchisees.[16] Even more ironically, many founders lose control anyway: They give way to professional managers as their organization grows.

Harnessing the Entrepreneurial Spirit

Raising capital and finding management—quickly—are reasons to start out by franchising. Once launched, the reasons to continue to franchise revolve around harnessing the drive and capabilities of an entrepreneur. We are talking about a business that is "programmable," that can be encapsulated in a formulaic, transferable business format. If you could transfer it to a franchisee, you could also transfer it to a manager employed by you (the company-owned outlet). Why choose a franchisee?

To simplify reality, there are two major ways a firm can motivate people. One is by monitoring them (making them employees, so as to be able to supervise them and apply sanctions and rewards). The other is to make them residual claimants (profit sharing). Residual claimants do not need as much monitoring. They will work anyway, out of desire for profit and fear of loss. *Franchising is a way to cut down monitoring costs by making people into residual claimants.*

Thus, the franchisee will be more motivated to exert sheer effort than will an employee manager. This explains why many franchises exist in businesses, such as many retailing sectors, where the jobs are relatively programmable but the hours are long and the margins are too low to pay supervisors well. Effort matters, and the business cannot pay someone enough to make sure effort is continuously put forth while maintaining minimum standards of behavior (accuracy, cleanliness, friendliness to customers, etc.). This is critical for service businesses, where production and distribution occur simultaneously, making it impossible to inspect goods before the customer sees them. A motivated person needs to be monitoring operations closely at all times.

Table 13.1   Sectors with substantial franchise presence, United States and France

Amusement
Automobiles:
    Equipment
    Rental
    Service
Building Products and Services
Business Services
Children's Products, including Clothing
Cleaning Services and Equipment
Educational Services
Employment Agencies
Health and Beauty (includes Hair Styling and Cosmetology)
Home Furnishings/Equipment
Lodging/Hotels
Maintenance
Miscellaneous Retail
Miscellaneous Services, including Training
Personal Services and Equipment
Pet Services
Photography and Video
Printing
Quick Services
Real Estate
Restaurants:
    Fast Food
    Traditional
Retail Food
Shipping and Packing
Travel

Source. Adapted from Shane, Scott and Maw-Der Foo (1999), "New Firm Survival: Institutional Explanations for New Franchisor Mortality," *Management Science* 45, no. 2 (February), pp. 142–159; and the French Federation of Franchising Web site, www.franchise-fff.com.

This point is apparent in Table 13.1, which lists sectors in which franchising has a strong presence.

There is a distinction between lack of effort and misdirected effort. The franchising contract is a good way to combat lack of effort, but it is often unsuccessful in solving the problem of misdirected effort. Franchisees often battle their franchisors because they have different ideas of how things should be done. Franchising cannot solve this problem, but it does create a mechanism that encourages the franchisor to take franchisees seriously and to consider whether they might, after all, be right. One franchisor offers a pithy summary[17] of what many feel to be the key issue: "You see, a manager will do what you want, but he won't work very hard. A franchisee will work hard, but he won't do what you want."

Not everyone agrees with this viewpoint. Starbucks is a highly successful chain of coffee shops.[18] Its fast growth and high coverage lead many people assume it is a franchised chain. Yet every store is a company outlet managed by a Starbucks employee. Howard Schultz, the founder, is sharply critical of franchising, arguing that it leads firms to expand too quickly without stopping to address problems as they arise. The result, he argues, is that errors (such as hiring the wrong people, losing control of operations, compromising on quality, or picking the wrong location) propagate through the system and become established. Starbucks is noted for its consistency of operations and its enthusiastic, committed store management. Schultz attributes this to offering stock options and argues that equity stakes in the overall business allow Starbucks to duplicate the enthusiasm and sense of ownership that franchisees bring to their business. Starbucks is proof that nothing about the industries in Table 13.1 makes franchising the only viable way to govern the channel.

There is more to franchising than inducing managers to keep managing even in the middle of the night on a holiday. A major reason to franchise is to use the franchisee as a consultant. Your franchisee-consultant works out implementation problems for you and generates new ideas for you. This argument holds that a franchisor has a general vision. To be implemented on a large scale, this vision must be adapted to local circumstances. As time goes by, the vision will need to be adapted to changes in its markets. The franchisor does not have the know-how to adapt locally and does not have the willingness to change the vision over time. Franchisees do.

An example occurs in Southeast Asia, where U.S.-style fast food has become quite popular. William Heinecke, an American raised in Thailand, approached Pizza Hut with the idea of opening a franchise outlet in Bangkok. Citing Asian's well-known dislike of cheese, Pizza Hut was skeptical but allowed Heinecke to go ahead. The franchisee's judgment proved to be stunningly good, with the result that Pizza Hut now has a substantial business in Thailand and Heinecke owns dozens of outlets.

This is an inversion of the usual notion of an all-knowing franchisor consenting to uplift the unsophisticated franchisee in return for fees and royalties. Instead, we have the image of some franchisees who are very sophisticated: They solve problems the national office does not even notice, and they come up with better ideas than does corporate. The job of corporate is to collect these ideas (screening out the lesser ones), adapt them to the entire chain, and then spread them to other franchisees. We can extend the idea of the sophisticated franchisee even further: Some franchisees may have a much better idea of the value of a prospective site than would a franchisor.

If that sounds unlikely, consider this: Most of the best-known images and product ideas of today's McDonald's were generated by franchisees.[19] For example, the fish burger was invented by a franchisee in a Catholic neighborhood as a way to bring customers in on Friday, when eating meat is discouraged. Although the franchisor has the original vision of the business format, over time franchisees further develop the vision collectively. In general, no single franchisee has a better format. The franchisor gathers, adapts, and diffuses the best ideas of the set of franchisees.

Harnessing the motivation of a capable person, then, is a major reason to franchise. Franchising is not only a means of finding motivated, capable managers. It is also a means of keeping them. For example, many large French retailers face slow growth in their home market. This has forced them to consider secondary locations, such as small towns that cannot support a large store and an employee manager. Seeking to find franchisees for these locations, many chains have rediscovered an excellent source of talent: their existing managers.

The result has been a boom in converting French employees to franchisees. Employees see the move to owning their own businesses as intrinsically satisfying. Franchisors see the move as a way to reduce risk and investment: both parties know each other. The one drawback is that employees usually lack the necessary capital. Most of them also lack some aspect of know-how: The manager of the produce section of a hypermarket will need training in finance, for example.

Franchisors are willing to bet on someone they know in order to retain that person's loyalty and know-how. Hence, French franchisors often favor their employees, giving them financial backing, unusual assistance to make the transition, and training. This can be overdone: Many employee managers are unable to make the shift to doing all the tasks themselves, without staff, and cannot adopt an entrepreneurial attitude toward risk. By assisting them too much, franchisors may inadvertently shift them to a role they are ill suited to undertake.[20]

Here, we have come full circle. We began with franchising as a way quickly to find good managers (without having to hire them) and to induce them to supply you with capital. Now we see franchising as a way to keep the managers you hired years ago, which necessitates that *you* give *them* the necessary capital. This is why Fast Retailing, the Japanese company behind Uniglo (a retailer of casual clothes) intends to operate up to 200 Uniglo outlets by converting proactive employees with over ten years experience into franchisees. The firm's founder, Tadashi Yanaii, believes that store managers should be independent and that franchising is a way to establish a win-win relationship.[21]

In short, franchising is more than a way to grow fast, to get capital, or to avoid overhead. Franchising is a versatile and generalized system of management motivation in marketing channels. It is easy to underestimate the power of franchising and to overestimate the value of controlling the operation via one's own employee managers. See Sidebar 13-2 for an example.

When Is Franchising Inappropriate?

Franchising is using a marketing channel that is almost a subsidiary. When is a subsidiary more appropriate? Chapter 9 on vertical integration covers this issue in detail. By and large, a subsidiary is more appropriate when the business format is highly unusual and rather difficult to codify and when it is difficult to ascertain whether the store is achieving the best possible results. As an example, Sidebar 13.3 profiles Truffaut, a garden supply center, and Buffalo Grill, a restaurant chain. Both chains vertically integrate much more than does their more conventional competition.

Frequently, franchising affords more control than is really necessary. As a business becomes more conventional and free riding on the brand becomes a less important issue, franchising may involve more responsibility than the company needs to assume. There are alternatives. For example, Pronuptia is a prominent maker of bridal gowns shown in Pronuptia stores the world over. These stores frequently start as a franchise and then develop into licenses or exclusive distribution.[22]

Sidebar 13.2

ADA discovers the benefits of franchising

ADA rents cars and trucks using a strong discount appeal. Its strategy is one of advertising a very low price, which often turns out to be far from the total price once the extras are factored in. ADA also offers low service. Initially, the firm kept ultralow costs by sticking to a niche (renting cars and light trucks in cities). The firm used franchising to grow fast, so fast that it saturated its home market of France. In the belief that it was essential to keep growing in France, ADA decided to open rental counters in airports and train stations, renting a broader assortment of cars as well as trucks. To run this new operation, management felt the need to "professionalize" its retail operations, so it staffed these sites with company personnel.

The results have been disappointing. ADA discovered that city dwellers who went to ADA counters were already well informed and needed little help. In contrast, travelers, who frequent airports and train stations, demanded more information and assistance. Because these locations are highly competitive, ADA had to add personnel, broaden its vehicle stock, and make its rental terms more flexible. Still, these counters suffered from lack of referrals from travel agencies, with which ADA has no connections.

As these counters sank into low levels of performance, employees deserted, leaving ADA with poor managers. Management sought to rectify the situation by adding overhead at corporate. Ultimately having gone to company stores to professionalize, ADA ended up conceding it could not compensate at headquarters for poor supervision at the rental site. The solution? Sell the troubled sites—to franchisees.[23]

THE HISTORICAL ROOTS OF FRANCHISING

Franchising is often considered a post–World-War-II phenomenon. But the roots of franchising go back much farther to ancient times in practice and to the Middle Ages in law. Franchising as we know it today can be readily traced to the late nineteenth century United States, when it was identified with soft drink bottling and with the retailing of gasoline, automobiles, and sewing machines. In business-to-business applications, the franchising concept was developed by the McCormick Harvesting Machine Company to sell directly to farmers, bypassing wholesalers.

Autos, sewing machines, and harvesters were relatively new, complex, mass-produced products that needed to be sold in huge volumes to gain economies of scale in manufacturing. Selling these machines at that scale required specialized marketing services that were unusual for their time: the extension of credit, plus demonstration and postsale repair. Firms in these industries could not hire and train their own dealers fast enough. They turned to near-subsidiaries as a way to grow quickly. Once growth was achieved, firms often turned away from their franchising operations and went into company-owned and managed outlets.[24] This is a trend that repeats itself, to be discussed in a later section.

The Authorized Franchise System: Moving the Product

What these sellers did was to induce dealers to acquire some of the identity of the producer and to concentrate on one product line. Fundamentally, dedicated dealers stocked a product and resold it, adhering to certain guidelines about what to offer the

Sidebar 13.3

Vertically integrating instead of franchising: Truffaut Garden Centers and Buffalo Grill Restaurants

Truffaut Garden Centers is a French retail chain. Founded in 1824 as a producer and wholesale grower by Charles Truffaut, the chain was still family owned when the founder's great-grandson paid a visit to the United States in the 1960s. Impressed by the large, full-line garden centers there, Georges Truffaut refocused his family firm. Abandoning production, Truffaut became a retail chain imitating the U.S. idea of offering all garden-related products from plants to fertilizer to lawn mowers under one roof. The novel concept pleased French consumers— which meant it was soon imitated.

Truffaut fell on hard times, was sold several times, and lost money. Early in the 1990s, the chain's new owners changed management, invested heavily, restructured, and reinvented the all-under-one-roof concept. Reasoning that gardening is fundamentally an emotional affair, Truffaut Garden Centers set out to "seduce" customers, to make them experience a thunderclap of emotional longing for a beautiful garden on their apartment window, balcony, or terrace or in their yard.

To seduce prospective customers, Truffaut's massive stores resemble greenhouses. Truffaut lavishes millions of francs annually on each store to create and recreate elaborate walks along garden paths throughout the greenhouse. These stores resemble a tourist destination: Only the price tags remind visitors that they are allowed to purchase. Visitors are drawn to the greenhouse/store to browse (for this purpose, Truffaut wins zoning variances permitting it to open when other stores are legally obliged to close, for example, on Sundays).

Visitors stroll along the long paths (some stores go up to 13,000 square meters, over 100,000 square feet, twice the size of competing stores). Along the way, they encounter thousands of plant varieties, appealingly displayed. They come across ponds, pergolas, fountains, benches, and landscape features. These items exist in kits: Competing stores display only the boxes. Truffaut displays the result. Visitors stroll to the edge of a pond, for example, and are reminded of their childhood at their grandparents' homes, playing near the concrete fish basins that were popular decades ago. Knowledgeable, helpful, low-pressure salespeople appear to explain that technology has made affordable ponds easy to install and maintain. Visitors become customers, and they come back over and over. In just over a decade, Truffaut, with only 40 stores in France, has become *the* reference for 7 million customers.

To create and build the habit of visiting (which almost invariably leads to purchasing), Truffaut mounts expensive marketing campaigns. An elaborate fidelity card gives regular customers rewards for purchases. Stores open their doors and invite their best customers to evening theme parties, such as Halloween (a new concept in France) and back-to-school. For the public, in-store events abound: all about rabbits, get to know the Newfoundland breed of dog, learn to do arts-and-crafts projects, and similar sessions. Why dogs, rabbits, and arts and crafts? People who like to garden are home oriented. They frequently have pets and in-home hobbies. To amortize its high fixed costs, Truffaut includes a pet center and devotes greenhouse space to crafts in the winter. Thus, visitors continue visiting year round, ready to fall in love with a new display and make an unplanned purchase.

The elements of this formula are unusual in France. In particular, high labor costs and inflexible labor laws lead French companies to minimize sales help. Yet, Truffaut spends heavily

Sidebar 13.3 (cont.)

Vertically integrating instead of franchising: Truffaut Garden Centers and Buffalo Grill Restaurants

on a large, well-trained sales force. Truffaut is also willing to incur the high fixed costs needed to build and maintain the greenhouses, set up and rotate the displays, keep the stores open long and unusual hours, hold an immense and varied inventory of perishables, and run recurring marketing campaigns.

This is why Truffaut prefers to own every store even though this means slower growth. In contrast, its largest competitor, Jardiland, is a franchisor. Jardiland's operations are more conventional; the formula is easier to transmit, and franchisees are less tempted to deviate from it. It is easier for the franchisor to tell if a store is not realizing its potential. Alternatively, Truffaut creates potential: It has enlarged the French garden market by its presence.

Buffalo Grill Restaurants show how the same situation can evolve into a franchisable concept. Buffalo Grill is a much-talked-about personal success story in France. It begins in the 1960s, when Christian Picart, a young man who had grown up in France under difficult circumstances, decided to seek his fortune in the United States. Working several hotel service and restaurant jobs (simultaneously), Picart observed firsthand the U.S. concept of a Wild West steak house. Returning to France, Picart adapted the concept and opened his first Buffalo Grill in 1980. Today, he owns the largest chain of theme restaurants in France. His rags-to-riches story rests on a formula that is highly unusual for France.

Picart took his Wild-West-in-France concept to an extreme, even by U.S. standards. A Buffalo Grill restaurant is instantly recognizable by its distinctive architecture: a large building resembling a saloon and covered by an enormous garish roof, bright red, emblazoned with the name in white. French zoning discourages such flamboyant, nontraditional architecture, but Picart will not open a restaurant unless he can get a zoning variance, no matter how desirable the site. He is helped by his insistence on locating where there is little competition: remote highways, industrial zones, and other underserved locations.

Inside each restaurant, the black-and red decor is almost painfully Wild Western (carved cowboy and Indian statues indicate the toilets, for example). The result is a fun, informal, inviting atmosphere, supported by large numbers of friendly personnel. Theme restaurants typically start well, then fade as the novelty of the theme wears off. But the real appeal of Buffalo Grill's limited menu is a combination of high-quality steaks and very low prices. This brings repeat customers: Proprietary processes (particularly for treating meat) and extremely rigorous cost control convert this formula into profits. Buffalo Grill's business format is elaborate, unusual, and precise. Low margins leave no room for deviation.

Having opened 260 restaurants (over 240 in France), Christian Picart has perfected his formula. One key to the formula is the architecture. The roof, for example, substitutes for advertising, of which the chain does virtually none. Building these large, customized restaurants costs millions of francs. Buffalo Grill guards the knowledge of the idiosyncrasies of these buildings by vertically integrating backward into architectural services. Similarly, the way Buffalo Grill cuts its meat is proprietary, so the chain is vertically integrated backward into meat cutting. This proved essential during the mad-cow-disease scare, when infected beef was discovered in the European food supply.

(continued)

Sidebar 13.3 (cont.)

Vertically integrating instead of franchising:
Truffaut Garden Centers and Buffalo Grill
Restaurants

Overnight, frightened customers decided to boycott beef. Buffalo Grill responded by offering unusual meats (bison, ostrich, and so forth). Competitors could not copy their action because Buffalo Grill's meat cutters used their unique experience to devise their own ways to cut these little-known meats. Customers reacted so well that these items became standard on the menu even after beef returned to favor.

The formula is unusual, but it is now well elucidated and thoroughly demonstrated. The essential parts (meat cutting and architecture) are owned by the firm. To date, most of the restaurants are also owned by the firm and run by employee managers. To continue his expansion, Christian Picart has started moving toward franchising. Many of his franchisees are drawn from the ranks of his managers. The best managers are rewarded for years of excellent service

by being offered a franchise. They are required to put up as much capital as they can, but the initial investment of 10 million francs is excessive. Therefore, Buffalo Grill cosigns bank loans for the difference, assuming responsibility in case of default. Because the restaurants are highly profitable, there is no shortage of interested managers or willing banks.

To date, among the 260 restaurants, Buffalo Grill counts about one third as franchisees, about half of whom are ex-managers of company-owned restaurants. A proprietary, unusual, and specialized concept has matured to become franchisable. With it, Christian Picart hopes to bring the Wild West *à la française* to Europe. Now that his concept is demonstrated to work well, he is poised to use franchising as his means to keep ownership of the idea. Bison and ostrich priced for a family budget in Prague? Why not?[25]

market. This stops somewhat short of licensing an entire business format. In particular, the producer's aim is to sell its product. The manufacturer seeks to maintain some semblance of control over how the brand name is presented for the purpose of increasing profits from the product directly. Producers make money on the margins they obtain by selling to their dealers rather than on fees and royalties.

This form of franchising has come to be called product and trade name franchising, or authorized franchise systems. Authorized dealers, distributors, resellers, agents (all these terms apply) meet minimum criteria the manufacturer establishes regarding the outlet's degree of participation in marketing flows. In these situations, a franchisor authorizes distributors (wholesalers or retailers or both) to sell a product or product line using its trade name for promotional purposes. Examples at the retail level are authorized tire, auto, computer, major appliance, television, and household furniture dealers whose suppliers have established strong brand names. Such authorization also can be granted at the wholesale level—for example, to soft drink bottlers and to distributors or dealers by manufacturers of electrical and electronics equipment.

What is usually referred to today as franchising is business format franchising. This is the licensing of an entire way of doing business under a brand name. For a franchisor, the reward for this activity is the generation of ongoing fees.

The Dividing Line: When Does Franchising Stop?

Establishing an authorized franchise system is a means for suppliers, without assuming financial ownership, to raise the probability that channel members will provide the appropriate type and level of service outputs to end-users. A major way in which organizers of authorized franchise systems have achieved this end is to specify or impose restrictions on how channel members can operate. As such, an authorized franchise system is a way to exercise power.

There are many ways to exercise power. How do we know when franchising stops and other channels begin? In some jurisdictions, the line is clear because legal requirements oblige any so-called franchisor to follow disclosure and reporting rules. These impose a significant legal cost on the franchisor.

But outside these jurisdictions, there is no sharp dividing line. Once vertical integration is eliminated, a gray area exists between franchising and many other forms of distribution. A franchisee, as imagined by Cyrus McCormick, the founder of the McCormick Harvesting Machine Company, was almost a company subsidiary. Logically, there are other ways to deal with an independent company yet simulate a company subsidiary. Therefore, it is sometimes difficult to say whether a channel is franchised or whether it is technically separable but led or dominated by an influential upstream channel member.

For example, a retailer cooperative or a wholesaler-sponsored voluntary group resembles franchising. Regulators have intervened in such disputes to ascertain whether franchising laws apply to these groups.[26] A key criterion is whether joining these groups is voluntary and whether the use of their services is optional. In franchising, these are not choices but are mandatory.

So just what is a franchise? The linguistic roots of the term *franchise* reflect McCormick's conceptualization of a dealer selling his harvesting machines. In both English and French, the term goes back to the Middle Ages, from which it draws two facets: freedom and privilege. A medieval franchise formally and contractually limited a sovereign's authority in some way (tax exemption, for example, or in the guarantee of certain rights). Thus, a franchise enlarged the freedom of the franchisee from the sovereign, just as dealers enjoyed more freedom from the McCormick Harvesting Machine Company than would a corporate division. The aspect of privilege comes from the benefits that should accrue from the granting of such an advantage.

What franchising is usually taken to mean today is the licensing of an entire business format. The European Union provides a good definition: a franchise is a *package of industrial or intellectual property rights*. The package relates to trade names, trademarks, shop signs, utility models, designs, copyrights, know-how, or patents. The package is to be exploited for the resale of goods or the provision of services to end-users. The EU points out that this definition uses three features to distinguish franchising:

1. The use of a common name or sign, with a uniform presentation of the premises
2. Communication of know-how from franchisor to franchisee
3. Continuing provision of commercial or technical assistance by the franchisor to the franchisee.

The EU exempts franchising from many of the regulations designed to encourage intra- and intercountry competition within the European Union. This exemption is made in recognition that it is critical to project a common identity in franchising and that doing so involves writing contracts that restrict competition. The exemption is justified from a consumer welfare standpoint because franchising should "combine the advantages of a uniform and homogeneous network, which ensures a constant quality of the products and services, with the existence of traders personally interested in the efficient operation of their business."[27]

We now return to this system of business format franchising and examine how it operates.

THE FRANCHISE CONTRACT

Giving and Taking Hostages, Or Why You Shouldn't Leave It to Lawyers

Unlike many business arrangements, franchising is tightly governed by elaborate and formal contracts. Many of these contracts run on for pages of intricate legal language. It is tempting for both franchisor and franchisee to leave the contract to the lawyers and simply presume that working arrangements will arise that will govern the relationship anyway. This is a dangerous error. In franchising, the contract really matters. In particular, three sections of a franchise contract determine who will enter the arrangement and how it will function.[28] These are:

1. The payment system. Particularly the lump-sum fee to enter the system, the royalty fee, and the initial investment. How these are calculated and how they may be adjusted over the contract duration are critical.
2. The real estate. Who holds the lease and how it may be transferred. This looks like a financing detail but is actually far more important.
3. Termination. Franchise arrangements anticipate a possible ending of the relationship and spell out how it would be conducted.

In the United States, where franchising has its fullest history, regulators and courts are concerned about whether it is socially beneficial. In particular, they are worried that franchisors (typically seen as large, powerful, and sophisticated) exploit franchisees (typically seen as small, weak, and naive). A major reason for this concern is that franchise contracts typically contain clauses that, on the face of it, are outrageously favorable to the franchisor. This implies that franchisors have better lawyers and more bargaining power.

Are these contracts actually unfair? Are franchisees really so weak and naive? Do they hire inferior lawyers? Or is something else happening?

In political affairs, two parties often safeguard an agreement by exchanging hostages. *The party that is in a better position to break its promises offers a hostage to the other side.* If this party (the poster of the hostage) reneges, the other party keeps the hostage. If both sides are tempted to break their promises, they exchange hostages (each side posts a hostage to be kept by the other in case of breach of promise).

Franchise contracts can be understood as attempts by each side to make sure the other side will live up to its promises.[29] *Contract clauses are used to post hostages.* Because both franchisor and franchisee are tempted to renege, each side will post some hostages. The franchisee is in a better position to renege, so it posts more hostages (accepts contracts that give great power to the franchisor). This is curious: The usual presumption is that the franchisee is in an excellent position to cheat the franchisor and must be stopped from so doing. To make sense of this, read on.

The Payment System

The franchisee usually pays a fixed fee, or lump-sum payment, to start up. If this were all, the franchisee would be in danger. The franchisor would be inclined to abscond, that is, collect the fee and then do nothing to help the franchisee.

The franchisee also makes an initial investment that covers acquiring inventory, obtaining and adapting the facility, purchasing tools and equipment, and advertising the opening of the outlet. If the store closed quickly, a good part of that investment would be lost. Fixtures and equipment, for example, might sell secondhand for half what the franchisee paid for them. Even worse, if they are specialized to the franchisor's decor (distinctive colors, patterns, emblazoned logos and slogans, etc.), they might resell for a quarter of their acquisition cost. That part of the initial investment that the franchisee cannot recover is a sunk cost.

The up-front fee and the unrecoverable part of the initial investment are at risk for the franchisee. They are hostages. If the franchisee does not carry out its promises and the business fails, the franchisee loses the hostages.

Once the franchisee has posted these hostages, the franchisor must post some hostages of its own. An excellent hostage is a royalty on sales (a variable fee). If the franchisor does not help the franchisee, sales suffer, and the franchisor shares the suffering by collecting less royalty income. Therefore, royalties motivate the franchisor to pay attention to the franchisee.[30]

Why a royalty on sales rather than on profit? After all, the franchisor's real function is to help the franchisee make money. The answer is that, in most cases, sales can be readily observed and verified. In contrast, profit is easy to manipulate and difficult to check.

By getting payments from franchisees, franchisors make money. *What is the best way to get money out of franchisees?* Put differently, if fixed fees and sales royalties are common, what should be their ratio? It can be argued that fixed and variable payments to the franchisor should be negatively correlated.[31] The rationale is that a franchisor charging a high fixed fee is sending two signals. The first signal is positive: My franchise is valuable. The second signal is negative: I am extracting as much as I can from you up front so that I can exploit you later (abscond, or "take the money and run"). To avoid sending this negative signal, franchisors can cut their up-front fee (sometimes to zero, even for well-known franchises)[32] and seek to make their money later by raising their royalty rates. Thus, they are sharing risk with their franchisees.

In so doing, the franchisors may be sharing too much risk. By forgoing up-front money now in favor of potential royalty payments later, franchisors take on the risk that franchisees will accept their assistance to set up the business (because this is a large part of the franchisor's role) and later try to renegotiate the contract to their advantage. This "opportunistic holdup" of the franchisor by the franchisee could take many forms, including negotiating for deferment or reduction of royalties, extra assistance, rent relief, and other considerations. Franchisors might renegotiate in order to avoid losing the money they invested to set up the franchisee in business.

In short, fear of holdup by the franchisee (renegotiating the deal once the business is running) drives the franchisor to ask for more up-front money in lieu of royalties. Fear of neglect by the franchisor drives the franchisee to demand the opposite.

How does it settle out? Evidence suggests little relation between the fixed fee and the royalty.[33] In terms of the sheer amount of the fixed fee, there is some indication that the franchisor typically concedes. It takes less up-front money than it would like and might reasonably demand. In return, the franchisee makes concessions on other aspects of the contract (discussed later). In addition, the franchisee makes heavy initial investments, much of which it cannot recover, especially if the investments are in franchise-specific decor and equipment or in merchandise that is difficult to return or resell. These initial investments are often much higher than the franchisor's fixed fee. By incurring this investment, the franchisee offers a hostage to assure the franchisor that it will exert its best efforts and stay in the business. This is a deterrent to mistreating the franchisor by renegotiating the contract at every opportunity.

A major reason to reduce up-front fixed fees is to enlarge the pool of applicants. A good candidate to be a franchisee possesses a certain profile (personality, background, management ability, and local knowledge) sought by the franchisor. If to this list one must add substantial personal wealth, the pool of qualified candidates shrinks dramatically.

Indeed, there is strong indication that many franchisors could ask for much higher *total* income than they do. This means they are also asking a lower royalty rate than they could. One estimate holds that McDonald's leaves several hundred thousand dollars "on the table" (i.e., in the franchisee's bank account) each time it grants a franchise.[34] Why would they do this? The answer is to *make the business precious to each franchisee.* By being generous, McDonald's gives the franchisee a great deal to lose. This greatly enhances the franchisee's desire to live up to its promises, which is exactly what franchising is designed to do.

In this vein, consider tied sales. This is a clause obliging franchisees to buy their inputs (products, supplies, etc.) from the supplier. For example, Avis and Budget in the United Kingdom require their franchisees to purchase from the franchisor the cars they rent out. Why not let the franchisees buy a car anywhere and see if they can make better deals on their own? After all, a Ford is a Ford. This issue is important to regulators, who see tie-ins as a hidden way to exploit franchisees by overcharging them for products and services they could buy elsewhere. If so, tie-ins are a disguised way to collect more fees on an ongoing basis.

On the other hand, overcharging franchisees for what they buy can go against the franchisor's interest if the franchisee can compensate by cheating in some other way. For example, a restaurant forced to buy overpriced ingredients from the franchisor might cut portion size or save food too long.

Who uses tied-sales clauses? Evidence indicates that many franchisors elect tied sales only when they need to facilitate quality control. Avis and Budget, for example, want to ensure that the cars being rented are fully equipped as promised. When the quality of inputs is difficult to measure on an ongoing basis, franchisors are more likely to use tied-sales clauses—and to price them fairly, so as to avoid resentment and allegations of profiteering. Where any other product would be satisfactory as an input, franchisors are less likely to write tied-sales clauses. When many, but not just any, other products would do, franchisors oblige franchisees to buy from sources they approve but not from the franchisor alone.

Who Will Be the Landlord?

An issue of particular interest to regulators is who collects the rent on the franchisee's premises. Many franchisors, such as McDonald's, take pains to ensure that they are the landlord. Failing that, they want to hold the right to lease the property to the franchisee. Therefore, they negotiate a lease with the property owner and then sublet to the franchisee. Their leases are frequently quite protective of the franchisor's rights, at the expense of the franchisee's rights.

Owning the land is a capital-intensive practice that absorbs much management attention and leads to frequent disputes. Why do it? A common explanation is that retailing depends on location, and the best locations are difficult to secure. This reasoning has it that owners of prime commercial locations would rather deal with franchisors than with a franchisee. Also, the franchisor may negotiate better than can a franchisee.

This would not explain why some franchisors insist on holding the lease for *all* their sites, even the lesser ones. Insistence on controlling the lease is best explained as a way to make termination of the franchisee a credible threat.[35] A noncompliant franchisee who is your tenant is easier to eject from your system if you can terminate the lease at the same time you terminate the franchisee. A franchisee who agrees to be a tenant and who also agrees to a lease that favors the landlord is a franchisee who is offering a hostage to the franchisor. This is particularly potent if the franchisee makes improvements to the property because these improvements can be appropriated by the landlord under many legal systems.

Leasing is not always a control device. Being the landlord or the lessor can be a tool for franchisors to assist franchisees by reducing their capital requirements or rents. Indeed, franchisors often defer rents on franchises that are in trouble. By design or by accident, however, franchisors who are landlords have a potent way to enforce termination of a franchisee. They can evict the franchisee while keeping the site for their operations.

Termination

Losing a franchisee is difficult and costly. For the franchisor, it is necessary to replace the franchisee (and, in the absence of leasing clauses, perhaps replace the location as well). The new franchisee must be brought up to norms, which takes time (and creates the opportunity cost of lost business). Knowing this, the franchisee might be tempted to hold up the franchisor (threaten to quit while negotiating a better deal). To a point, the franchisor will concede, just to avoid having to replace the franchisee.

Not surprisingly, many franchisors make it expensive (difficult) for the franchisee to leave them. As already noted, franchisees are less willing to walk away from a lucrative business (low royalties on a good business) and to walk away from other investments they have made (such as franchise-specific decor). Other contract devices make it even more difficult to quit.

In the United Kingdom, many contracts require franchisees to find their own replacements. The franchisee must find a candidate quickly, *and* the candidate must be acceptable to the franchisor. Otherwise, the franchisor can impose a candidate.

The franchisees must pay a transfer fee, a sum that is lower if they find their own replacement (saving the franchisor the trouble). Franchisors often insert a right-of-first-refusal clause giving them the right to take the franchisee's contract if they match any offer the franchisee can find.

This protects the franchisor against a franchisee who threatens to sell to an unsuitable buyer. It also gives the franchisor some ability to abuse franchisees by denying them the right to liquidate their business at a fair value in a timely way. In the United States, a number of states regulate termination precisely to prevent such abuse. In the United Kingdom, where regulation is less pervasive in franchising, another safeguard is needed. The parties find it in arbitration: Arbitration clauses are very common.

Why Contracts Do Not Vary within a System

Franchise contracts have surprisingly little variance over outlets. One would expect that every contract would quote different terms of trade, as no two franchisees face the same situation. However, franchisors tend to have a single contract (with only minor variations) and a single price. They offer their contracts on a take-it-or-leave-it basis.

Contracts also do not vary much over time. Adjustments occur occasionally, particularly in the price (royalties and/or fixed fees): The price rises as the franchisor becomes better established. Otherwise, contracts are surprisingly stable.[36] Part of the reason is that contracts tend to be for fairly long periods, fifteen years being common in the United States. Another reason is that tailoring contracts incurs high legal fees, especially in jurisdictions with high disclosure requirements. Still another reason is the importance to franchisors of being perceived as fair, as treating franchisees equitably. By offering the same contract to all, the franchisor avoids appearing to practice discrimination. This threat seems to loom larger than the possible loss of flexibility or the appearance of arbitrariness.

Safeguards Outside the Contract

Ultimately, the contract is a delicate balancing act. Each side has incentives to cheat the other. Franchisors can take the money and do nothing to help (abscond). Franchisees operate their own businesses and are difficult to monitor and direct. This means they can dishonor their promises to comply with the franchisor's rules, abuse the brand name, and fail to offer their best efforts (noncompliance, free riding, shirking). In writing a contract, the objective is to create a self-enforcing agreement, that is, an arrangement that neither side wants to violate. They comply without being monitored or threatened because the contract arranges their incentives so that cheating is not in their own interest.

The trouble is that every clause that stops one side from cheating creates a new way for the other side to cheat. *Every effort to balance the power creates a new possibility for imbalance.* This is true of most business arrangements between independents. Often, businesses do not try to solve the problem by means other than writing elaborate contracts. Franchisors and franchisees, however, take a great risk if they permit themselves to operate in this way. The two parties are agreeing to join their fates for years. The franchisor is sacrificing its secrets and its trademarks. The franchisee is sacrificing its autonomy. Their arrangement is elaborate and forward looking. Their contracts must be, as well.

Franchise contracts can be understood as an effort to balance, roughly, the interests of both sides. Where one side is tempted to cheat, a clause is created to block

Table 13.2   The franchise contract

The *International Franchise Guide* of the *International Herald Tribune* suggests that any franchise contract should address the following subjects.

- Definition of terms
- Organizational structure
- Term of initial agreement
- Term of renewal
- Causes for termination or nonrenewal
- Territorial exclusivity
- Intellectual property protection
- Assignment of responsibilities
- Ability to subfranchise
- Mutual agreement on pro forma cash flows
- Development schedule and associated penalties
- Fees, front end and ongoing
- Currency and remittance restrictions
- Remedies in case of disagreement

Source: Moulton, Susan L., ed. (1996), *International Franchise Guide*, (Oakland, CA: Source Books Publications).

cheating. Often, that same clause gives too much power to the other side, creating the need for another clause to rectify the excesses of the first, and so on.

Contracts become complex fast, and in spite of their complexity they probably are not correctly calibrated at the end of the process. No contract can specify all contingencies and craft the proper solution for all problems. Nonetheless, a franchise contract should be thorough and forward looking. Table 13.2 suggests the issues that should be covered in some form in a franchise contract.

When Do Franchisors Enforce Their Contracts?

What else besides contracts can safeguard the relationship? The answer that comes up over and over is *reputation*. Franchisors who take a long-term view of their businesses worry, and rightly so, about creating a bully-boy image, of being seen as harsh, oppressive, or greedy. They worry for fear of losing current franchisees or their cooperation and of being unable to attract new franchisees. Most of all, they worry about being classed as a fly-by-night franchisor who is out to make money quickly through fees and lucrative tie-in sales and then abandon its franchisees. Such franchisors are swindlers. The others, those who wish to build a business, make it a point to treat franchisees correctly and to project that they do so. Their reputation is worth more to franchisors than the short-term gains they might extract by invoking harsh contract terms to win disputes with their franchisees.

This is why franchisors do not always enforce the contracts they have so carefully written. Instead, they weigh the costs and benefits of punishing each act of noncompliance and tolerate quite a few. Table 13.3 sketches the likelihood of an established franchisor taking action.

Table 13.3   When do franchisors enforce the franchise contract?

Consider the scenario of a well-established franchisor that has built a network of franchisees. In theory, such a franchisor should be quick to punish transgressions, such as

- Sourcing from a supplier of one's own choice rather than suppliers approved by the franchisor
- Failing to maintain the look and ambiance of the premises
- Violating the franchisor's standards and procedures
- Failing to pay advertising fees—or even the franchisor's royalty

Such violations are surprisingly frequent. When do franchisors exercise their legitimate right to enforce their contracts by punishing the franchisee? Research indicates* franchisors weigh the costs and benefits, taking into account the system-investments they need to protect their own power and the countervailing power of the franchisee and the franchise network. In particular, in their actions franchisors appear to consider what signals they are sending to franchisees, both current and potential, by what they tolerate and what they enforce. With this in mind, franchisors pick their battles rather than enforcing their contracts every time they are violated.

When it is particularly costly to enforce, franchisors are more likely to overlook a violation. This is more probable in the following circumstances.

- The franchisees have a very dense, tightly knit network among themselves. Hence, the franchisor fears a reaction of solidarity, with other franchisees siding with the violator.
- The violator is a central player in the franchisee's network—with one exception, to be presented below.
- The franchisor suffers from performance ambiguity, meaning its information systems are not sensitive enough to be sure of the situation. Such a franchisor cannot monitor well and, therefore, cannot be sure its case against the violator is strong.
- The franchisor has built strong relational governance, in which the system operates on norms of solidarity, flexibility, and exchange of information. Such a franchisor does not want to risk ruining these norms, and has other ways to deal with the violation in any case.

These are the costs of enforcing the contract. But under certain circumstances the benefits of enforcement outweigh them. The franchisor is more likely to take punitive action to enforce its contract when:

- The violation is critical, such as missing a large royalty payment or operating a very shabby facility in a highly visible location. This is particularly the case when the franchisee is a central player in the network. Ordinarily, central players are protected (as noted above) because the franchisor fears a system backlash, but when a central player violates the contract in a critical way, franchisors choose to enforce because it sends a strong signal that the rules are the rules. Put another way, tolerating a major violation by a central player would signal other franchisees that the contract is just a piece of paper with no real weight.
- The violator is a master franchisee, that is, has multiple units. Here, the risk is that the violation propagates across this franchisee's units and becomes a large-scale problem if the franchisor does not enforce the contract.

Table 13.3   (cont.)

- The franchisor has invested a great deal in the franchise *system* (as opposed to this particular franchisee). The franchisor needs to protect its investment and the capabilities it has created while building the system. This is true even when the franchisor does enjoy strong relational governance. The franchisor will risk upsetting a given relationship to protect its system investments.
- The franchisor is large.
- Mutual dependence in the franchisee-franchisor relationship is high (so that it can withstand the conflict that enforcement will create).
- The franchisor is much more powerful than the franchisee (so that the franchisor can coerce the franchisee to tolerate enforcement).

Taken together, the franchisor clearly weighs the power of both sides and the impact of each act of enforcement on its entire franchise system. Franchisees thus have more power than appears to be the case if one examines each dyad (franchisor/franchisee) in isolation.

*Antia, Kersi D. and Gary L. Frazier (2001), "The Severity of Contract Enforcement in Interfirm Channel Relationships," *Journal of Marketing*, 65, no. 4 (October), pp. 67–81.

WHY FRANCHISE SYSTEMS INCLUDE COMPANY OUTLETS

Franchisee-owned and company-owned outlets are usually considered equal alternatives. The reasoning is that one or the other will fit the situation but not both. Why, then, do so many franchisors also have company-owned stores, often doing exactly the same thing as franchises in exactly the same markets? A franchising system without any company-owned stores is somewhat unusual.[37] Among U.S. firms that franchise, on average 30 percent of their outlets are company owned.[38] What is the explanation?

Variation in Situations

The obvious explanation is that some markets are different from others. If so, company outlets and franchisee outlets should serve different types of markets. In what respect, then, are they different?

A popular supposition is that some markets require monitoring from the franchisor.[39] The reasoning is that the franchisee is tempted to cheat when repeat business is low (i.e., when business is transient). For example, a fast-food restaurant on a superhighway should draw heavily on people passing through only once. If this location were franchised, the franchisee would be tempted to cheat (e.g., cutting costs by serving stale food). Travelers would be drawn to the restaurant by the franchisor's brand name. The franchisee would damage brand equity but would not suffer the usual consequences (lost future sales) because the customer would not return anyway. To protect its brand equity from such free riding, the franchisor should own the outlet. (As noted earlier, the other franchisees should welcome this decision.) However, apart from the restaurant on a highway, it is difficult to think of situations that demand the company substitute monitoring for the motivation of an entrepreneur. This leads us to another explanation.

Temporary Franchises and Temporary Company Stores

One explanation for the simultaneous existence of franchise and company-owned stores is that some of the stores are temporary. This reasoning has it that circumstances at one point in time create a need for one form or the other.

Franchisors usually start out with some outlets of their own, where they formulate the business format and develop the brand name. This gives them something to sell to franchisees. If they skirt this step and start franchising early, they cannot attract many franchisees and must write generous contracts. So franchisors start out with company stores. Then they add franchisees, usually at a high rate. The company stores are a necessity during the franchisor's founding stages.

The general question is this: Once the business is underway, why add *any* company stores? Sometimes the cause is accidental or transient: A franchisee has a problem, and the franchisor buys out the location. This can be done to conceal franchisee problems for purposes of system morale (or, in the United States, to avoid a lawsuit). Or it can be to help a profitable franchisee who needs to exit quickly (say, for health reasons). Or it may be to hold the location. For all these motives, the company outlet is temporary. It is sold as soon as a new franchisee can be found.

A variation of this idea occurs in Italy, where opening a retail store in a particular sector (say, food retailing) requires a sector-specific license from the local authorities. These licenses are limited in supply, hence valuable. This is an obstacle for Italian franchisors. If they wish to expand quickly, they may be obliged to accept an undesirable franchisee simply because the individual holds one of the licenses to sell that product category in an area. Forecasting conflict with the license holder, the franchisor declines to franchise. Instead, it elects to use its corporate influence to get a license for itself, which means running a company outlet for some time. This leads to a pattern in Italian franchising of system growth by divesting corporate assets. The franchisor operates the outlet, learns from the experience, then divests the outlet by selling out to a suitable franchisee. There is some indication that divestment costs the franchisor little: The newly franchised store cooperates with management much as the company store did but often with better operating results.[40]

Ultimately, the idea of temporary franchisees or temporary company stores does not go very far in explaining why many franchisors maintain both systems. As they grow, most franchisors add new company outlets, albeit at a lower rate than they add franchisees.[41] Those systems that grow the fastest do so by favoring franchisees over company units. (These systems in turn have lower failure rates, to be discussed later).[42] So there must be permanent reasons for having both types—the plural form.

The Plural Form: Exploiting the Synergy of Having Both Company and Franchisee Outlets

Simultaneously and *deliberately* maintaining both company and franchised outlets to do the same thing is the strategy of using the plural form.[43] The principle is that franchisors can manage the duality of their organization (simultaneously vertically integrated and outsourced) by drawing on the strengths of each system to offset the weaknesses of the other. They do this in four ways.

First, the plural form in franchising enables franchisors to build a control system that creates functional rivalry between the two forms. This works because franchisors monitor their own units very heavily. They do so with:

> ➤ Elaborate management information systems that generate detailed daily reports on every aspect of the outlets' operations
> ➤ Frequent, elaborate, unannounced field audits covering hundreds of items and requiring hours to complete
> ➤ Mystery shoppers, who are paid professional auditors posing as customers (see Chapter 6 on expertise power)

Company managers of the outlets tolerate this heavy, invasive control mechanism because they are paid a salary for observing the rules. Top management tells them what to do, and they do it. They are not held accountable for making profit.

In contrast, these practices are less invasively implemented, less frequent, less thorough, and simply less often used with franchisees. Rather than telling franchisees what to do, franchisor managers attempt to persuade them. Titles and terms are telling here: Company-store managers report to district managers, but franchisees work with (do not report to) franchise consultants. The information and experience gained from this heavy control mechanism in company stores help the franchisor to stay in touch with the business it purports to master.

A second advantage of plural systems is that *each form benchmarks the other*. Franchisors encourage competition, comparing the performance of company and franchisee outlets and encouraging each type to do better than the other type. Because company and franchisee outlets do exactly the same thing (which is seemingly senseless), direct comparisons are possible, which heightens the competition.

A third advantage of the plural form is that the franchisor can create career paths for personnel to go back and forth between the company side and the franchisee side of the house. In so doing, the franchisor can accommodate its personnel while at the same time creating a means of socializing everyone on both sides of the house. One career path rises through the company side only by dealing with company outlets as a manager, then a supervisor, then a corporate executive. Another path rises through the franchise side only by starting a unit, adding new ones, and growing into a mini-hierarchy. (Some are not so mini: One major U.S. restaurant chain has a franchisee who owns over 400 units, which is more than many other restaurant chains number in their entirety.)

Three other career paths are noteworthy because they connect the franchisee and company-owned sides of the franchisor.

1. Company people become franchisees: This is a surprisingly common path. Company people like it because they can develop into entrepreneurs, often with less capital than an outsider would need. Franchisors like it because their franchisee community is seeded with people they know they can work with.

2. Company-unit managers become franchisee consultants: This is a shift from running a company store (being on salary, following the rules) to working persuasively with franchisees. The jobs are very different (like a promotion from a factory supervisor to a diplomatic post). The transition can be difficult, but former company store managers have credibility with franchisees because of their hands-on experience.

3. Company managers become franchisee managers: This is a move from the franchisor's hierarchy to managing in a multiunit franchisor. This move from one organization to another, still in a management position, is an important way in which mini-hierarchies mimic the franchisor's organization.

The beauty of these three border-crossing career paths is that they solidly unite the franchisor and franchisee by creating a means of exchanging personnel regularly on a large scale. This vehicle enables franchisees and franchisors to socialize each other and develop bonds.

The fourth advantage of the plural form is that each side engages in teaching the other side, which helps create a *mutual strategy*. It is commonly believed that franchisors set the strategy and then convince franchisees to adhere to it. In plural forms, each side (company and franchisee) tries ideas, then attempts to persuade the other side. In the process, strategy is formed by rigorous debate. Plural forms create more options and debate them more candidly and thoroughly than do unitary forms. In the process of debate, the ideas are refined and each side becomes committed to them. Thus, debate creates commitment to new initiatives.

Why not have only franchisees and simply give them a free hand to try things and then transmit best practices across franchisees? Company stores are good *laboratories*: The company can test rigorously, absorbing the risk of failure itself. For example, Dunkin' Donuts experiments with new products and processes in its own stores. This is a sort of test market: DD can assure that the test is conducted properly and that feedback is entirely candid. The franchisor also can experiment at its own expense without putting a franchisee at risk if the chain experiments with a bad idea. Once the new product or process has been perfected, DD can point to its own success to encourage franchisees to adopt the change themselves.

Why not have only company stores and then use the stores to generate ideas? One answer is that store managers do not generate ideas: They follow rules. Ideas come from the franchisor's central data base of store operations. To determine how to refine and implement them requires the active involvement of motivated entrepreneurs. Further, as noted earlier, many ideas come from entrepreneurs as they cope with local circumstances: competition, labor force, and customers. For example, the popularity of Indian food in London has led McDonald's to add curry and spice to its British menus.[44] Ideas like this can come from corporate but are more likely to come from local owners adapting to local competition and tastes.

In short, plural forms complement each other in ways that make the chain stronger and that make both franchisors and franchisees better off. Of course, this depends on active management. Having company and franchisee units simultaneously is beneficial if both sides work to make it so and appreciate the benefits of a "dual personality." Absent this, simultaneously entertaining both forms can actually be destructive.

Exploiting Franchisees: Redirection of Ownership

To this point, the explanations for a dual system have been benevolent. However, a malevolent explanation has attracted substantial attention from regulators and from scholars.[45] The premise is that franchisors would rather have company outlets than franchisees in order to control the operation closely and to appropriate all the profits generated by the marketing channel. (This, of course, assumes a company system would be as profitable. This is a heroic assumption, given the franchisee's entrepreneurial motivation, but it is an assumption the franchisor might be tempted to make.) Given this premise, the owner of a trademark might franchise anyway, but only to build the business. Once established, the franchisor would be tempted to use its profits to buy back franchises. If the franchisees do not agree, the franchisor might attempt to appropriate their property (e.g., by fabricating a reason to invoke a termination clause, end a lease, etc.).

This sinister scenario projects that over time, franchisors will build the fraction of company owned units, especially in the most lucrative locations (e.g., urban commercial districts). The logic here is that franchisors use franchisees to build the system, then expropriate them. The idea is euphemistically labeled the redirection of ownership hypothesis. Fortunately, the evidence does not suggest that this happens systematically. However, anecdotal evidence and court cases indicate that it does happen.

An example is Zannier, a retailer that covers the children's clothing market in France using thirteen different brand names and a variety of routes to market (hypermarkets, single-brand boutiques, multibrand boutiques, both company owned and franchisee owned). Zannier's strategy is to lock up the market by covering every viable position. To get there, the company used franchisees to grow quickly. Zannier eventually paid damages to settle legal challenges created by franchisees, who charged that once the franchisor had grown large and successful, it used pricing tactics and restrictive contract terms to squeeze out more than 200 of its franchisees in favor of other channels, including company-owned stores.[46]

ONGOING CHALLENGES FACING THE FRANCHISOR

The preceding section focuses on the decision to franchise and the strategic choices that follow: the form of the contract, the balancing of company and franchisee units, and the use of multiunit franchisees. These are policy issues at the corporate level. But what really makes franchising work is the daily behavior of people at the field level. Once a franchisor gets past its founding stages, it often finds that these operating issues overwhelm all others. In this section, we look at some of the challenges a franchisor faces once the system is launched.

Survival

This presumes that franchisors do, in fact, survive past launch. Franchisors have very high failure rates. Various estimates have it that some three quarters of the hundreds of franchisors launched in the 1980s in the United States survived fewer than ten years.[47] For every high-profile franchisor like McDonald's, which makes franchisees wealthy, several business formats and brand names have gone out of business, stripping franchisees of their wealth. Many of these build to a substantial size over a number of years before collapsing. Although some of the franchisors failed in spite of their best efforts, others failed because they set out to defraud their franchisees, just as they might defraud any other investor. For example, the Malaysian and Thai governments have departments that help citizens become franchisees, and franchising appears ready to boom in India. Justifiably, these governments are concerned that their citizens will be cheated by unscrupulous would-be franchisors.[48]

Which franchisors are most likely to survive? Evidence indicates that success forecasts success.[49] The older the system and the more units it has, the greater its odds of continuing to age (not going out of business). For a prospective franchisee, these established franchisors may offer the most expensive franchises, but they also carry lower risk of system failure. Evidence indicates that four years is a threshold: Franchise systems that are at least four years old have a sharply lower probability of failing than do younger systems.[50]

Survival is also more likely if the franchisor can attract a favorable rating from a third party. For example, in the United States, the magazine *Entrepreneur* surveys franchisors, collecting information from them. The magazine insists on verifying some of the information, then adds subjective judgments to compile proprietary ratings of hundreds of franchisors. This rating is a good predictor of franchisor survival many years later. Perhaps the magazine's staff is especially prescient, but a more likely explanation is that the ranking acts like a third-party certification, which helps the franchisor be seen as a legitimate player in its operating environment. This, in turn, helps the franchisor acquire the resources needed to survive. This is worth considering: Many entrepreneurs attach a low priority to certification and will not cooperate with certifying bodies.

Gaining and Keeping a Cooperative Atmosphere

A critical issue in franchising is that franchisees see the benefits they derive when the outlet is new. Once it is underway, they may question whether they are receiving continuing value in return for their royalties. A typical attitude is expressed by one franchisee:[51]

> It does not bring in much business, and whatever business it does bring in, I suppose it helps people feel more secure. But right now, I feel it's my business—and that's my name on the front because the numbers would be the same.

Franchising's inherent conflict between being one's own boss and being almost a subsidiary becomes prominent once the business gains ground. Franchisors must respond by earning the franchisee's continuing cooperation and goodwill. How can they do so?

Franchisees are more cooperative when they sense a solid relationship between themselves and their franchisor. Strong relationships with franchisors can thrive, even in high-pressure environments, such as many intensely competitive retail industries. Several conditions encourage franchisees to hold feelings of solidarity with the franchisor.[52] Stronger bonds exist when:

- Franchisees feel their franchisor encourages them to innovate (try new methods, develop ideas, solve problems)
- Franchisees feel a team spirit among themselves, getting on well internally and taking an interest in each other
- Franchisees feel that good performance is recognized by the franchisor
- Franchisees feel the franchisor is fair, setting reasonable objectives and not terminating franchisees without good reason
- Franchisees feel they control their own business, setting standards and making decisions as they see fit

This last point is paradoxical. By definition, franchisees do *not* control their own businesses. They have sold a substantial amount of autonomy in return for the franchise package. Franchising is inherently asymmetric, with franchisees being highly dependent on the franchisor. Yet, franchisees are entrepreneurs and feel the entrepreneur's need to be the boss.[53] The job of a franchisor's manager is to exert influence without appearing to threaten the franchisee's autonomy. This is a difficult balancing act, requiring diplomacy and persuasive skills. It is why franchisors tend to resolve serious conflicts by searching for integrative, win-win solutions, in which franchisee and franchisor collectively craft a mutually acceptable solution.[54]

Inherent Goal Conflict

A structural source of conflict built into every franchising system is the clash of goals between franchisee and franchisor. This clash is due to the difference between what each side puts into the business and what each side gets out of it. For the franchisor, higher sales are always better. Higher sales mean higher variable fees, therefore more income. This, in turn, enables more promotion, which raises brand equity. More brand equity increases the fees (fixed and variable) that can be charged and enlarges the pool of prospective store managers and franchisees.

For a franchisee in a given trading area, more sales means more profit—up to a point (see Figure 13.1). The franchisee breaks even at sales of B*. After B*, profits rise with sales, but gaining higher sales necessitates adding costs (new units, longer

Figure 13.1   Typical sales-to-profit relationships for franchisors and franchisees

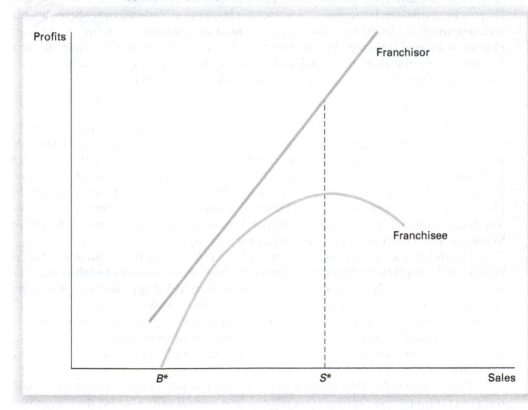

Source: Adapted from Carmen, James M. and Thomas A. Klein (1986), "Power, Property, and Performance in Franchising," *Research in Marketing* 8, pp. 71–130.

hours, etc.) that are subject to diminishing returns. After point S* in sales, profits turn down. Past this point, franchisees and franchisors have incongruent goals, which will create intense conflict

In short, franchisors seek to maximize sales, while franchisees seek to maximize profits. This incongruity of goals appears vividly as chains expand. Seeking to maximize system sales, franchisors are motivated to saturate a market area by authorizing new outlets. In the process, they often encroach on existing outlets and thereby cannibalize their own franchisees. For example, McDonald's grew to be, indirectly, the largest private employer in Brazil by adding hundreds of franchisees. Once touted by McDonald's as a model operation, Brazil has become a trouble spot for the franchisor, which dismissed the head of its Brazilian operation after franchisees sued, claiming McDonald's had undermined them by opening too many stores.[55]

Events like this hurt the franchisor's reputation with its franchisees, reducing morale, but the financial gains from authorizing new outlets tempt the franchisor to encroach anyway.[56] Systematic evidence suggests that this is exactly what franchisors do. As their system grows, they locate new outlets close enough to existing outlets to hurt their revenue—as long as the new outlet adds enough revenue to raise total system royalties. In contrast, vertically integrated firms (all company-owned outlets) are careful to space their new outlets far enough away from their existing outlets to avoid cannibalizing an existing outlet's revenue stream.[57]

Here we have a built-in dilemma. Franchisors want to grow, even to the point of encroaching on their franchisees. How can the franchisor cover a market densely without alienating its franchisees? One solution is to offer new sites to existing nearby franchisees or to give them the right of first refusal to a new location near them. If there are economies of scale in operating multiple sites, the franchisee is in position to gain from them. This idea leads us to a paradox: the multiunit franchisee.

Multiunit Franchising: Handicap or Advantage?

Thus far, we have asked whether a franchisor would deal with a manager (company owned) or an individual owner-manager (franchisee) or both for each unit. Curiously, many franchisors do neither.[58] Rather than dealing with a different individual for each location, they deal with the same individual (or a company) for multiple locations. This is multiunit franchising. There are a number of variations of the idea, but the principle is that the manager of a unit is not the owner but an employee of the owner. The franchisee owns more than one unit and must hire its own employees to run the locations. This arrangement is common and is growing.

On the face of it, this system is difficult to rationalize. If the purpose of franchising is to replace lackluster employee managers of an outlet with motivated owner-managers, multiunit franchising is nonsensical. All it appears to do is to put a layer of franchisee management between the franchisor and the person running the outlet. The master franchisee is monitoring the monitor (the store manager). Why would the franchisee do a better job of managing the store manager than would the franchisor? If the franchisor is willing to permit multiunit franchising, why not own the units itself?

This issue is little understood at present. There is some evidence that franchisors resort to multiunit franchising to grow faster and to deal with markets they know very little. For example, U.S. franchisors heavily favor multiunit operators to open operations in Africa and the Middle East.[59] Doing so may simply postpone problems, which is why there is some indication that franchisors that use multiunits fail more frequently than those that insist that franchisees own and manage their stores.[60] This slows growth but may make the system healthier.

In this regard, McDonald's prefers (but does not require) single-unit franchising. Perhaps as a result, it has virtually no presence in Africa.[61] In contrast, competitor Burger King[62] embraced multiunit franchising early in its history and used it to grow fast. Eventually, the chain had to confront fundamental flaws in its market strategy and operations—flaws that had been masked by fast growth. The franchisor became embroiled in wrangling with its powerful multiunit franchisees. This created a spiral of conflict that hardened into embittered, lasting mediocre relations. Ultimately, the chain suffered severely and was surpassed by McDonald's.

Before dismissing multiunit franchising, however, we should examine its positive side. This positive side is underappreciated at present. A multiunit franchisee commonly creates an organization structure that mimics the franchisor's structure. The multiunit franchisee also imitates the franchisor's practices. These "mini-hierarchies" simplify things enormously for the franchisor. They allow the franchisor to deal with one organization, the multiunit franchisee. At the same time, the multiunit operators replicate the franchisor's management practices and policies in their own organizations. In so doing, multiunit franchisees reduce the enormous job of managing hundreds of relationships into a more tractable management problem.

An example is Kentucky Fried Chicken (KFC). The franchisor has more than 3,500 U.S. restaurants. More than half of them are owned by only seventeen people. If KFC can convince only seventeen franchisees of the merits of an idea, it influences almost 1,800 restaurants. Moreover, if these seventeen franchisees accept an idea, they exert a powerful influence on the opinions of the remaining franchisees.

Of course, if mini-hierarchies are to be helpful to the franchisor, it is critical to have their cooperation and to have them replicate the franchisor. Many large restaurant chains appear to have mastered this process, demonstrating that multiunit franchising can be a viable and valuable strategy. One important feature is that prospective franchisees are carefully screened, given a trial period, and observed. If they do not satisfy the franchisor, they are not allowed to open more units.

The explanation of multiunits, however, involves much more. Evidence from fast food restaurants suggests that many small things (such as the fastest way to make a pepperoni pizza) make a big difference in such highly competitive businesses. This sort of know-how is acquired by experience and transmitted by example, but personnel turnover is very high (indeed, the difficulty of getting good personnel to dedicate themselves to these businesses is part of why they are franchised in the first place). Thus, personnel go down the learning curve, then leave, taking their knowledge with them. The result is that when a new pizza restaurant opens it starts with low profits because it is at the top of a learning curve. Personnel learn, then leave, so the knowledge gained depreciates fast.

Multiunit franchisees can be understood as a vehicle for preserving and spreading knowledge. They do so among their own stores by holding meetings, making phone calls, and using other means of communication. This in turn creates personal ties, which speeds the spread of knowledge. In many franchise networks, little knowledge transfer occurs across franchises unless the franchisor steps in to do it. This means the *value of multiunit franchises is to spread learning curves by actively lobbying to disseminate know-how across its own locations.*[63]

Furthermore, much of the knowledge of how to operate a franchise is tacit and idiosyncratic and tends to be specific to a local area. This can be seen by studying the failure rates of these businesses. Even in codified and standardized (programmable) businesses, such as pizza restaurants, local experience matters and lowers failure rates of franchisees. This local experience can be brought to a given outlet by the franchisor or by the multiunit franchisee—indeed, there is an extra impact when both the franchisor and the multiunit franchisee have considerable experience in a limited market area. What is striking is that distant experience, whether gained by the franchisor or the multiunit franchisee, is less helpful than local congenital experience.[64]

This explains an empirical regularity about how franchisors build the empires of many of their multiunit franchisees. When franchisors that use multiunit franchising decide to cover a site, they have a tendency to award it to the franchisee who owns the next closest unit to the site. In this way, franchisors appear to appreciate the power of contiguity—having units owned by one person next to each other without intermingling units owned by different people. Research shows[65] that franchisors tend to allow franchisees to build large networks of stores that appear on a map as an unbroken mass, uninterrupted by other franchisees of the same chain or by company-owned stores of the franchisor. This is particularly the case if the next site to be developed is not only contiguous but has a demographic profile similar to the rest of the multiunit-owner's stores. This suggests that owning clusters of stores makes it easier for franchisees to monitor their monitors (store managers) and to amortize their human capital connected to an area. Another advantage of contiguous stores under one owner is that the customer base is more likely to be served by the same owner in any store. This curbs free riding.

Other Ways to Gain Cooperation

On a daily basis, what can franchisors do to gain cooperation? An important tool is to offer genuine assistance—and remind the franchisee of it. Franchisees are more cooperative when they attribute their successes to the aid of the franchisor and attribute their failures to themselves.[66]

Another factor that helps makes franchising run smoothly is formalization. Being explicit about who is responsible for doing what greatly improves the functioning of a franchise system. It does so by increasing coordination and reducing resentment.

SUMMARY

Franchising a business format is a way to grow quickly while investing in building brand equity. For the franchisee, it is a system for gaining assistance and reducing risk. By paying fees, entrepreneurs purchase the services of a corporate backer, a coach, a problem solver, and an enforcement agency that polices the way the brand is presented. For the franchisor, the system is a way to acquire capital and management quickly and to harness the motivation and capability of an entrepreneur.[67] For businesses that can be put into a format and transmitted, franchising is an excellent solution to the problems of monitoring employee managers.

Part of the codification of the formula is writing a complex contract specifying rights and duties. These contracts are crafted to give both sides good reason to abide by their agreement. Many franchisors price their franchises lower than the market will bear. In so doing, they increase the applicant pool and give their franchisees a reason—the profit motive—to stay in the business. They also signal via lower lump-sum entry fees that they do not intend to take the franchisees' money and fail to provide promised services. But franchisors frequently bind their franchisees with clauses that award control of the property to the franchisor, and they limit the franchisees' ability to terminate their business easily. These contracts vary surprisingly little over franchisees and over time in a franchise system. They serve to give the franchisor a means to punish noncompliance, which allows the protection of brand equity but also reinforces the franchisee's dependence on the franchisor. Part of that dependence rests on the franchisee's heavy investment in franchise-specific assets, which have a low resale value outside the business. Franchisors cannot rely entirely on their contracts to run the system. They must also develop a reputation for fair dealings with their franchised channel. This requires the franchisor not to exploit the franchisees' dependence opportunistically.

Franchise systems typically mix company-owned and franchised outlets. This gives the franchisor a laboratory and a classroom to train personnel, try out ideas, and refine the business format. Dual or plural systems also permit the franchisor to achieve synergies between the two sides of its business. This can be achieved by permitting multiunit franchising but encouraging the owners to build mini-hierarchies to mimic the franchisor. Plural forms permit the franchisor to collect, adapt, and spread new products and practices. Plural forms can insure vigorous debate and build commitment to new initiatives. Some degree of rivalry motivates both sides of the operation to improve.

Failure rates of franchisors are very high. Survival becomes more likely as a system grows, ages, and acquires certification by third parties. Part of the challenge of aging is retaining the franchisees' cooperation. This is enhanced by building a sense of solidarity, seeking win-win solutions to major conflicts, offering genuine assistance, and formalizing roles and duties. But conflict is inevitable, in part because of a built-in clash of goals. Franchisees pursue profit, franchisors pursue sales, and the two goals collide as operations become large. In particular, franchisors are tempted to saturate markets and cannibalize their own franchisees.

Multiunit franchising, where one person owns many outlets, is surprisingly common and rather difficult to understand. In principle, it dilutes the owner's motivation, increases the franchisee's power, and inserts another level of hierarchy between the store manager and the franchisor. Still, multiunit franchising is common and often results in blocks of contiguous outlets owned by the same person. Used like this, multiunit franchising may be an effective way to monitor the monitors and to capture and spread local knowledge while obliging multiunit franchisees to bear the cost of free riding. This is because these areas capture entire customer bases, so that other units in the franchisee's market will suffer if the brand name is abused.

The complexity and risk of franchising should lead channel managers to consider other solutions. Frequently, the level of control afforded by franchising is simply not necessary. Other means to achieve cooperation are available. These are discussed in the other chapters of this book. Nonetheless, franchising affords a very high level of control. Franchising is an effective way to create incentives to perform tasks according to a standard without needing to monitor operations constantly.

By the 1970s, it was clear that franchising had become a permanent force, not just a fad, in structuring distribution channels in the United States. Today, it is clear that the same is true worldwide. Franchising has become an institution so stable and so pervasive that it is the single most common way to become an entrepreneur in North America, in Europe, and in Asia.[68] The dynamism of this channel institution is remarkable. Franchising is an institution that deserves serious consideration by any manager in any marketing channel.

Take-Aways

- Franchising is a marketing channel structure intended to convince end-users that they are buying from a vertically integrated manufacturer when, in fact, they may be buying from a separately owned company.
- Franchising a business format is a way to grow quickly while investing in building brand equity.
  - For the franchisor, the system is a way to acquire capital and management quickly and to harness the motivation and capability of an entrepreneur. For programmable businesses (those that can be put into a format and transmitted), franchising is an excellent solution to the problems of monitoring employee managers.
  - For the franchisee, it is a system for gaining assistance and reducing risk. By paying fees, entrepreneurs purchase the services of a corporate backer, a coach, a problem solver, and an enforcement agency that polices the way the brand is presented.
- Part of the codification of the formula is writing a complex contract specifying rights and duties. These contracts are crafted to give both sides good reason to abide by their agreement.
  - Many franchisors price their franchises lower than the market will bear. In so doing, they increase the applicant pool and give their franchisees a reason—the profit motive—to stay in the business.
  - Franchisors frequently bind their franchisees with clauses that award control of the property to the franchisor, and they limit the franchisees' ability to terminate their business easily.
  - These contracts give the franchisor a means to punish noncompliance, which allows the protection of brand equity but also reinforces the franchisee's dependence on the franchisor.
  - Franchisors must not exploit the franchisees' dependence opportunistically. This is one reason why franchisors do not enforce their contracts every time franchisees violate them. Instead, they weigh the costs and benefits and select which battles they will fight with franchisees who fail to comply.

- Franchise systems typically mix company-owned and franchised outlets. This gives the franchisor a laboratory and a classroom to train personnel, try out ideas, and refine the business format.
- Failure rates of franchisors are very high. Survival becomes more likely as a system grows, ages, and acquires certification by third parties.
- Survival and prosperity are enhanced by building a sense of solidarity, seeking win-win solutions to major conflicts, offering genuine assistance, and formalizing roles and duties.
- Conflict is inevitable, in part because of a built-in clash of goals.
- Multiunit franchising, where one person owns many outlets, is surprisingly common and rather difficult to understand.
- The complexity and risk of franchising should lead channel managers to consider other solutions.

DISCUSSION QUESTIONS

1. Write a plan for starting your own franchising operation. What would be the essential elements of the plan? What specific points would you include in the contractual arrangement you establish with your franchisees?

2. In 1988, Vidal Herrera founded a U.S. company, Autopsy/Post Services, to perform autopsies in Los Angeles.[69] An autopsy is a medical examination of a corpse, including dissection and tests of tissue and body fluids. The purpose is to ascertain the cause of death. Autopsy/Post Services will autopsy a body for a flat $2,000, more if the body has been exhumed (removed from burial) or if extra tests are ordered. Since 1988, Herrera's business has grown larger than he can handle.

   Clients include insurance companies, government bodies (who have the right to demand autopsies when the cause of death is unknown or may be criminal), family members, and medical providers (such as hospitals). An autopsy is requested to discover or to verify a cause of death and is considered good medical practice. Autopsies contribute to medical research. Many medical conditions (such as toxic shock syndrome and congenital heart disease) were discovered by autopsy, permitting researchers to develop treatments.

   Unfortunately, autopsies can be expensive, costing from several hundred to several thousand dollars. Also, conflicts of interest can arise: The logical party to suggest an autopsy is the provider of medical care, but the autopsy's results may disagree with the provider's estimation of the cause of death (one study shows autopsies disagree with the attending physician almost half the time). Thus, the provider may hesitate to suggest an autopsy. Autopsies are frequently requested by someone who suspects negligence or other malpractice or who wishes to have tests performed (e.g., genetic tests) to answer a troubling question.

   Autopsies are being performed at a declining rate in the United States (and in the world), but Vidal Herrera nonetheless believes the market potential is considerable. Herrera plans to franchise Autopsy/Post Services to achieve rapid growth. If you were medically qualified, would you buy a franchise from him? What factors would you consider? How would you evaluate his offer? What would make you inclined to sign onto his franchise system? What would cause you to refuse?

3. What are the ways in which a franchise contract motivates a franchisee to cooperate with the franchisor? What are the positive and negative aspects of these contracts from the franchisee's viewpoint? From the franchisor's viewpoint? Now turn the question around. What are the ways a franchise contract motivates a franchisor to treat franchisees fairly?

4. In the McDonald's example, trace the ways in which franchisee and franchisor influence each other. Who has the greater power and why?

5. "The franchisor wants to own the very best locations. These are money makers, and their prime locations make them an advertisement for the brand. They have to be just perfect." Debate this statement.

6. Some companies disdain franchising because it means putting an intermediary between themselves and their customers. Their attitude is that one less intermediary is one less person to remunerate. Hence, they prefer to own their stores themselves. Are they right? Why would a firm with great brand equity (or the intention to build it) entrust its stores to a franchisee?

7. There are two ways to become a multiunit franchisee. One is sequential development: Franchisees are given new sites to develop after they master existing sites. The other is area development: An individual signs an agreement to open a stated number of outlets in a stated time period in a given geographical area and in return is given exclusive rights to the area. Which method is better?

8. The policy of developing multiunit franchisees by giving them contiguous sites is in many ways very costly and cumbersome. What are the costs and benefits of contiguity? Is the policy worth its price?

9. Franchising is often thought of as a retail activity, but B2B franchising is now flourishing. If it is a good idea, why has it spread more slowly than B2C franchising?

ENDNOTES

1. We thank Rupinder Jindal and Rozenn Perrigot for helpful discussions in preparation for this chapter.

2. Spelling note: *franchisor* is U.S. English, while *franchiser* is British English. This textbook adopts the U.S. convention, but many documents, particularly in Europe, specify *franchiser*.

3. Bradach, Jeffrey L. (1998), *Franchise Organizations* (Boston, MA: Harvard Business School Press).

4. Alon, Ilan (2004), "Global Franchising and Development in Emerging and Transitioning Markets," *Journal of Macromarketing* 24, no. 2 (December), pp. 156–167.

5. Dant, Rajiv P. and Patrick J. Kaufmann (2003), "Structural and Strategic Dynamics in Franchising," *Journal of Retailing* 79, no. 2 (Summer), pp. 63–75.

6. Clicquet, Gerard (2000), "Plural Form Networks and Retail Life Cycle: An Exploratory Investigation of Hotel Franchised/Company-Owned Systems in France," *Journal of Business and Entrepreneurship* 12, no. 2 (Summer), pp. 75–98.

7. Welch, Lawrence S. (1989), "Diffusion of Franchise System Use in International Operations," *International Marketing Review* 6, no. 5, pp. 7–19.

8. *Economist* (2000), "The Tiger and the Tech," *Economist*, February 5, pp. 70–72.

9. A master reference is Blair, Roger D. and Francine Lafontaine (2005), *The Economics of Franchising* (Cambridge: Cambridge University Press).

10. This information is drawn from multiple sources: Kaufmann, Patrick J. and Francine Lafontaine (1994), "Costs of Control: The Source of Economic Rents for McDonald's Franchisees," *Journal of Law and Economics* 37, no. 3 (October), pp. 417–453; Love, John F. (1986), *McDonald's: Behind the*

Golden Arches (New York: Bantam Books); Wattenz, Eric (1999), "La Machine McDonald's," *Capital* 7, no. 9 (September), pp. 48–69; and Piétralunga, Cédric (2004), "Les Recettes Qui Ont Fait Rebondir McDo," *Capital* 11, no. 6 (June), pp. 28–32.

11. Reinartz, Werner J. and V. Kumar (1999), "Store-, Market-, and Consumer-Characteristics: The Drivers of Store Performance," *Marketing Letters* 10, no. 1 (February), pp. 5–22.

12. Combs, James G. and David J. Ketchen (1999), "Can Capital Scarcity Help Agency Theory Explain Franchising? Revisiting the Capital Scarcity Hypothesis," *Academy of Management Journal* 42, no. 2 (April), pp. 196–207.

13. Norton, Seth W. (1988), "An Empirical Look at Franchising as an Organizational Form," *Journal of Business* 61, no. 2 (April), pp. 197–218.

14. Gimeno, Javier, Timothy B. Folta, Arnold C. Cooper, and Carolyn Y. Woo (1997), "Survival of the Fittest? Entrepreneurial Human Capital and the Persistence of Underperforming Firms," *Administrative Science Quarterly* 42, no. 4 (December), pp. 750–783.

15. Shane, Scott A. (1996), "Hybrid Organizational Arrangements and Their Implications for Firm Growth and Survival: A Study of New Franchisors," *Academy of Management Journal* 39, no. 1 (February), pp. 216–234.

16. Dant, Rajiv P. (1995), "Motivation for Franchising: Rhetoric Versus Reality," *International Small Business Journal* 14, no. 1 (October–December), pp. 10–32.

17. Birkeland, Peter M. (2002), *Franchising Dreams* (Chicago, IL: The University of Chicago Press).

18. Schultz, Howard and Dori Jones Yang (1997), *Pour Your Heart Into It: How Starbucks Built a Company One Cup at a Time* (New York: Hyperion).

19. Minkler, Alanson P. (1992), "Why Firms Franchise: A Search Cost Theory," *Journal of Institutional and Theoretical Economics* 148, no. 1 (Spring), pp. 240–249.

20. Aoulou, Yves and Olivia Bassi (1999), "Une Opportunité de Cassière à Saisir," *LSA* 29, no. 14 (March 18), pp. 42–47.

21. Reported with comment in the February 27, 2004, weekly newsletter of IF Consulting (www.i-f.com).

22. Reidboym, Marc and Sabine Germain (2001), "La Franchise Francaise," *LSA* 31, no. 16 (March 22), pp. 28–30.

23. Michel, Caroline (2002), "Ada, le Dernier échec de Papy Rousselet," *Capital* 10, no. 8 (August), pp. 32–33.

24. Chandler, Alfred D. (1977), *The Visible Hand: The Managerial Revolution in American Business* (Cambridge, MA: Belknap Press).

25. Truffaut is featured in *Capital* (1999), "Le Jardinier Truffaut A La Main Verte," *Capital* 7, no. 7 (July) pp. 44–45. Buffalo Grill is described in Guérin, Jean-Yves (1999), "Buffalo Grill: Le Cow-Boy Est un Radin," in *L'Essentiel du Management* Vol. 8, issue 7 (July), pp. 20–24.

26. Federal Trade Commission (1983), "Franchise Rule Exemption for Wholesale Grocers Announced by Federal Trade Commission," *FTC News Note* 25, no. 83 (March 18), p. 3.

27. European Commission (1997), Green Paper on Vertical Restraints in EU Competition Policy, Brussels, Directorate General for Competition, p. 44.

28. Dnes, Antony W. (1993), "A Case-Study Analysis of Franchise Contracts," *Journal of Legal Studies* 22, no. 2 (June), pp. 367–393. This reference is the basis for much of this section and the source of comparative statements about franchising in the United Kingdom.

29. Klein, Benjamin (1995), "The Economics of Franchise Contracts," *Journal of Corporate Finance* 2, no. 1 (Winter), pp. 9–37.

30. Agrawal, Deepak and Rajiv Lal (1995), "Contractual Arrangements in Franchising: An Empirical Investigation," *Journal of Marketing Research* 32, no. 2 (May), pp. 213–221.

31. Lal, Rajiv (1990), "Improving Channel Coordination through Franchising," *Marketing Science* 9, no. 4 (Fall), pp. 299–318.

32. The Economist Intelligence Unit (1995), "Retail Franchising in France," *EIU Marketing in Europe* (December), pp. 86–104.

33. Lafontaine, Francine (1992), "Agency Theory and Franchising: Some Empirical Results," *Rand Journal of Economics* 23, no. 2 (Summer), pp. 263–283.

34. Kaufmann, Patrick J. and Francine Lafontaine (1994), "Costs of Control: The Source of Economic Rents for McDonald's Franchisees," *Journal of Law and Economics* 37, no. 2 (October), pp. 417–453.

35. Klein, Benjamin (1980), "Transaction Cost Determinants of 'Unfair' Contractual Arrangements," *American Economic Review* 70, no. 2 (May), pp. 356–362.

36. Lafontaine, Francine and Kathryn L. Shaw (1998), "Franchising Growth and Franchisor Entry and Exit in the U.S. Market: Myth and Reality," *Journal of Business Venturing* 13, no. 2 (March), pp. 95–112.

37. Lafontaine and. Shaw (1998), previously cited.

38. Carney, Mick and Eric Gedajlovic (1991), "Vertical Integration in Franchise Systems: Agency Theory and Resource Explanations," *Strategic Management Journal* 12, no. 8 (November), pp. 607–629.

39. Brickley, James A. and Frederick H. Dark (1987), "The Choice of Organizational Form: The Case of Franchising," *Journal of Financial Economics* 18, no. 2 (June), pp. 401–420.

40. Baroncelli and Manaresi (1997), previously cited.

41. Lafontaine, Francine and Patrick J. Kaufman (1994), "The Evolution of Ownership Patterns in Franchise Systems," *Journal of Retailing* 70, no. 2 (Summer), pp. 97–113.

42. Shane, Scott A. (1996), "Hybrid Organizational Arrangements and Their Implications for Firm Growth and Survival: A Study of New Franchisors," *Academy of Management Journal* 39, no. 1 (February), pp. 216–234.

43. Bradach, Jeffrey L. (1997), "Using the Plural Form in the Management of Restaurant Chains," *Administrative Science Quarterly* 42, no. 2 (June), pp. 276–303. This source is the basis for this section and is an excellent guide to the working operations of large chain franchisors.

44. *Economist* (1999), "Britain: In the Pink," *Economist* 352, no. 8131 (August 7), pp. 46-47.

45. This discussion is based on Dant, Rajiv P., Audehesh K. Paswan and Patrick J. Kaufman (1996), "What We Know About Ownership Redirection in Franchising: A Meta-Analysis," *Journal of Retailing* 72, no. 4 (Winter), pp. 429–444.

46. Bouillin, Arnaud (2001), "Comment Zannier Verrouille Son Marche," *Management* 11, no. 6 (June), pp. 28–30.

47. Shane (1996) and Lafontaine (1992), previously cited.

48. Reported with comment in the April 2, 2004, weekly newsletter of IF Consulting (www.i-f.com).

49. Shane, Scott and Maw-Der Foo (1999), "New Firm Survival: Institutional Explanations for New Franchisor Mortality," *Management Science* 45, no. 2 (February), pp. 142–159.

50. Shane (1996), previously cited.

51. Birkeland (2002), previously cited.

52. Strutton, David, Lou E. Pelton, and James R. Lumpkin (1995), "Psychological Climate in Franchising System Channels and Franchisor–Franchisee Solidarity," *Journal of Business Research* 34, no. 2 (October), pp. 81–91.

53. Dant, Rajiv P. and Gregory T. Gundlach (1999), "The Challenge of Autonomy and Dependence in Franchised Channels of Distribution," *Journal of Business Venturing* 14, no. 1 (January), pp. 35–67.

54. Dant, Rajiv P. and Patrick L. Schul (1992), "Conflict Resolution Processes in Contractual Channels of Distribution," *Journal of Marketing* 56, no. 1 (January), pp. 38–54.

55. Jordan, Miriam and Shirley Leung (2003), "McDonald's Faces Foreign Franchisees' Revolt," *Dow Jones Business News*, October 21, p. 6.

56. Kaufmann, Patrick J. and V. Kasturi Rangan (1990), "A Model for Managing System Conflict During Franchise Expansion," *Journal of Retailing* 66, no. 2 (Summer), pp. 155–173.

57. Kalnins, Arturs (2004), "An Empirical Analysis of Territorial Encroachment

Within Franchised and Company-Owned Branded Chains," *Marketing Science* 23, no. 4 (Fall), pp. 476–489.

58. Kaufmann, Patrick J. and Rajiv Dant (1996), "Multiunit Franchising: Growth and Management Issues," *Journal of Business Venturing* 11, no. 5 (September), pp. 343–358.

59. Dant, Rajiv P. and Nada I. Nasr (1998), "Control Techniques and Upward Flow of Information in Franchising in Distant Markets: Conceptualization and Preliminary Evidence," *Journal of Business Venturing* 13, no. 1 (January), pp. 3–28.

60. Shane, Scott A. (1998), "Making New Franchise Systems Work," *Strategic Management Journal* 19, no. 7 (July), pp. 697–707.

61. *Economist* (1999), "Through a Glass, Drunkenly," Economist, May 8, p. 90.

62. McLamore, James W. (1998), *The Burger King: Jim McLamore and the Building of an Empire* (New York: McGraw-Hill).

63. Darr, Eric D., Linda Argote, and Dennis Epple (1995), "The Acquisition, Transfer, and Depreciation of Knowledge in Service Organizations: Productivity in Franchises," *Management Science* 41, no. 11 (November), pp. 1,750–1,762.

64. Kalnins, Arturs and Kyle J. Mayer (2004), "Franchising, Ownership, and Experience: A Study of Pizza Restaurant Survival," *Management Science* 50, no. 12 (December), pp. 1,716–1,728.

65. Kalnins, Arturs and Francine Lafontaine (2004), "Multiunit Ownership in Franchising: Evidence From the Fast-Food Industry in Texas," *Rand Journal of Economics* 35, no. 4 (Winter), pp. 749–763.

66. Anand, Punam and Louis W. Stern (1985), "A Sociopsychological Explanation for Why Marketing Channel Members Relinquish Control," *Journal of Marketing Research* 22, no. 4 (November), pp. 365–376.

67. Rubin, Paul H. (1990), *Managing Business Transactions* (New York: The Free Press).

68. *Economist* (2000), "The Tiger and the Tech," *Economist*, February 5, pp. 70–72.

69. *Economist* (1999), "United States: Autopsies: Dial One Yourself," *Economist* 350, no. 8100 (January 2), p. 29.

Logistics and Supply Chain Management

Learning objectives

After reading this chapter you will be able to:

▨ Define supply chain management and state its boundaries

▨ Describe the critical elements of efficient consumer response and quick response

▨ Relate a brand's characteristics to the need for its supply chain to be market responsive versus physically efficient

▨ Understand why channel management is needed to implement the supply chain management paradigm in an organization

THE IMPACT OF LOGISTICS AND SUPPLY CHAIN MANAGEMENT

Logistics concerns the processing and tracking of factory goods during warehousing, inventory control, transport, customs documentation, and delivery to customers.[1] In the 1980s, new ideas from the consulting industry prompted a shift to the broader concept of *supply chain management (SCM)*. SCM covers any physical input, not just finished goods, and implicates *every* element of the value-added chain, not just the manufacturer or other single member of the chain of value added.[2] The premise of SCM is that routes to market (downstream) should coordinate with manufacturing processes (upstream). Going backward, or upstream, SCM encompasses not only inventories of finished goods but also work in process (WIP) and raw materials all the way back to the suppliers of the suppliers of the suppliers. Going forward, or downstream, SCM encompasses all channel members down to and including the customers of the customers. At the extreme, supply chain management means signaling the very beginning of the chain of value-added what to do and when to do it as a function of what is happening at the very end of the chain of distribution. Thus, transactions at the grocery checkout counter could pass through multiple steps, ultimately to be used to suggest to a farmer what to plant—and to the farmer's suppliers what to fabricate. This is the extreme (some would say utopian, or even ludicrous) version of SCM.

Today, logistics is widely considered to be part of supply chain management.[3] Indeed, a new concept in tune with concerns for the environment has emerged: reverse logistics (see Sidebar 14.1 for a description).

Over time, the flow and storage of goods has been made much more efficient. It is estimated that in the 1960s, U.S. firms spent 15–30 percent of every sales dollar to pay for product flows: Today, that average has been reduced to around 8 percent.[4] Key to achieving this performance is coordination not only across functional silos within the firm but across the many firms in a value-added chain. For supply chain management requires that every player in a channel sends information or places orders that trigger behavior by *any and every other player*, including those downstream. That behavior is not just a matter of stockpiling or moving inventories. It may be marketing behavior. For example, what is going in the warehouse may signal a supplier not to offer a promotion this month or to offer one price instead of another price. Inventory management may result in a change of assortment, with some SKUs being eliminated and others being added, to be produced to the express specifications of a single customer.

These decisions are about marketing and about channel management. That logistics should influence marketing—which is one premise of SCM—is a revolutionary idea to many managers. What is this revolution called supply chain management? Is it what its proponents claim—the ultimate in satisfying the buyer *and* cutting costs? Is it ludicrous, the idea of a channel's becoming more effective (better meeting the buyer's service output demands) while simultaneously cutting costs? This is the promise of SCM.

Ultimately, logistics (and the larger concept of SCM) is a vast, varied, and complex discipline in itself. Perhaps this is why logistics is often treated as a highly technical field, amenable to the methods of operations research. This should not deter managers from using their judgment and from relying on simple tools, such as graphs and spreadsheets, to make logistical decisions. Nonetheless, formal methods are often a powerful aid to the manager. These are covered in a number of texts and articles on logistics. This chapter focuses on the role of the logistics or supply chain manager and the need for this role to be heavily involved in the management of marketing channels.

This chapter overviews SCM, first in general terms and then in two formulations: efficient consumer response (ECR) and quick response (QR). These two models of SCM are often confused: They are in fact extremely different. After contrasting them, the chapter explains when each is appropriate and then closes on a critical question: What must a firm do to realize the promise of SCM?

RESPONDING EFFICIENTLY

SCM[5] is an organizing concept that starts with customer service and argues that this results from the cumulative efforts of the entire channel. *Customer service cannot be interpreted as the sole responsibility of any single channel member.* The guiding principle is to unify product flows and information flows up and down the production and distribution chain. Doing this requires (1) a market orientation, focused on the last customer,

Sidebar 14.1

Reverse logistics

Forward or ordinary logistics refers to the physical distribution of products from the factory to end-users. Reverse logistics turns the process around. A reverse supply chain performs a series of activities required to retrieve a used product from a final customer and either dispose of it or reuse it. A number of producers are building reverse supply chains for a variety of motives. Some companies are forced to do so by pressure from environmental regulators or from customers. But others see it as an opportunity for profit. For example, a leader in reverse logistics is Bosch, which sells its hand tools both as new and remanufactured and turns a profit while saving bulky, long-lasting power tools from being discarded. Chapters 3 on flows and 5 on gap analysis show examples of reverse channels of distribution.

Reverse supply chains cover five key steps in sequence:

1. Product acquisition. This may be the most difficult step and typically requires working with downstream channel members such as distributors and retailers.

2. Reverse logistics. Transporting the used merchandise, which is also difficult because it is not factory packaged and can be physically dispersed. Some firms outsource this stage to specialists.

3. Inspection and disposition. Includes testing, sorting, and grading, which is slow and labor intensive. Some firms streamline this step with bar codes and sophisticated tracking. Firms must decide what to do with each item: Deciding early in the process may be key to doing this step well.

4. Reconditioning components or remanufacturing the item entirely.

5. Selling and distributing recycled components or products. This demands a large investment in what might be an entirely new channel to an entirely different market.

Often, these products are remanufactured, which means they go back to the manufacturer and are upgraded to the quality standards of new products. They can also be used for components. An interesting issue here is who should collect the used product from the end-users and get them back to the manufacturer. The auto industry favors third-party specialists (dismantling centers) to collect used cars and send the dismantled parts and materials back to manufacturers to be recycled in whole or in part. Makers of consumer goods often use retailers. For example, Kodak collects disposable cameras, paying the retailer a fixed fee and transportation costs. Manufacturers can do the job themselves, which is typical in the document industry. Xerox collects end-of-lease copiers itself, while Hewlett-Packard collects computers and peripherals and Canon collects consumables (cartridges). While all these methods can work, the retailer has a certain advantage due to its proximity to the customer and its ability to amortize its investment in the forward supply chain in building its reverse supply chain.

Compared to the logistics of manufacturing and marketing new goods, reverse logistics are less predictable in both timing and quality levels. Consequently, costs can soar. One way to contain costs is to work with the forward supply chain to build in features that will help the eventual reverse supply chain. For example, new products can be designed on a platform that assumes inputs from used products. For this reason, Bosch builds sensors into new tools that will come into play when the products are returned, to signal at the inspection and grading stage whether each motor is worth saving. These closed-loop systems (in which forward activities anticipate and interlock with eventual reverse activities) may be the key to making reverse supply chains work well. That would be a boon for the preservation of the earth's limited resources.[6]

(2) effective channel management to enable smooth transfers of product and information, and (3) effective logistics. SCM is a paradigm, that is, a set of common values, beliefs, and tools that unite a group of people engaged in related tasks. Let us begin with the roots of SCM in the grocery industry.

Efficient Consumer Response

Efficient consumer response (ECR) is a landmark in marketing channels. It is a movement that has wrought radical change in the U.S. grocery industry and that has spread to other sectors and countries. Its success is surprising, given how different it is from the usual operating methods of most channels.

The origin of ECR is fear. In 1992, the U.S. grocery store industry was feeling threatened by the rapid growth of nongrocery outlets, such as drug stores.[7] These alternative format (alternative to a supermarket) stores were aggressively adding food to their assortments, and the consumer was responding positively. A principal threat was seen to be Wal-Mart, which was beginning its (now very successful) move from mass merchandising to a hypermarket concept (merchandise and groceries). This is why in 1992 two grocery trade associations commissioned a study of grocery methods. The report strongly criticized existing grocery channels and proposed a radical and complex series of changes to these channels. This program of change was named according to its objective: to achieve efficient (as opposed to wasteful) consumer (the final buyer) response (supplying *only* what is *desired*).

As initially proposed, the idea was to focus on four areas where the industry as a whole had (and still has) great potential for improvement. The four areas are:

1. *A continuous replenishment program (CRP).* The goal is to end the bullwhip effect, covered in Chapter 3 on flows. The bullwhip effect is a systematic distortion of information that causes channel members to overreact to small changes in end-user demand. The method is to use purchase data captured via scanners from the final buyer to inform all upstream supply chain members of demand, right back to the suppliers of suppliers. This requires massive standardization of codes and methods and implementation of *electronic data interchange* (EDI). EDI is the interchange of information over secure communication circuits from one company's computers to another company's computers in a standard format (so no human intervention is needed). Using EDI, purchase orders can be dispatched and payments can be made automatically, for example. EDI involves large investments in proprietary systems that render documents readable to all players while protecting data security. Although tens of thousands of firms use EDI, others are moving to Internet-based alternatives based on the XML programming technology, in the hope that Web platforms will be cheaper and more flexible yet safe from computer hackers.[8]

2. *Efficient pricing and promotions.* A scourge of the grocery industry is poorly calibrated promotions that wreak havoc with pricing and buyer behavior. At the consumer level, excessively generous promotions (such as one free for one purchased) create demand spikes and degrade brand equity. Nontargeted promotions encourage price comparisons and brand switching purely for temporary price cuts. At the wholesale level, manufacturer promotions lead to huge demand spikes. These push factory production up too high, then down too low. This, in turn, pushes inventory up too high (resulting in spoiled food) or down too low (running out of stock).

3. *Changes in product introduction.* Thousands of new product introductions, most of which fail, are endemic to grocery retailing. ECR calls for combining market research

commissioned by channel members in order more accurately to forecast new product success on a store-by-store basis or based on reasonable store groupings (store clusters).

4. *Changes in merchandising.* The idea, as with changes in product introduction, is to combine research for finding better ways to merchandise brands and their associated categories (e.g., snack foods, pet food, soups) store by store or cluster by cluster.

Over time, these ideas have been developed and expanded. ECR has become an umbrella term that now encompasses a variety of means by which pure grocers combat alternative format stores and by which any channel member can improve its competitiveness in marketing fast moving consumer goods (FMCG).

Obstacles to Efficient Consumer Response

The list of obstacles to ECR is formidable.[9] At a physical level, ECR requires agreement on codes and on a huge number of EDI choices or their closest Web equivalents. In general, ECR requires standardization of methods. For example, crossdocking is a way to minimize warehousing in the process of making up assortments of varied goods destined for a single store. It is a delicate exercise that is difficult to pull off if channel members cannot agree on a number of issues. This is one instance of why ECR implementation is a long and expensive affair.

One of the greatest barriers to ECR is the necessity of trusting other channel members. Trust and good working relationships are necessary for the information exchange, joint planning, and joint actions that underpin efforts to make the entire grocery channel respond to consumers while cutting waste. Trust is based on equity. The fundament of ECR is that channel members share risk and information to produce gains for the channel as a whole and then share the gains equitably. Opportunism (reneging on a promise to compensate all players fairly) is fatal to ECR.

In spite of such challenges, ECR exists and has made great progress. Trade publications of many industries overflow with discussions of how to create ECR in their sectors. ECR has become, for many, synonymous with supply chain management.

That ECR began in the grocery industry is miraculous. When the ECR initiative was unveiled at a trade conference in 1993, few in the audience were confident that the traditionally adversarial relations in these marketing channels could be set aside. The cooperation and transparency that ECR requires had to be created. The power of example is critical, and here the example is the now legendary arrangement between Wal-Mart and P&G (see Chapter 8 on strategic alliances). Ironically, Wal-Mart's entry into the food business is what drove the grocery industry to devise ECR in the first place.

ECR also requires considerable change in the internal operations of a channel member.[10] Jobs are lost and roles are redefined when EDI rationalizes supply chains. People representing many different functions in the organization (sales, marketing, finance, purchasing, production, shipping, warehousing, accounting) must work together in project teams to create tremendous organizational change. And teamwork must become permanent. Salespeople and purchasing agents, for example, are replaced by multifunctional teams on the buyer's side and the seller's side. Each side is expected to understand the other's business. These are wrenching changes.

RESPONDING RAPIDLY

Rapid response, or *quick response* (QR), is another approach to supply chain management.[11] It appears similar to, and is often compared with, ECR. A closer look reveals that the two are really quite different. QR originated in the early 1980s in the fashion industry, where it has seen its greatest development. Many of the original developments are attributed to Benetton, the Italian retailer of knitwear.

In some ways, QR is like ECR. The fundamental pull-system idea—let the consumer tell the entire channel what to make and what to ship, then do it quickly—is the same. The emphasis on interfirm cooperation, data analysis, data transmission, inventory management, and waste reduction also is the same. The fundamental difference is in the volatile, unpredictable nature of what is being sold. For FMCG categories, such as toothpaste, consumers know well in advance what they want and what they do not want. ECR enables them to tell the retailer and the suppliers readily.

In fashion, consumers do not know what they want until the moment they are ready to buy it. This is because they do not know what will be fashionable and whether the next fashion will appeal to them. In fashion retailing, consumers see and try an item, *then* form an opinion, and they change their minds readily. Benchmarks are difficult to find, in part because of lack of standardization (for example, of sizes) in the industry. Routinely, retailers put out a line of clothing and then discover consumer reaction. If the sizes tend to run bigger or smaller than normal, the retailer will have the wrong size assortment. If one fabric or color or variation pleases more than another, retailers will find themselves with too much of one item and not enough of another. Fashion is perishable: Consumers will not wait months for restock of a desirable item, and items that sell poorly must be marked down quickly in order to get rid of them at all.

Historically, store buyers forecasted fashion demand well in advance and committed to orders, sometimes six seasons before the items would be sold. This is a push system (make to forecast). Over time, consumer fashion tastes have become so difficult to forecast that many fashion retailers have adopted the opposite strategy: Try something in a small way and see if it works. If it sells, stock more, and quickly. But stock how? Manufacturers need lead time. By the time fashion is discovered, it is too late to order up more.

This is the impetus for quick response. The essence of QR is in manufacturing. QR involves keeping manufacturing flexible as to what to make and how much to make. In contrast, ECR is more focused on how much to make and when to put it into a warehouse. There is no need to keep manufacturing flexible to produce variations of toothpaste, and there is little harm in stockpiling it for a while. Demand can be steadied (e.g., by restraining promotions), thus heading off production surges. However, it is critical to keep clothing fabrication flexible to produce more of the latest hot dress or jacket in the popular sizes of this season's hit colors and fabrics. Production volume must be scaled up or down dramatically, and setups from one item to another should be quick. The items produced should be out the factory's door and to the customer rapidly.

Thus, while ECR focuses on shipments and promotions, QR focuses more on manufacturing. QR firms are heavy users of flexible manufacturing techniques. Much of ECR is about pricing and promotion, which do not figure at all in QR. The objective is always the same: Catch the fashion and charge for it. When mistakes are made (which should be a frequent event), catch the mistake soon and mark it down quickly—but modestly. Then mark down again what is left—quickly. In this way, drastic markdowns are reduced: These become necessary to move out merchandise that has been around well after people realized they did not want it.

Sidebar 14.2 profiles Zara, a leading example of quick response. One notable aspect of Zara is how well the marketing and channel strategy meshes with its supply chain management. Zara clothing is relatively inexpensive, which shows that QR need not mean charging premium prices. The real key is to avoid deep discounts on unwanted goods.

Given the intricacy of the production process, QR puts a great strain on the myriad fashion channel members, particularly the subcontractors in manufacturing. To keep up trusting relationships and open information transmission among so many players is difficult. The uncertainty of the demand environment also puts a strain on the system, making it hard to issue guarantees.

This is why some vertical integration is commonly used to achieve QR in fashion. Vertical integration is not total but occurs in two functions: design of the merchandise and retailing. Design is wholly owned because it is the key to manufacturing. Retailing is wholly owned in order to have stores to serve as test sites, observatories, and transmitters of fast, thorough information. (Benetton, for example, is largely franchised but keeps some stores under company ownership.) With their own stores, integrated providers (e.g., The Gap) can quickly alter prices, raising them to stave off stockouts on surprise winners (while rushing more into production) or lowering them before which items are losers has become obvious to consumers. This is quick response indeed.

How quick does response have to be? This depends on how fashionable the goods are. The less demand is influenced by fashion trends, the more the supply chain looks conventional. For moderately priced staple clothing, for example, it is neither necessary nor profitable to have a hyper-responsive supply chain. A good system of regional warehouses will suffice to fill surprise inventory gaps, and long lead times for production and transportation are employed to cut costs without penalty.[12]

PUTTING IT ALL TOGETHER: WHAT IS THE RIGHT SUPPLY CHAIN?

To this point, we have seen building blocks of supply chain management and have seen them put together in different ways to serve different environments. Which model is better: QR (keep manufacturing design flexible, do not focus on minimizing transportation costs) or ECR (fix design, control costs tightly)? Both are pull systems but differ in how and when they react.

Physical Efficiency versus Market Responsiveness

A good starting point in choosing a supply chain model is the nature of demand for a brand.[13] A functional brand of a product is a staple that people buy in many outlets and that serves basic, stable needs. Thus, the brands have stable, predictable demand and long life cycles. This invites competition, which creates low margins. In contrast, an innovative brand of a product is new and different. This enables it to earn higher margins. The sales cycle of the innovative product/brand is short and unpredictable, in part because such brands are quickly imitated and their advantage dissipated. Fundamentally, an innovative product faces unpredictable demand, has a

Sidebar 14.2

Zara, the master of quick response

In the 1960s, Armancio Ortega was a salesperson in a woman's clothing store in rural Spain. The thrifty client base was unwilling to spend on fanciful indulgences. Noticing that an expensive pink bathrobe in the window of the store created attention and desire but no buyers, Ortega decided to try a novel strategy of copying coveted fashionable items and selling them at a very low price. He turned his family's living room into a workshop and convinced his brother, sister, and fiancée to make inexpensive copies of fashionable clothes. The strategy worked so well that Ortega founded a manufacturing company in 1963. After twelve years of patient experimentation and system building, he vertically integrated forward into retailing, opening his first retail store in the same town as his original employer. Disappointed that his first choice of name (Zorba, after a character in the film *Zorba the Greek*) was trademarked, Armancio Ortega compromised and named his store Zara.

Today, Ortega is the wealthiest person in Spain. He is the majority owner of Inditex, a large and profitable vertically integrated clothing retailer selling under multiple brand names targeting multiple segments. Zara, the flagship, accounts for three quarters of the group's revenue and holds over 600 stores in over 40 countries. The secret of Zara's success is quick response (QR). Rather than being forecast driven, Zara is demand led.

Zara's much admired and analyzed supply chain begins in its three design centers (women, men, and children). These centers turn out new products continuously, not just for each fashion season. Competitors generate 2,000 to 4,000 new garments a year. Zara generates 11,000, introducing them in a steady barrage of new styles. Indeed, the time from the designer's sketch to putting the stock in the stores is a stunningly short 15 days.

In each design center, a staff of stylists (clothes designers) searches for ideas of what will connect with its clientele based on forecasting not only what customers are buying but also on what they might want to buy. The ideas can come from anywhere. Teams of trend-spotters travel the world, seeing what many different types of people are currently wearing and what physical possibilities exist (fabrics, cuts, accessories, and so forth). Stylists use this input, as well as examining magazines about fashion, celebrities, entertainment, and lifestyle. They are looking for ideas to copy, such as a dress worn by singer Victoria Beckham, photographed in a celebrity magazine. Information also comes in from stores about what is currently selling.

Stylists work in teams to use all this information to create prototypes. Each prototype is reviewed by three teams: stylists, salespeople, and fabric purchasing agents. All three groups need to agree for a model to launch, beginning the fifteen-day countdown to having the item in the stores. The objective is to capture the buyer's imagination in the same way that expensive pink bathrobe inspired Spanish window shoppers in 1963. But in Zara, the clothes are affordable, sparking impulse purchase. How?

The secret is to avoid the twin costs of holding inventory and marking down unsold items, which in fashion tend to be critical. Zara, whose stores are largely in Europe, is vertically integrated backward into production of many clothes and sources the rest largely from makers also located in Europe. This collocation allows Zara to move much faster than European competitors, who source from Asian countries to reduce production costs. Zara thus incurs higher labor costs, but it controls production costs by the principle of postponement (converting work-in-process inventory to finished-goods inventory only at the last possible moment).

(*continued*)

Sidebar 14.2 (cont.)

Zara, the master of quick response

The key is to order raw fabric early and hold it (because fabric cannot be quickly manufactured) and dye and finish it closer to the time of sale. Zara and its suppliers operate formidable manufacturing centers that create the goods and sort them according to their destination city (where Zara will have multiple stores).

While these goods are moving by truck to enormous, modern warehouses, store managers consult personal digital assistants (PDAs, pocket-sized computers) that display photos of the proposed new merchandise. Using their sense of their clientele in their part of the city, they quickly reject or accept. Then the merchandise is rushed by truck or air freight to the accepting store. Why the rush? A major reason is that Zara stores have virtually no place to store inventory: They must be supplied just in time. Why? The stores are located in prime, expensive shopping districts, in space that is too valuable to use as a warehouse. In turn, to keep costs down while selling inexpensive clothes out of prestigious addresses, Zara does no advertising, counting entirely on word of mouth (WOM).

Relying on WOM demands that customers have an appealing experience every time they visit. To control the shopping experience, a staff of builders designs and constructs every store based on the store manager's reactions to ideas proposed by a model store. In this way, Zara adapts locally while maintaining a consistent look.

To complete the cycle, items that do not sell are swiftly noted, removed, and rushed to another location, where they have a better chance of succeeding. The quickly changing assortment brings browsers back: in Spain, clients visit the average clothing store three or four times a year but visit Zara 17 times a year. These visits create WOM, which restarts the cycle: fresh retail sales, store feedback to stylists, new prototype, manufacturing fast from

postponed work-in-progress fabric inventory, rushing finished product in, selling out or rushing out, beginning again.

This is indeed quick response to the market. Zara is agile—but it is *not* lean (everywhere). It spends more than competitors do on transportation (all that rushing and moving inventory around) even though production is relatively nearby. It also spends more than competitors do on labor (due to European costs). But these costs are more than offset by savings in inventory (holding, markdowns) and the ability to support a marketing strategy that rests on the experience created by each shop's ambiance and prime location rather than on advertising.

Zara's success has been much noted, and a certain myth has built around it. The myth is that it is a state-of-the-art marvel in information technology. While Zara is indeed heavily computerized, it is not a model of the latest in information technology and spends much less than do most retailers on IT as a percentage of sales. In particular, Zara does *not* have

- An elaborate customer relationship management (CRM) system
- Sophisticated planning and scheduling software to convert demand information into production requirements
- Logistics software to run the distribution centers
- Extranets across factories and intranets across stores
- Enterprise resource process software to underpin the whole infrastructure
- A large information technology department
- A formal technology budget

Zara does not even have personal computers in its stores: Dedicated terminals collect basic sales and inventory information, which is transmitted to headquarters by store managers (not by intranet) daily. All this does not mean

Sidebar 14.2 (cont.)

Zara, the master of quick response

Zara shuns IT. Indeed, it has been early to adopt computerization, thanks to insistence by Armancio Ortega himself (who today is still heavily involved in design and not interested in taking retirement). The current CEO is a former IT manager, a testament to Zara's comfort with computerization.

The key is that Zara adopts IT only as internal managers see fit. For example, Zara was early to adopt PDAs (personal digital assistants) to replace faxes and relies on them heavily, obliging managers to use them to place orders and refusing to allow orders to be phoned in. In other ways, however, Zara prefers not to automate but to leave decision making in the hands of field personnel, particularly the store managers. These managers play a much greater role than in competing retailers. They have considerable latitude in some areas (such as ordering merchandise) but zero latitude in other areas (such as pricing).

Zara can take a minimalist approach to IT in part because the products have few components and do not need to be tracked or maintained after purchase. As analyst Andrew McAfee puts it, Zara works because of its minimalist attitude toward IT, not in spite of it. IT is used to aid judgment, not to make judgments. Computerization is standardized, targeted to where managers see a business case for it. All technology initiatives come from within Zara and complement its processes rather than usurp them. And IT is not imposed by specialists on reluctant managers: The managers are well versed in computerization, and the IT personnel are well versed in Zara's business.

In short the logistics of quick response rest on thoughtful management using IT as a tool rather than as a substitute for human judgments.[14]

short product life cycle, and is hard to forecast. It has high margins but also higher markdowns and stockouts (due to changing tastes and forecast errors). Because these products are differentiated, they often exist in many variations. Functional products have the reverse profile.

Figure 14.1 summarizes the contrasts between these two end points of a spectrum.

The key to supplying functional goods is to hold down three types of costs: (1) manufacturing, (2) holding inventory, and (3) transportation. These costs all involve handling a good and are observable physical costs tracked by accountants. Efficient manufacturing and logistics are crucial. They matter because low margins make cost consciousness important and because predictable demand simplifies decision making. ECR fits in this spirit, as do many methods of manufacturing that are based on tight planning and management of supplies. Here, the most important information flow occurs inside the chain from retailers back to suppliers of manufacturers.

Supply chains for these products need to be physically efficient. At the factory, this means running at high capacity. In the warehouse, it means fast-turning inventory. Products are designed once and for all to make them easy to manufacture and to maximize their performance. Cost and quality are the criteria used to select suppliers.

	Highly Functional Products ⟶	Highly Innovative Products
Demand	Predictable	Unpredictable
Forecast error	Low	High
Product variety (variants of basic models)	Low	High
Contribution margin	Low	High
Markdowns due to obsolescence	None or low	High
Frequency of stockout	Low	High

Figure 14.1   Types of goods for supply chain management

Source: Adapted from Fisher, Marshall L. (1997), "What Supply Chain Is Right for Your Product?" *Harvard Business Review* 78 (March–April), pp. 105–116.

Innovative goods demand the opposite. The greatest risk with these products is to miss the market by having the wrong item at the wrong time at the wrong price. The key to innovative goods is speed: Demand cannot be estimated, only noted as it begins to surge. Hence, the point of sale is a critical information flow. For innovative goods, the opportunity cost of a stockout is very high, given the high margins. By the time the stockout is rectified, the item may have lost favor, leaving the supplier with drastically devalued stocks.

Supply chains for innovative products need to be market responsive. To do this, product design must be modular to postpone final assembly as long as possible. Performance and cost are less critical here and can be sacrificed somewhat to achieve modularity. Suppliers are selected for quality and flexibility, not lowest cost. The manufacturing system keeps buffer stocks of supplies, just in case. Finally, reducing the lead time needed to fill an order is an obsession, even though this raises transportation and fulfillment costs.

These differences are summarized in Figure 14.2. Market responsiveness and physical efficiency are two end points on a continuum, along which a supply chain philosophy can be fitted.

An intriguing element here is that where a brand falls on the spectrum from highly functional to highly responsive depends on the brand's marketing strategy. Thus, the same product category can have more innovative or more functional brands, each calling for a different supply chain. For example, in cars, some brands are very conservative and stable, often appealing to a buyer who resists change. Other brands have an ephemeral, faddish appeal. The more functional brand needs a more physically efficient supply chain and does not need to be so market responsive. The more innovative brand needs more market responsiveness and can afford less physical efficiency in its supply chain.

	Physically Efficient Supply Chain (Functional Goods) ⟶	Market-Responsive Supply Chain (Innovative Goods)
Objective	Cut costs of manufacturing, holding inventory, transportation.	Respond quickly as demand materializes.
Consequences of failure	Low prices and higher costs create margin squeeze.	Stockouts of high-margin goods. Heavy markdowns of unwanted goods.
Manufacturing goods	Run at high capacity utilization rate.	Be ready to alter production (quantity and type) swiftly. Keep excess production capacity.
Inventory	Minimize everywhere.	Keep buffer stocks of parts and finished goods.
Lead times	Can be long, because demand is predictable.	Must be short.
Supplies should be	Low cost. Adequate quality.	Fast, flexible. Adequate quality.
Product design	Design for ease of manufacture and to meet performance standards.	Design in modules to delay final production.

Figure 14.2   Two kinds of supply chains

Source: Adapted from Fisher, Marshall L, (1997) "What Supply Chain Is Right for Your Product?" *Harvard Business Review* 78 (March–April), pp. 105–116.

Supply Chain Management: Why Only Now?

On paper, supply chain management is an eminently sensible idea. Yet SCM is more a slogan than a reality at many companies, and the methods needed to make pull systems work are still very difficult to implement. Pull systems in channels are so different from push systems that making the changeover is a very challenging task. Barriers to implementation, internal and external, are everywhere. What does a company need to build a supply chain management mentality into its marketing channels? Experience and data suggest that two elements are critical.

1. An internal culture of cross-functional integration (as opposed to functional silos).

2. Effective channel management. This means trust, good working relations, good design, the judicious exercise of power—in short, the implementation of the principles described in this book.

Sidebar 14.3

How to build Triple-A supply chains

What should be a supply chain's objective? Hau L. Lee, a prominent figure in supply chain management, argues that focusing on a single objective (e.g., efficiency or cost cutting or even speed) is dangerous because people are guided to sacrifice higher objectives (such as product quality) to achieve them. Instead, Lee argues that a great supply chain can become simply an expensive and unprofitable project unless it has all three properties of a triple-A system. Lee offers suggestions for how to achieve each property.[15]

Agility: Fast response to any change in volume, variety, specification, or situation. Ways to make a supplier chain more agile include:

- Forge collaborative relationships with suppliers
- Design for postponement, which means pushing back the time when one must finalize the product
- Keep buffer inventories of items that are not difficult to stock (and more generally, keep some slack resources in the system to respond to emergencies, such as a natural disaster)
- Invest in good, dependable logistics systems

- Ensure that there is a good deal of information flowing up and down in the chain
- Have a fallback plan and a crisis management team in anticipation of emergencies

Adaptability: Ability to change to meet large permanent shifts in the environment. Ways to make a supplier chain more adaptable include:

- Continuously add new suppliers; use intermediaries (such as consultants or trade associations) to find them
- Evaluate the needs of ultimate customers, not just immediate consumers
- Insist on flexible product designs
- Monitor world economies to notice trends
- Monitor technical and product life cycles to notice changes

Alignment: Individuals and organizations have compatible incentives. Ways to make a supplier chain better aligned include:

- Exchange information freely within and across organizations
- Give suppliers and customers clear roles, tasks, and responsibilities
- Practice the equity principle

The very best supply chains are "triple-A" systems: agile, adaptable, and aligned.[16] *Agile* systems respond fast to changes in volume, variety, or specifications. Such systems cope well with emergencies, such as a fire or an earthquake. *Adaptable* systems change to follow major shifts in the environment, such as major shifts in customer expectations or available technologies. *Aligned* systems give all parties compatible incentives, so that not only employees within divisions but companies in supply chains have reasons to coordinate. Sidebar 14.3 suggests how to achieve these three vital properties: Many suggestions are matters of good channel management in and of themselves.

SUMMARY

Logistics involves the processing and tracking of factory goods during warehousing, inventory control, transport, customs documentation (a small issue or a nonissue inside trading zones), and delivery to customers. Changes in logistics can create astonishing increases in effectiveness and in efficiency. Many companies have dramatically altered their manufacturing processes and have reaped great rewards from so doing. Now they are turning to their marketing channels and applying the same principles (such as pull systems and electronic information sharing), looking to achieve another wave of gains. Most businesses need an example to follow: Good examples of better logistics are becoming abundant. Moreover, changes in logistics are becoming more and more feasible.

This leads to the idea of supply chain management, a paradigm that starts with customer service and argues that this results from the cumulative efforts of the entire channel. Customer service cannot be interpreted as the sole responsibility of any single channel member. The guiding principle is to unify product flows and information flows up and down the production and distribution chain. Doing this requires (1) a market orientation, focused on the last customer; (2) effective channel management, to enable smooth transfers of product and information; and (3) effective logistics.

To many people, the principles of supply chain management are epitomized in efficient consumer response. As initially proposed, the idea is to focus on four areas where the industry as a whole had (and still has) great potential for improvement. These are (1) continuous replenishment, (2) efficient pricing and promotions, (3) changes in product introduction, and (4) changes in merchandising. Improvements in each of these areas are based on the entire channel's sharing information and working together to devise ways to cut needless and baffling variety, redirect promotions to build brand equity, balance stocks, and eliminate the bullwhip effect (oscillating inventories with a tendency to accumulate upstream).

Another kind of pull system is quick response. The objective here is to manage the supply chain for products whose demand is difficult to predict. QR puts the emphasis on flexible manufacturing to react to trends detected in point-of-sale data. To gain the information and flexibility, many channel members choose to own some stores (for the demand information) and to employ designers (for the ability to reset a production process quickly).

A spectrum from more functional to more innovative products can be used to determine which supply chain philosophy is most appropriate for a given brand. Innovative brands (whose demand is fundamentally volatile) need supply chains that respond quickly to market signals. Functional products (whose demand is stable) need a supply chain that holds down physical costs. Both types of supply chains have become more feasible with the development of new technologies and with changes in management practice. One of the cornerstones of good supply chain management is effective marketing channel management.

DISCUSSION QUESTIONS

1. Give three examples of more innovative products (for SCM purposes) and three examples of more functional products. Give at least one example of two brands (one more innovative, one more functional) in the same product category (e.g., automobiles). What is the right supply chain for the more innovative products, and why? How does this differ from the more functional products?

2. In your opinion, what is the greatest obstacle to implementing the principles and practices of supply chain management?

3. The Zara sidebar argues that quick response can be done without state-of-the-art information technology. Do you agree? Is the Zara case unusual? Would Zara be better off by introducing SCM hardware and software that it currently lacks? Does the Zara example generalize to other situations?

4. Some companies have adopted reverse logistics systems under pressure from government regulation. Should this idea be generalized to all products? To all firms? What are the arguments pro and con? If you were a supply chain manager for an automobile maker, how might you go about responding to such legislation? What could you do to create an efficient reverse supply chain?

ENDNOTES

1. The authors are grateful to Frédéric Dalsace, to Enver Yücesan, and to the late Xavier de Groote. Over the years, they have been a source of instruction, guidance, and inspiration in the domain of logistics and supply chain management. Errors and omissions remain the responsibility of the authors.

2. Lambert, Douglas M. and Martha C. Cooper (2000), "Issues in Supply Chain Management," *Industrial Marketing Management* 29, no. 1 (January), pp. 65–83.

3. Lancioni, Richard A. (2000), "New Developments in Supply Chain Management for the Millennium," *Industrial Marketing Management*, 29, no. 1 (January), pp. 1–6.

4. Ballou, Ronald H., Stephen M. Gilbert, and Ashok Mukherjee (2000), "New Managerial Challenges from Supply Chain Opportunities," *Industrial Marketing Management* 29, no. 1 (January), pp. 7–18.

5. Sautter, Elise Truly, Arnold Maltz, and Kevin Boberg (1999), "A Customer Service Course: Bringing Marketing and Logistics Together," *Journal of Marketing Education* 21, no. 2 (August), pp. 138–145.

6. Guide, Daniel R. and Luk N. Van Wassenhove (2002), "The Reverse Supply Chain," *Harvard Business Review* 80, no. 2 (February), pp. 25–26; and Savaskan, R. Canan, Shantanu Bhattacharya, and Luk N. Van Wassenhove (2004), "Closed-Loop Supply Chain Models with Product Remanufacturing," *Management Science* 50, no. 2 (February), pp. 239–252.

7. Triplett, Tim (1994), "More U.S. Grocers Turning to ECR to Cut Waste," *Marketing News* 28, no. 19 (September 12), pp. 3–5; and *Oil and Gas Investor* (1998), "Lessons Learned from the Grocery Industry," *Oil and Gas Investor* (Second Quarter), p. 23.

8. Cooke, James (2002), "EDI: What Lies Ahead," *Modern Materials Handling*, 10, no. 3, pp. 1–3.

9. O'Sullivan, Denis (1997), "ECR: Will It End in Tears?" *Logistics Focus* 5 (September), pp. 2–5; and Puget, Yves (1999), "Les Quatre Niveaux de la 'Supply Chain,'" *LSA* 19, no. 22 (October), p. 71.

10. Ellinger, Alexander E. (2000), "Improving Marketing/Logistics Cross-Functional Collaboration in the Supply Chain," *Industrial Marketing Management* 29, no. 1 (January), pp. 85–96.

11. Richardson, James (1996), "Vertical Integration and Rapid Response in Fashion Apparel," *Organization Science* 7, no. 4 (July–August), pp. 400–412.

12. van Ryzin, Garrett and Siddarth Mahajan (1999), "On the Relationship between Inventory Costs and Variety Benefits in Retail Assortments," *Management Science*, 45, no. 11 (November), pp. 1496–1509; and Dvorak, Robert E. and Frits van Paasschen (1996), "Retail Logistics: One Size Doesn't Fit All," *The McKinsey Quarterly*, 2, no. 2, pp. 120–129.

13. This section is based on Fisher, Marshall L. (1997), "What Is the Right Supply Chain for Your Product?" *Harvard Business Review* 78, no. 2 (March–April), pp. 105–116.

14. This sidebar is based on a variety of sources: Bialobos, Chantal (2003), "Zara, le Marchand de Fringues le Plus Rapide de l'Europe," *Capital* 12, no. 12

(December), pp. 38–42; McAfee, Andrew (2004), "Do You Have Too Much IT?" *Sloan Business Review* 45, no. 3 (Spring), pp. 18–22; *Fortune* (2000), "Zara Has a Made-to-Order Plan for Success," *Fortune* 142, no. 5 (September 4), p. 80–82; and Christopher, Martin (2000), "The Agile Supply Chain," *Industrial Marketing Management* 29, no. 1 (January), pp. 37–44.

15. Lee (2004), previously cited.
16. Lee, Hau L. (2004), "The triple-A Supply Chain," *Harvard Business Review* 82, no. 10 (October), pp. 102–112.

Company Index

Name Index

Ross, William T., 240n48, 285n14, 327n17
Rotch, William, 32n25, 105n9
Roux, Annette, *123*
Rubin, Paul H., 419n12, 559n67
Rublin, Lauren R., 375n41
Rumelt, Richard R., 240n42
Ruppersberger, Gregg, 517n88
Ryzen, Garrett van, 574n12

S

Sakano, Tomoaki, 242n70
Sallis, James, 329n57
Samiee, Saeed, 516n31
Saranow, Jennifer, 67n11, 195n16
Saunders, Carol, 240n25
Sautter, Elise Truly, 574n5
Savaskan, R. Canan, 574n6
Sa Vinhas, Alberto, 153n58, 286n23, 286n27
Savitt, Ronald, 483nn1–4, 483nn6–7
Sawhney, Kirti, 150n1
Scammon, Debra L., 151n11, 419n17, 423n93
Scheer, Lisa K., 241n53, 241n60, 242n71, 287n42, 287n44, 328n38
Scheffman, David T., 375n40
Scheier, Robert L., 65–66n3, 104–5n4, 105n5, 193–4n8
Scherer, F. M., 420n28, 421n64, 422n84
Scherrer, Matthieu, 151n23
Schlesinger, Jacob M., 65–66n3
Schmeltzer, John, *42*, 65n1, 104n1, 193n6
Schul, Patrick L., 558n54
Schultz, Howard, 529, 557n18
Schurr, Paul H., 240n46, 285n6, 329n48
Schwartz, Marius, 152n42
Scully, Gerald W., 516n25
Segal, David, 423n90
Sellerin, Raphael, 374n4
Selnes, Fred, 329n57
Serra, Matt, *253–54*
Sethuraman, Rajagopalan, 327n15, 482n53
Sexton, Richard J., 516n28
Sexton, Terri A., 516n28
Seyed-Mohamed, Nazeem, 240n44
Shane, Scott A., 528, 557n15, 558n42, 558n47, 559n61, 558nn49–50
Shankar, Venkatesh, 152–3n51
Sharpe, Anita, 420n34
Shaw, Kathryn L., 558nn36–37
Sheffet, Mary Jane, 151n11, 419n17, 423n93
Sherman, Mark, 31n15

Shervani, Tasadduq, 150n1, 152n50, 286n24
Shi, Christiana Smith, 478n61, 478nn57–59
Shocker, Allan D., 152n33
Shugan, Steven M., 152n48, 239n4
Siguaw, Judy A., 327n15
Silva-Risso, Jorge, 153n54
Simmons, Carolyn J., 152n32
Simonian, Haig, 419n5
Simonin, Bernard L., 153n65, 375n25
Simpson, James T., 242n69
Simpson, Penny M., 327n15
Singh, Harbir, 329n45
Skinner, Steven J., 240n47, 241n55
Smith, Ethan, 194n11
Smith, Laurie P., 285n16
Snyder, Edward A., 375n34
Soberman, David A., 30n9, 286n35
Song, Lisa, 475n21
Southam, Hazel, 151n27
Spagat, Elliot, 153n64
Spekman, Robert, 287n51, 375n36
Spencer, Jane, 105n7, 194n9
Spiller, Pablo T., 375n40
Spriggs, Mark T., 421n60
Spurgeon, Devon, 475n11
Staelin, Richard, 286n34, 375n35, 420n48
Stampfl, Ronald W., 475n2
Stanek, Steve, 67n14, 67n20
Steenkamp, Jan-Benedict E. M., 239nn22–23, 241n53, 241n60, 241n67, 285n9, 287nn41–42, 287n44, 328n32, 328n36, 329n38
Steiner, Robert L., 150n7
Steinhauer, Jennifer, *441*
Stern, Gabriella, 477n55
Stern, Louis W., 32n27, 32n28, 192n2, 193n3, 193n5, 195n17, 239n7, 239n11, 240n35, 241n65, 242n71, 285nn1–2, 287nn47–48, 374n9, 559n66
Stock, James R., 105n8
Stoll, Neal R., 420n47
Stremersch, Stefan, 329n60
Stringer, Kortney, 31n11
Stroud, Jerri, 423n90
Strutton, David, 558n52
Stump, Rodney, 328n28
Stumpf, Edward, 516n29
Sturdivant, Frederick D., 192n2, 195n17
Subramani, Mani R., 241n57
Sullivan, Mary W., 152n46, 286n33, 405, 420n42, 421n50, 422n81
Summers, John O., 241n66, 241n68
Superville, Darlene, 477nn44–45
Sweeney, Daniel J., 475n2, 477n50, 477n54

Swift, Gustavus, 357
Szymanski, David M., 374n14

T

Tacchini, Sergio, 368–69
Talukdar, Debabrata, 153n52
Tanouye, Elyse, 420n35, 423n99
Taylor, Alex, 152n36, 241n56, 285n10, 328n29
Taylor, Robert E., 422n82
Tedeschi, Bob, 476n30
Tellis, Gerard J., 151n21
Terpstra, Vern, 153n65, 375n25
Thayer, Warren, 421n50
Thomas, Andrew R., 329n42
Thomas, Kenneth W., 275, 287n54
Thomas-Graham, Pamela A., 286n28
Thomson, Simon, 30n9
Thouanel-Lorant, Patricia, 151n15
Thunder, David, 418n4
Tibben-Lembke, Ronald S., 105n7, 194n9
Tkacik, Maureen, 285nn17–18
Tomlinson, Richard, 374n18
Toosi, Nahal, 477nn44–45
Torode, Christina, 153n57
Trachtenberg, Jeffrey A., 193n7, 194n9
Trinkle, Bob, 374–5n24, 517n44
Triplett, Tim, 574n6
Troy, Mike, 31n10
Truffaut, Charles, *532*
Truffaut, Georges, *532*
Tucker, Emma, 419nn5–6, 421n68
Turcsik, Richard, 421n68

V

Van Den Bulte, Christophe, 329n60
Vander, Nat, 476n26
van Ryzin, Garett, 105n6
Varadarajan, P. Rajan, 374n14
Varon, Elana, 65–66n3, 104–5n4, 193–4n8
Vecchio, Leonardo Del, 368
Venkatraman, N., 241n57
Villard, Nathalie, 374n2
Villas-Boas, Miguel, 286n32
Vogelstein, Fred, 375n39
Vurva, Richard, 516n16

W

Wagoner, Rick, 251
Walker, Orville C., Jr., 285n11, 374n16, 376n49
Walsh, M. Ann, 375n46
Wassenhove, Luk N. Van, 574n6

Subject Index